Learning and Appl
Autodesk Inventor 2009
Step-by-Step

L. Scott Hansen, Ph.D.

Associate Professor of Engineering Technology
College of Computing, Integrated Engineering
and Technology
Southern Utah University
Cedar City, Utah

Industrial Press, Inc
New York

Copyright © 2008 by Industrial Press Inc., New York.

ISBN (978-0-8311-) 3365-8

Third Edition, August 2008

Sponsoring Editor: John Carleo
Cover Design: Janet Romano

Printed in the United States of America. All right reserved. This book, or any parts thereof, may not be reproduced, stored in a retrieval system, or transmitted in any form with-out the permission of the publisher.

Limits of Liability and disclaimer of Warranty
The author and publisher make no claim of warranty, written, expressed, assumed or implied.

Industrial Press Inc.
989 Avenue of the Americas, 19th Floor
New York, NY 10018

10 9 8 7 6 5 4 3 2 1

Note to the Reader

This book provides clear and concise applied instruction in order to help you develop a mastery of *Autodesk Inventor*. Almost every instruction includes a graphic illustration to aid in clarifying that instruction. Software commands appear in **bold** or in "quotation marks" for everyone who prefers not to read every word of the text. Most illustrations also include small pointer arrows and text to further clarify instructions.

This book was written for classroom instruction or self study, including for individuals with no 3D solid modeling experience at all. You will begin at a very basic level, but by the time you finish you will be completing complex functions.

For any organization requiring additional help, I am available for onsite training. Please contact me at: hansens@suu.edu

Scott Hansen
Cedar City, Utah

Table of Contents

Chapter 1 Getting Started 1

    Create a simple sketch using the Sketch Panel. 6
    Dimension a sketch using the General Dimension command. 11
    Extrude a sketch in the Part Features Panel using the Extrude command. 38
    Create a fillet in the Part Features Panel using the Fillet command 40
    Create a hole in the Part Features Panel using the Extrude command 44
    Create a counter bore in the Part Features Panel using the Hole command ... 52

Chapter 2 Learning More Basics. 67

    Revolve a sketch in the Part Features Panel using the Revolve command. ... 86
    Create a hole in the Part Features Panel using the Extrude command 99
    Create a series of holes in the Part Features Panel using the
        Circular Hole command 111

Chapter 3 Learning To Detail Part Drawings 121

    Create an Orthographic view using the Drawing Views Panel. 163
    Create a Solid Model using the Edit Views command 174

Chapter 4 Advanced Detail Drawing Procedures 181

    Create an Auxiliary View using the Drawing Views Panel 187
    Create a Section View using the Drawing Views Panel 193
    Dimension views using the Drawing Annotation Panel 197
    Create Text using the Drawing Annotation Panel. 205

Chapter 5 Learning To Edit Existing Solid Models 215

    Edit the part using the Sketch Panel 245
    Edit the part using the Extrude command 251
    Edit the part using the Fillet command. 264

Chapter 6 Advanced Design Procedures 275

    Learn to use the X, Y, and Z Planes 284
    Learn to use the Wireframe viewing command 288
    Learn to project geometry to a new sketch. 290
    Learn to use the Shell command. 302

Chapter 7 Introduction To Assembly View Procedures. **351**

    Learn to import existing solid models into the Assembly Panel. 353
    Learn to constrain all parts in the Assembly Panel. 368
    Learn to edit/modify parts while in the Assembly Panel 396
    Learn to assign colors to different parts in the Assembly Panel. 412
    Learn to drive constraints to simulate motion. 418
    Learn to create an .avi or .wmv file while in the Assembly Panel 426

Chapter 8 Introduction To The Presentation Panel **429**

    Learn to import existing solid models into the Presentation Panel. 442
    Learn to design parts trails in the Presentation Panel 446

Chapter 9 Introduction to Advanced Commands **455**

    Learn to create a sweep using the Sweep command 456
    Learn to create a loft using the Loft command 468
    Learn to create a coil using the Coil command 489

Chapter 10 Introduction to the Design Accelerator **493**

    Learn to Create a Disc Cam 499
    Learn to constrain a Disc Cam in an Assembly file 508
    Learn to edit a Disc Cam 514
    Learn to animate a Disc Cam using the Drive Constraint command 521

Chapter 1 Getting Started

Objectives:
- Create a simple sketch using the Sketch Panel
- Dimension a sketch using the General Dimension command
- Extrude a sketch in the Part Features Panel using the Extrude command
- Create a hole in the Part Features Panel using the Extrude command
- Create a fillet in the Part Features Panel using the Fillet command
- Create a counter bore in the Part Features Panel using the Hole command

Chapter 1 includes instruction on how to design the part shown below.

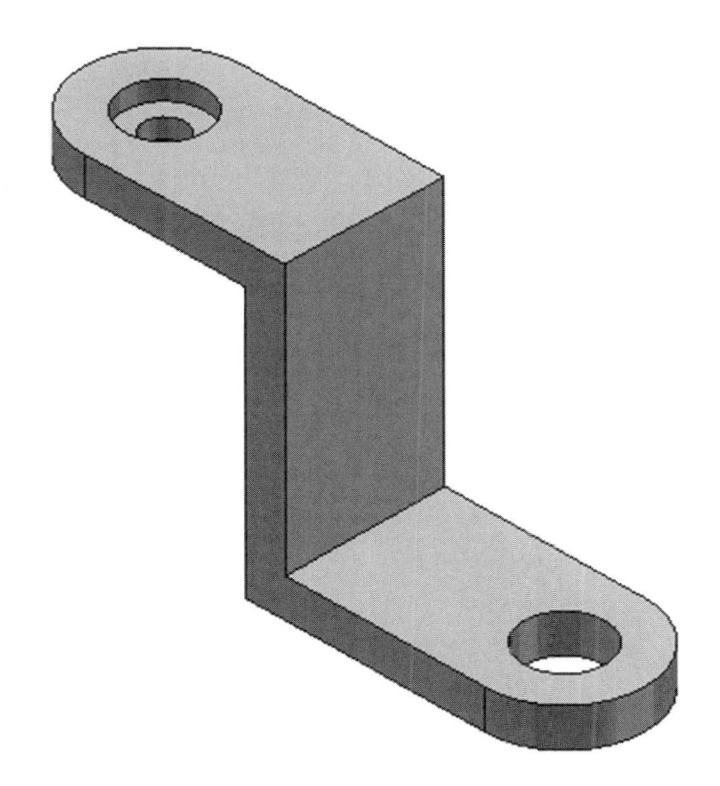

Chapter 1: Getting Started

1. Start Inventor by moving the cursor to the **start** button in the lower left corner of the screen. Click the left mouse button once.

2. A pop up menu of the programs that are installed on the computer will appear. Scroll through the list of programs until you find Autodesk Inventor Professional 2009.

3. Move the cursor over **Autodesk Inventor Professional 2009** and left click once.

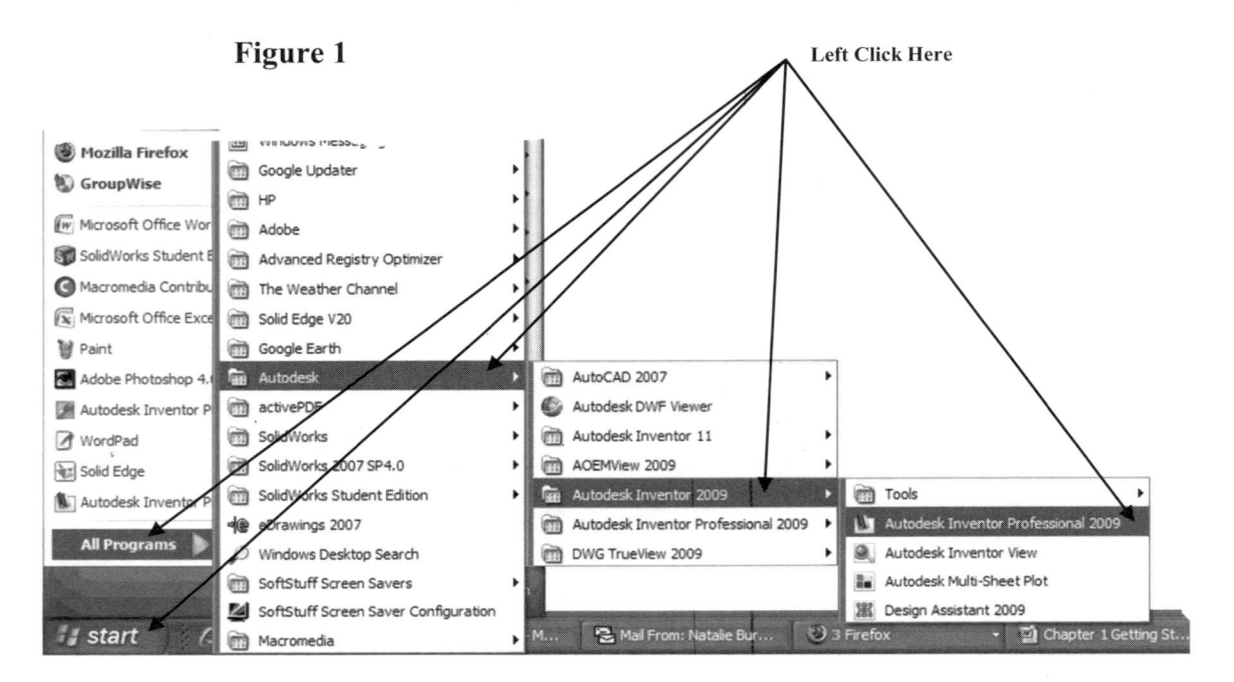

Figure 1

4. Autodesk Inventor Professional 2009 will open (load up and begin running).

Chapter 1: Getting Started

5. The Autodesk Inventor Professional 2009 startup banner will appear briefly as shown in Figure 2.

Figure 2

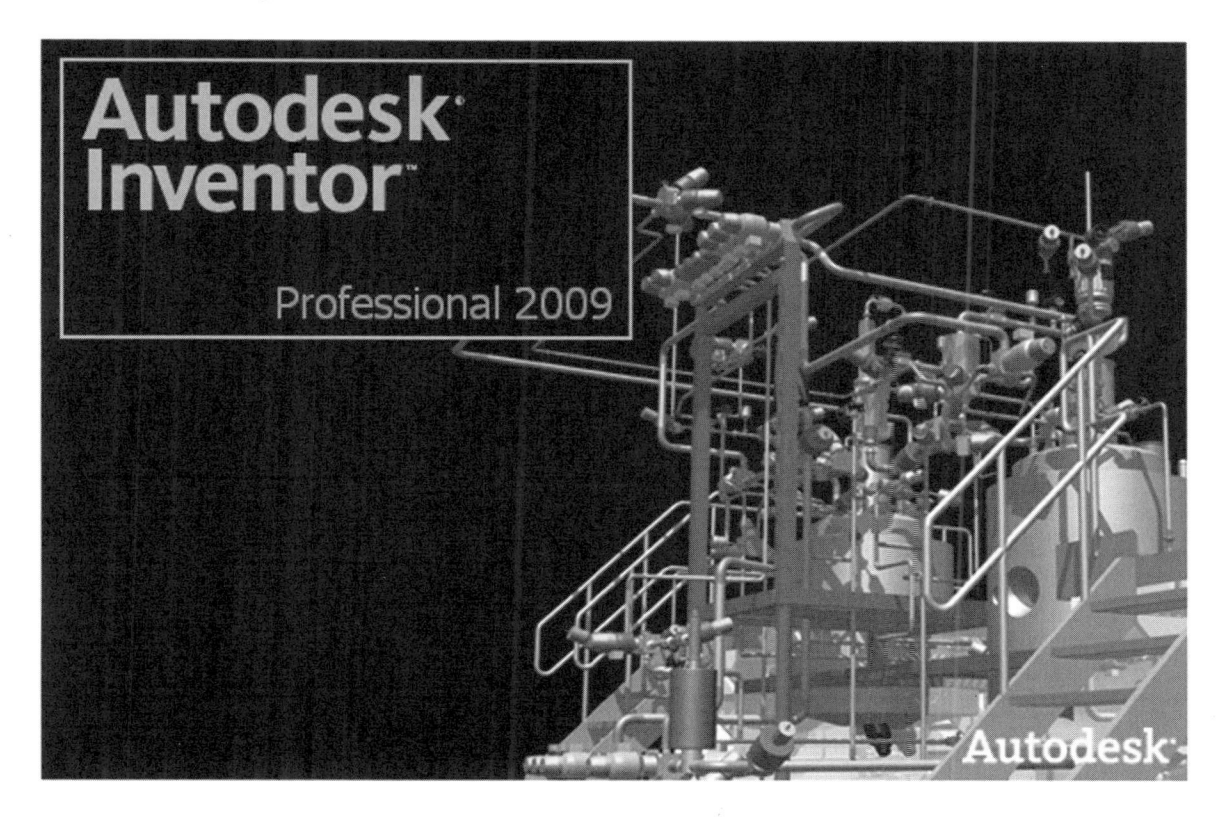

Chapter 1: Getting Started

6. The Open dialog box will appear. Left click on the white piece of paper located beneath the text "Quick Launch" as shown in Figure 3.

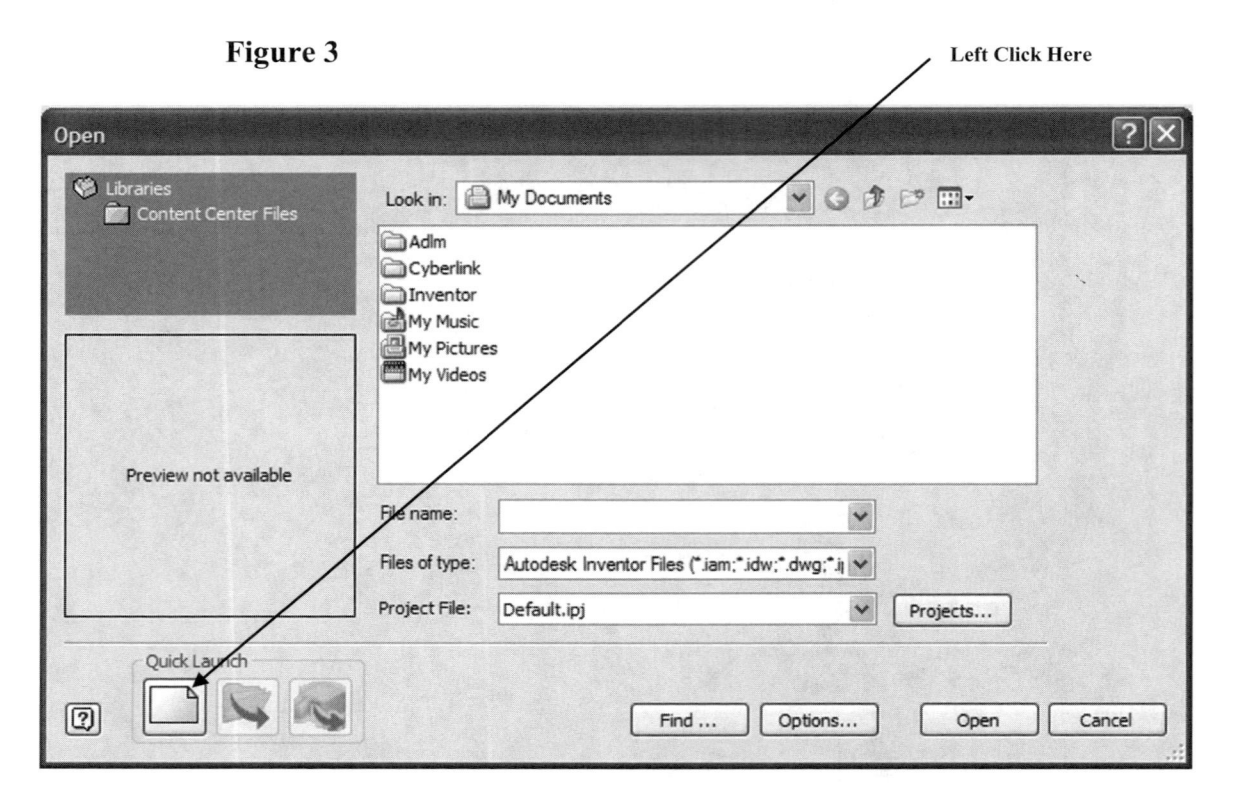

Figure 3

Left Click Here

4

Chapter 1: Getting Started

7. The New File dialog box will appear. When starting any new drawing left click on the Quick Launch icon if the New File dialog box does not appear.
Left click on the **English** tab at the upper left corner of the dialog box. After left clicking on the **English** tab, left click on **Standard (in).ipt** as shown in Figure 4.

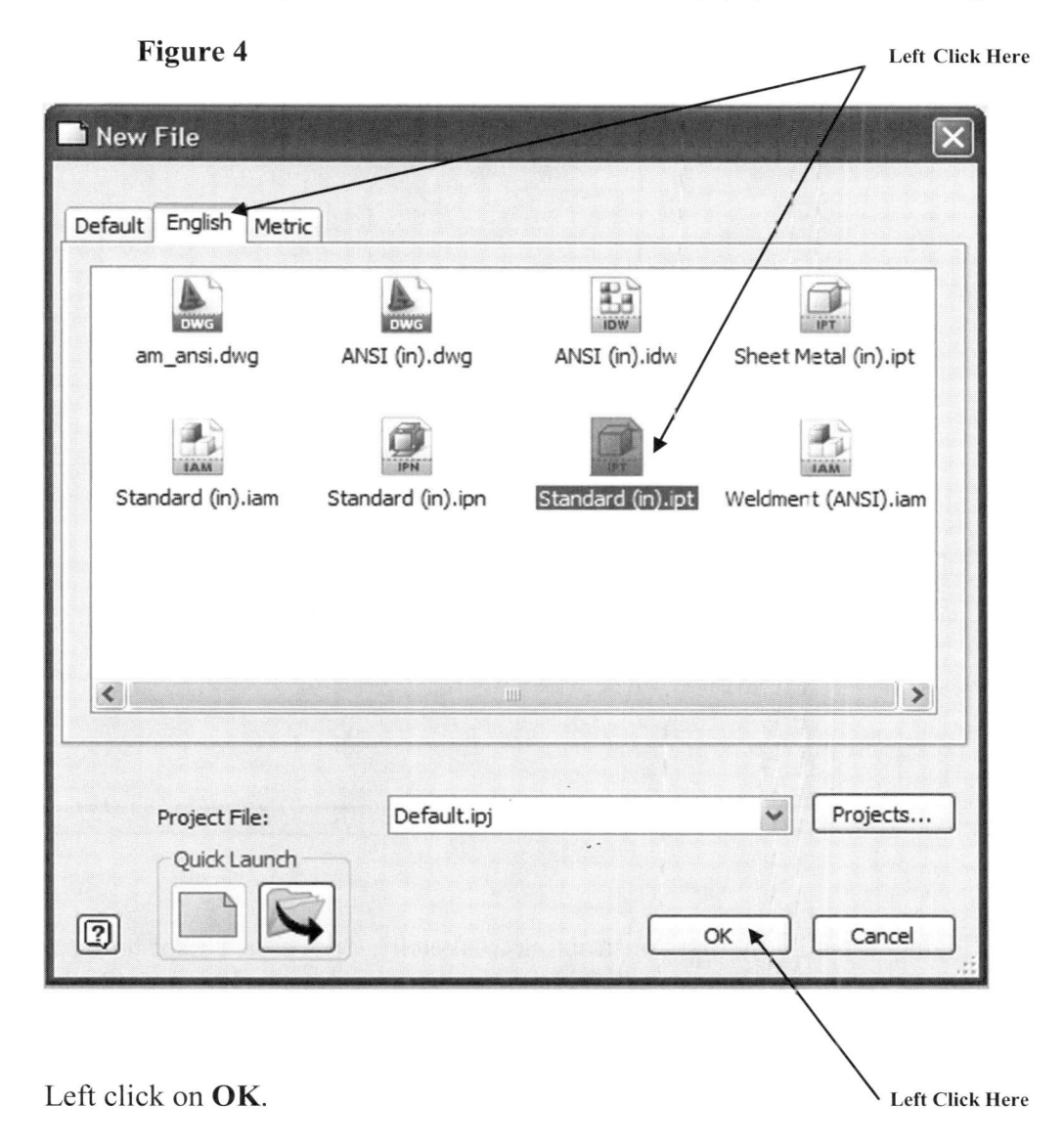

Figure 4

8. Left click on **OK**.

Chapter 1: Getting Started

9. Inventor is now ready for use. The screen should look similar to Figure 5.

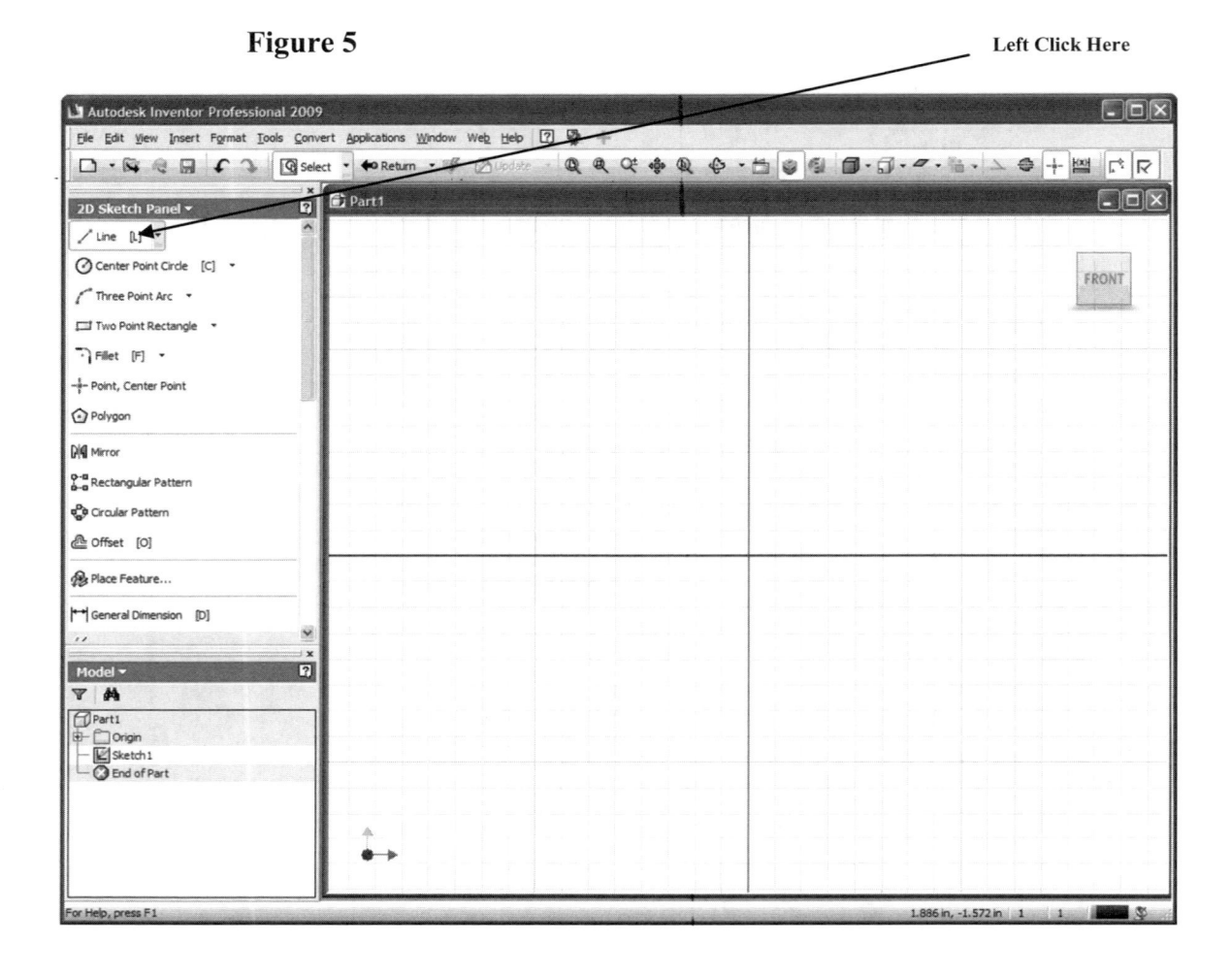

    Figure 5

10. Begin a drawing by first constructing a "sketch". Move the cursor to the upper left corner of the screen and left click on **Line** as shown in Figure 5. To know what any icon or command will do, move the cursor over the icon or command and wait a few seconds. A yellow banner will appear describing the icons or commands function.

11. Move the cursor somewhere in the lower left portion of the screen and left click once. This will be the beginning end point of a line.

12. Move the cursor towards the lower right portion of the screen and left click once as shown in Figure 6.

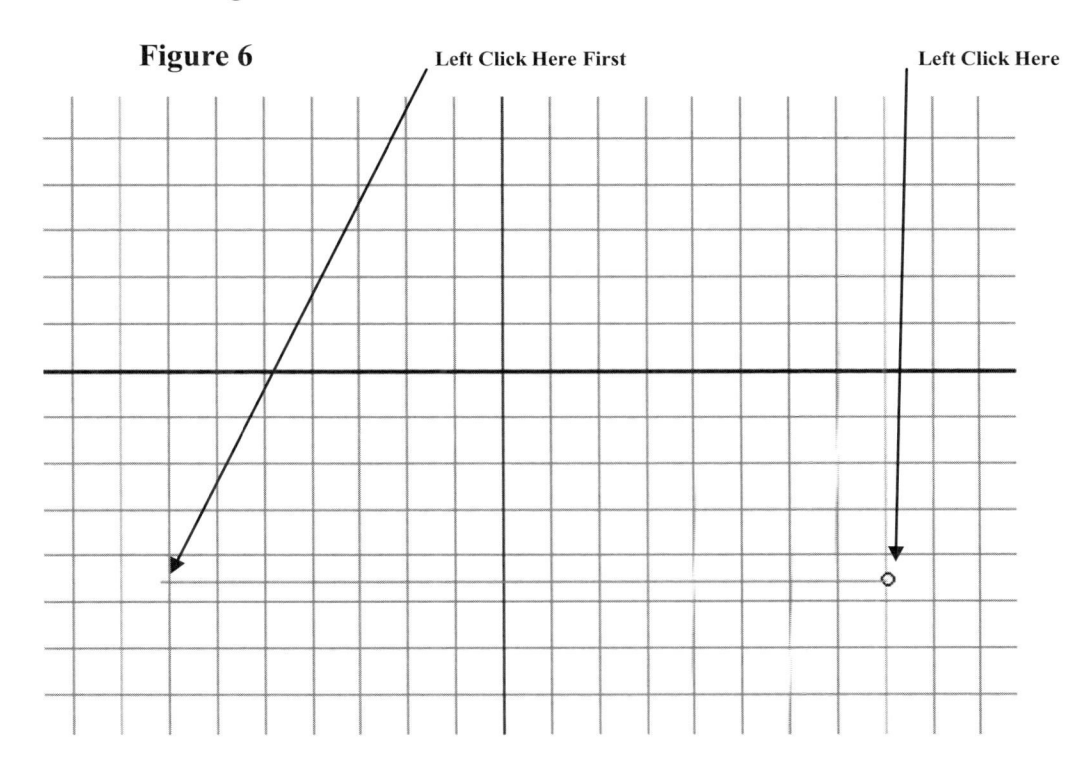

Figure 6   Left Click Here First   Left Click Here

13. While the line is still attached to the cursor, move the cursor towards the top of the screen and left click once as shown in Figure 7.

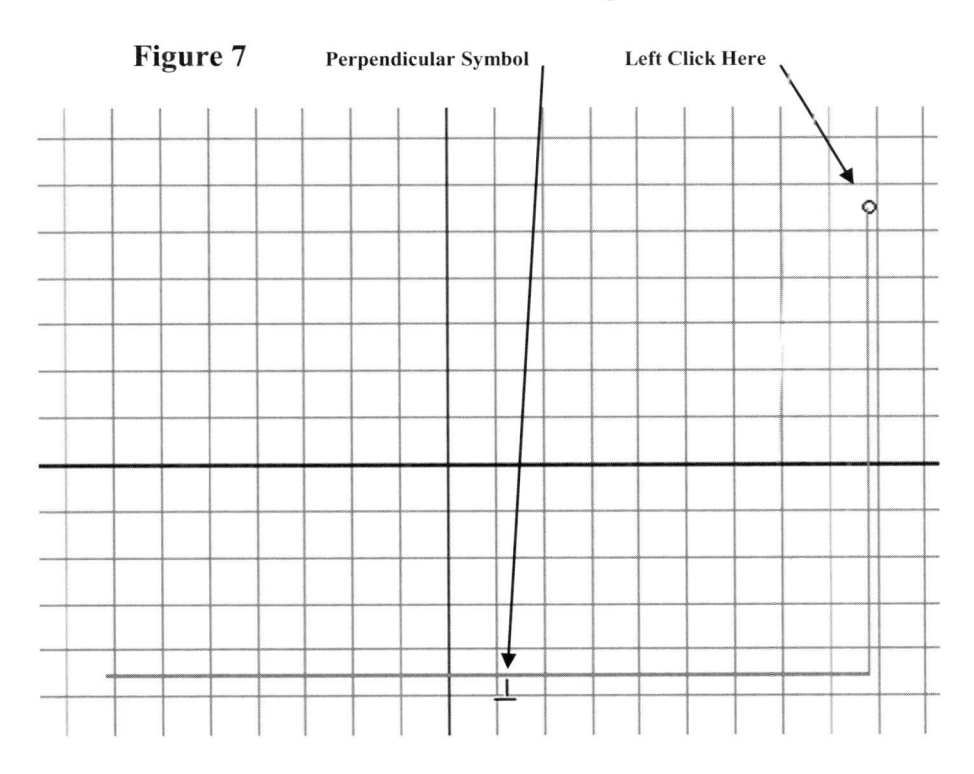

Figure 7   Perpendicular Symbol   Left Click Here

Chapter 1: Getting Started

14. Notice the "perpendicular" symbol that is displayed at the side of the screen.

15. This signifies that the vertical line is exactly 90 degrees (perpendicular) to the horizontal line.

16. With the line still attached to the cursor, move the cursor towards the left side of the screen as shown in Figure 8.

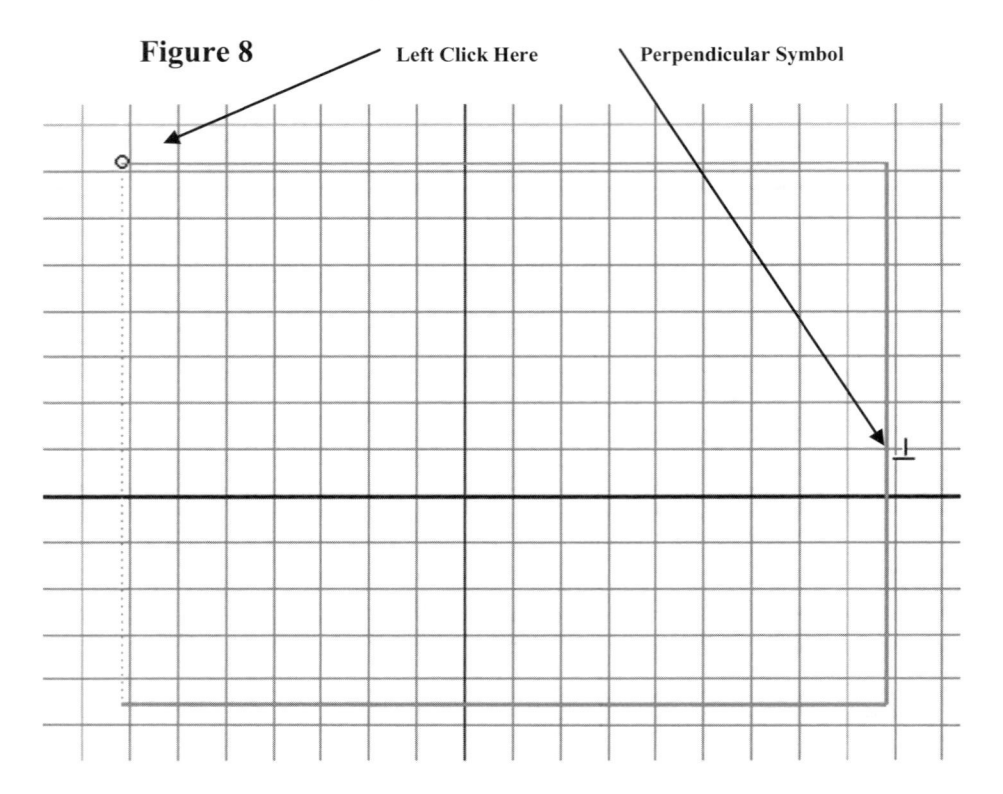

Figure 8 — Left Click Here — Perpendicular Symbol

17. Notice the line of small dots connecting the first and last points together. Left click once when the small dots appear as shown in Figure 8.

18. This will form a 90 degree box. Move the cursor down towards the original starting point. Ensure that a green dot appears (as shown in Figure 9) at the intersection of the two lines. This indicates that Inventor has "snapped" to the intersection of the lines. After the green dot appears, left click once. Notice the perpendicular symbol beneath the bottom of the box.

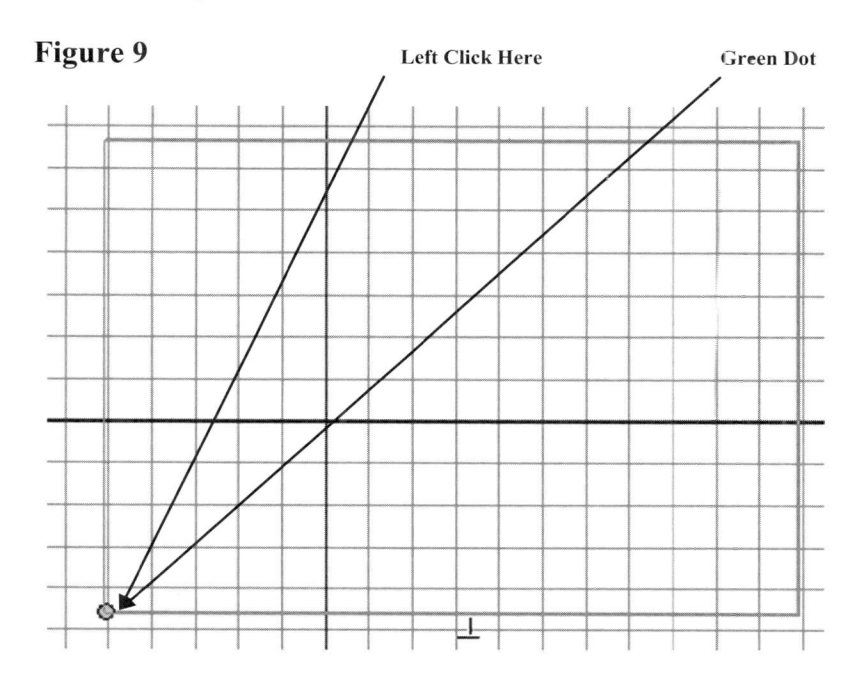

Figure 9

Left Click Here   Green Dot

19. Your screen should look similar to Figure 10.

Figure 10

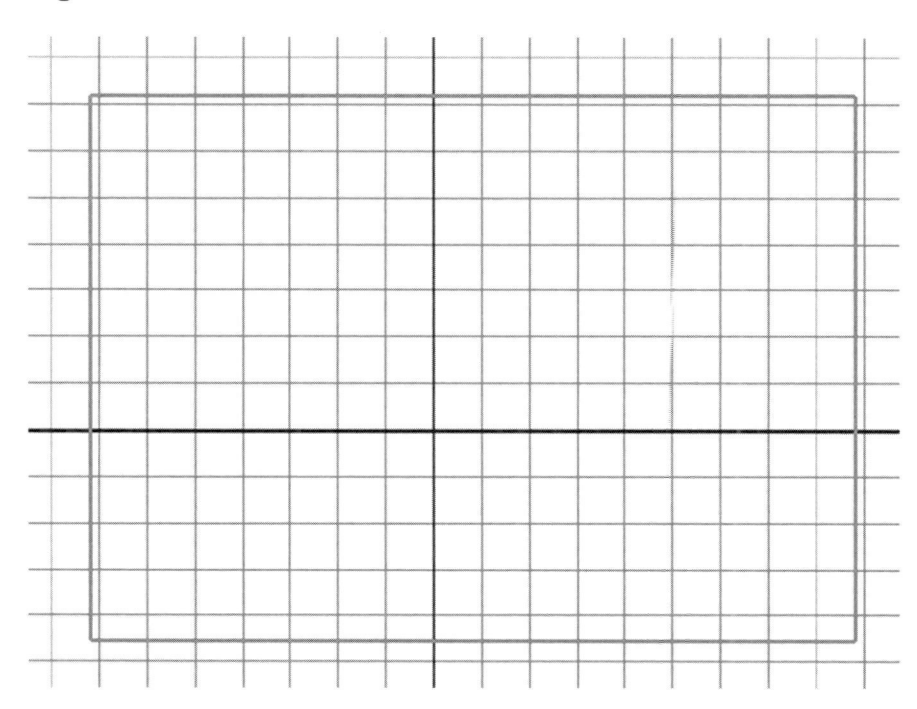

Chapter 1: Getting Started

20. Dimension the lines to the proper length. Before doing this use the keyboard and press **Esc** once or twice while the command is still active. Inventor will "get out" of the Line command. Alternatively, right click around the drawing. A pop up menu will appear. Left click on **Done [Esc]** as shown in Figure 11.

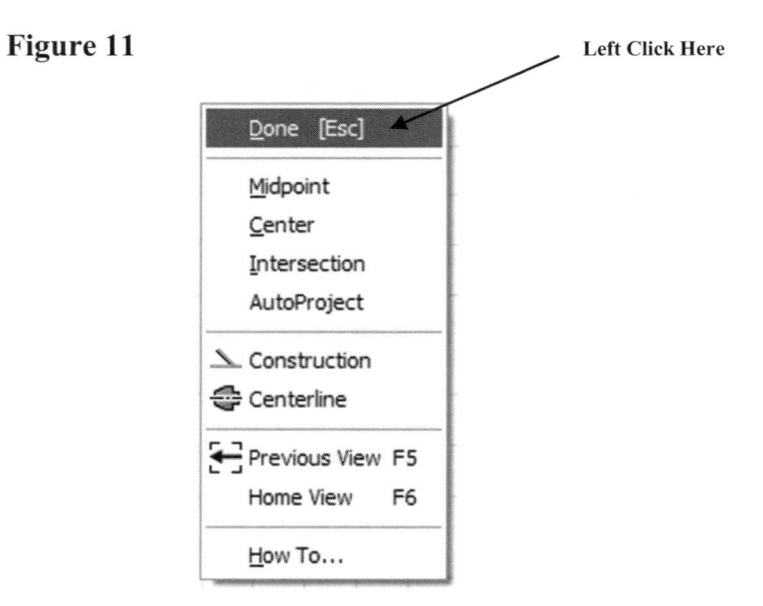

Figure 11

Chapter 1: Getting Started

21. Move the cursor to the middle left portion of the screen and left click on **General Dimension** as shown in Figure 12.

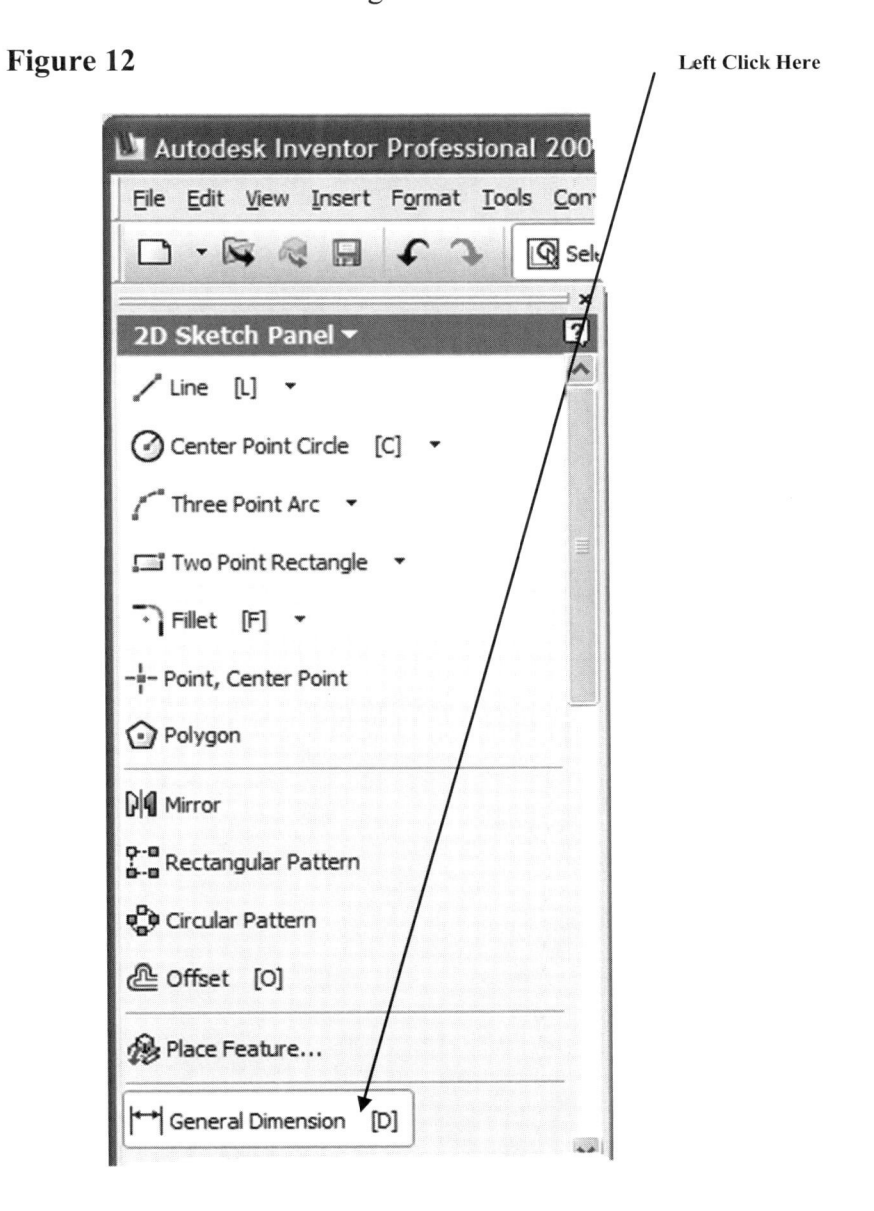

Figure 12   **Left Click Here**

11

Chapter 1: Getting Started

22. After selecting **General Dimension** move the cursor over the bottom horizontal line. The line will turn red as shown in Figure 13. Select the line by left clicking anywhere on the line **or** on each of the end points. To use the end points of the line, move the cursor over one of the end points. A small red square will appear. Left click once and move the cursor to the other end point. Another red square will appear. Left click once. The dimension will now be attached to the cursor. Move the cursor up and down to verify it is attached.

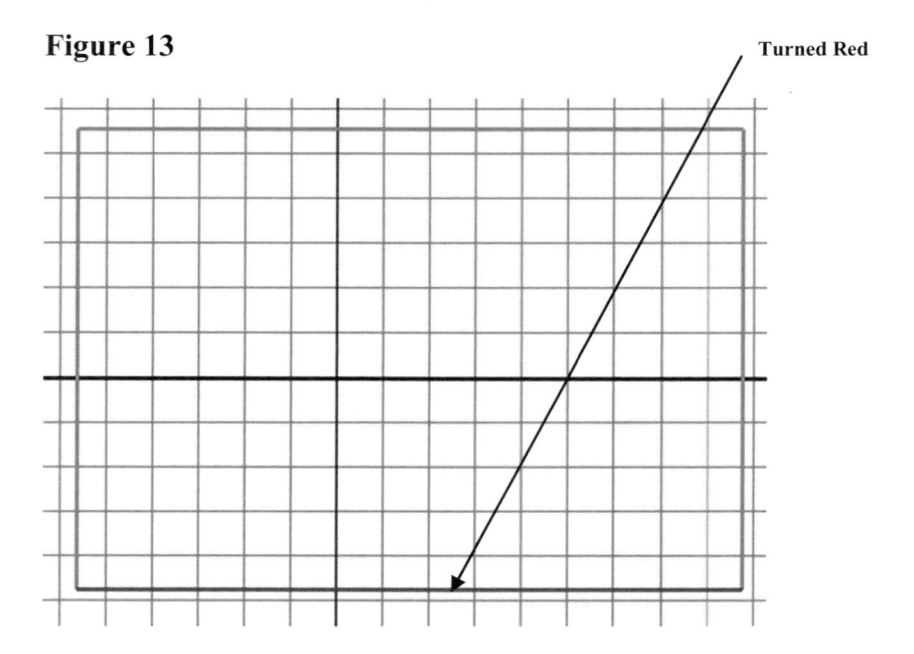

Figure 13   **Turned Red**

Chapter 1: Getting Started

23. Move the cursor down. The actual dimension of the line will appear as shown in Figure 14.

Figure 14   **Left Click Here**

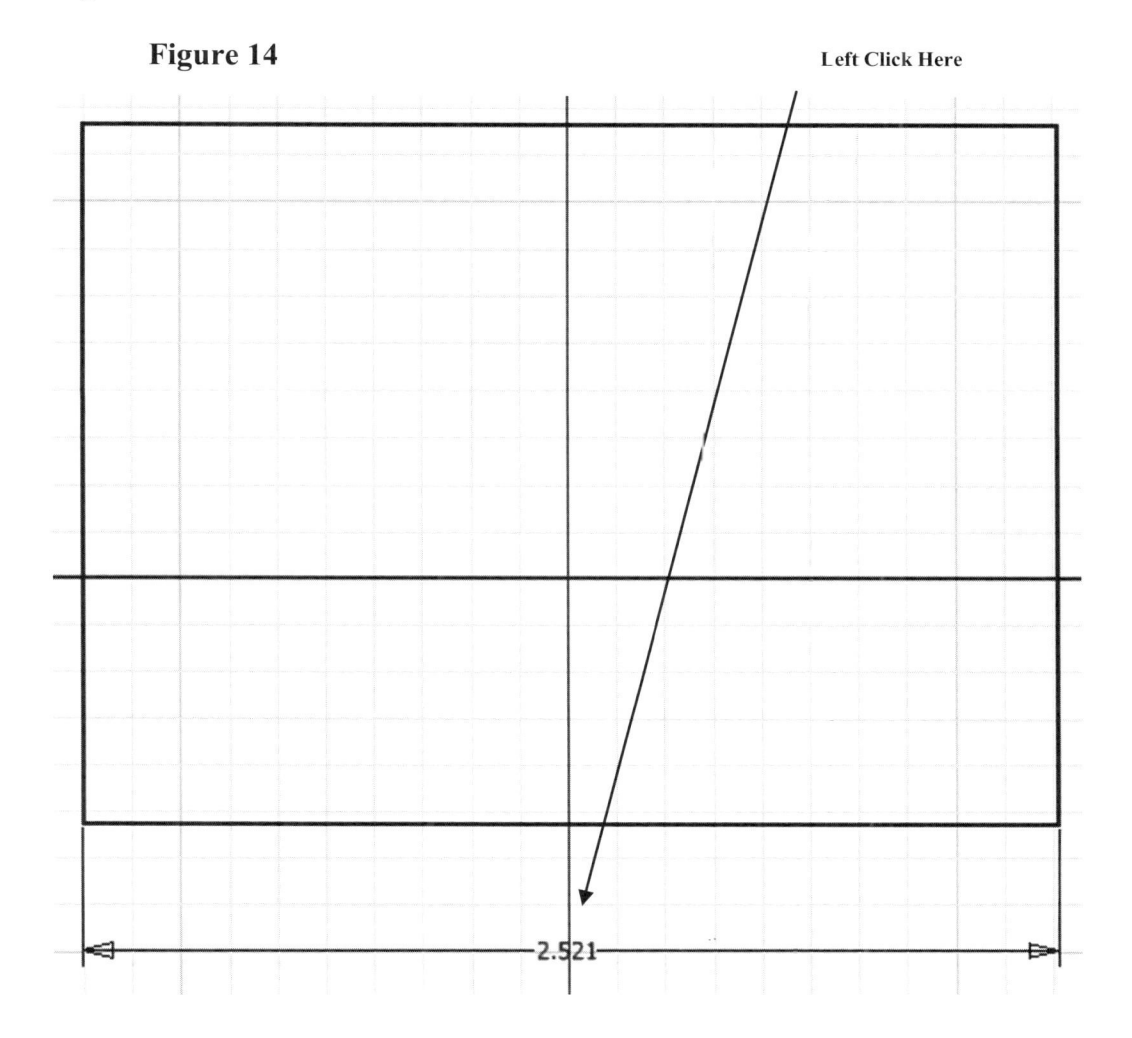

Chapter 1: Getting Started

24. Move the cursor to where the dimension will be placed and left click once. While the dimension is still in red, left click once. The Edit Dimension dialog box will appear as shown in Figure 15.

25. To edit the dimension, type **2.00** in the Edit Dimension dialog box (while the current dimension is highlighted) and press **Enter** on the keyboard.

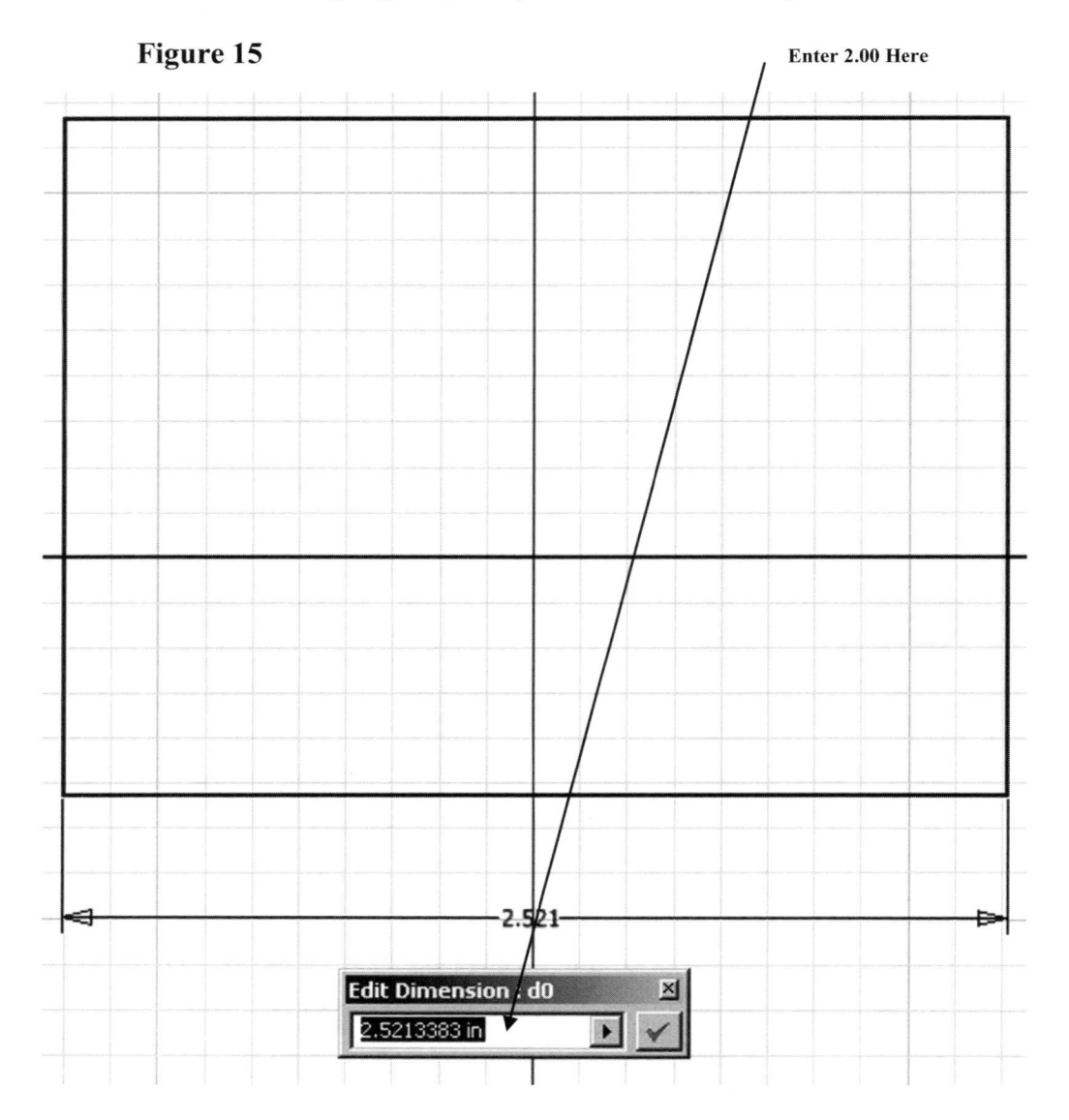

Figure 15

14

Chapter 1: Getting Started

26. The dimension of the line will become 2 inches as shown in Figure 16.

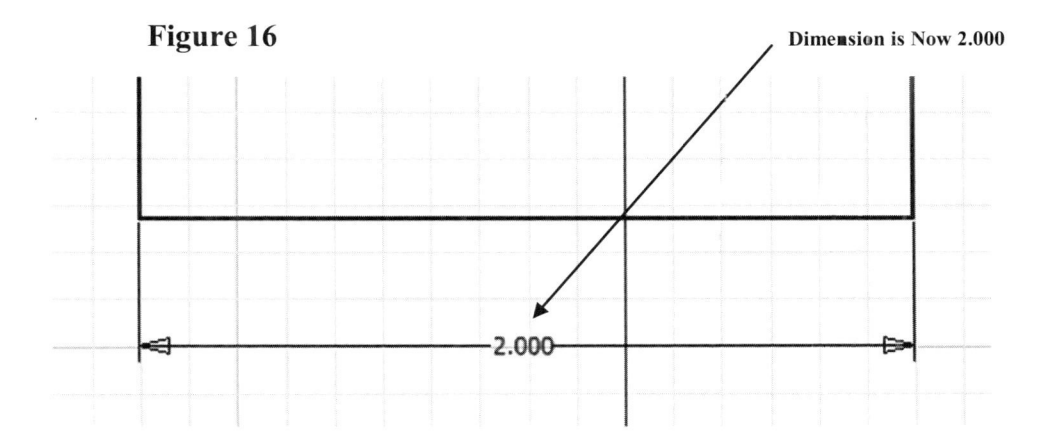

Figure 16

Dimension is Now 2.000

27. Select **General Dimension** as shown in Figure 17.

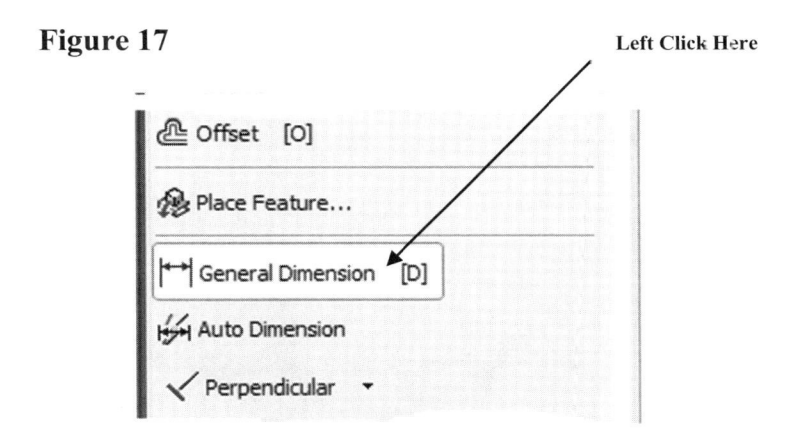

Figure 17

Left Click Here

15

Chapter 1: Getting Started

28. After selecting **General Dimension** move the cursor over the right side vertical line. The line will turn red as shown in Figure 18. Left click once on the line.

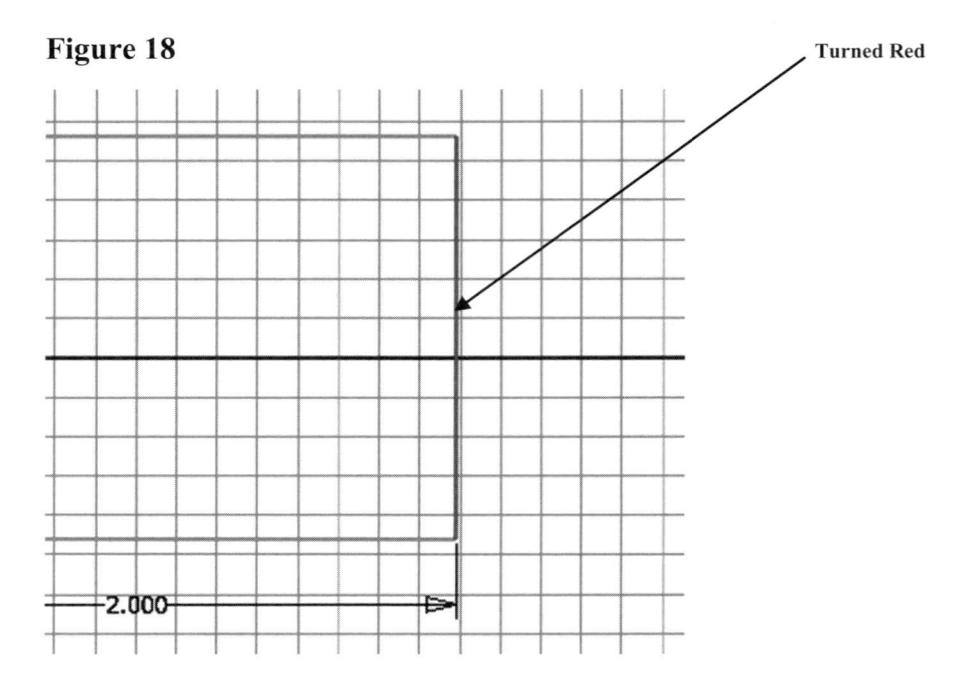

Figure 18   Turned Red

Chapter 1: Getting Started

29. The dimension is attached to the cursor. Move the cursor up and down to verify it is attached. Move the cursor to the right of the line where the dimension will be placed and left click once. While the dimension is still red, left click the mouse once. The Edit Dimension dialog box will appear as shown in Figure 19.

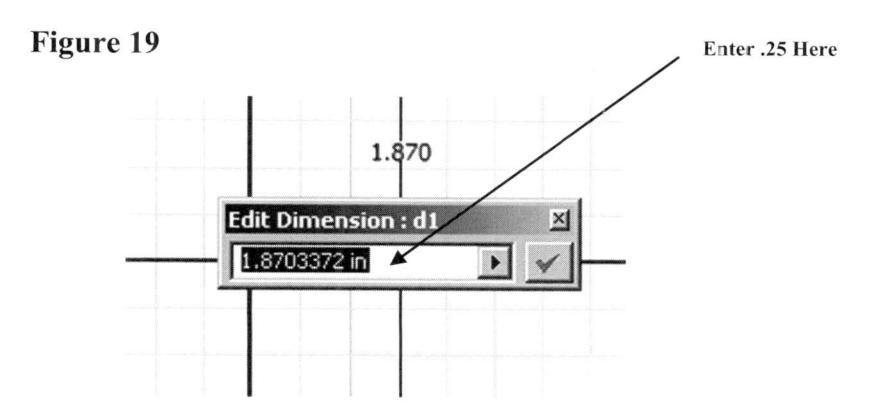

Figure 19

Enter .25 Here

30. To edit the dimension, enter **.25** in the Edit Dimension dialog box (while the current dimension is highlighted) and press **Enter** on the keyboard.

31. The screen should look similar to Figure 20.

Figure 20

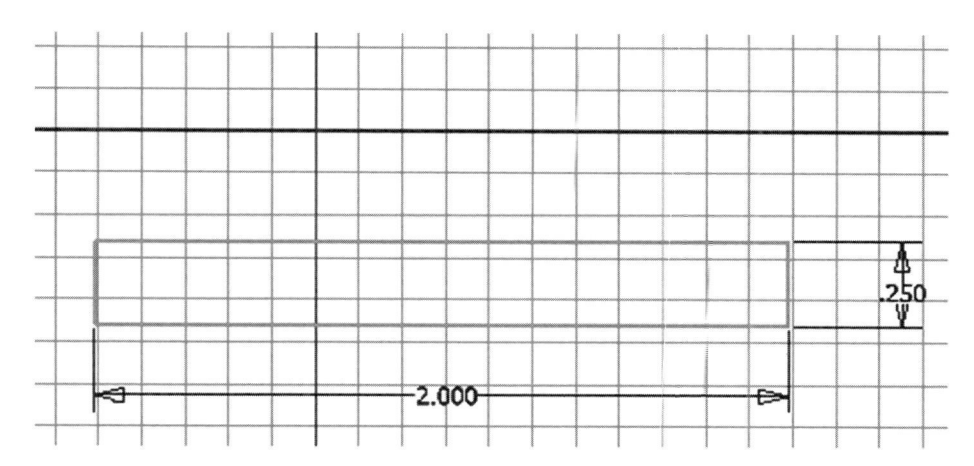

17

Chapter 1: Getting Started

32. Move the cursor to the upper left corner of the screen and left click on **Line** as shown in Figure 21.

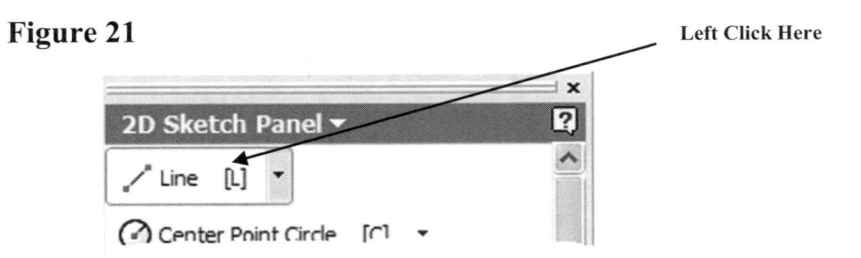

Figure 21

Left Click Here

33. Move the cursor to the upper left corner of the box and left click once as shown in Figure 22.

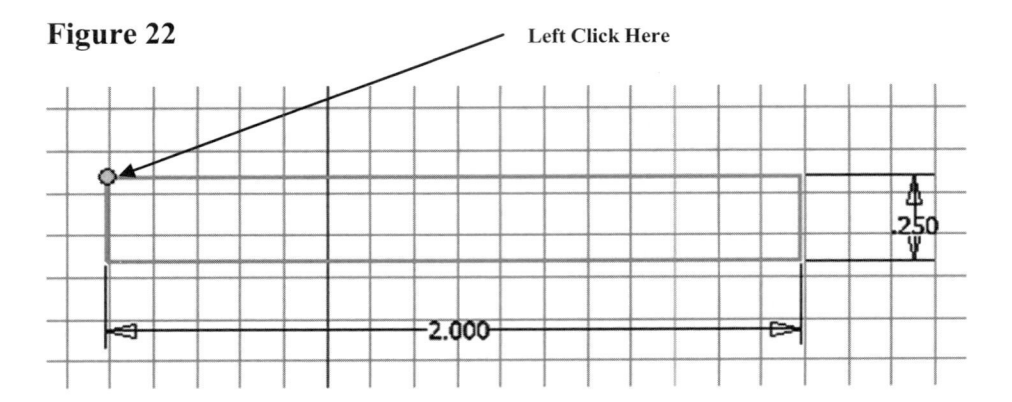

Figure 22

Left Click Here

34. Move the cursor upward to create a vertical line as shown in Figure 23.

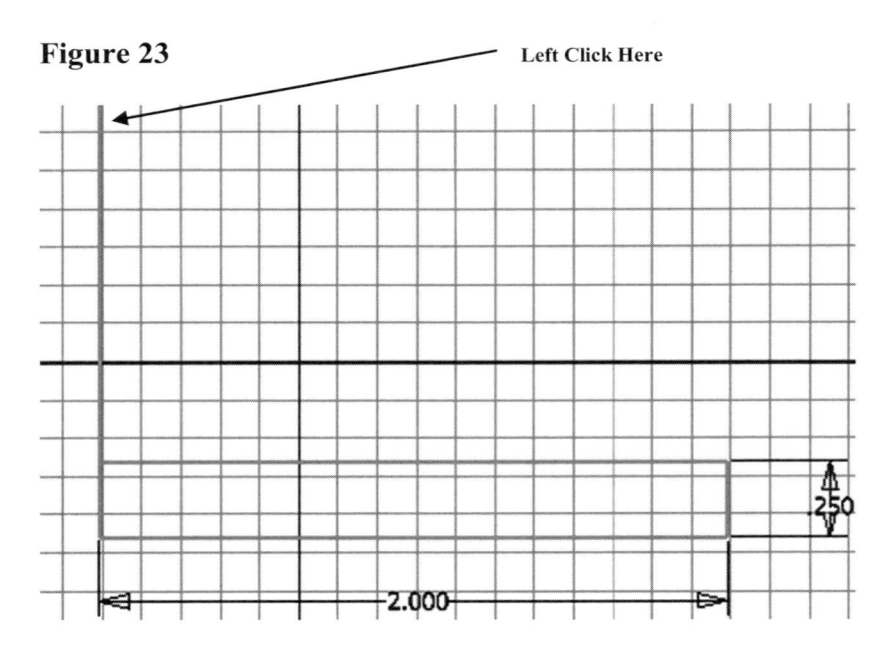

Figure 23

Left Click Here

Chapter 1: Getting Started

35. With the line still attached to the cursor, left click once then move the cursor to the left side of the screen similar to what is shown in Figure 24.

Figure 24 — Left Click Here

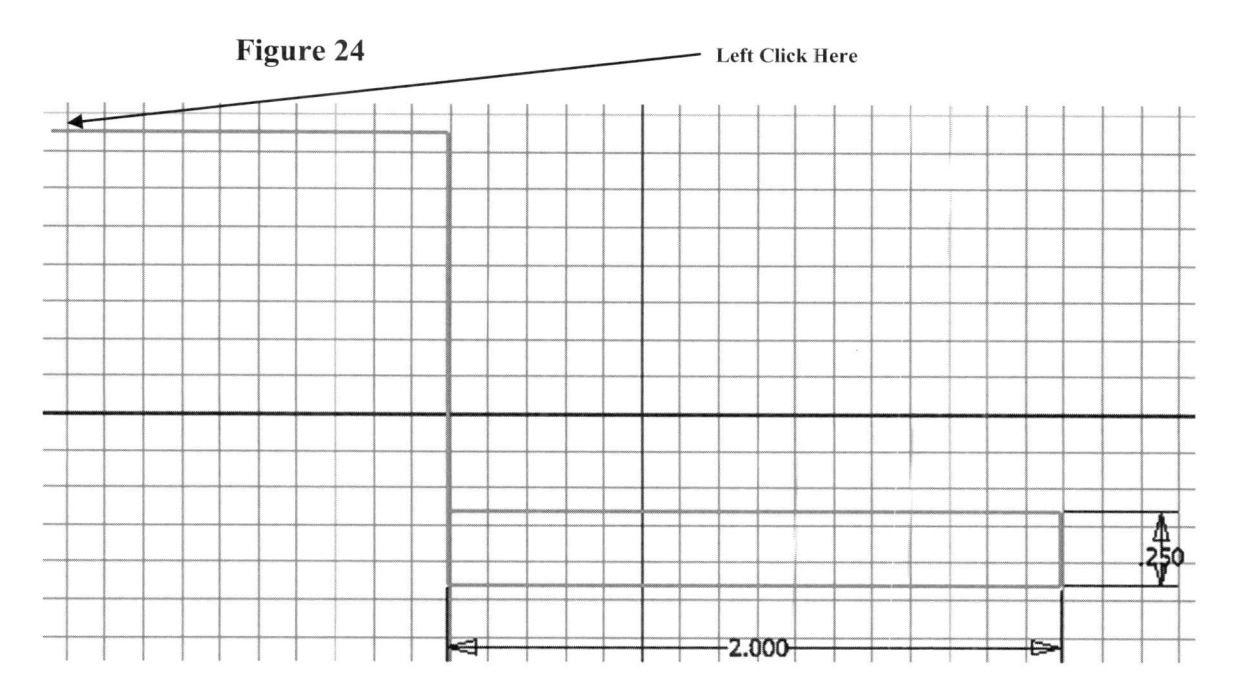

36. With the line still attached to the cursor, left click once then move the cursor to the top of the screen similar to what is shown in Figure 25.

Figure 25 — Left Click Here

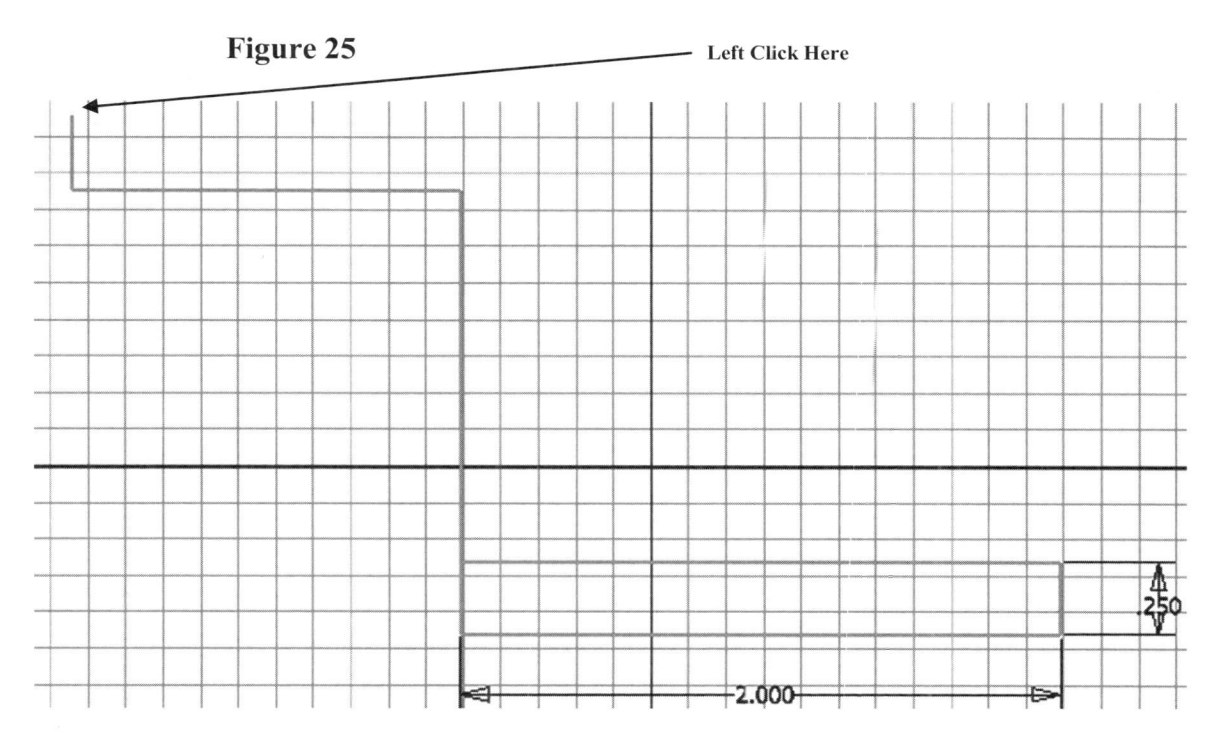

Chapter 1: Getting Started

37. With the line still attached to the cursor, left click once then move the cursor to the right side of the screen as shown in Figure 26. Notice the Perpendicular symbol.

Figure 26   Perpendicular Symbol   Left Click Here

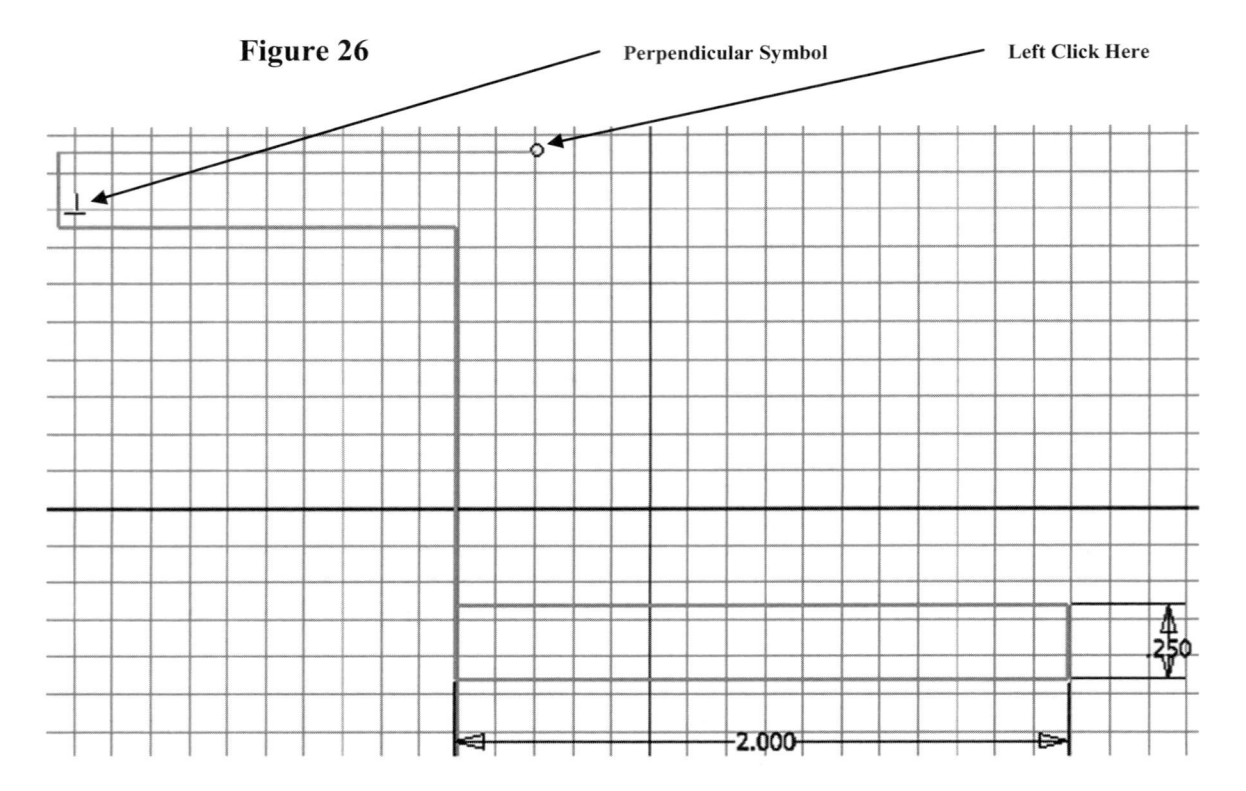

Chapter 1: Getting Started

38. With the line still attached to the cursor, left click once then move the cursor down towards the bottom of the screen similar to what is shown in Figure 27. Notice a yellow dot appearing at the intersection of the two lines. Once the left mouse button is clicked the yellow dot will briefly turn green. This indicates that the lines are all connected.

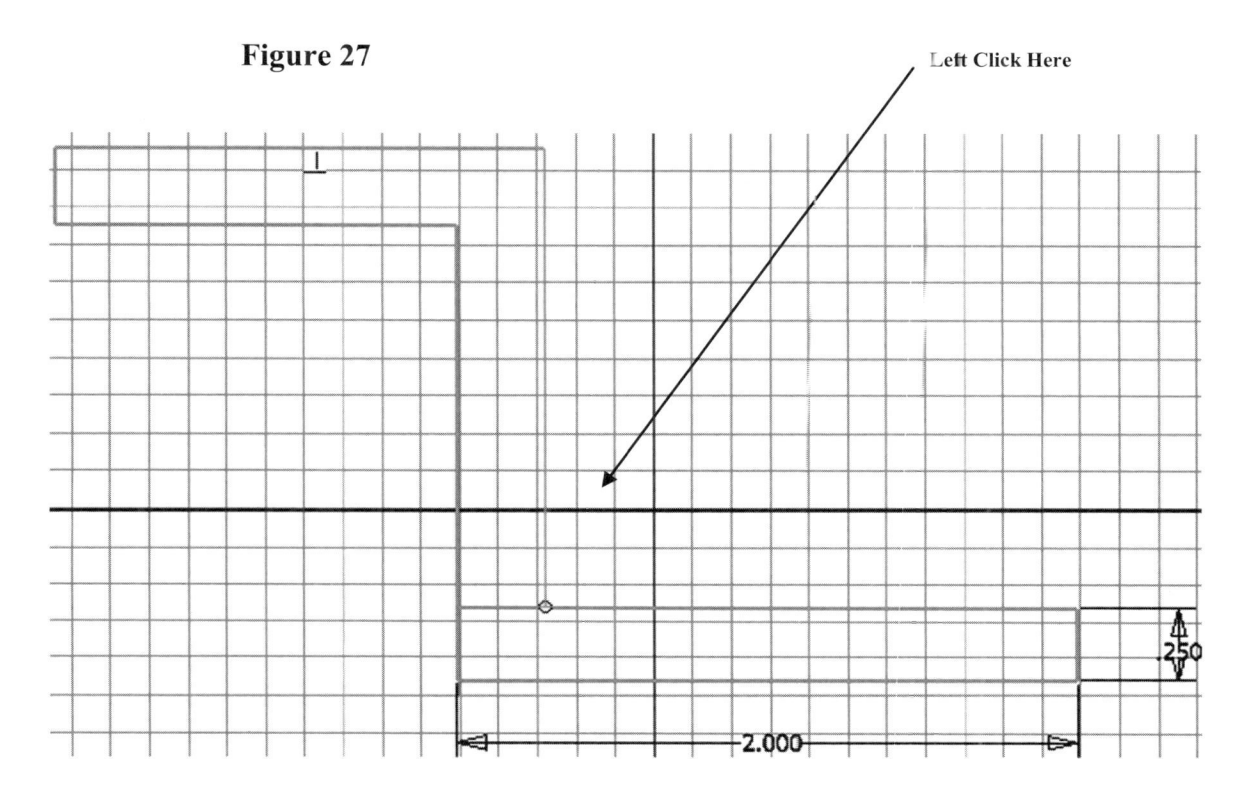

Figure 27

Left Click Here

39. Move the cursor to the middle left portion of the screen and left click on **Trim** as shown in Figure 28.

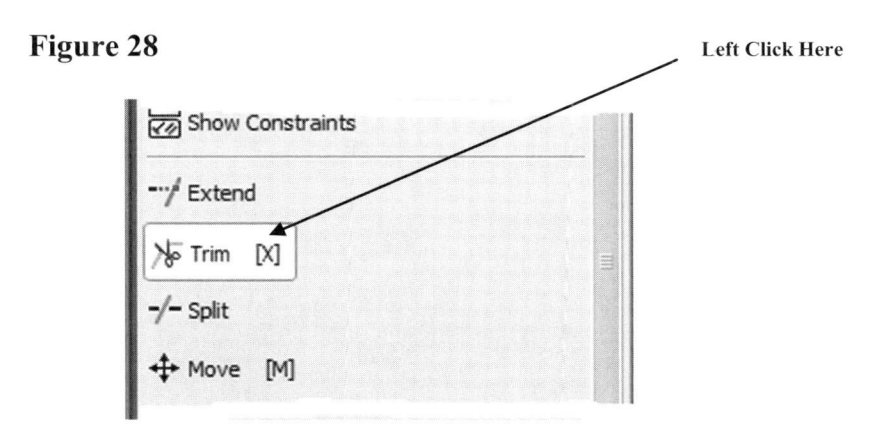

Figure 28

Left Click Here

21

Chapter 1: Getting Started

40. Move the cursor over the portion of the line that is shown in Figure 29. The line will become dashed. Inventor is guessing that this line will be trimmed.

Figure 29

Line Becomes Dashed

41. While the line is dashed, left click on the dashed portion. The line will be trimmed as shown in Figure 30.

Figure 30

Line is Trimmed

42. Move the cursor over the line in the lower left corner of the drawing as shown in Figure 31. The line will turn red. This particular line will have to be deleted so that the line above can be extended the full length.

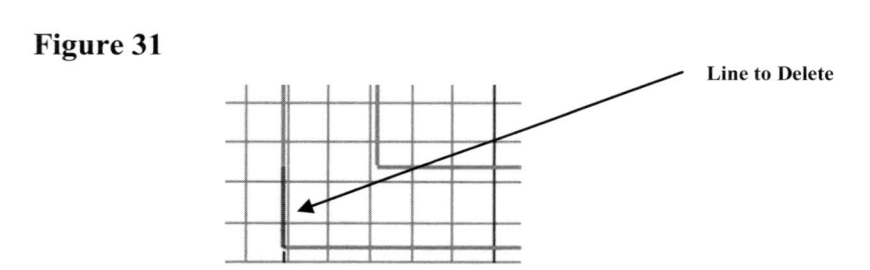

Figure 31

Line to Delete

Chapter 1: Getting Started

43. After the line turns red, right click the mouse. A pop up menu will appear as shown in Figure 32.

Figure 32

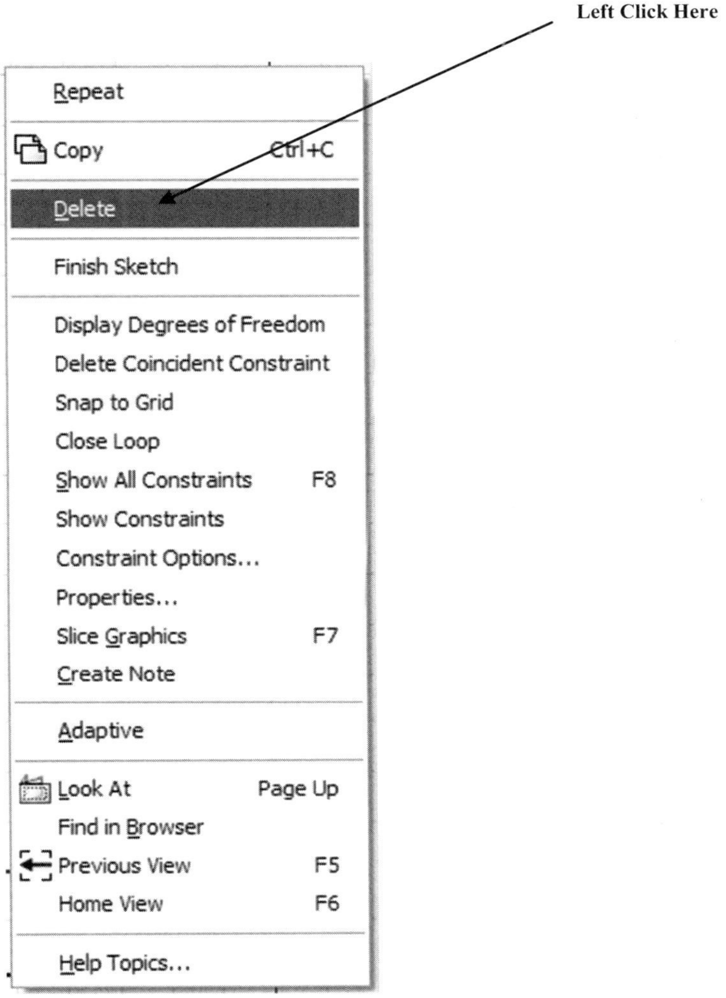

Left Click Here

44. Left click on **Delete**.

45. The line will be deleted as shown in Figure 33.

Figure 33

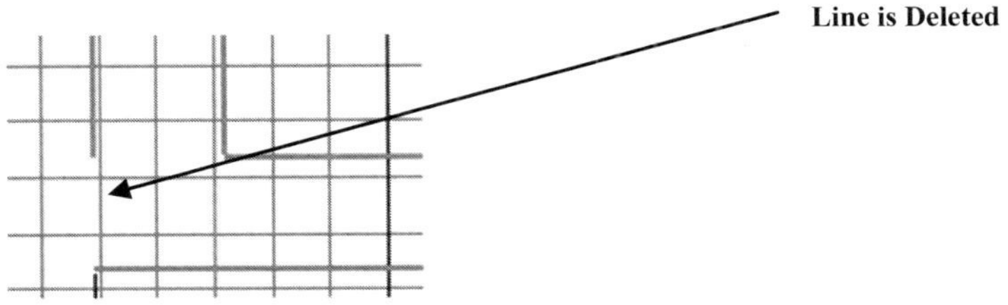

Line is Deleted

23

Chapter 1: Getting Started

46. Move the cursor to the middle left portion of the screen and left click on **Extend** as shown in Figure 34.

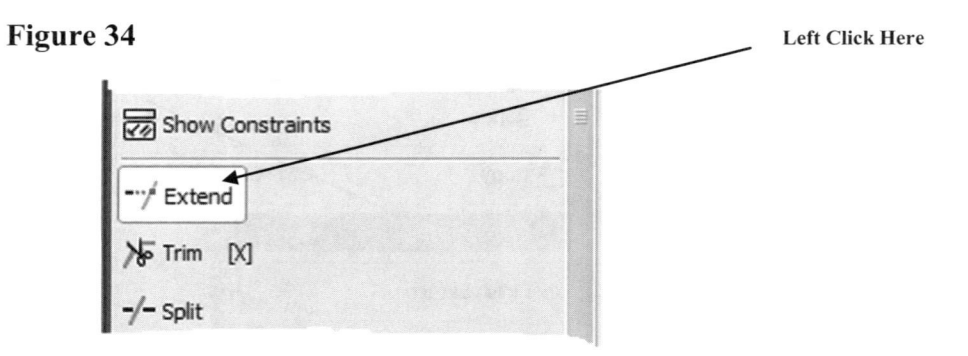

Figure 34   **Left Click Here**

47. Move the cursor to the line above the recently deleted line. This is the line that will be extended. After the cursor is over the line it will turn red and extend a line downward, as shown in Figure 35.

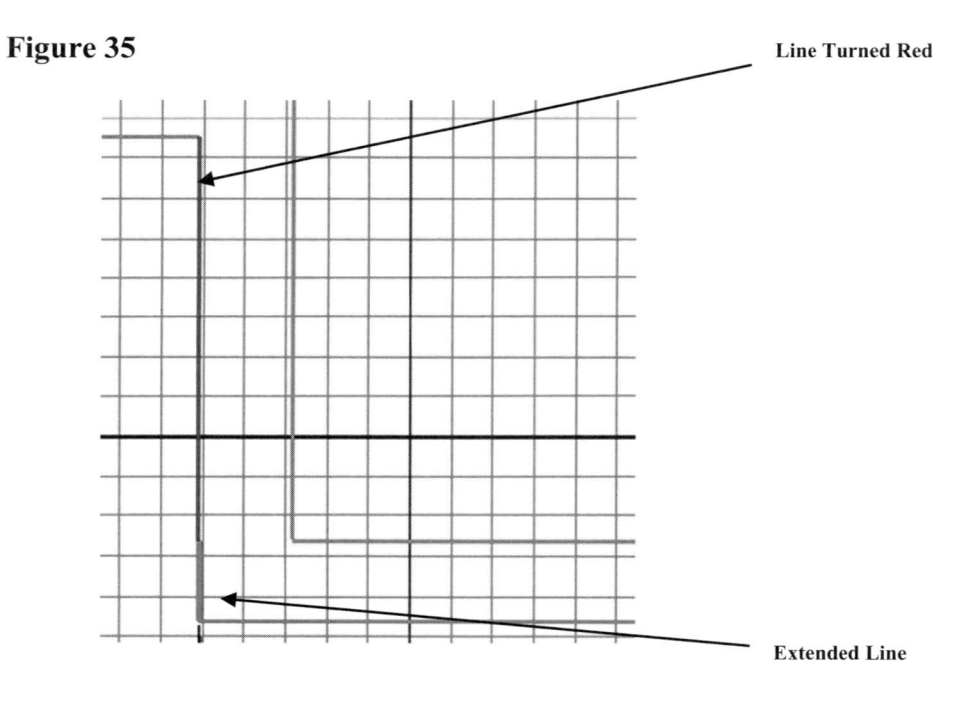

Figure 35   **Line Turned Red**

Extended Line

Chapter 1: Getting Started

48. After the extended line appears, left click the mouse. The line will extend creating one continuous line as shown in Figure 36.

Figure 36

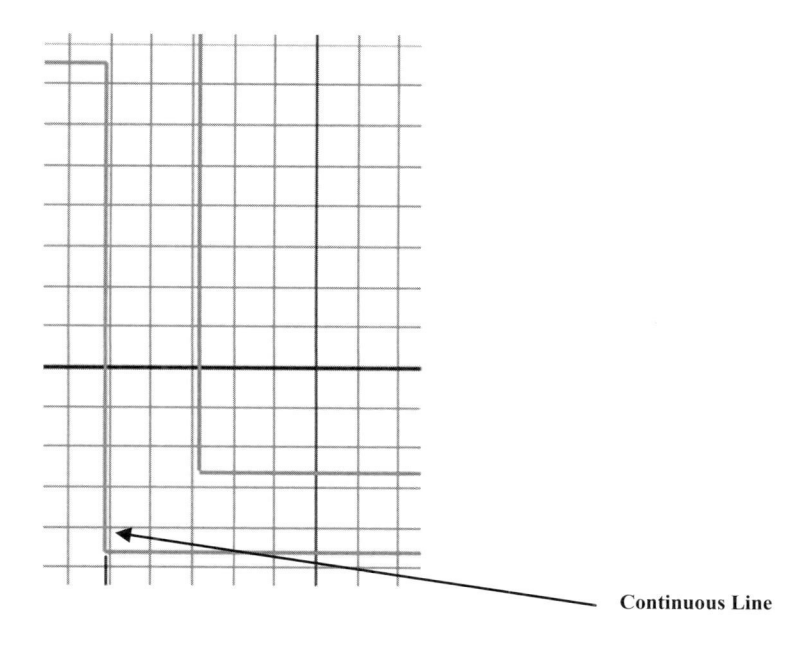

Continuous Line

49. Move the cursor to the middle left portion of the screen and left click on **General Dimension** as shown in Figure 37.

Figure 37

Left Click Here

Chapter 1: Getting Started

50. After selecting **General Dimension** move the cursor over the left side vertical line. The line will turn red as shown in Figure 38. Left click on the line.

Figure 38

Line Turned Red

51. The dimension is attached to the cursor. Move the cursor back and forth to verify it is attached. Move the cursor to the left side of the line where the dimension will be placed and left click once. While the dimension is still red, left click the mouse once. The Edit Dimension dialog box will appear as shown in Figure 39.

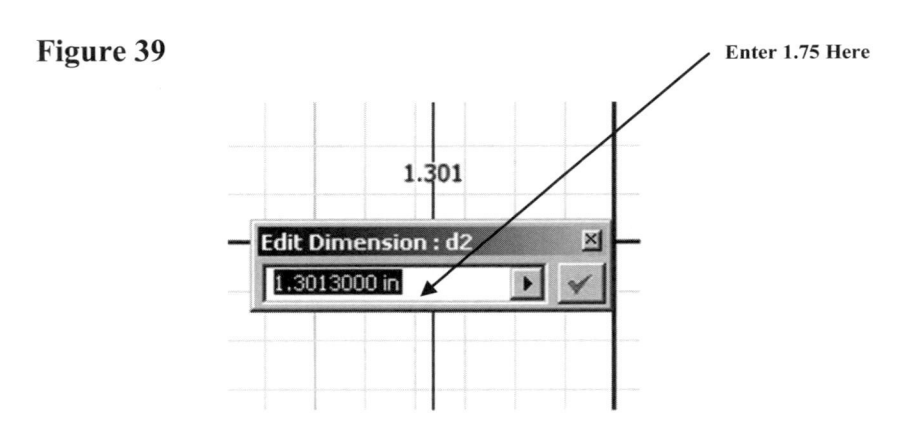

Figure 39

Enter 1.75 Here

52. To edit the dimension, enter **1.75** in the Edit Dimension dialog box (while the current dimension is highlighted) and press **Enter** on the keyboard.

Chapter 1: Getting Started

53. The dimension is now 1.750 as shown in Figure 40.

Figure 40

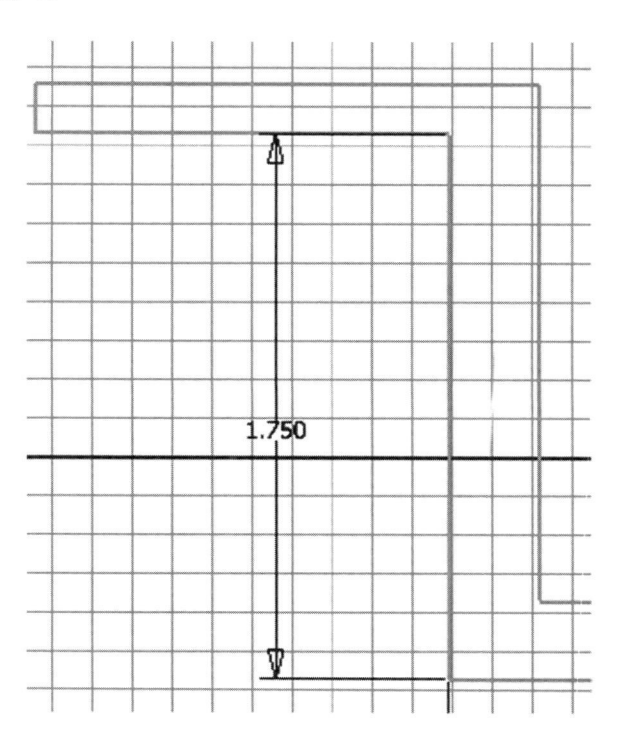

54. Move the cursor to the middle left portion of the screen and left click on **General Dimension** as shown in Figure 41.

Figure 41　　　　　　　　　　　　　　　　　　　　　　Left Click Here

27

Chapter 1: Getting Started

55. After selecting **General Dimension** move the cursor over the left side vertical line. The line will turn red as shown in Figure 42. Left click on the line.

Figure 42

Turned Red

56. The dimension is attached to the cursor. Move the cursor up and down to verify it is attached. Move the cursor to the left side of the line where the dimension will be placed and left click once. While the dimension is still red, left click the mouse once. The Edit Dimension dialog box will appear as shown in Figure 43.

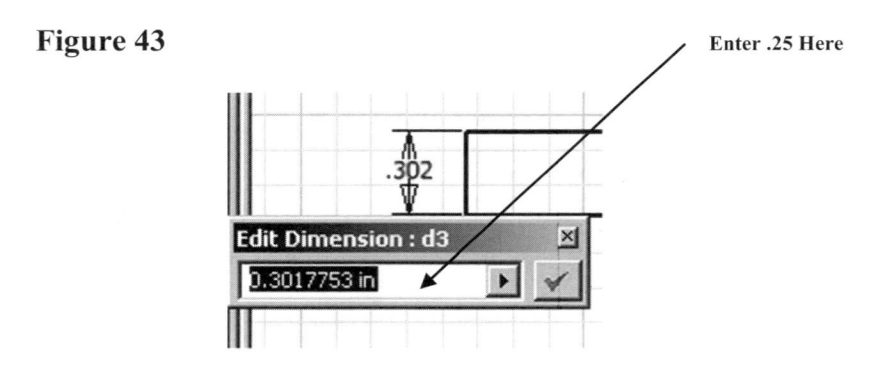

Figure 43

Enter .25 Here

57. To edit the dimension, enter **.250** in the Edit Dimension dialog box (while the current dimension is highlighted) and press **Enter** on the keyboard.

Chapter 1: Getting Started

58. The dimension is now .250 as shown in Figure 44.

Figure 44

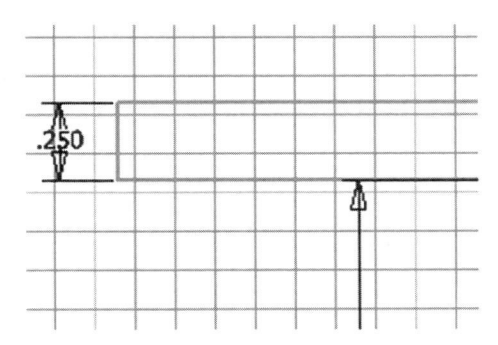

59. Move the cursor to the middle left portion of the screen and left click on **General Dimension** as shown in Figure 45.

Figure 45

Left Click Here

60. After selecting **General Dimension** move the cursor over the top horizontal line. The line will turn red as shown in Figure 46. Left click on the line.

Figure 46

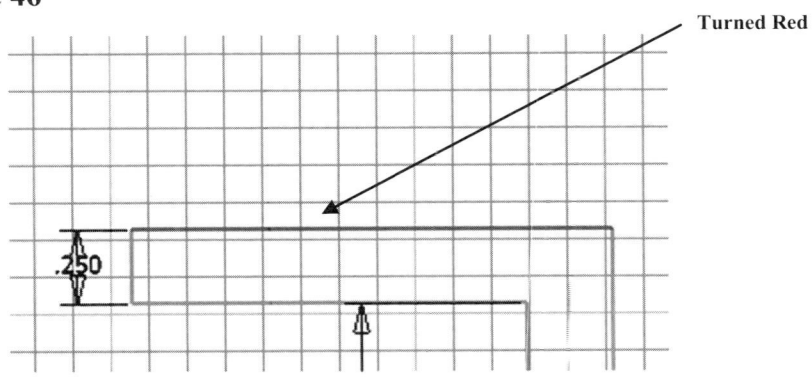

Turned Red

Chapter 1: Getting Started

61. The dimension is attached to the cursor. Move the cursor up and down to verify it is attached. Move the cursor above the line where the dimension will be placed and left click once. While the dimension is still red, left click the mouse once. The Edit Dimension dialog box will appear as shown in Figure 47.

Figure 47

Enter 1.75 Here

62. To edit the dimension, enter **1.750** in the Edit Dimension dialog box (while the current dimension is highlighted) and press **Enter** on the keyboard. The dimension is now 1.750 as shown in Figure 48.

Figure 48

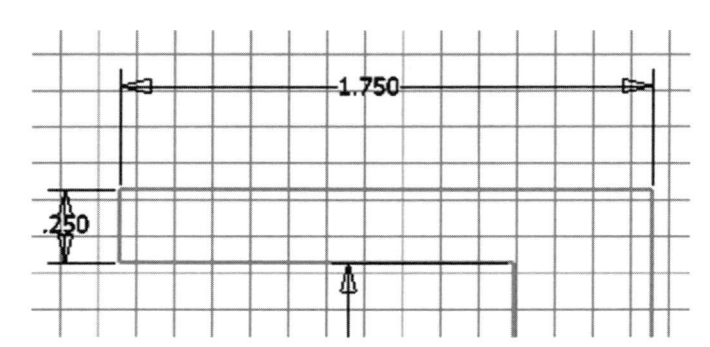

Chapter 1: Getting Started

63. Move the cursor to the middle left portion of the screen and left click on **General Dimension** as shown in Figure 49.

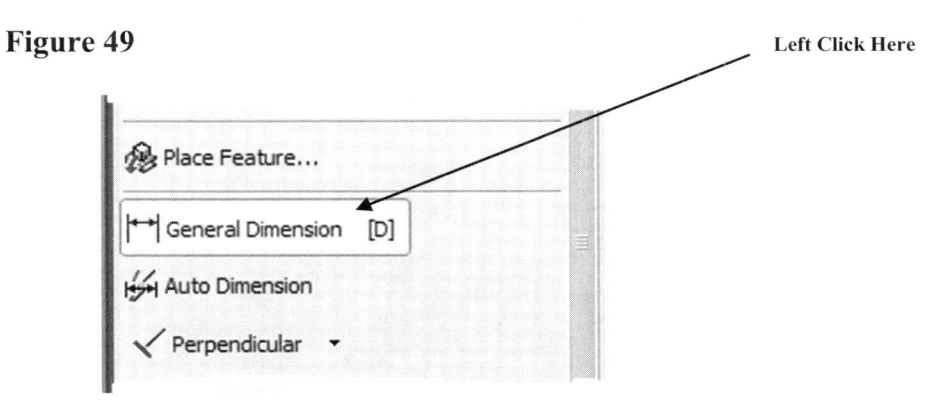

Figure 49

Left Click Here

64. After selecting **General Dimension** move the cursor over one of the two vertical lines. The line will turn red as shown in Figure 50. Left click once on the line.

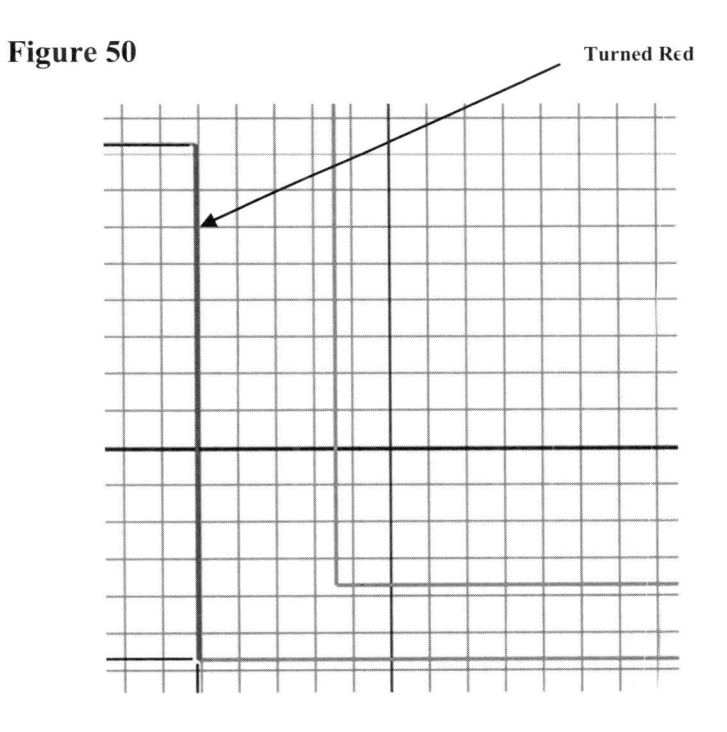

Figure 50

Turned Red

31

Chapter 1: Getting Started

65. Move the cursor to the other vertical line and left click after it turns red as shown in Figure 51.

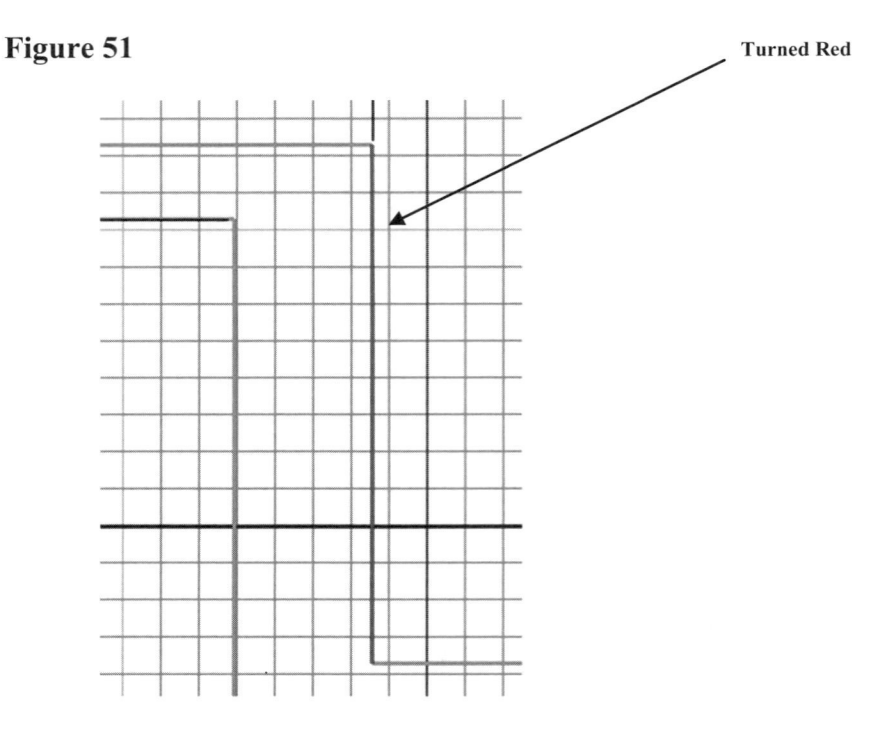

Figure 51

Turned Red

66. The dimension is attached to the cursor. Move the cursor up and down to verify it is attached. Move the cursor above the upper lines where the dimension will be placed and left click once. While the dimension is still red, left click the mouse once. The Edit Dimension dialog box will appear as shown in Figure 52.

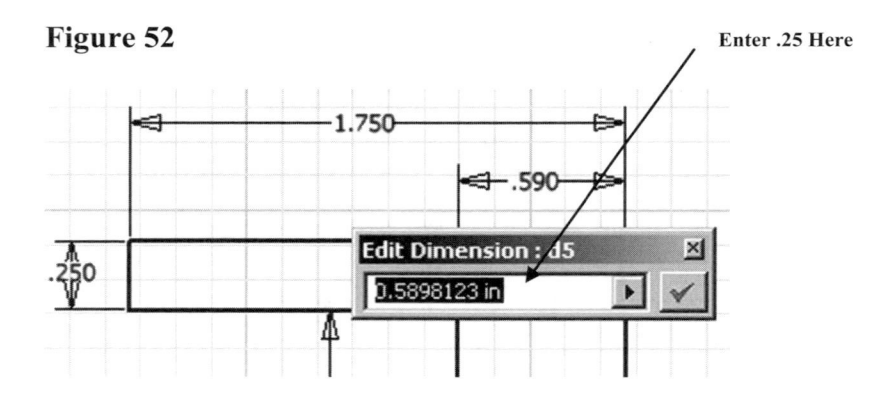

Figure 52

Enter .25 Here

67. To edit the dimension, enter **.25** in the Edit Dimension dialog box (while the current dimension is highlighted) and press **Enter** on the keyboard.

Chapter 1: Getting Started

68. Your screen should look similar to Figure 53.

Figure 53

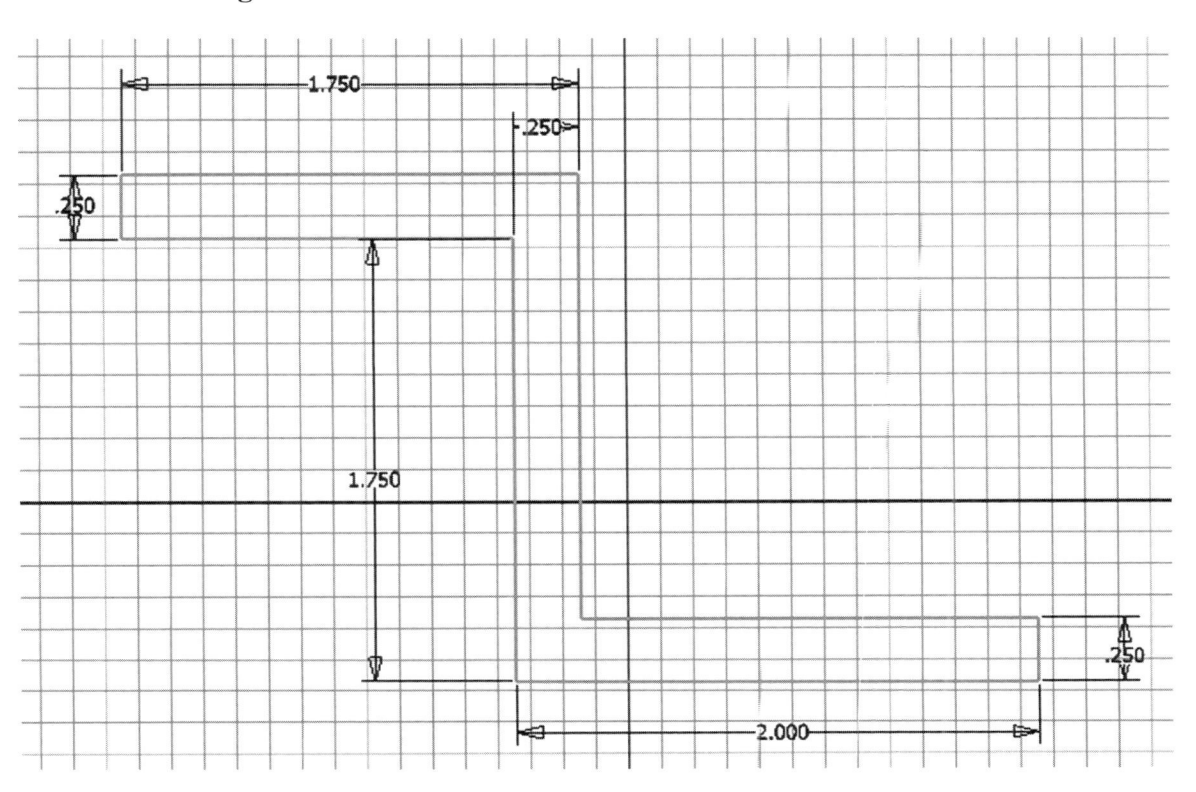

69. After the sketch is complete it is time to extrude the sketch into a solid. First press the **Esc** key to ensure that no commands are active.

Chapter 1: Getting Started

70. After you have verified that no commands are active, right click anywhere on the sketch. A pop up menu will appear. Left click on **Finish Sketch** as shown in Figure 54.

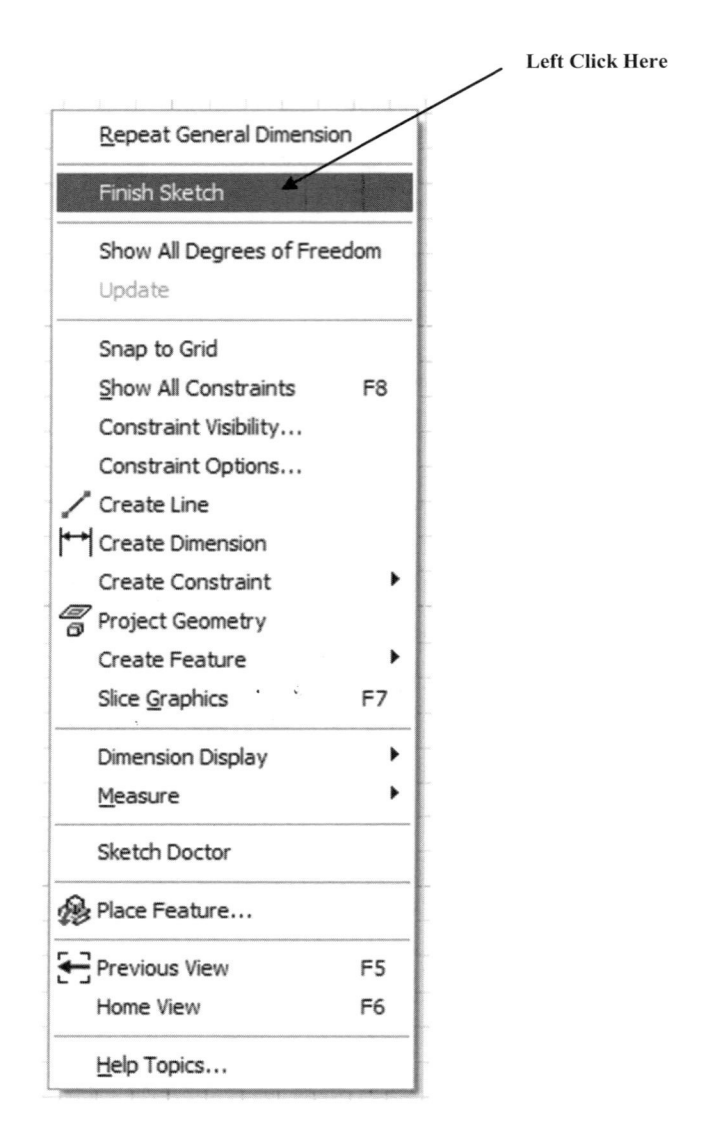

Figure 54

Left Click Here

71. Inventor is now out of the Sketch Panel and into the Part Features Panel. Notice that the commands at the left of the screen are now different. To work in the Part Features Panel a sketch must be present and have no opens (non-connected lines). If there are any opens in the sketch an error message will appear. Your screen should look similar to Figure 55.

Figure 55

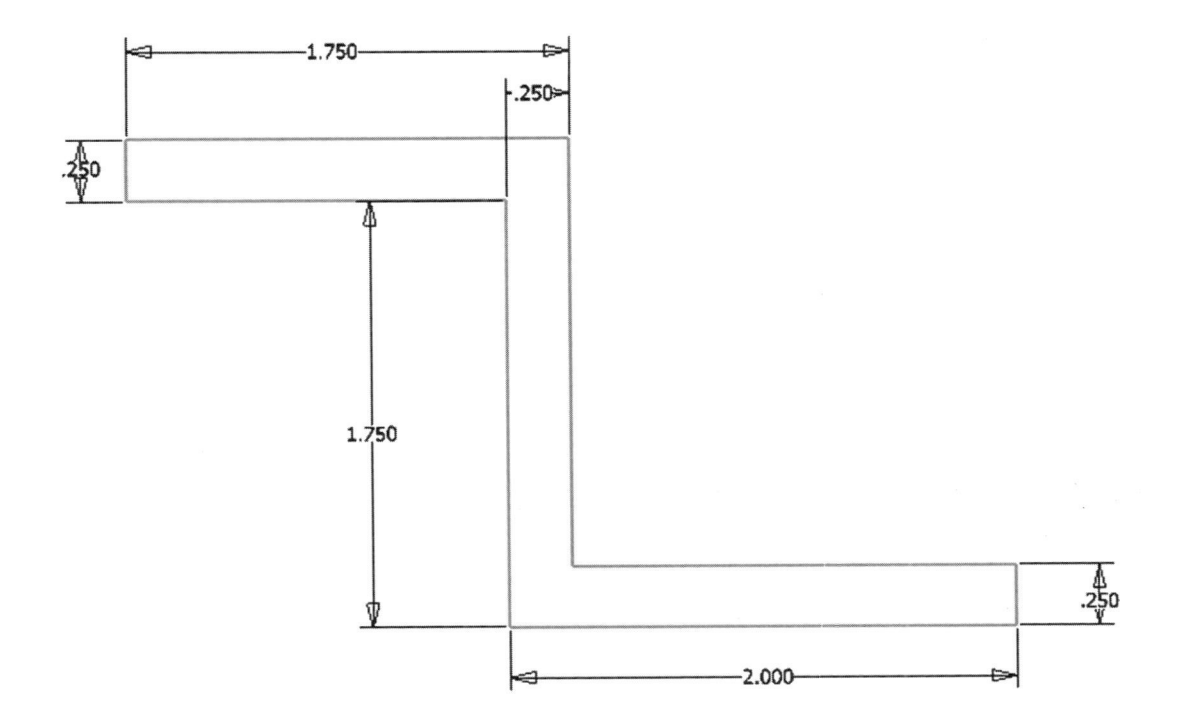

Chapter 1: Getting Started

72. Right click anywhere on the sketch. A pop up menu will appear. Left click on **Home View** (also known as **Isometric View**) as shown in Figure 56.

Figure 56   Left Click Here

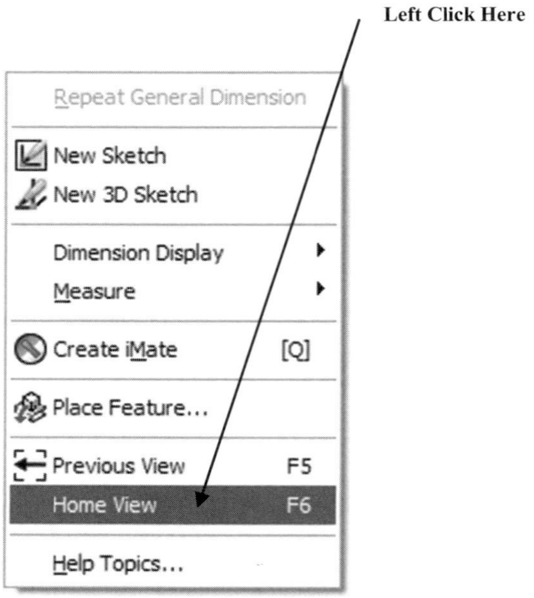

Chapter 1: Getting Started

73. The view is now isometric as shown in Figure 57.

Figure 57

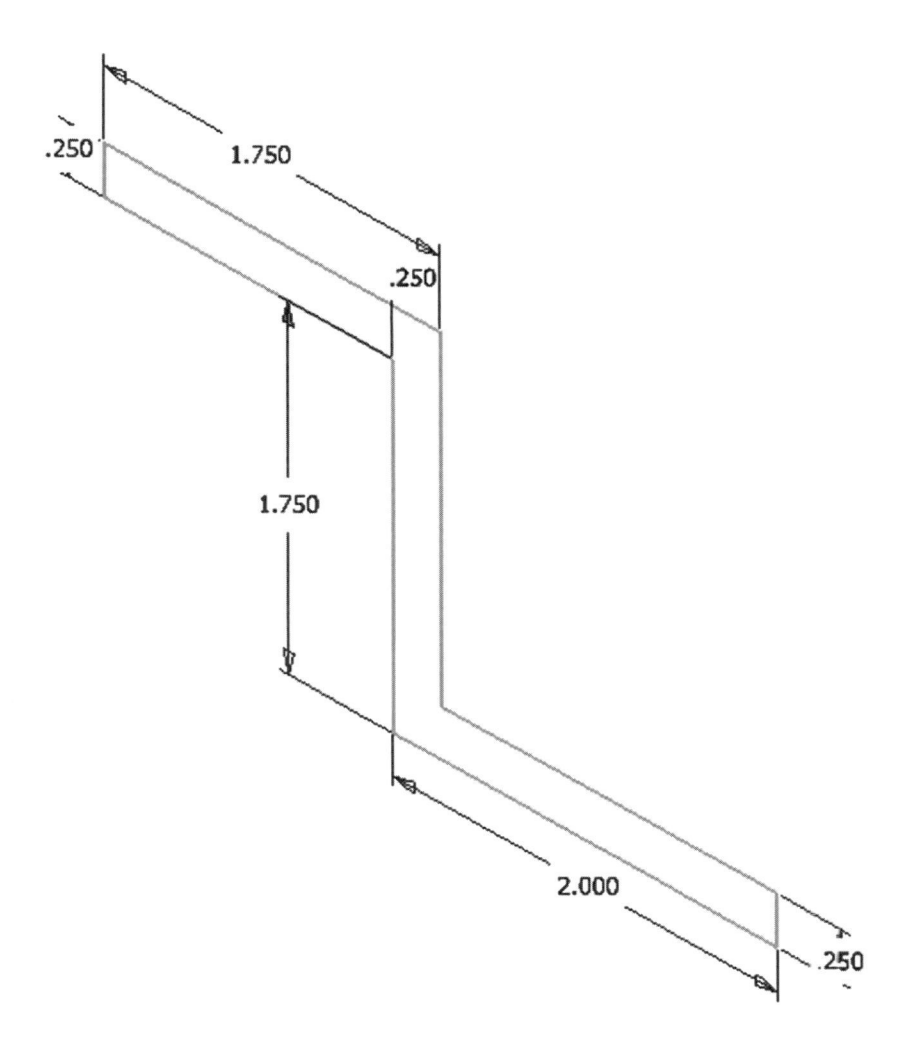

Chapter 1: Getting Started

74. Move the cursor to the upper left portion of the screen and left click on **Extrude.** The Extrude dialog box will appear. Inventor also provides a preview of the extrusion. If Inventor gave you an error message there are opens (non-connected lines) somewhere on the sketch. Check each intersection for opens by using the **Extend** and **Trim** commands. Your screen should look similar to Figure 58.

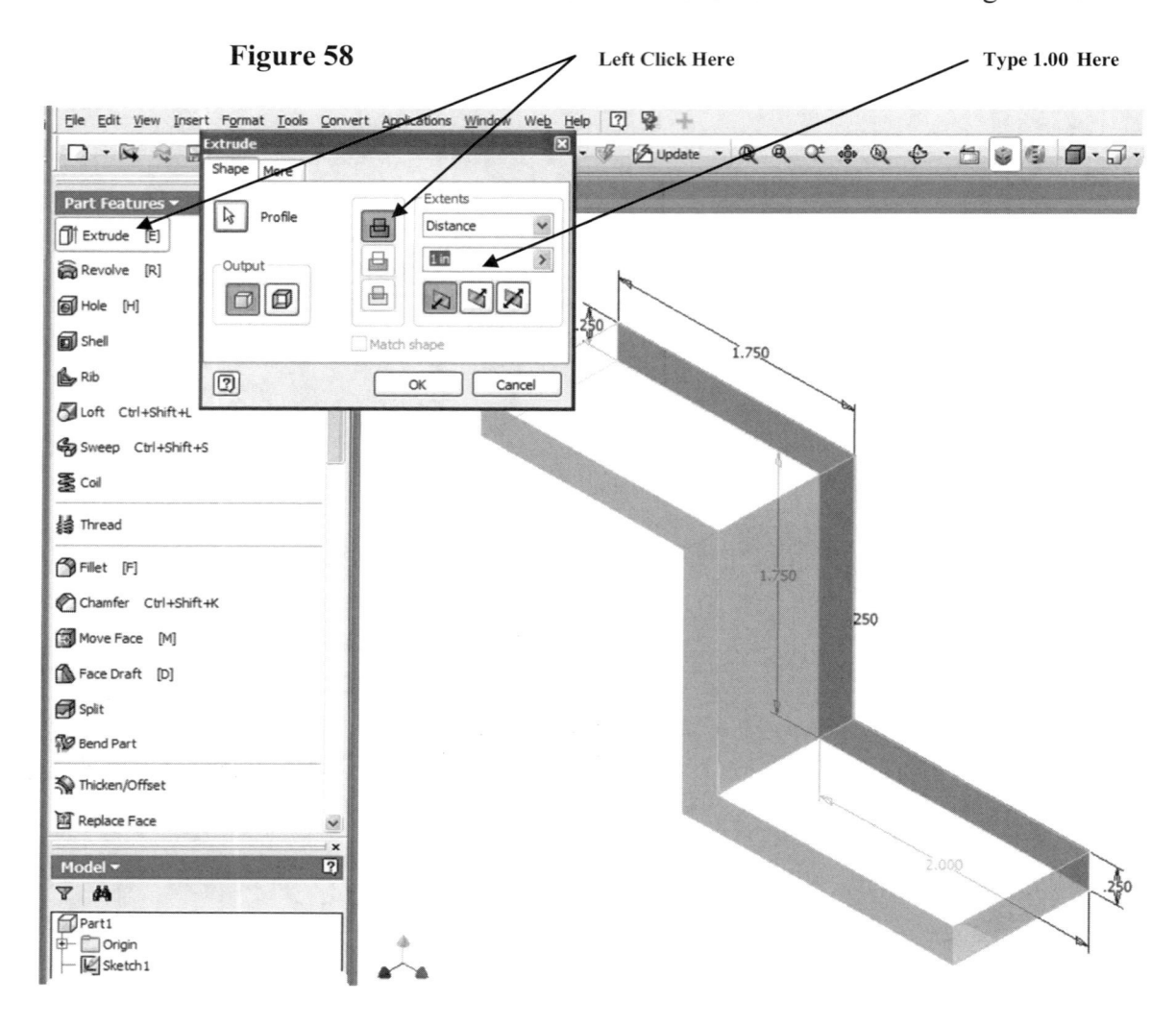

Figure 58

75. While the text located under "Distance" is still highlighted, enter **1.000** and left click on **OK**. Inventor will create a solid from the sketch as shown in Figure 58.

76. Your screen should look similar to Figure 59.

Figure 59

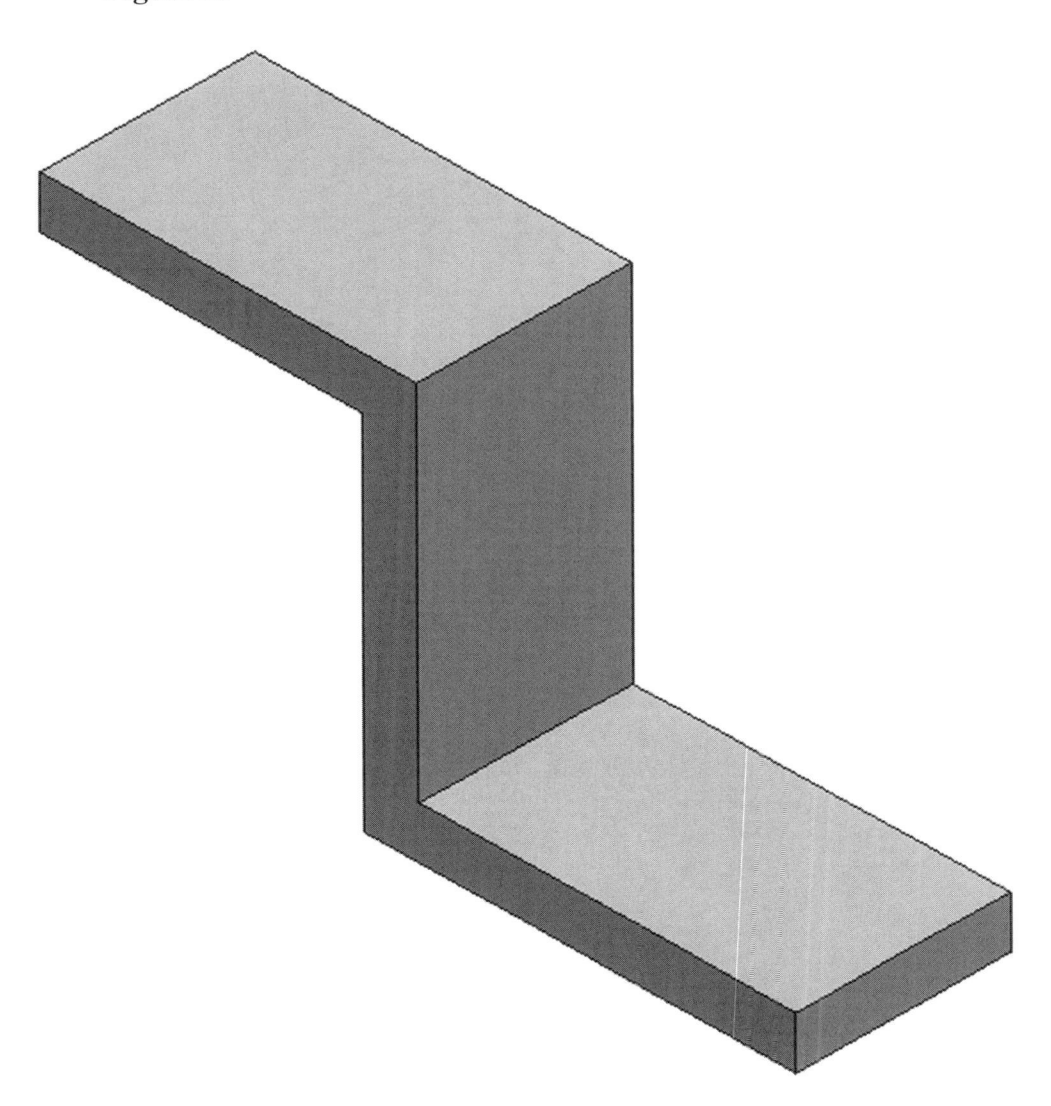

Chapter 1: Getting Started

77. Move the cursor to the middle left portion of the screen and left click on **Fillet**. The Fillet dialog box will appear as shown in Figure 60.

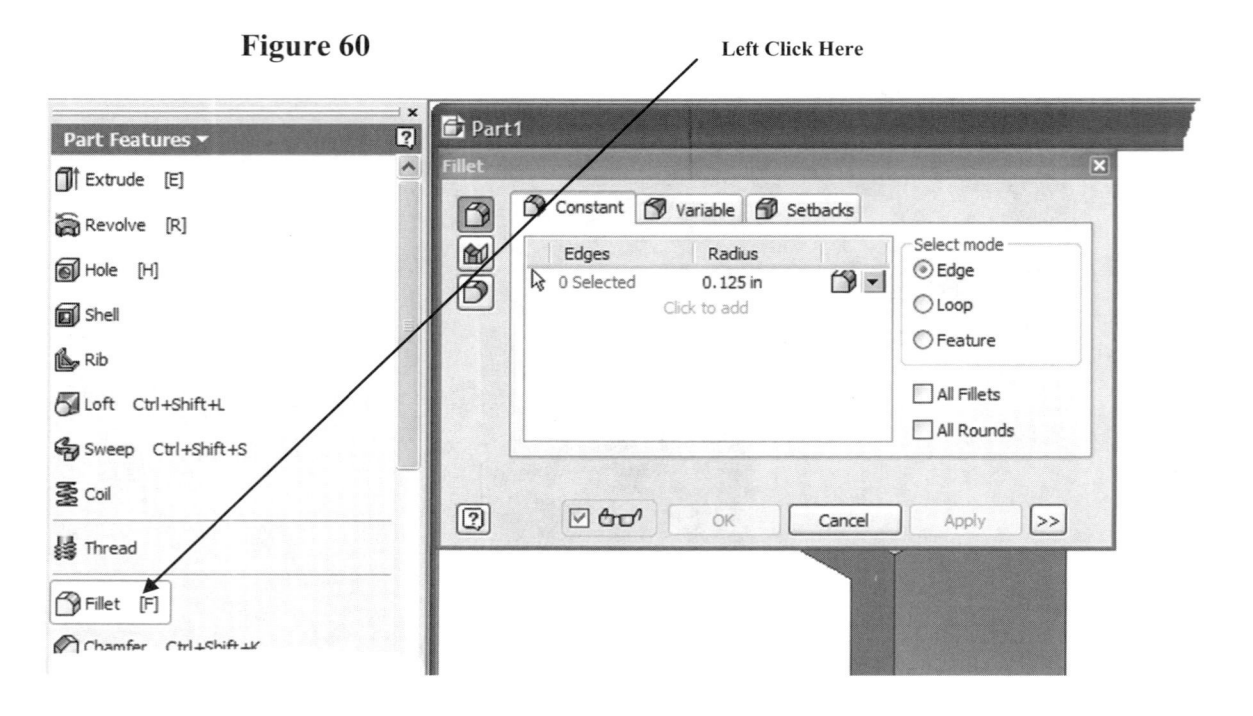

Figure 60

78. Move the cursor to the lower left edge of the part. After the edge turns red, left click once as shown in Figure 61.

Figure 61

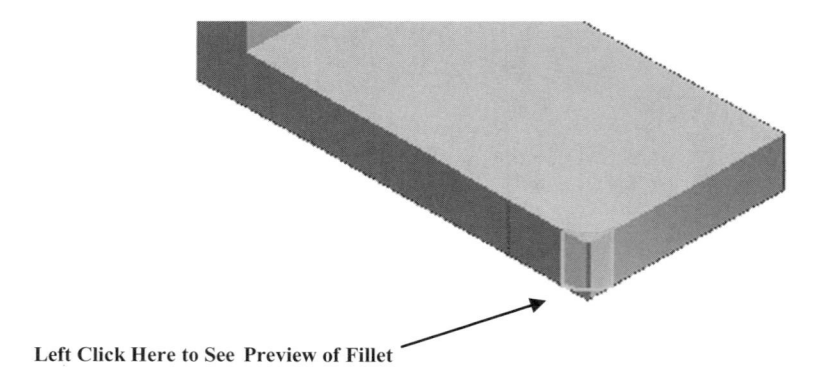

Chapter 1: Getting Started

79. Notice the red lines illustrating a preview of the fillet. Left click on the opposite edge as shown in Figure 62.

Figure 62

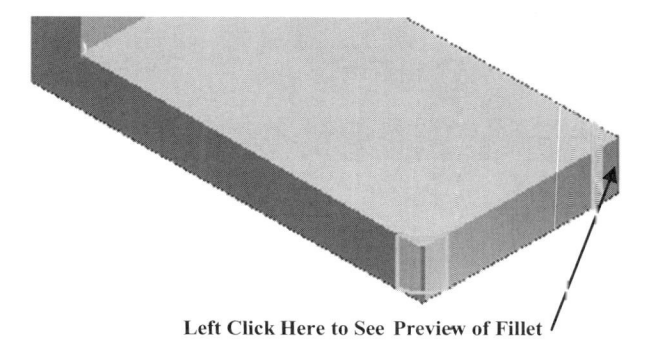

Left Click Here to See Preview of Fillet

80. Left click on the two upper remaining edges. Even though the far upper edge is not visible, move the cursor to the location of the edge and Inventor will find it as shown in Figure 63.

Figure 63

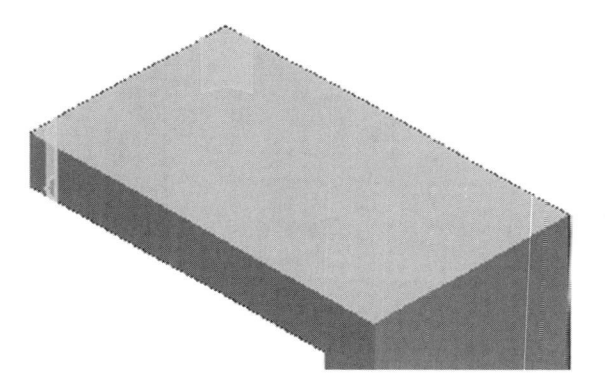

41

Chapter 1: Getting Started

81. Move the cursor to the dimension located under the text "Radius" and highlight the dimension. After the dimension is highlighted, type **.5** and press **Enter** on the keyboard. Notice the preview of the fillet Inventor provides in Figure 64.

Figure 64

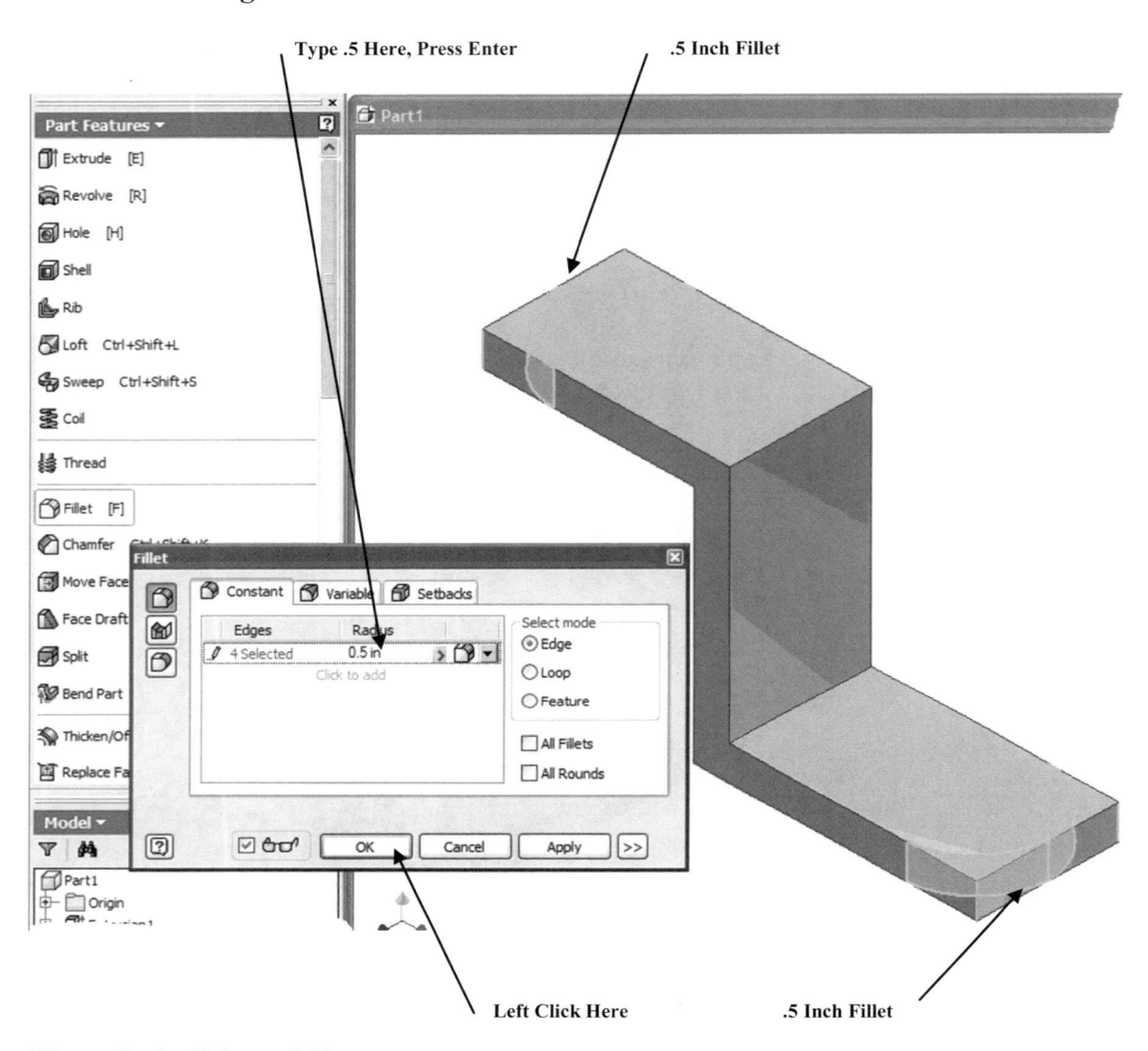

82. Left click on **OK**.

42

83. Your screen should look similar to Figure 65.

Figure 65

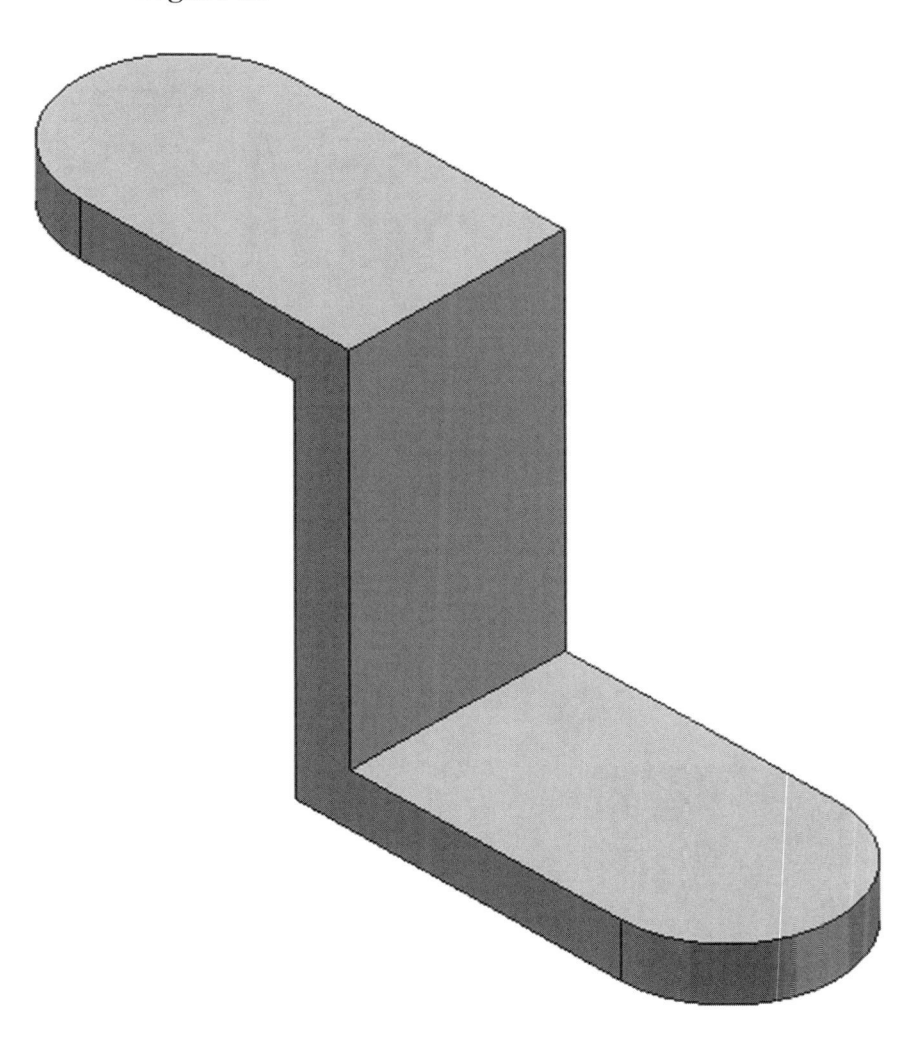

Chapter 1: Getting Started

84. The next task will include cutting a hole in each of the ends. To accomplish this, a sketch will need to be constructed on each surface. Move the cursor to the surface that will have the new sketch as shown in Figure 66. Notice the edges of the surface are red.

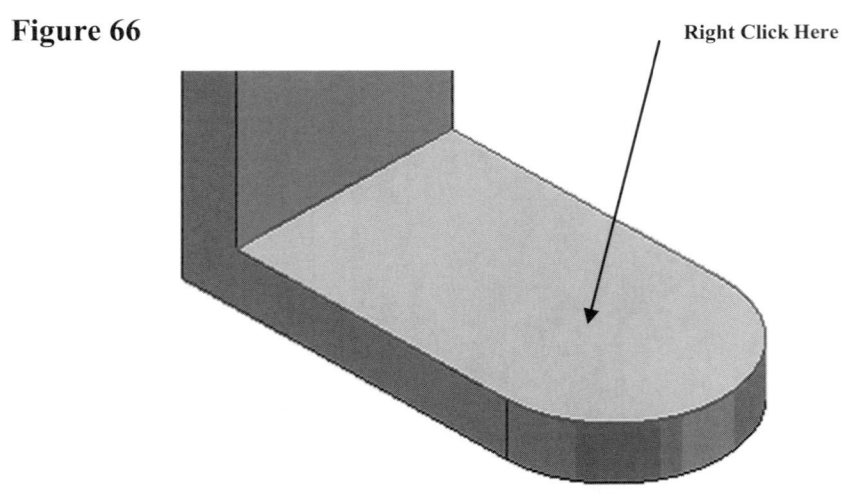

Figure 66

Right Click Here

85. After the edges of the surface turn red, right click on the surface. The surface will change color. A pop up menu will also appear. Left click on **New Sketch** as shown in Figure 67.

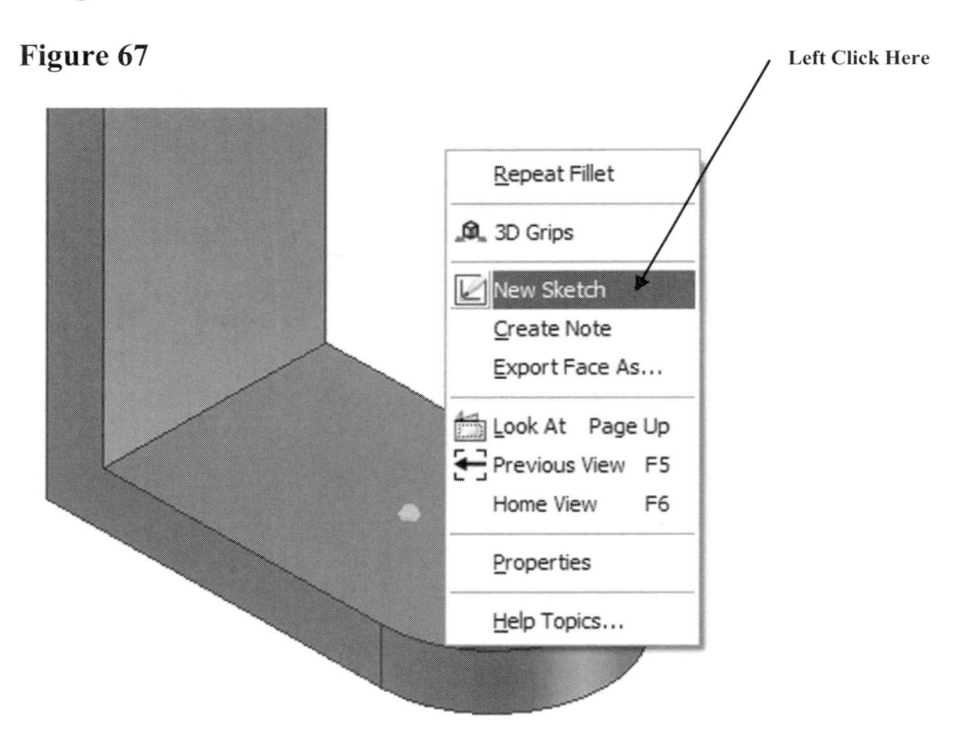

Figure 67

Left Click Here

44

Chapter 1: Getting Started

86. Inventor will create a "sketch" on that particular surface. Notice the menu to the left has changed back to the options available in the sketch panel. Inventor has now returned to the sketch panel.

87. Your screen should look similar to Figure 68.

Figure 68

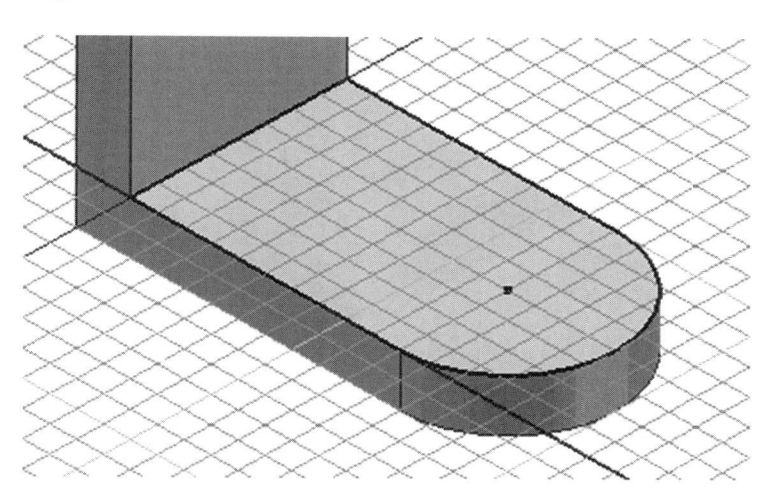

88. Move the cursor to the middle left portion of the screen and left click on **Center Point Circle** as shown in Figure 69.

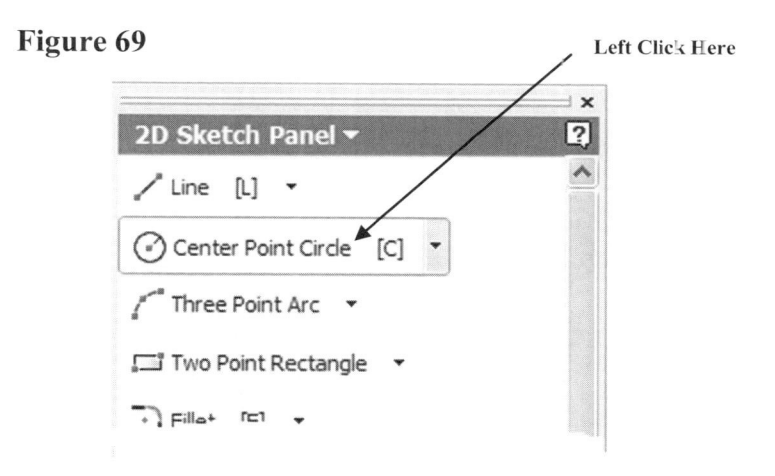

Figure 69

45

Chapter 1: Getting Started

89. Move the cursor along the edge of the fillet until a green dot appears. The dot will appear at the center of the radius as shown in Figure 70.

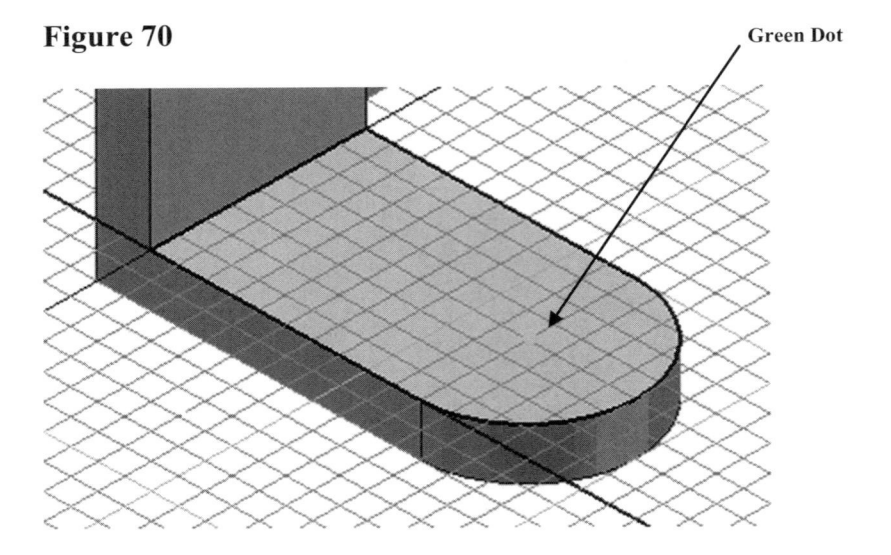

Figure 70

Green Dot

90. After the green dot appears, left click once. This will be the center of a circle, which will later become a thru hole. Move the cursor out to the side. The hole will become larger. Move the cursor out far enough to create a hole size similar to Figure 71.

Figure 71

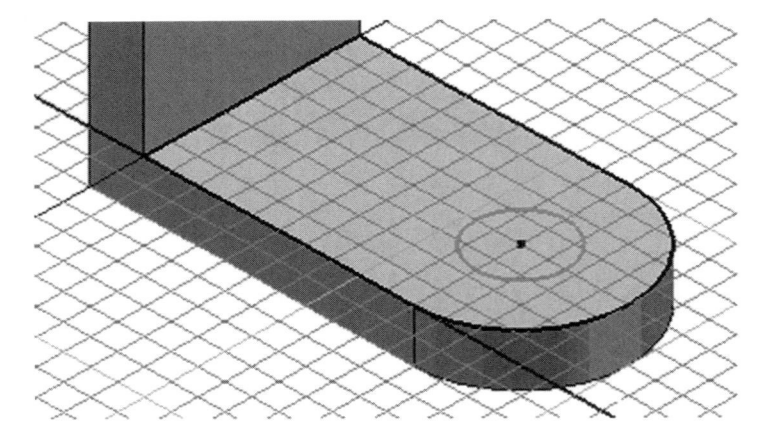

91. After the hole size looks similar to Figure 71, left click once.

Chapter 1: Getting Started

92. Move the cursor to the middle left portion of the screen and left click on **General Dimension** as shown in Figure 72.

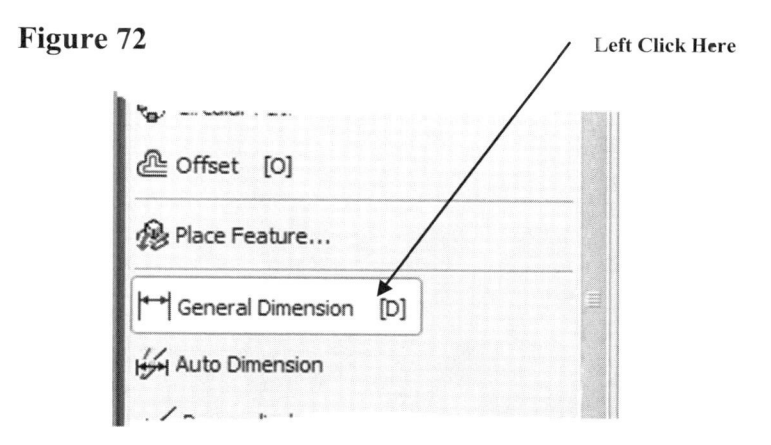

Figure 72

93. Left click on the edge (not the center) of the circle as shown in Figure 73. The circle will turn red.

Figure 73

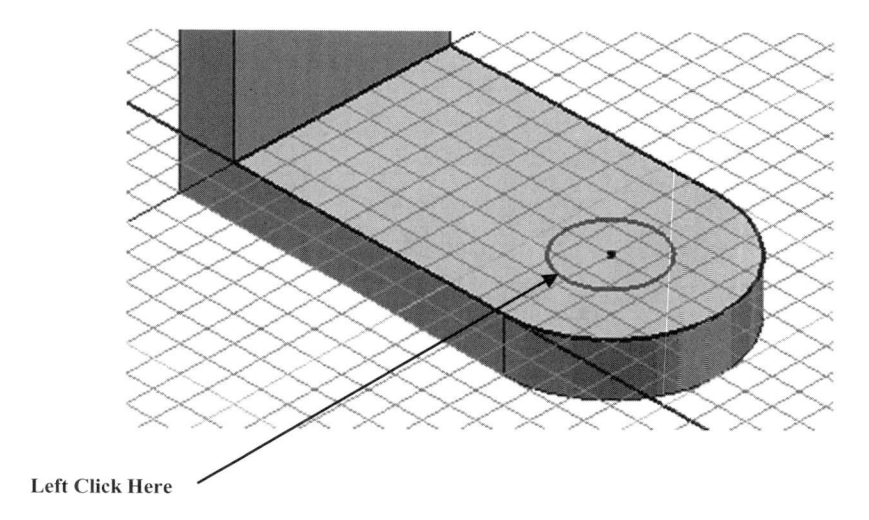

Chapter 1: Getting Started

94. As soon as the dimension appears, it is attached to the cursor. Move the cursor up and down to verify it is attached. Move the cursor to where the dimension will be placed and left click once as shown in Figure 74.

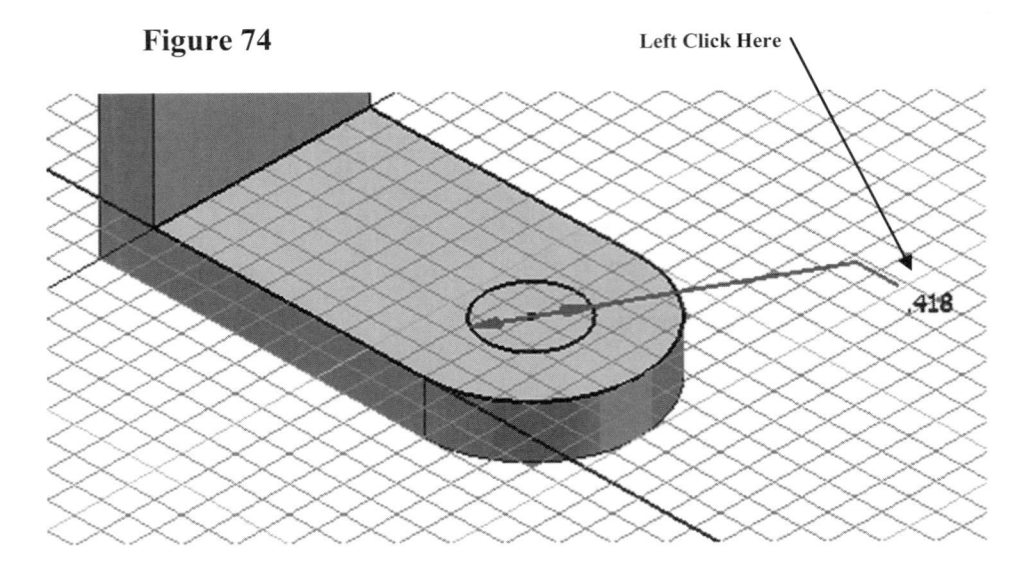

Figure 74

95. While the dimension is still red, left click the mouse once. The Edit Dimension dialog box will appear as shown in Figure 75.

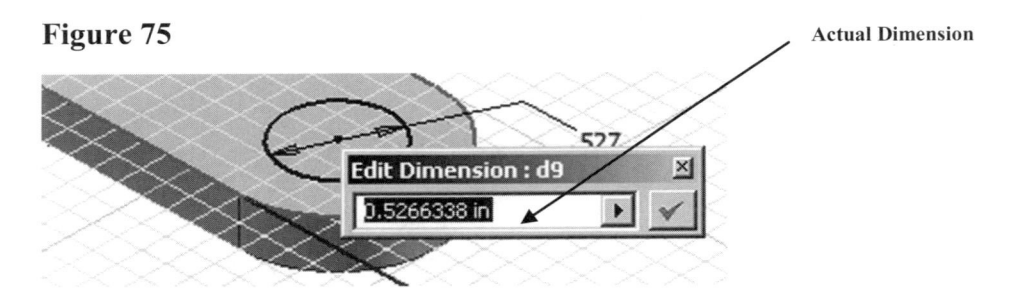

Figure 75

96. Type **.50** in the Edit Dimension dialog box and press **Enter** on the keyboard. The diameter of the hole will become .50 inches. Press the **Esc** key to ensure that no commands are active.

Chapter 1: Getting Started

97. Right click anywhere on the drawing. A pop up menu will appear. Left click on **Finish Sketch** as shown in Figure 76.

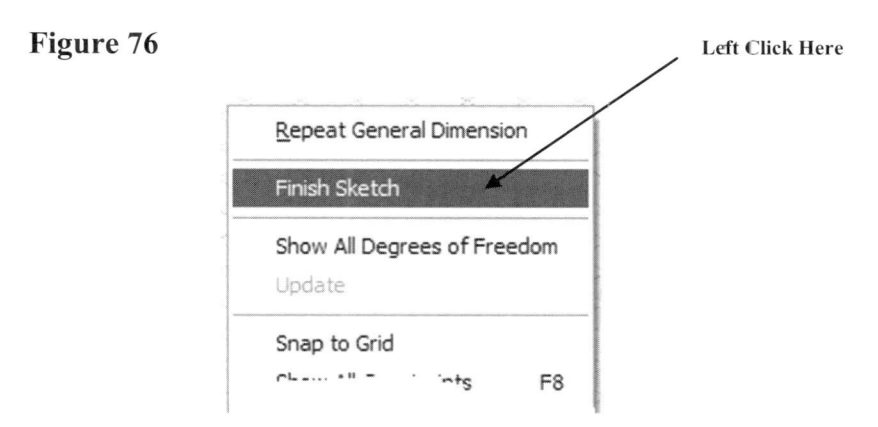

Figure 76

Left Click Here

98. Inventor is now out of the Sketch Panel and into the Part Features Panel. Notice that the commands at the left of the screen are now different. To work in the Part Features Panel a sketch must be present and have no opens (non-connected lines). If there are any opens in the sketch an error message will appear. Your screen should look similar to Figure 77.

Figure 77

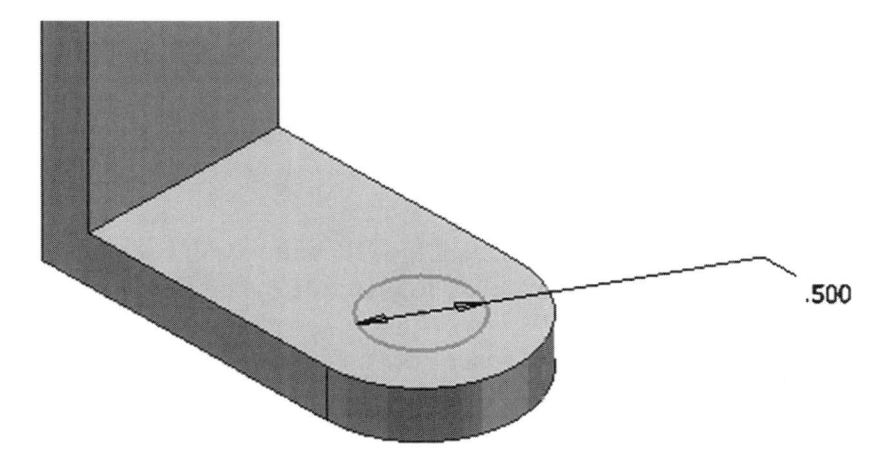

.500

Chapter 1: Getting Started

99. Move the cursor to the middle left portion of the screen and left click on **Extrude**. The Extrude dialog box will appear. If the OK icon is not active, ensure that the **Profile** icon at the left side of the Extrude dialog box has been selected. Now move the cursor over the circle in the drawing. After the circle turns red, left click once. Your screen should look similar to Figure 78.

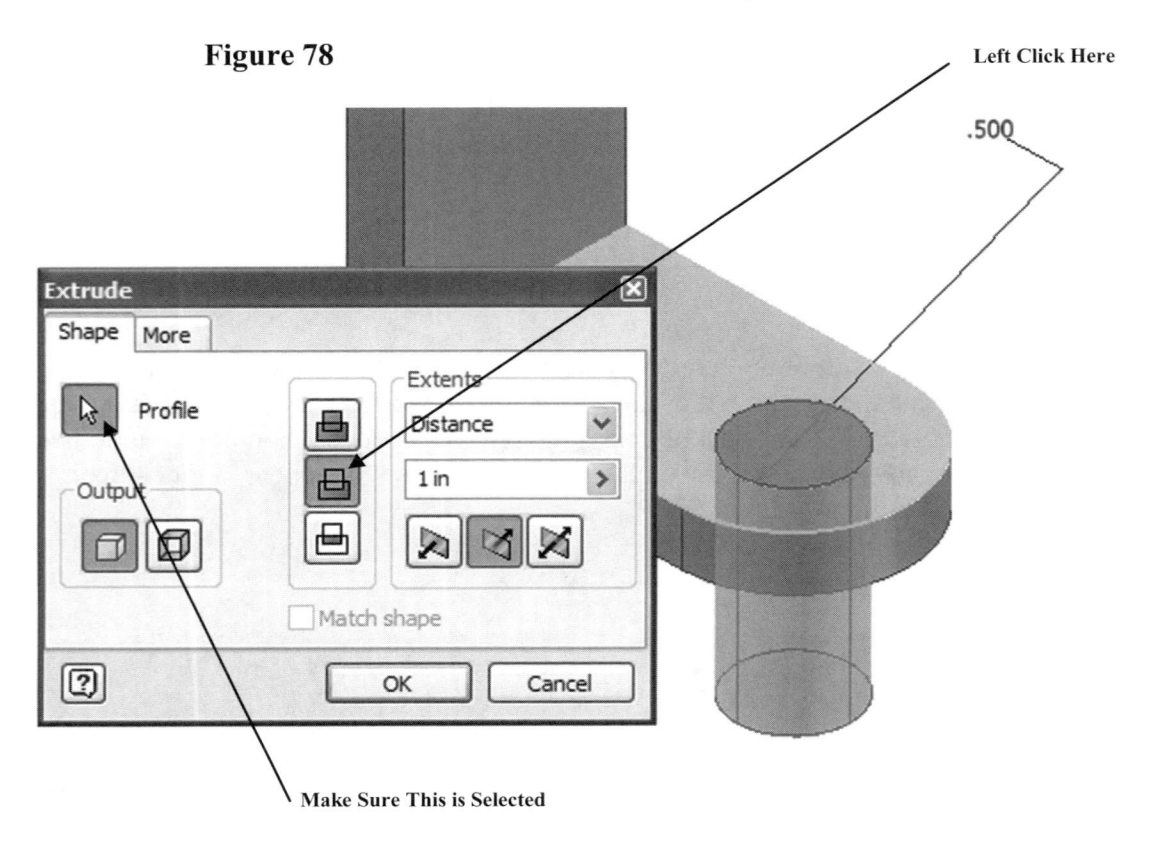

Figure 78

100. After the circle has been selected, the OK button will become active as shown in Figure 78. Inventor is now ready to **Extrude** the circle.

101. This time we will extrude "space" or "air" rather than material as was done to create the bracket.

Chapter 1: Getting Started

102. With this in mind, left click on the "Cut" icon located in the middle of the Extrude dialog box as shown in Figure 79.

Figure 79

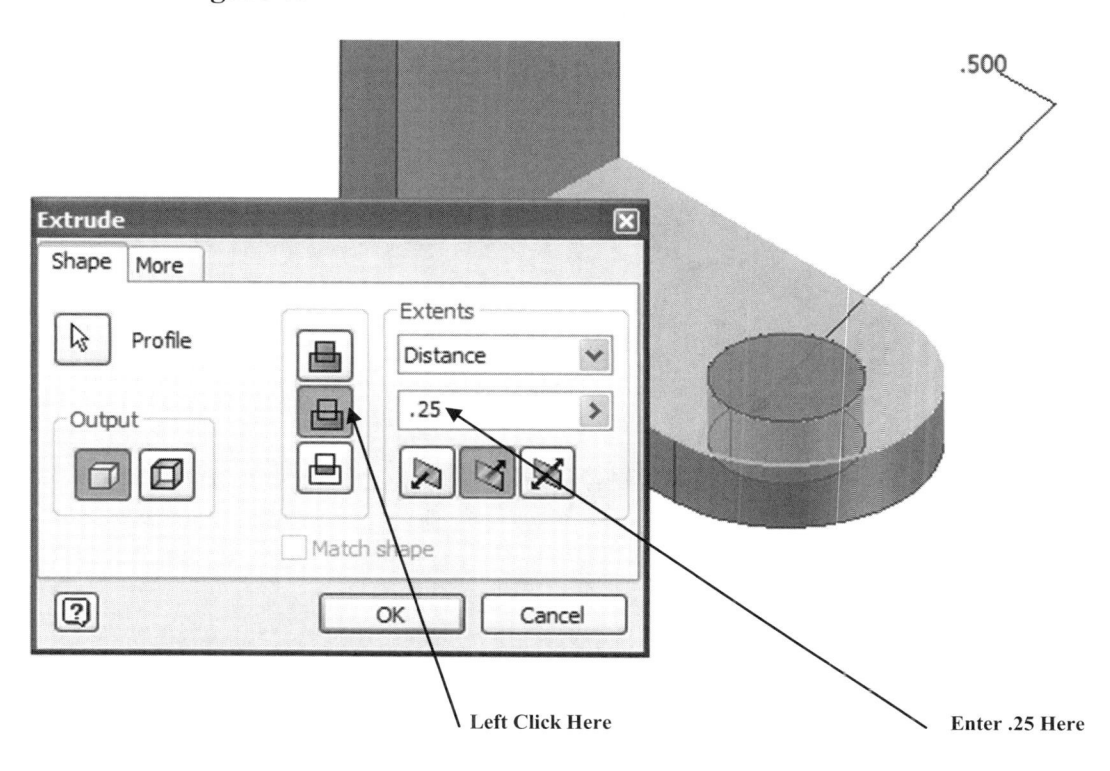

Left Click Here   Enter .25 Here

103. Enter **.25** for the distance as shown in Figure 79. Inventor will provide a preview of the extrusion. Red signifies that Inventor will cut material inside the circle and will form a hole through the part. Left click **OK**.

104. You should have a thru hole in the part similar to Figure 80.

Figure 80

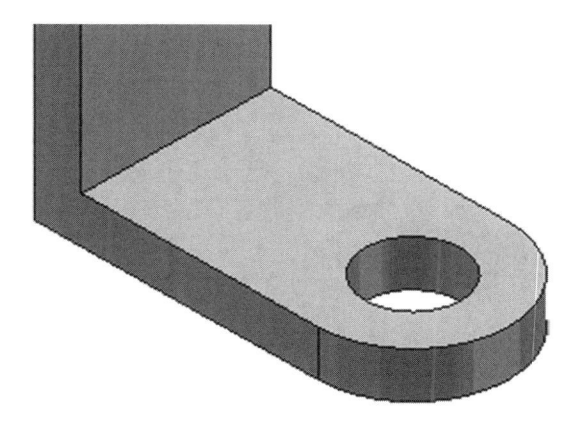

Chapter 1: Getting Started

105. Another method of creating a hole is to use the Point, Center Point command.

106. To use the Point, Hole Center command, Inventor will need to be in the Sketch Panel. Change to the Sketch Panel by moving the cursor to the top portion of the part. The outer edges of the part will turn red. Right click on the surface as shown in Figure 81.

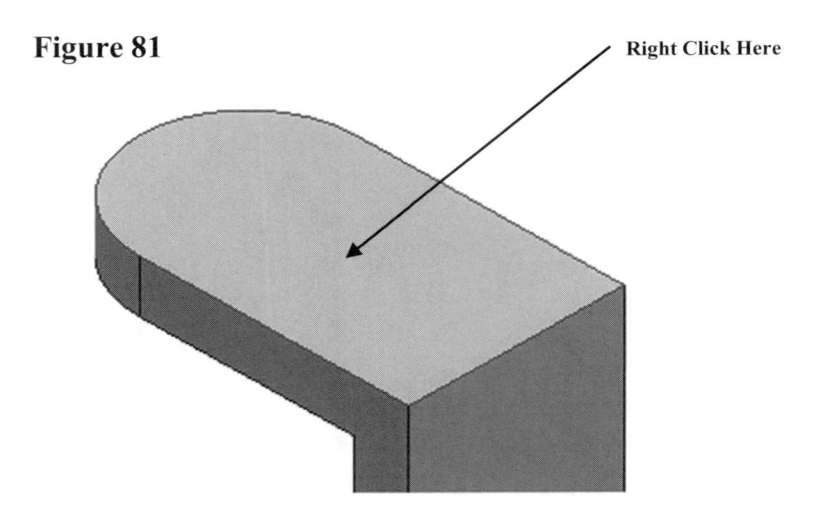

Figure 81 Right Click Here

107. The surface will change color. A pop up menu will also appear as shown in Figure 82.

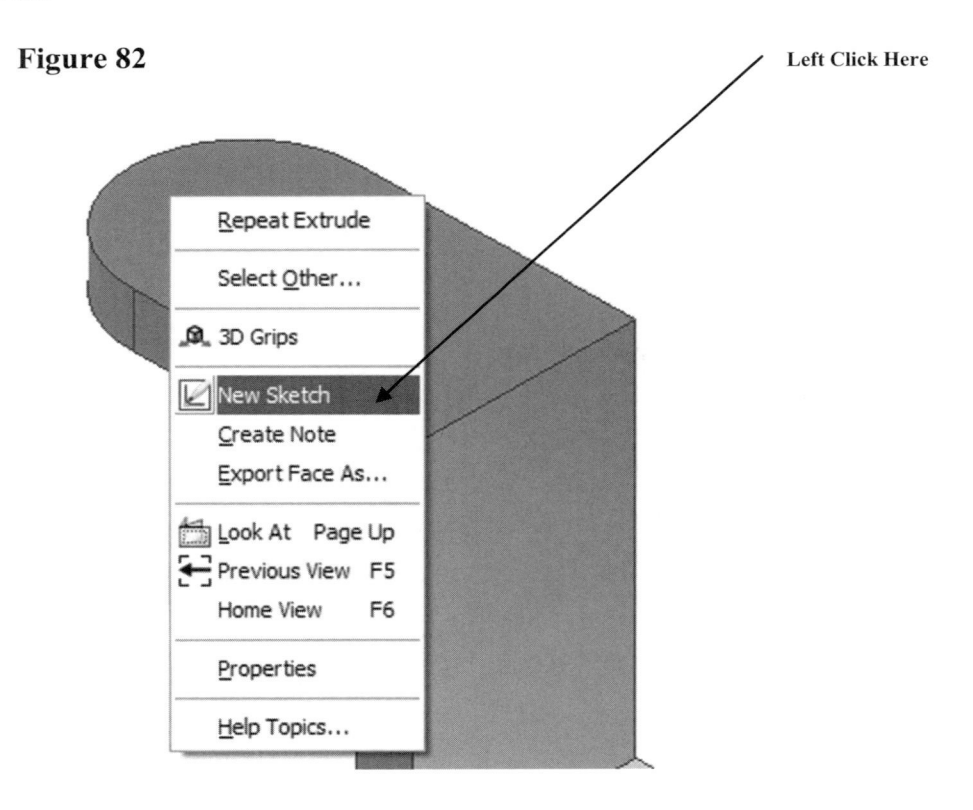

Figure 82 Left Click Here

52

Chapter 1: Getting Started

108. Left click on **New Sketch**. Inventor will return to the Sketch Panel as shown in Figure 83.

Figure 83

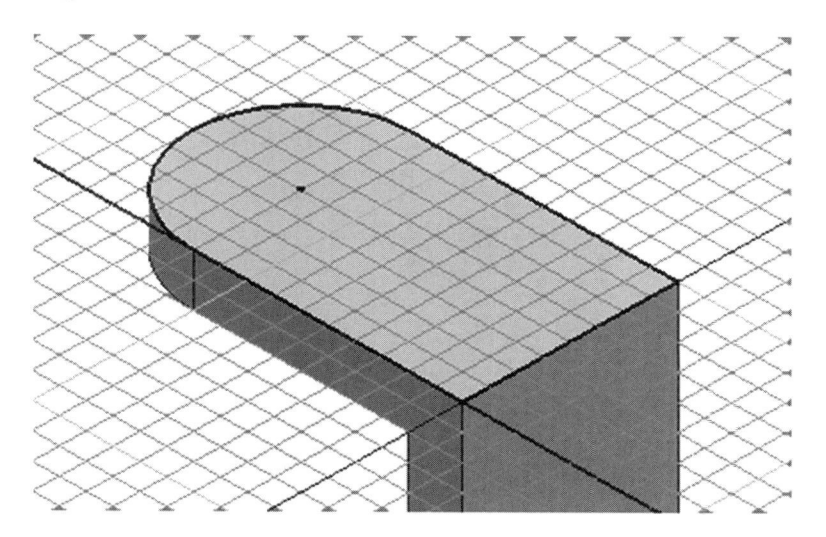

109. Move the cursor to the middle left portion of the screen and left click on **Point, Center Point** as shown in Figure 84.

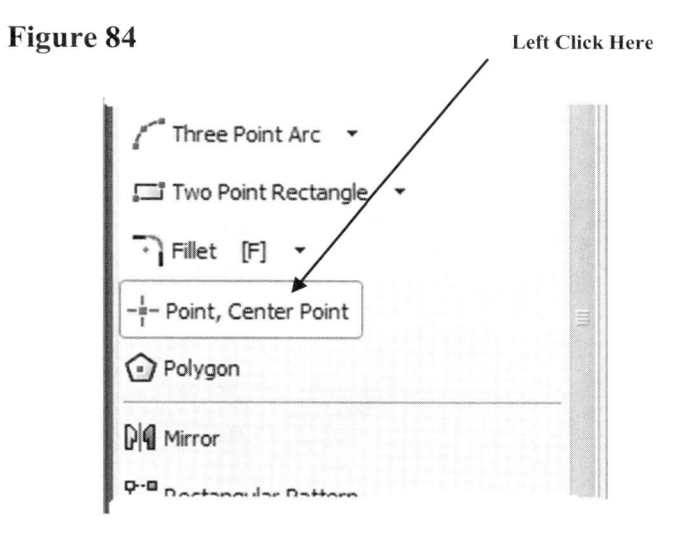

Figure 84

Left Click Here

53

Chapter 1: Getting Started

110. Move the cursor along the edge of the fillet until a green dot appears. The dot will appear at the center of the radius as shown in Figure 85. Left click on the green dot.

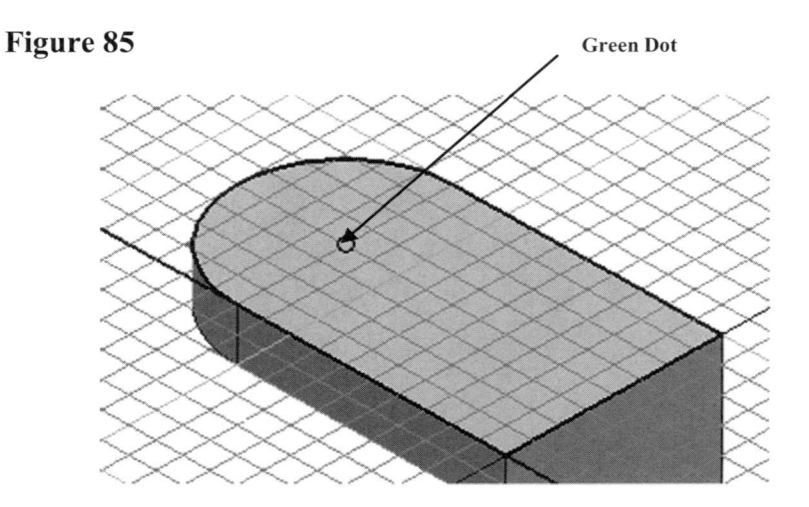

Figure 85   Green Dot

111. After left clicking on the center point, Inventor will place a small center marker on the center of the fillet radius as shown in Figure 86. Press the **Esc** key once.

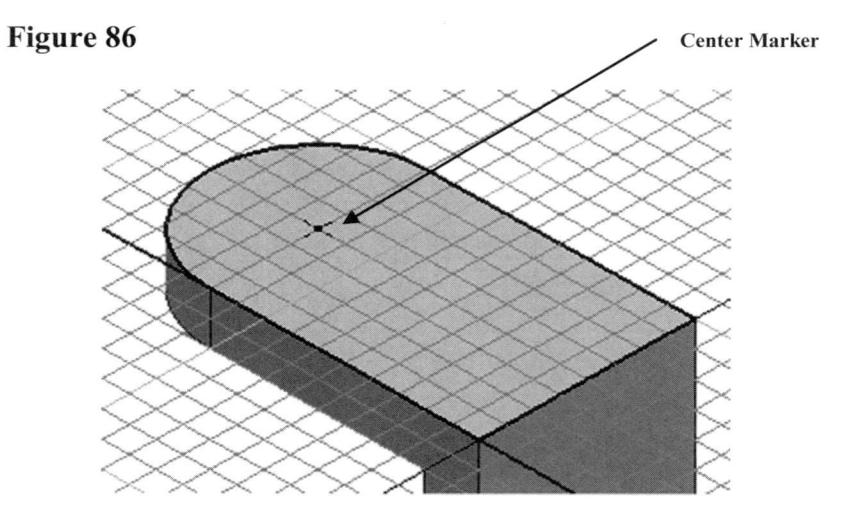

Figure 86   Center Marker

Chapter 1: Getting Started

112. Right click anywhere on the drawing. A pop up menu will appear. Left click on **Finish Sketch** as shown in Figure 87.

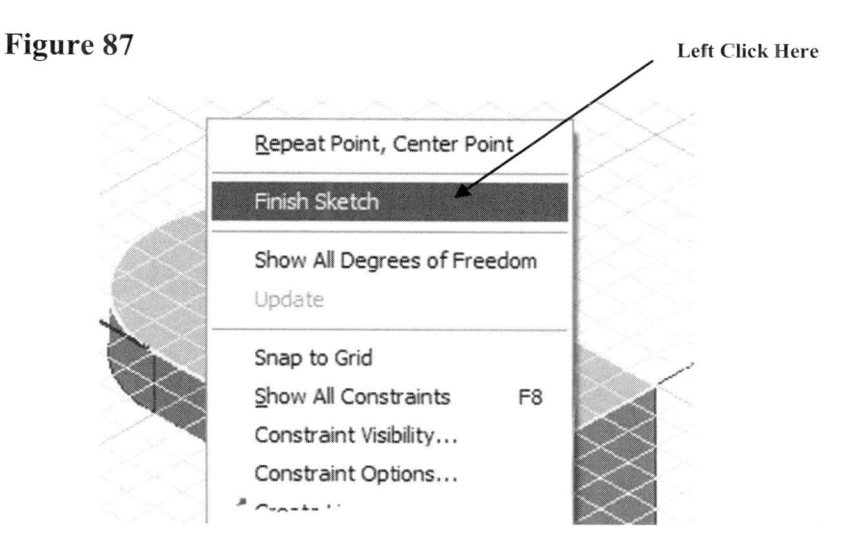

Figure 87

113. Inventor is now out of the Sketch Panel and into the Part Features Panel. Notice that the commands at the left of the screen are now different. To work in the Part Features Panel a sketch must be present and have no opens (non-connected lines). If there are any opens in the sketch an error message will appear. Your screen should look similar to Figure 88.

Figure 88

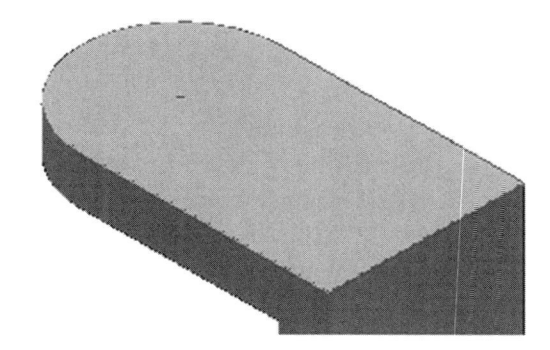

55

Chapter 1: Getting Started

114. Move the cursor to the middle left portion of the screen and left click on **Hole**. The Holes dialog box will appear as shown in Figure 89.

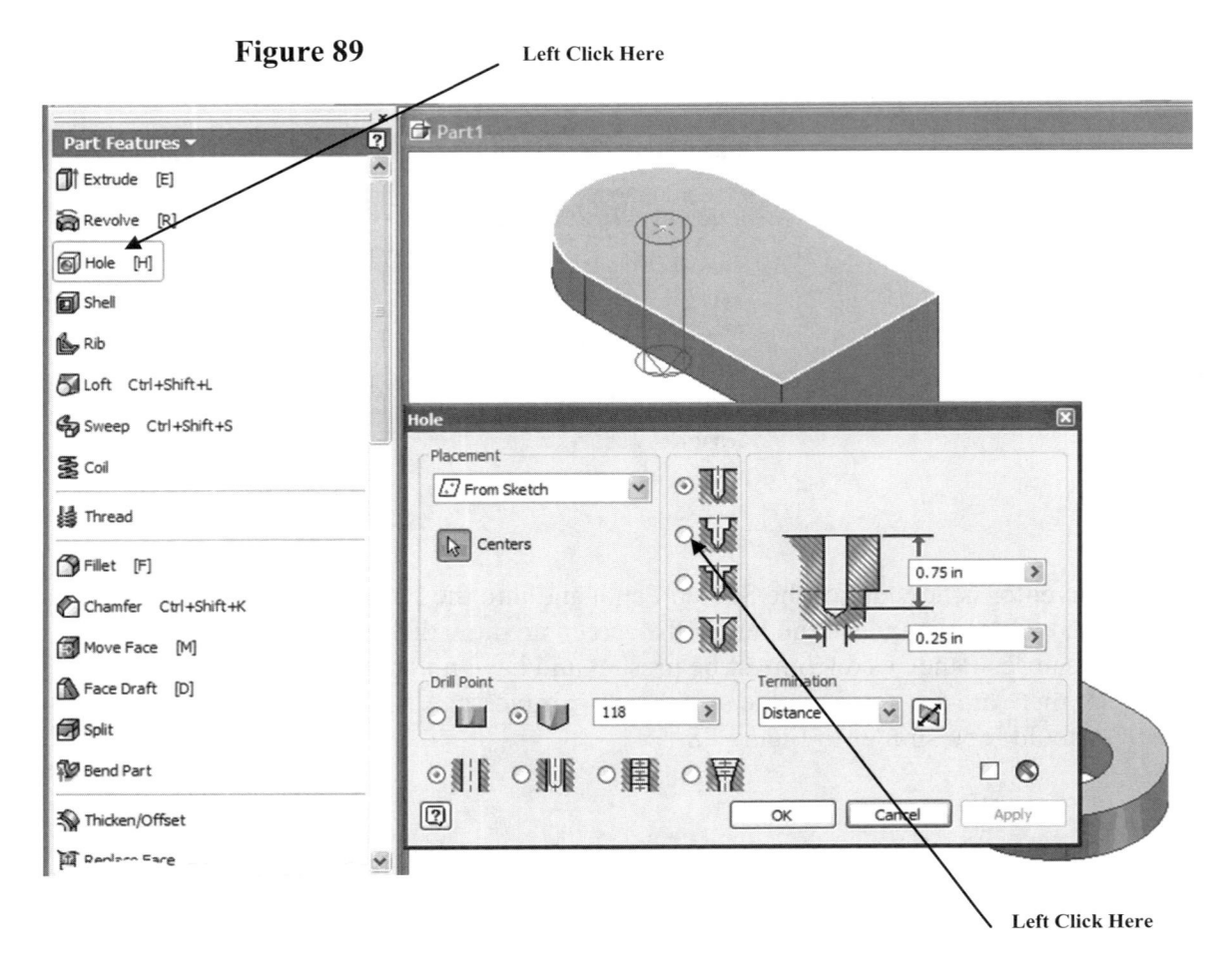

Figure 89

115. Left click on the middle of the dialog box and place a dot as shown in Figure 89. This is the "Counter Bore" icon. A preview and dimensions of the hole type are provided on the right side of the Holes dialog box. Select one of the other hole types and watch the preview of the hole in the right side of the Holes dialog box change.

56

Chapter 1: Getting Started

116. To edit the dimensions of the counter bore hole use the cursor to highlight the desired dimension as shown in Figure 90. Notice the preview of the hole type on the part illustrated in red.

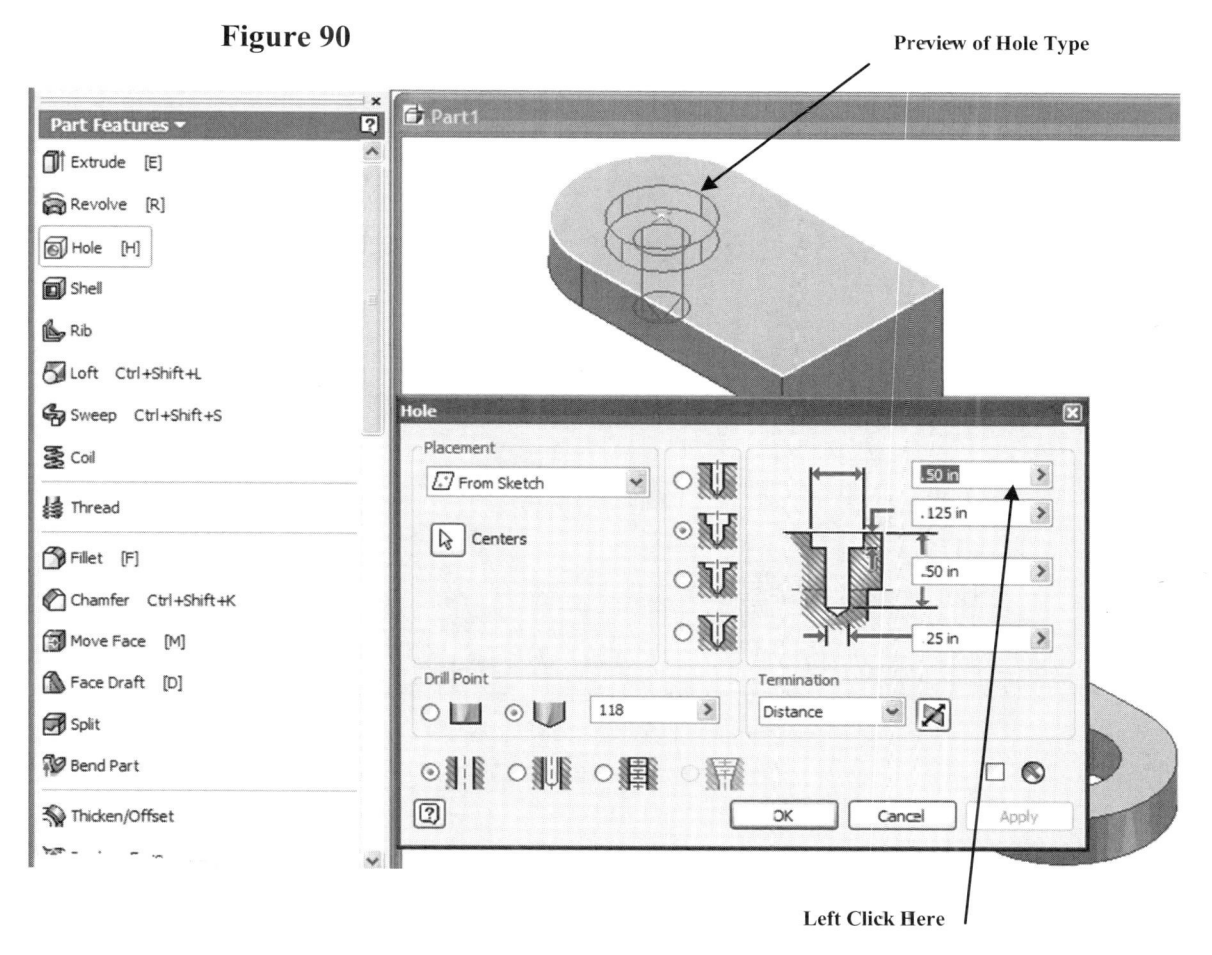

Figure 90

117. After highlighting the dimension, type in **.50** (if .50 is not already typed in) for the counter bore diameter.

Chapter 1: Getting Started

118. Type in **.125** for the counter bore depth, **.50** for the overall depth, **.25** for the hole diameter and left click on **OK** as shown in Figure 91.

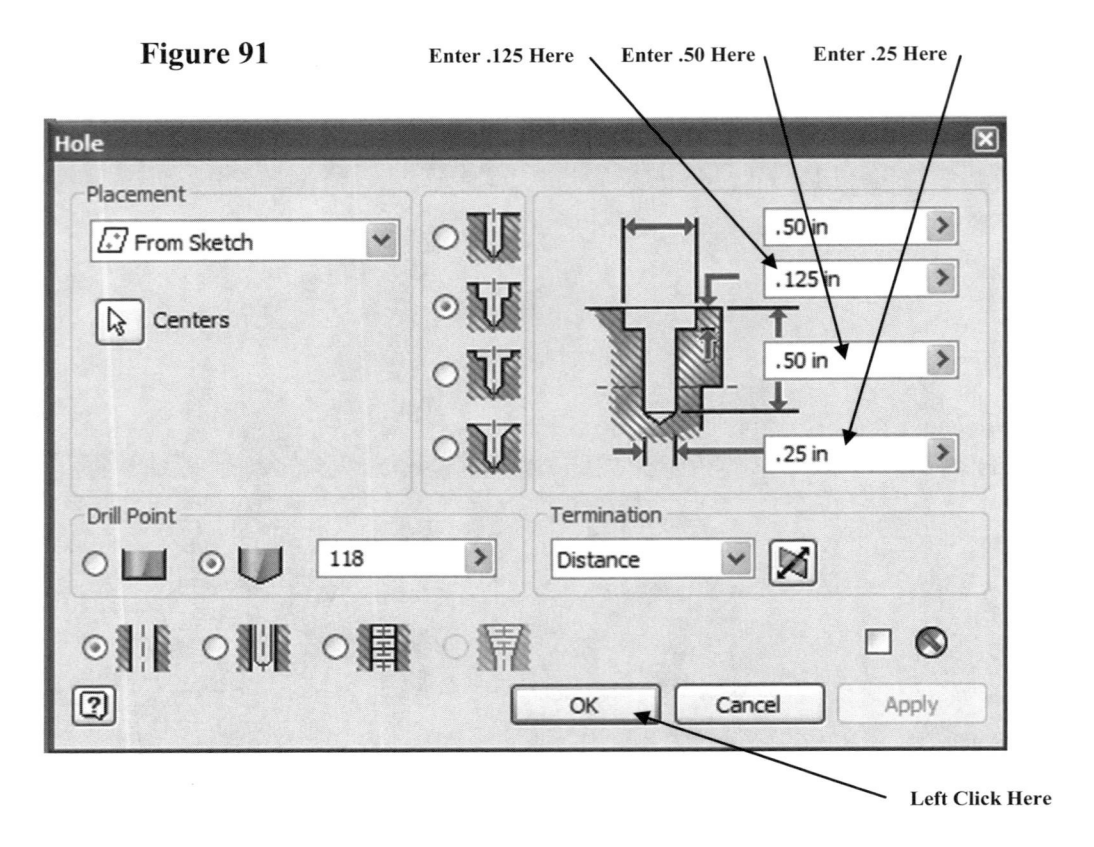

Figure 91

Enter .125 Here   Enter .50 Here   Enter .25 Here

Left Click Here

119. Your screen should look similar to Figure 92.

Figure 92

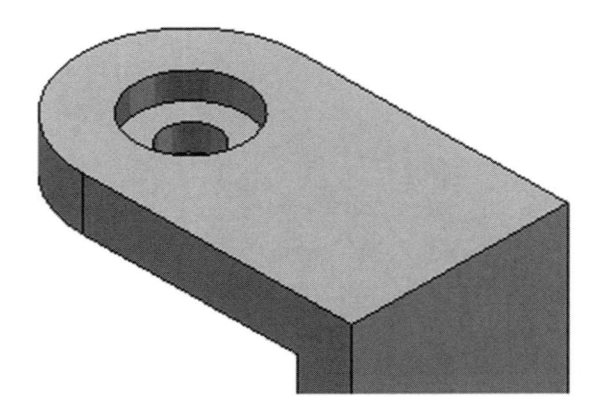

58

Chapter 1: Getting Started

120. To ensure that the hole is correct move the cursor to the top portion of the screen and left click on the "Orbit" (also known as the "Rotate") icon as shown in Figure 93.

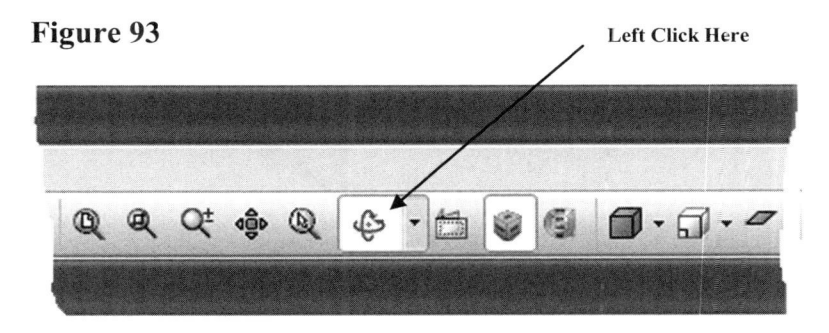

Figure 93

121. The Orbit/Rotate command will become active. Left click anywhere inside the white circle, hold the left mouse button down, and drag the cursor upward. The part will rotate upward as shown in Figure 94.

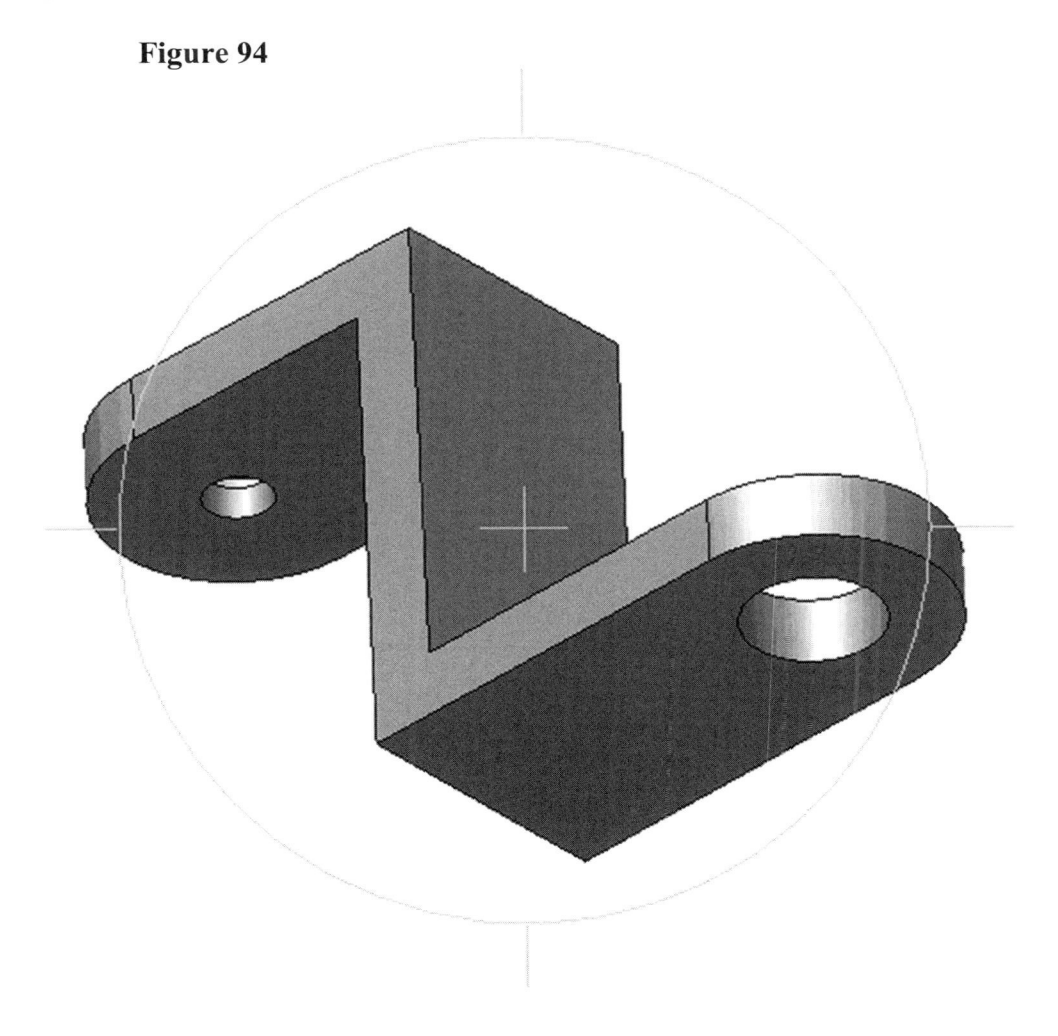

Figure 94

Chapter 1: Getting Started

122. Holding the left mouse button down keeps the part attached to the cursor. To view the part in Isometric, right click anywhere on the screen and left click on **Home View** from the pop up menu as shown in Figure 95.

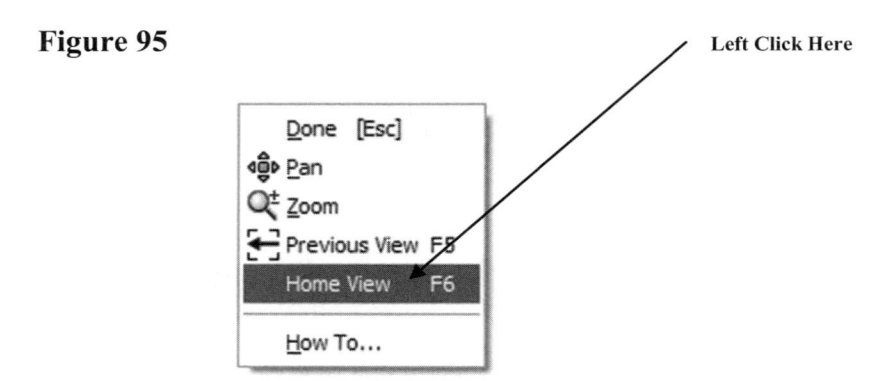

Figure 95

Left Click Here

123. As long as the white circle is present, the Orbit/Rotate command is still active. To get out of the Orbit/Rotate command either use the keyboard and press **Esc** once or twice, or right click anywhere on the screen and left click on **Done [Esc]** from the pop up menu shown in Figure 96.

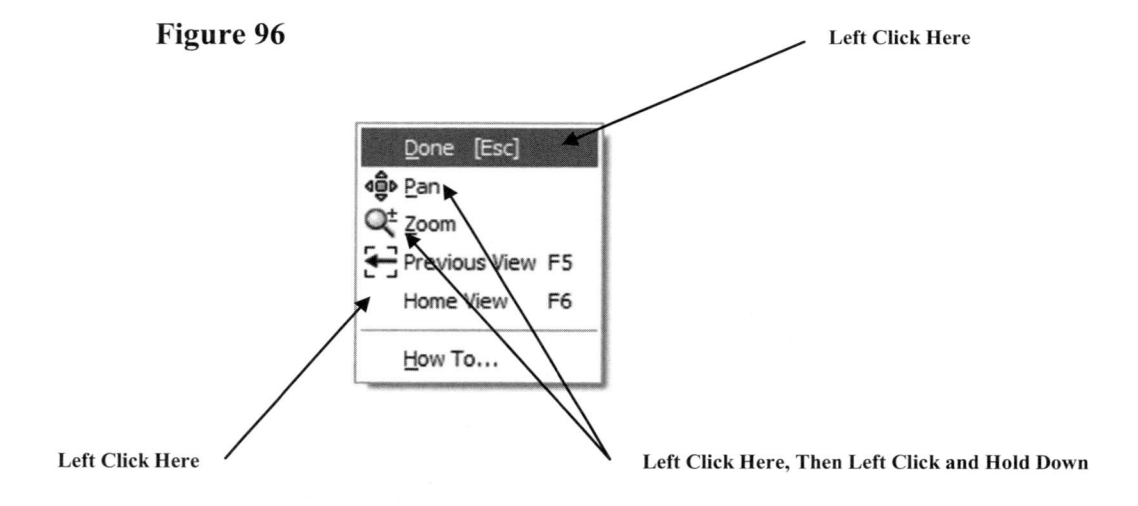

Figure 96

Left Click Here

Left Click Here

Left Click Here, Then Left Click and Hold Down

Chapter 1: Getting Started

124. Other commands for viewing are located in the pop up menu or at the top of the screen as shown in Figures 96 and 97.

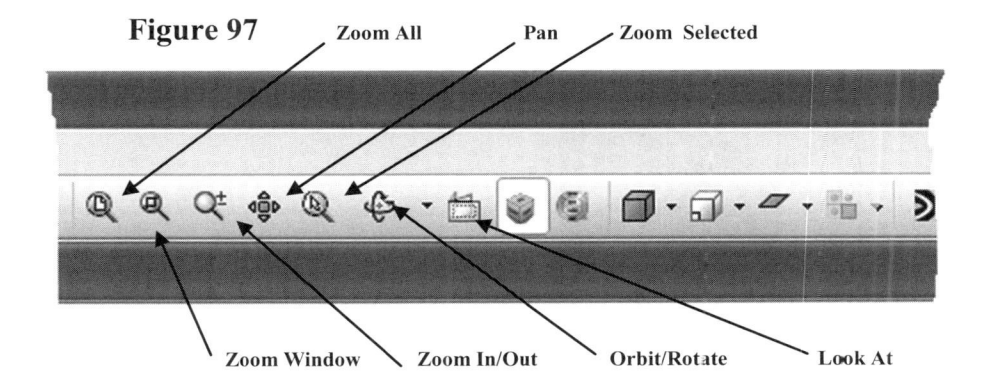

Figure 97 — Zoom All — Pan — Zoom Selected

Zoom Window — Zoom In/Out — Orbit/Rotate — Look At

125. The Zoom Window command works by using the cursor to draw a window around an area you want to zoom in on. After selecting the "Zoom Window" icon hold the left mouse button down, drag a diagonal box around the desired area, and release it when the proper amount of zoom is achieved.

126. The Zoom In/Out command works similar to the Zoom Window command. Start by selecting the "Zoom In/Out" icon. Left click on the drawing and hold the left mouse button down while moving the cursor up and down until the proper amount of zoom is achieved.

127. The Pan command works similar to the Zoom In/Out command. Start by selecting the "Pan" icon. Left click on the drawing and hold the left mouse button down while moving the cursor up and down or side to side. Release the mouse button once the desired view is achieved.

128. The Look At command works similar to the Pan command. Start by selecting the "Look At" icon. Left click on any surface you want to view perpendicularly.

Chapter 1: Getting Started

Drawing Activities

Problem 1

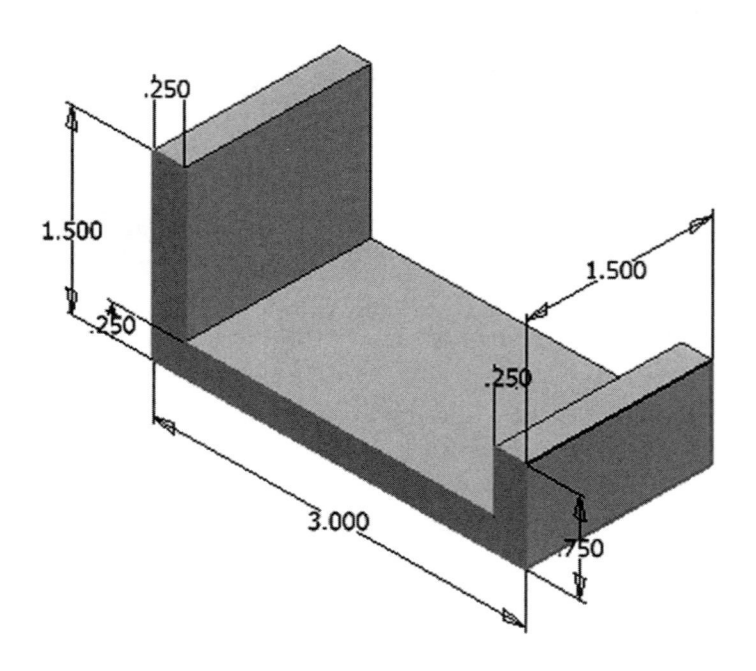

Problem 2

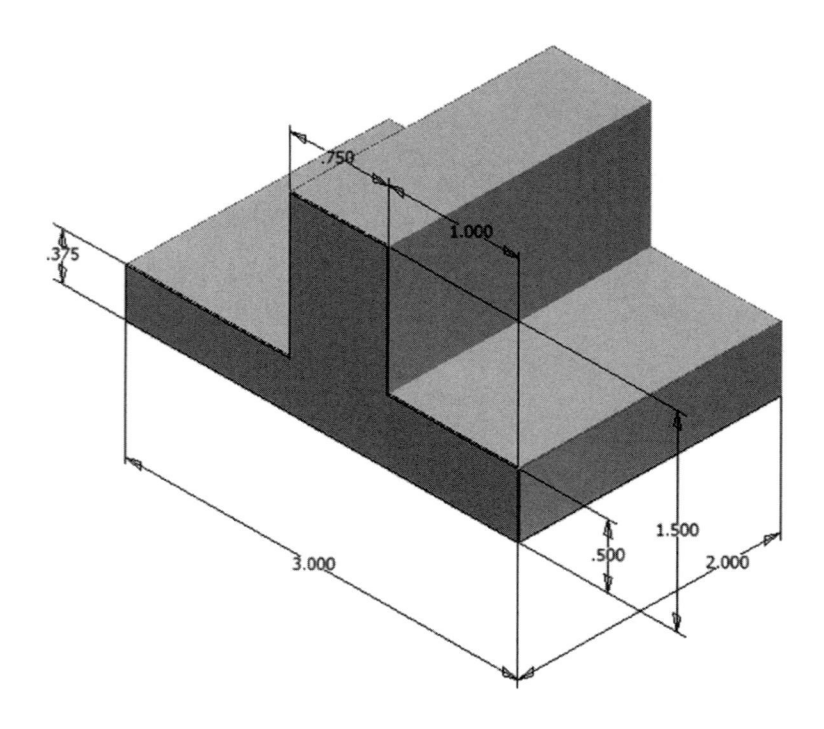

Problem 3

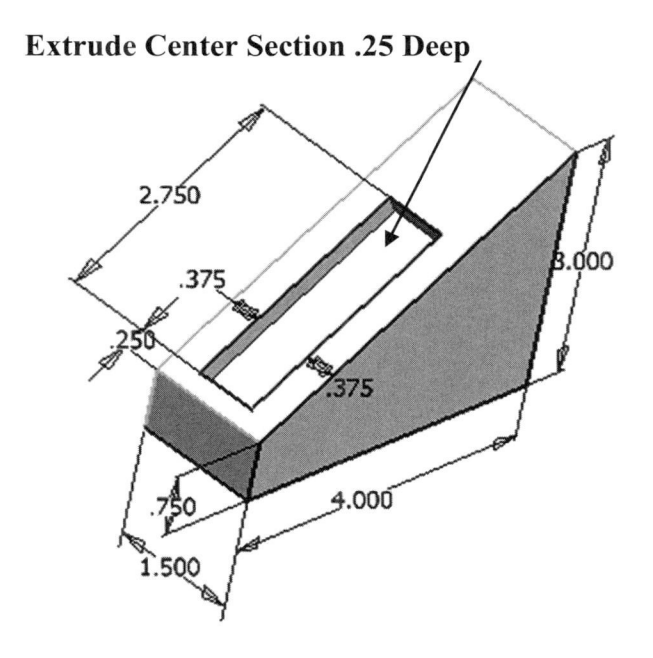

Extrude Center Section .25 Deep

Problem 4

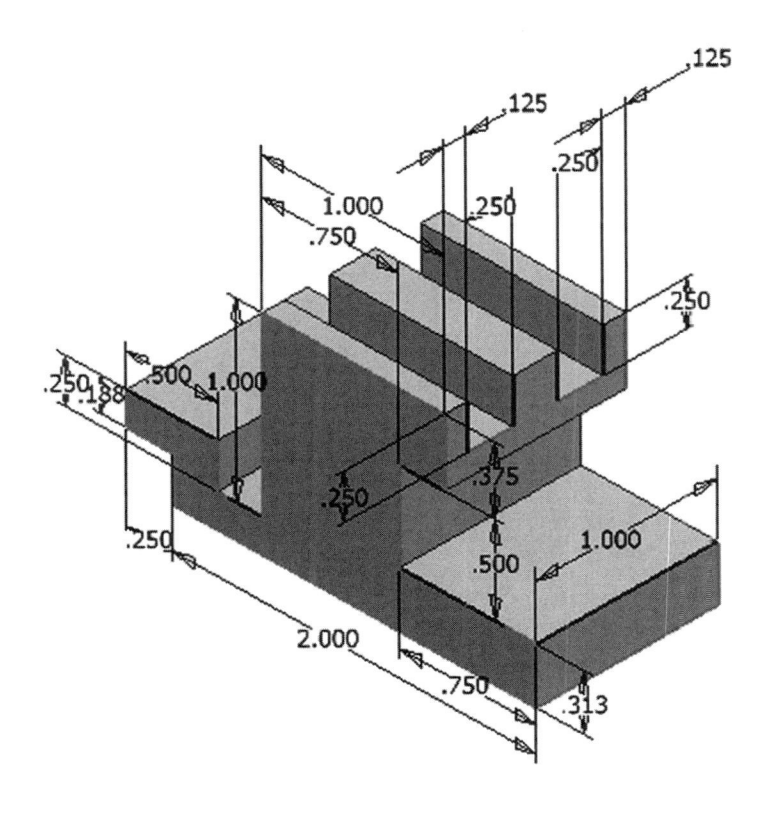

Chapter 1: Getting Started

Problem 5

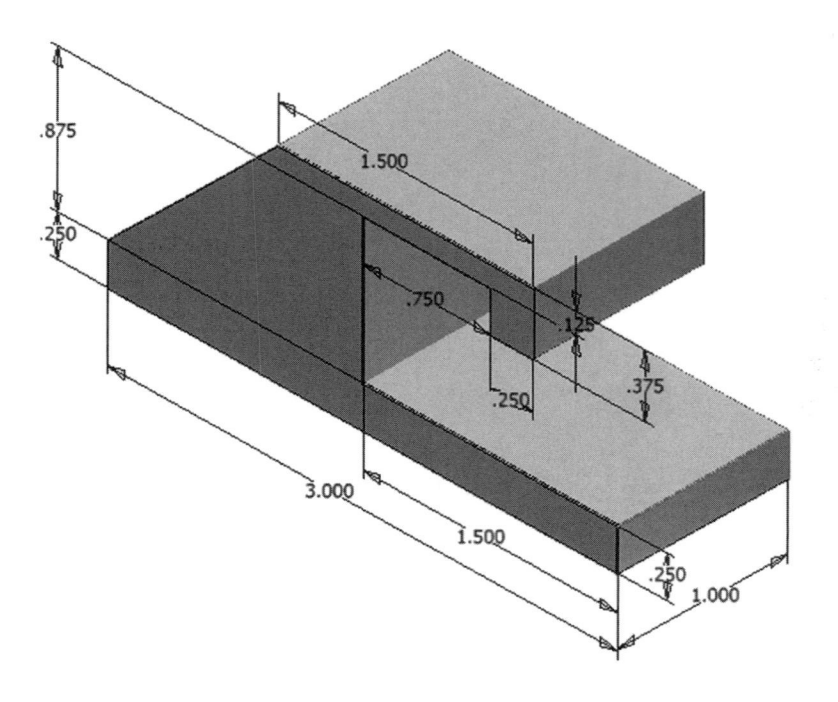

Problem 6

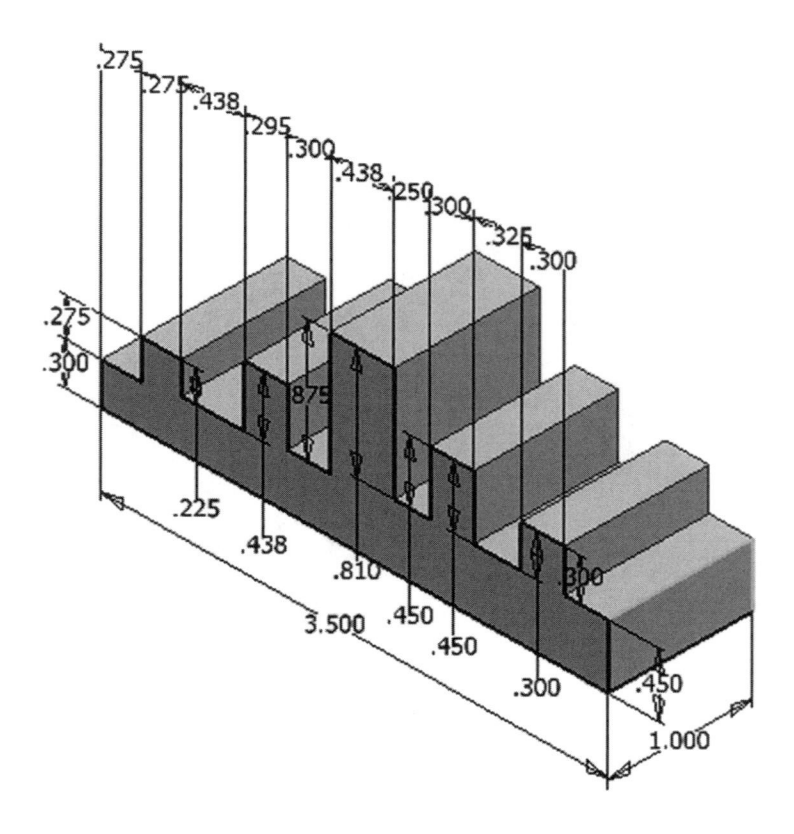

Problem 7

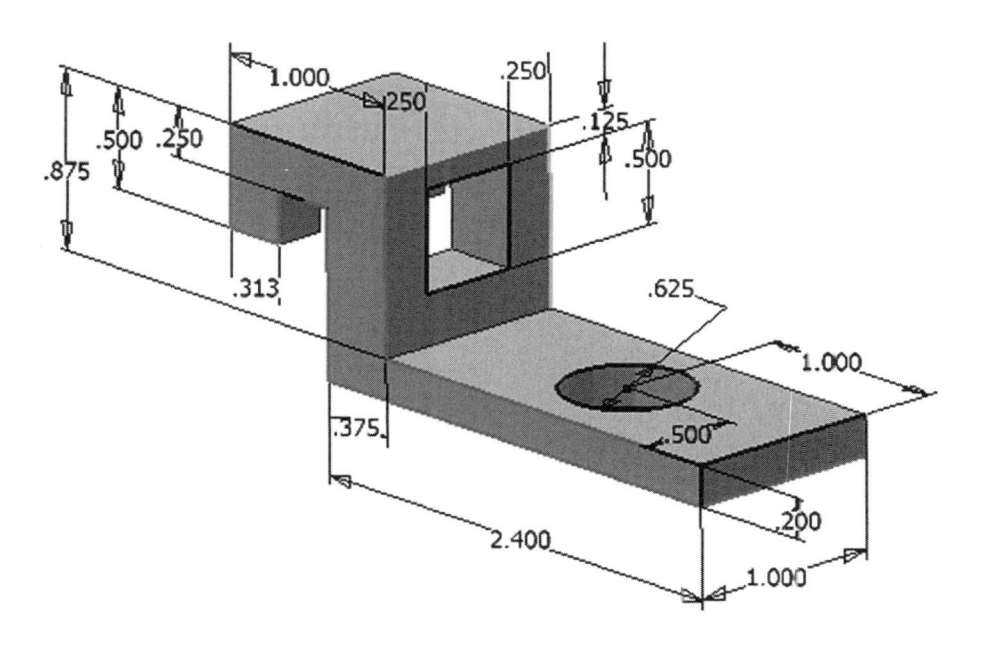

Problem 8

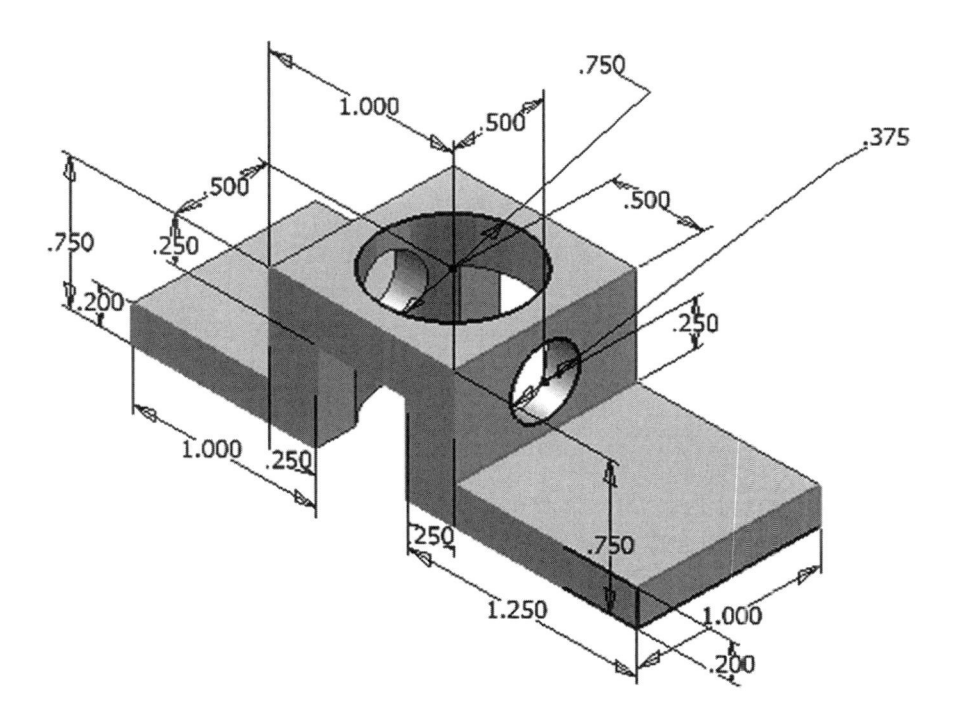

Chapter 2 Learning More Basics

Objectives:
- Create a simple sketch using the Sketch Panel
- Dimension a sketch using the General Dimension command
- Revolve a sketch in the Part Features Panel using the Revolve command
- Create a hole in the Part Features Panel using the Extrude command
- Create a series of holes in the Part Features Panel using the Circular Hole command

Chapter 2 includes instruction on how to design the part shown below.

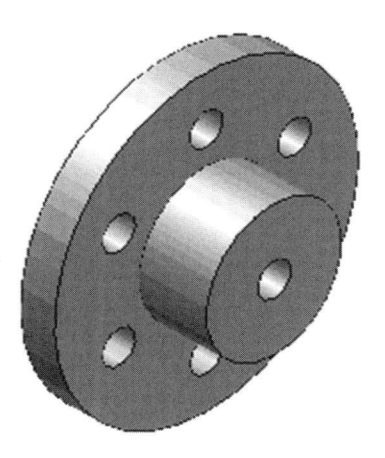

Chapter 2: Learning More Basics

1. Start Autodesk Inventor 2009 by referring to "Chapter 1 Getting Started".

2. After Autodesk Inventor 2009 is running, begin a new sketch.

3. Move the cursor to the upper left corner of the screen and left click on **Line** as shown in Figure 1.

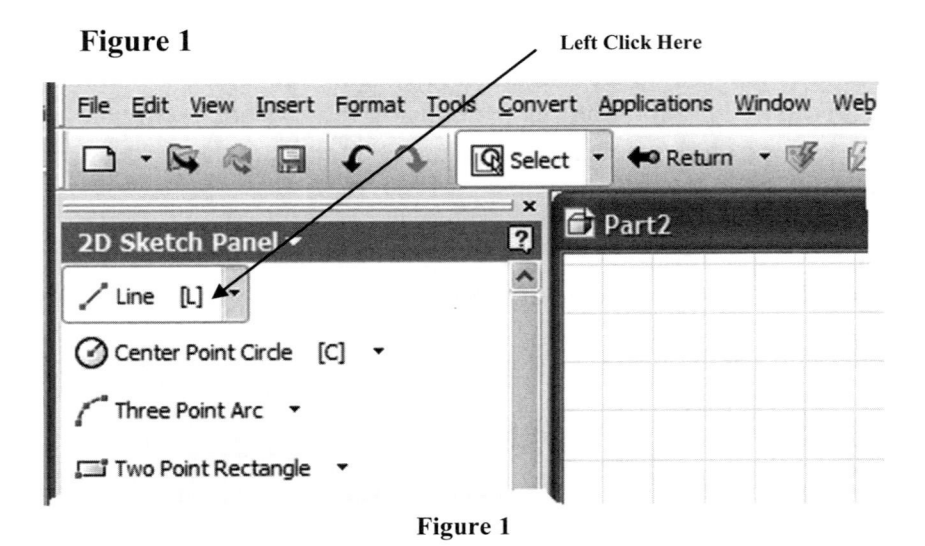

Figure 1

4. Move the cursor somewhere in the lower left portion of the screen and left click once. This will be the beginning end point of a line as shown in Figure 2.

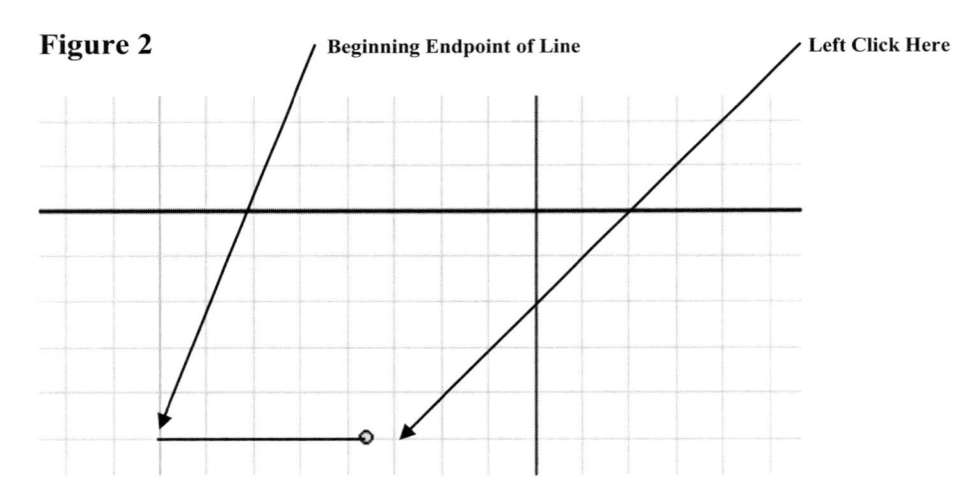

Figure 2

5. Move the cursor to the right and left click once as shown in Figure 2.

68

Chapter 2: Learning More Basics

6. Move the cursor up and left click once as shown in Figure 3.

Figure 3

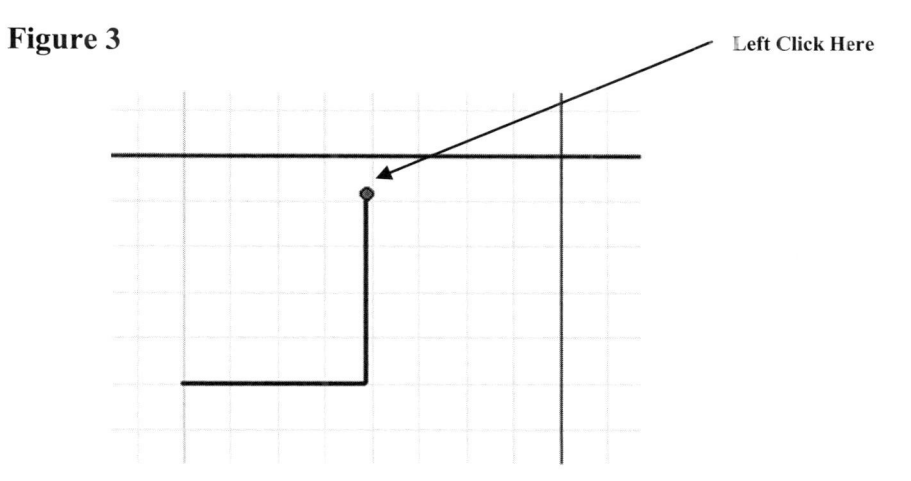

Left Click Here

7. Move the cursor to the right and left click once as shown in Figure 4.

Figure 4

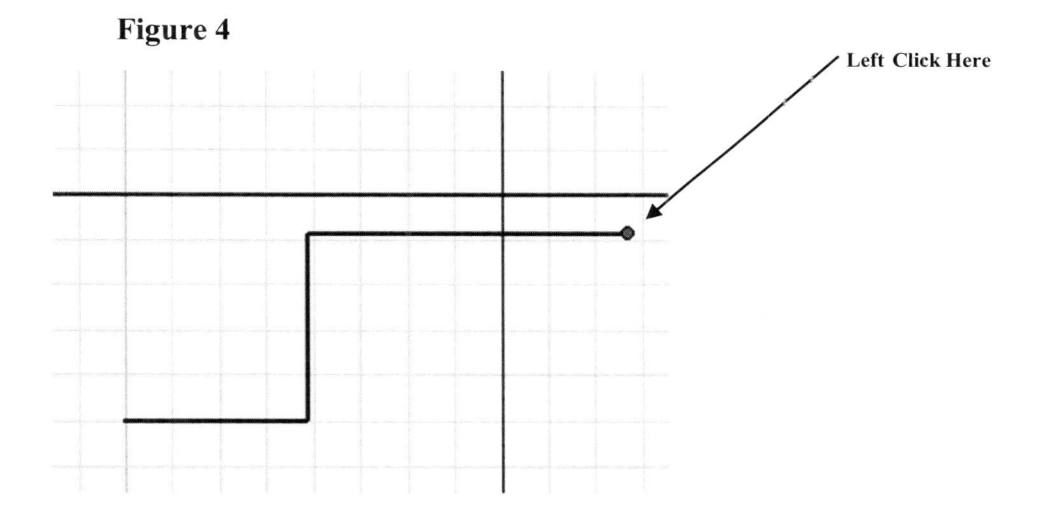

Left Click Here

Chapter 2: Learning More Basics

8. Move the cursor up and left click once as shown in Figure 5.

Figure 5

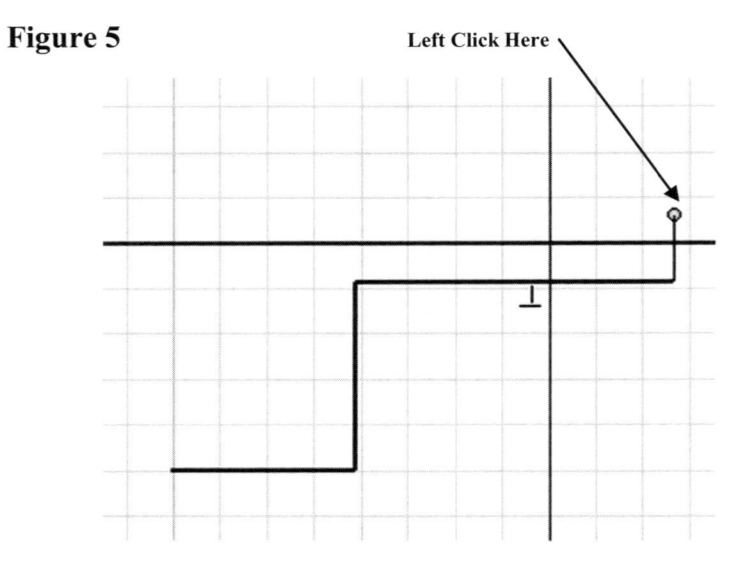

9. Move the cursor to the left and left click once. Ensure the dots between the first end point and the last end point appear as shown in Figure 6.

Figure 6

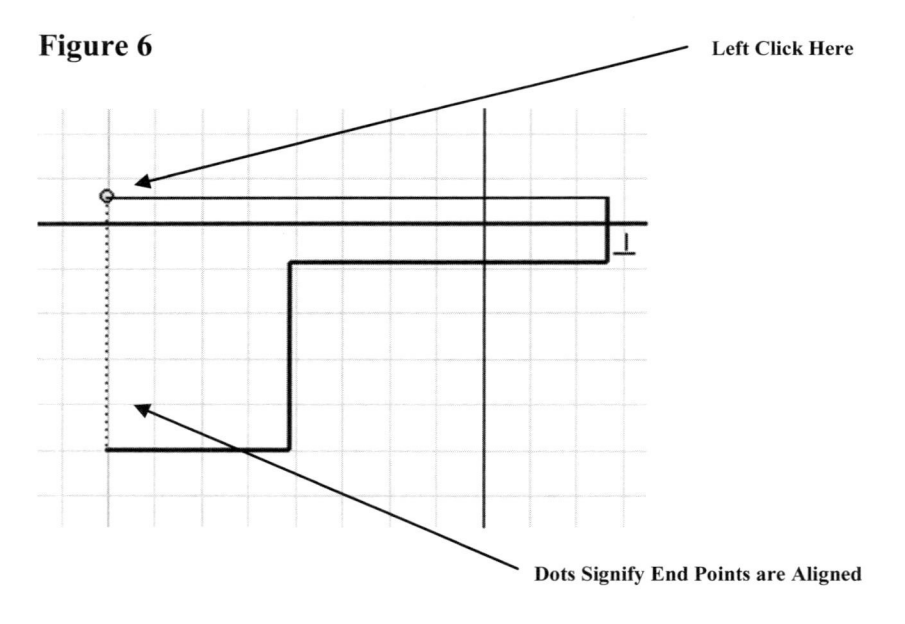

70

Chapter 2: Learning More Basics

10. Move the cursor back to the original starting end point and left click once as shown in Figure 7. Press the **Esc** key on the keyboard.

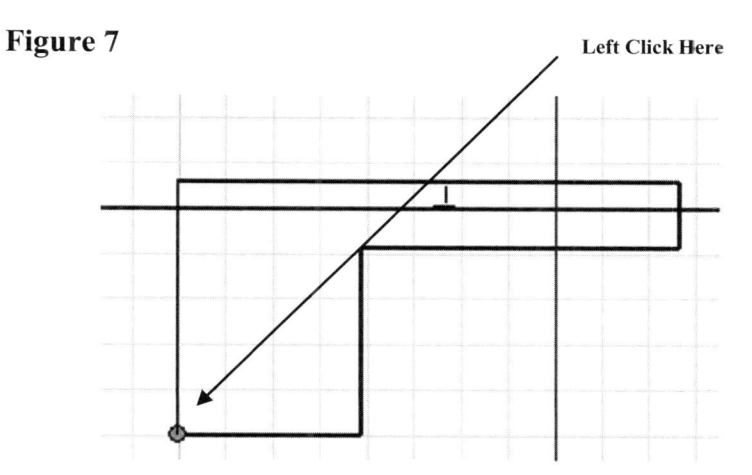

Figure 7

Left Click Here

11. Move the cursor to the middle left portion of the screen and left click on **General Dimension** as shown in Figure 8.

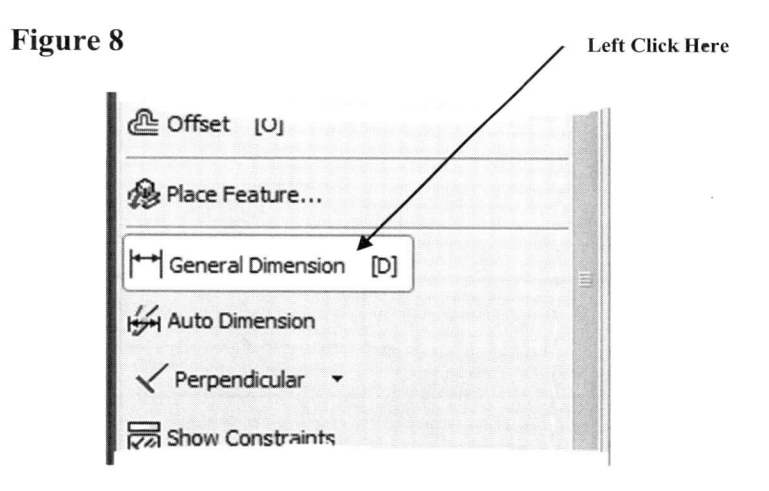

Figure 8

Left Click Here

Chapter 2: Learning More Basics

12. After selecting **General Dimension** move the cursor over the bottom horizontal line. The line will turn red as shown in Figure 9. Select the line by left clicking anywhere on the line **or** on each of the end points. To use the end points of the line, move the cursor over one of the end points. A small red square will appear. Left click once and move the cursor to the other end point. After the red square appears, left click once. The dimension will be attached to the cursor.

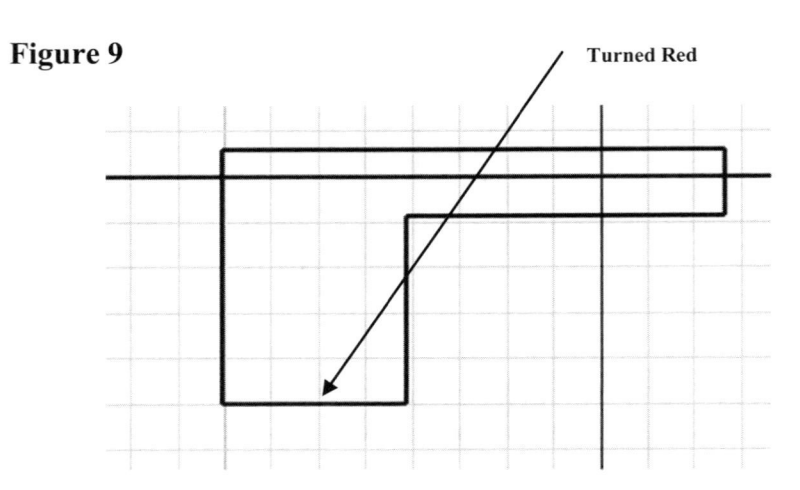

Figure 9   Turned Red

13. Move the cursor down. The actual dimension of the line will appear as shown in Figure 10.

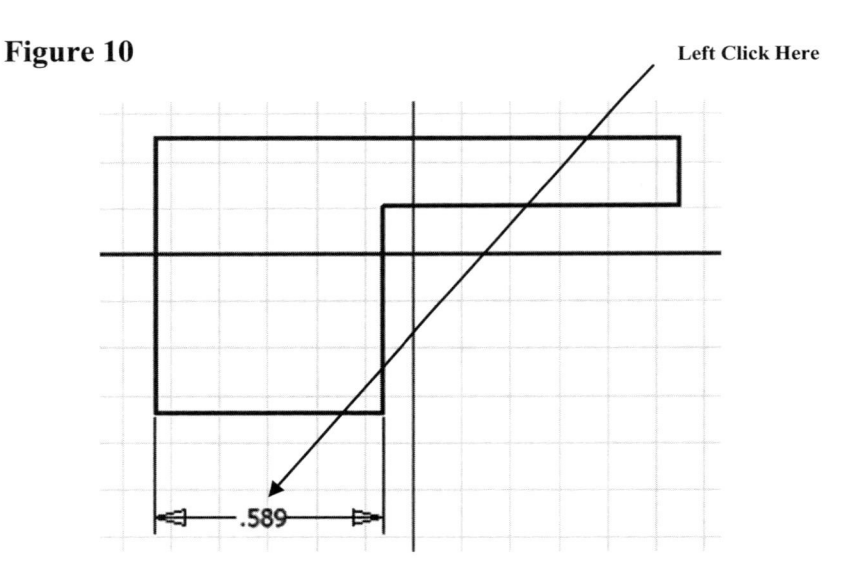

Figure 10   Left Click Here

72

Chapter 2: Learning More Basics

14. Move the cursor to where the dimension will be placed and left click once. While the dimension is still in red, left click once. The Edit Dimension dialog box will appear as shown in Figure 11.

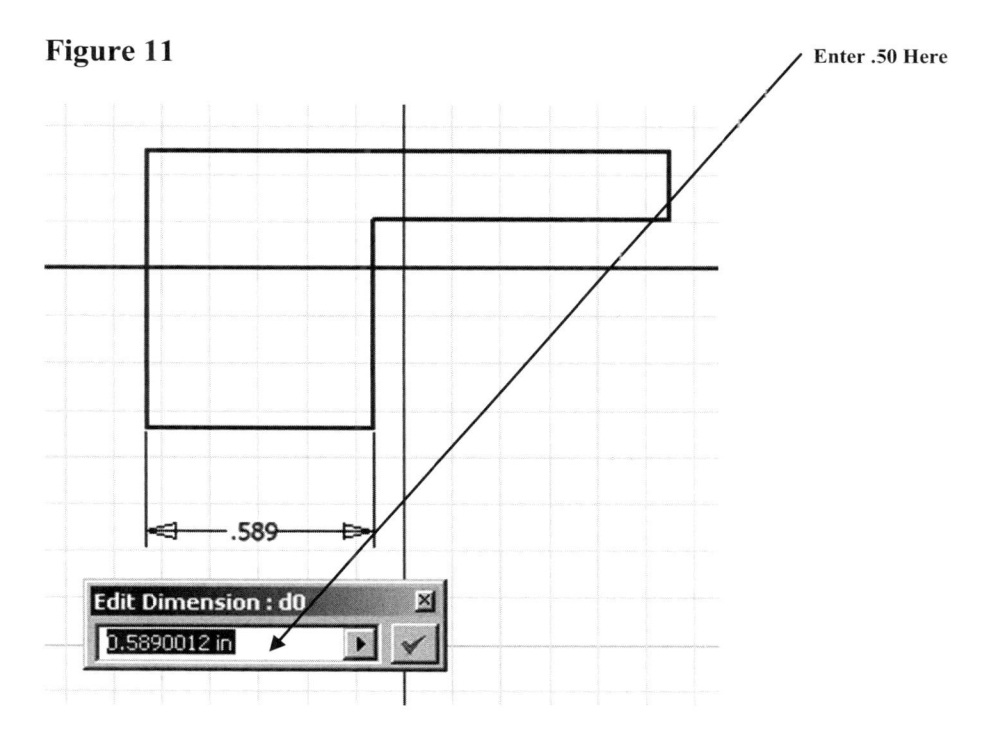

Figure 11

Enter .50 Here

15. To edit the dimension, type **.5** in the Edit Dimension dialog box (while the current dimension is highlighted) and press **Enter** on the keyboard.

16. The dimension of the line will become .5 inches as shown in Figure 12.

Figure 12

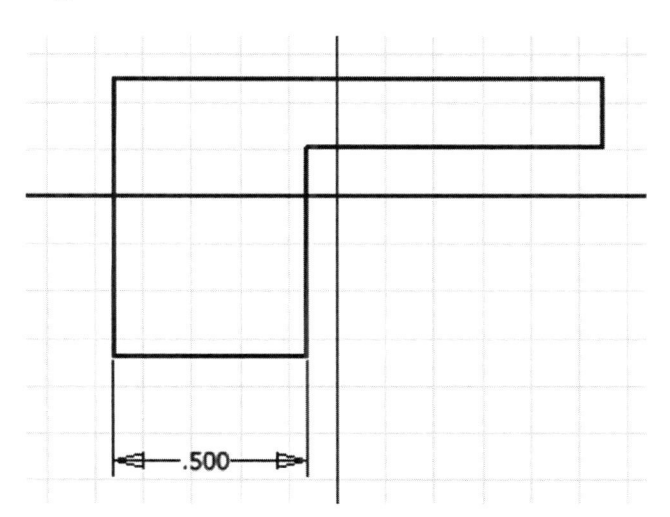

Chapter 2: Learning More Basics

17. To view the entire drawing move the cursor to the middle portion of the screen and left click once on the "Zoom All" icon as shown in Figure 13.

Figure 13　　　　　　　　　　　　Left Click Here

18. The drawing will "fill up" the entire screen. If the drawing is still too large left click on the "Zoom" icon as shown in Figure 14. After selecting the Zoom icon, hold the left mouse button down and drag the cursor up and down to achieve the desired view of the sketch.

Figure 14　　　　　　　　　　　　Left Click Here

19. Move the cursor to the middle left portion of the screen and left click on **General Dimension** as shown in Figure 15.

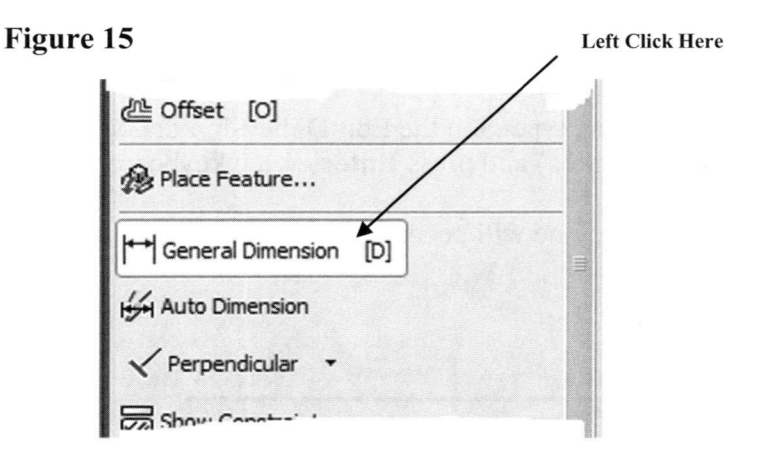

Figure 15　　　　　　　　　　　　Left Click Here

74

Chapter 2: Learning More Basics

20. After selecting **General Dimension** move the cursor over the vertical line. The line will turn red as shown in Figure 16. Select the line by left clicking anywhere on the line **or** on each of the end points. To use the end points of the line, move the cursor over one of the end points. A small red square will appear. Left click once and move the cursor to the other end point. After the square red dot appears, left click once. The dimension will be attached to the cursor.

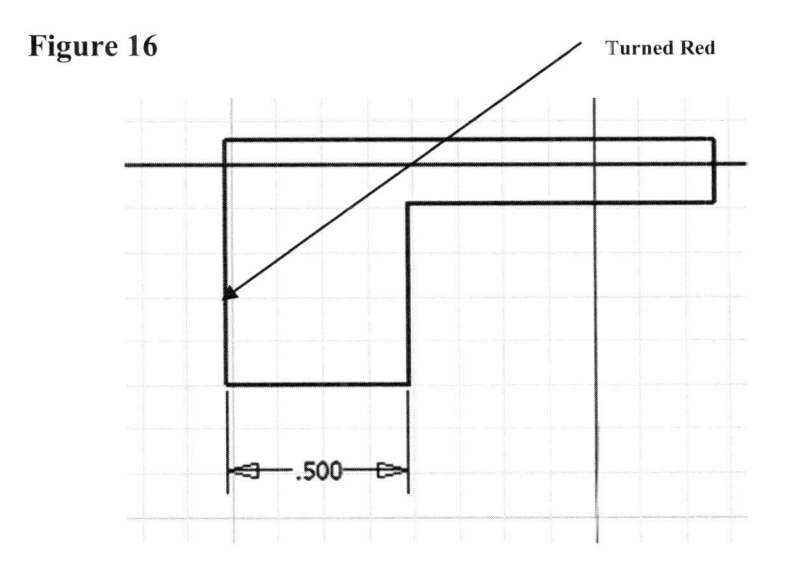

Figure 16   Turned Red

21. Move the cursor to the side. The actual dimension of the line will appear as shown in Figure 17.

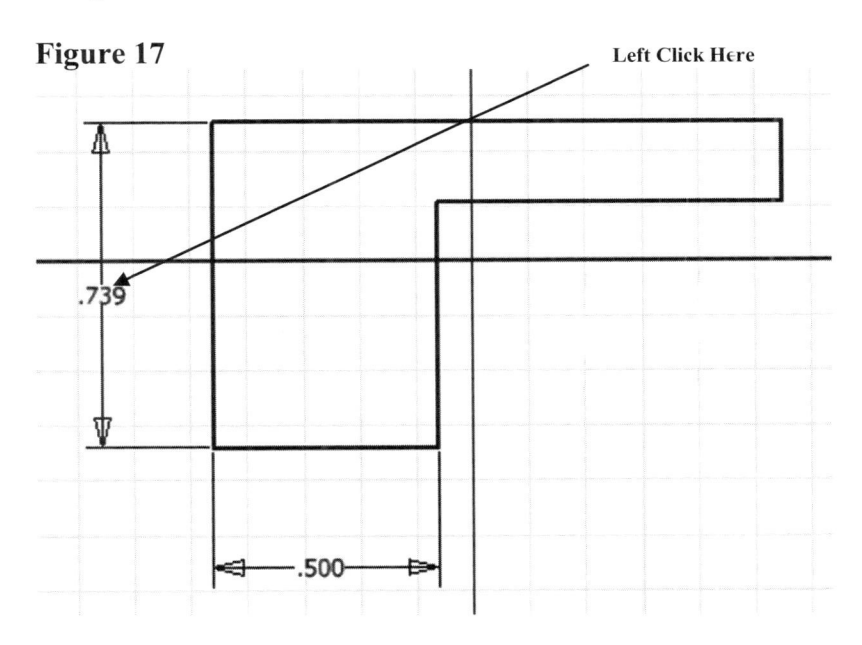

Figure 17   Left Click Here

75

Chapter 2: Learning More Basics

22. Move the cursor to where the dimension will be placed and left click once. While the dimension is still in red, left click once. The Edit Dimension dialog box will appear as shown in Figure 18.

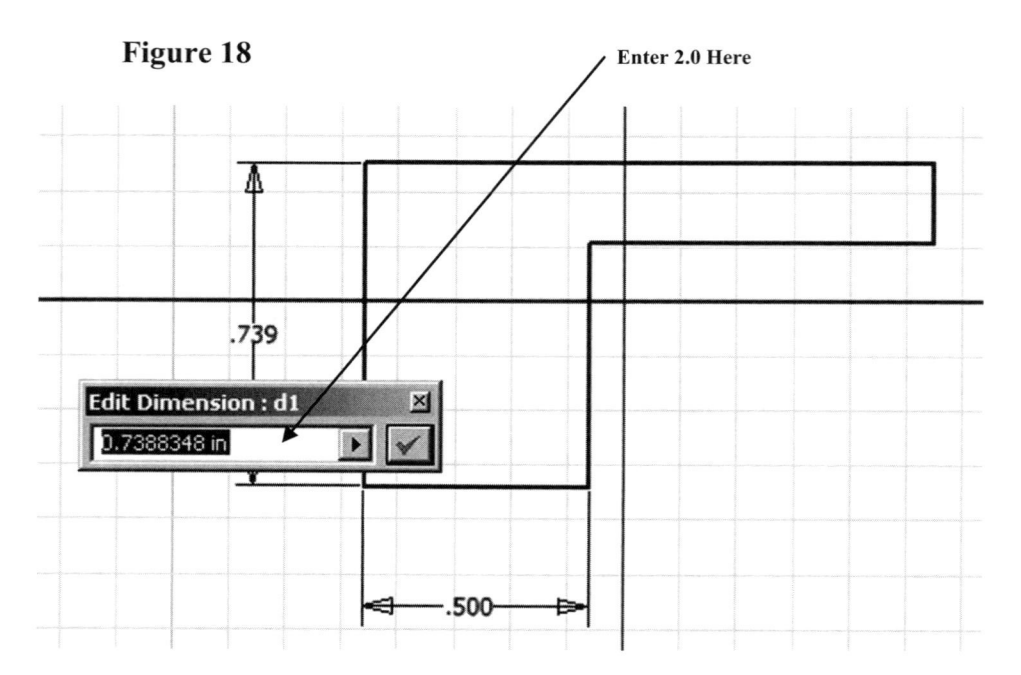

Figure 18

23. To edit the dimension, Enter **2.0** in the Edit Dimension dialog box (while the current dimension is highlighted) and press **Enter** on the keyboard.

24. The dimension of the line will become 2.0 inches as shown in Figure 19. Use the Zoom icons to zoom out if necessary.

Figure 19

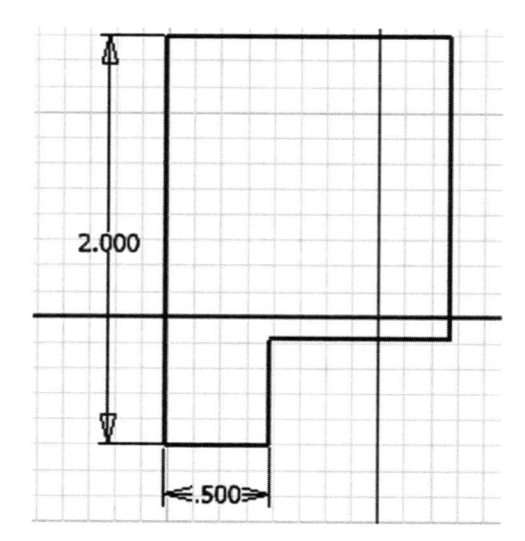

76

Chapter 2: Learning More Basics

25. Move the cursor to the middle left portion of the screen and left click on **General Dimension** as shown in Figure 20.

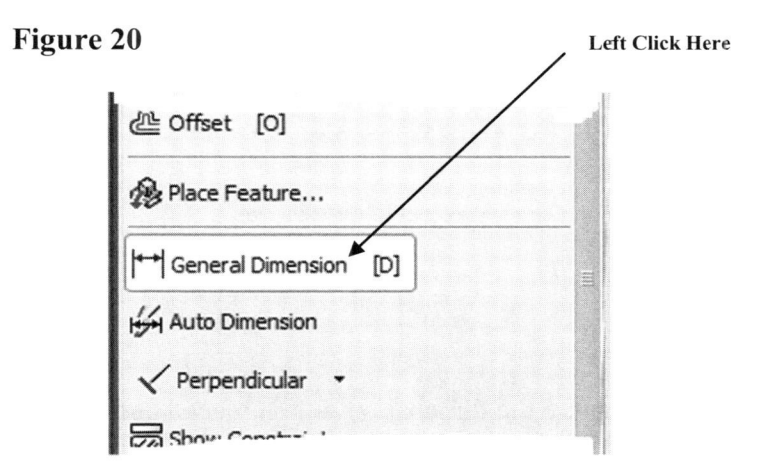

Figure 20

Left Click Here

26. After selecting **General Dimension** move the cursor over the top horizontal line. The line will turn red as shown in Figure 21. Select the line by left clicking anywhere on the line **or** on each of the end points. To use the end points of the line, move the cursor over one of the end points. A small red square will appear. Left click once and move the cursor to the other end point. After the red square appears, left click once. The dimension will be attached to the cursor.

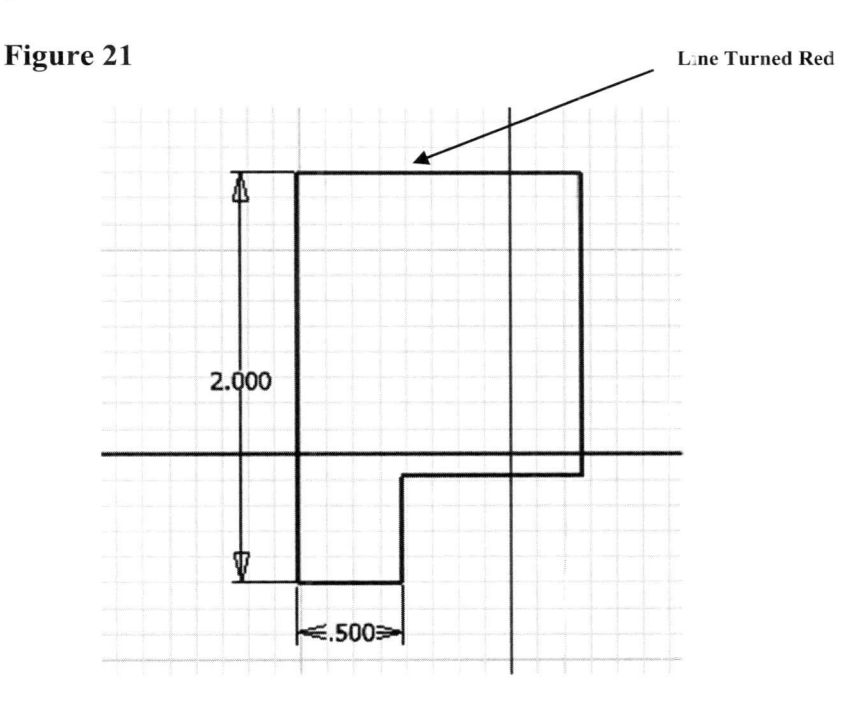

Figure 21

Line Turned Red

Chapter 2: Learning More Basics

27. Move the cursor up. The actual dimension of the line will appear as shown in Figure 22.

Figure 22

Left Click Here

28. Move the cursor to where the dimension will be placed and left click once. While the dimension is still in red, left click once. The Edit Dimension dialog box will appear as shown in Figure 23.

Figure 23

Enter 1.5 Here

29. To edit the dimension, Enter **1.5** in the Edit Dimension dialog box (while the current dimension is highlighted) and press **Enter** on the keyboard.

30. The dimension of the line will become 1.5 inches as shown in Figure 24. Use the Zoom icons to zoom out if necessary.

Figure 24

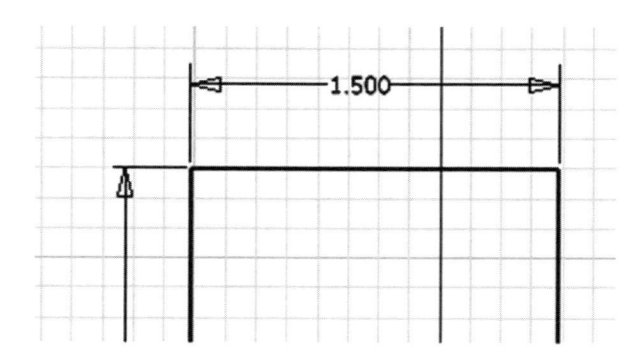

Chapter 2: Learning More Basics

31. Move the cursor to the middle left portion of the screen and left click on **General Dimension** as shown in Figure 25.

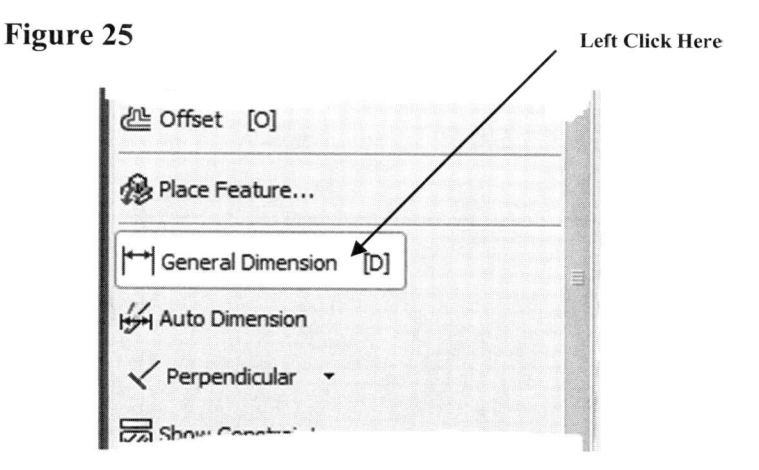

Figure 25

Left Click Here

- Offset [O]
- Place Feature...
- General Dimension [D]
- Auto Dimension
- Perpendicular
- Show Constr...

32. After selecting **General Dimension** move the cursor over the right side vertical line. The line will turn red as shown in Figure 26. Select the line by left clicking anywhere on the line **or** on each of the end points. To use the end points of the line, move the cursor over one of the end points. A small red square will appear. Left click once and move the cursor to the other end point. After the red square appears, left click once. The dimension will be attached to the cursor.

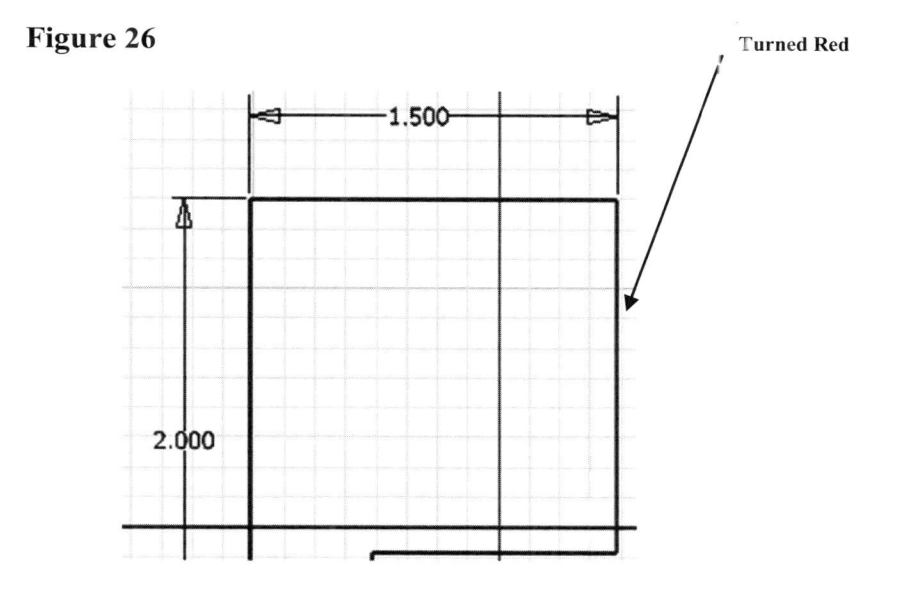

Figure 26

Turned Red

1.500

2.000

79

Chapter 2: Learning More Basics

33. Move the cursor up. The actual dimension of the line will appear as shown in Figure 27.

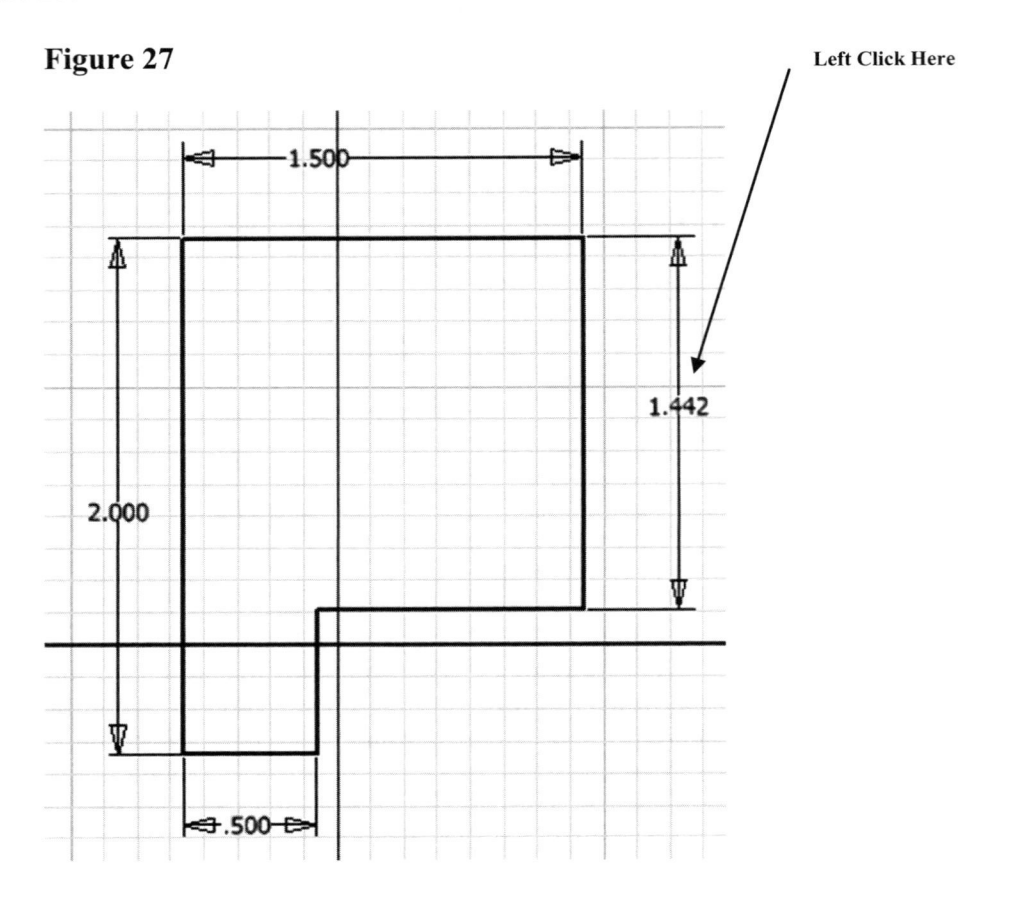

Figure 27

Chapter 2: Learning More Basics

34. Move the cursor to where the dimension will be placed and left click once. While the dimension is still in red, left click once. The Edit Dimension dialog box will appear as shown in Figure 28.

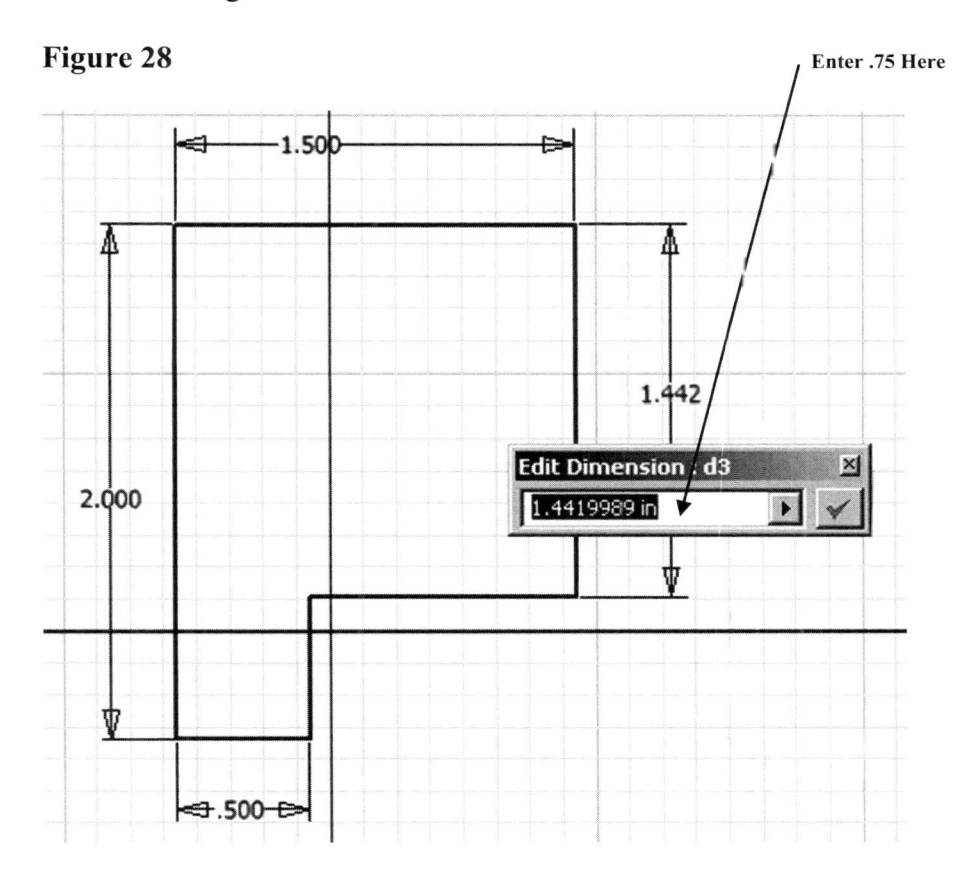

Figure 28

35. To edit the dimension, Enter **.75** in the Edit Dimension dialog box (while the current dimension is highlighted) and press **Enter** on the keyboard.

Chapter 2: Learning More Basics

36. The dimension of the line will become .75 inches as shown in Figure 29. Use the Zoom icons to zoom out if necessary.

Figure 29

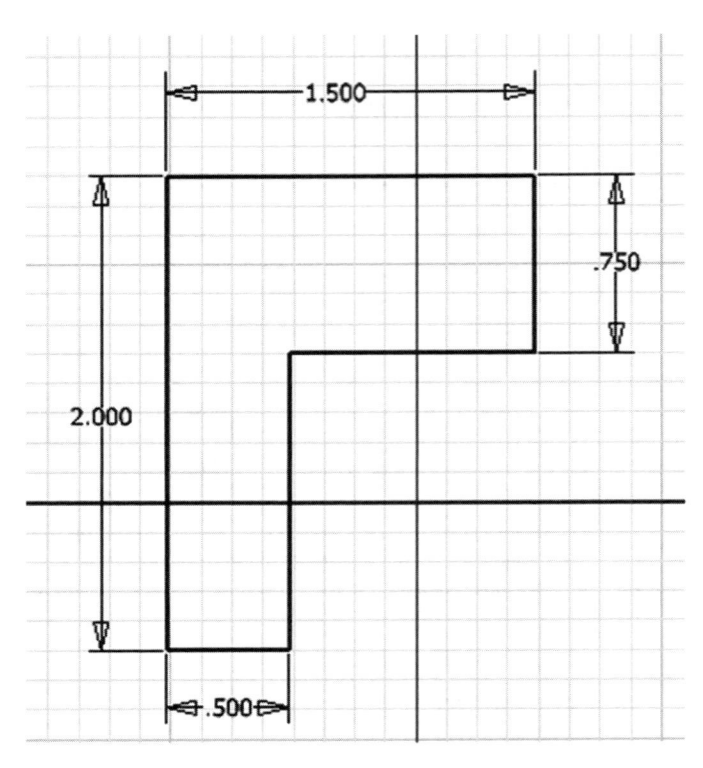

37. Move the cursor to the upper left corner of the screen and left click on **Line** as shown in Figure 30.

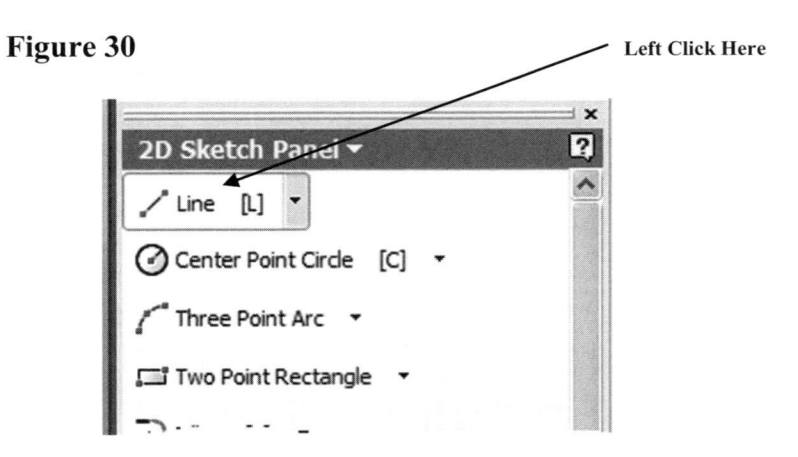

Figure 30

Chapter 2: Learning More Basics

38. Draw a line parallel to the top horizontal line as shown in Figure 31.

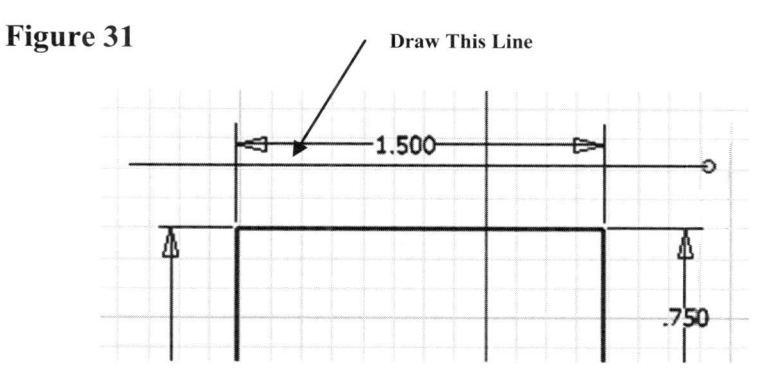

Figure 31

39. Dimension the line as shown in Figure 32.

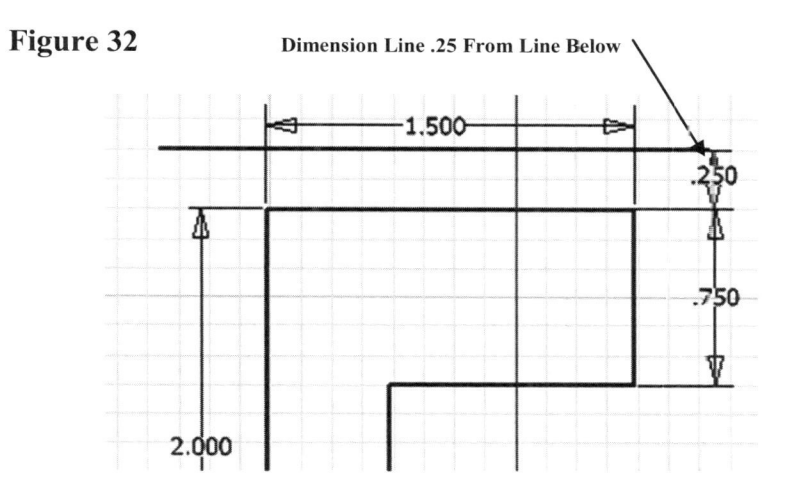

Figure 32

40. Using the keyboard, press **ESC** once or twice or right click around the drawing. A pop up menu will appear. Left click on **Done [Esc]** as shown in Figure 33.

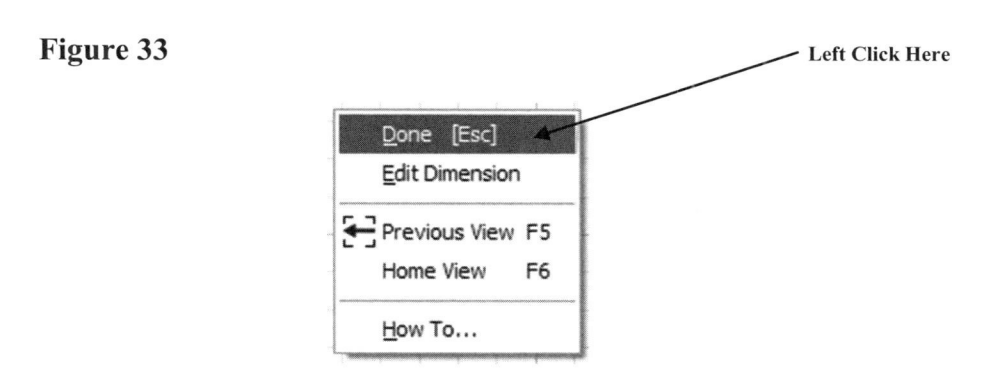

Figure 33

Chapter 2: Learning More Basics

41. After the sketch is complete it is time to revolve the sketch into a solid.

42. After you have verified that no commands are active, right click anywhere on the sketch. A pop up menu will appear. Left click on **Finish Sketch** as shown in Figure 34.

Figure 34

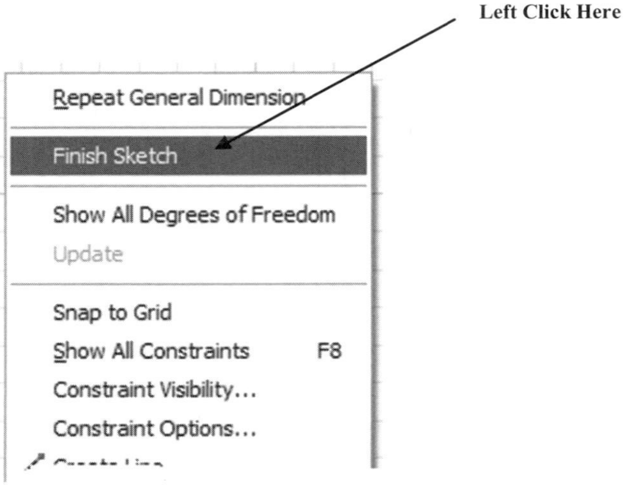

43. Inventor is now out of the Sketch Panel and into the Part Features Panel. Notice that the commands at the left of the screen are now different. To work in the Part Features Panel a sketch must be present and have no opens (non-connected lines). If there are any opens in the sketch an error message will appear. Your screen should look similar to Figure 35.

Figure 35

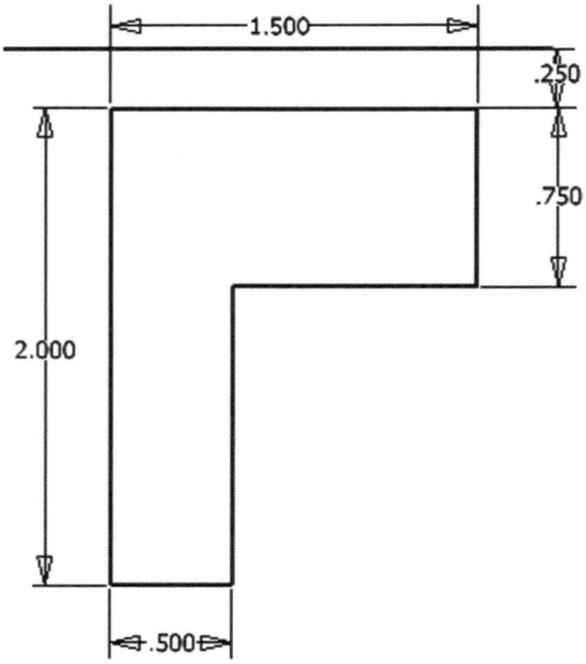

Chapter 2: Learning More Basics

44. Right click around the sketch. A pop up menu will appear. Left click on **Isometric/Home View** as shown in Figure 36.

Figure 36

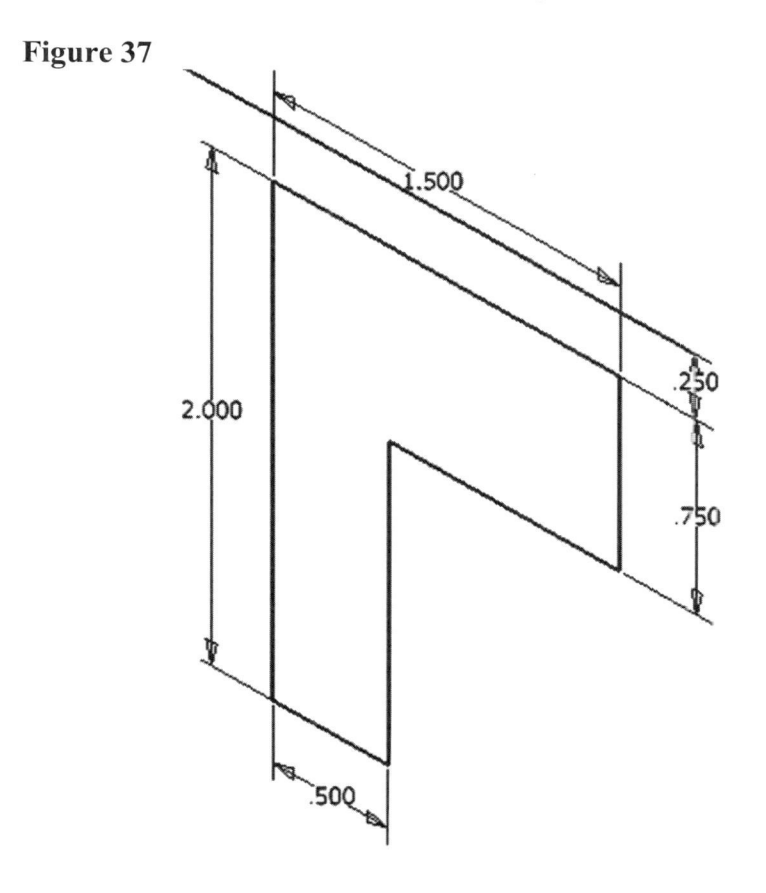

45. The view will become isometric as shown in Figure 37.

Figure 37

85

Chapter 2: Learning More Basics

46. Move the cursor to the middle left portion of the screen and left click on **Revolve**. The Revolve dialog box will appear. Inventor also provides a preview of the revolve. If Inventor gave you an error message, there are opens (non-connected lines) somewhere on the sketch OR the view is not Isometric. Check each intersection for opens by using the **Extend** and **Trim** commands and make sure the view is Isometric. Your screen should look similar to Figure 38.

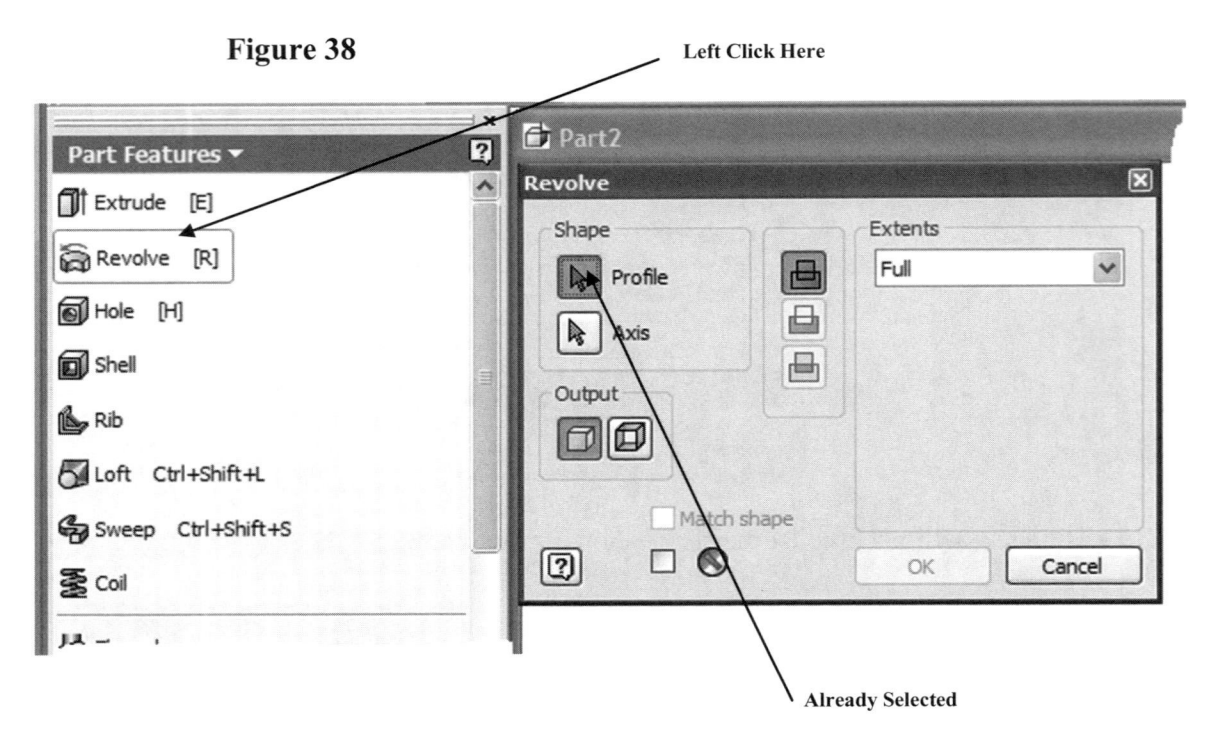

Figure 38

47. Notice that the Profile icon has already been selected. Because there is only one profile present, Inventor assumes that particular profile will be selected. If the drawing contained more than one profile, you would have to first select the profile icon in the revolve dialog box then use the cursor to select the desired profile.

Chapter 2: Learning More Basics

48. Move the cursor inside the profile causing it to turn red and left click once as shown in Figure 39.

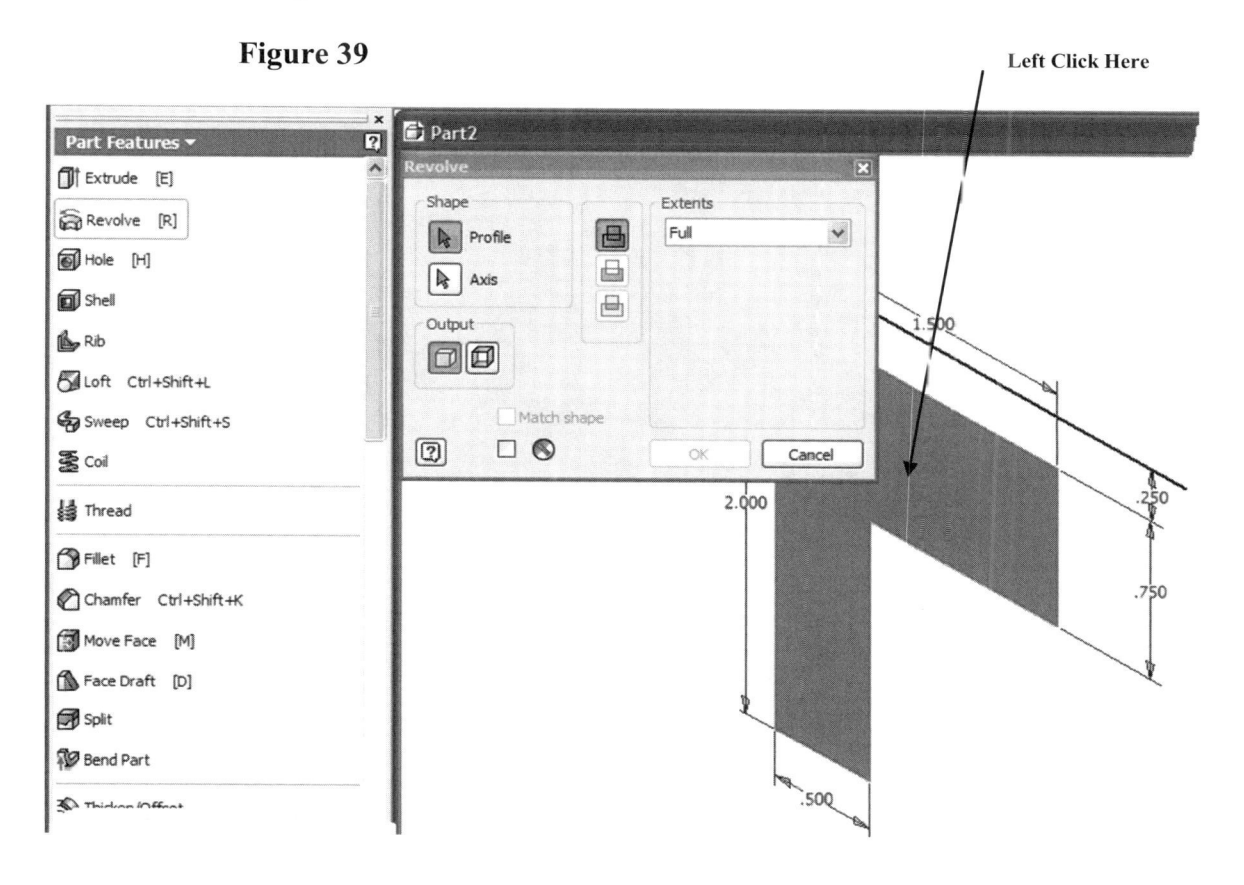

Figure 39

Chapter 2: Learning More Basics

49. Left click on **Axis** in the dialog box as shown in Figure 40.

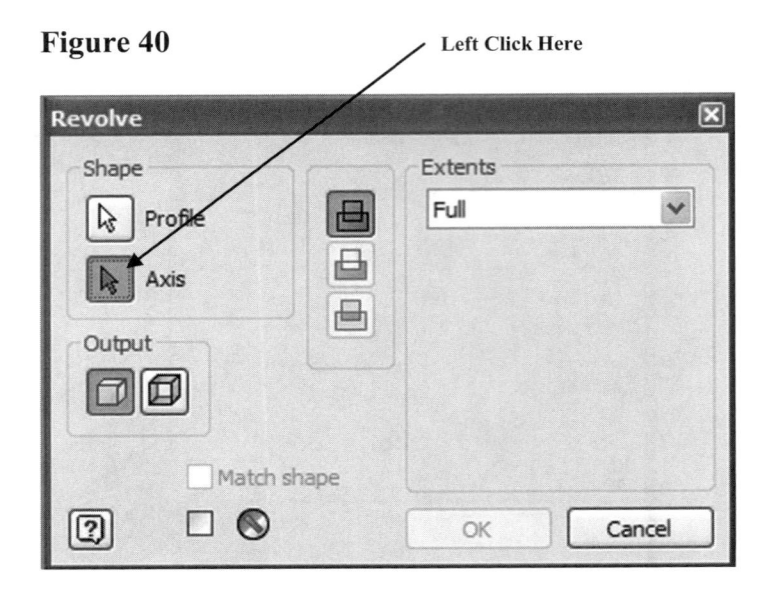

Figure 40

Chapter 2: Learning More Basics

50. Move the cursor over the axis line (the line located just above the top horizontal line). The line will turn red. Left click on the line as shown in Figure 41.

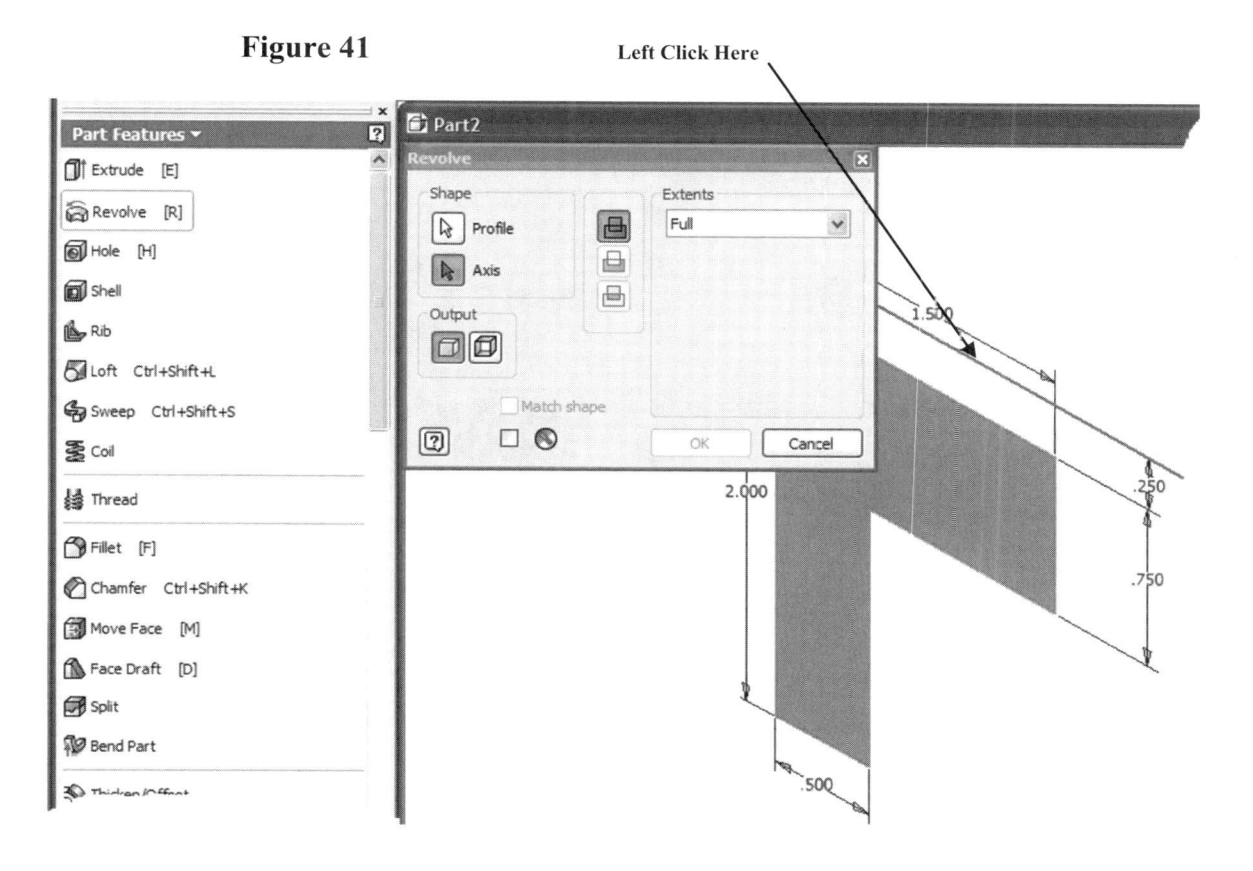

Figure 41

Chapter 2: Learning More Basics

51. A preview of the revolve will appear as shown in Figure 42.

   Figure 42

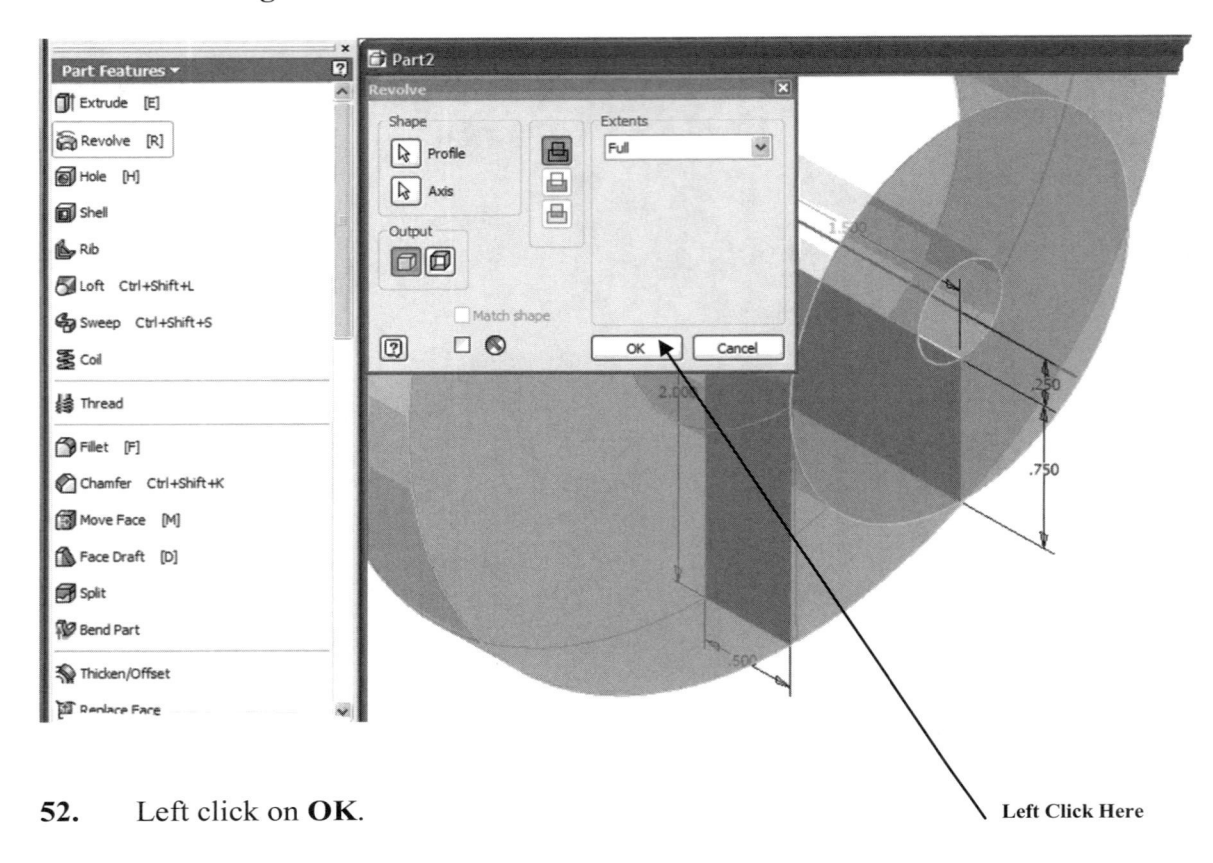

   Left Click Here

52. Left click on **OK**.

Chapter 2: Learning More Basics

53. Your screen should look similar to Figure 43. You may have to use the zoom out command to view the entire part.

Figure 43

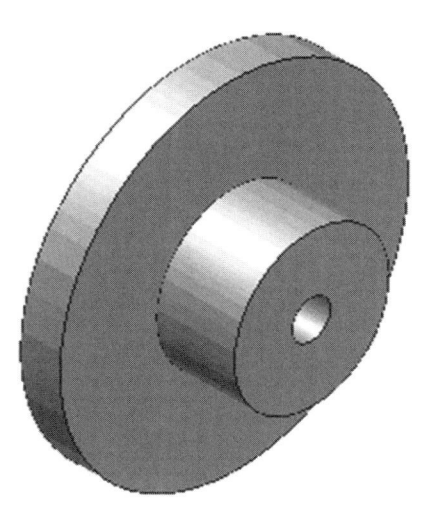

54. Move the cursor to the edge of the part causing the edges to turn red. After the edges become red, right click on the surface as shown in Figure 44.

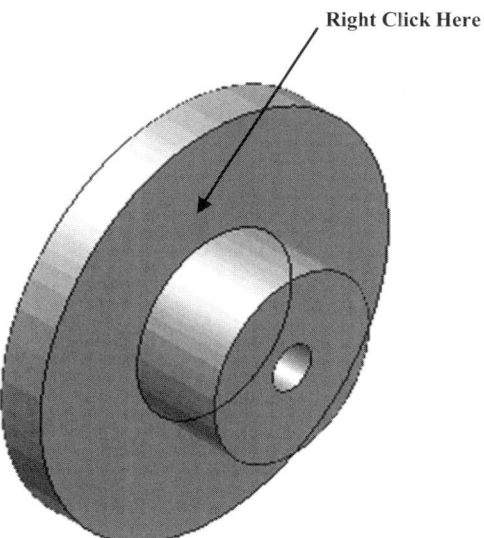

Figure 44 Right Click Here

91

Chapter 2: Learning More Basics

55. The surface will turn blue and a pop up menu will appear. Left click on **New Sketch** as shown in Figure 45.

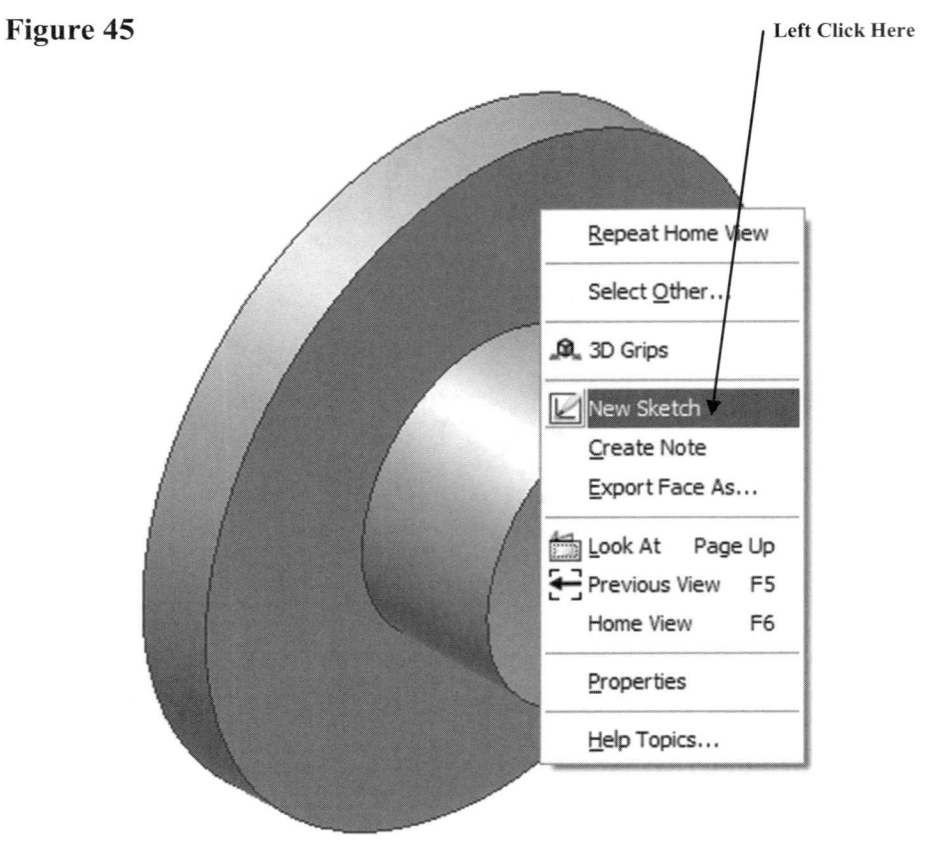

Figure 45

56. Inventor will begin a new sketch on the selected surface. Your screen should look similar to Figure 46.

Figure 46

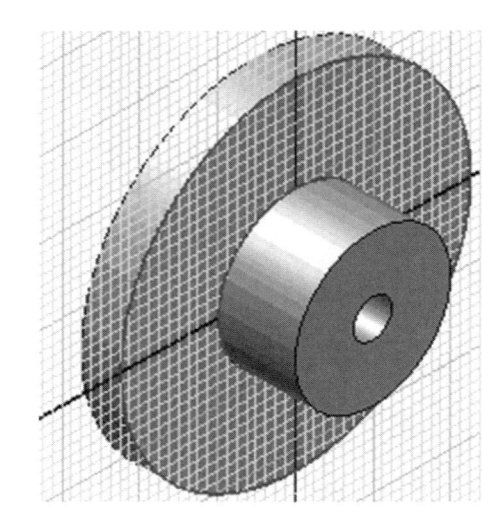

Chapter 2: Learning More Basics

57. To gain a better look at the selected surface, move the cursor to the top center portion of the screen and left click on the "Look At" icon. You can also left click on the "Right" portion of the View Cube as shown in Figure 47. The View Cube can also be used to rotate the part around (by holding the left mouse button down) similar to using the Orbit/Rotate icon.

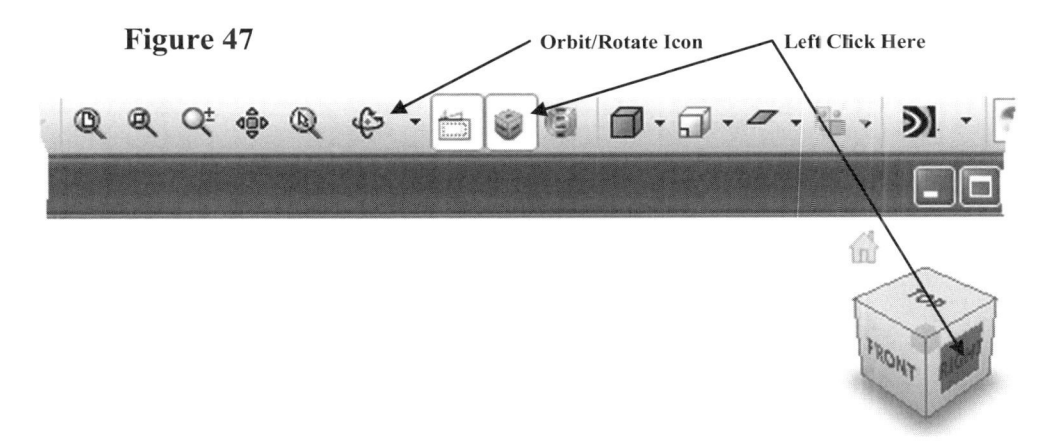

Figure 47

58. Left click on the surface the new sketch will be constructed on as shown in Figure 48.

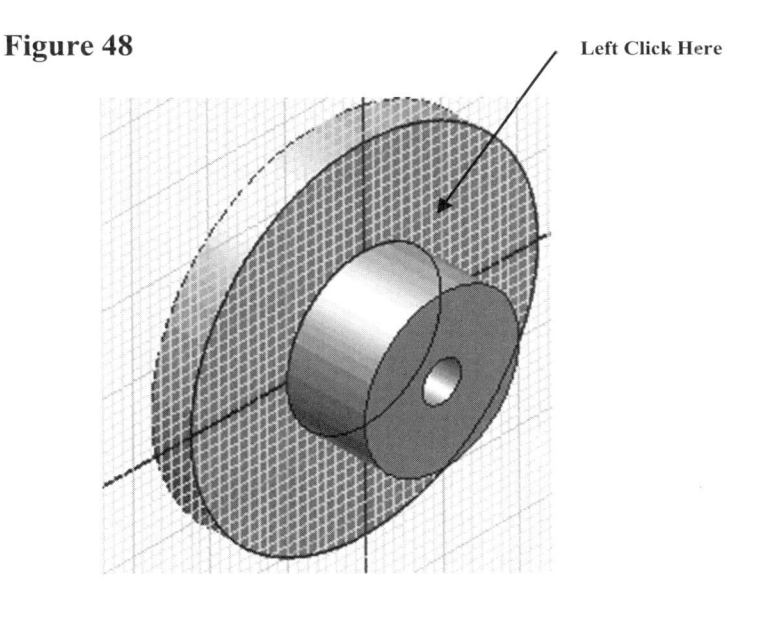

Figure 48

Chapter 2: Learning More Basics

59. Inventor will rotate the part to provide a perpendicular view of the selected surface as shown in Figure 49.

Figure 49

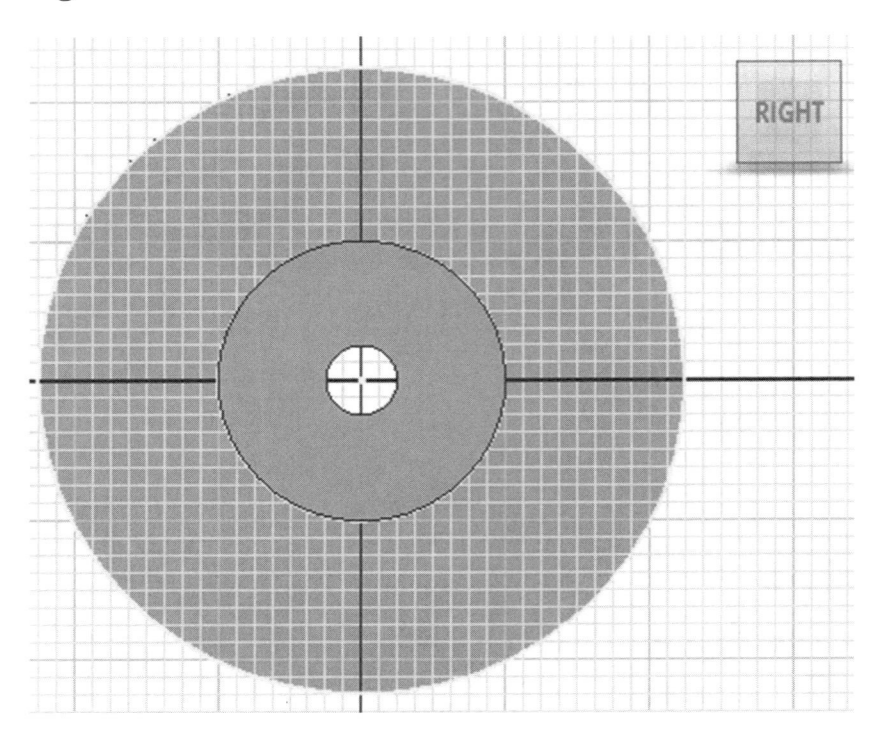

60. Move the cursor to the upper left corner of the screen and left click on **Line** as shown in Figure 50.

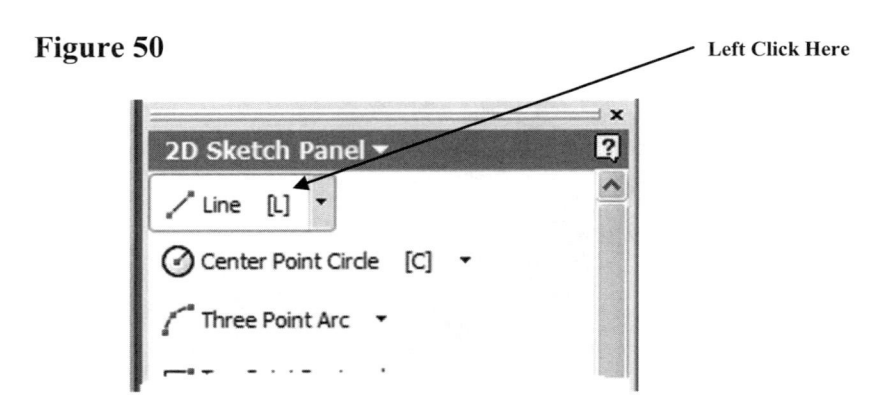

Figure 50

Chapter 2: Learning More Basics

61. Left click on the center of the hole. Ensure that a green dot appears as shown in Figure 51.

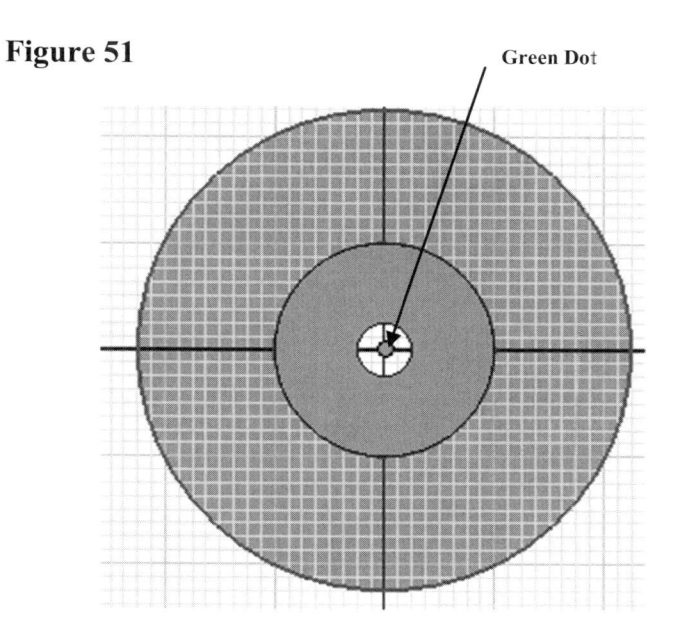

Figure 51

Green Dot

62. Move the cursor straight up and left click as shown in Figure 52.

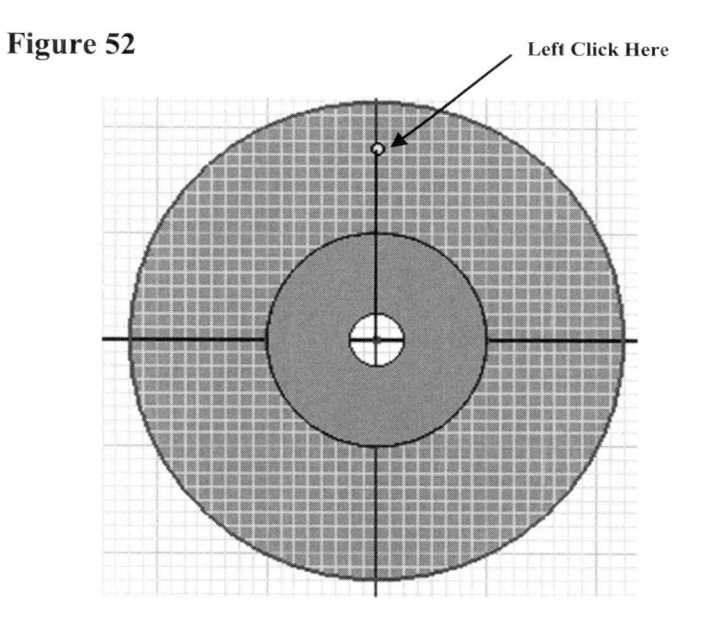

Figure 52

Left Click Here

Chapter 2: Learning More Basics

63. Right click. A pop up menu will appear. Left click on **Done [Esc]** as shown in Figure 53.

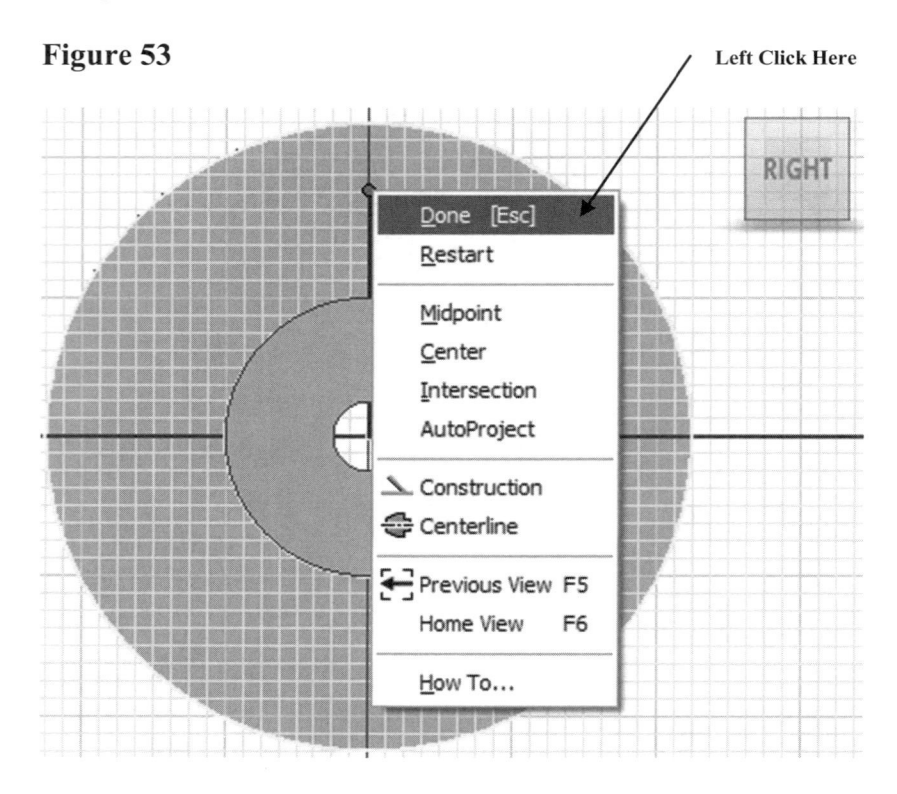

Figure 53

64. Move the cursor to the middle left portion of the screen and left click on **General Dimension** as shown in Figure 54.

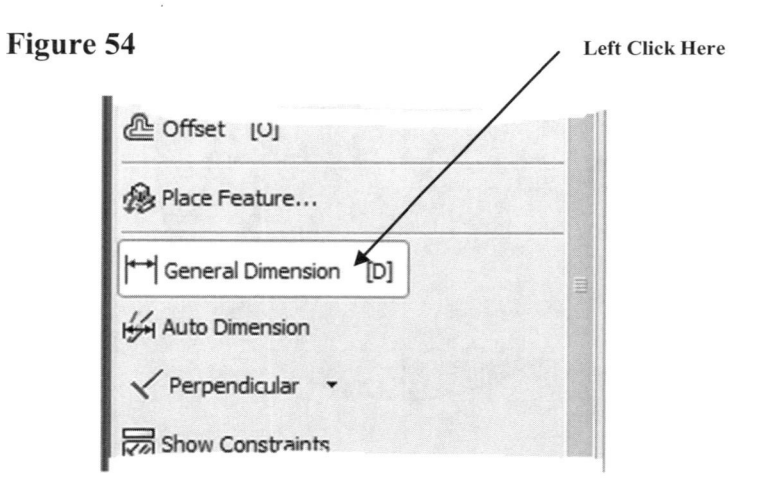

Figure 54

Chapter 2: Learning More Basics

65. After selecting **General Dimension** move the cursor to the line that was just drawn. The line will turn red as shown in Figure 55. Select the line by left clicking anywhere on the line **or** on each of the end points. To use the end points of the line, move the cursor over one of the end points. A small red square will appear. Left click once and move the cursor to the other end point. After the red square appears, left click once. The dimension will be attached to the cursor.

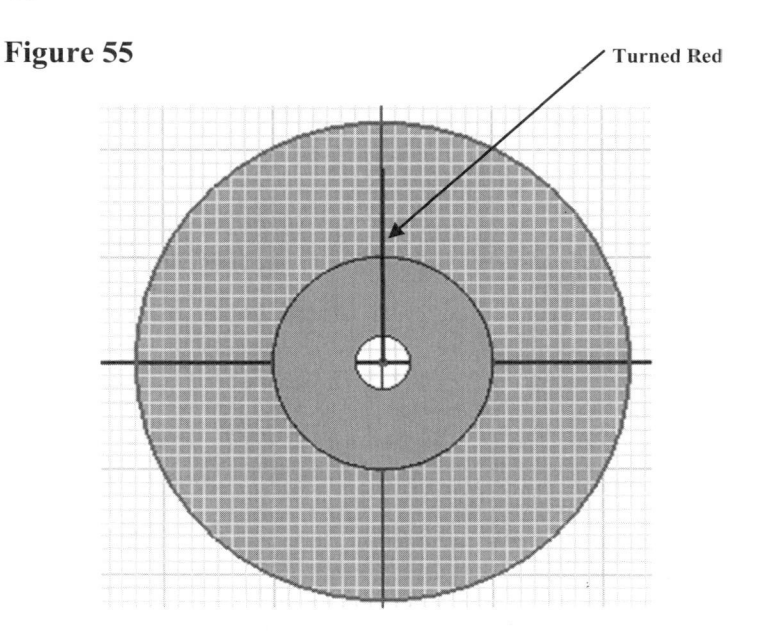

Figure 55

66. Move the cursor to the side. The actual dimension of the line will appear as shown in Figure 56.

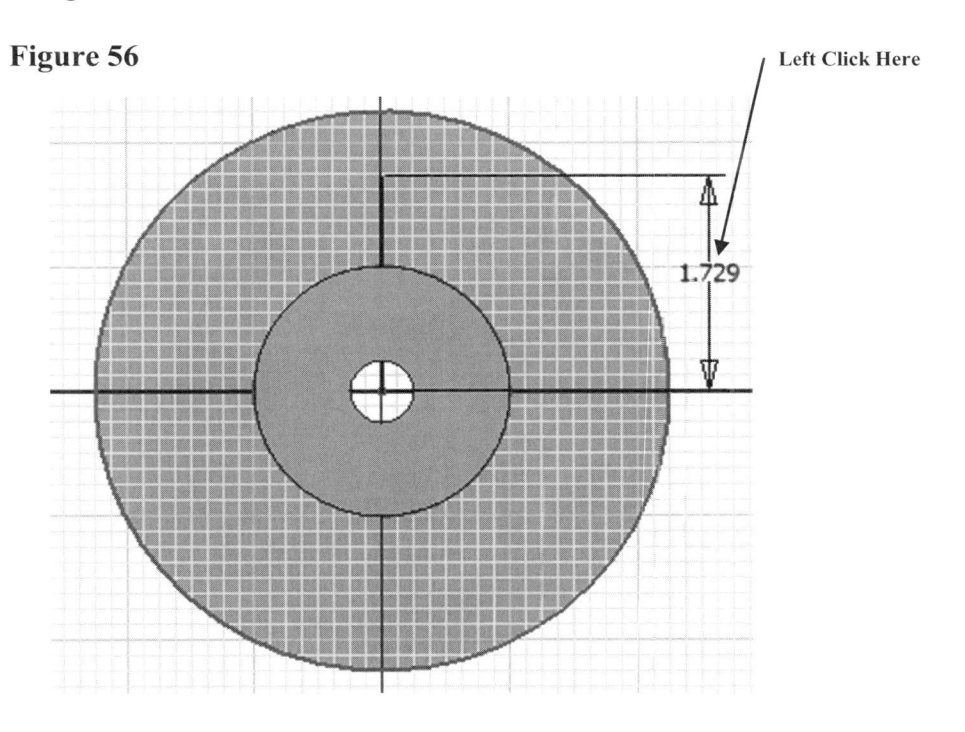

Figure 56

Chapter 2: Learning More Basics

67. Move the cursor to where the dimension will be placed and left click once. While the dimension is still in red, left click once. The Edit Dimension dialog box will appear as shown in Figure 57.

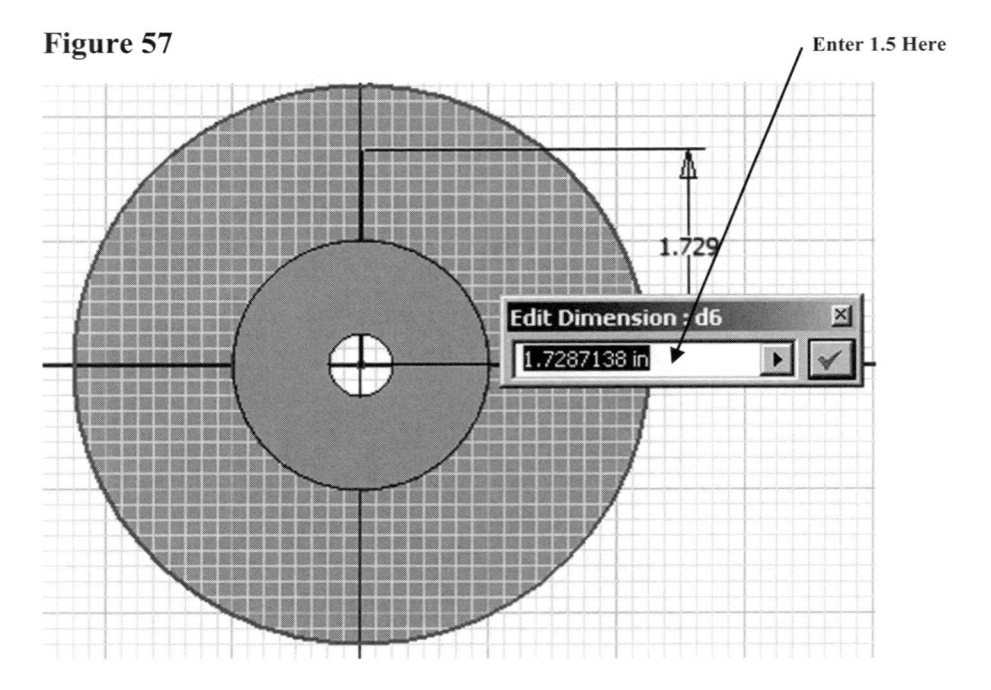

Figure 57

68. To edit the dimension, Enter **1.5** in the Edit Dimension dialog box (while the current dimension is highlighted) and press **Enter** on the keyboard.

69. The dimension of the line will become 1.5 inches as shown in Figure 58. Use the Zoom icons to zoom out if necessary.

Figure 58

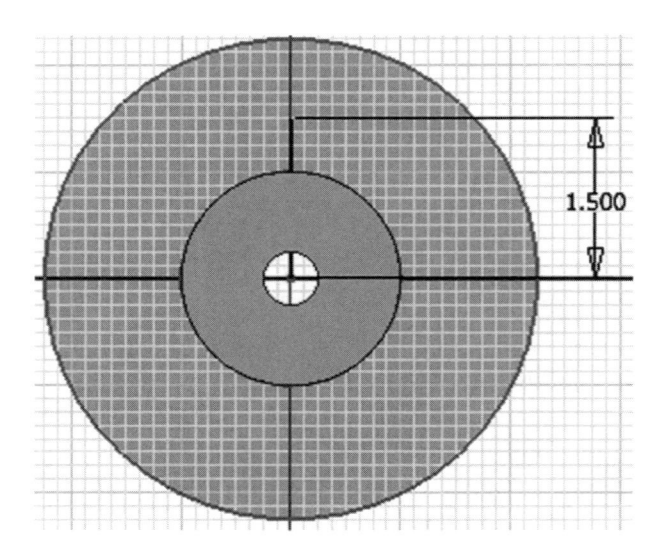

Chapter 2: Learning More Basics

70. Move the cursor to the middle left portion of the screen and left click on **Center Point Circle** as shown in Figure 59.

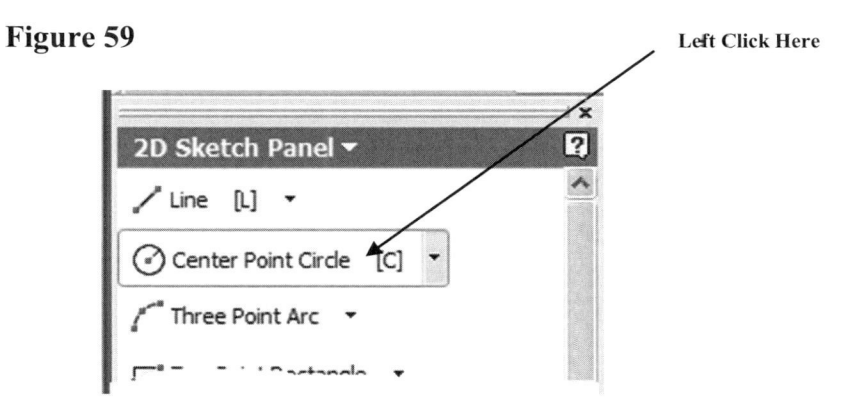

Figure 59

Left Click Here

71. Left click on the end point of the line as shown in Figure 60.

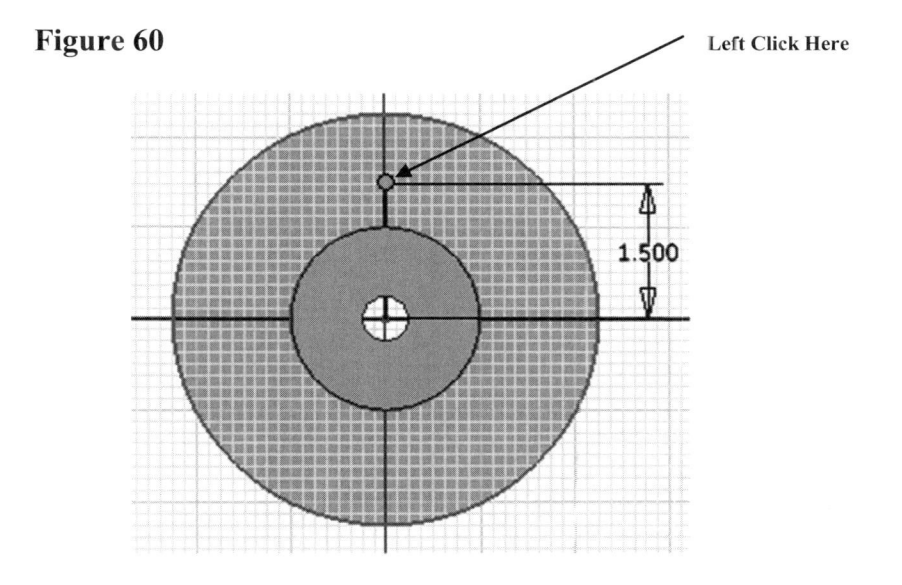

Figure 60

Left Click Here

99

Chapter 2: Learning More Basics

72. Move the cursor out to the right to create a circle as shown in Figure 61.

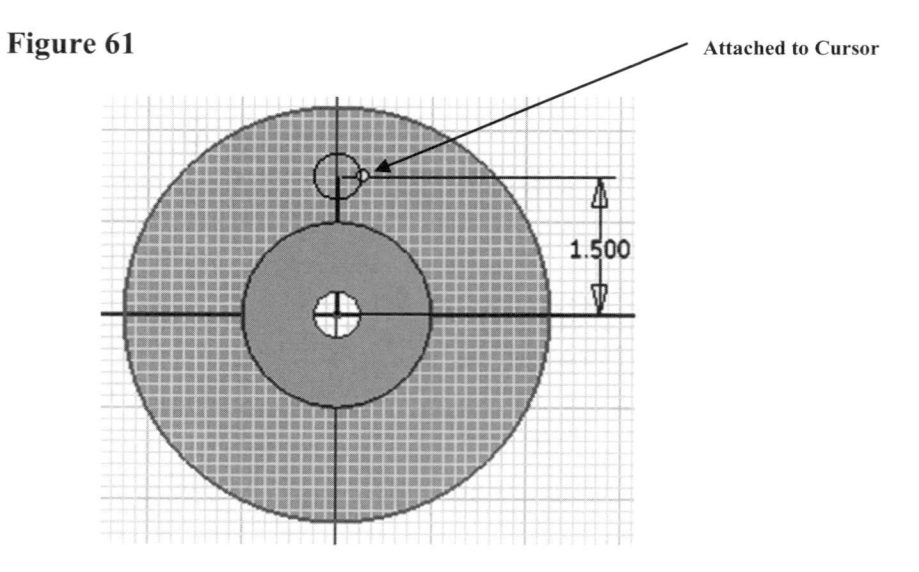

Figure 61

73. Left click as shown in Figure 62.

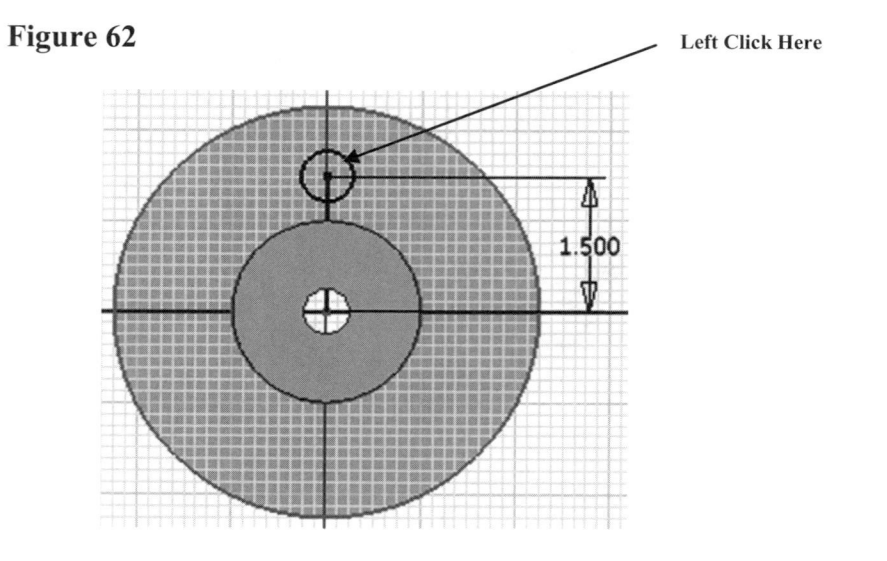

Figure 62

Chapter 2: Learning More Basics

74. Move the cursor to the middle left portion of the screen and left click on **General Dimension** as shown in Figure 63.

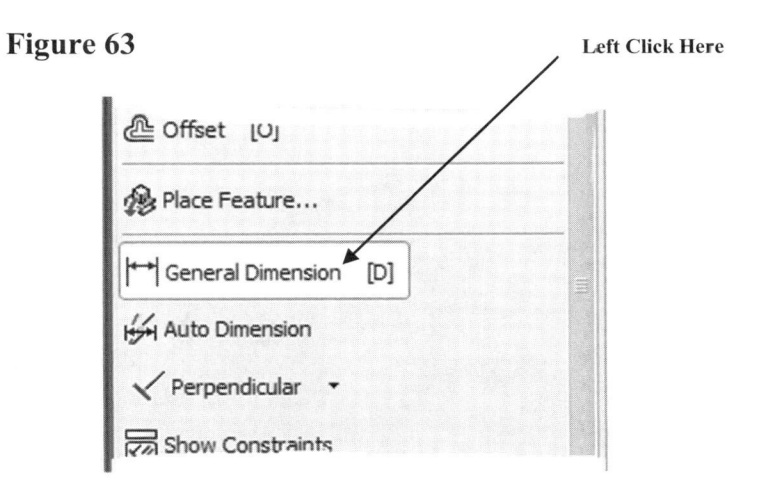

Figure 63

Left Click Here

75. After selecting **General Dimension** move the cursor to the circle that was just drawn. The circle will turn red. Select the circle by left clicking anywhere on the circle (not the center) as shown in Figure 64. The dimension will be attached to the cursor.

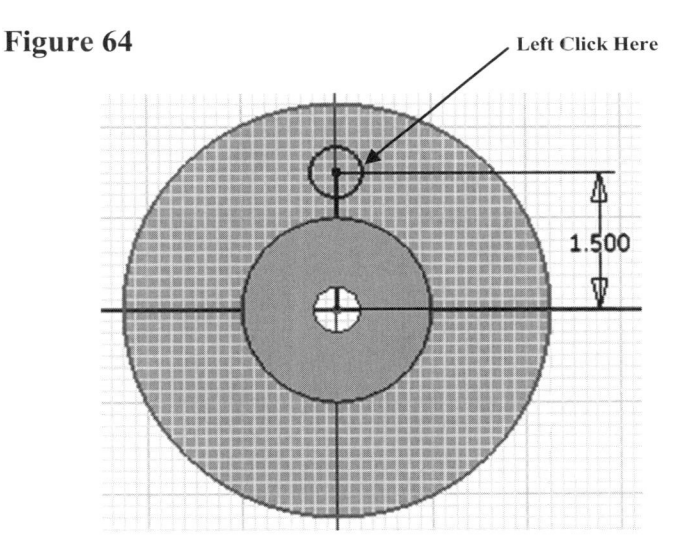

Figure 64

Left Click Here

1.500

Chapter 2: Learning More Basics

76. Move the cursor to the side. The actual dimension of the line will appear as shown in Figure 65.

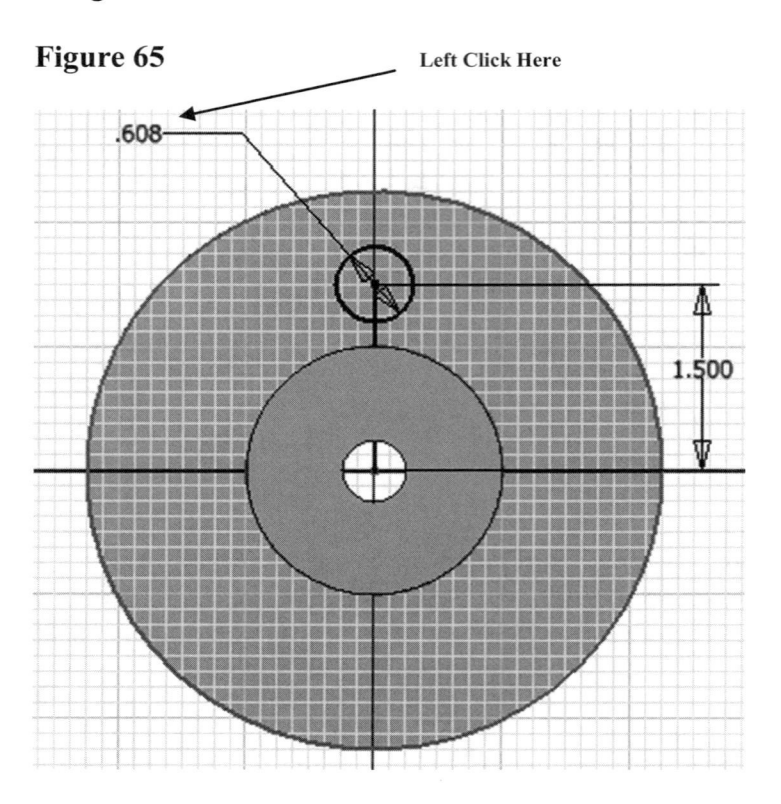

Figure 65

Left Click Here

Chapter 2: Learning More Basics

77. Move the cursor to where the dimension will be placed and left click once. While the dimension is still in red, left click once. The Edit Dimension dialog box will appear as shown in Figure 66.

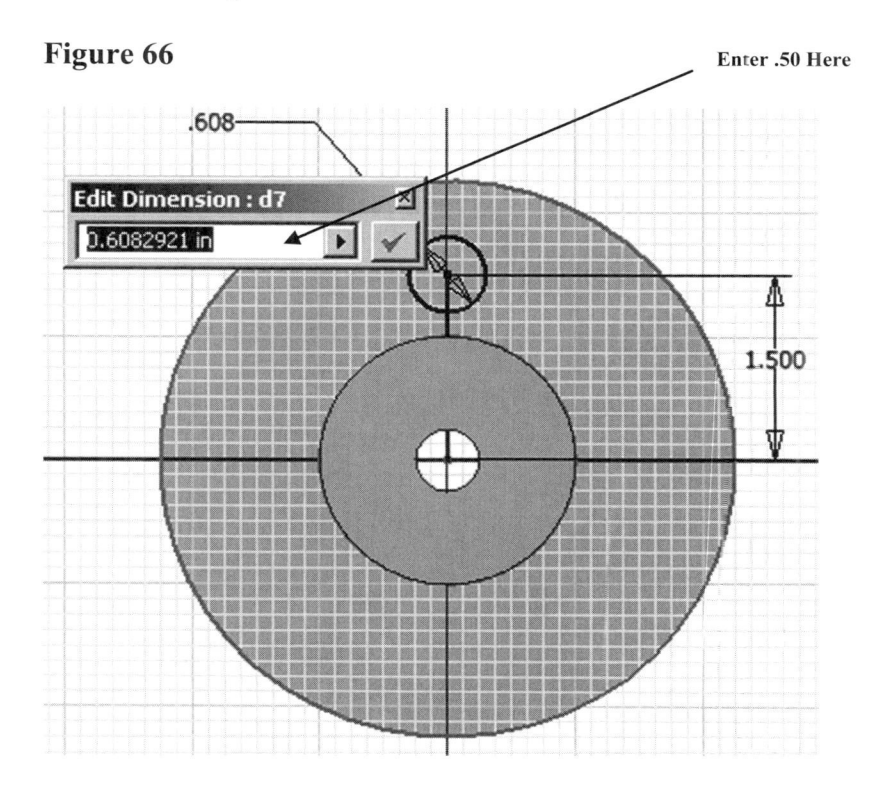

Figure 66

78. To edit the dimension, Enter **.50** in the Edit Dimension dialog box (while the current dimension is highlighted) and press **Enter** on the keyboard. Press the **Esc** key once or twice.

Chapter 2: Learning More Basics

79. The dimension of the line will become .50 inches as shown in Figure 67. Use the Zoom icons to zoom out if necessary.

Figure 67

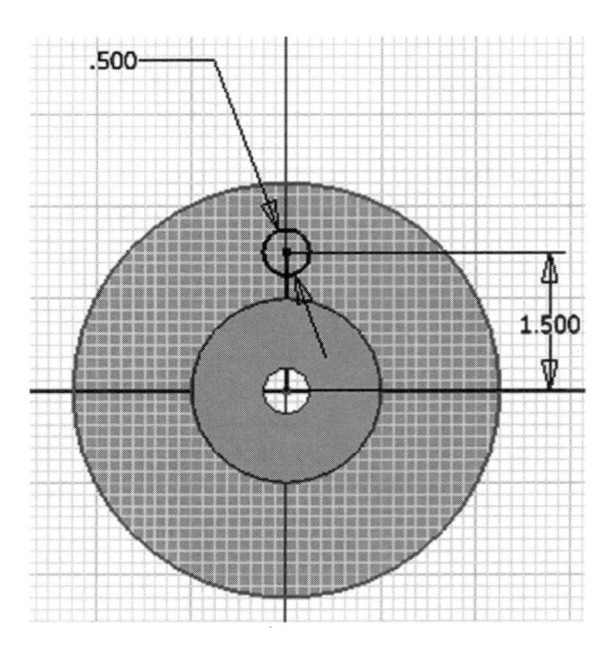

80. Move the cursor to the line that was used to locate the center of the circle. The line will turn red as shown in Figure 68.

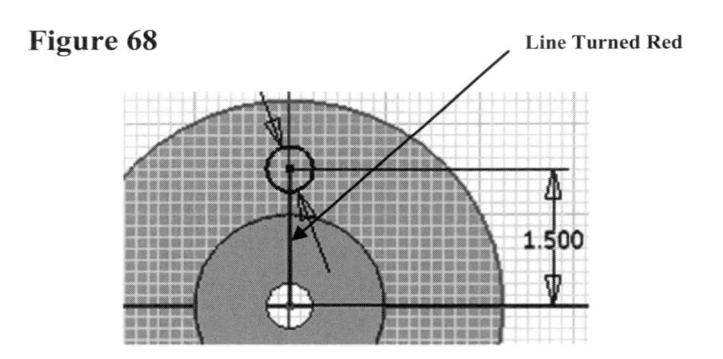

Figure 68 Line Turned Red

Chapter 2: Learning More Basics

81. Right click on the line after it turns red. A pop up menu will appear as shown in Figure 69.

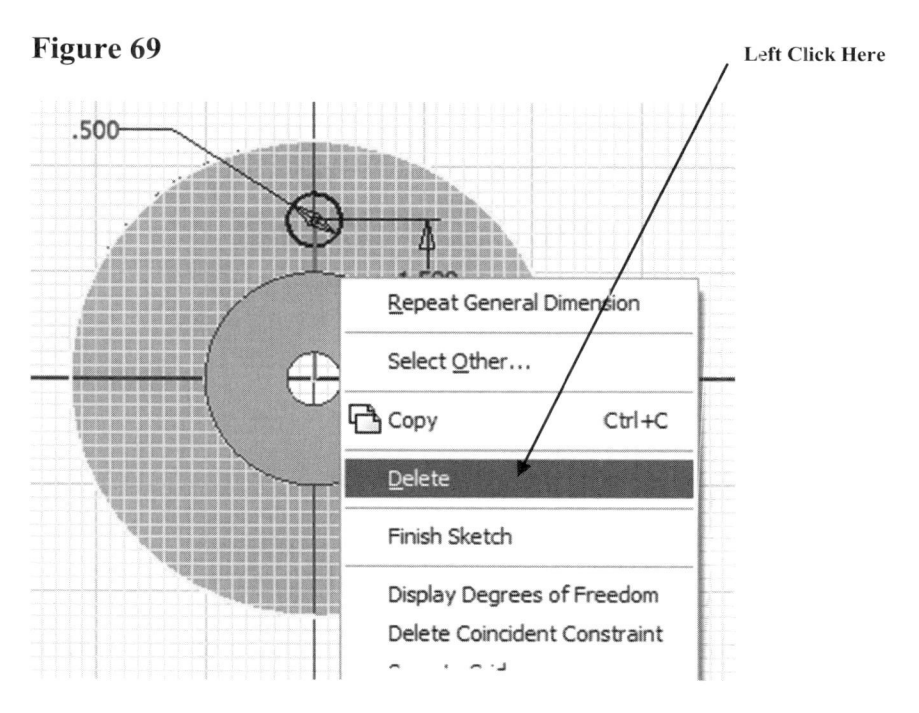

Figure 69

82. Left click on **Delete** as shown in Figure 69.

83. If any commands are still active, use the keyboard to press **Esc** once or twice, or right click around the drawing. A pop up menu will appear. Left click on **Done [Esc]** as shown in Figure 70.

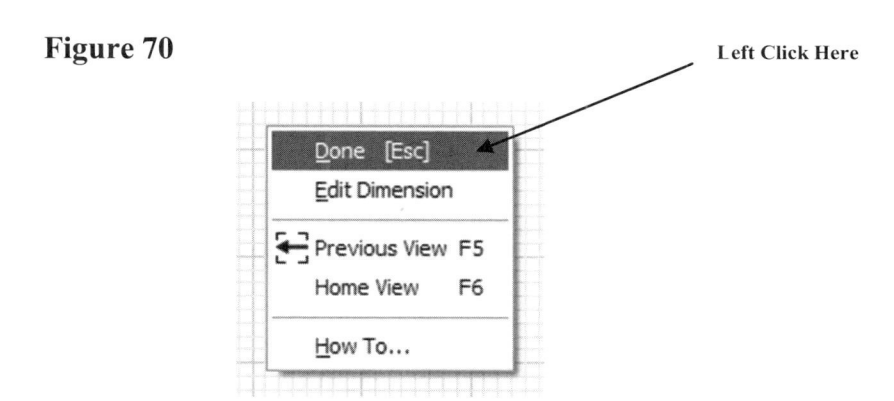

Figure 70

105

Chapter 2: Learning More Basics

84. After you have verified that no commands are active, right click anywhere on the sketch. A pop up menu will appear. Left click on **Finish Sketch** as shown in Figure 71.

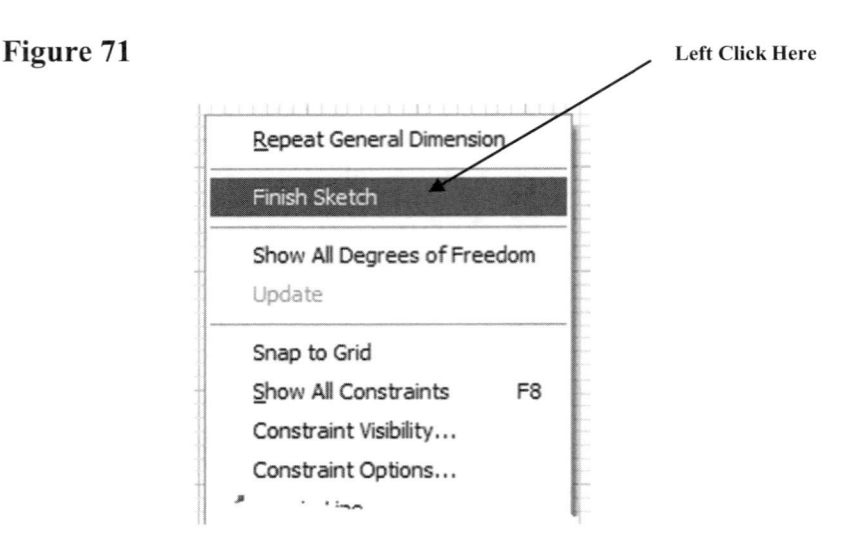

Figure 71

Left Click Here

- Repeat General Dimension
- Finish Sketch
- Show All Degrees of Freedom
- Update
- Snap to Grid
- Show All Constraints   F8
- Constraint Visibility…
- Constraint Options…

85. Inventor is now out of the Sketch Panel and into the Part Features Panel. Notice that the commands at the left of the screen are now different. To work in the Part Features Panel a sketch must be present and have no opens (non-connected lines). If there are any opens in the sketch an error message will appear. Your screen should look similar to Figure 72.

Figure 72

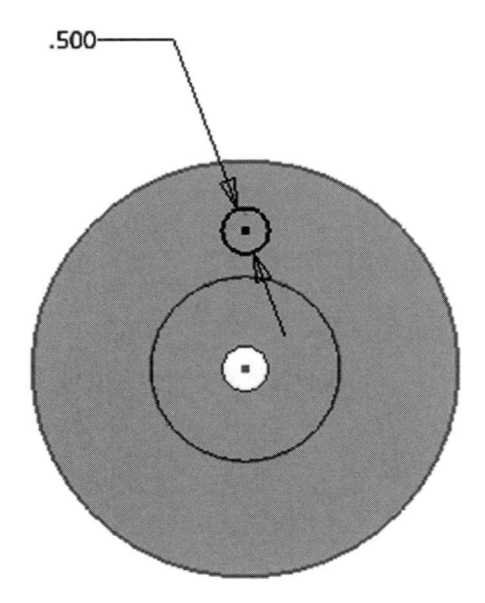

106

Chapter 2: Learning More Basics

86. Right click around the part. A pop up menu will appear. Left click on **Isometric/Home View** as shown in Figure 73.

Figure 73

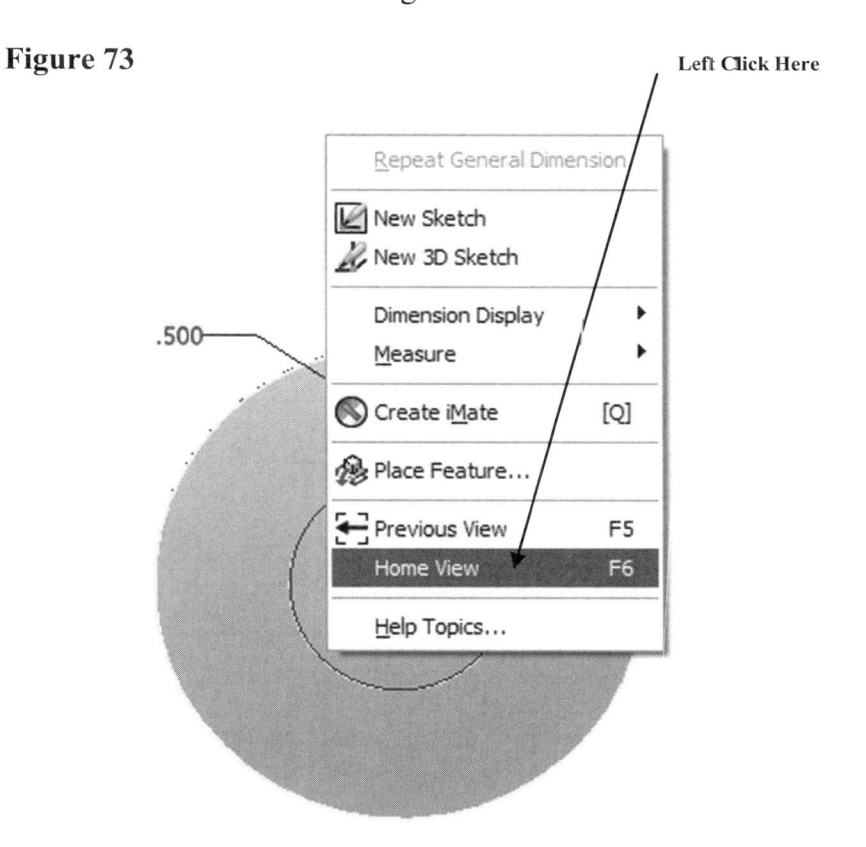

87. The view will become isometric as shown in Figure 74.

Figure 74

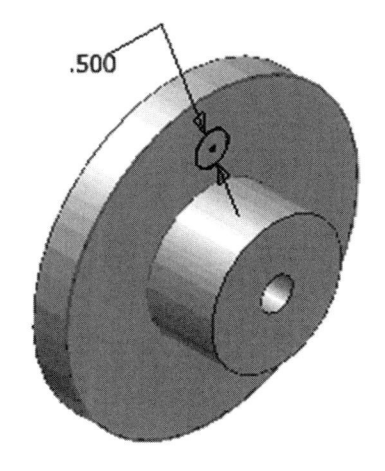

Chapter 2: Learning More Basics

88. Move the cursor to the middle left portion of the screen and left click on **Extrude**. The Extrude dialog box will appear as shown in Figure 75.

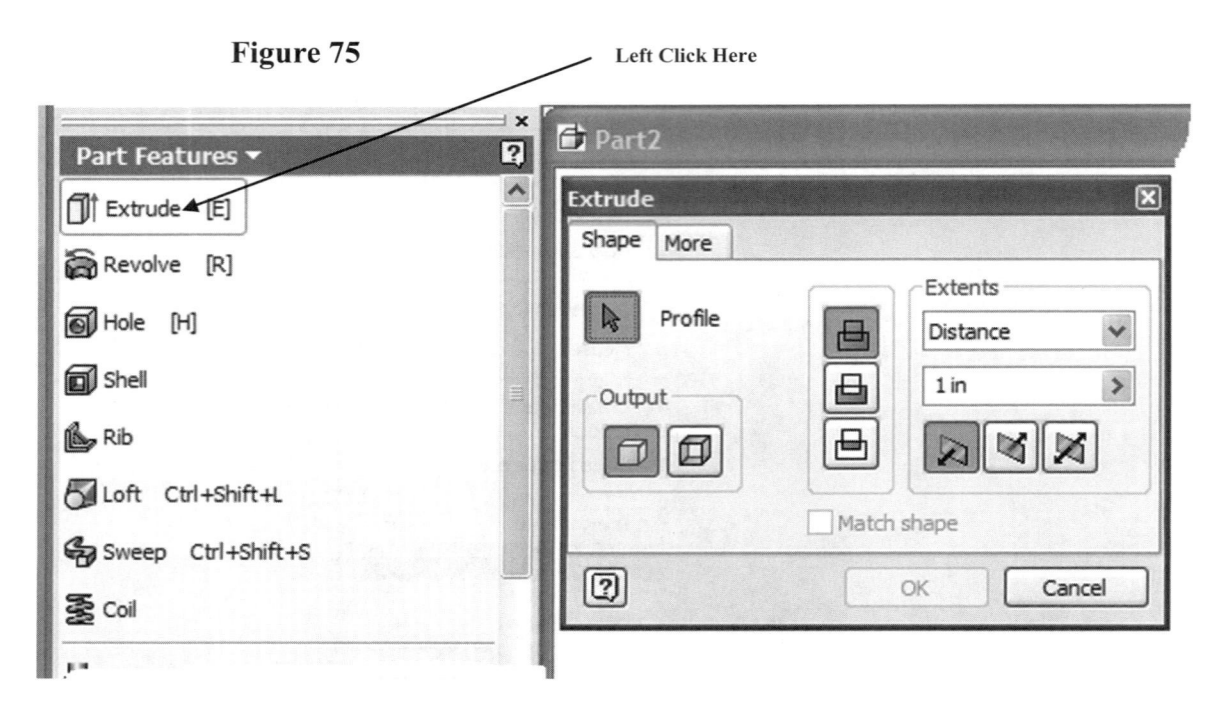

Figure 75 — Left Click Here

89. Move the cursor to the center of the circle causing it to turn red as shown in Figure 76.

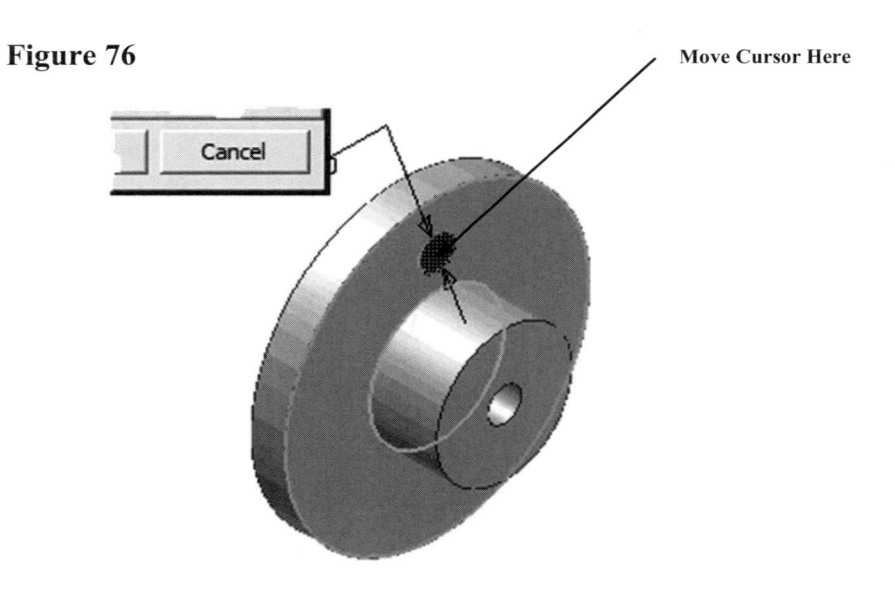

Figure 76 Move Cursor Here

108

Chapter 2: Learning More Basics

90. After the hole turns red, left click once. Select the "Cut" icon in the Extrude dialog box. Select the "Direction" icon to ensure the extrusion occurs in the right direction as shown in Figure 77.

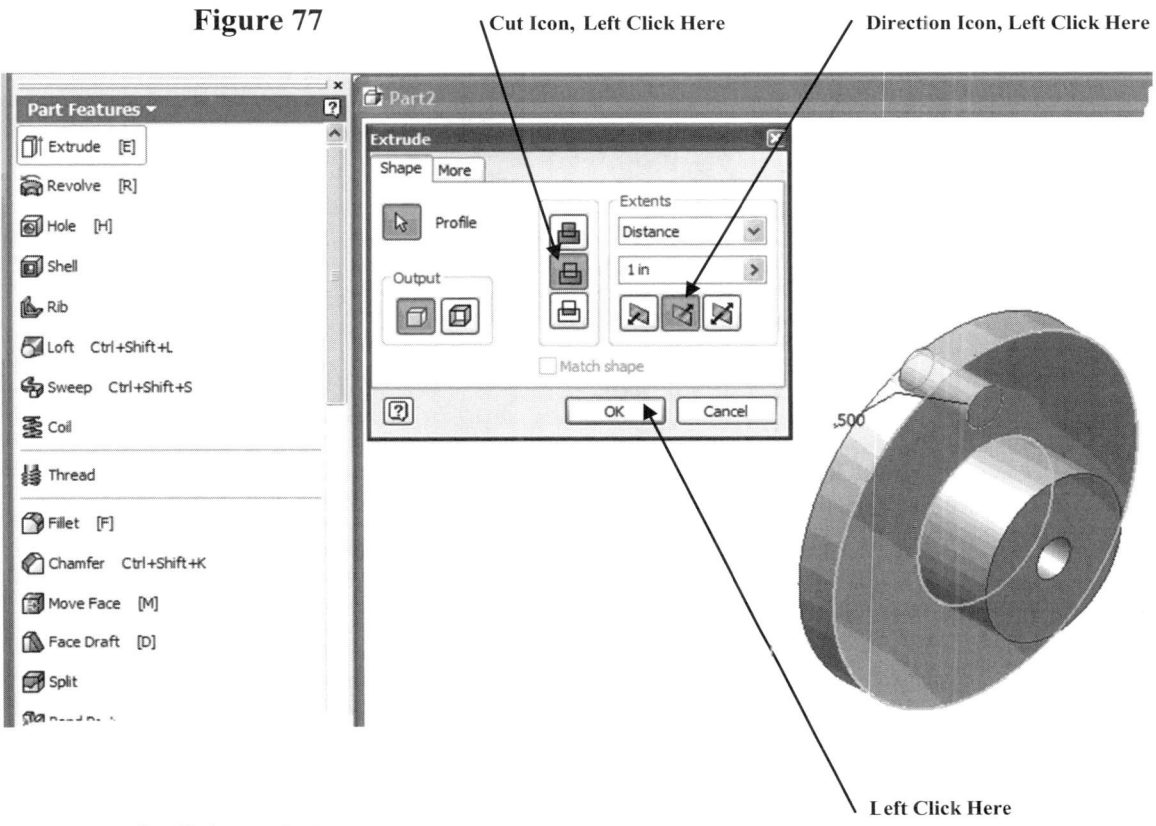

Figure 77

91. Left click on **OK**.

Chapter 2: Learning More Basics

92. Your screen should look similar to Figure 78.

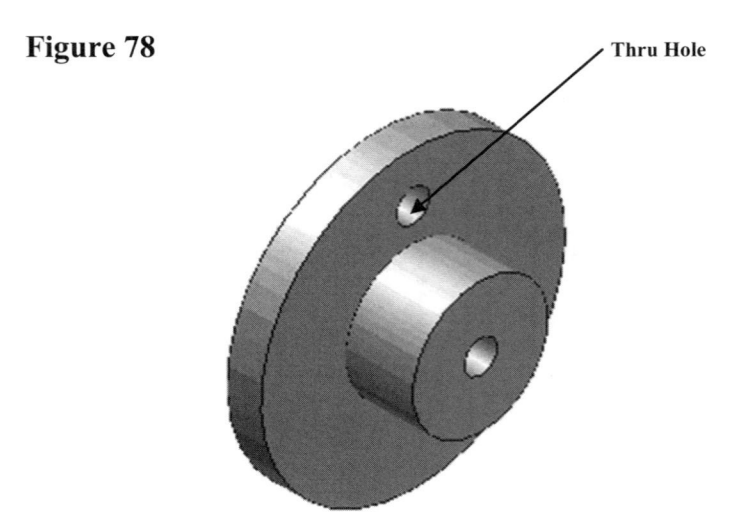

Figure 78   Thru Hole

93. Move the cursor to the middle left portion of the screen and left click on **Circular Pattern**. You may have to scroll down to see the command. The Circular Pattern dialog box will appear as shown in Figure 79.

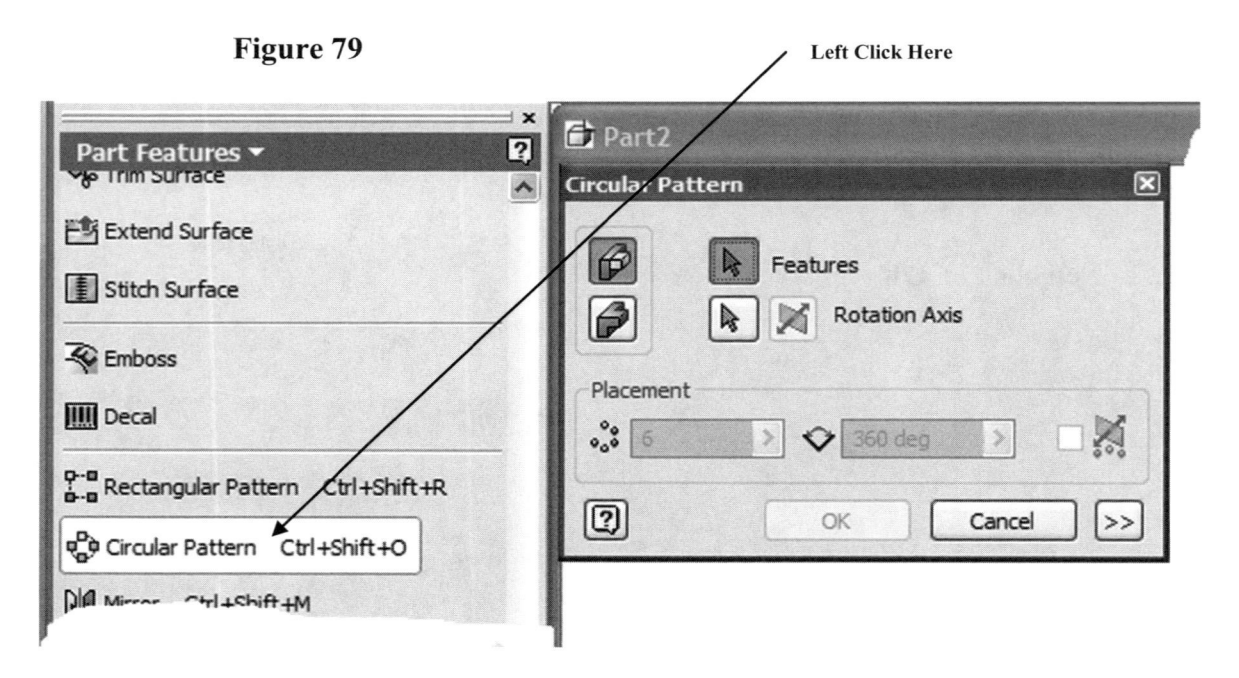

Figure 79   Left Click Here

110

Chapter 2: Learning More Basics

94. Move the cursor to the center of the hole causing red dashed lines to appear.
The part must be displayed in Home/Isometric view for Inventor to find the hole.
Left click as shown in Figure 80.

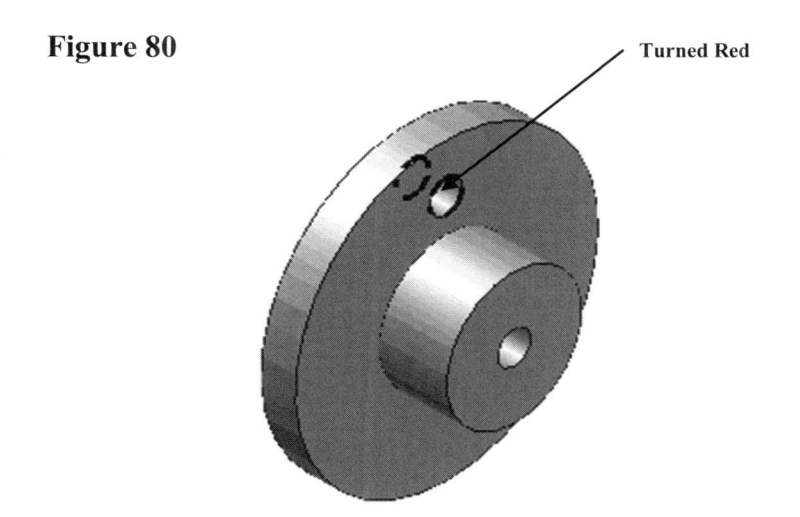

Figure 80 — Turned Red

95. Left click on **Rotation Axis** in the dialog box as shown in Figure 81.

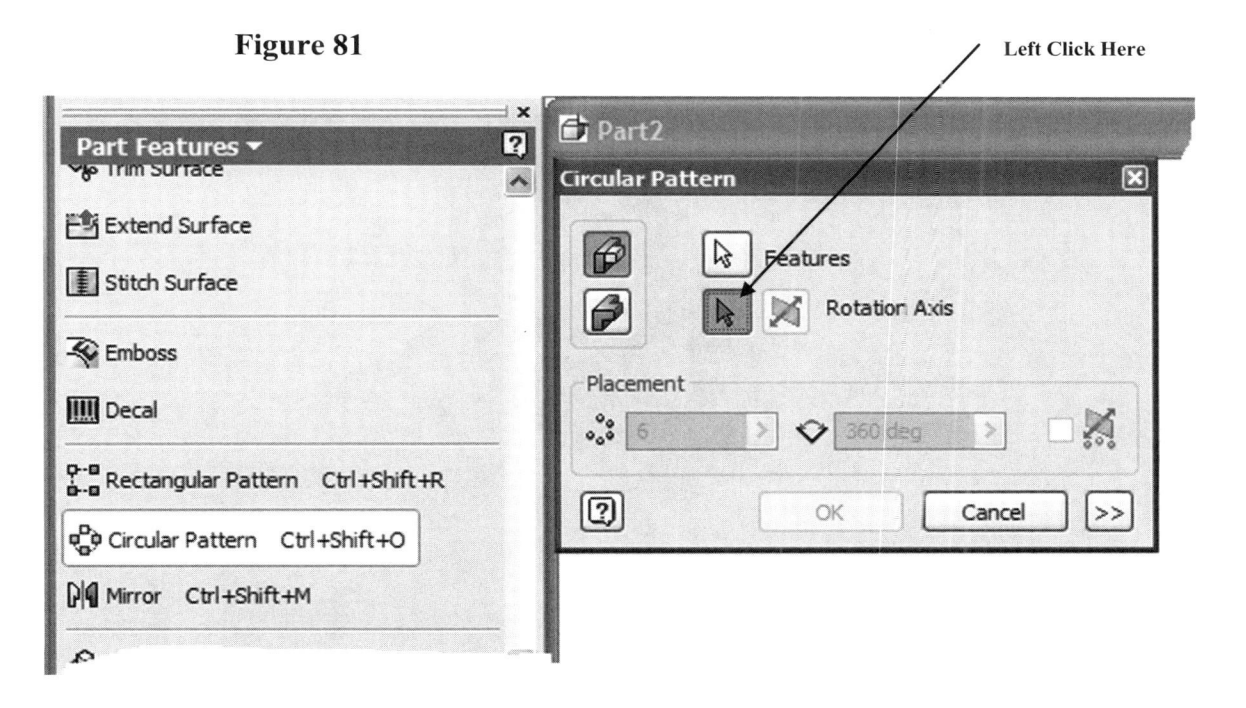

Figure 81 — Left Click Here

111

Chapter 2: Learning More Basics

96. Move the cursor to the edge of the part. The edges will turn red as shown in Figure 82.

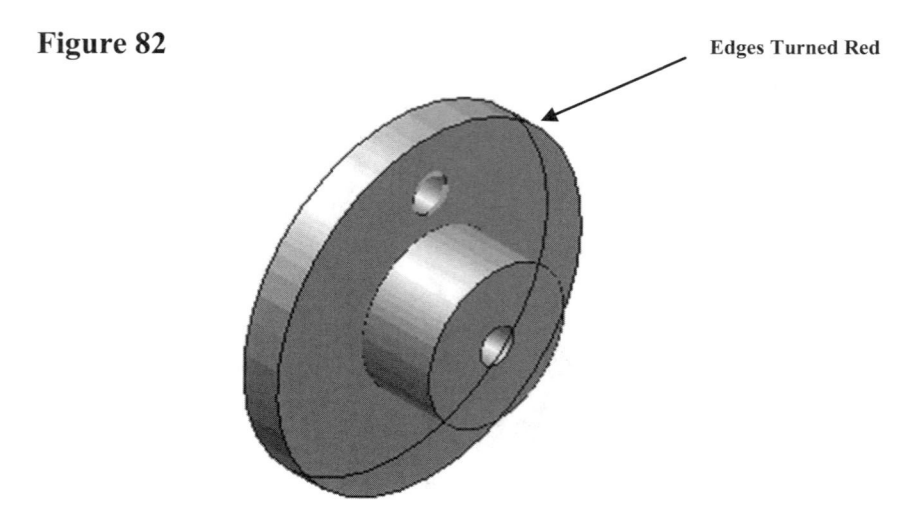

Figure 82

Edges Turned Red

97. After the edges turn red, left click once. Inventor will provide a preview of the hole pattern as shown in Figure 83.

Figure 83

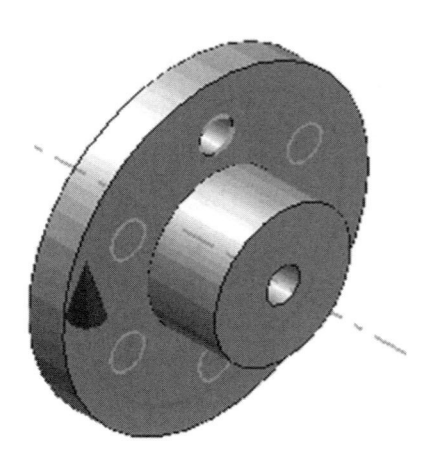

98. There are options in the Circular Pattern dialog box that are used for dictating the number of holes to be produced and the number of degrees betweens the holes. Verify that **6** is displayed for the number of holes. Verify that **360 deg** is displayed for the number of degrees. Left click on **OK** as shown in Figure 84.

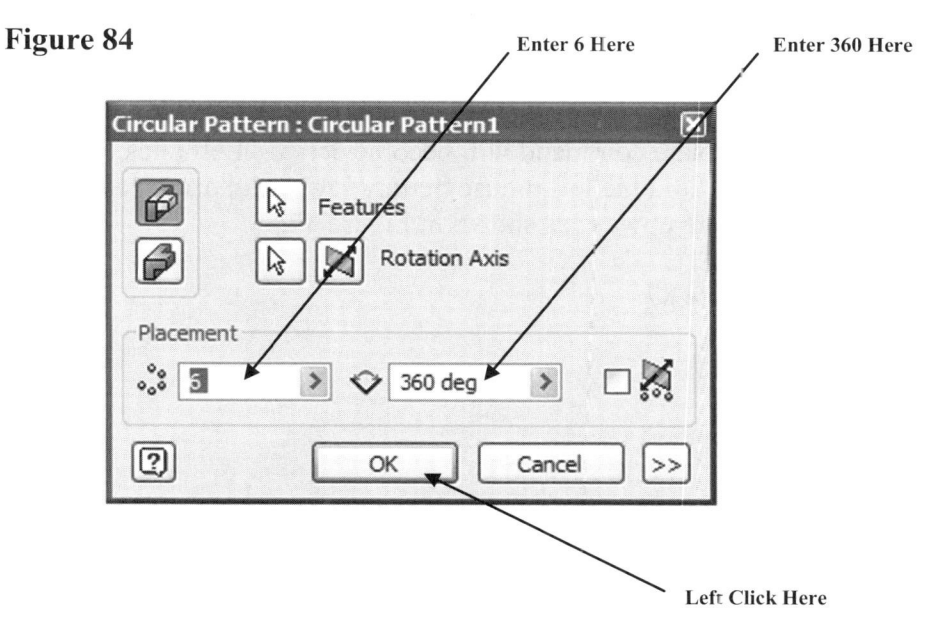

   Figure 84

99. Your screen should look similar to Figure 85.

   Figure 85

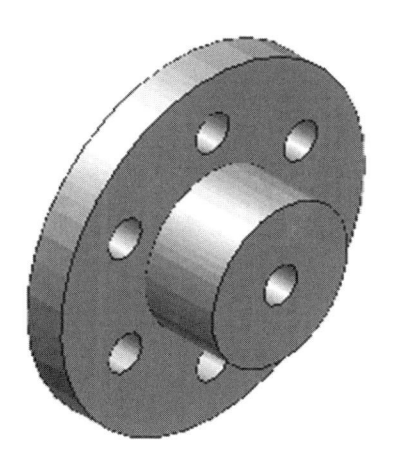

Chapter 2: Learning More Basics

100. To ensure that the holes are correct, move the cursor to the top portion of the screen and left click on the "Orbit/Rotate" icon as shown in Figure 86.

Figure 86

101. The Orbit/Rotate command will become active. Left click anywhere inside the white circle, hold the left mouse button down, and drag the cursor upward. The part will rotate upward as shown in Figure 87.

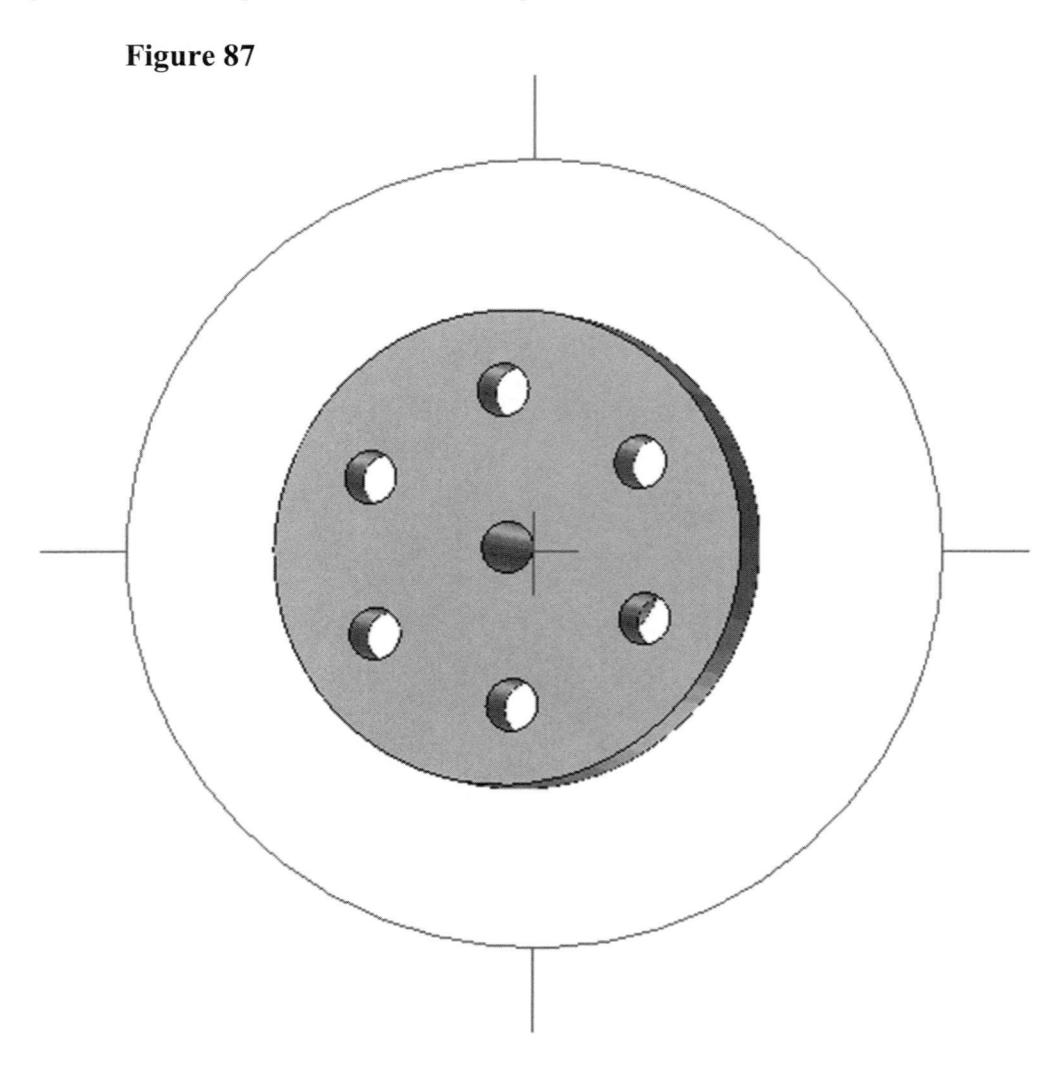

Figure 87

Chapter 2: Learning More Basics

102. Holding the left mouse button down keeps the part attached to the cursor. To view the part in Isometric, right click anywhere on the screen and left click on **Isometric/Home View** as shown in Figure 88.

Figure 88

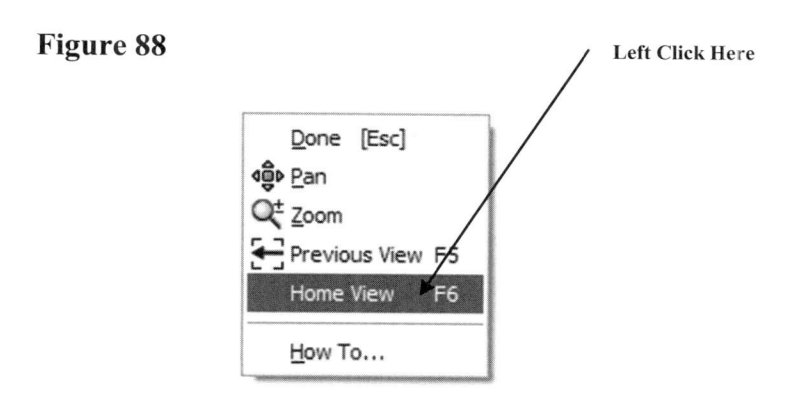

Left Click Here

103. As long as the white circle is present, the Orbit/Rotate command is still active. To get out of the Orbit/Rotate command either use the keyboard and press **Esc** once or twice, or right click anywhere on the screen. A pop up menu will appear. Left click on **Done [Esc]** as shown in Figure 89.

Figure 89

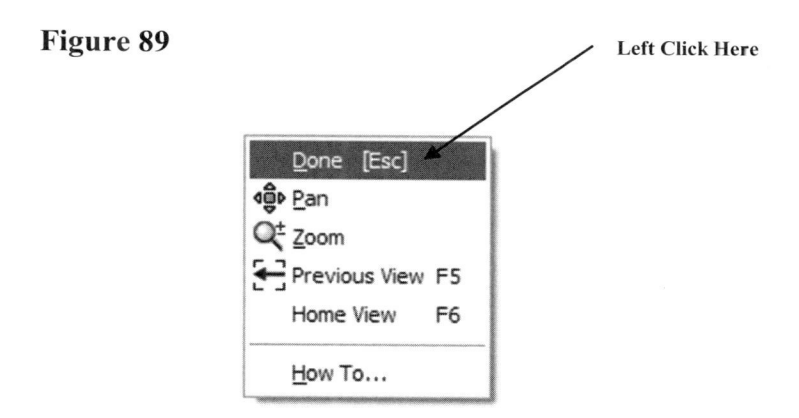

Left Click Here

Chapter 2: Learning More Basics

104. Other commands for viewing are located in the pop up menu or at the top of the screen as shown in Figures 90.

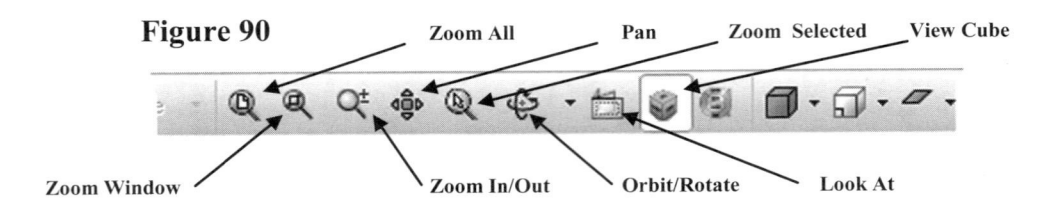

Figure 90   Zoom All   Pan   Zoom Selected   View Cube

Zoom Window   Zoom In/Out   Orbit/Rotate   Look At

105. The Zoom Window command works by using the cursor to draw a window around an area you want to zoom in on. After selecting the "Zoom Window" icon, hold the left mouse button down, drag a diagonal box around the desired area, and release it when the proper amount of zoom is achieved.

106. The Zoom In/Out command works similar to the Zoom Window command. Start by selecting the "Zoom In/Out" icon. Left click on the drawing, hold the left mouse button down, and drag the cursor up and down until the proper amount of zoom is achieved.

107. The Pan command works similar to the Zoom In/Out command. Start by selecting the "Pan" icon. Left click on the drawing, hold the left mouse button down, and drag the cursor up and down or side to side. Release the mouse button once the desired view is achieved.

108. The Look At command works similar to the Pan command. Start by selecting the "Look At" icon. Left click on any surface you want to view perpendicularly.

109. The View Cube icon turns the view cube off and on. The view cube is located in the upper right portion of the screen. The view cube functions very similar to the Rotate command. Left clicking (holding the left mouse button down) on the view cube in the upper right portion of the screen allows the user to either rotate the part around manually or to view the part in any of the standard views. The View Cube and icon are shown in Figure 91.

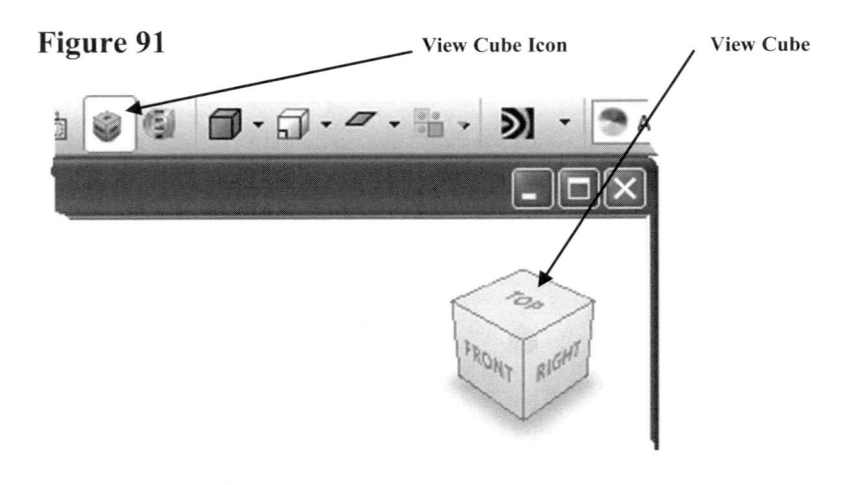

Figure 91   View Cube Icon   View Cube

Drawing Activities

Problem 1

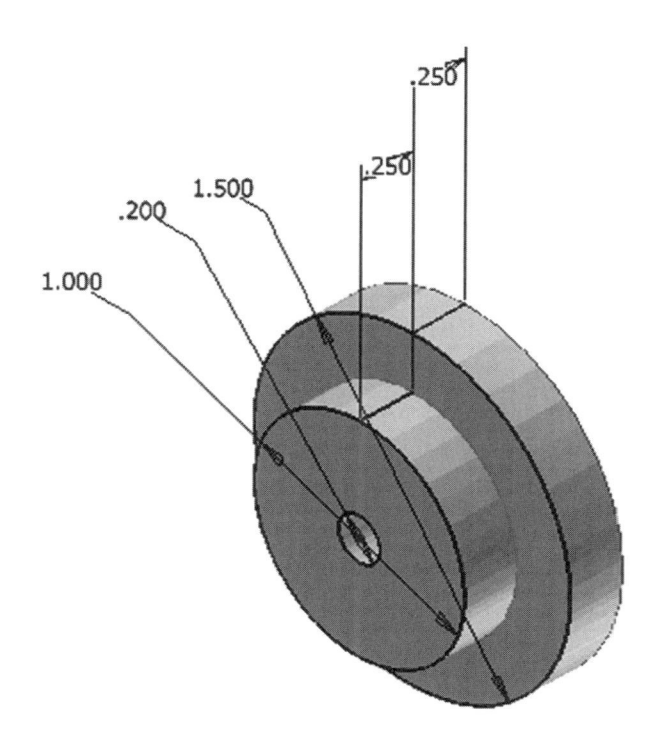

Problem 2

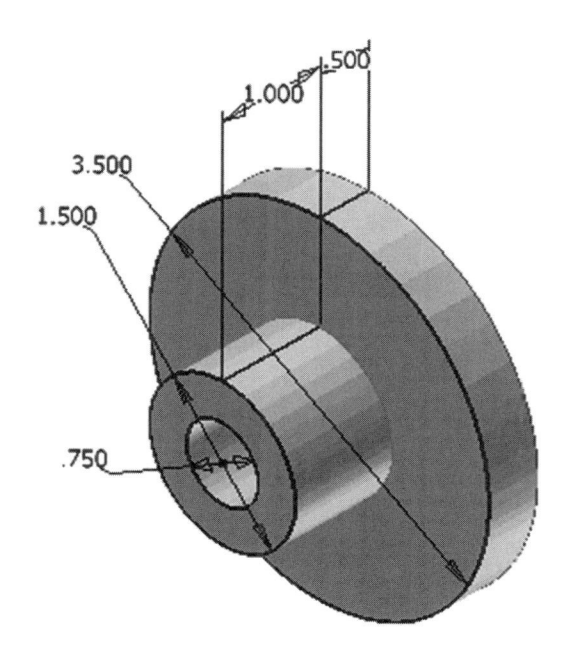

Chapter 2: Learning More Basics

Problem 3

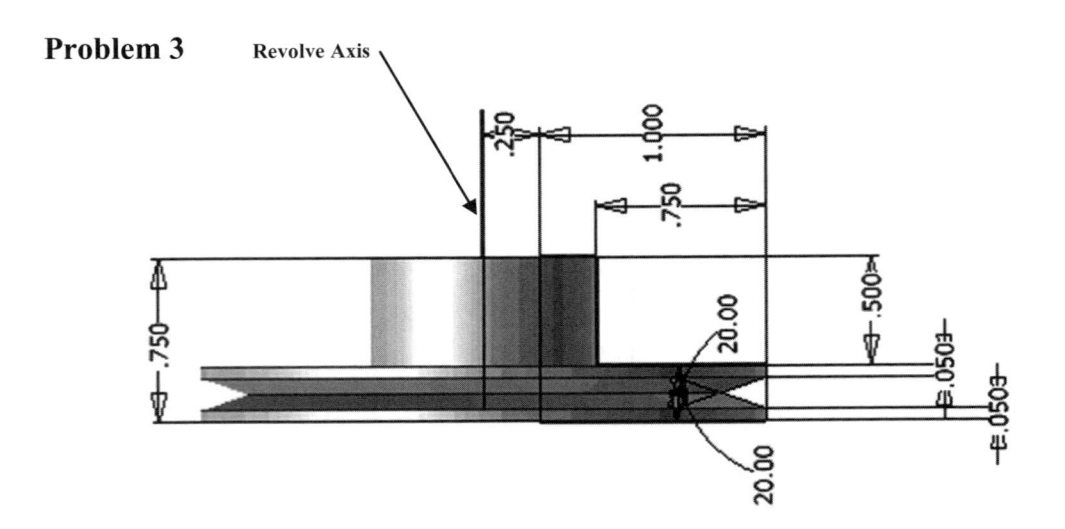

Revolve Axis

.250
1.000
.750
.750
.500
.0503
.0503
20.00
20.00

Problem 4

Revolve Axis

1.250
.063
.750
.125
.188

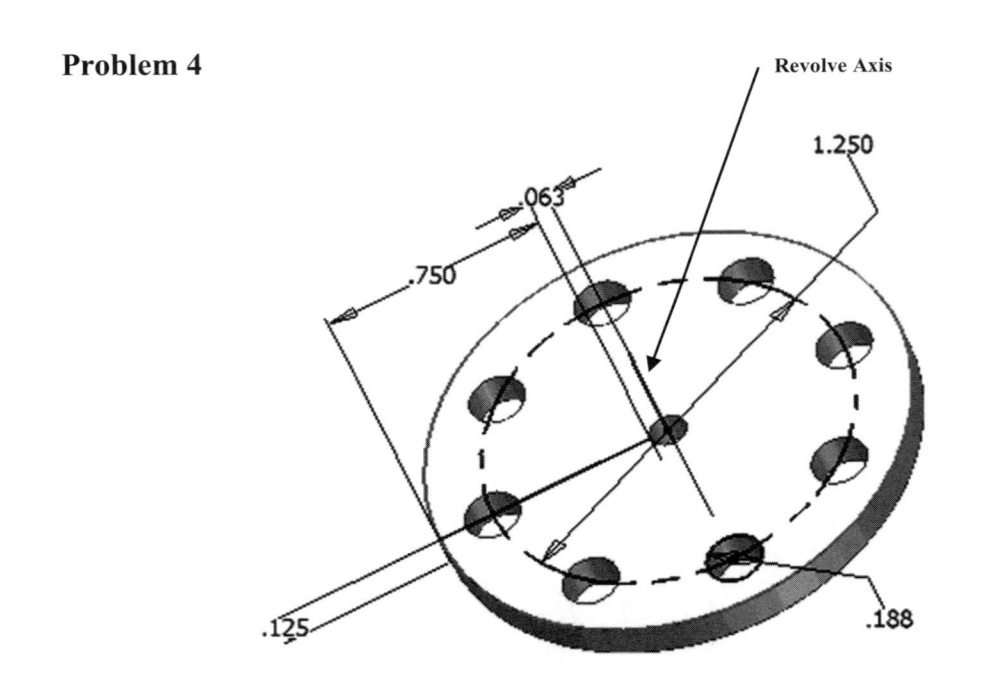

Problem 5

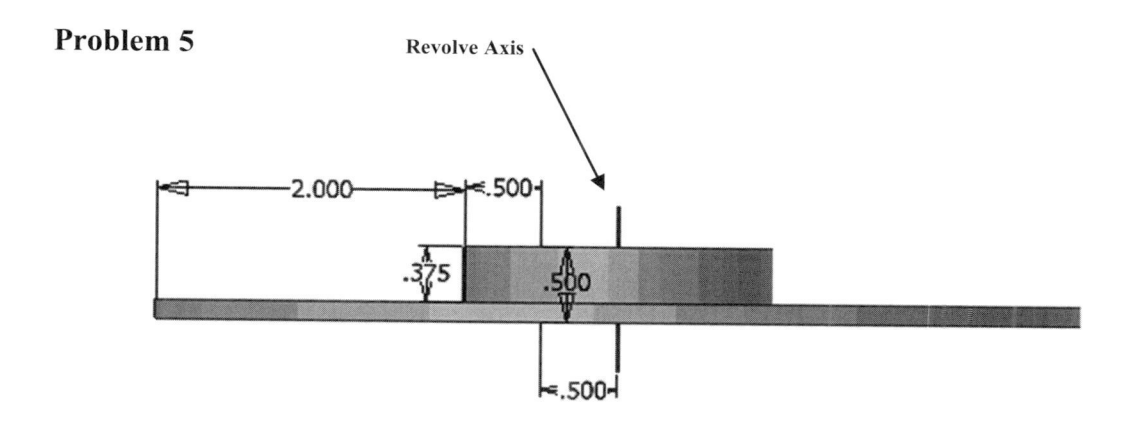

Revolve Axis

2.000 .500 .375 .500 .500

Problem 6

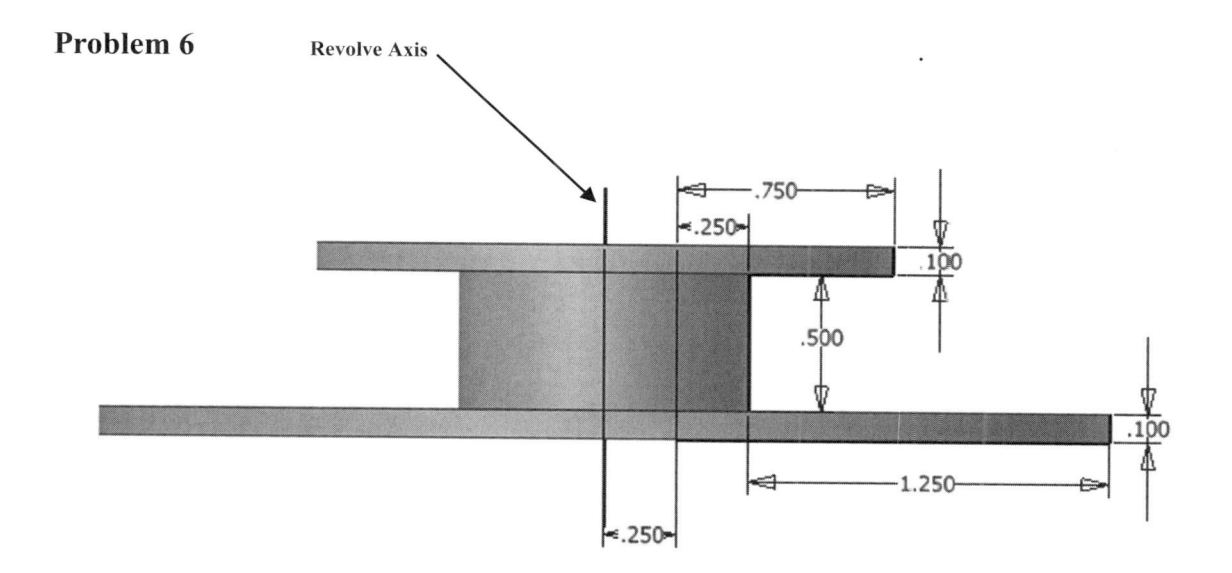

Revolve Axis

.750 .250 .100 .500 .100 1.250 .250

Chapter 2: Learning More Basics

Problem 7

Revolve Axis

.20 .250
1.000
.250
.125
.375
.375
.200
.750
.100
.375

Problem 8

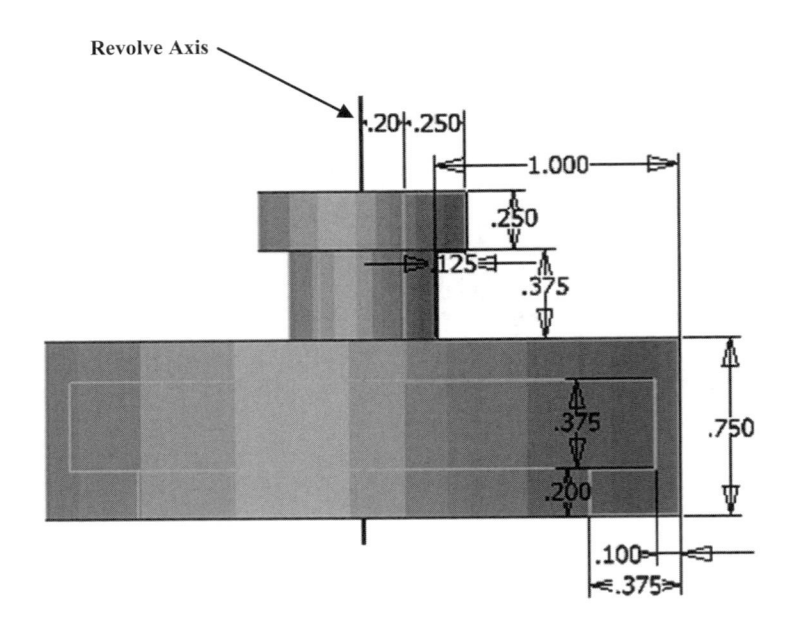

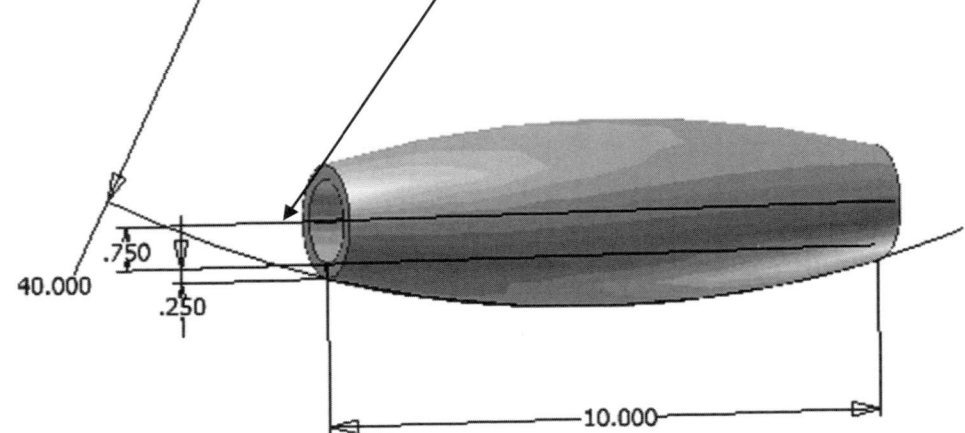

Revolve Axis

40.000
.750
.250
10.000

Chapter 3 Learning To Create a Detail Drawing

Objectives:
- Create a simple sketch using the Sketch Panel
- Extrude a sketch into a solid using the Part Features Panel
- Create an Orthographic view using the Drawing Views Panel
- Create a Solid Model using the Edit Views command

Chapter 3 includes instruction on how to design the parts shown below.

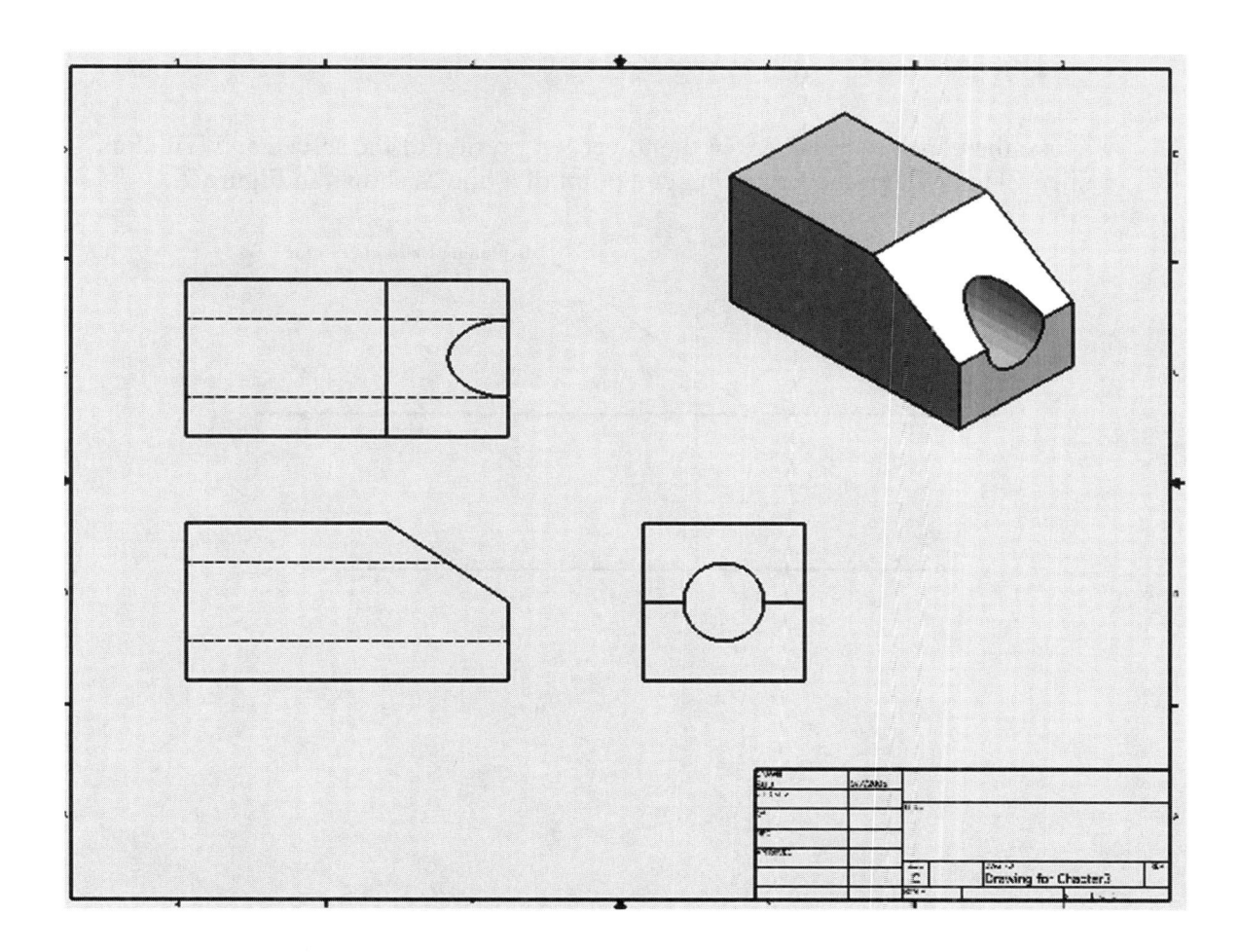

Chapter 3: Learning To Detail Part Drawings

1. Start Autodesk Inventor 2009 by referring to "Chapter 1 Getting Started".

2. After Autodesk Inventor 2009 is running, begin a new sketch.

3. Move the cursor to the upper left corner of the screen and left click on **Line** as shown in Figure 1.

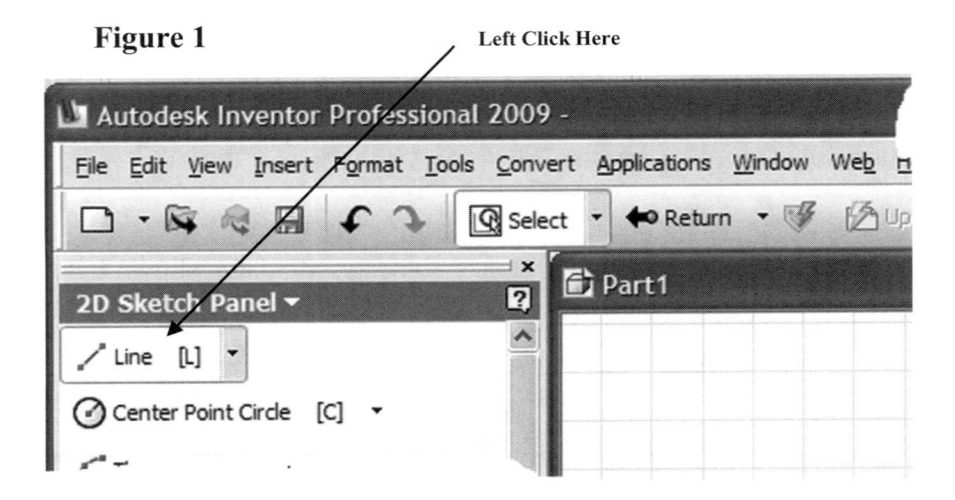

Figure 1

Left Click Here

4. Move the cursor somewhere in the lower left portion of the screen and left click once. This will be the beginning end point of a line as shown in Figure 2.

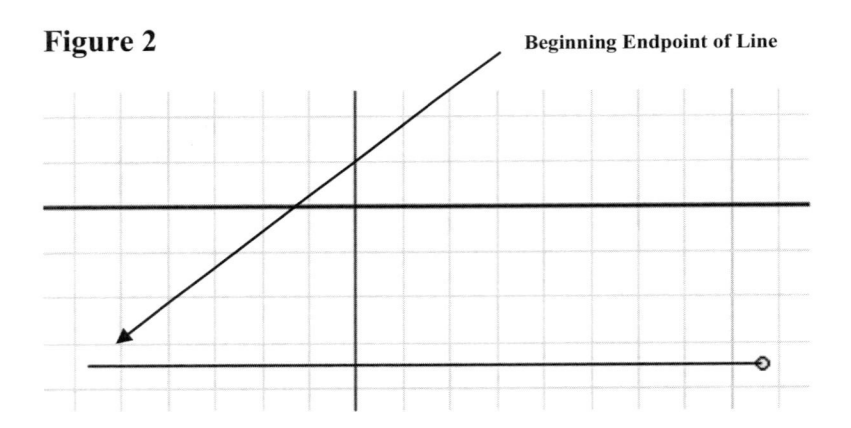

Figure 2

Beginning Endpoint of Line

Chapter 3: Learning To Detail Part Drawings

5. Move the cursor to the right and left click once as shown in Figure 3.

Figure 3

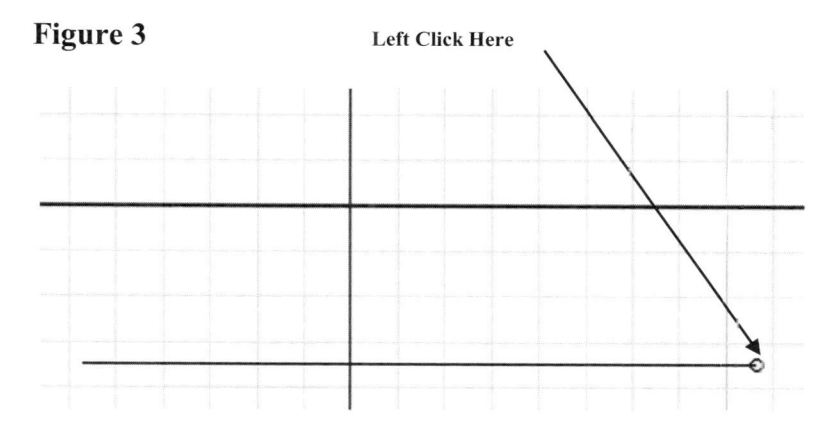

6. Move the cursor upward and left click once as shown in Figure 4.

Figure 4

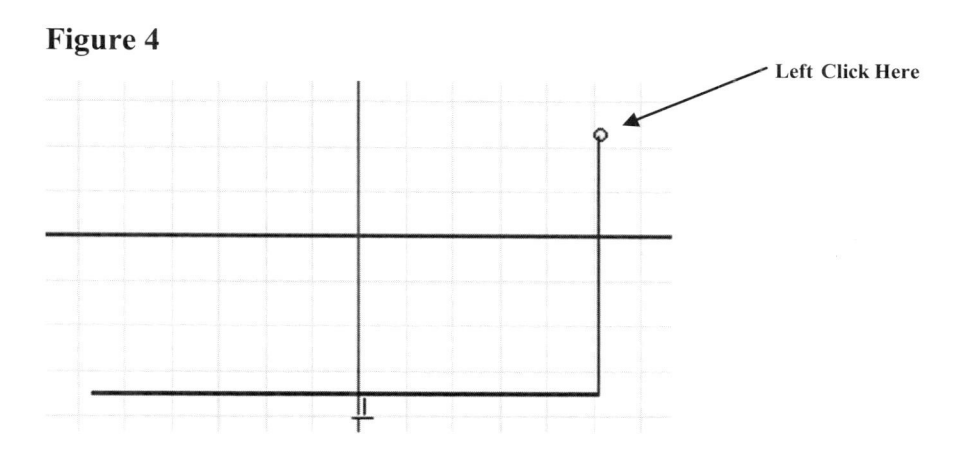

7. Move the cursor to the left, wait for the dots to appear, then left click once as shown in Figure 5.

Figure 5

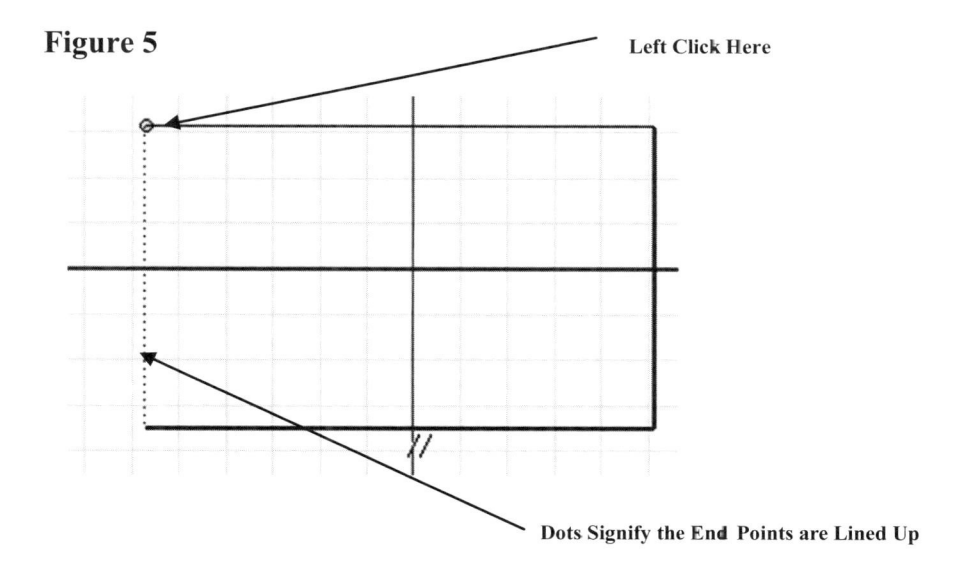

Chapter 3: Learning To Detail Part Drawings

8. Move the cursor back to the original starting end point. A green dot will appear. Left click once. Your screen should look similar to Figure 6. Press the **Esc** key once or twice.

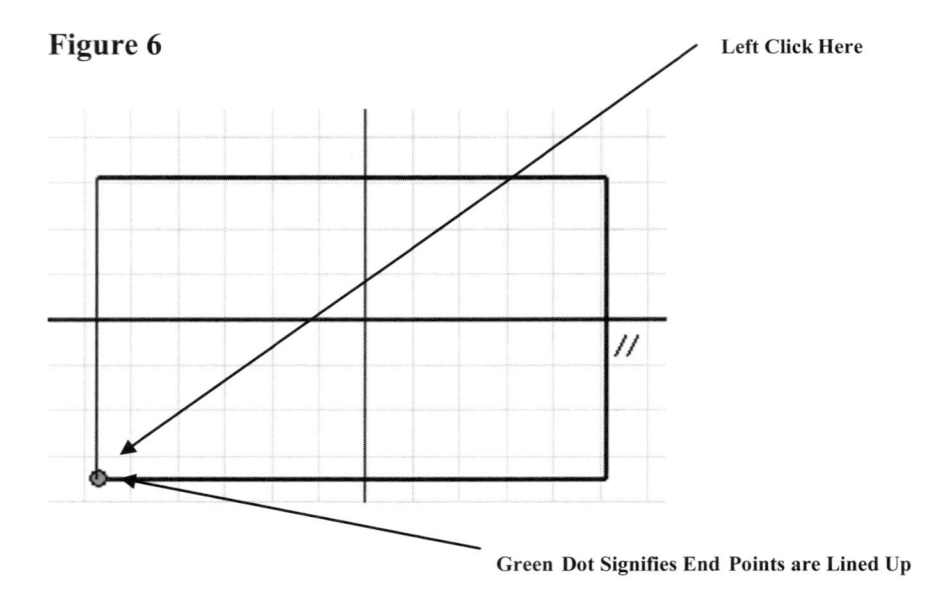

Figure 6

Left Click Here

Green Dot Signifies End Points are Lined Up

9. Move the cursor to the middle left portion of the screen and left click on **General Dimension** as shown in Figure 7.

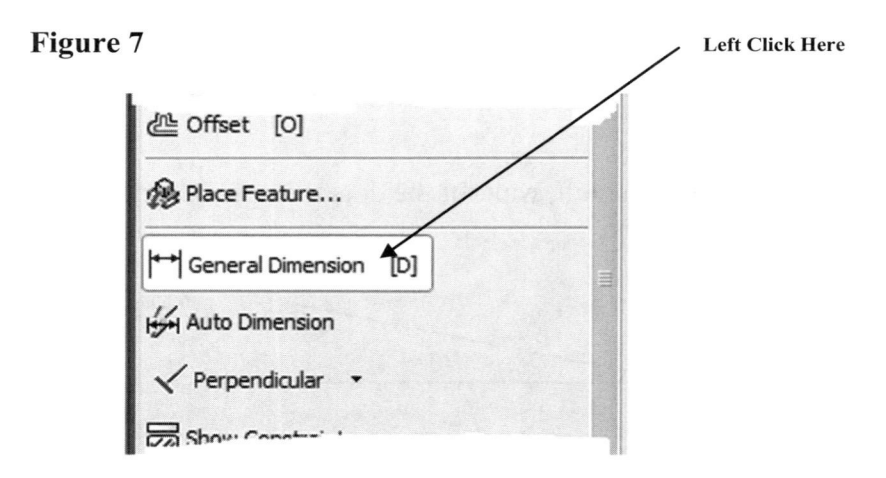

Figure 7

Left Click Here

124

Chapter 3: Learning To Detail Part Drawings

10. After selecting **General Dimension** move the cursor over the bottom horizontal line until it turns red as shown in Figure 8. Select the line by left clicking anywhere on the line **or** on each of the end points. The dimension will be attached to the cursor.

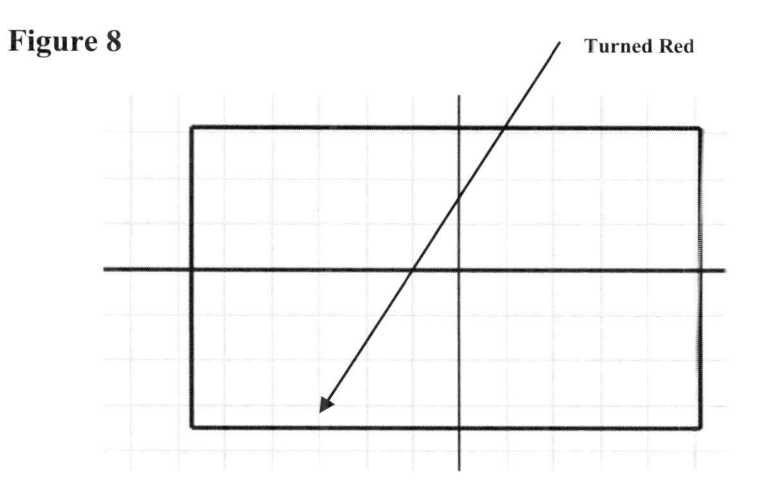

Figure 8

Turned Red

11. Move the cursor down. The actual dimension of the line will appear as shown in Figure 9.

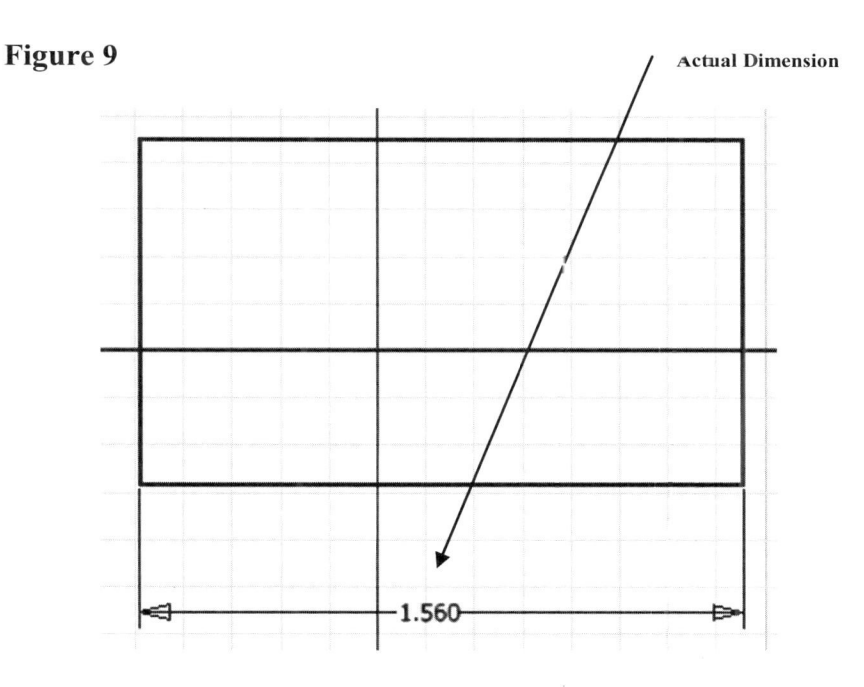

Figure 9

Actual Dimension

1.560

Chapter 3: Learning To Detail Part Drawings

12. Move the cursor to where the dimension will be placed and left click once. While the dimension is still in red, left click once. The Edit Dimension dialog box will appear as shown in Figure 10.

Figure 10

Enter 2.00 Here

13. To edit the dimension, type **2.00** in the Edit Dimension dialog box (while the current dimension is highlighted) and press **Enter** on the keyboard.

14. The dimension of the line will become 2.00 inches as shown in Figure 11.

Figure 11

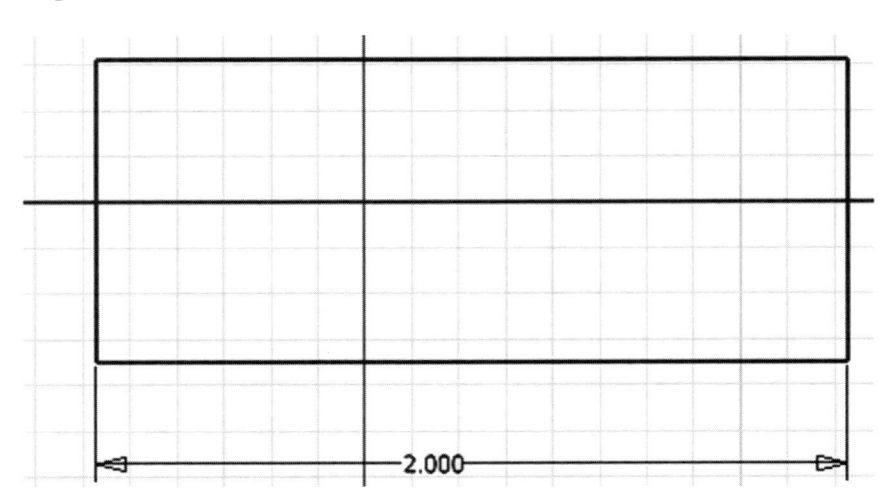

Chapter 3: Learning To Detail Part Drawings

15. To view the entire drawing move the cursor to the middle portion of the screen and left click once on the "Zoom All" icon as shown in Figure 12.

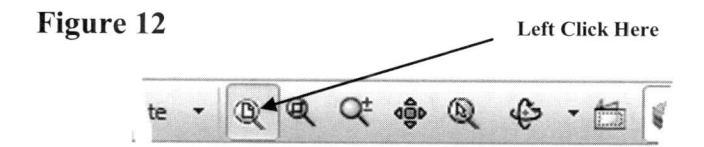

Figure 12

16. The drawing will "fill up" the entire screen. If the drawing is still too large, left click on the "Zoom" icon as shown in Figure 13. After selecting the Zoom icon, hold the left mouse button down and drag the cursor up and down to achieve the desired view of the sketch.

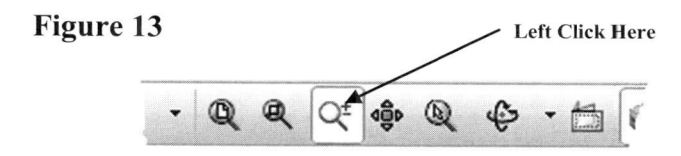

Figure 13

17. Move the cursor to the middle left portion of the screen and left click on **General Dimension** as shown in Figure 14.

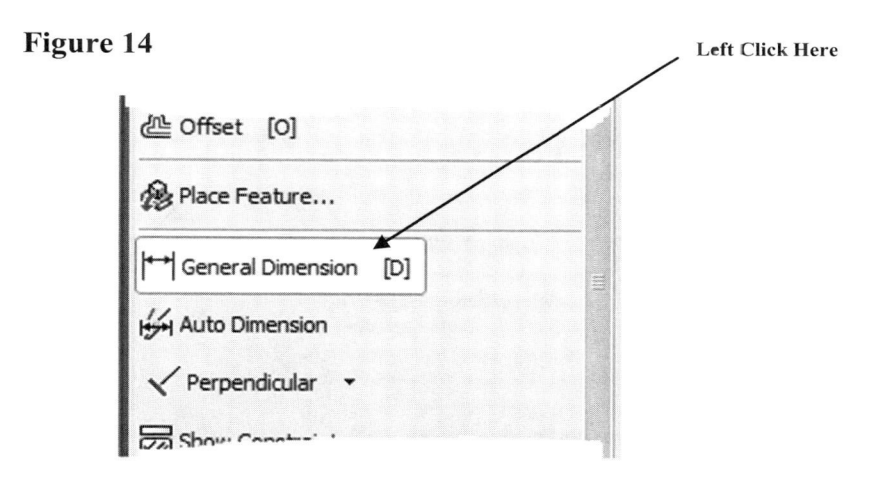

Figure 14

Chapter 3: Learning To Detail Part Drawings

18. After selecting **General Dimension** move the cursor over the right side vertical line. The line will turn red as shown in Figure 15. Select the line by left clicking anywhere on the line **or** on each of the end points. The dimension will be attached to the cursor.

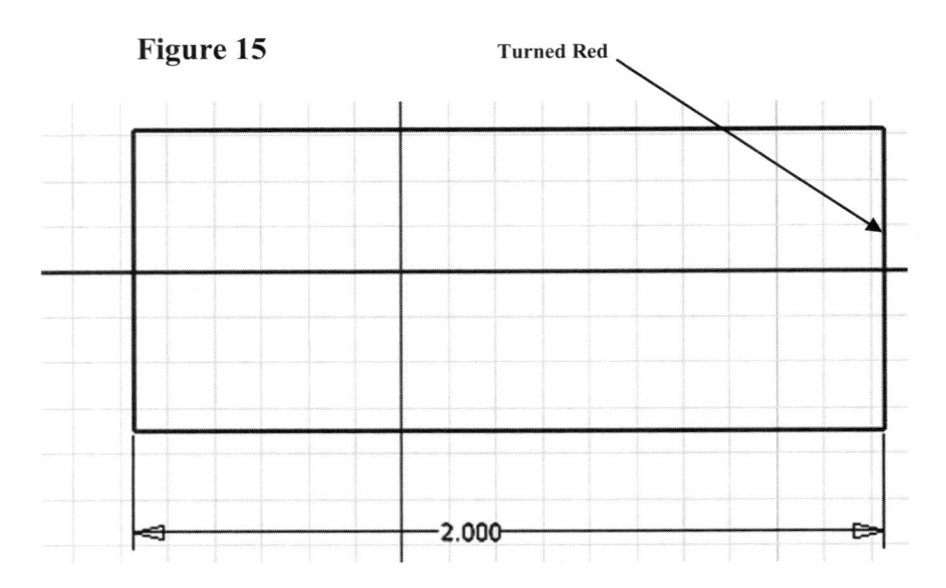

Figure 15　　　　　　　　　Turned Red

19. Move the cursor to the side. The actual dimension of the line will appear as shown in Figure 16.

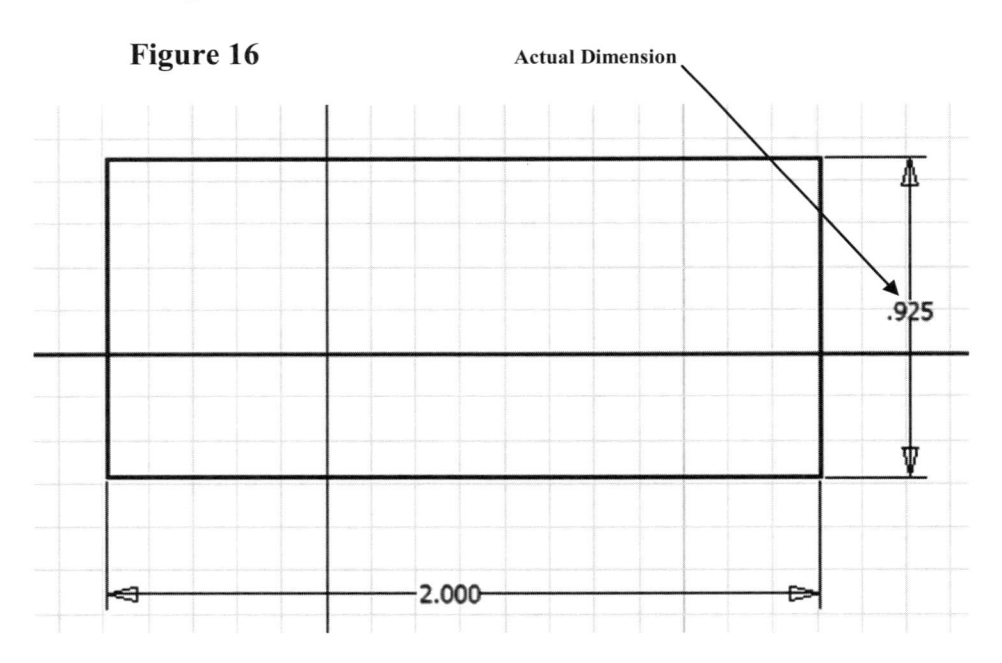

Figure 16　　　　　　　　　Actual Dimension

128

Chapter 3: Learning To Detail Part Drawings

20. Move the cursor to where the dimension will be placed and left click once. While the dimension is still in red, left click once. The Edit Dimension dialog box will appear as shown in Figure 17.

Figure 17

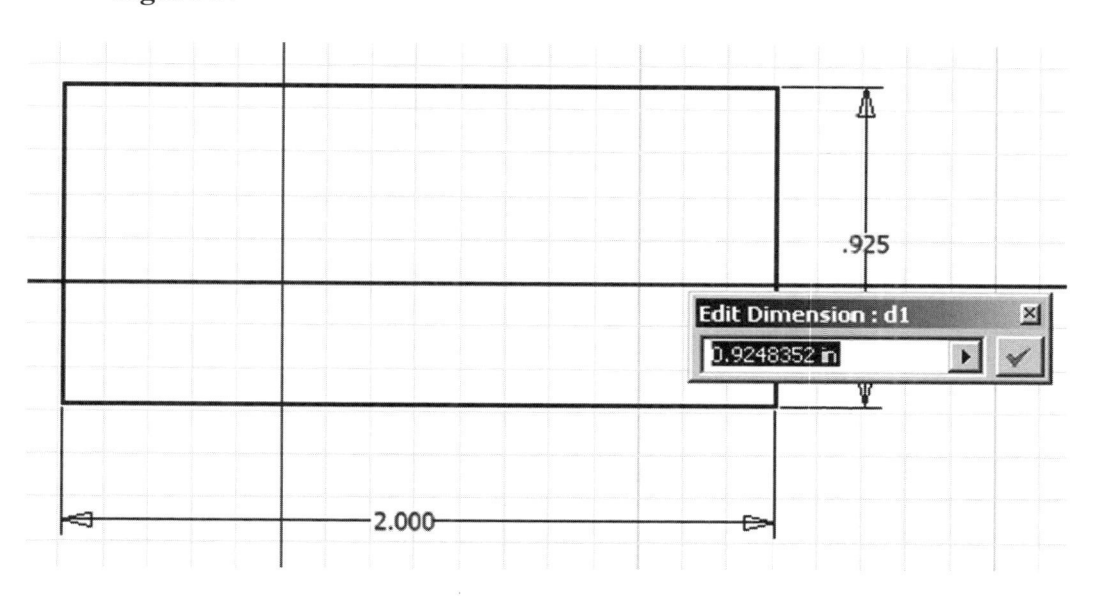

21. To edit the dimension, type **1.00** in the Edit Dimension dialog box (while the current dimension is highlighted) and press **Enter** on the keyboard.

22. The dimension of the line will become 1.00 inches as shown in Figure 18. Use the Zoom icons to zoom out if necessary.

Figure 18

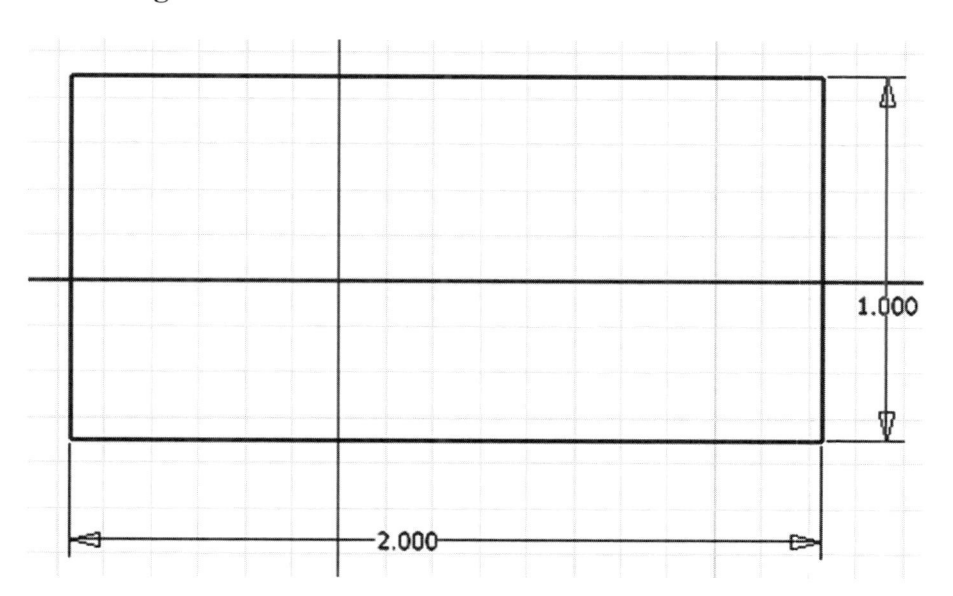

Chapter 3: Learning To Detail Part Drawings

23. Move the cursor to the middle left portion of the screen and left click on **General Dimension** as shown in Figure 19.

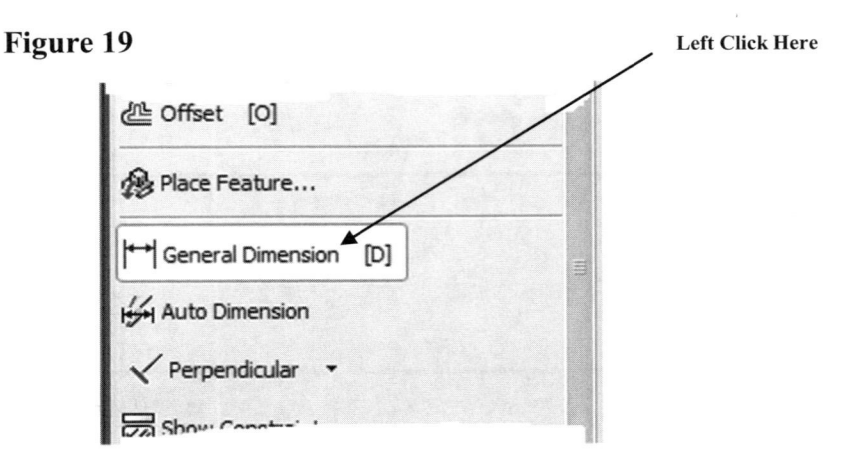

Figure 19   **Left Click Here**

24. After selecting **General Dimension** move the cursor over the top horizontal line. The line will turn red as shown in Figure 20. Select the line by left clicking anywhere on the line **or** on each of the end points. The dimension will be attached to the cursor.

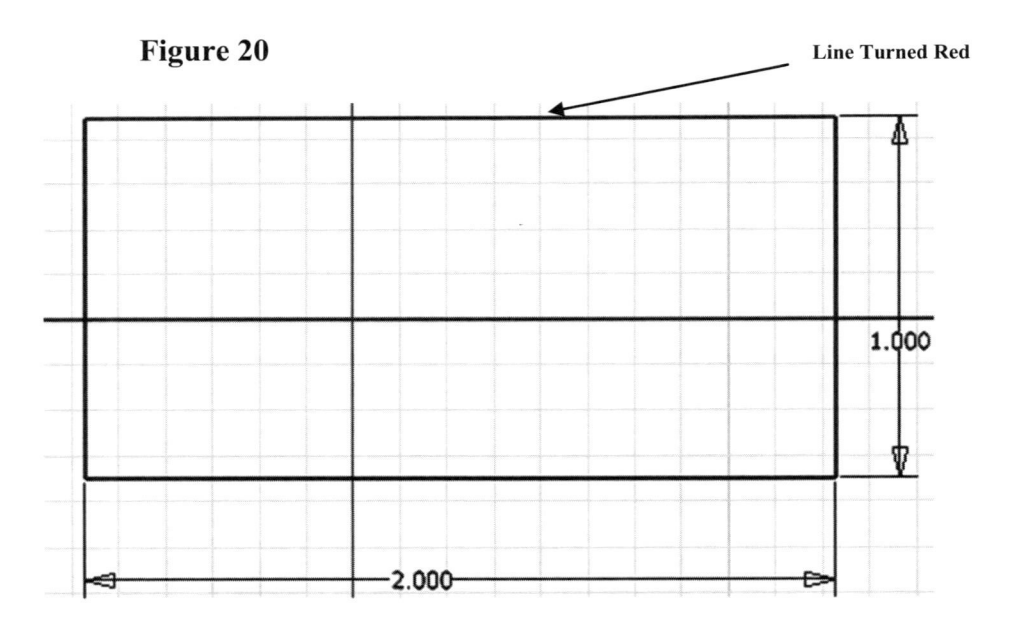

Figure 20   **Line Turned Red**

130

25. Move the cursor up. The actual dimension of the line will appear as shown in Figure 21.

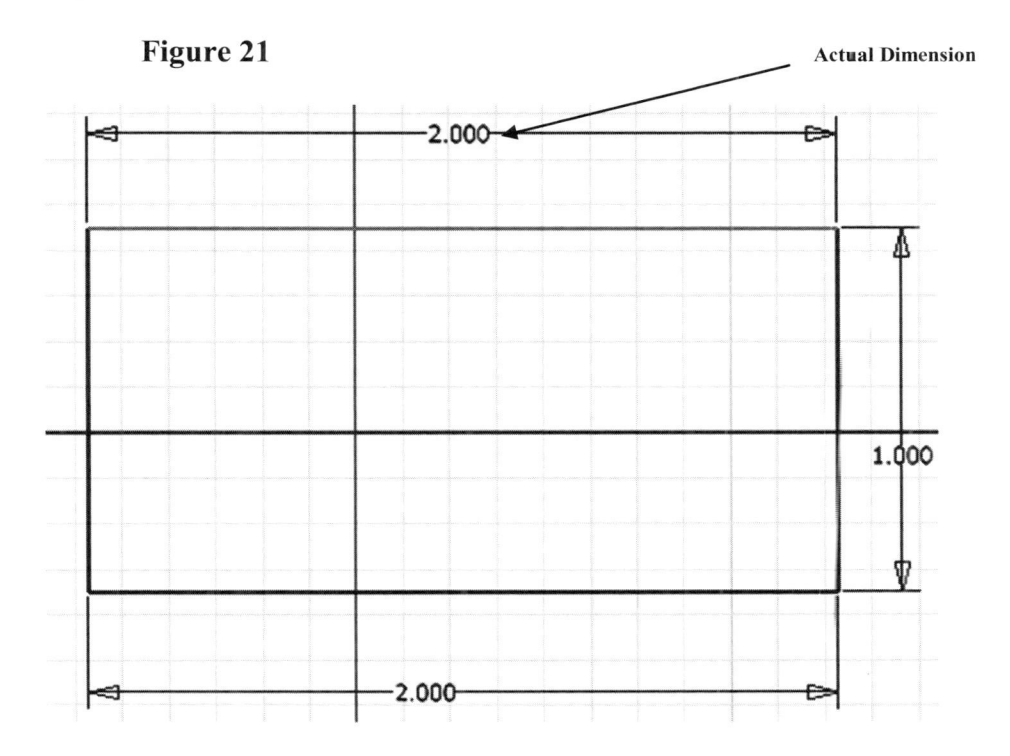

Figure 21

26. Notice that the dimension is exactly 2.000. Move the cursor to where the dimension will be placed and left click once. The Create Linear Dimension dialog box will appear as shown in Figure 22.

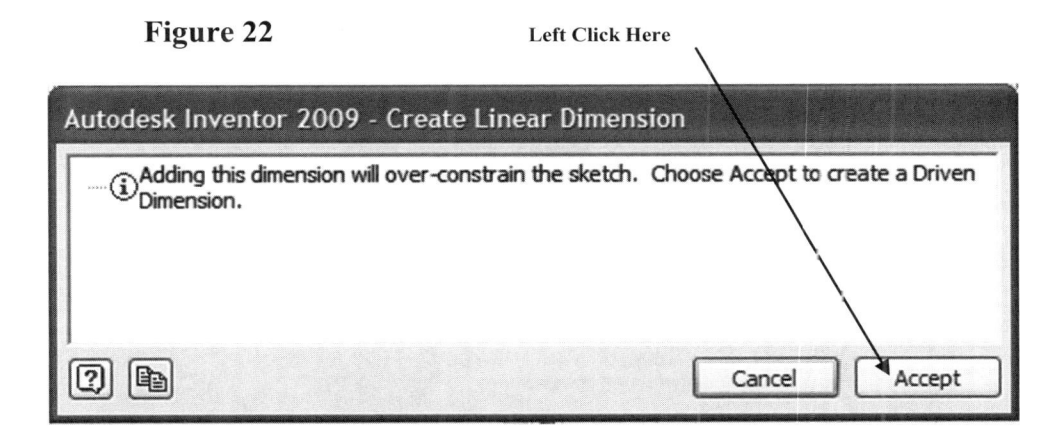

Figure 22

27. This dimension will over-constrain the sketch because the sketch has been constrained with 90 degree angles when it was constructed. Left click on **Accept**. The dimension will be a driven dimension meaning it cannot be used to edit or change the length of the line.

Chapter 3: Learning To Detail Part Drawings

28. The driven dimension appears in parenthesis as shown in Figure 23.

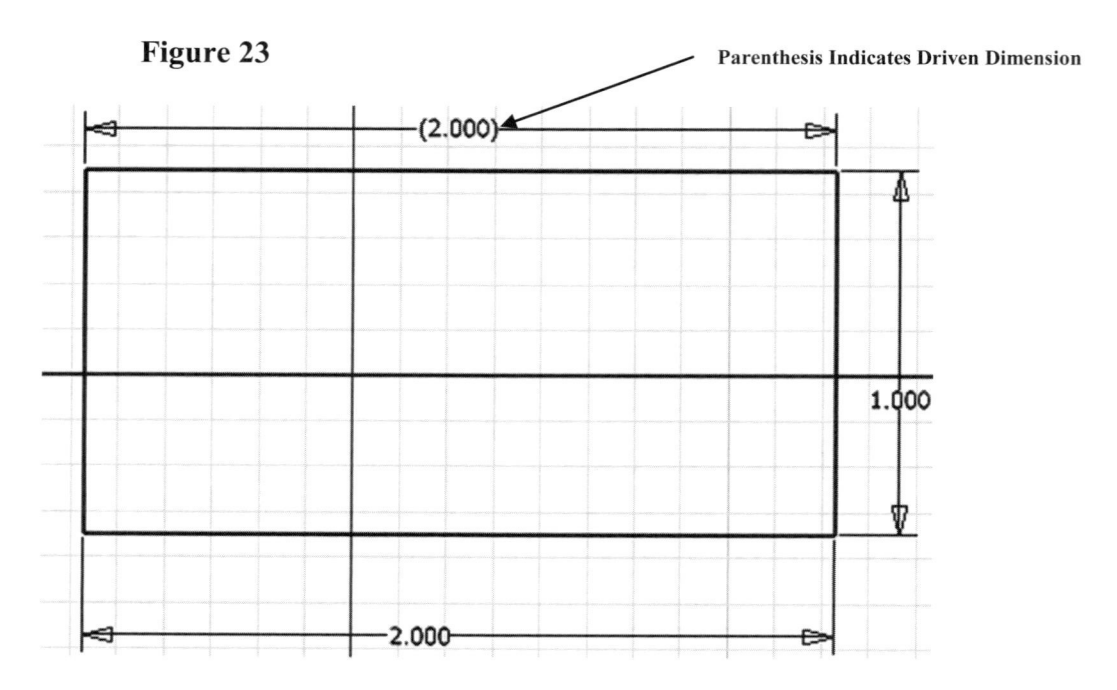

Figure 23

Parenthesis Indicates Driven Dimension

29. Dimensioning the far left line would also result in a driven dimension. Because of this, the dimensioning portion is complete.

30. After the sketch is complete it is time to extrude the sketch into a solid. Right click anywhere on the drawing. A pop up menu will appear. Left click on **Done [Esc]** as shown in Figure 24.

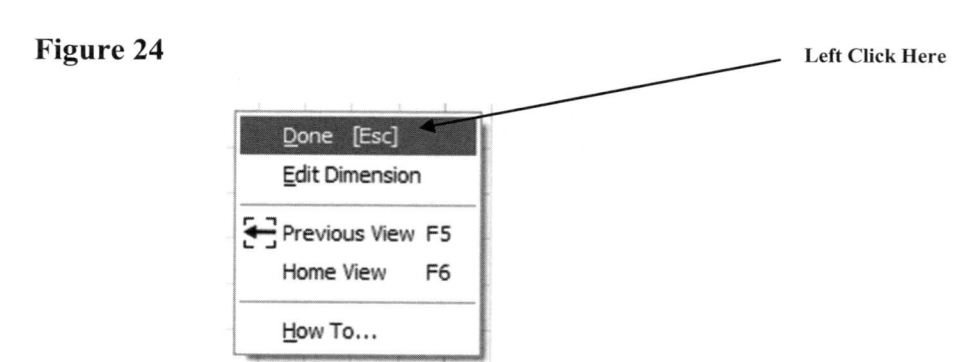

Figure 24

Left Click Here

Chapter 3: Learning To Detail Part Drawings

31. After you have verified that no commands are active, right click anywhere on the sketch. A pop up menu will appear. Left click on **Finish Sketch** as shown in Figure 25.

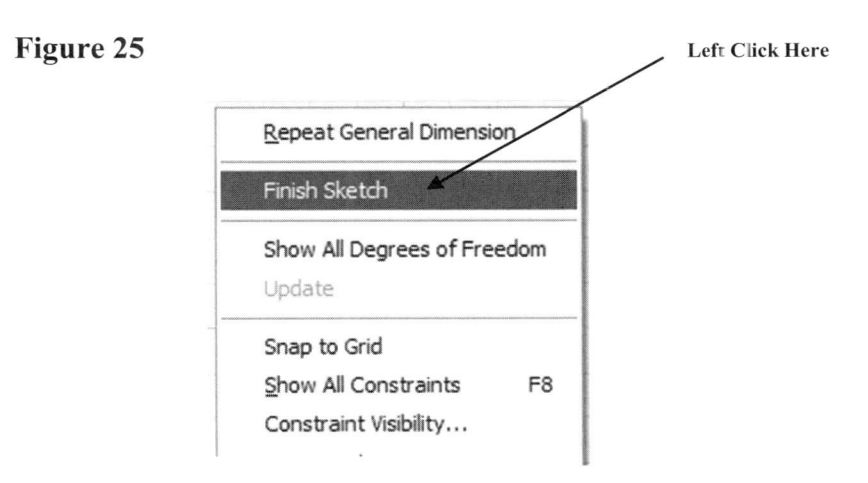

Figure 25

32. Inventor is now out of the Sketch Panel and into the Part Features Panel. Notice that the commands at the left of the screen are now different. To work in the Part Features Panel a sketch must be present and have no opens (non-connected lines). If there are any opens in the sketch an error message will appear. Your screen should look similar to Figure 26.

Figure 26

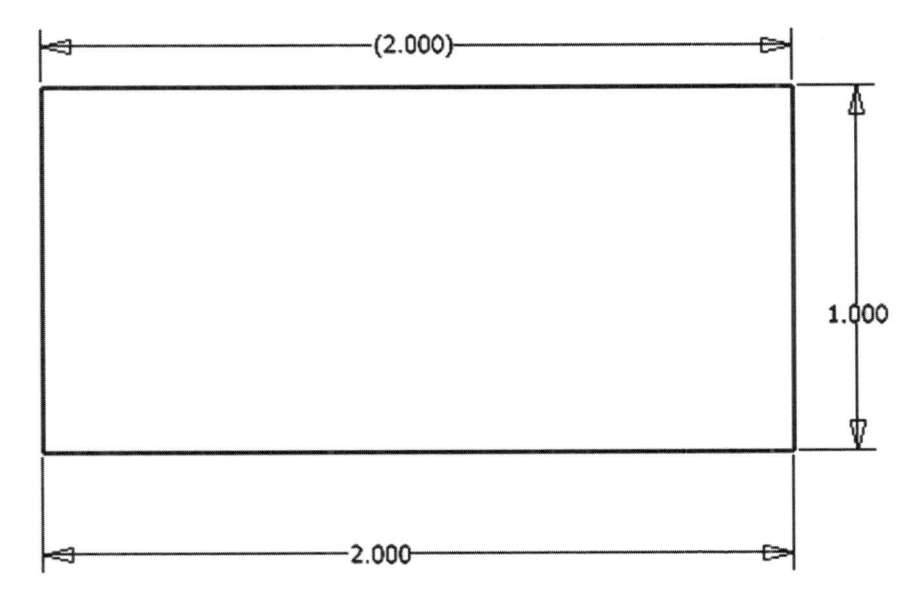

Chapter 3: Learning To Detail Part Drawings

33. Right click around the sketch. A pop up menu will appear. Left click on **Isometric/Home View** as shown in Figure 27.

Figure 27

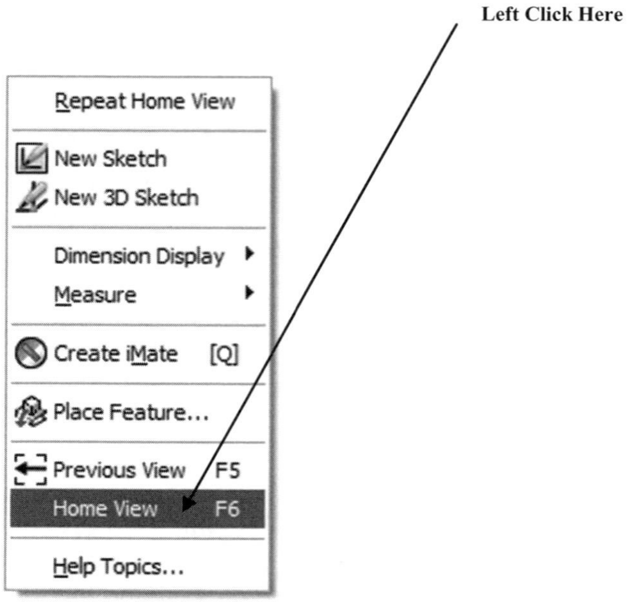

Left Click Here

34. The view will become isometric as shown in Figure 28.

Figure 28

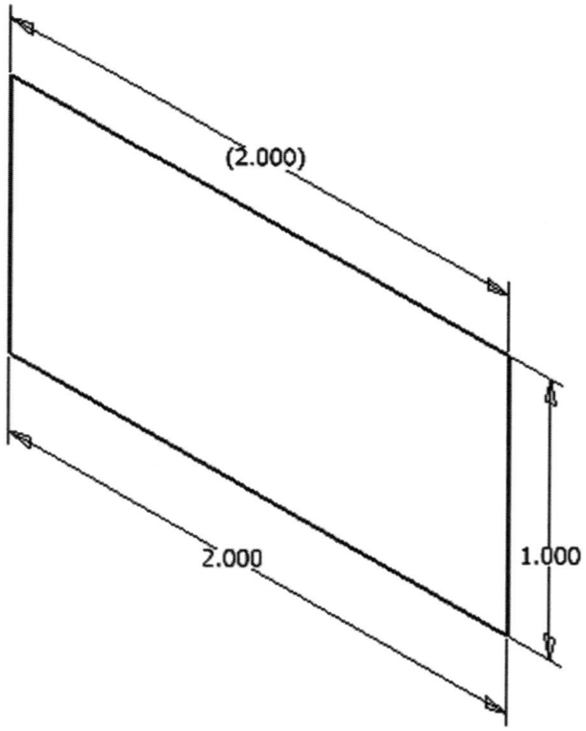

Chapter 3: Learning To Detail Part Drawings

35. Move the cursor to the middle left portion of the screen and left click on **Extrude**. The Extrude dialog box will appear. Inventor also provides a preview of the extrusion. If Inventor gave you an error message there are opens (non-connected lines) somewhere on the sketch. Check each intersection for opens by using the **Extend** and **Trim** commands. Your screen should look similar to Figure 29.

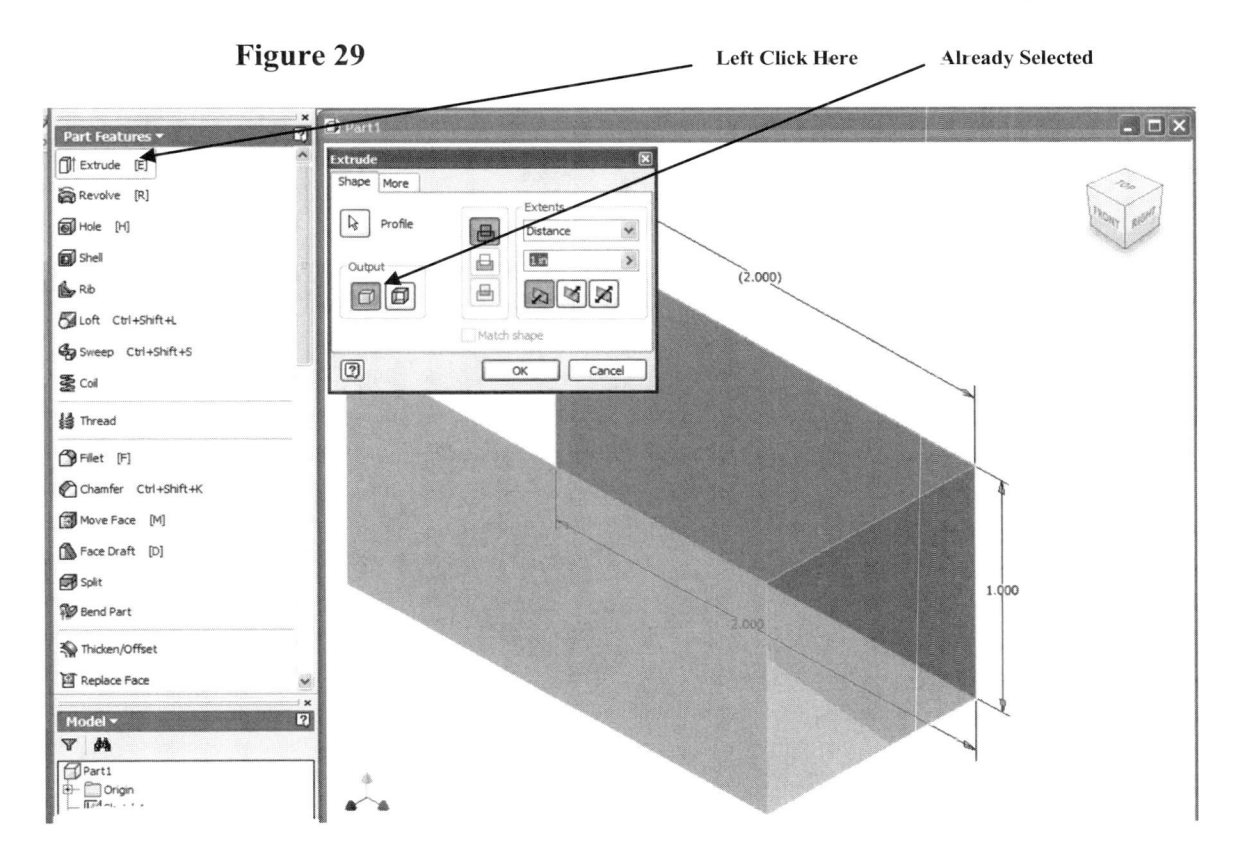

Figure 29

36. Because there is only one profile present, Inventor assumes that particular profile will be selected. If the drawing contained more than one profile, you would have to first select the Profile icon in the extrude dialog box then use the cursor to select the desired profile.

135

Chapter 3: Learning To Detail Part Drawings

37. Left click on **OK**. Your screen should look similar to Figure 30. You may have to use the zoom out command to view the entire part.

Figure 30

Chapter 3: Learning To Detail Part Drawings

38. Move the cursor to the middle left portion of the screen and left click on **Chamfer**. The Chamfer dialog box will appear as shown in Figure 31.

Figure 31

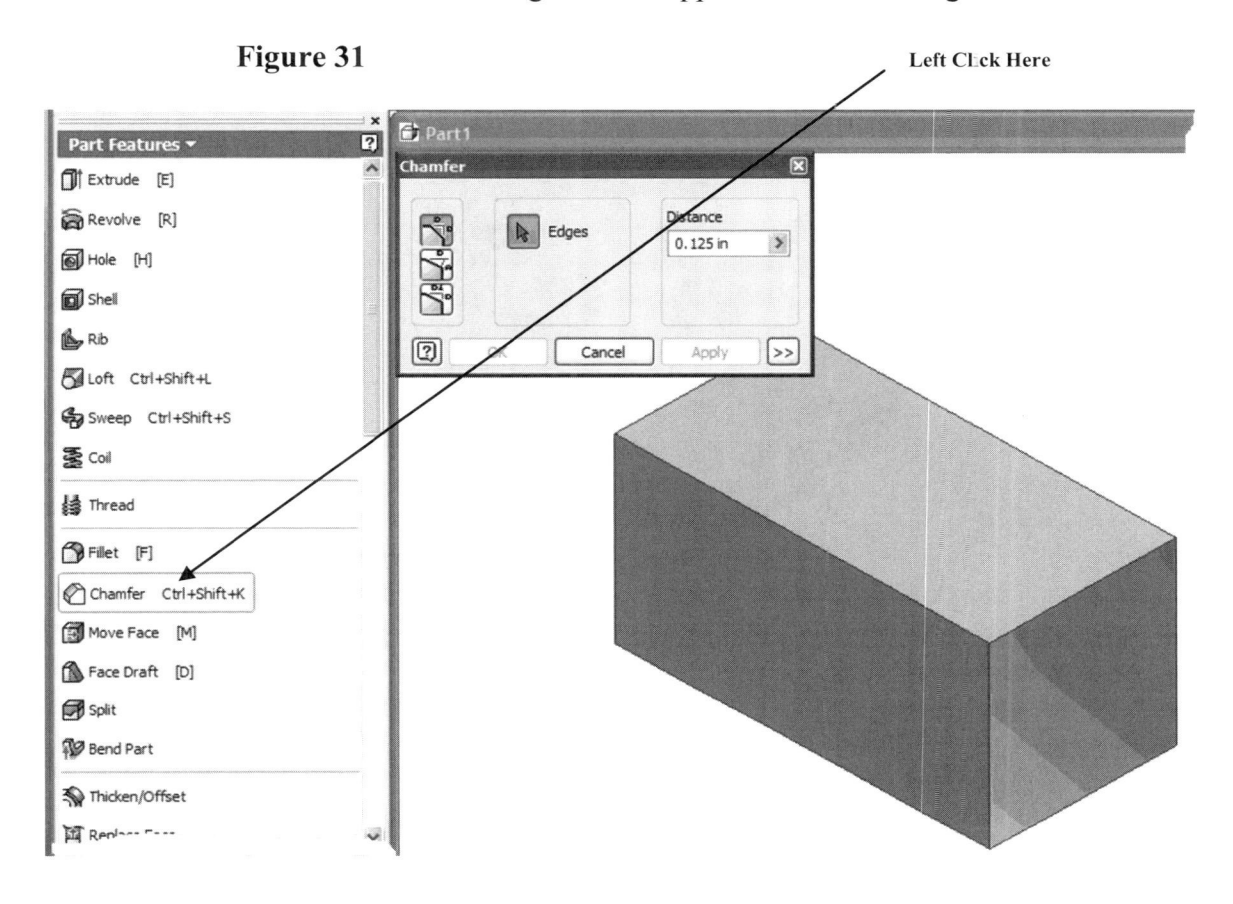

39. After selecting **Chamfer,** left click on the "Two Distance Chamfer" icon as shown in Figure 32.

Figure 32

137

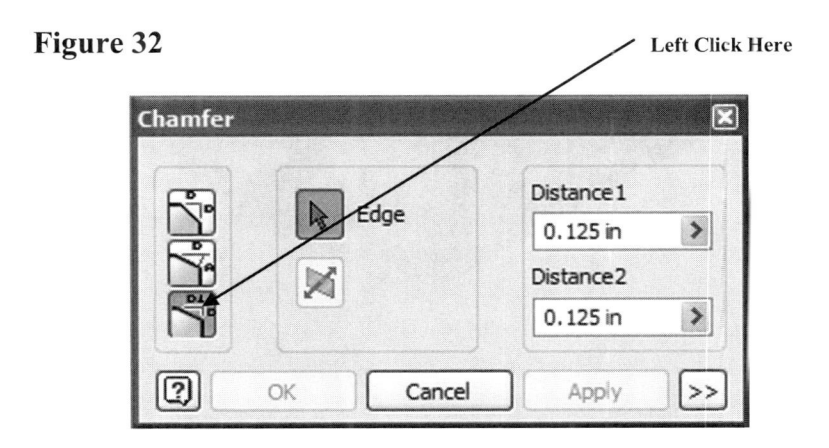

Chapter 3: Learning To Detail Part Drawings

40. Move the cursor to the front upper corner. A red line will appear as shown in Figure 33.

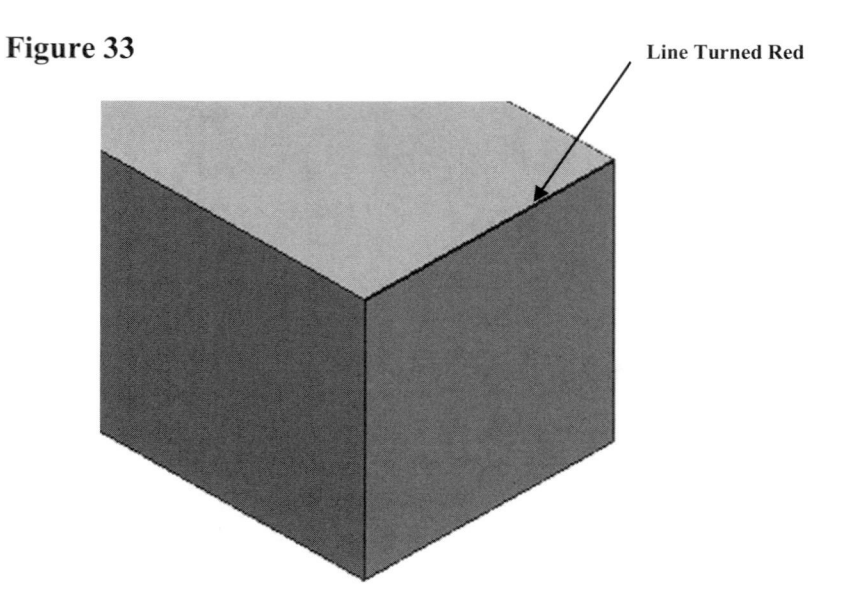

Figure 33

Line Turned Red

41. Inventor will provide a preview of the anticipated chamfer as shown in Figure 34.

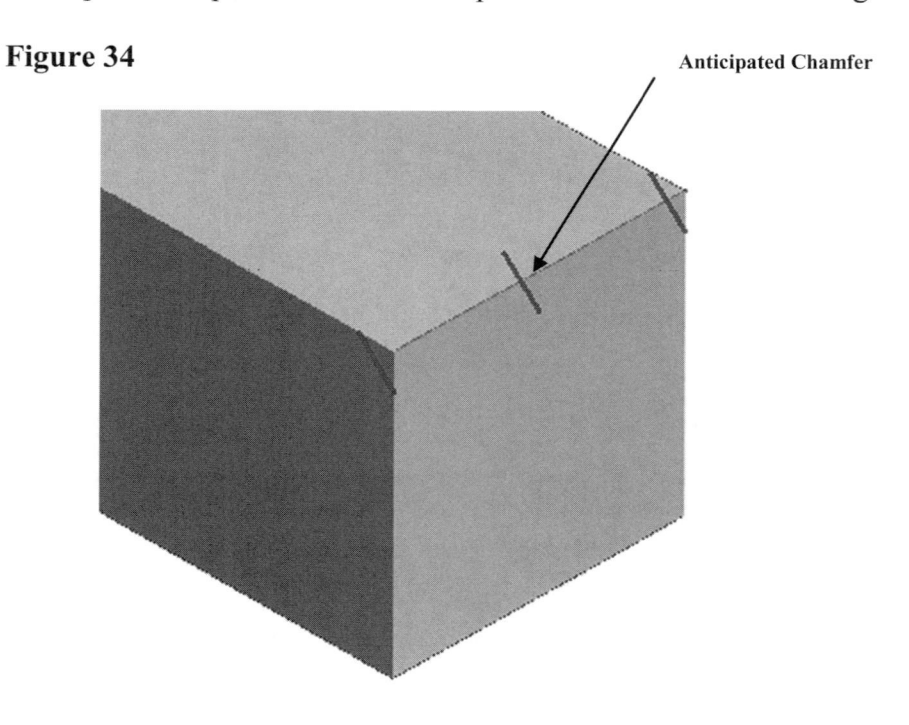

Figure 34

Anticipated Chamfer

Chapter 3: Learning To Detail Part Drawings

42. Move the cursor to Distance 1 in the dialog box and highlight the text. Enter **.5** in the dialog box. Inventor will provide a preview of the chamfer as shown in Figure 35.

Figure 35

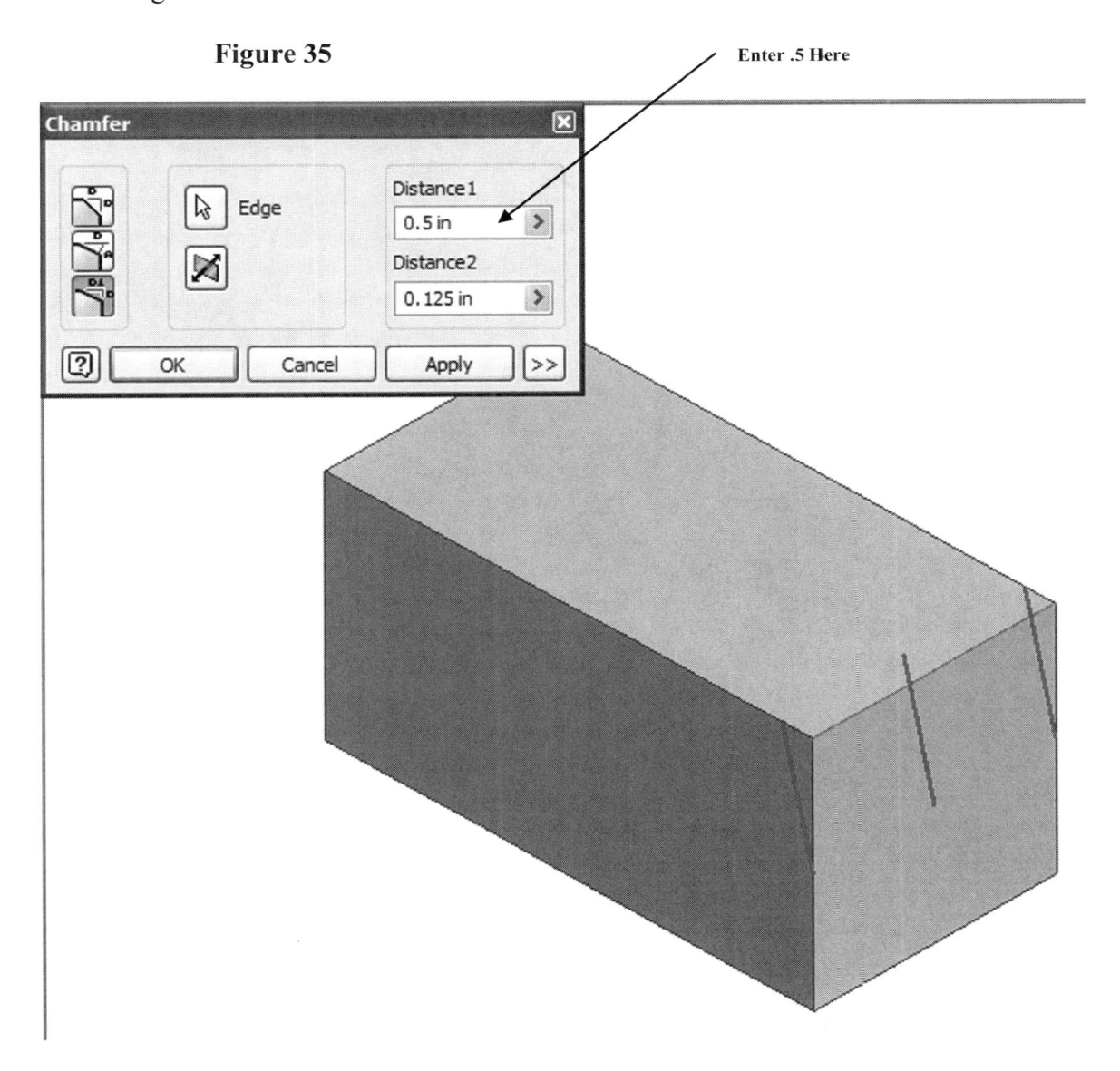

Enter .5 Here

Chapter 3: Learning To Detail Part Drawings

43. Move the cursor to Distance 2 in the dialog box and highlight the text. Enter **.75** in the dialog box. Inventor will provide a preview of the chamfer as shown in Figure 36.

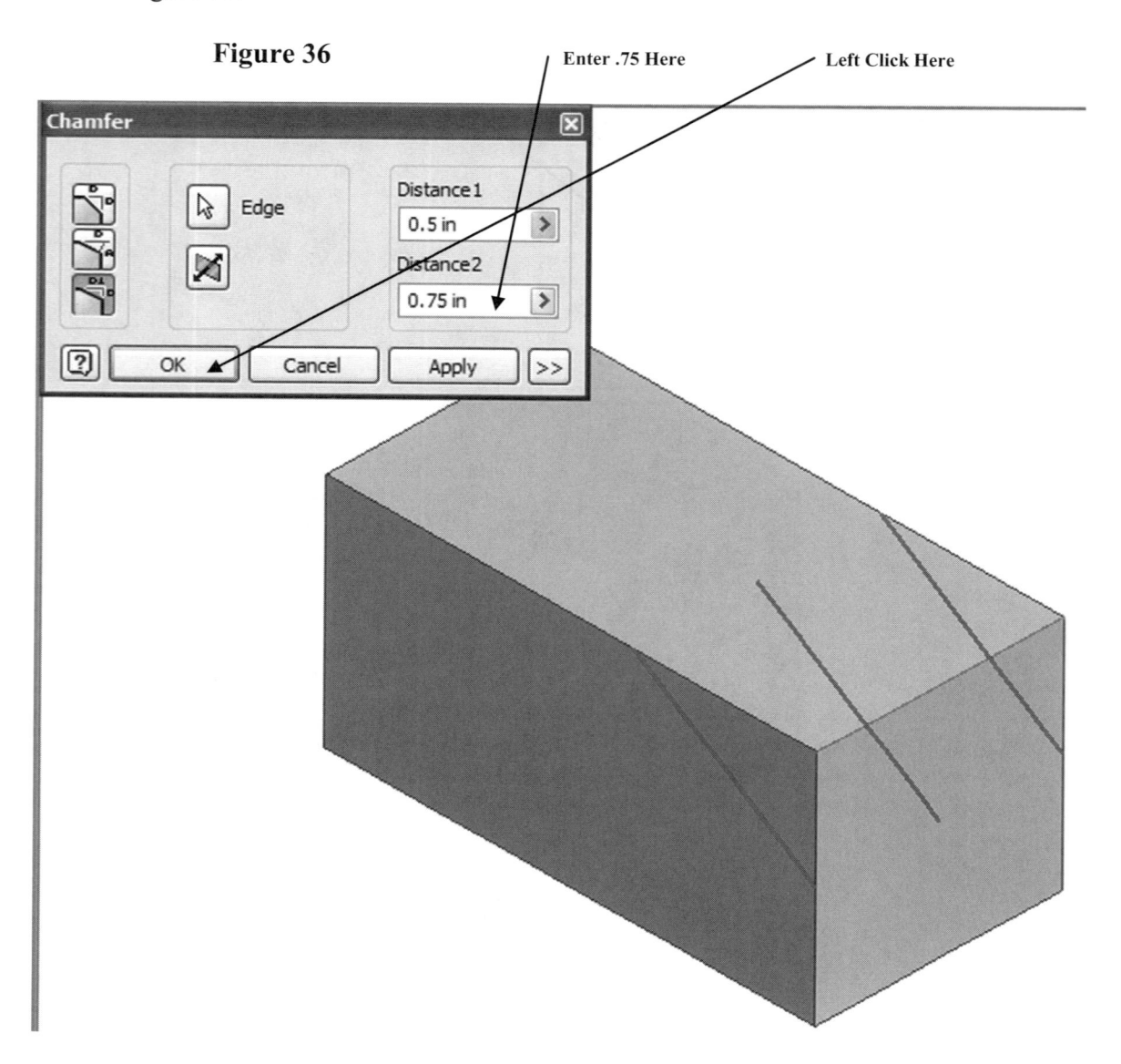

Figure 36

Enter .75 Here

Left Click Here

140

Chapter 3: Learning To Detail Part Drawings

44. Left click on **OK**. Your screen should look similar to Figure 37.

Figure 37

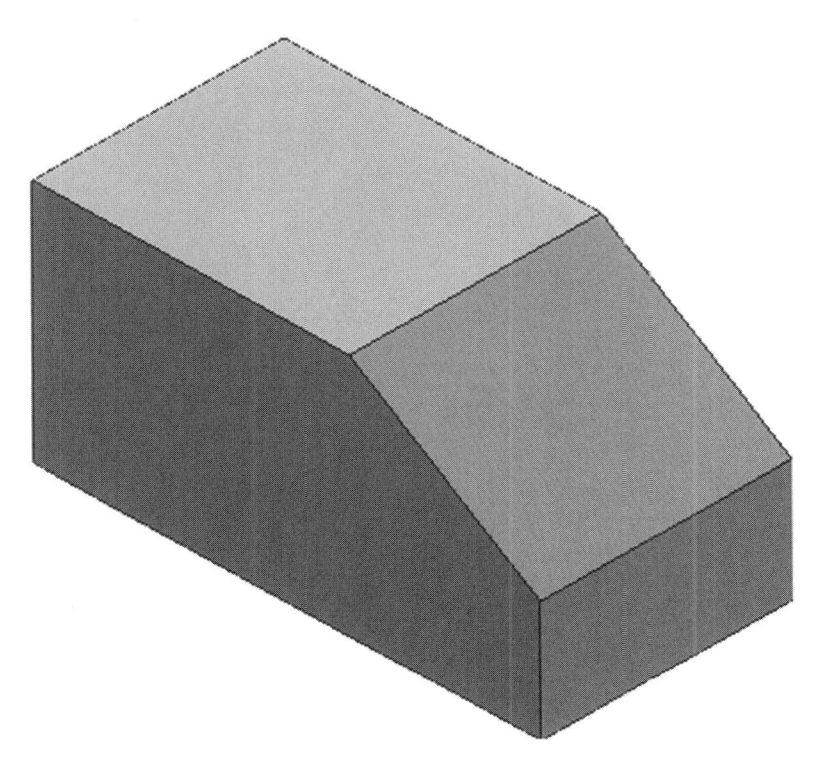

45. Move the cursor to the upper middle portion of the screen and left click on "Orbit/Rotate" as shown in Figure 38.

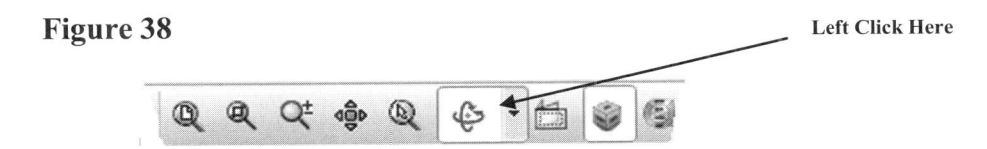

Figure 38

Left Click Here

Chapter 3: Learning To Detail Part Drawings

46. A white circle will appear around the part as shown in Figure 39.

Figure 39

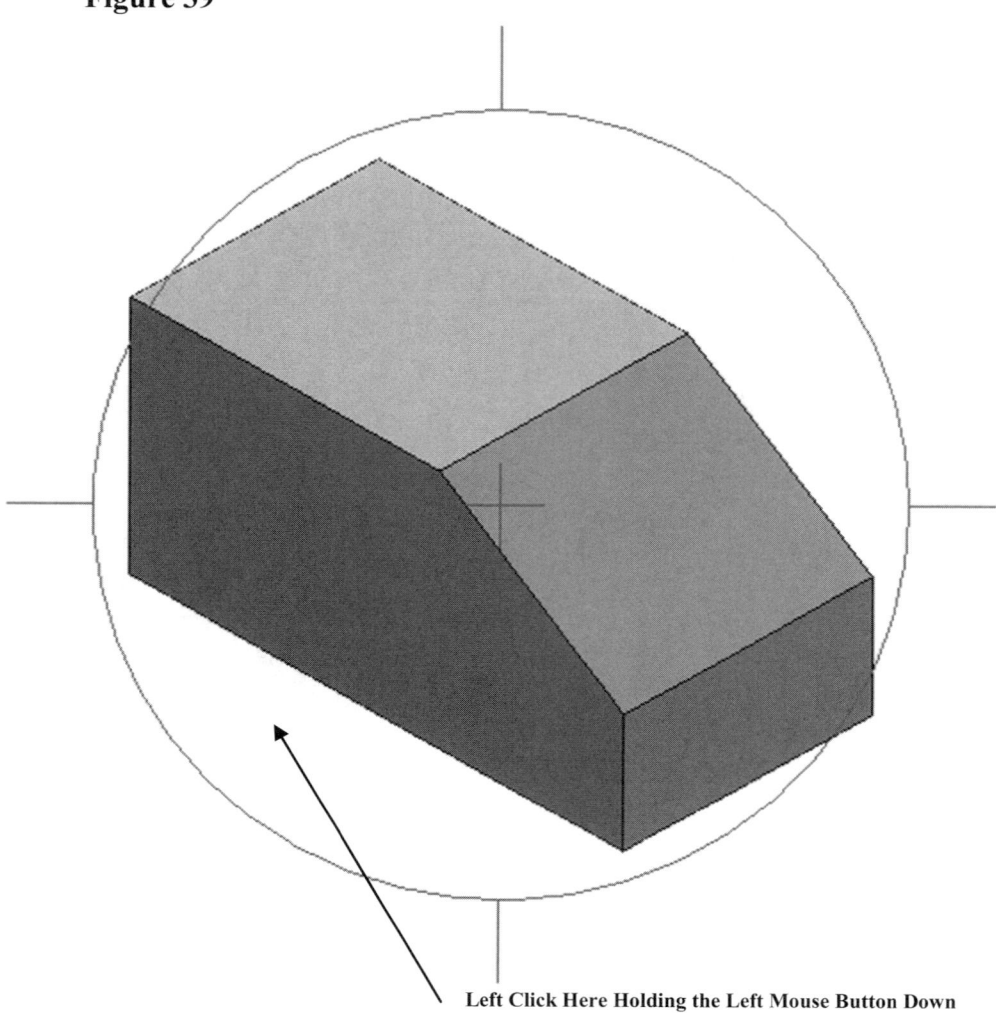

Left Click Here Holding the Left Mouse Button Down

47. Left click (holding the left mouse button down) inside the lower left portion of the circle.

Chapter 3: Learning To Detail Part Drawings

48. While holding the left mouse button down, drag the cursor to the right to gain access to the backside of the part as shown in Figure 40.

Figure 40

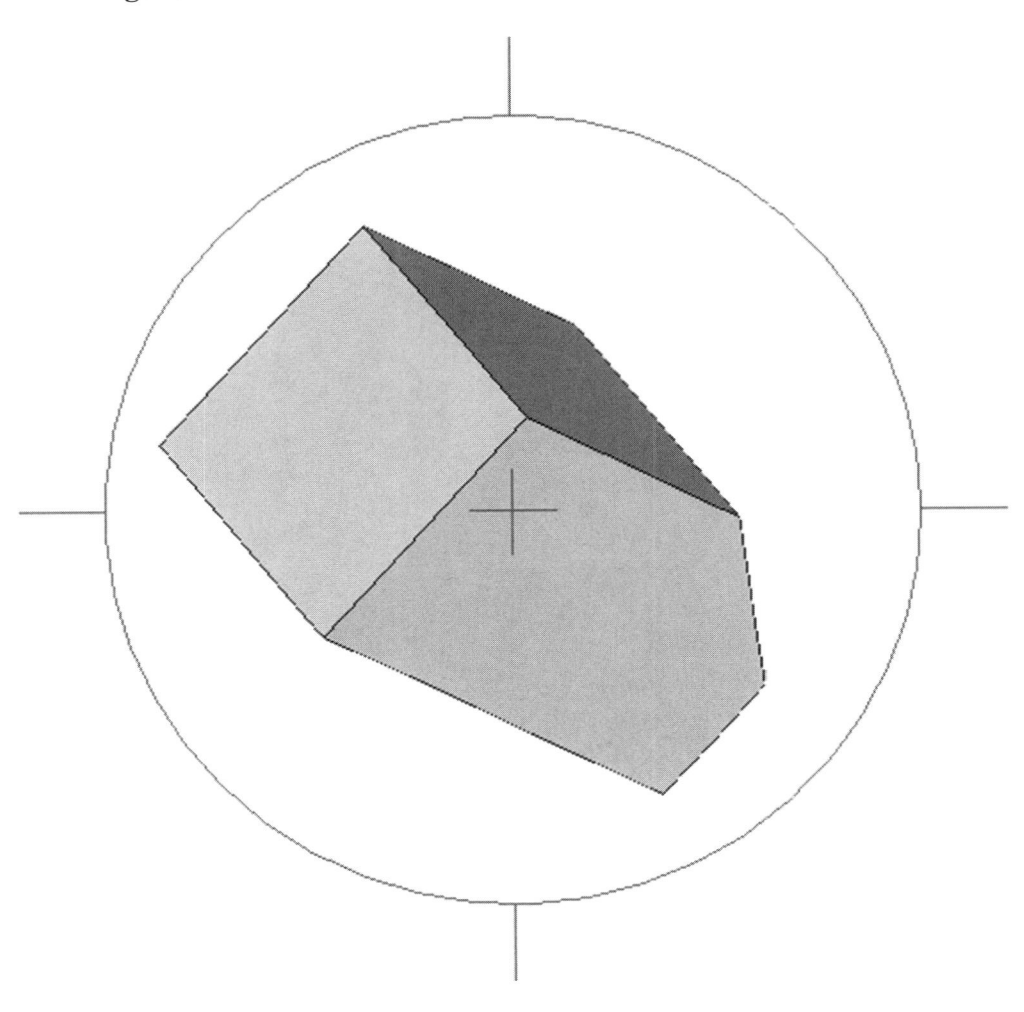

Chapter 3: Learning To Detail Part Drawings

49. Right click inside the circle. A pop up menu will appear. Left click on **Done [Esc]** as shown in Figure 41.

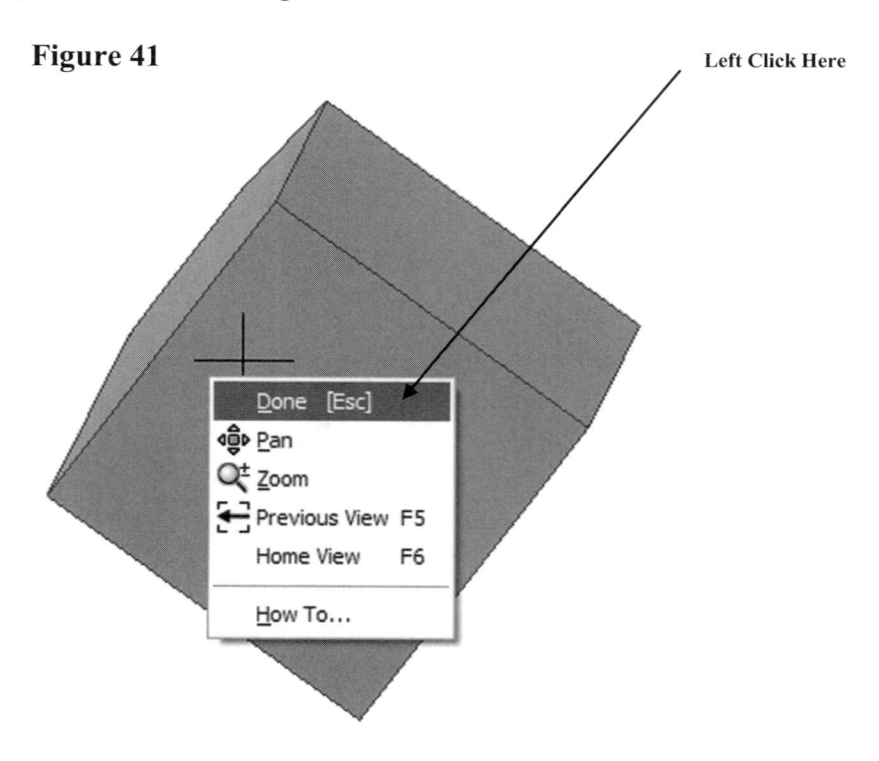

Figure 41

Left Click Here

50. Move the cursor to the upper middle portion of the screen and left click on the "Look At" icon as shown in Figure 42.

Figure 42

Left Click Here

Chapter 3: Learning To Detail Part Drawings

51. Move the cursor to the backside surface causing it to turn red and left click as shown in Figure 43.

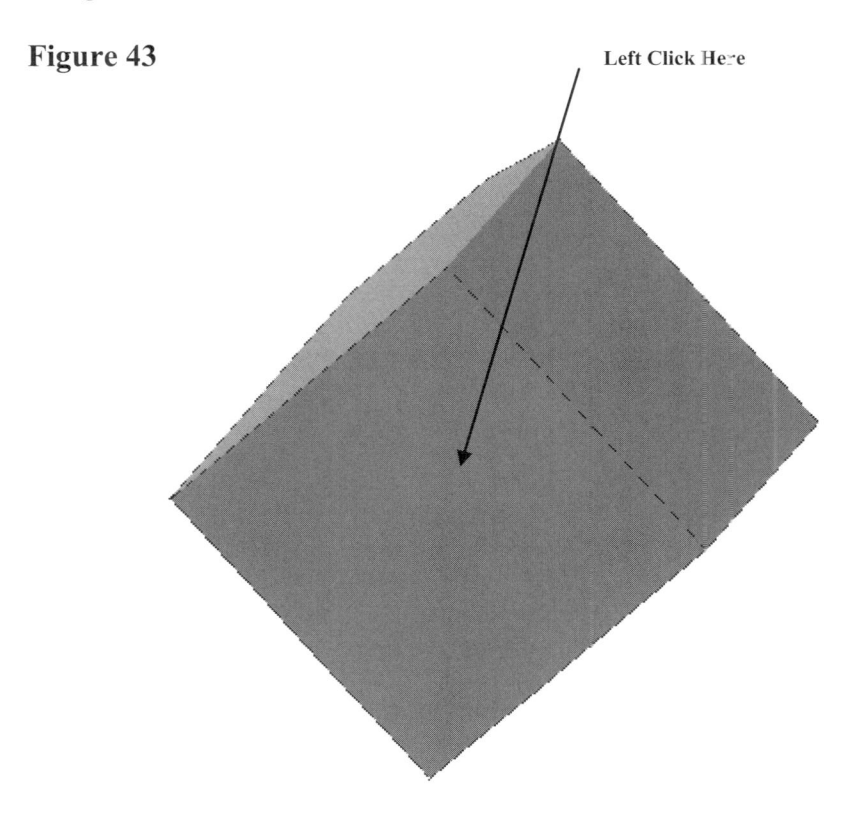

Figure 43

Left Click Here

52. Inventor will rotate the part providing a perpendicular view of the surface as shown in Figure 44.

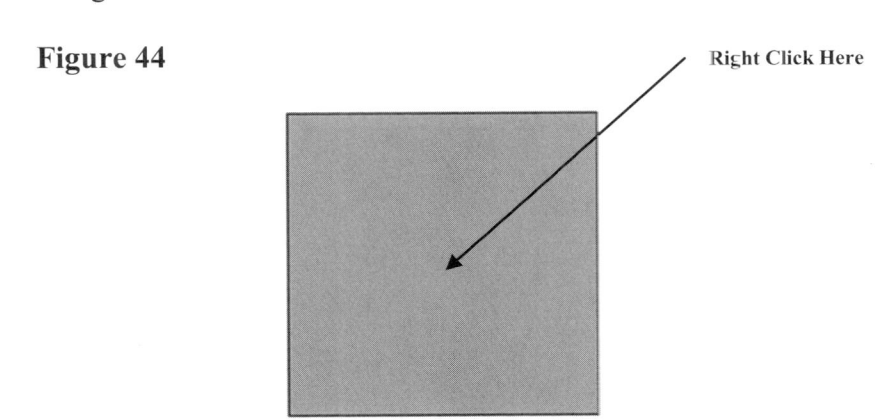

Figure 44

Right Click Here

Chapter 3: Learning To Detail Part Drawings

53. Right click anywhere on the surface. A pop up menu will appear. Left click on **New Sketch** as shown in Figure 45.

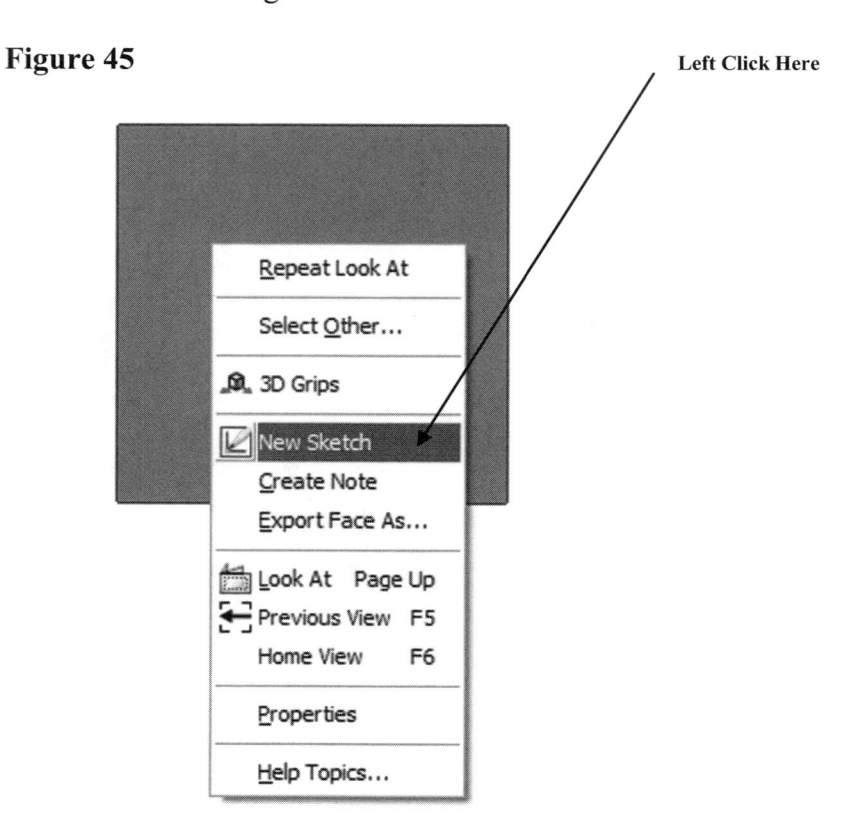

Figure 45

Left Click Here

54. A new sketch will appear on the surface as shown in Figure 46.

Figure 46

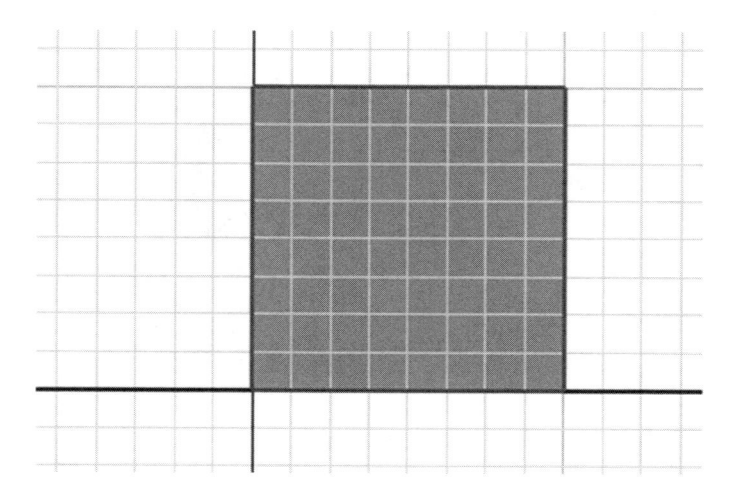

Chapter 3: Learning To Detail Part Drawings

55. Move the cursor to the upper left portion of the screen and left click on **Center Point Circle** as shown in Figure 47.

Figure 47 Left Click Here

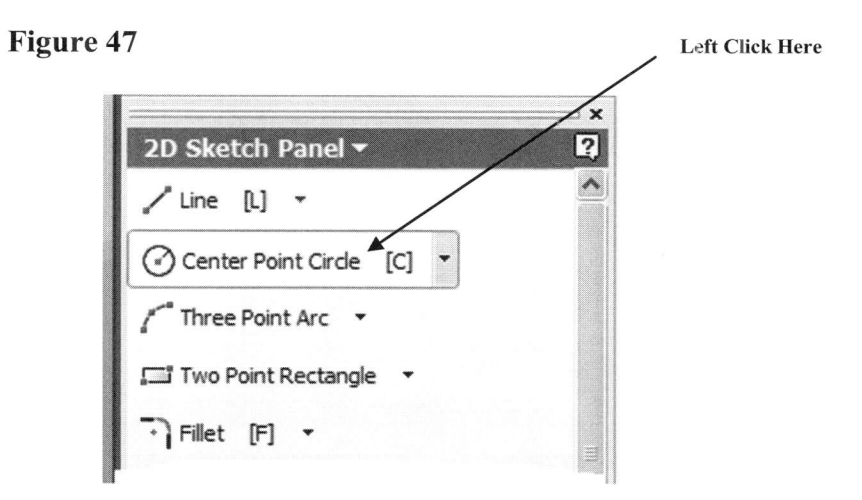

56. Left click on the backside surface as shown in Figure 48.

Figure 48 Left Click Here

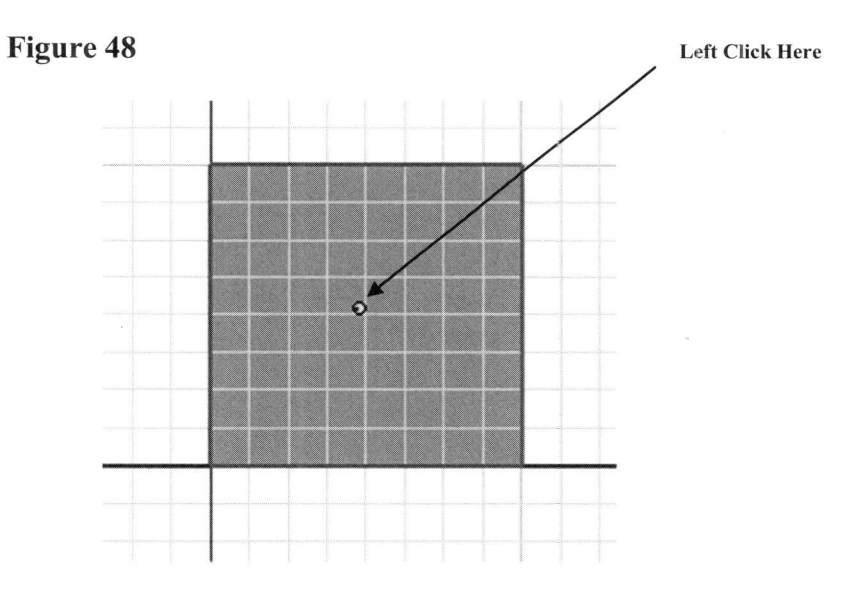

Chapter 3: Learning To Detail Part Drawings

57. Move the cursor to the side forming a circle and left click as shown in Figure 49.

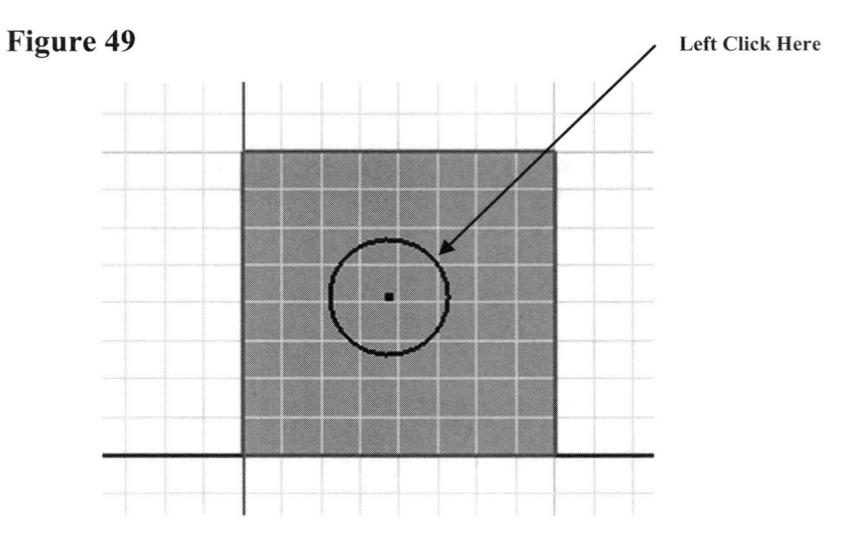

Figure 49

Left Click Here

58. Move the cursor to the middle left portion of the screen and left click on **General Dimension** as shown in Figure 50.

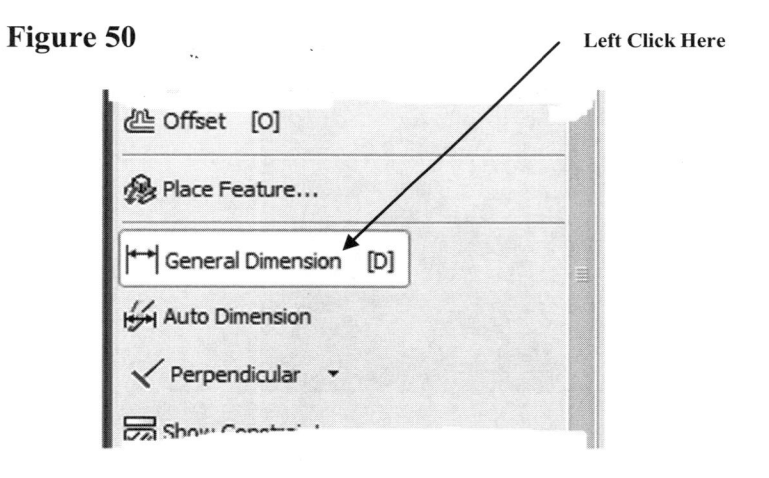

Figure 50

Left Click Here

Chapter 3: Learning To Detail Part Drawings

59. After selecting **General Dimension** move the cursor over the circle until it turns red as shown in Figure 51. Select the circle by left clicking on the edge of the circle.

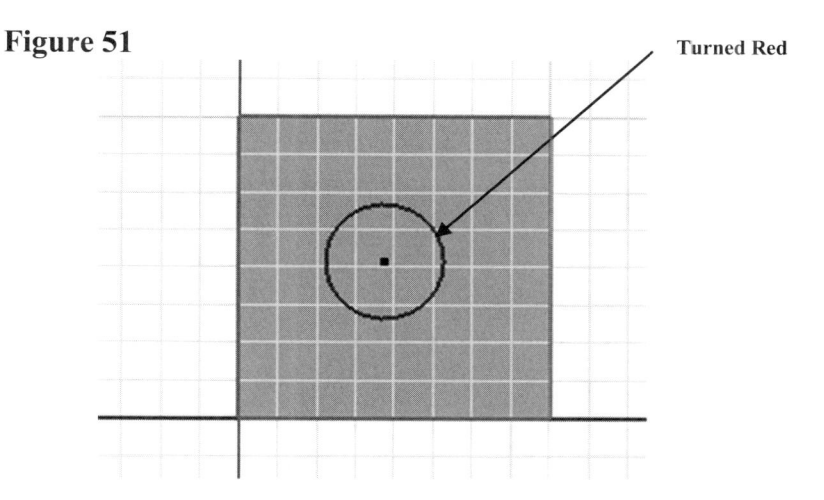

Figure 51 Turned Red

60. The dimension will be attached to the cursor. Move the cursor out to the right as shown in Figure 52.

Figure 52

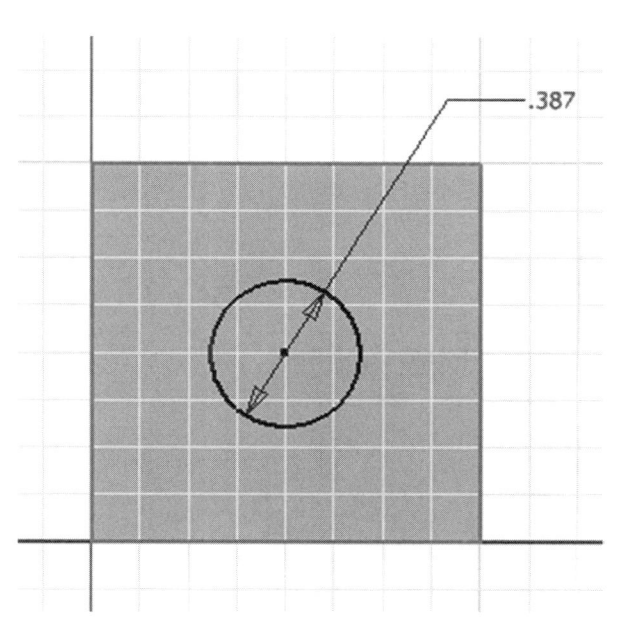

61. The actual dimension of the circle will appear as shown in Figure 52.

Chapter 3: Learning To Detail Part Drawings

62. Move the cursor to where the dimension will be placed and left click once. While the dimension is still in red, left click once. The Edit Dimension dialog box will appear as shown in Figure 53.

Figure 53

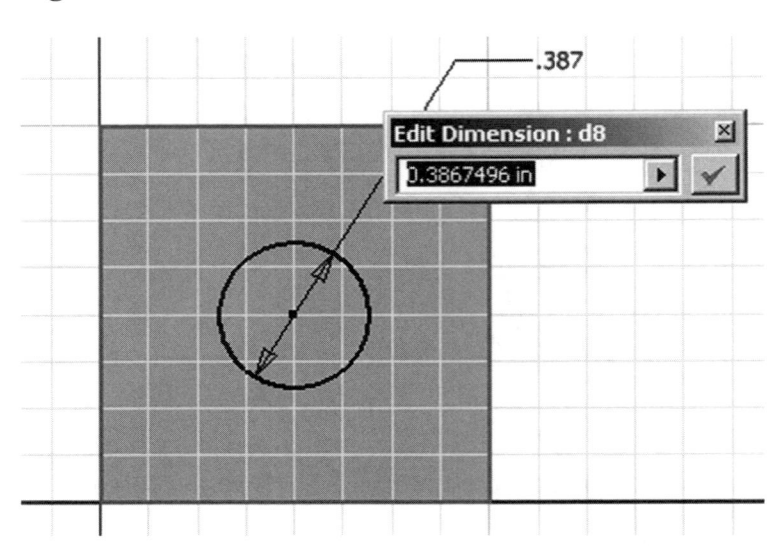

63. To edit the dimension, type **.5** in the Edit Dimension dialog box (while the current dimension is highlighted) and press **Enter** on the keyboard.

64. Your screen should look similar to Figure 54.

Figure 54

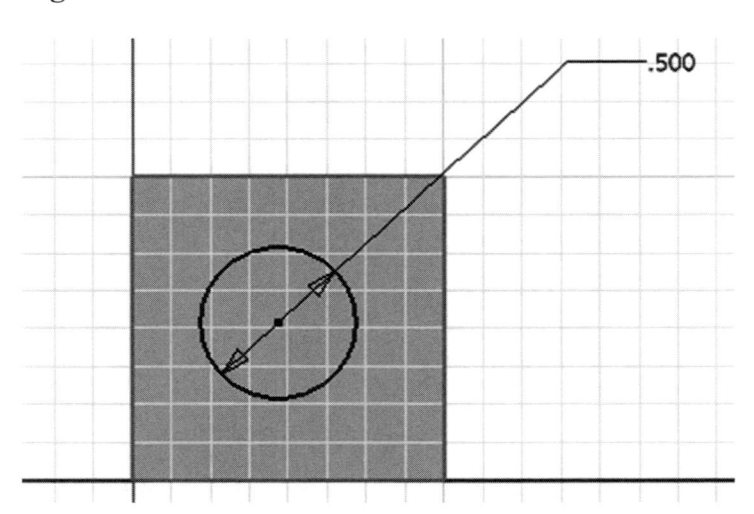

150

Chapter 3: Learning To Detail Part Drawings

65. Move the cursor to the middle left portion of the screen and left click on **General Dimension** as shown in Figure 55.

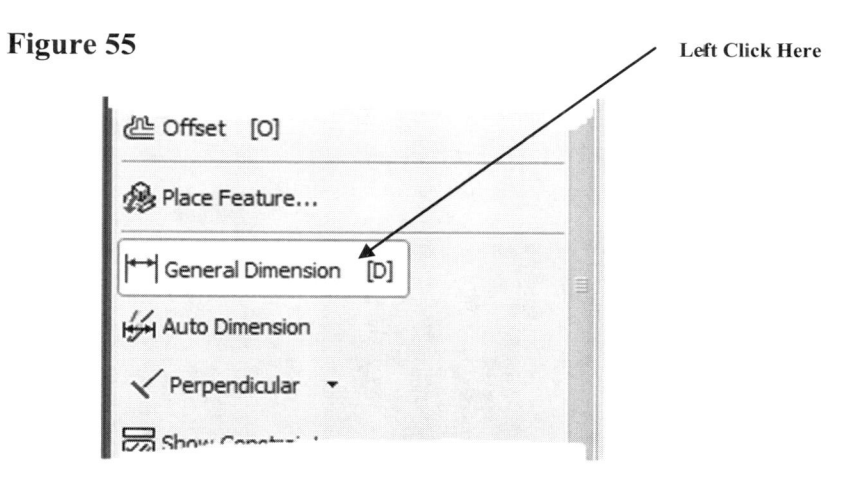

Figure 55

66. After selecting **General Dimension** move the cursor over the center of the circle until it turns red and left click as shown in Figure 56.

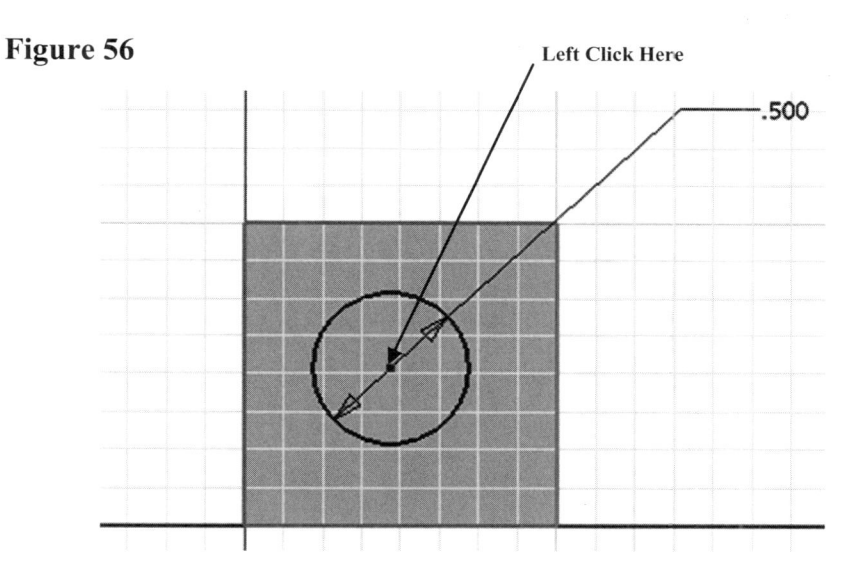

Figure 56

Chapter 3: Learning To Detail Part Drawings

67. Left click on the left side of the part as shown in Figure 57.

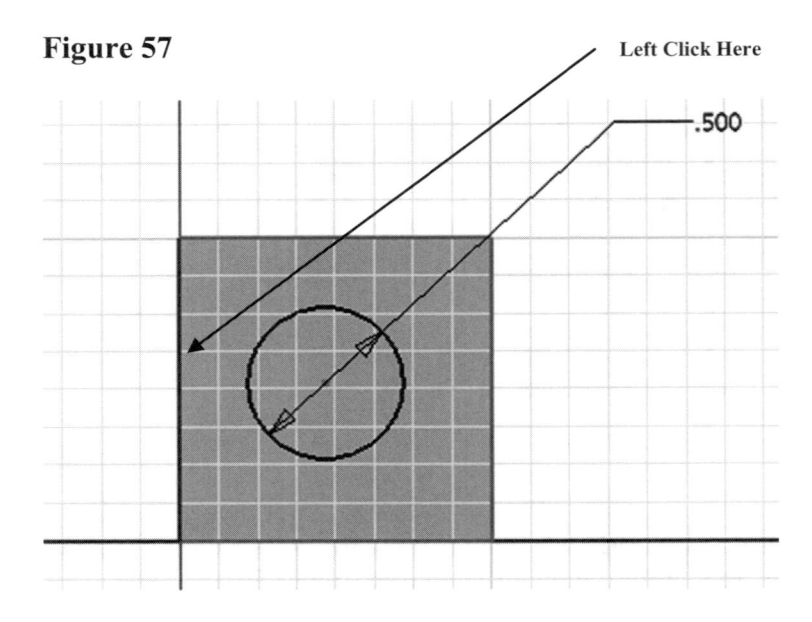

Figure 57

68. The dimension will be attached to the cursor. Move the cursor up as shown in Figure 58.

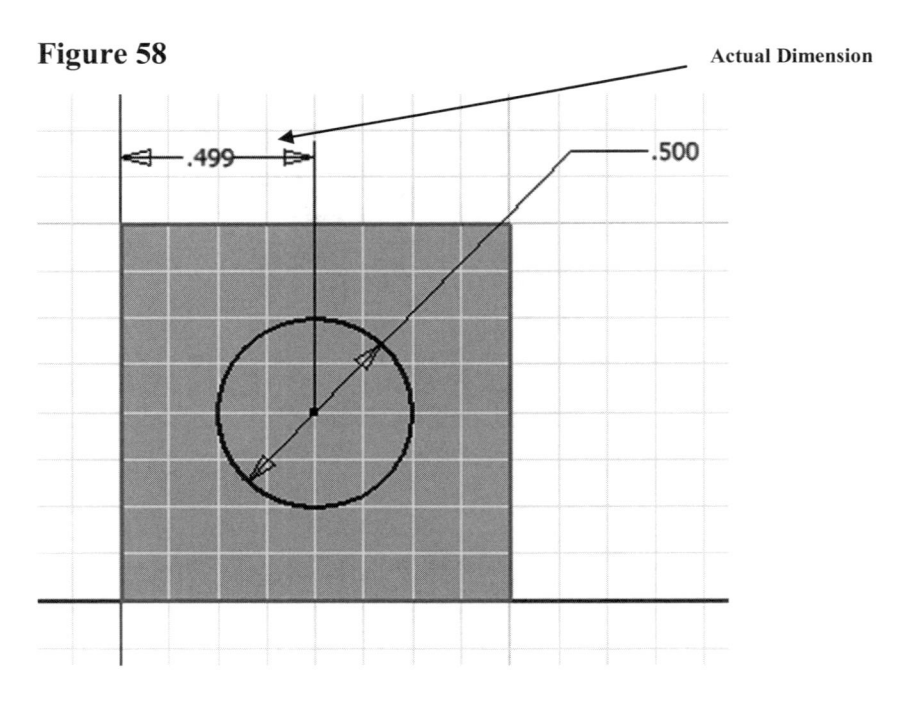

Figure 58

69. The actual dimension of the circle will appear as shown in Figure 58.

152

Chapter 3: Learning To Detail Part Drawings

70. Move the cursor to where the dimension will be placed and left click once. While the dimension is still in red, left click once. The Edit Dimension dialog box will appear as shown in Figure 59.

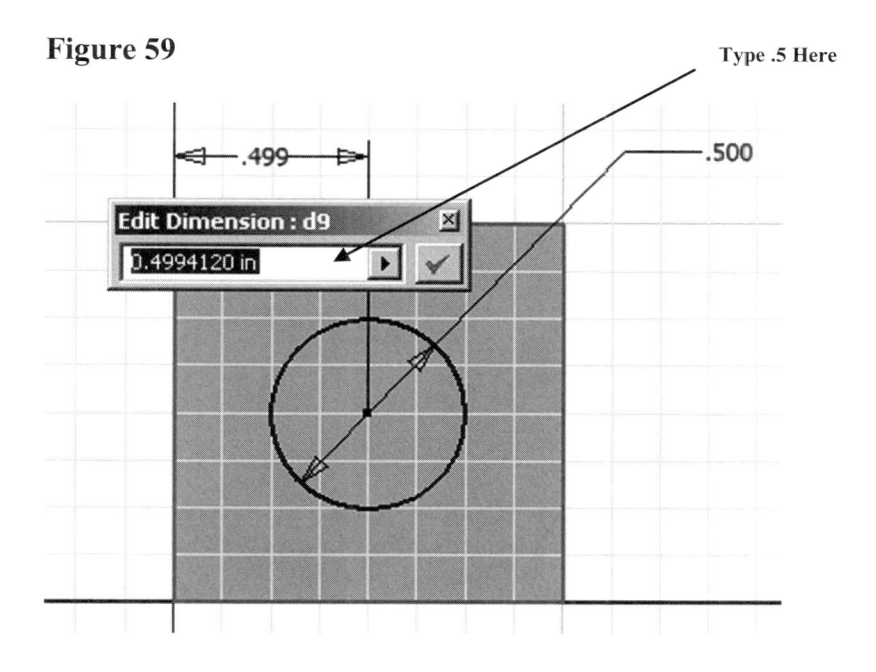

Figure 59

71. To edit the dimension, type **.5** in the Edit Dimension dialog box (while the current dimension is highlighted) and press **Enter** on the keyboard.

72. Your screen should look similar to Figure 60.

Figure 60

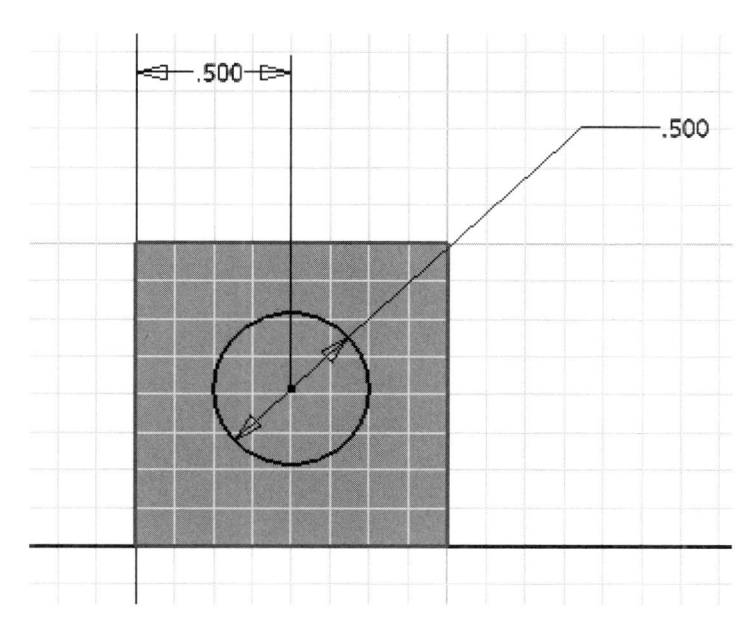

153

Chapter 3: Learning To Detail Part Drawings

73. Move the cursor to the middle left portion of the screen and left click on **General Dimension** as shown in Figure 61.

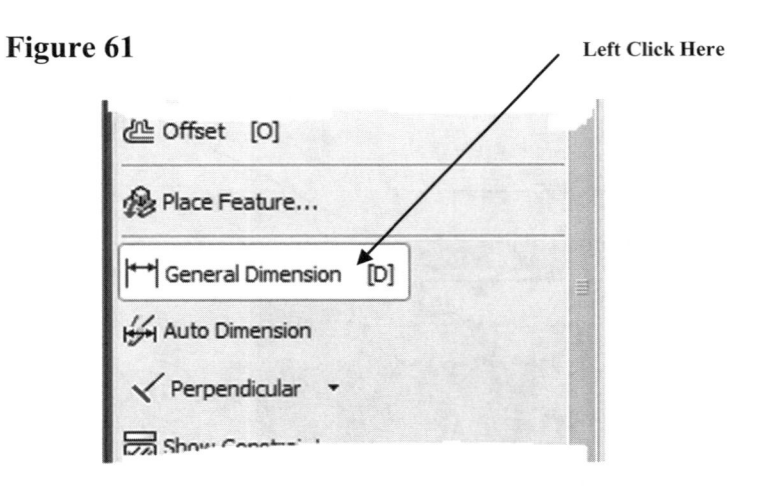

Figure 61

Left Click Here

- Offset [O]
- Place Feature...
- General Dimension [D]
- Auto Dimension
- Perpendicular
- Show Constr...

74. After selecting **General Dimension** move the cursor over the center of the circle until it turns red and left click as shown in Figure 62.

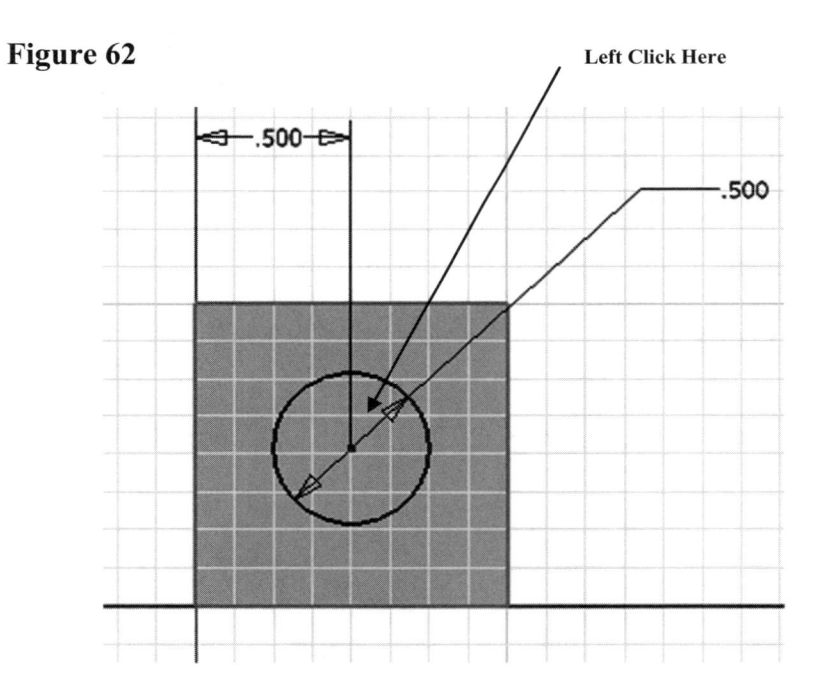

Figure 62

Left Click Here

.500

.500

Chapter 3: Learning To Detail Part Drawings

75. Left click on the bottom side of the part as shown in Figure 63.

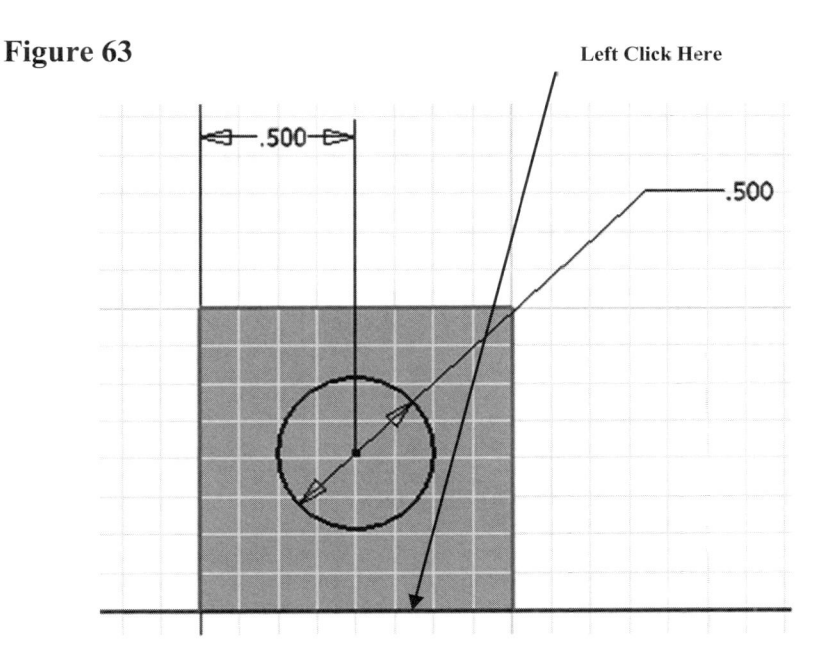

Figure 63

76. The dimension will be attached to the cursor. Move the cursor to the side as shown in Figure 64.

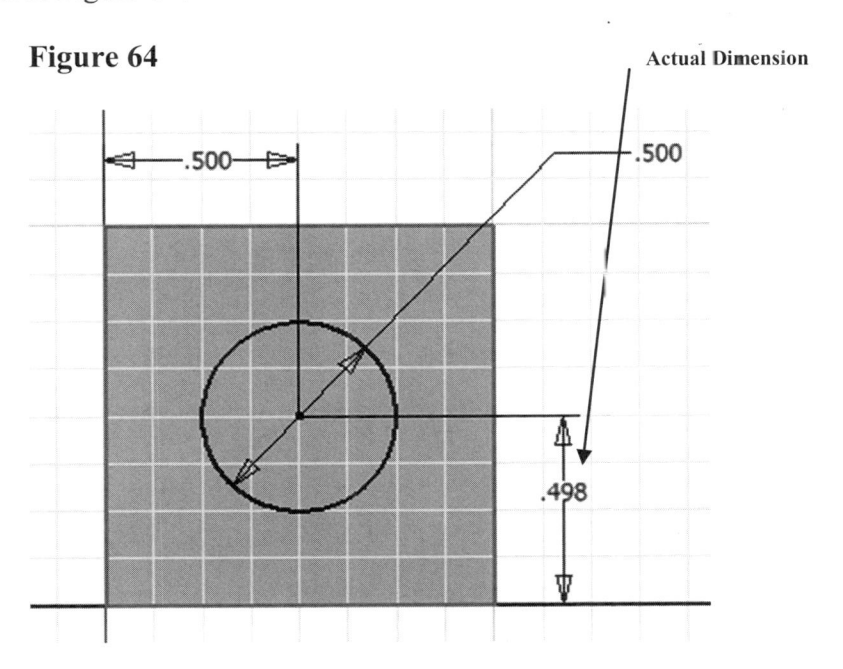

Figure 64

77. The actual dimension will appear as shown in Figure 64.

Chapter 3: Learning To Detail Part Drawings

78. Move the cursor to where the dimension will be placed and left click once. While the dimension is still in red, left click once. The Edit Dimension dialog box will appear as shown in Figure 65.

Figure 65

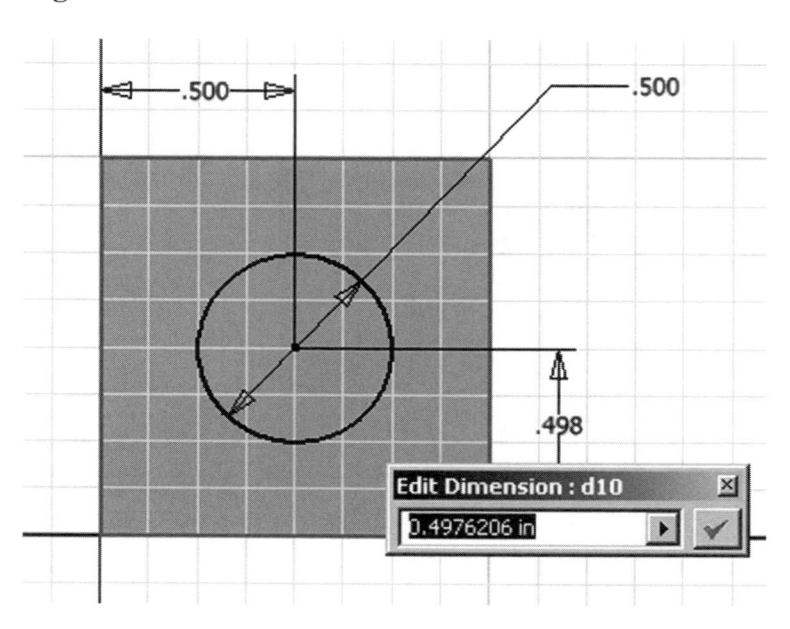

79. To edit the dimension, type **.5** in the Edit Dimension dialog box (while the current dimension is highlighted) and press **Enter** on the keyboard. Press the **Esc** key once or twice.

80. Your screen should look similar to Figure 66.

Figure 66

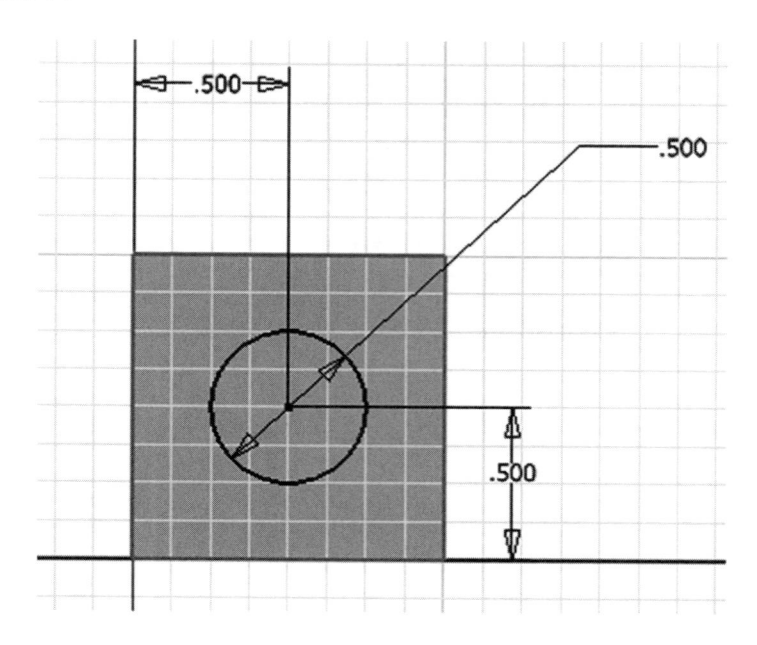

156

Chapter 3: Learning To Detail Part Drawings

81. After the sketch is complete it is time to extrude a hole through the solid.

82. After you have verified that no commands are active, right click anywhere on the sketch. A pop up menu will appear. Left click on **Finish Sketch** as shown in Figure 67.

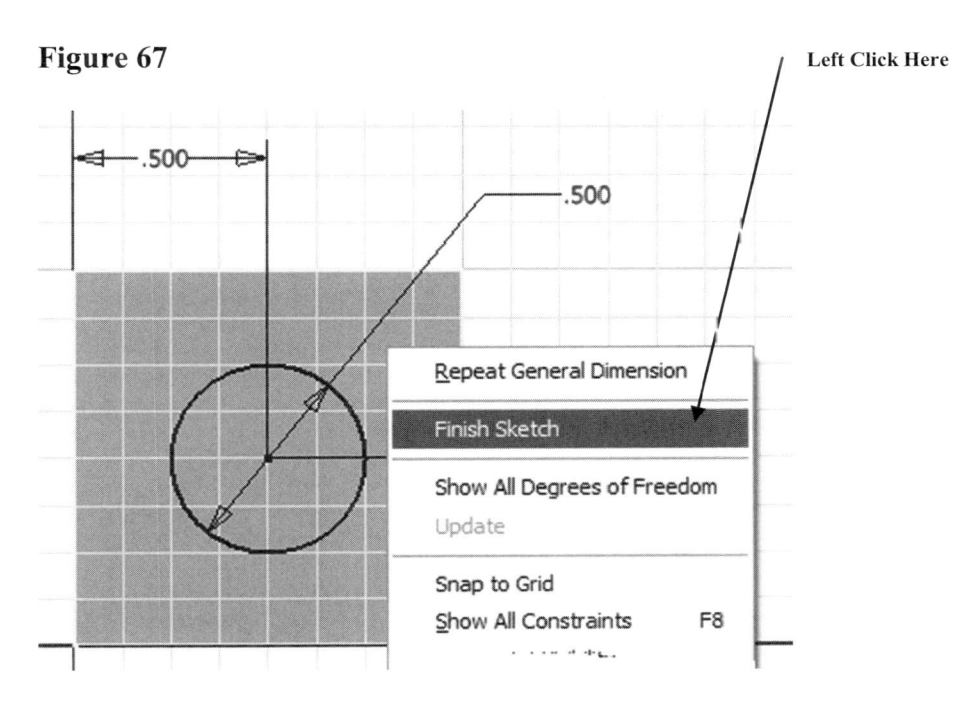

Figure 67

Chapter 3: Learning To Detail Part Drawings

83. Inventor is now out of the Sketch Panel and into the Part Features Panel. Notice that the commands at the left of the screen are now different. To work in the Part Features Panel a sketch must be present and have no opens (non-connected lines). If there are any opens in the sketch an error message will appear. Your screen should look similar to Figure 68.

Figure 68

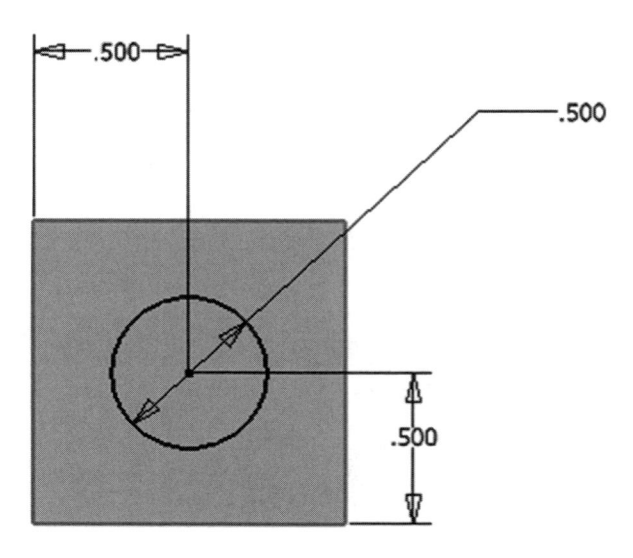

84. Move the cursor to the upper middle portion of the screen and left click on the "Rotate" icon as shown in Figure 69.

Figure 69   Left Click Here

158

Chapter 3: Learning To Detail Part Drawings

85. A white circle will appear around the part as shown in Figure 70.

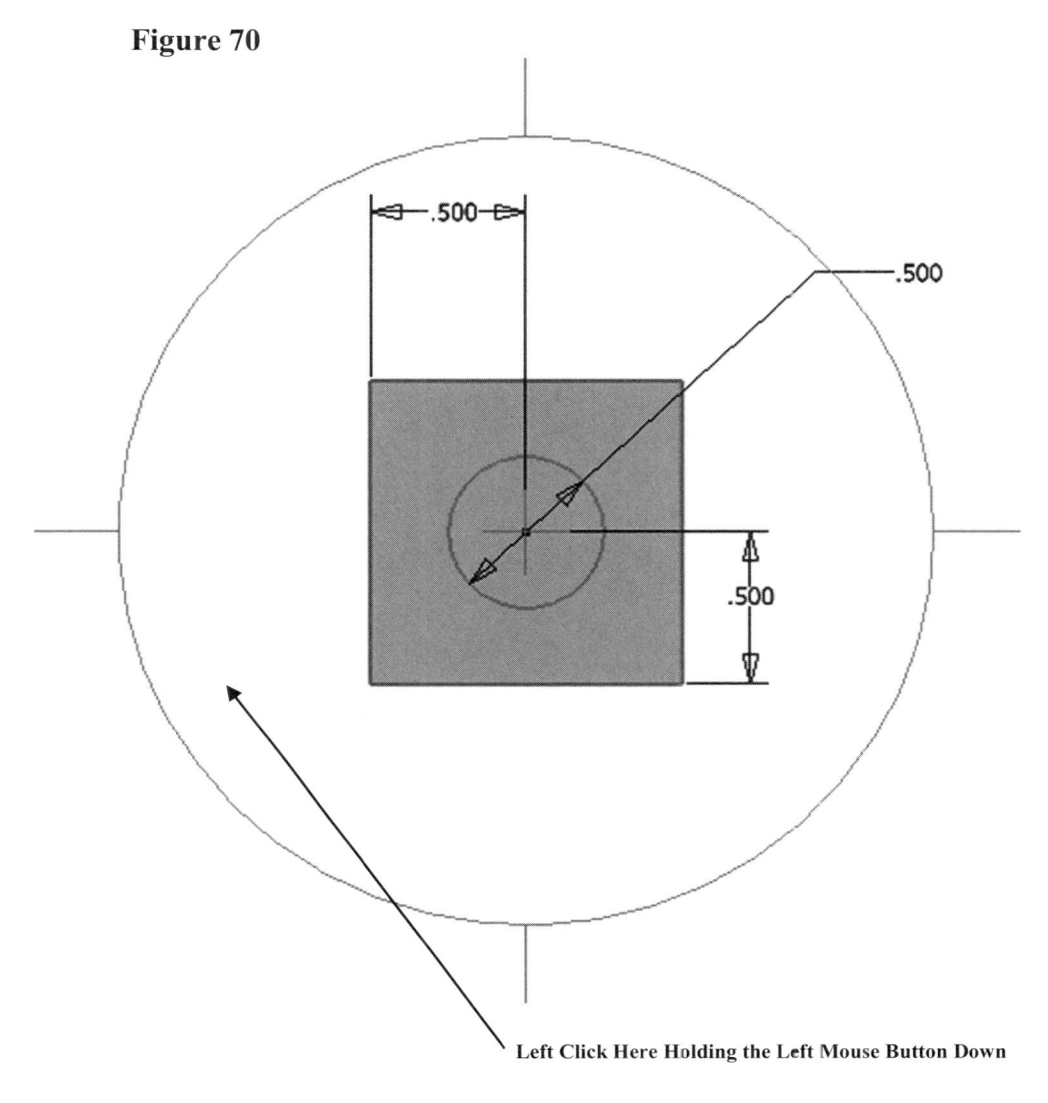

Figure 70

Left Click Here Holding the Left Mouse Button Down

86. Left click (holding the left mouse button down) inside the lower left portion of the circle.

Chapter 3: Learning To Detail Part Drawings

87. While holding the left mouse button down, drag the cursor to the right to gain an isometric view of the part as shown in Figure 71.

Figure 71

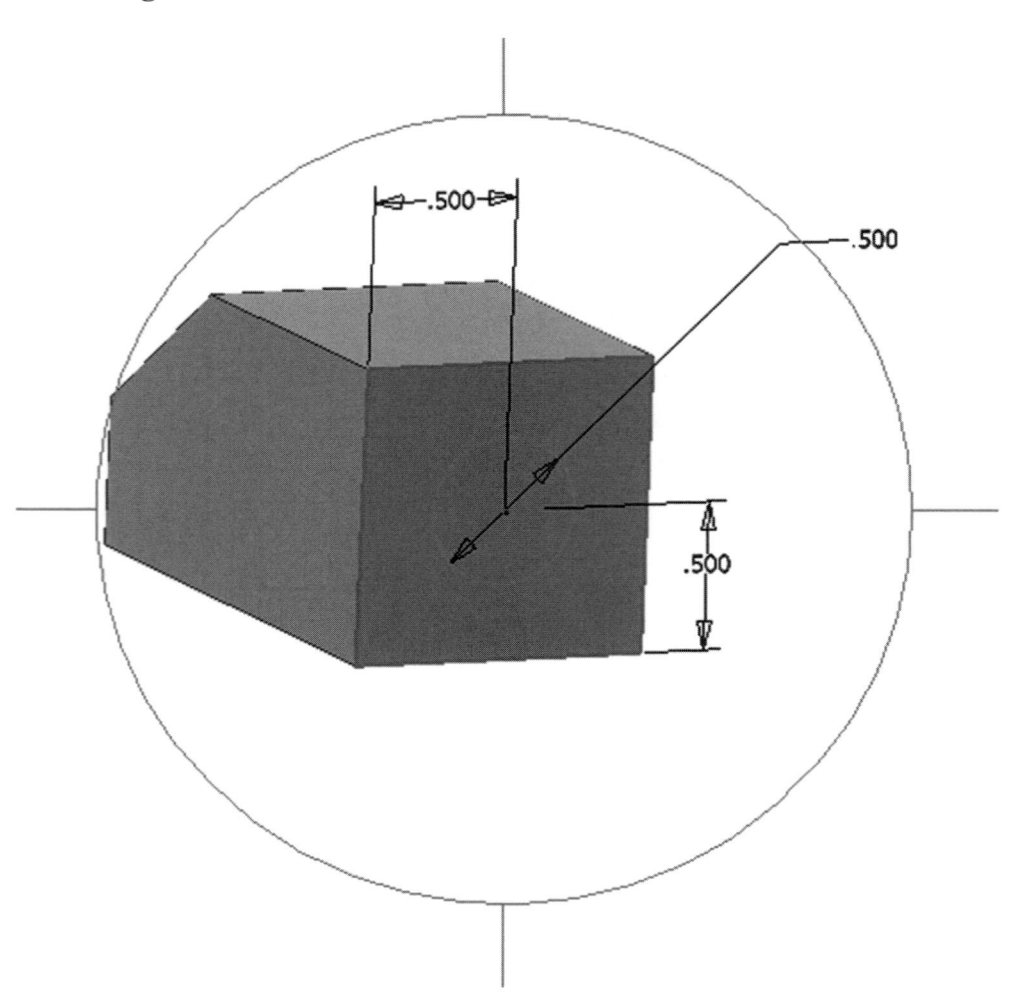

Chapter 3: Learning To Detail Part Drawings

88. Move the cursor to the middle left portion of the screen and left click on **Extrude**. The Extrude dialog box will appear. Inventor also provides a preview of the extrusion. If Inventor gave you an error message, there are opens (non-connected lines) somewhere on the sketch. Check each intersection for opens by using the **Extend** and **Trim** commands. Your screen should look similar to Figure 72.

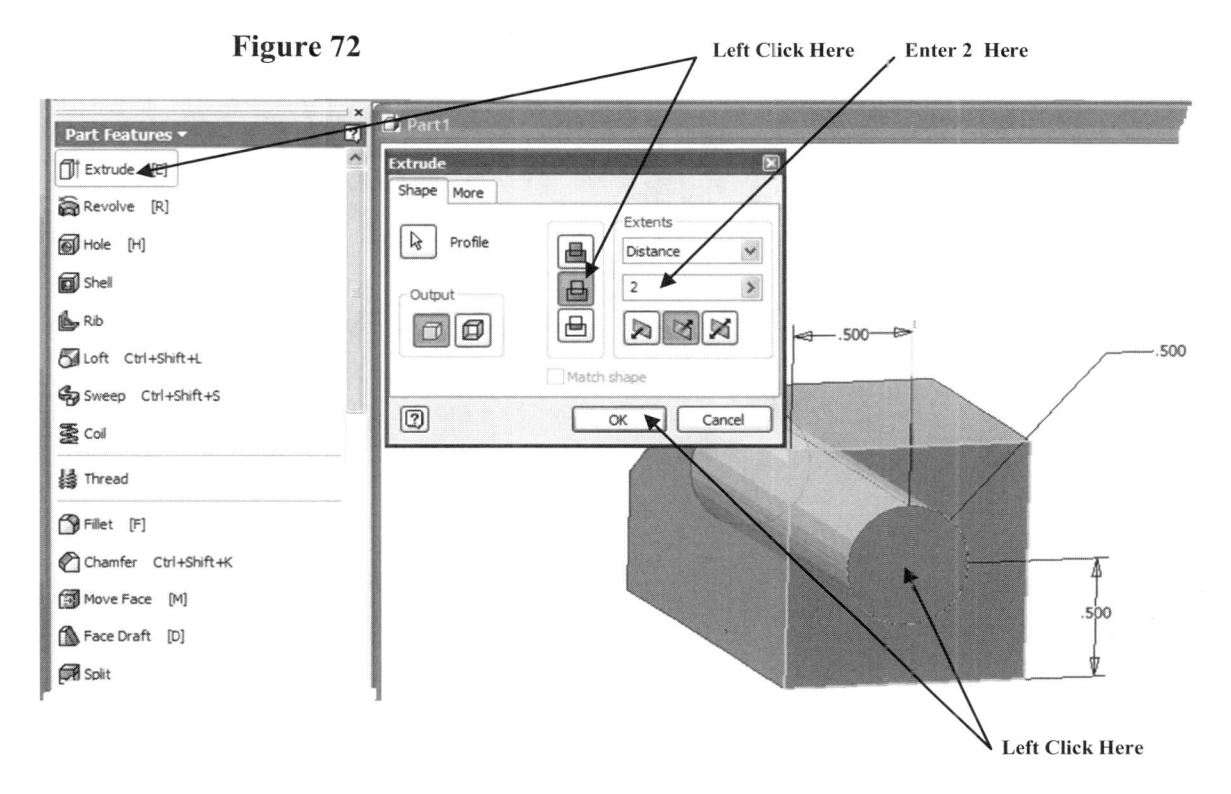

Figure 72

89. Left click on the "Cut" icon in the middle of the dialog box.

90. Left click in the center of the circle causing it to turn red as shown in Figure 72.

91. Enter **2** under distance for the depth of the extrusion and left click **OK**.

161

Chapter 3: Learning To Detail Part Drawings

92. Right click anywhere on the part. A pop up menu will appear. Left click on **Isometric/Home View** as shown in Figure 73.

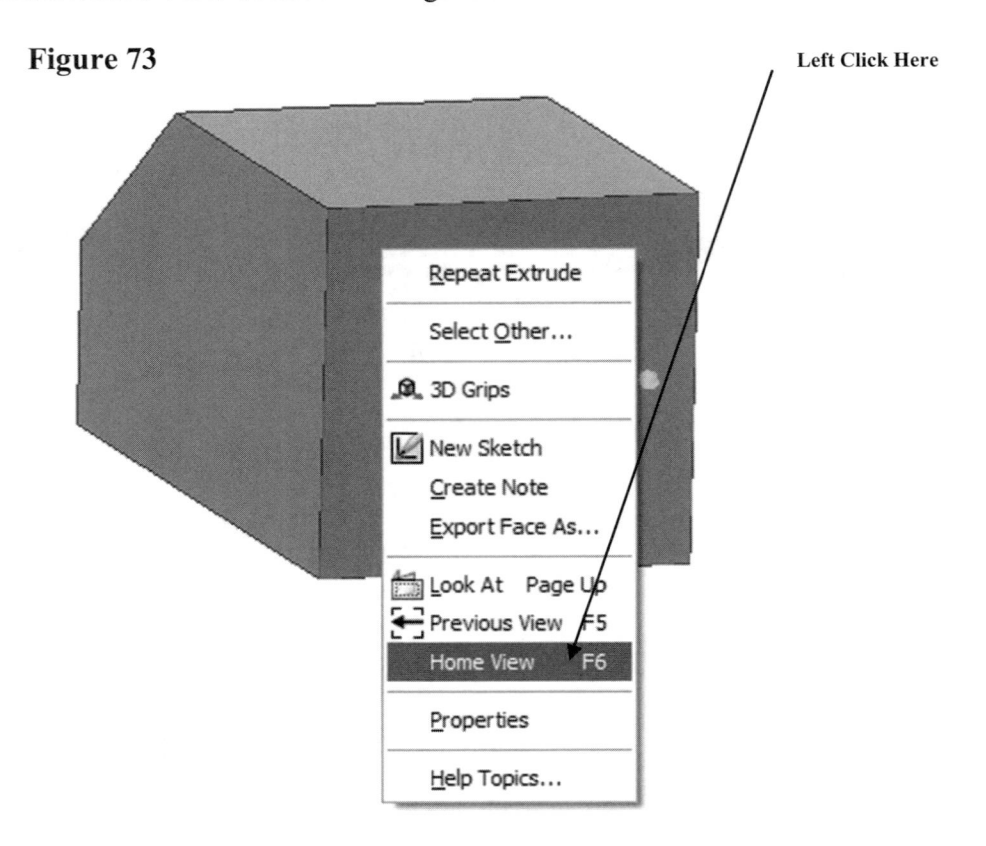

Figure 73

Left Click Here

93. Your screen should look similar to Figure 74.

Figure 74

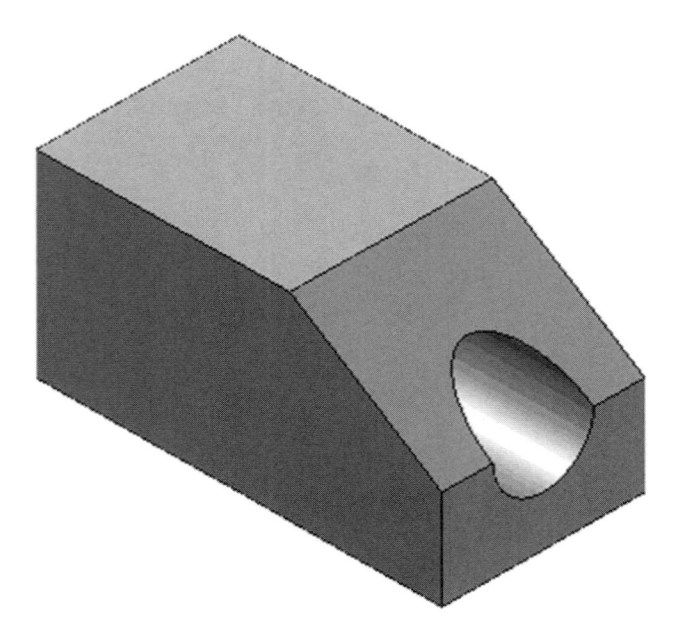

Chapter 3: Learning To Detail Part Drawings

94. Save the part file for easy retrieval to be used in the following section. Do not close the part file.

95. After the part file has been saved, move the cursor to the upper left portion of the screen and left click on the "New" icon as shown in Figure 75.

Figure 75

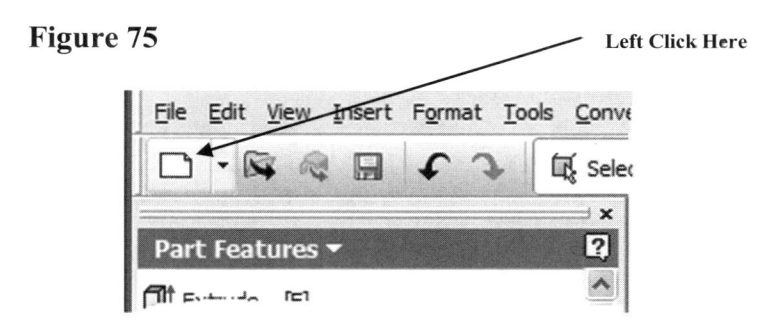

96. The New File dialog box will appear. Left click on **English** as shown in Figure 76.

Figure 76

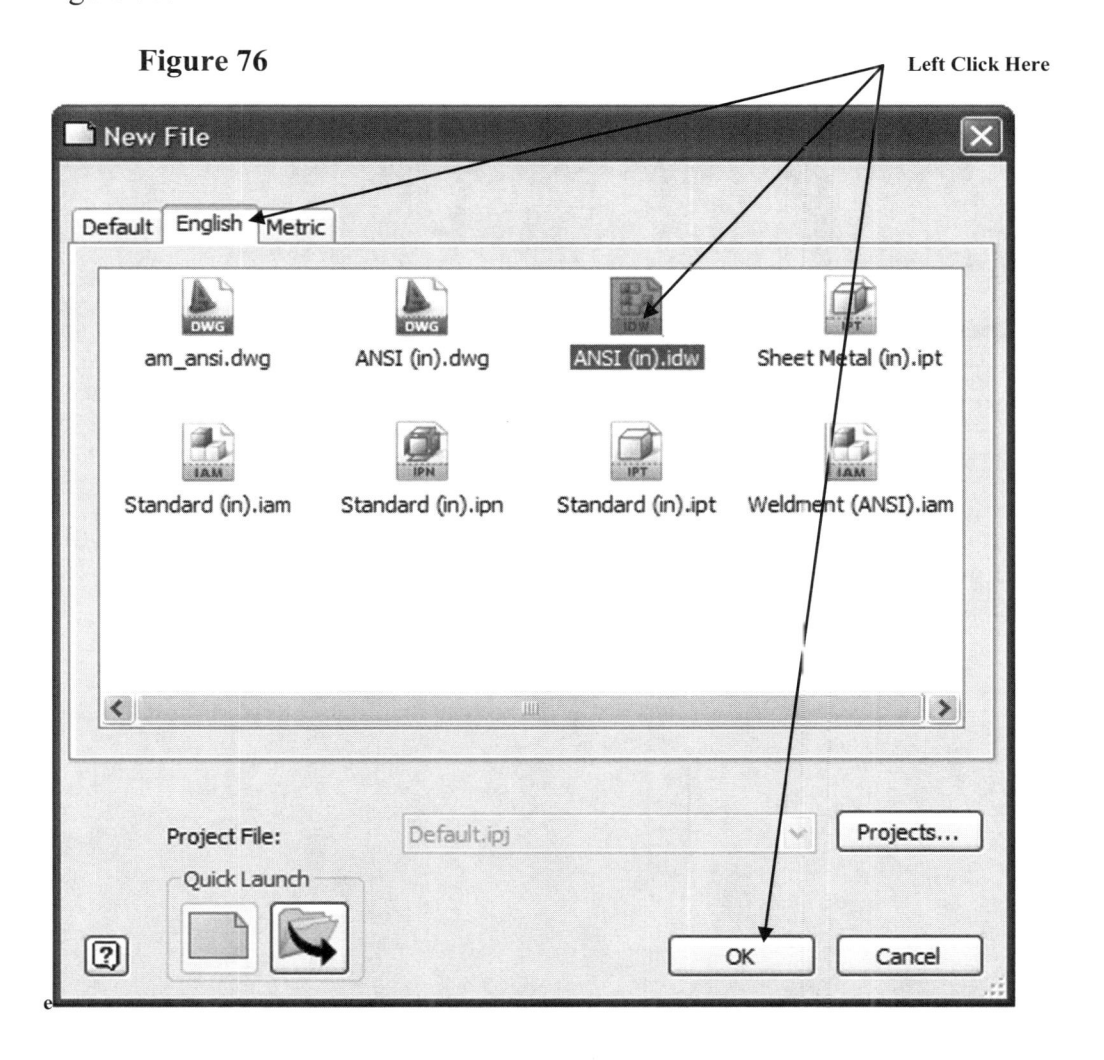

163

Chapter 3: Learning To Detail Part Drawings

97. Left click on **ANSI (in).idw**.

98. Left click on **OK**.

99. Your screen should look similar to Figure 77.

> **Figure 77**

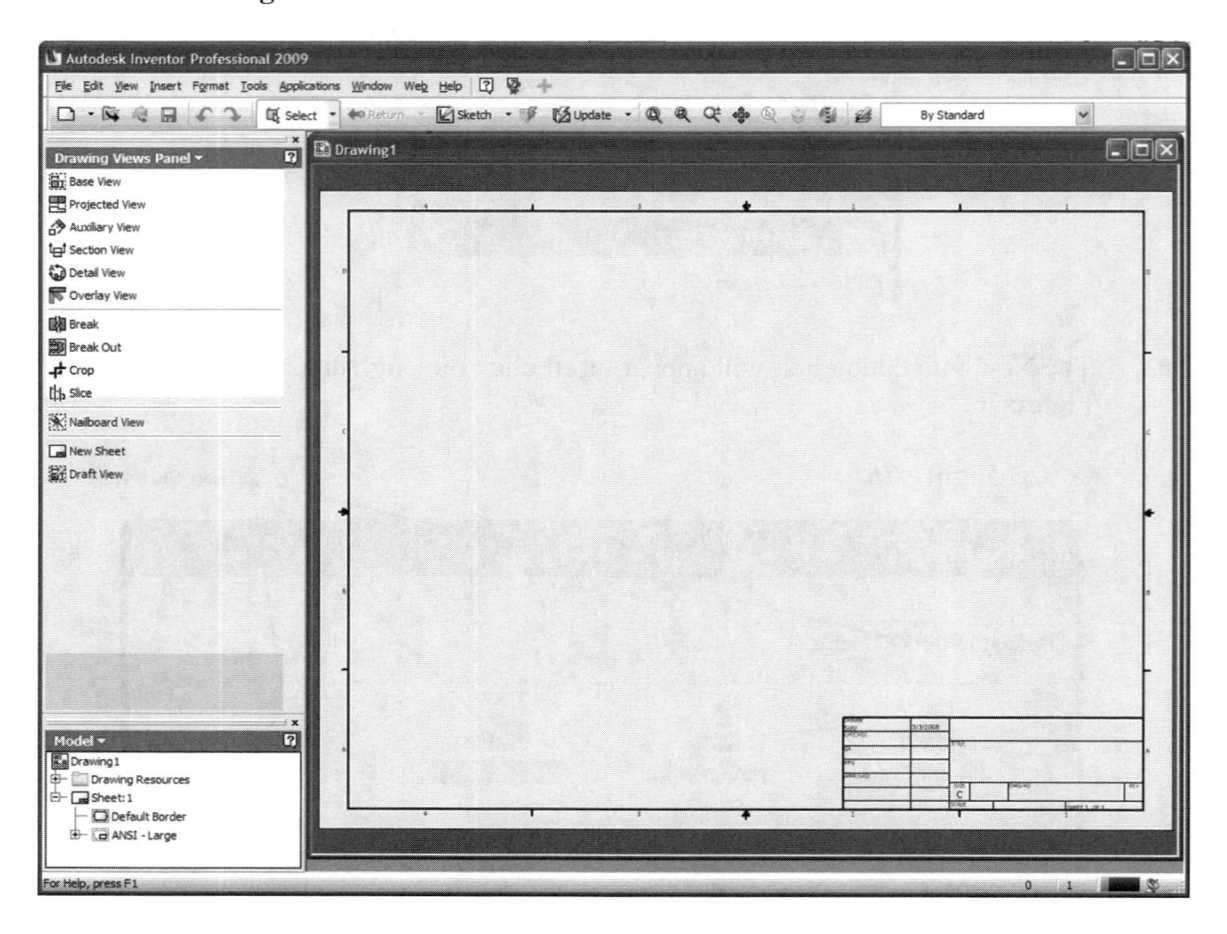

100. Inventor is now in the Drawing Views Panel. Notice the commands at the left are now different.

Chapter 3: Learning To Detail Part Drawings

101. Move the cursor to the upper left portion of the screen and left click on **Base View** as shown in Figure 78.

Figure 78

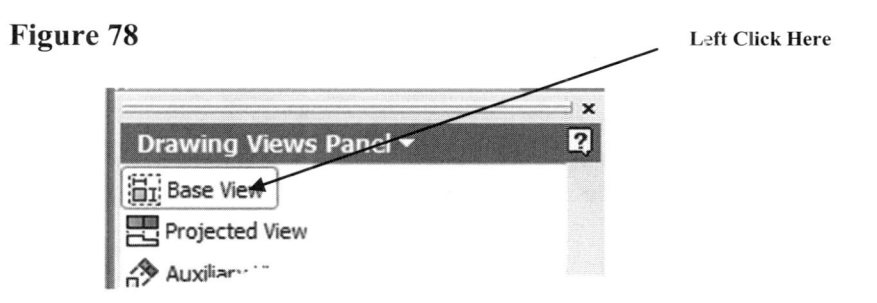

Left Click Here

102. The drawing of the wedge block should appear attached to the cursor. Move the cursor around to verify it is attached. If the part does not appear attached to the cursor, use the "Explore" icon to locate the part file as shown in Figure 79.

Figure 79

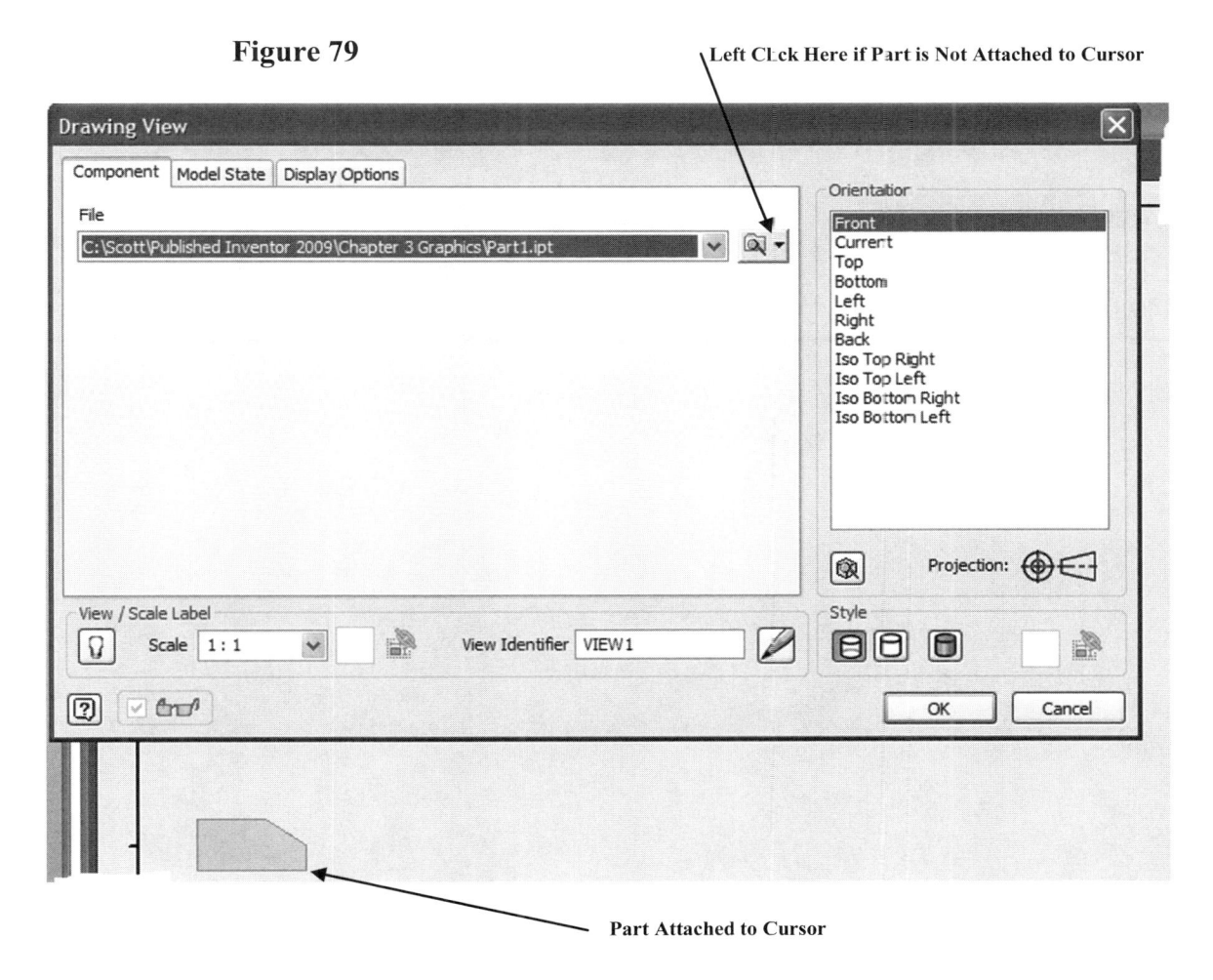

Left Click Here if Part is Not Attached to Cursor

Part Attached to Cursor

165

Chapter 3: Learning To Detail Part Drawings

103. Different views can be selected for the front, top, and side views. Select the desired view from the Orientation selection box as shown in Figure 80. To understand how the orientation selection works, left click on **Top** or **Left** to have the top view or left view as the front (base) view.

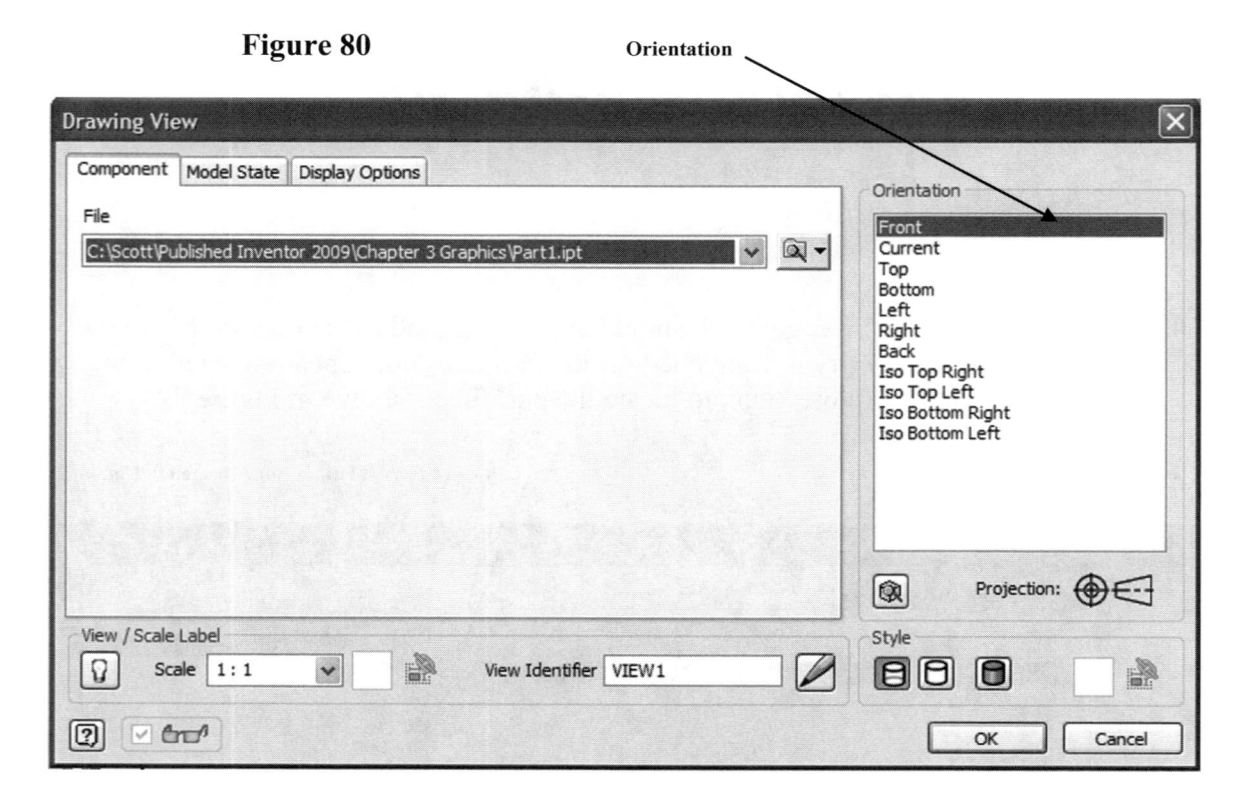

Figure 80

104. Select the **Front** view for the base view. Left click on the **Scale** drop down box and set the drawing scale to **4:1** as shown in Figure 81.

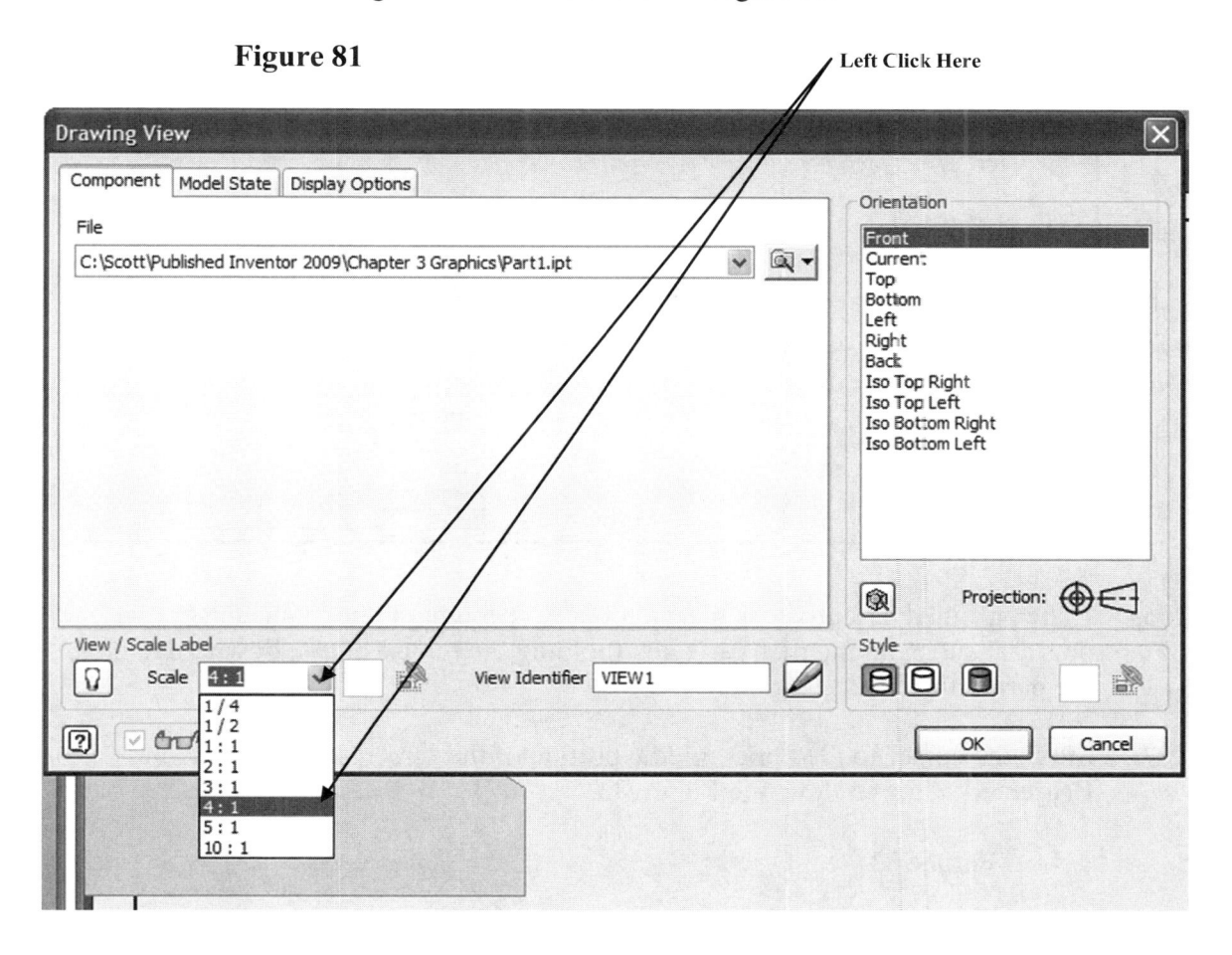

Figure 81

Chapter 3: Learning To Detail Part Drawings

105. Place the part just above the title block that is in the lower right corner of the screen and left click once. This will place the part as shown in Figure 82.

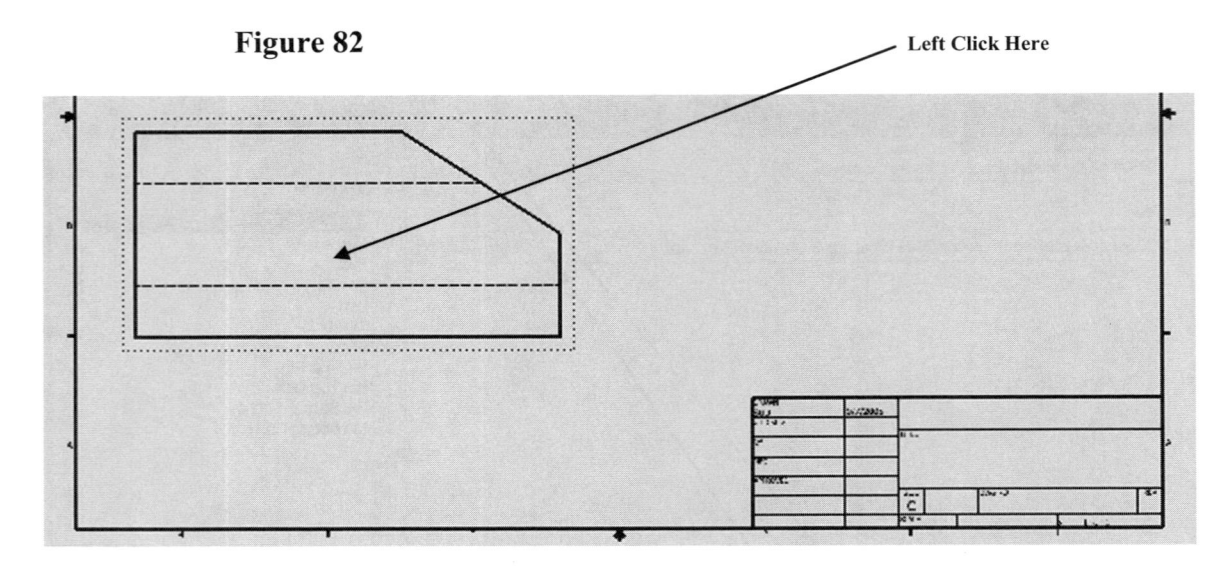

Figure 82 — Left Click Here

106. If the part inadvertently was placed too low or too high, move the cursor over the dots that surround the part, left click (holding the mouse button down), and drag the part to the desired location.

107. Move the cursor to the upper middle portion of the screen and left click on **Projected View** as shown in Figure 83.

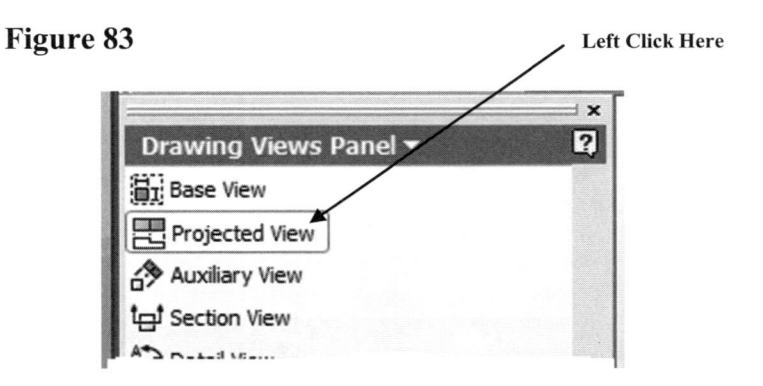

Figure 83 — Left Click Here

Chapter 3: Learning To Detail Part Drawings

108. The part will be attached to the cursor. Move the cursor upward and left click as shown in Figure 84.

Figure 84

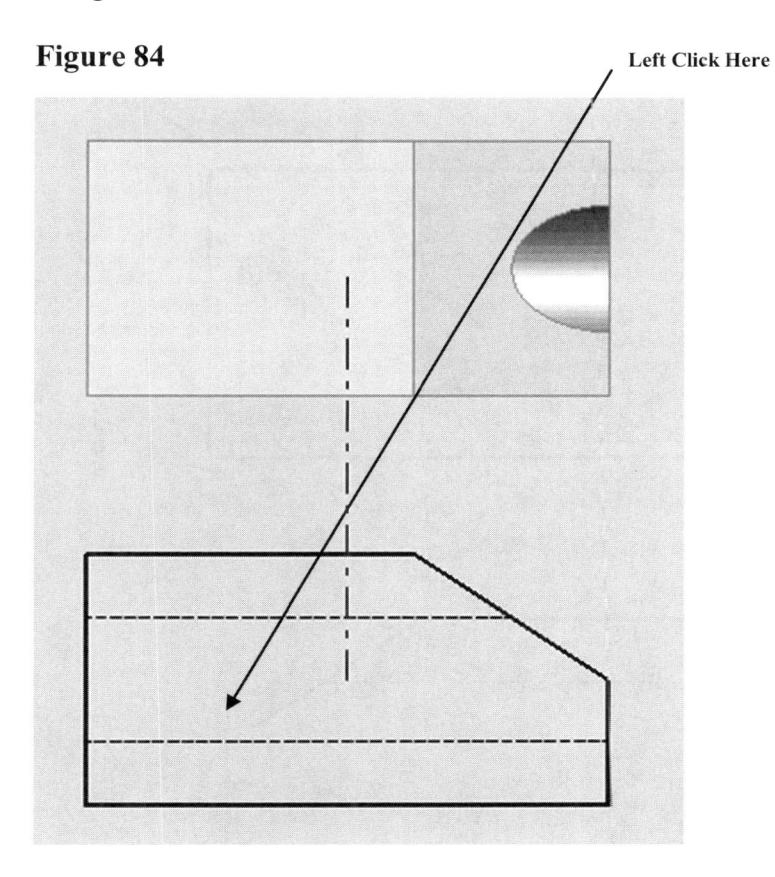

Left Click Here

169

Chapter 3: Learning To Detail Part Drawings

109. Place the part the desired distance from the front (base) view and left click once. Notice the black lines around the top view as shown in Figure 85. This indicates that the view has been placed.

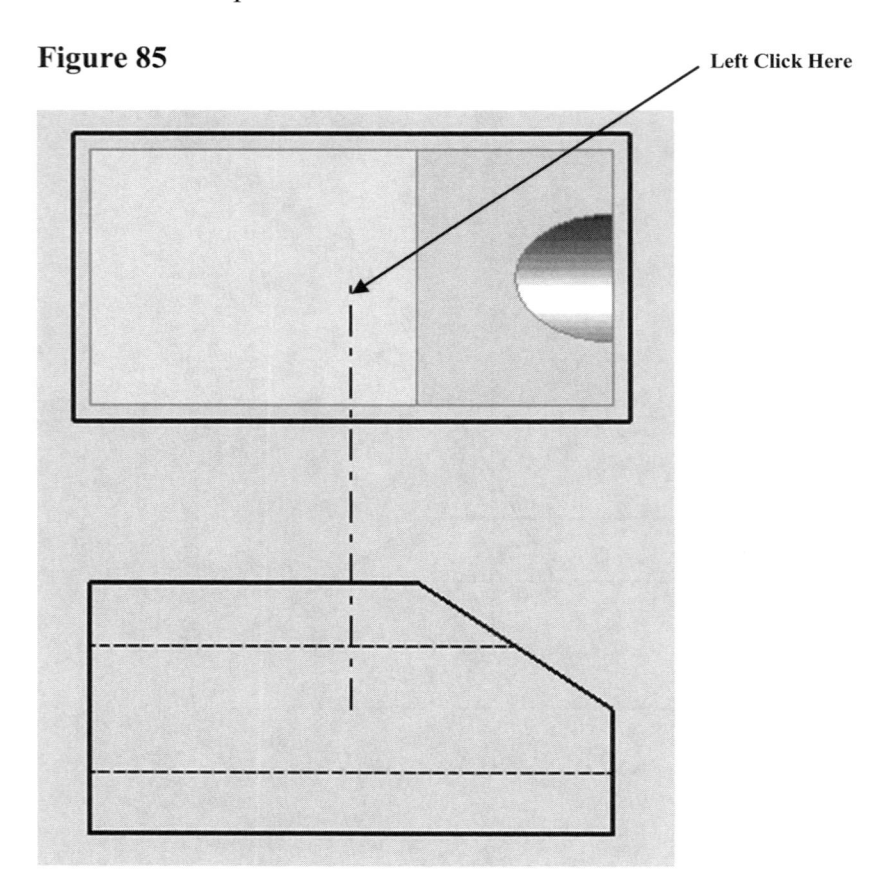

Figure 85

Left Click Here

Chapter 3: Learning To Detail Part Drawings

110. Move the cursor over to the upper right corner of the page and left click once as shown in Figure 86.

Figure 86

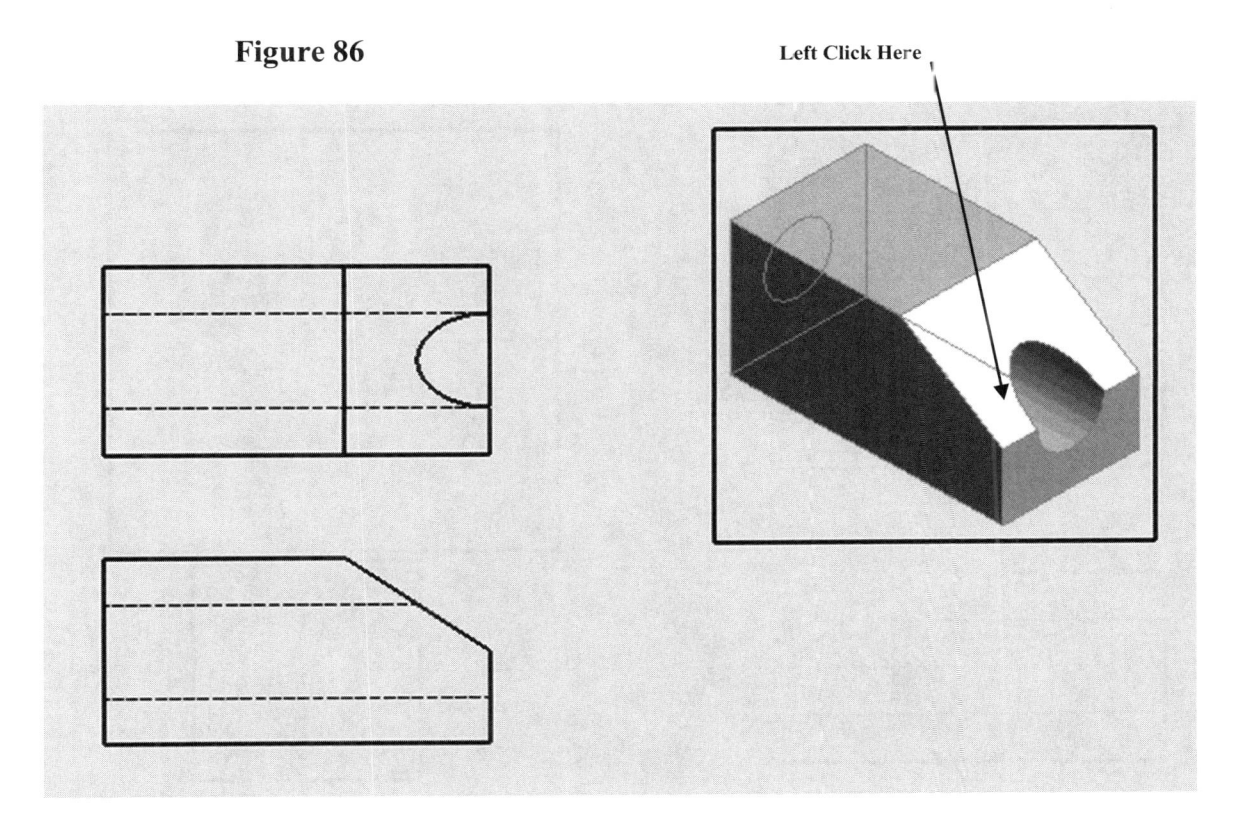

Left Click Here

Chapter 3: Learning To Detail Part Drawings

111. Move the cursor down to where the side view will be located and left click once as shown in Figure 87.

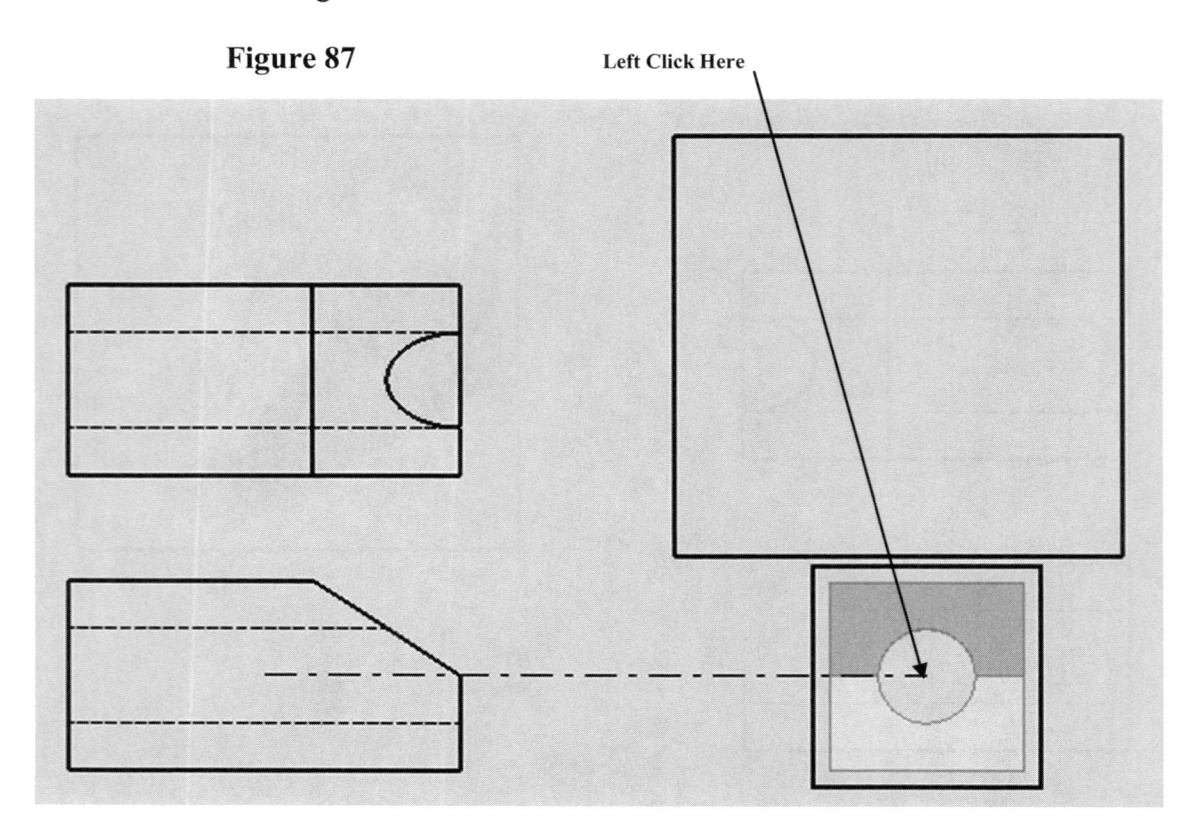

Figure 87   Left Click Here

112. Right click on the last view created (side view). A pop up menu will appear. Left click on **Create** as shown in Figure 88.

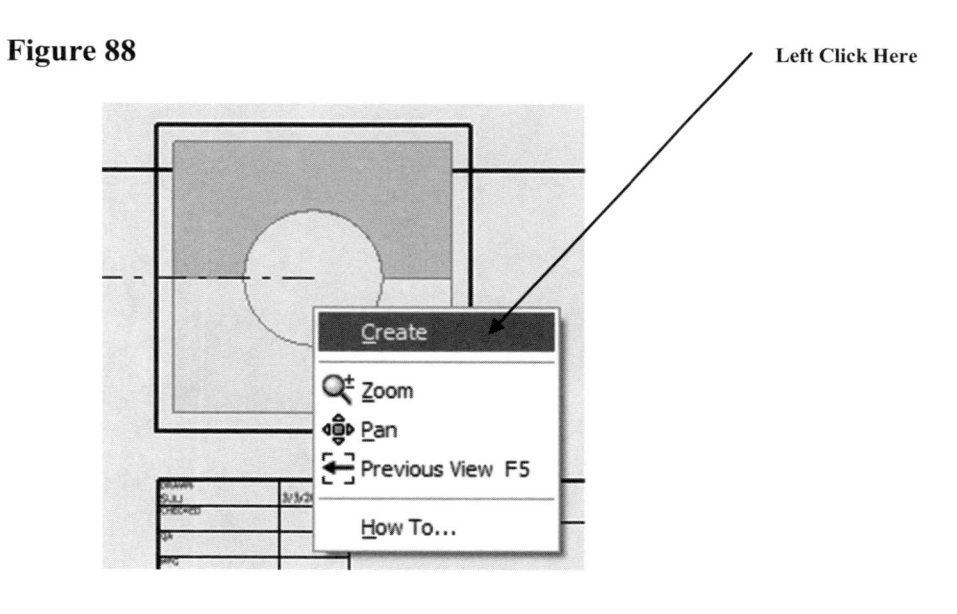

Figure 88   Left Click Here

172

113. Your screen should look similar to Figure 89.

Figure 89

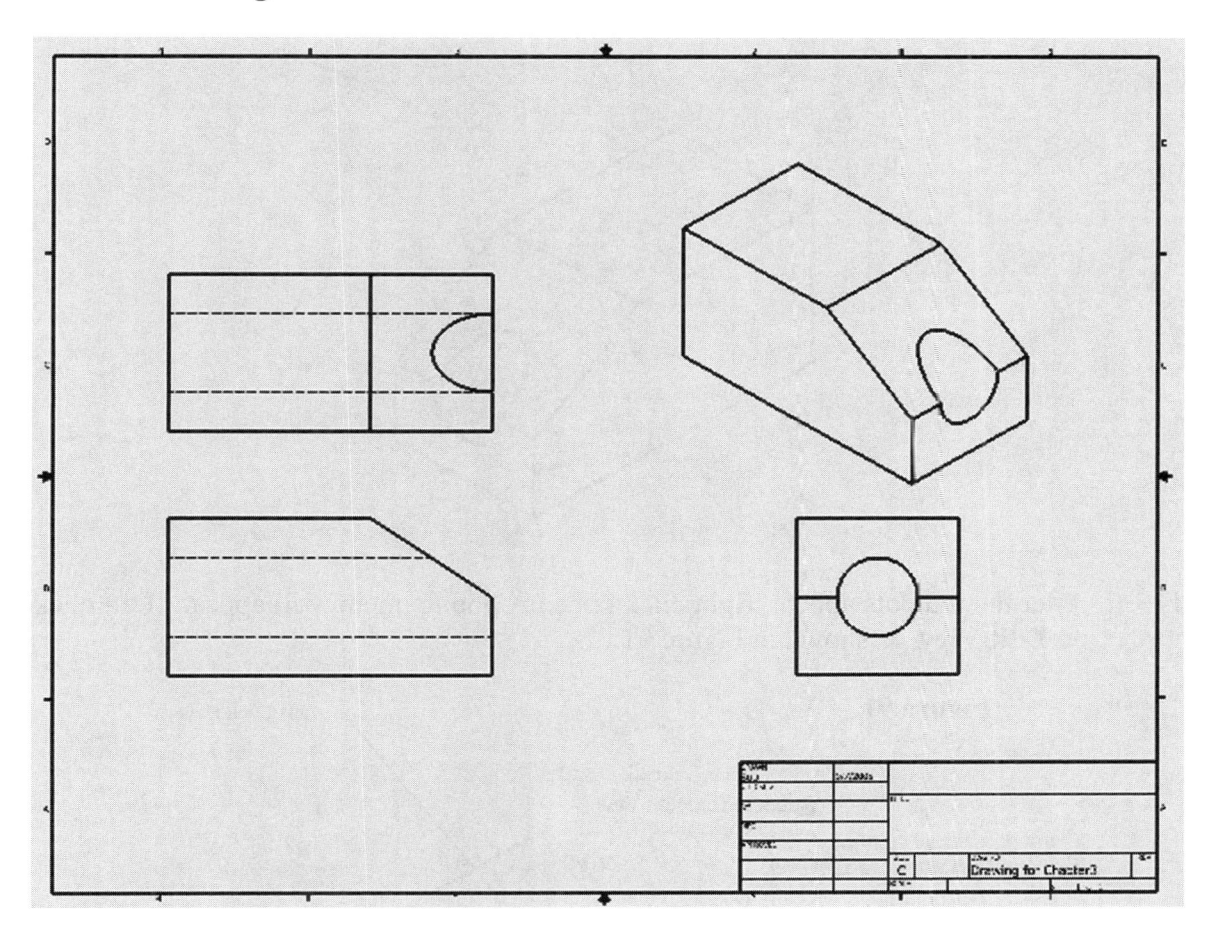

Chapter 3: Learning To Detail Part Drawings

114. Move the cursor over the isometric view in the upper right corner of the drawing. Red dots will appear as shown in Figure 90.

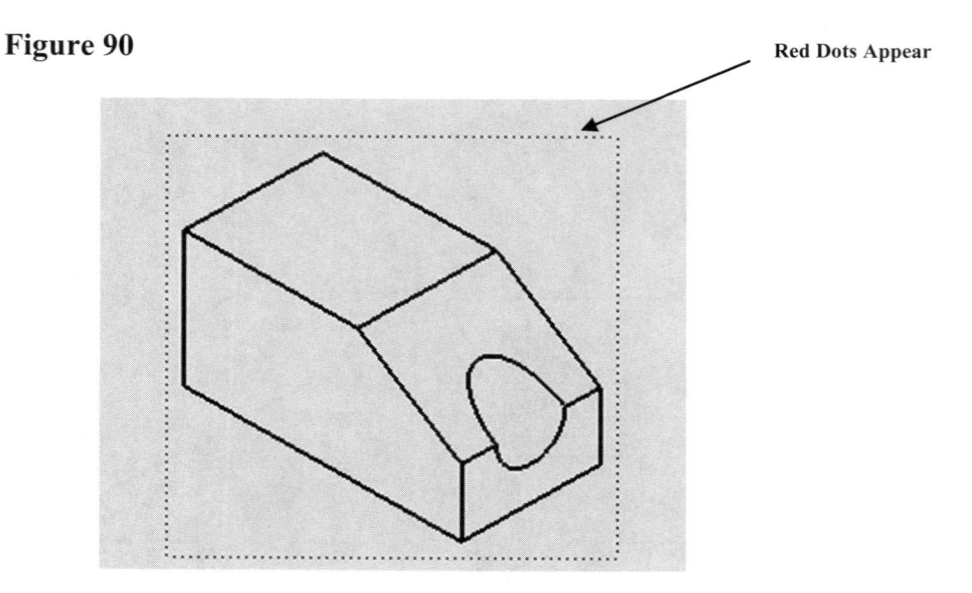

Figure 90

Red Dots Appear

115. After the red dots appear, right click once. A pop up menu will appear. Left click on **Edit View** as shown in Figure 91.

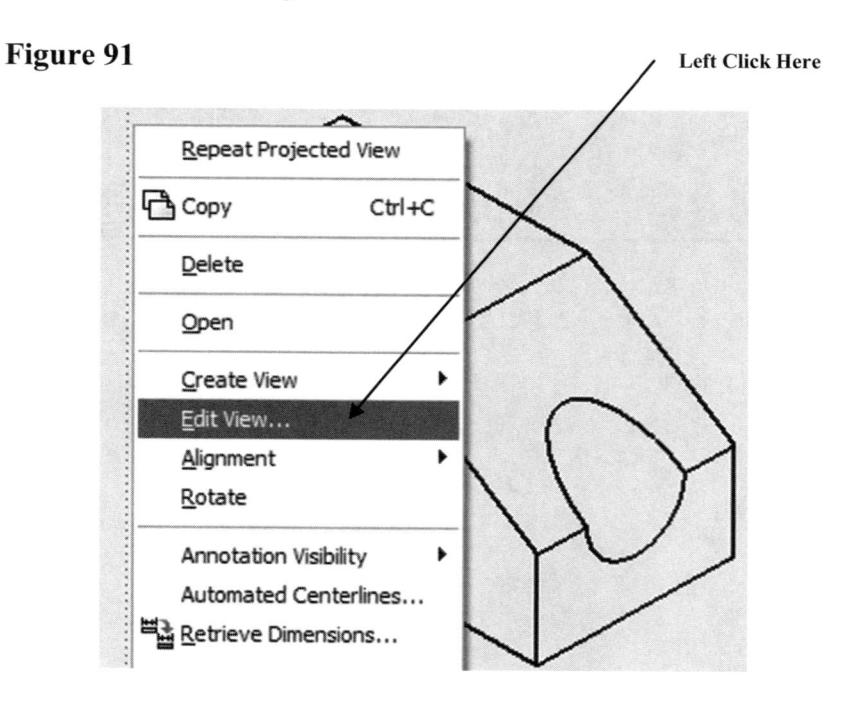

Figure 91

Left Click Here

174

Chapter 3: Learning To Detail Part Drawings

116. The Drawing View dialog box will appear. Left click on the "blue barrel" under Style as shown in Figure 92.

Figure 92

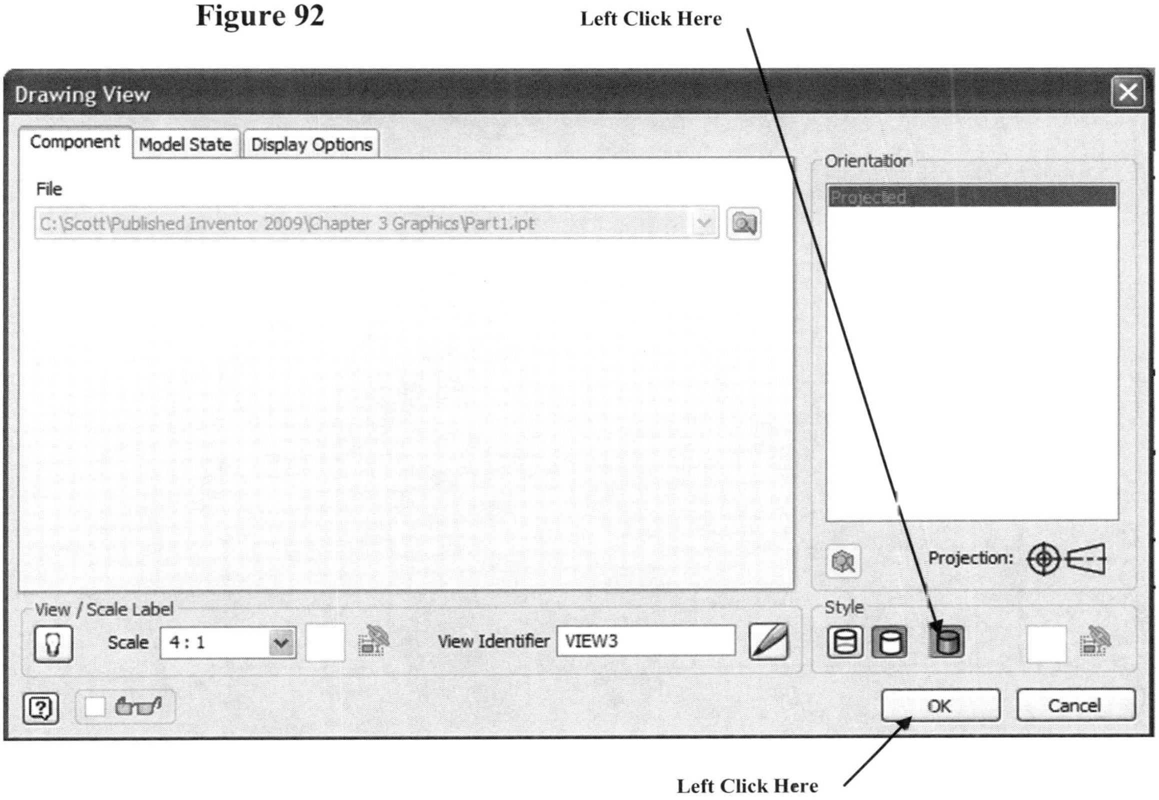

117. Left click on **OK**.

118. The isometric view will become a miniature solid model as shown in Figure 93.

Figure 93

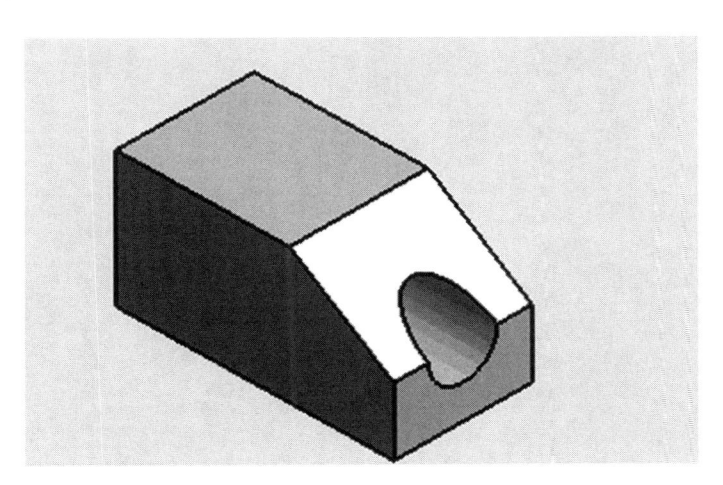

Chapter 3: Learning To Detail Part Drawings

119. Your screen should look similar to Figure 94.

Figure 94

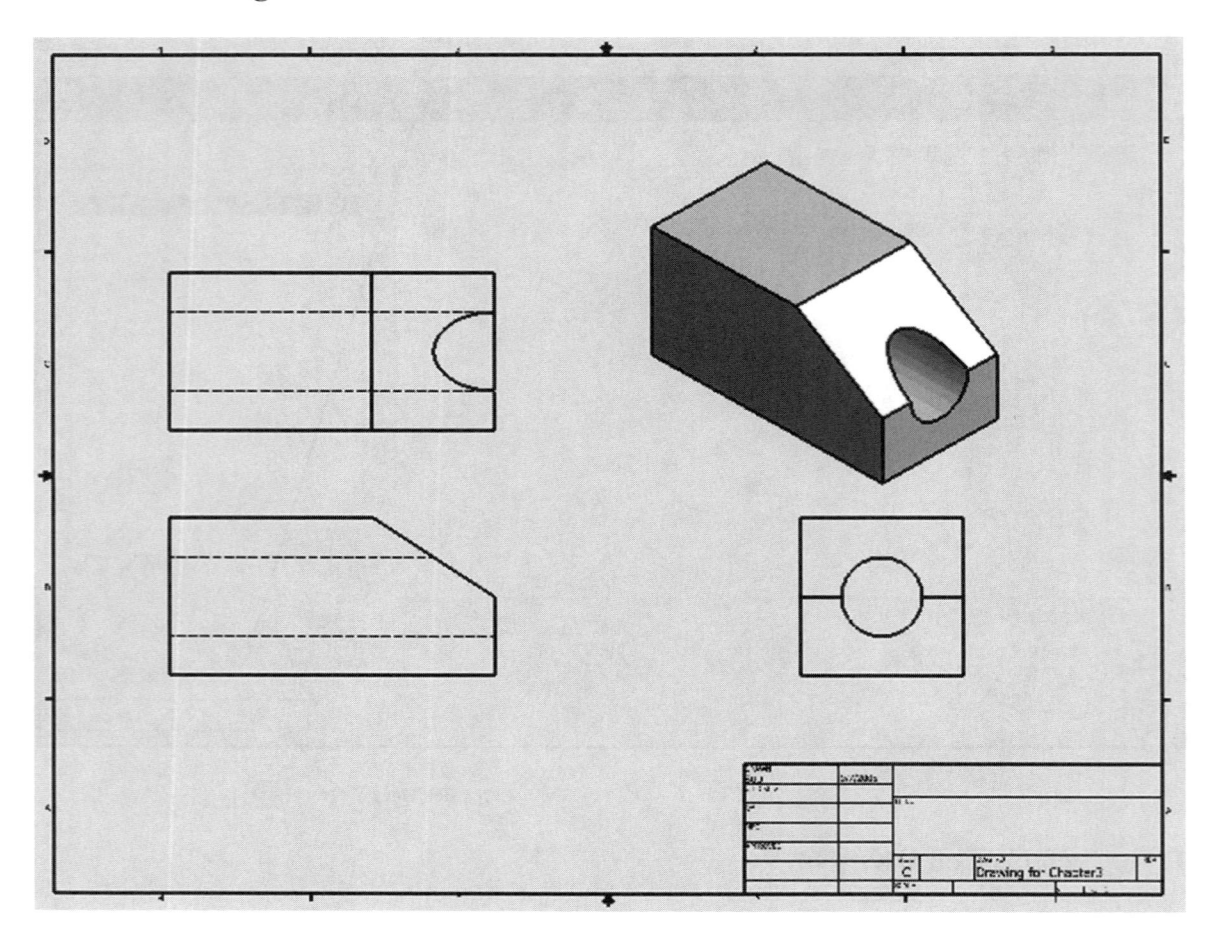

120. Save the part file for easy retrieval. This part will be used in the following chapter.

Drawing Activities

Use these problems from Chapters 1 and 2 to create 3 view orthographic view detail drawings.

Problem 1

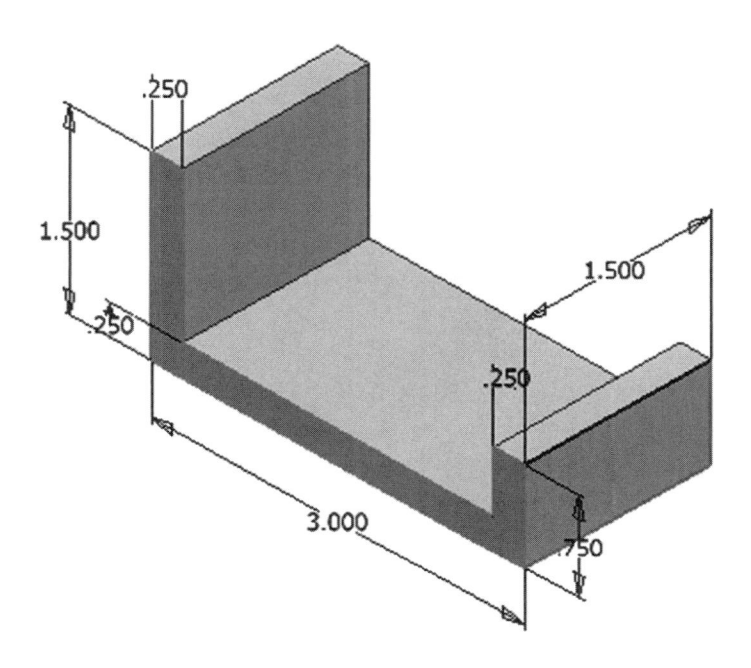

Problem 2

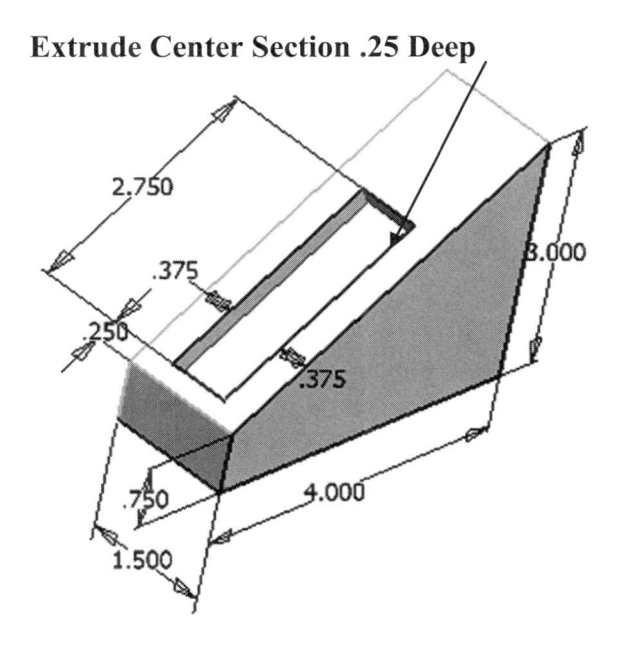

Extrude Center Section .25 Deep

Chapter 3: Learning To Detail Part Drawings

Problem 3

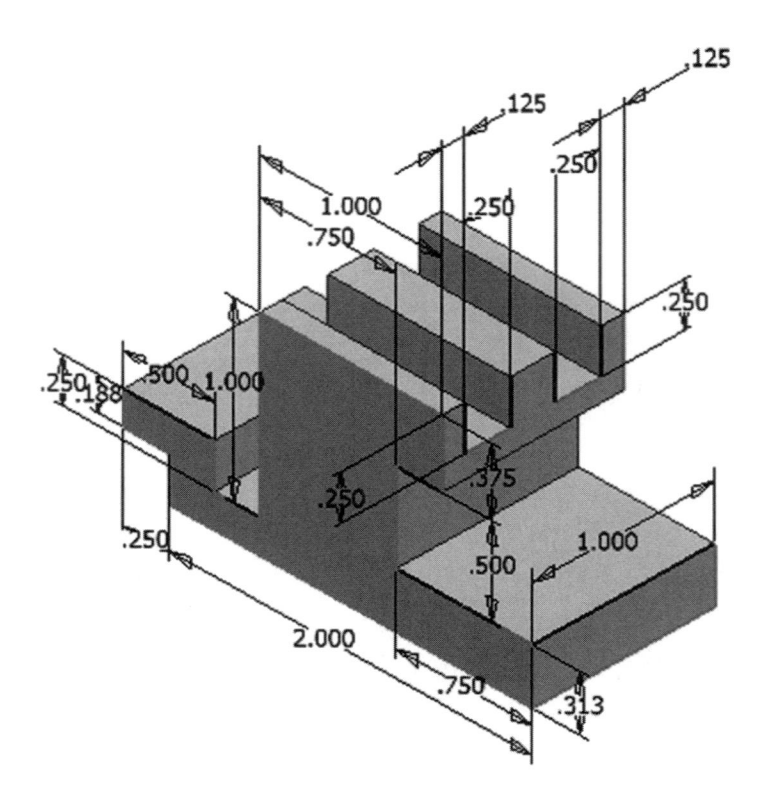

Problem 4

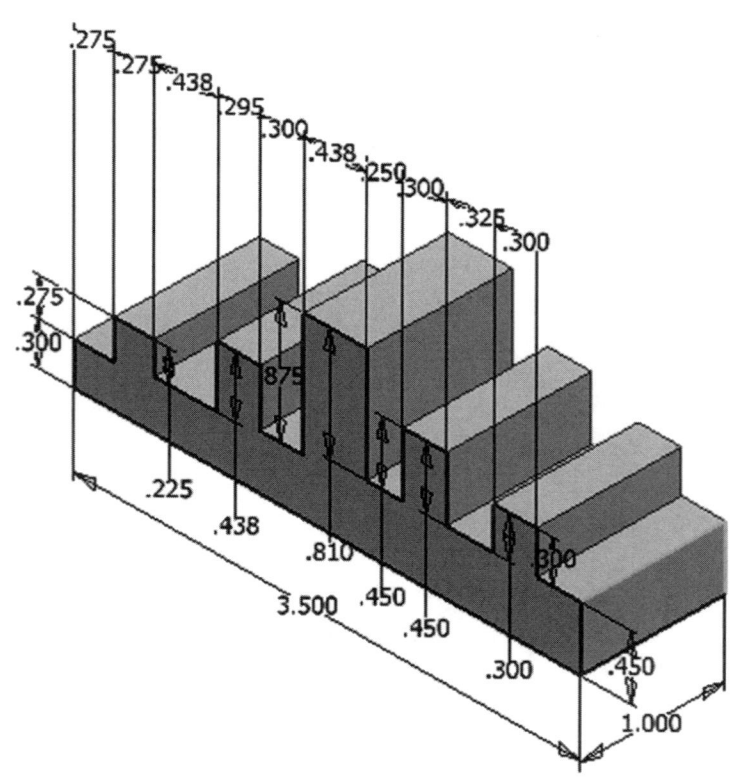

Problem 5

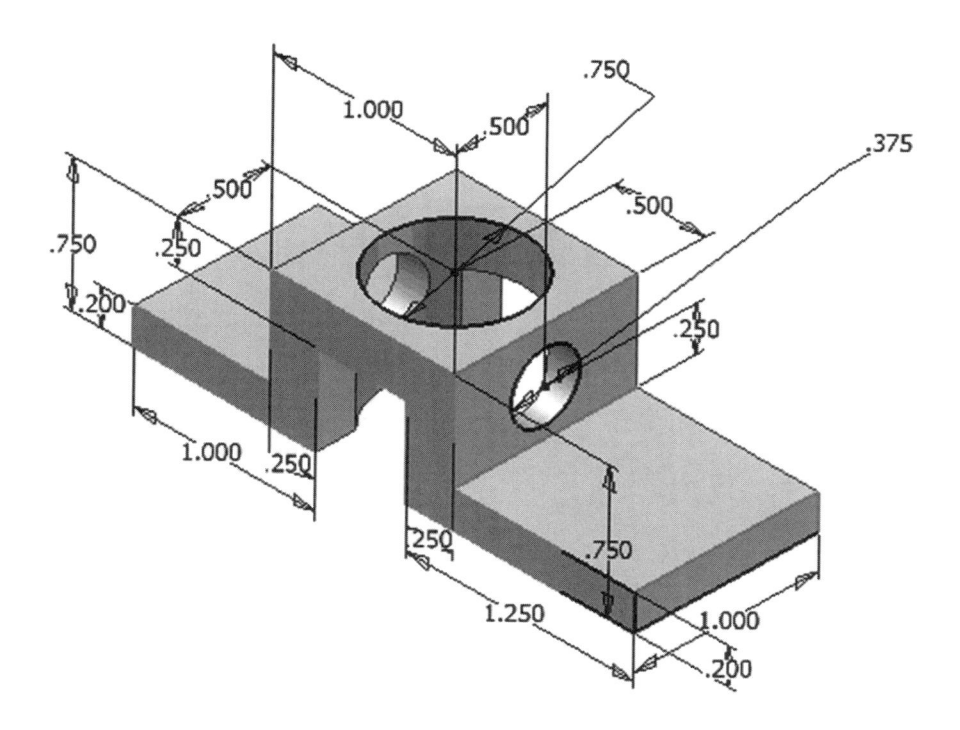

Problem 6

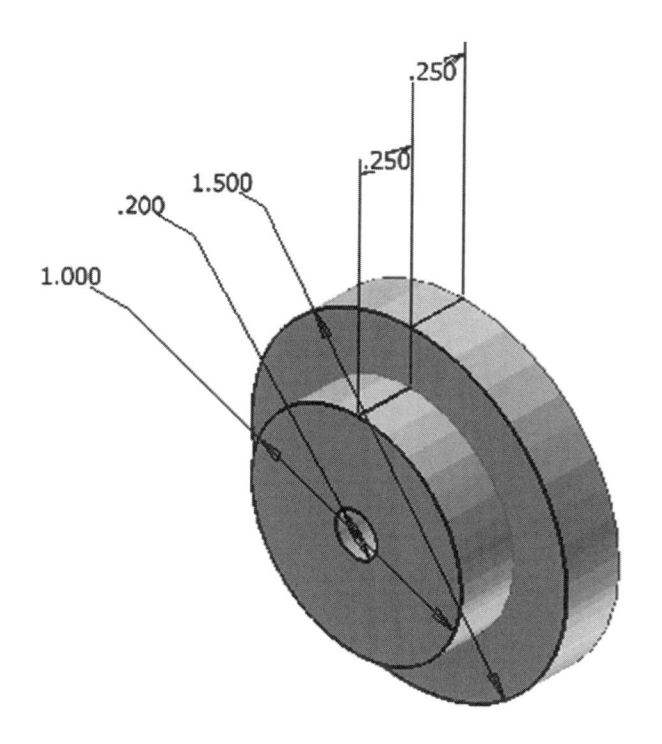

Chapter 3: Learning To Detail Part Drawings

Problem 7

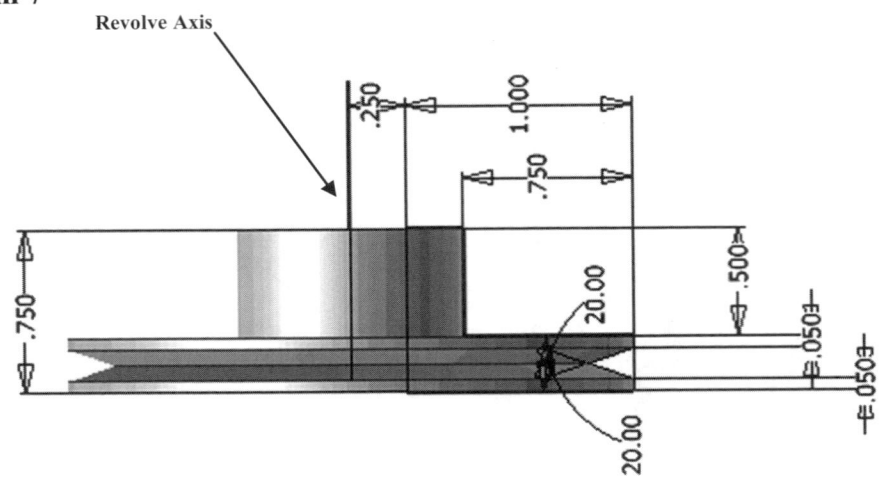

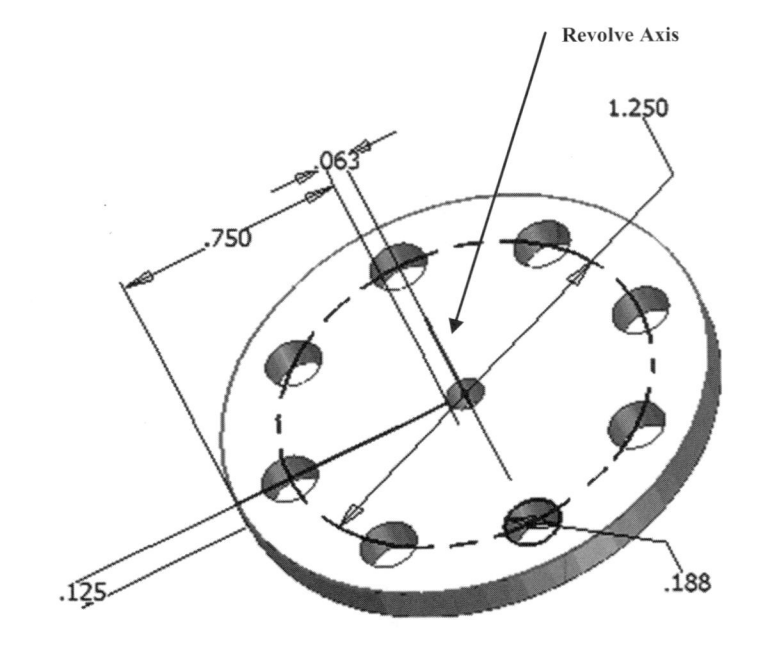

Problem 8

Chapter 4 Advanced Detail Drawing Procedures

Objectives:
- Create an Auxiliary View using the Drawing Views Panel
- Create a Section View using the Drawing Views Panel
- Dimension views using the Drawing Annotation Panel
- Create Text using the Drawing Annotation Panel

Chapter 4 includes instruction on how to create the drawings shown below.

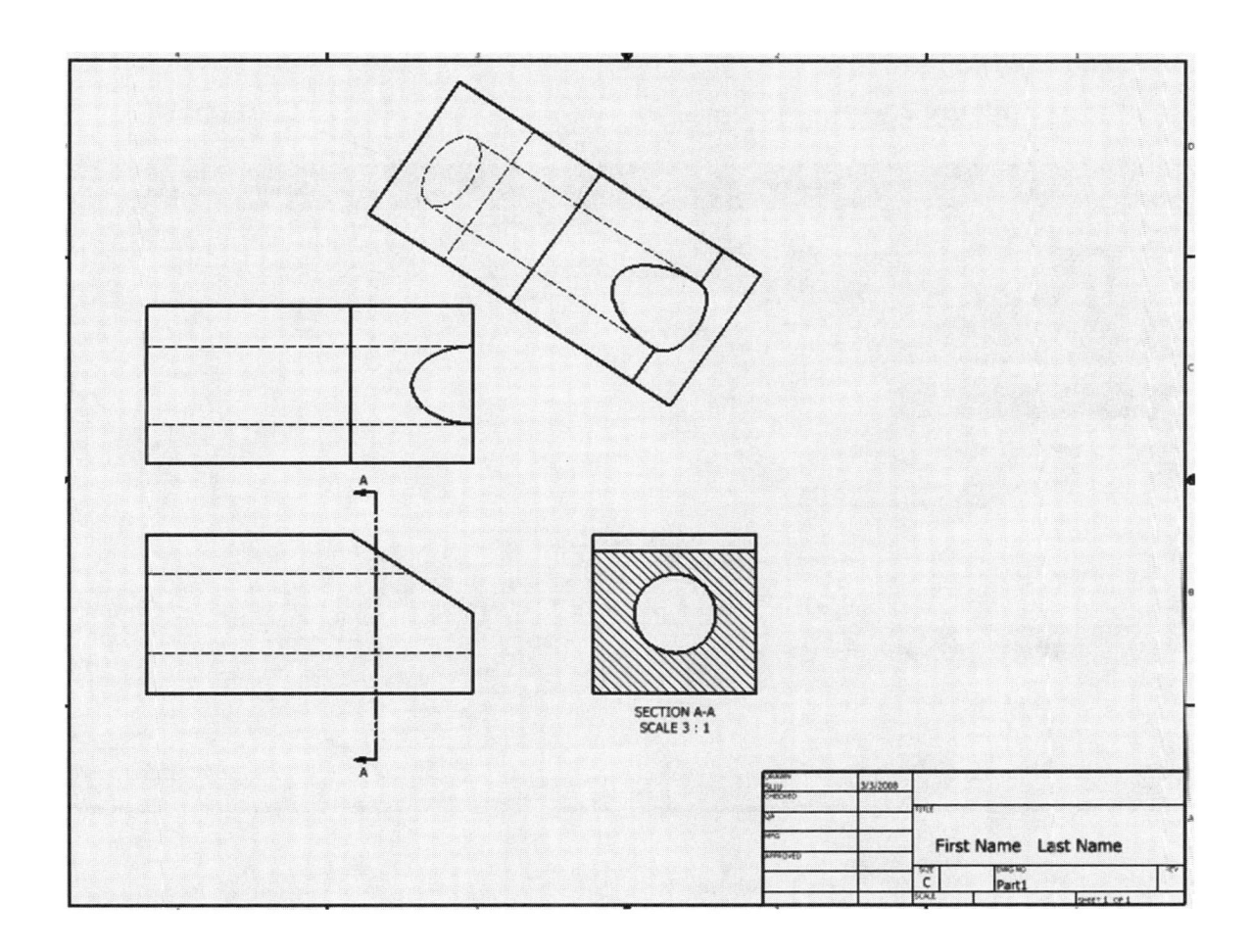

Chapter 4: Advanced Detail Drawing Procedures

1. Start Autodesk Inventor 2009 by referring to "Chapter 1 Getting Started".

2. After Autodesk Inventor 2009 is running, open the .idw file that was created in Chapter 3. Move the cursor to the upper left corner of the screen and left click on the "Open" icon as shown in Figure 1.

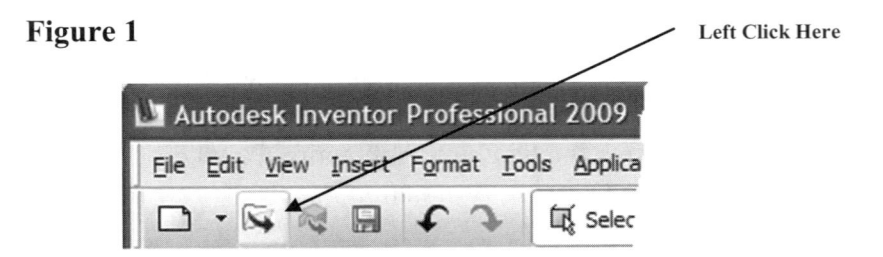

Figure 1   Left Click Here

3. The Open dialog box will appear. Left click on the drawing that was created in Chapter 3. Left click on **Open**. If a Preview of the part is not displayed, left click **Part1.idw** again as shown in Figure 2.

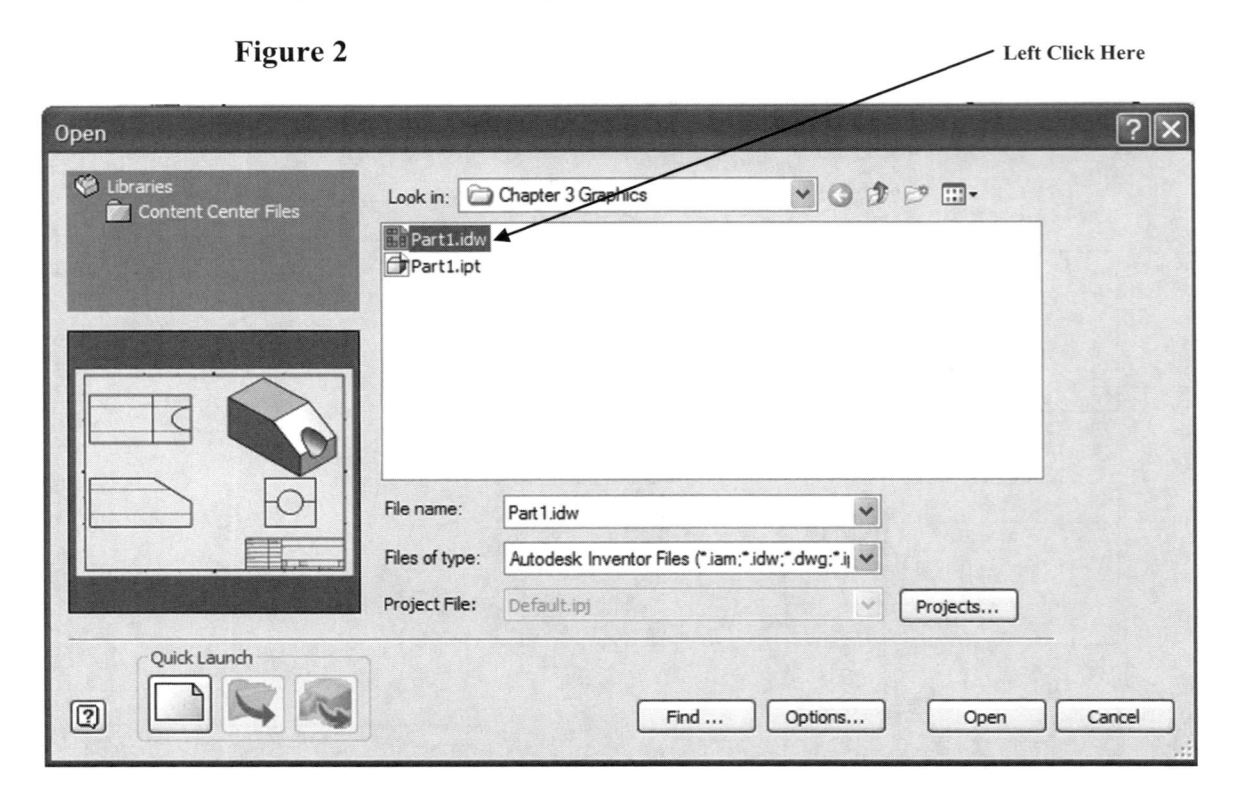

Figure 2   Left Click Here

182

Chapter 4: Advanced Detail Drawing Procedures

4. Left click on **Open** as shown in Figure 3.

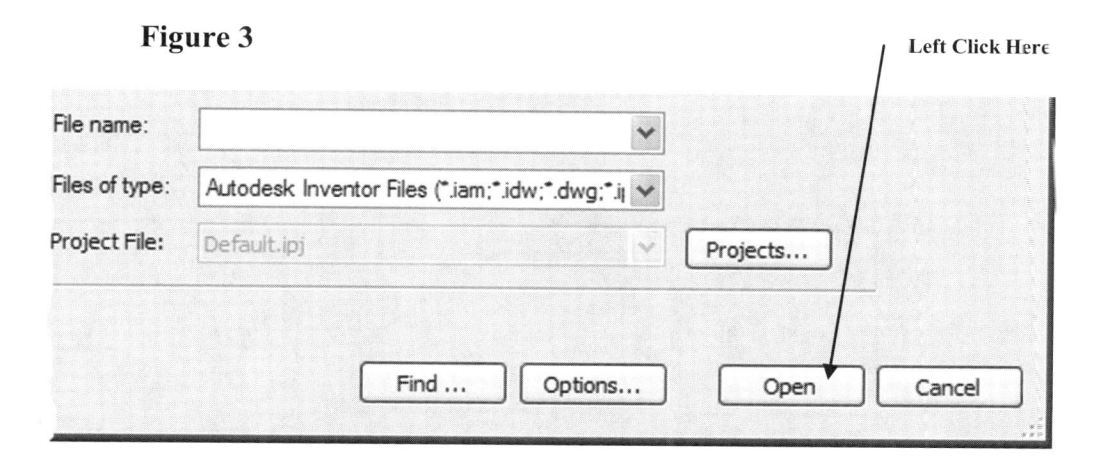

Figure 3

5. After you have the .idw file open, move the views closer together to provide additional room on the drawing. Start by moving the cursor over the top view causing dots to appear around the view. After the dots appear, left click on the dots (holding the left mouse button down) and drag the view down closer to the front (base) view as shown in Figure 4.

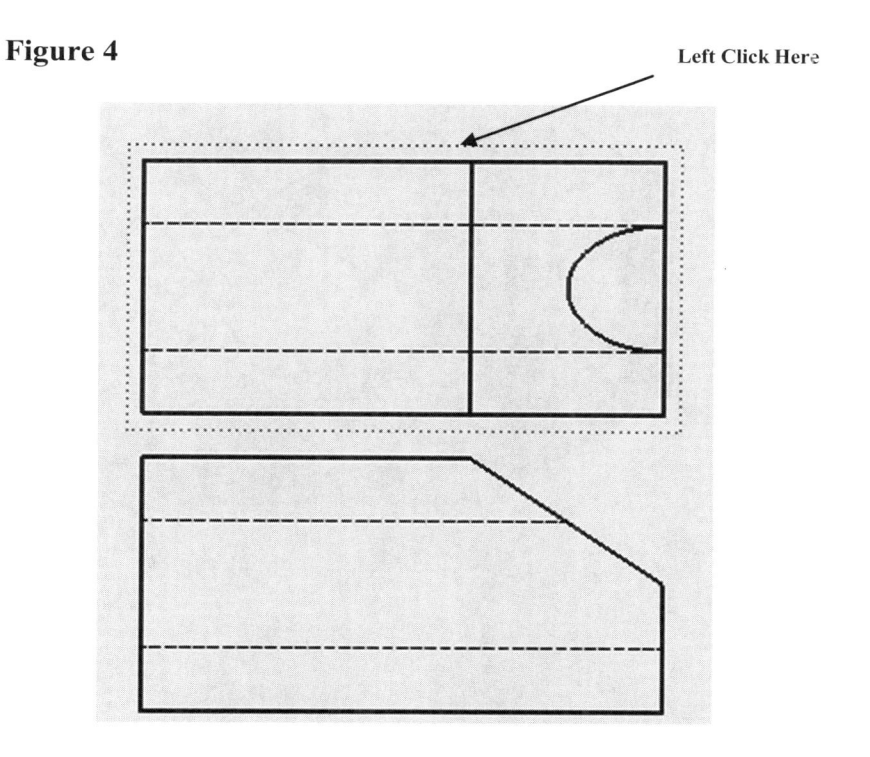

Figure 4

Chapter 4: Advanced Detail Drawing Procedures

6. Move the side view closer to the front (base) view. Start by moving the cursor over the side view causing dots to appear around the view. After the dots appear, left click on the dots (hold the left mouse button down) and drag the view closer to the front (base) view as shown in Figure 5.

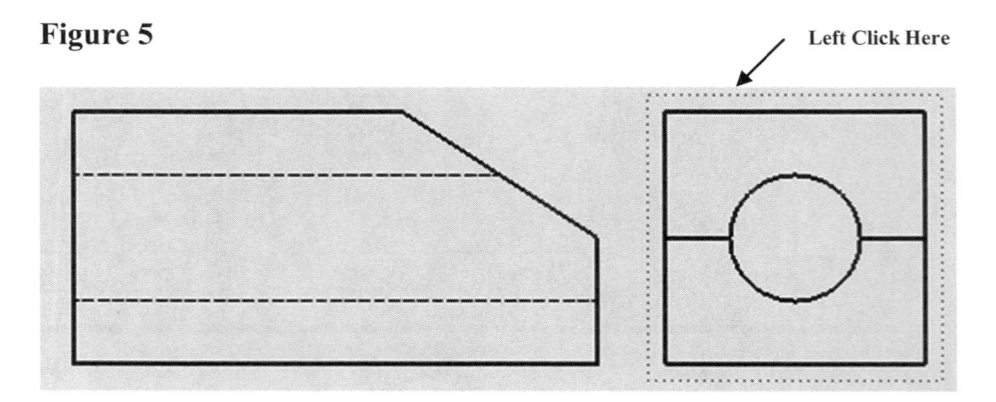

Figure 5

7. You will need to delete the isometric view that was created in Chapter 3. Move the cursor near the isometric view causing red dots to appear. Right click. A pop up menu will appear. Left click on **Delete** as shown in Figure 6.

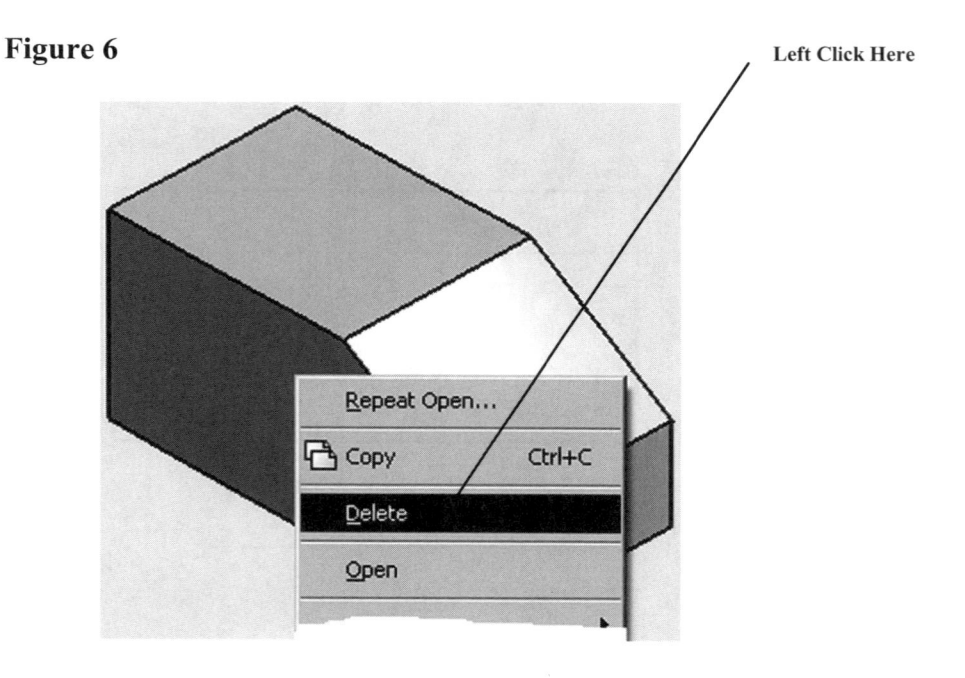

Figure 6

Chapter 4: Advanced Detail Drawing Procedures

8. The Delete dialog box will appear. Left click on **OK** as shown in Figure 7.

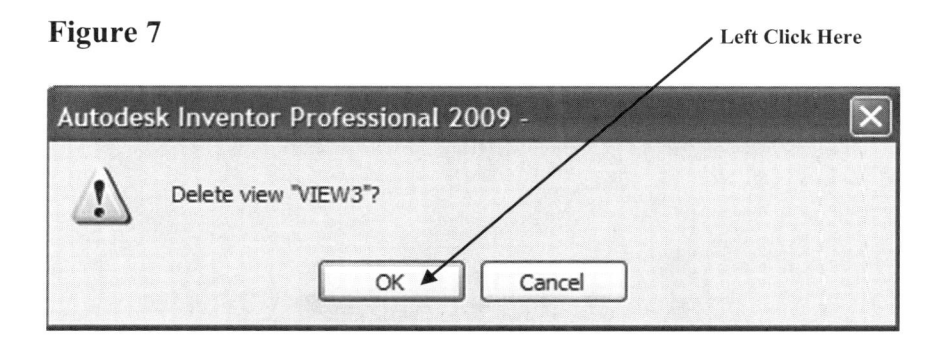

Figure 7

Left Click Here

9. There will now be more room to work. Your screen should look similar to Figure 8.

Figure 8

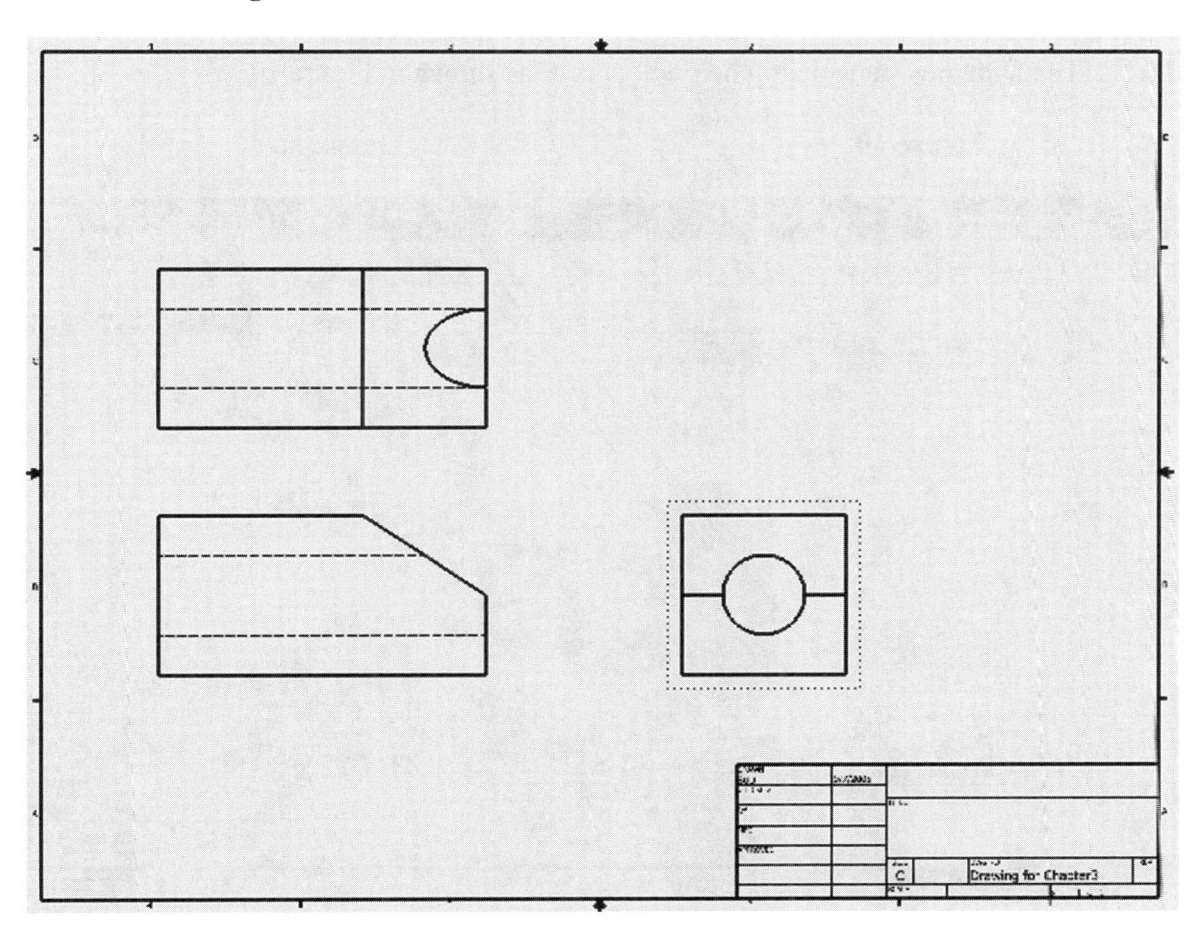

185

Chapter 4: Advanced Detail Drawing Procedures

10. To provide more space on the drawing, the drawing view scale will have to be reduced. Right click on the front (base) view. A pop up menu will appear. Left click on **Edit View** as shown in Figure 9.

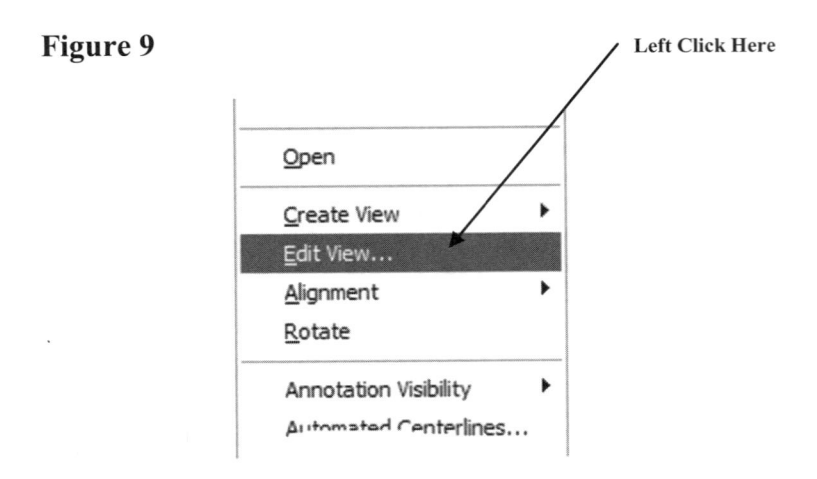

Figure 9

Left Click Here

11. The Drawing View dialog box will appear as shown in Figure 10.

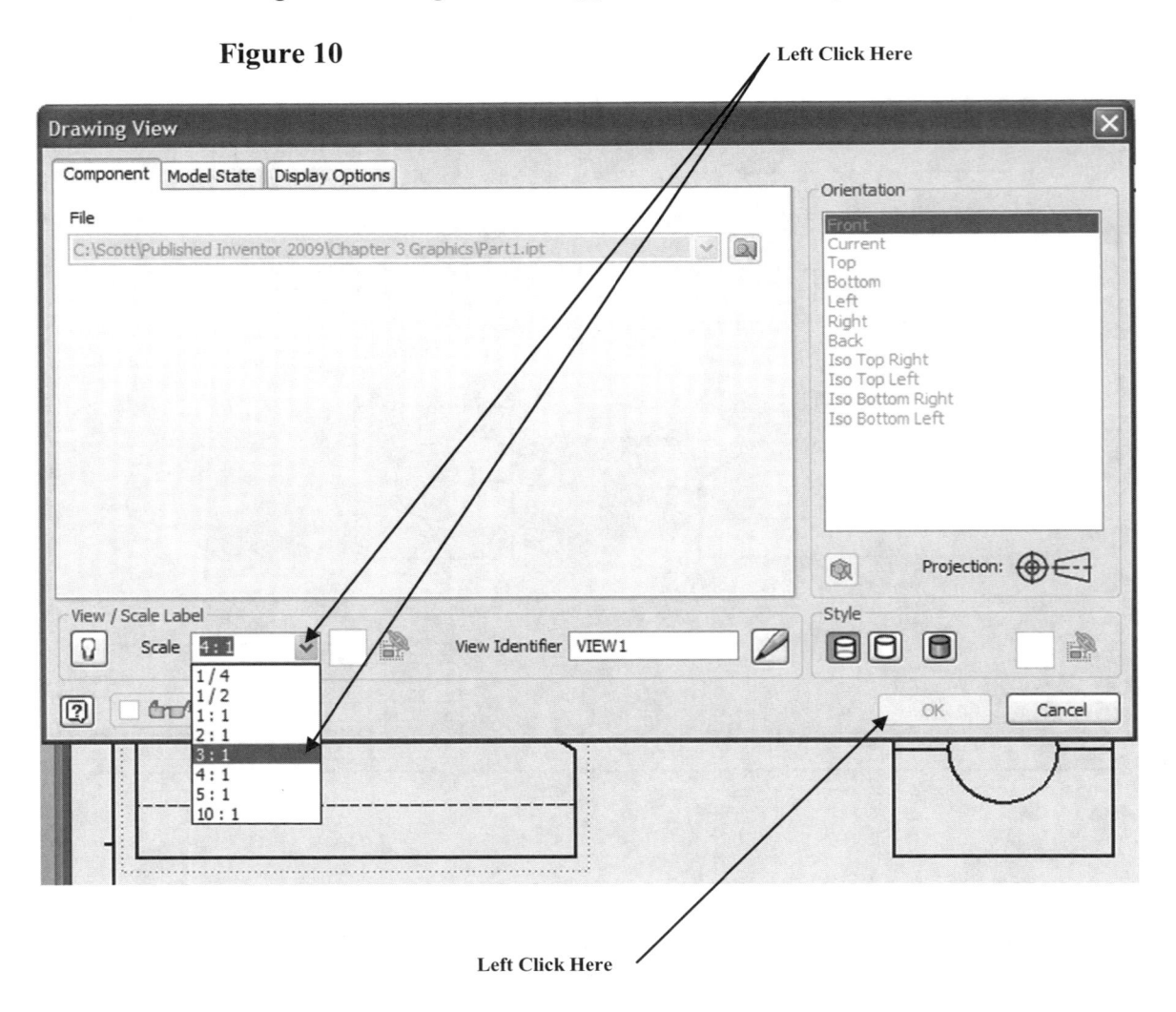

Figure 10

Left Click Here

Left Click Here

186

Chapter 4: Advanced Detail Drawing Procedures

12. Change the Scale to **3:1** and left click on **OK**. Your screen should look similar to Figure 11.

Figure 11

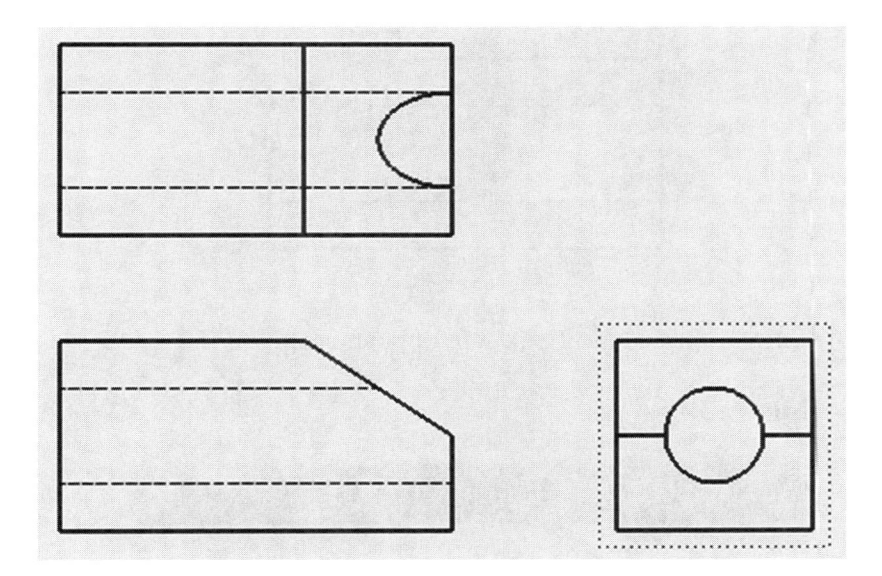

13. Move the cursor to the upper middle portion of the screen and left click on **Auxiliary View** as shown in Figure 12.

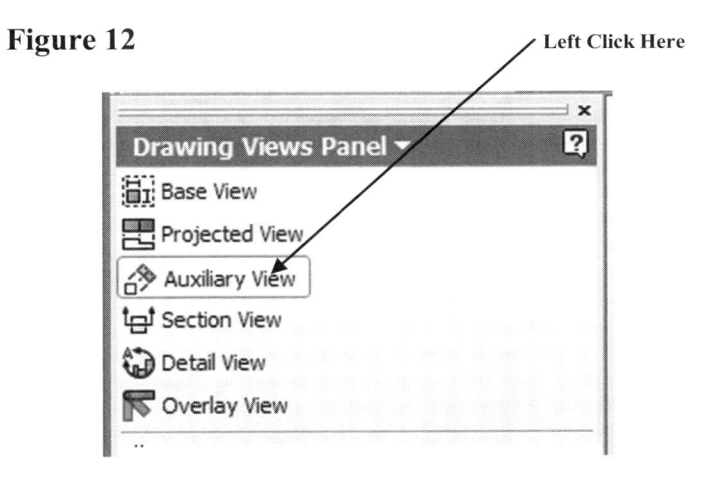

Figure 12

Chapter 4: Advanced Detail Drawing Procedures

14. Move the cursor to the front (base) view causing red dots to appear around the view. Left click once as shown in Figure 13.

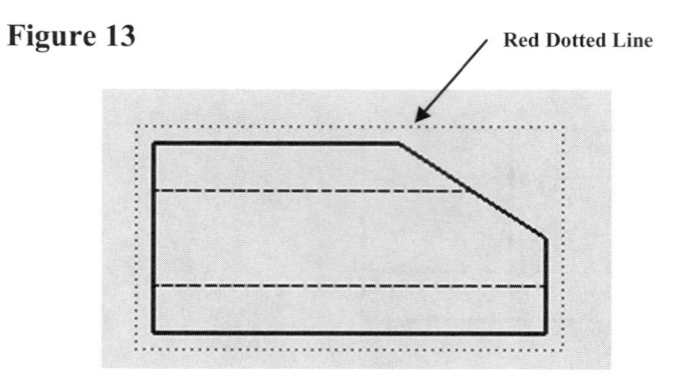

   Figure 13

15. The Auxiliary View dialog box will appear as shown in Figure 14.

   Figure 14

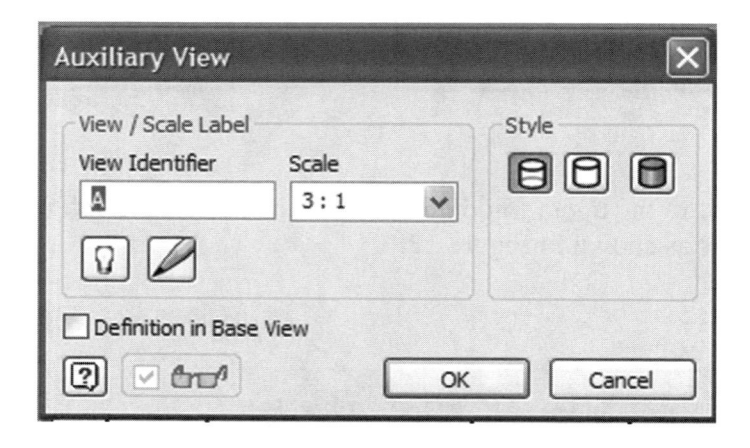

16. Move the cursor over the wedge line causing it to turn red. Left click as shown in Figure 15.

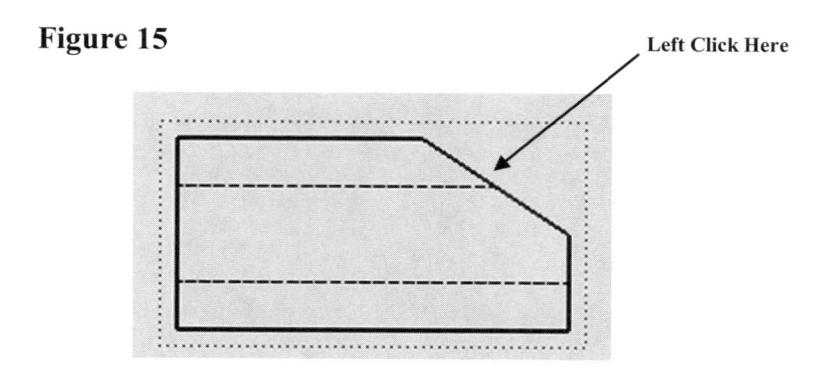

   Figure 15

188

Chapter 4: Advanced Detail Drawing Procedures

17. Inventor will create an auxiliary view from the selected surface. The view will be attached to the cursor as shown in Figure 16.

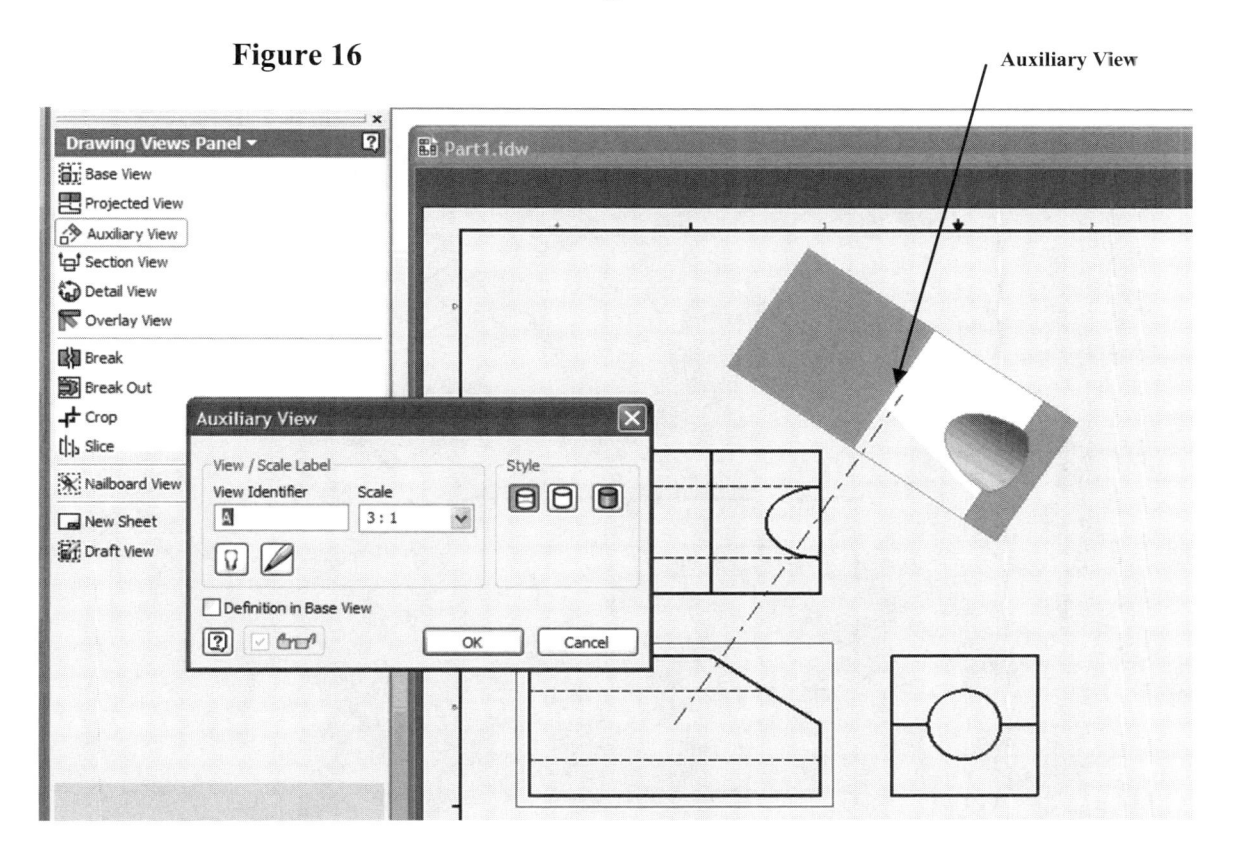

Figure 16

Chapter 4: Advanced Detail Drawing Procedures

18. Move the cursor towards the upper right and left click. The Auxiliary View dialog box will close as shown in Figure 17.

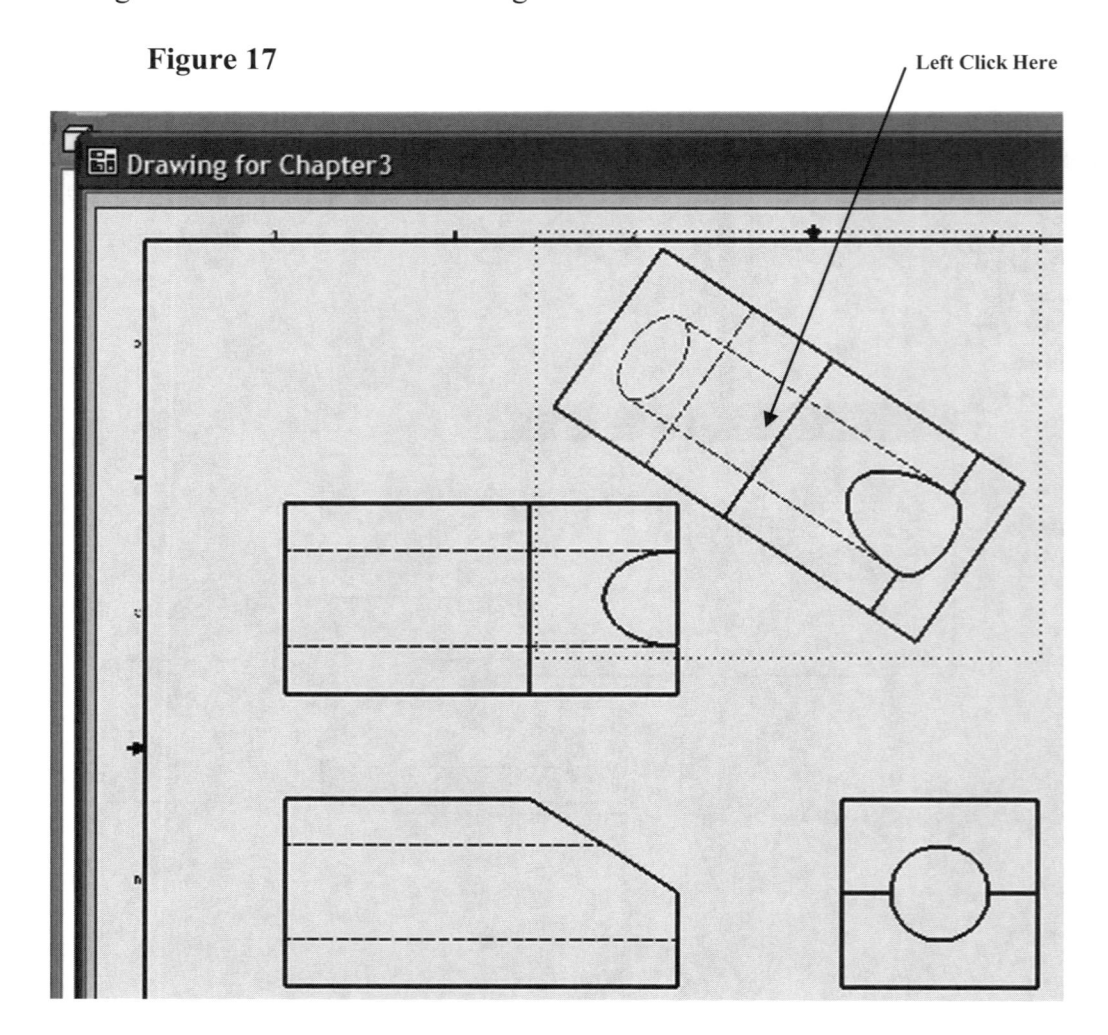

Figure 17

Chapter 4: Advanced Detail Drawing Procedures

19. Your screen should look similar to Figure 18.

   Figure 18

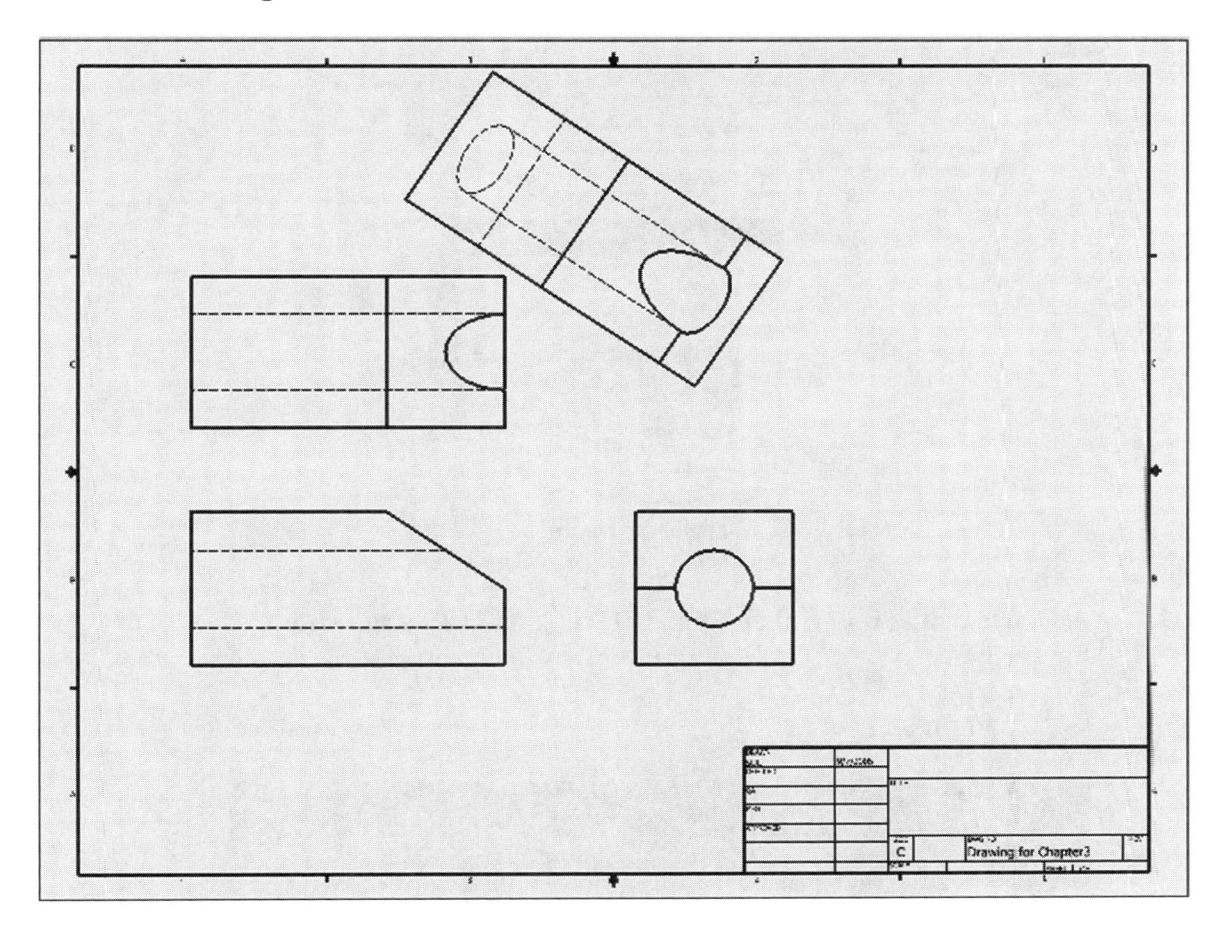

20. Move the cursor to the side view causing red dots to appear as shown in Figure 19.

   Figure 19   Red Dots

191

Chapter 4: Advanced Detail Drawing Procedures

21. Right click on the view. A pop up menu will appear. Left click on **Delete** as shown in Figure 20.

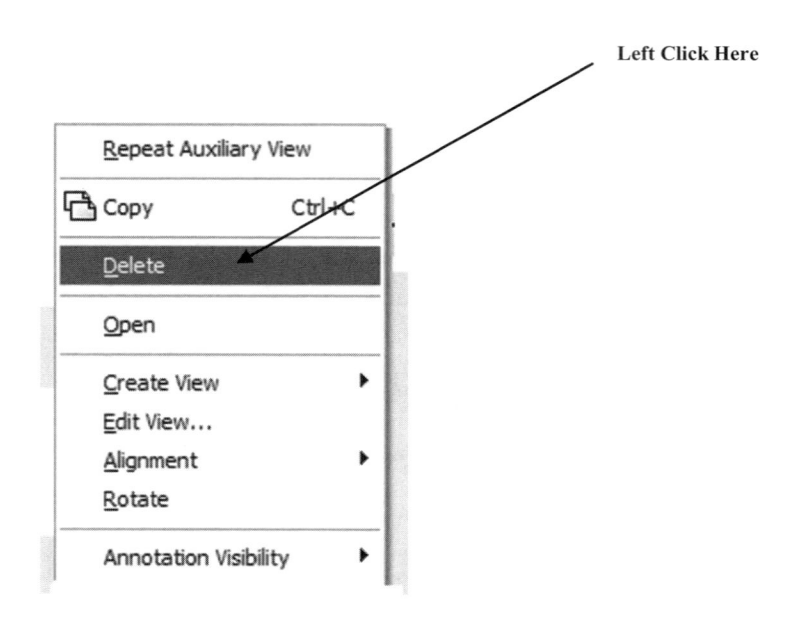

Figure 20

Left Click Here

22. A Delete dialog box will appear. Left click on **OK** as shown in Figure 21.

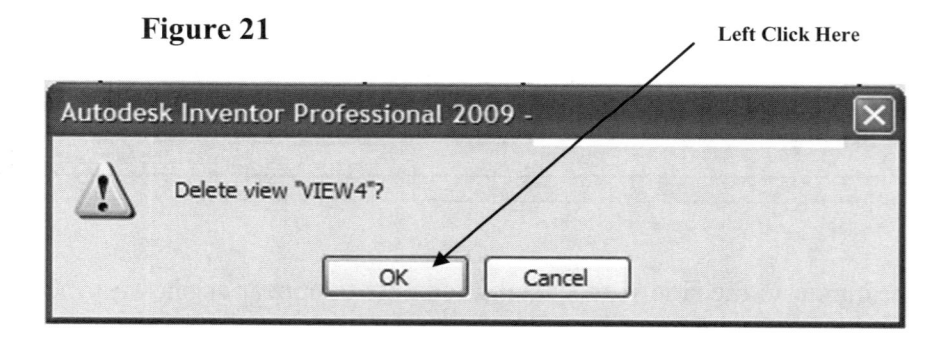

Figure 21

Left Click Here

Chapter 4: Advanced Detail Drawing Procedures

23. Move the cursor to the upper left portion of the screen and left click on **Section View** as shown in Figure 22.

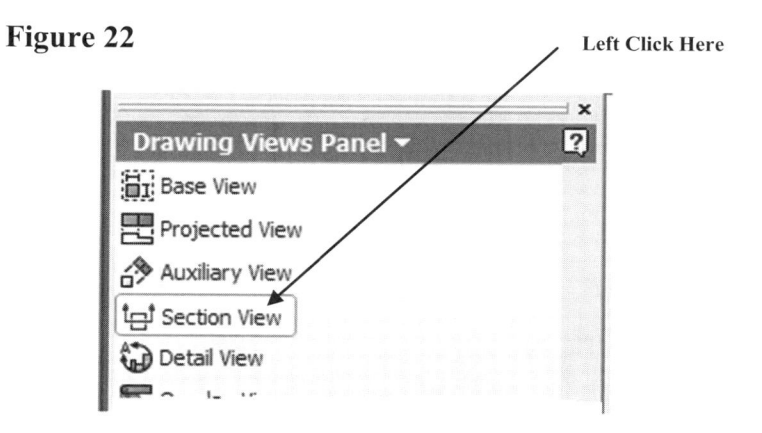

Figure 22

Left Click Here

24. Move the cursor over the front view causing red dots to appear around the view as shown in Figure 23.

Figure 23

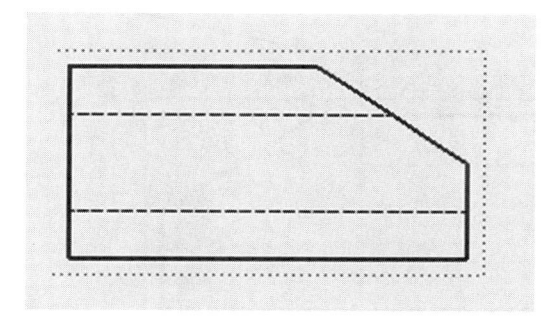

25. Left click on the view causing the red dots to turn into a solid red line as shown in Figure 24.

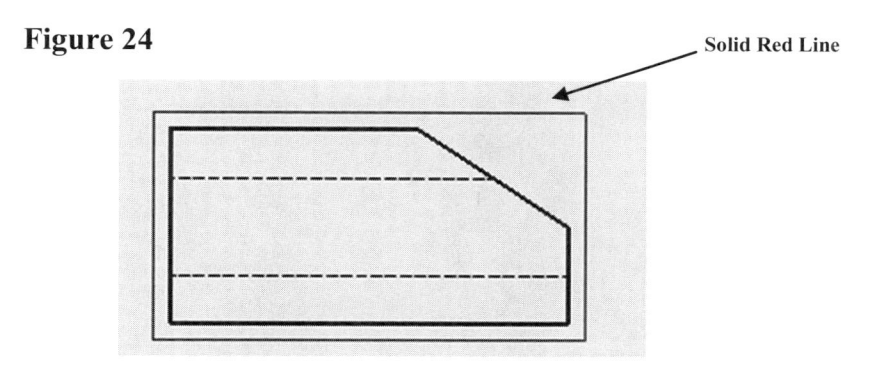

Figure 24

Solid Red Line

Chapter 4: Advanced Detail Drawing Procedures

26. Move the cursor around outside the red line and wait for the dotted line to appear as shown in Figure 25. It may take a few seconds before the line appears.

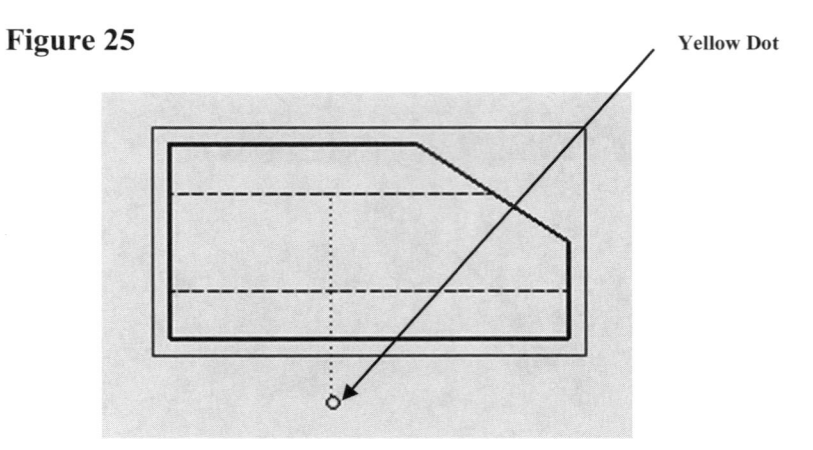

Figure 25 Yellow Dot

27. Left click on the yellow dot, move the line up, and left click as shown in Figure 26.

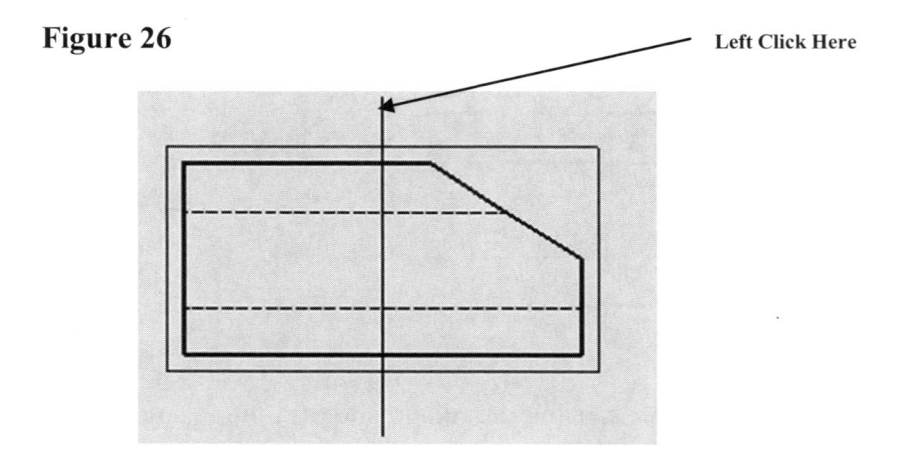

Figure 26 Left Click Here

Chapter 4: Advanced Detail Drawing Procedures

28. Right click in the same location. A pop up menu will appear. Left click on **Continue** as shown in Figure 27.

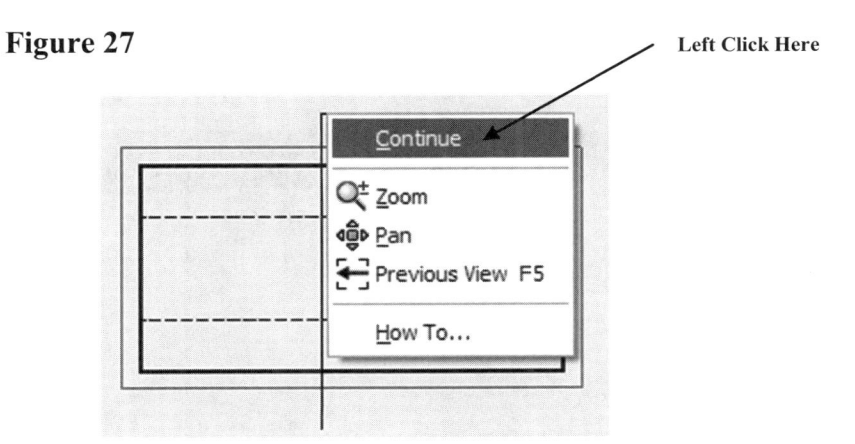

Figure 27

Chapter 4: Advanced Detail Drawing Procedures

29. The Section View dialog box will appear as shown in Figure 28. The section view will be attached to the cursor. Move the cursor to the right where the side view used to be located and left click. The Section View dialog box will close.

Figure 28

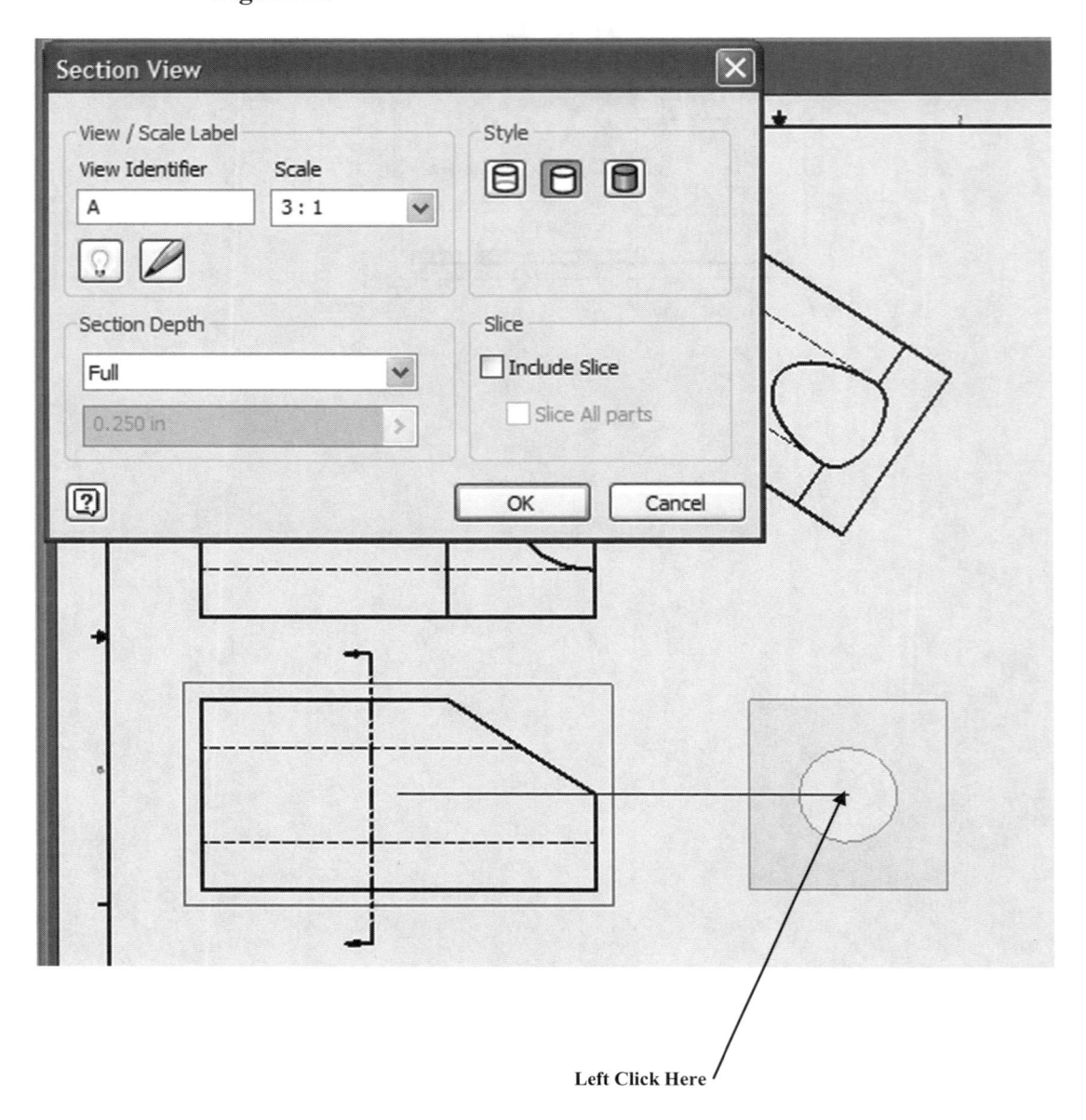

Left Click Here

Chapter 4: Advanced Detail Drawing Procedures

30. Inventor will create a section view to the right as shown in Figure 29.

Figure 29

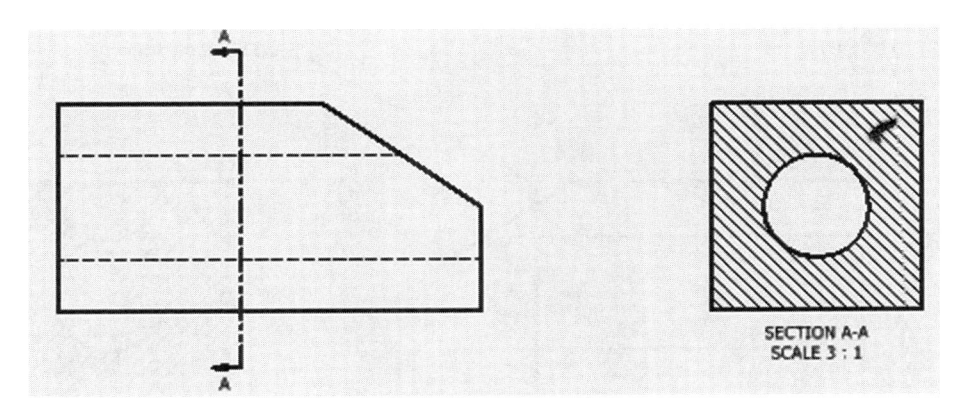

31. Inventor will create a side view that represents wherever the cutting plane line cuts through the part. Move the cursor over the cutting plane line causing it to turn red as shown in Figure 30.

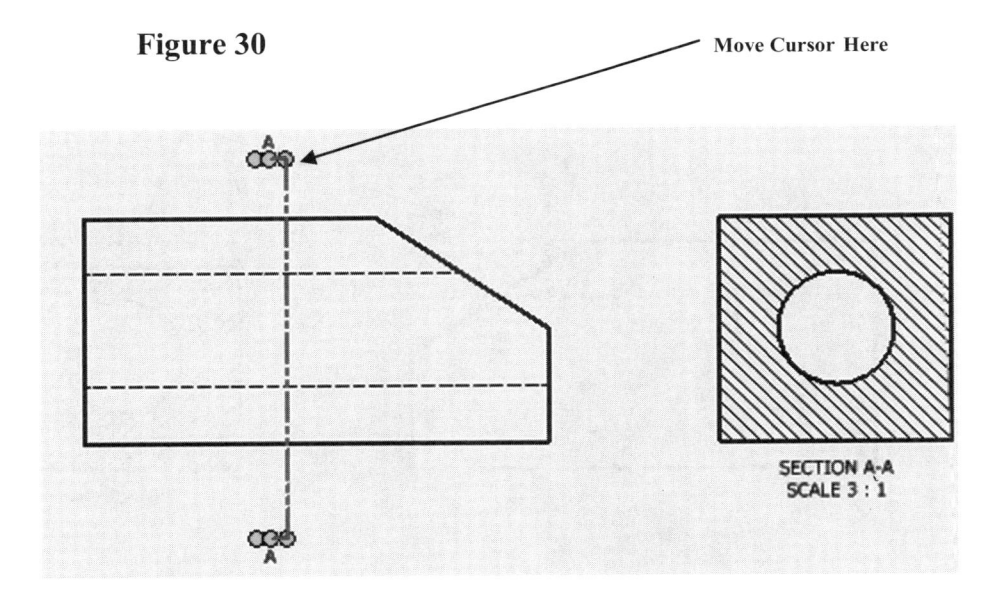

Figure 30   Move Cursor Here

197

Chapter 4: Advanced Detail Drawing Procedures

32. Once the line becomes highlighted (turns red) left click (holding the left mouse button down) and drag the cursor to the right. The cutting plane line will become a normal looking line while attached to the cursor as shown in Figure 31.

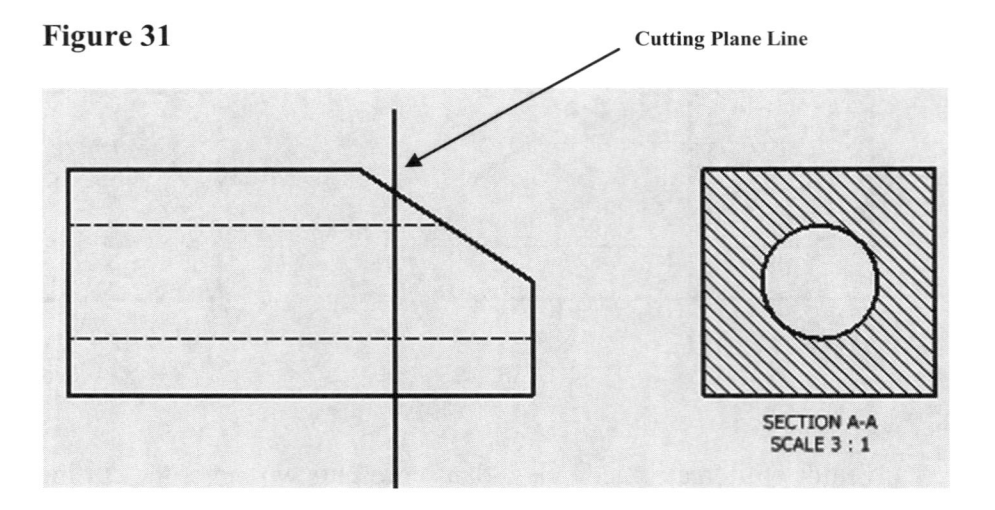

Figure 31

33. Once the cutting plane line has been moved to a new location release the left mouse button. The side view now reflects the new location of the cutting plane line as shown in Figure 32.

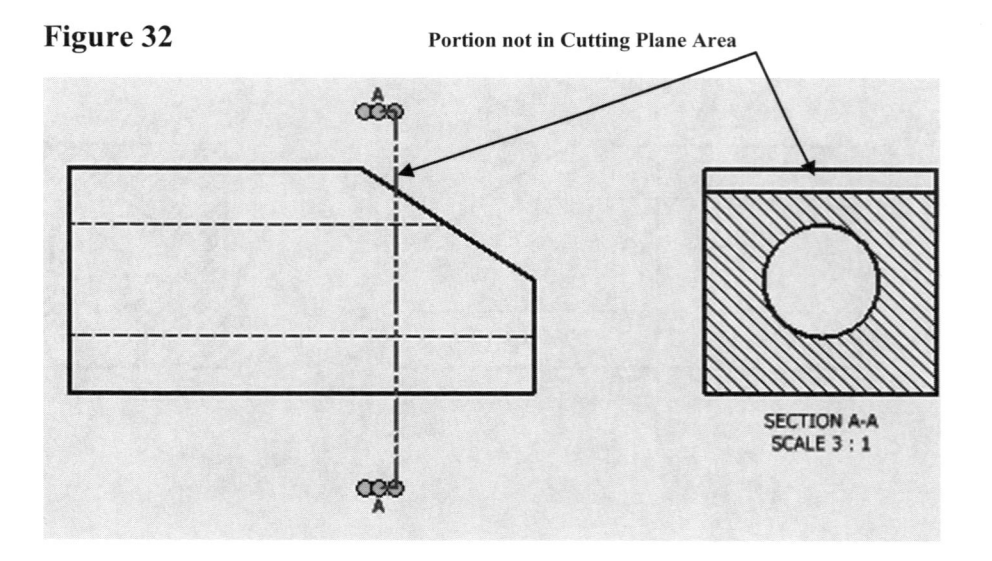

Figure 32

198

Chapter 4: Advanced Detail Drawing Procedures

34. Left click anywhere around the part. This will cause the cutting plane line to return to it's original appearance as shown in Figure 33.

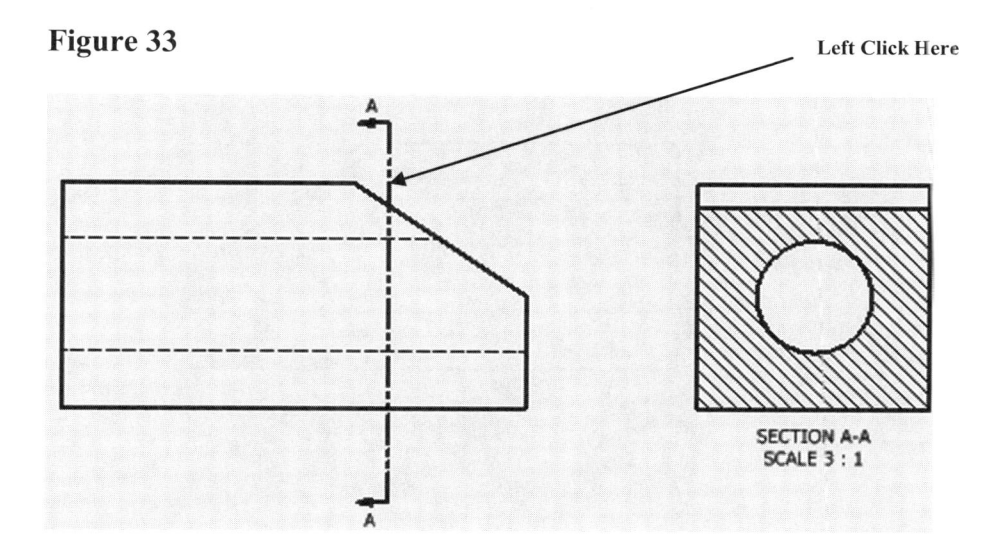

Figure 33

Left Click Here

35. Move the cursor to the middle left portion of the screen and left click on **Break** as shown in Figure 34.

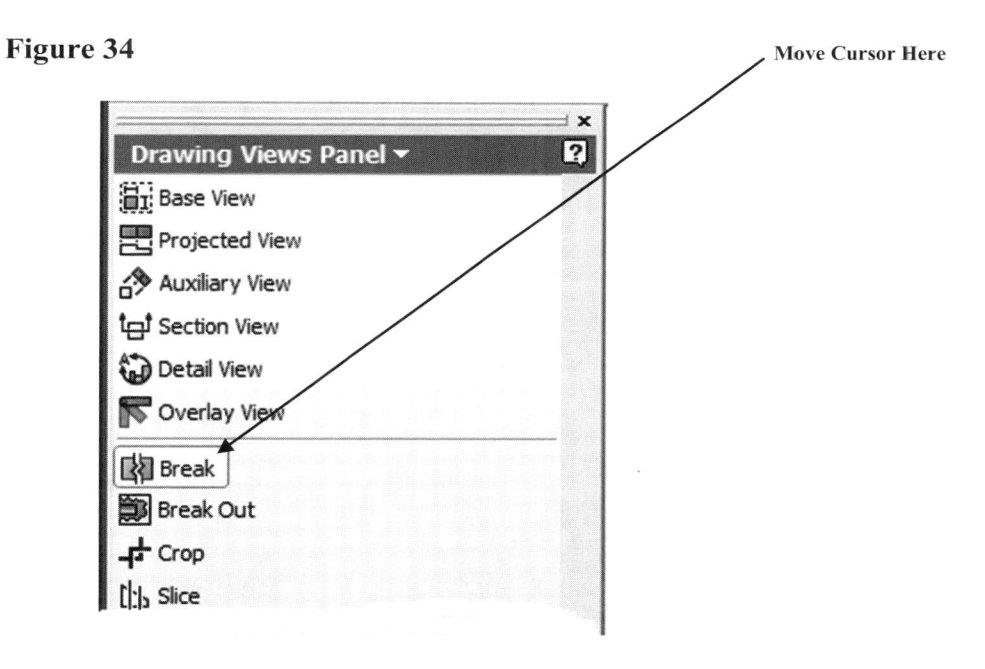

Figure 34

Move Cursor Here

199

Chapter 4: Advanced Detail Drawing Procedures

36. Move the cursor to the front view and left click once as shown in Figure 35.

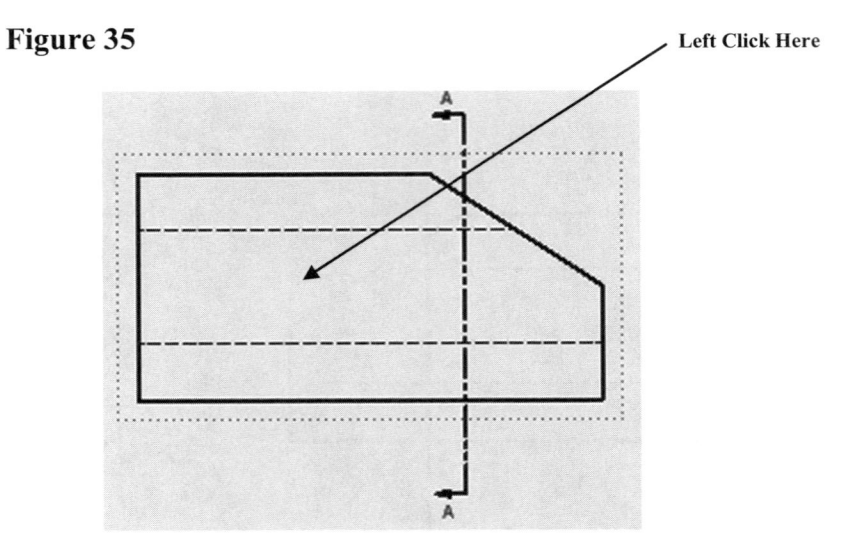

Figure 35

Left Click Here

37. The Break Dialog box will appear. The Break symbol will also be attached to the cursor as shown in Figure 36.

Figure 36

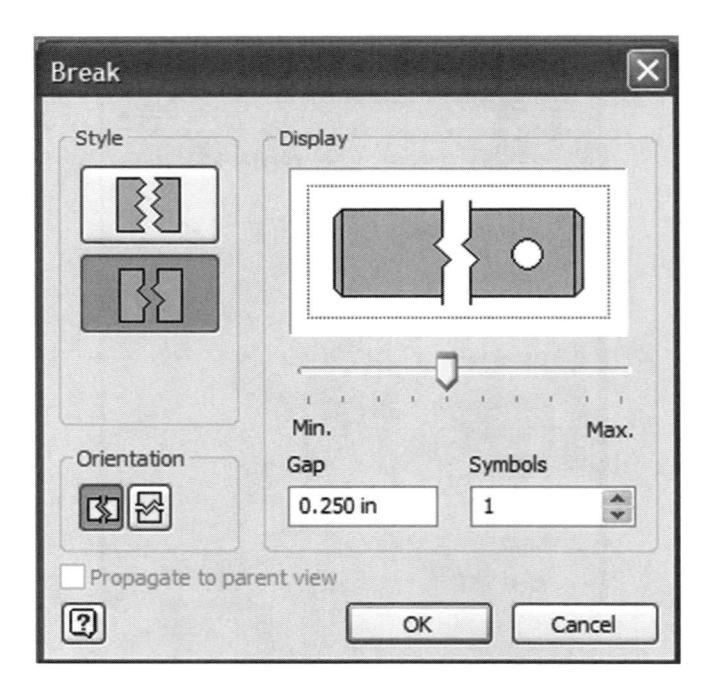

200

Chapter 4: Advanced Detail Drawing Procedures

38. Left click on the part causing a red box to appear as shown in Figure 37.

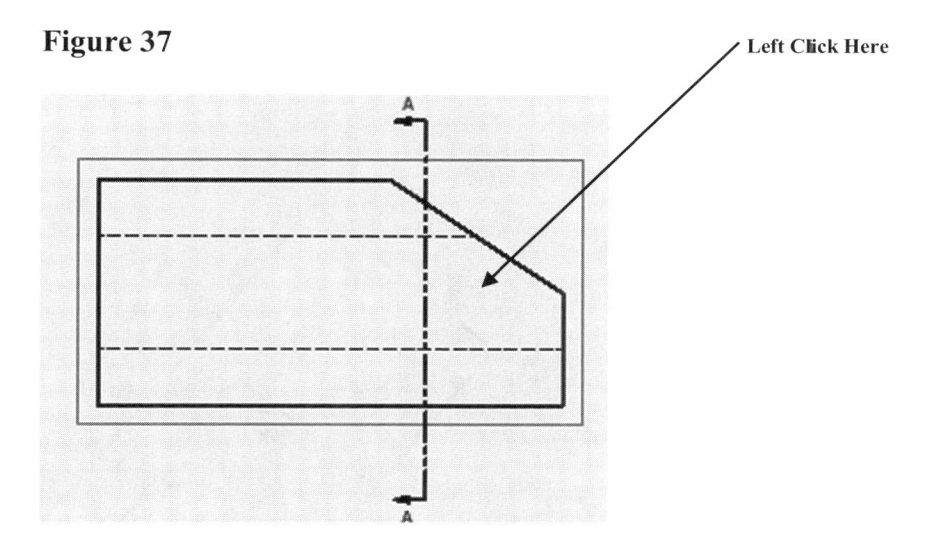

Figure 37   Left Click Here

39. Move the cursor to the left side of the cutting plane line and left click once. Move the cursor to the left. Another line will appear next to the first line. These two lines represent the size of the gap that Inventor will create in the part. A third line will be attached to the cursor. This line represents how much of the part will be removed from the view. Move the cursor to the far left portion of the part and left click as shown in Figure 38.

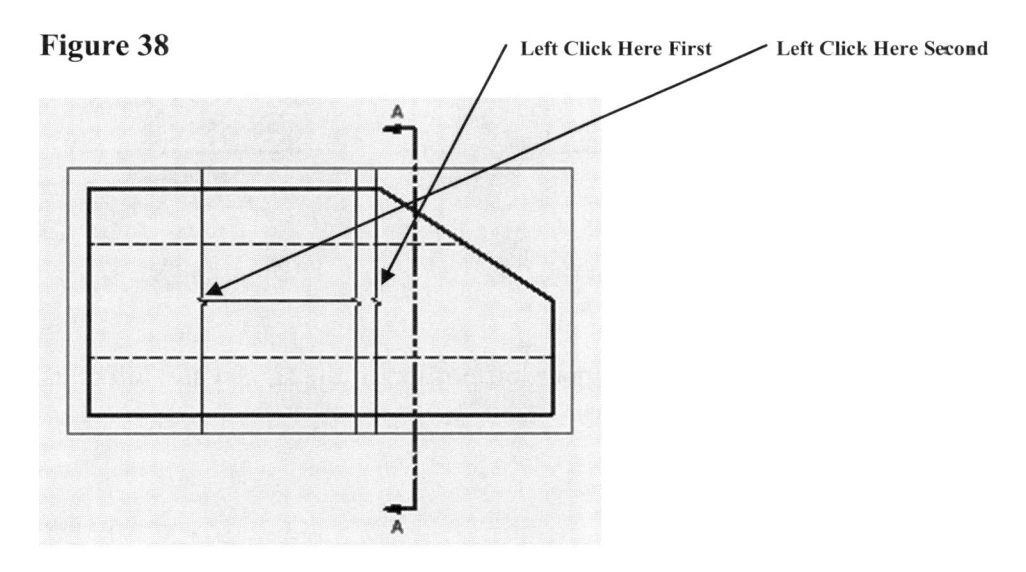

Figure 38   Left Click Here First   Left Click Here Second

201

Chapter 4: Advanced Detail Drawing Procedures

40. Inventor will remove sections from both the front and top views. The location of the cutting plane line will also move as shown in Figure 39.

Figure 39

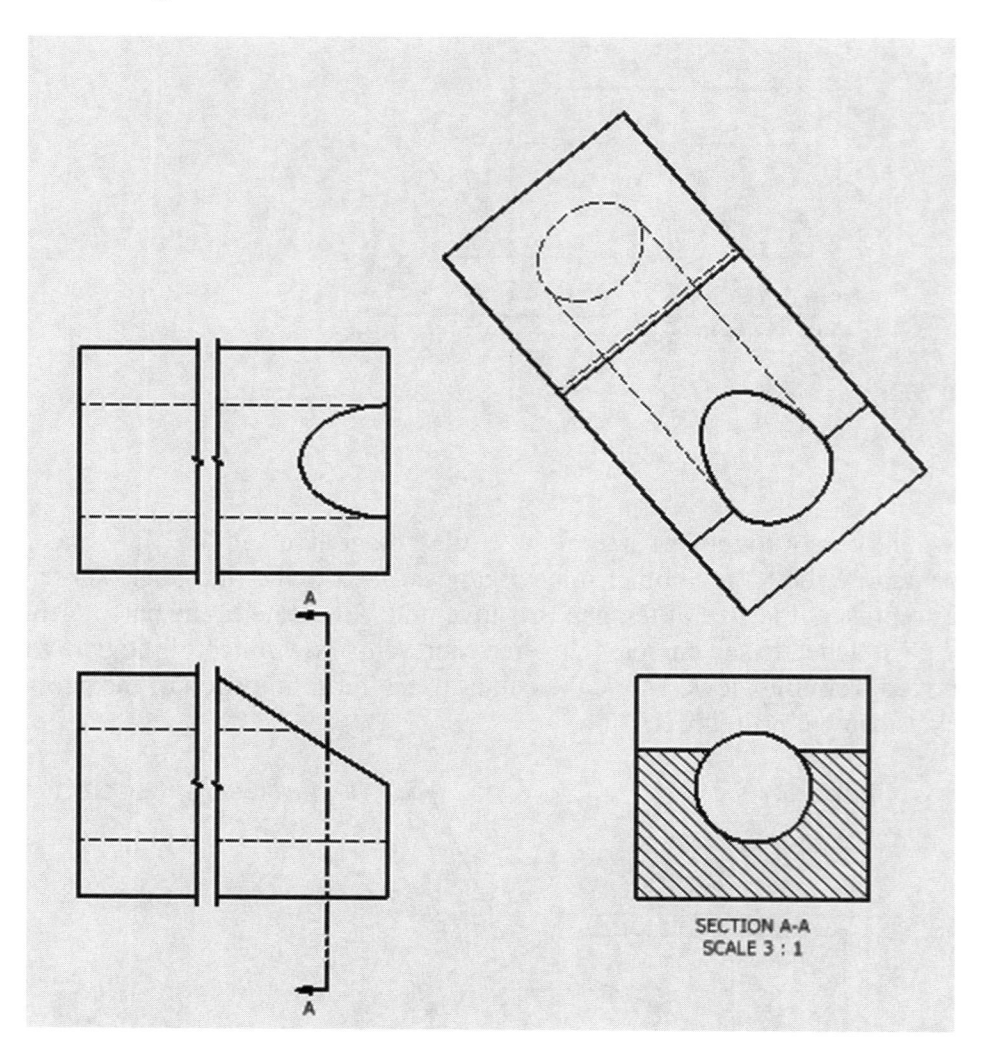

41. Move the cursor to the upper left portion of the screen and left click on **Undo** as shown in Figure 40.

Figure 40 — Left Click Here

Chapter 4: Advanced Detail Drawing Procedures

42. Move the cursor to the upper left portion of the screen and left click on **General Dimension** as shown in Figure 41.

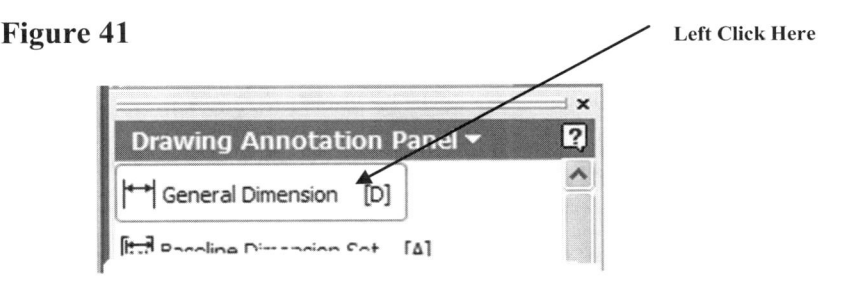

Figure 41

Left Click Here

43. Move the cursor over the left side vertical line causing it to turn red as shown in Figure 42. Select the line by left clicking anywhere on the line **or** on each of the end points. The dimension will be attached to the cursor.

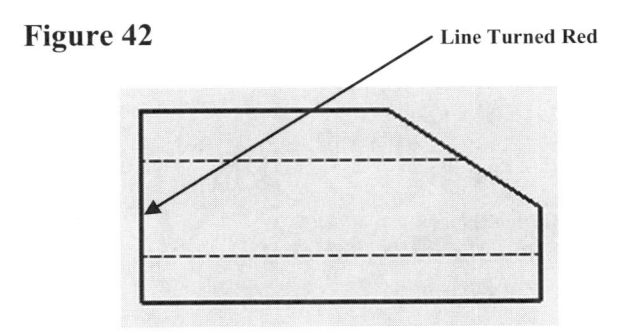

Figure 42

Line Turned Red

44. Move the cursor to the left and left click once. The actual dimension of the line will appear as shown in Figure 43.

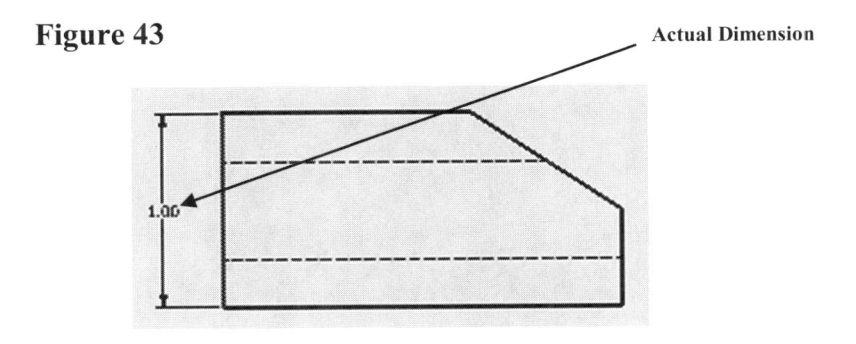

Figure 43

Actual Dimension

45. Finish dimensioning the part to your own satisfaction. When the part is satisfactorily dimensioned, save the file to a location where it can easily be retrieved.

Chapter 4: Advanced Detail Drawing Procedures

46. To delete an unwanted dimension, move the cursor over the dimension. The dimension will turn red and several green dots will appear as shown in Figure 44.

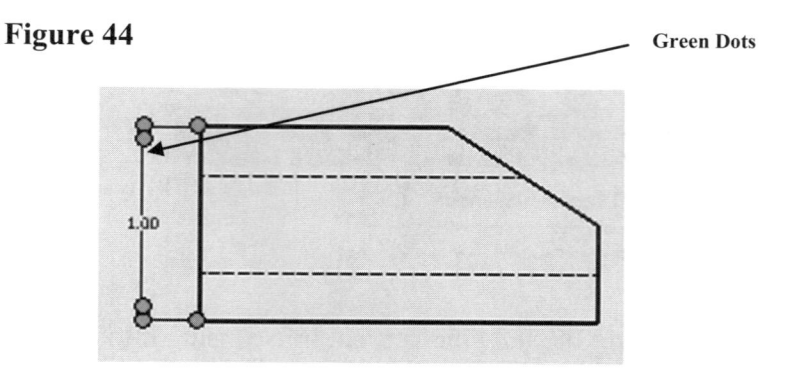

Figure 44

Green Dots

47. Right click on the dimension. A pop up menu will appear. Left click on **Delete** as shown in Figure 45.

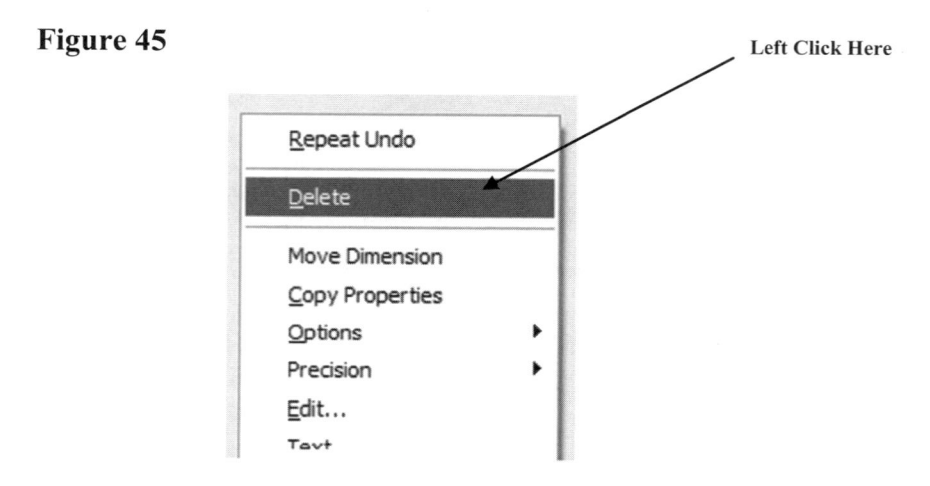

Figure 45

Left Click Here

Chapter 4: Advanced Detail Drawing Procedures

48. Move the cursor to the middle left portion of the screen and left click on **Text** as shown in Figure 46.

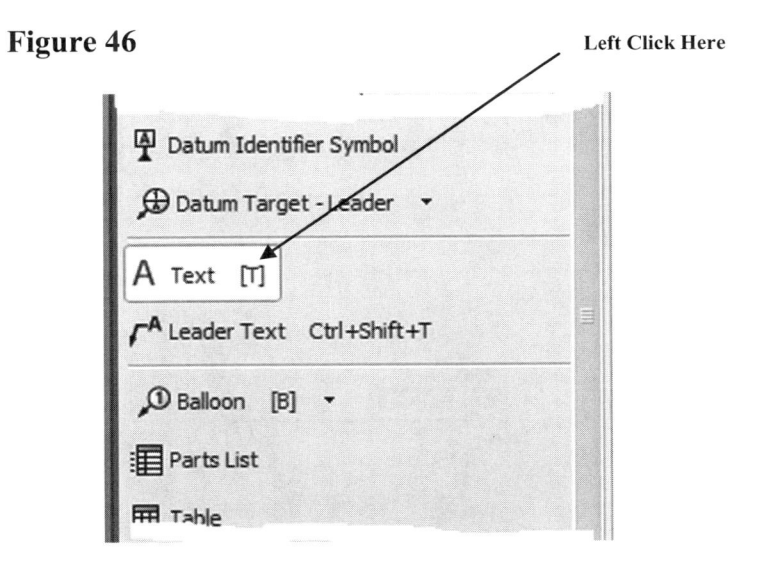

Figure 46   Left Click Here

49. Move the cursor to the title block location as shown in Figure 47. Left click once when the yellow dot appears.

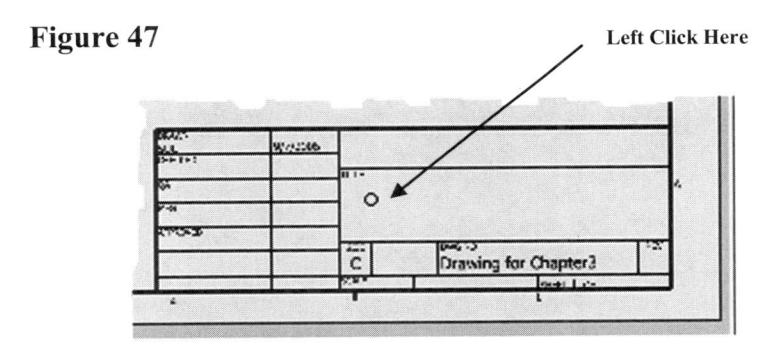

Figure 47   Left Click Here

Chapter 4: Advanced Detail Drawing Procedures

50. The Format Text dialog box will appear. Left click on the drop down box and change the text height to **.240** inches as shown in Figure 48.

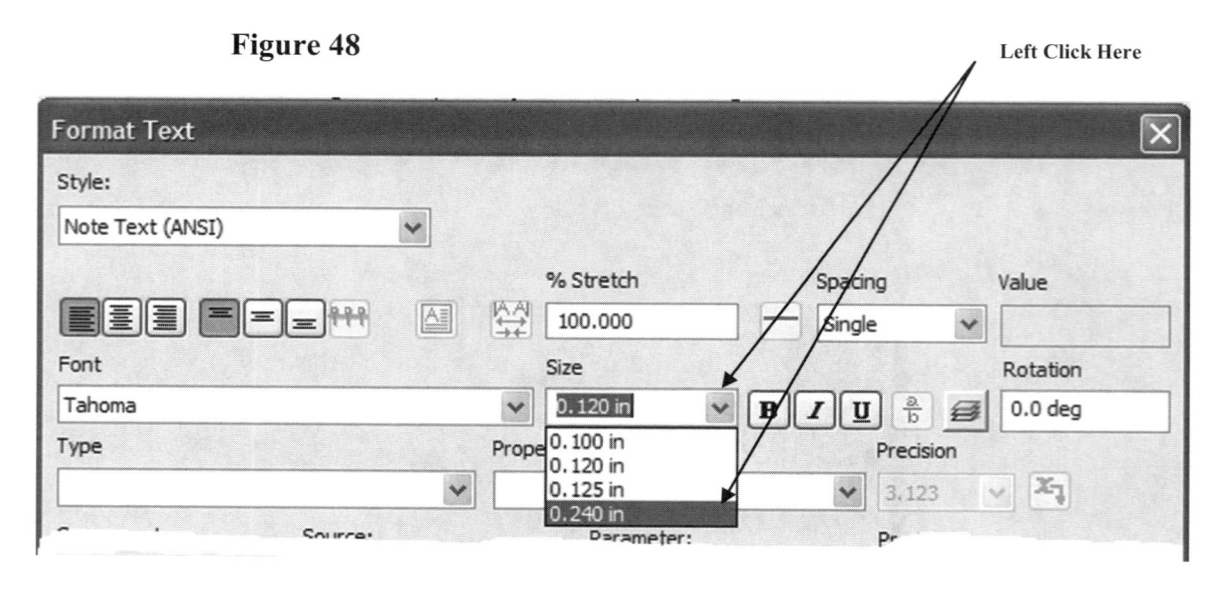

Figure 48

51. Move the cursor to the open area located in the lower half of the Format Text dialog box and type your first and last name. Text will appear near the flashing cursor as shown in Figure 49.

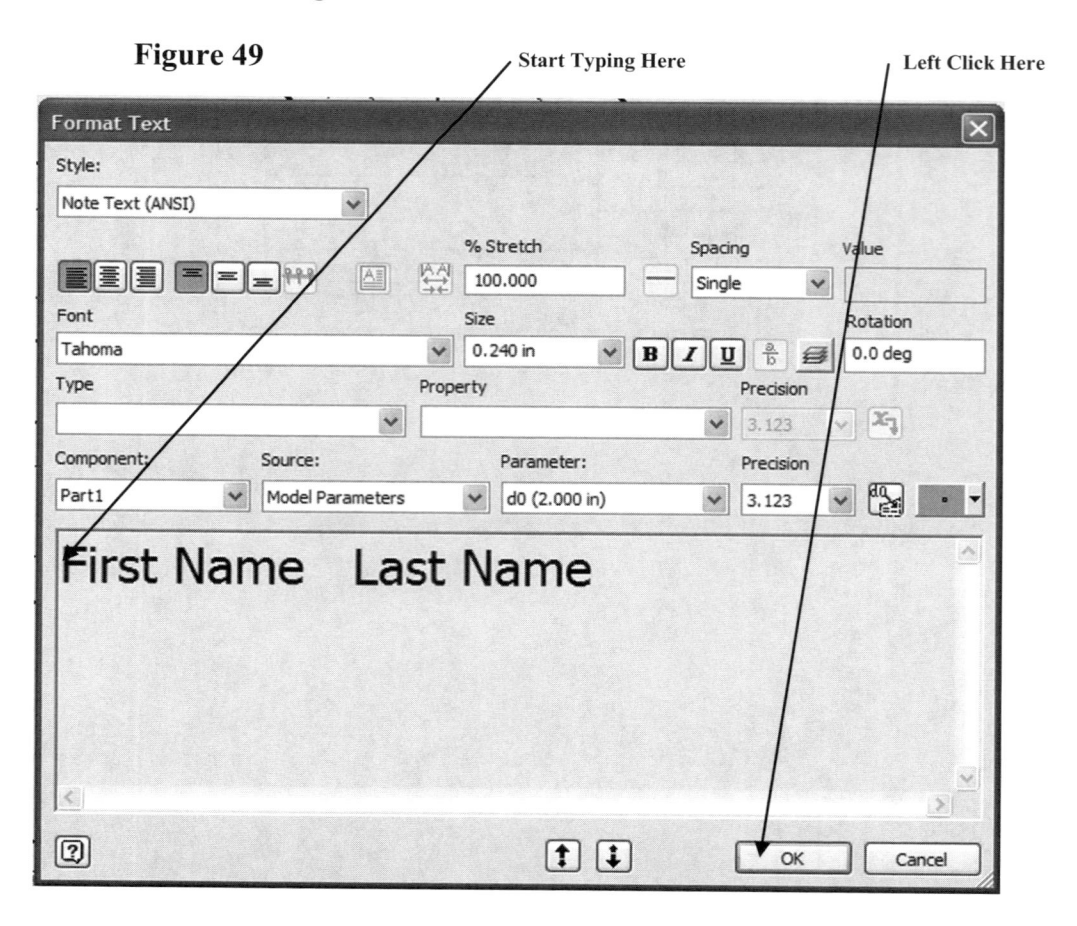

Figure 49

206

Chapter 4: Advanced Detail Drawing Procedures

52. After text has been entered, left click on **OK** as shown in Figure 49.

53. The Format Text dialog box will close.

54. Text will appear in the title block as shown in Figure 50.

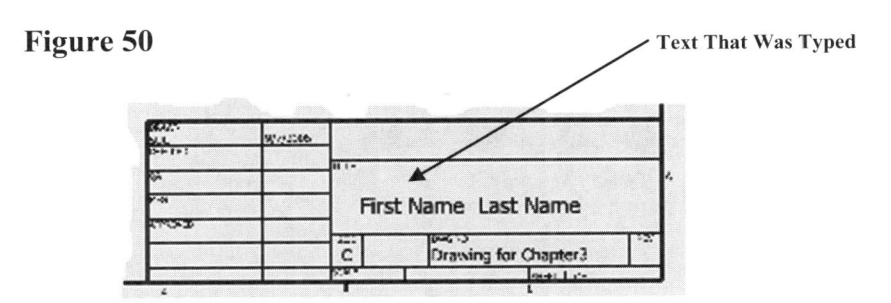

Figure 50

55. Right click near the text. A pop up menu will appear as shown in Figure 51.

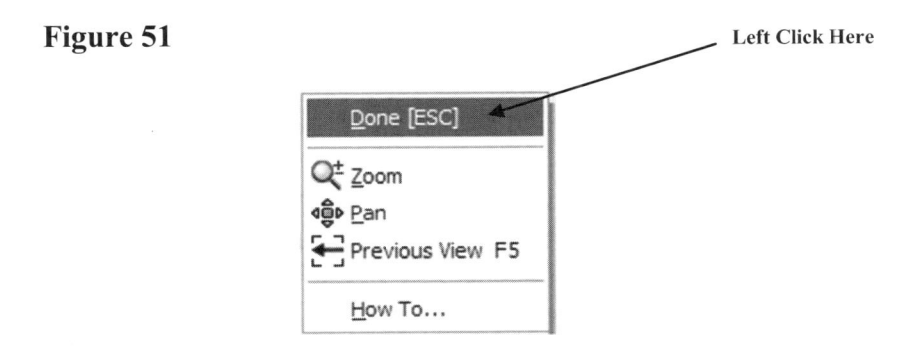

Figure 51

56. If the text needs to be moved, move the cursor over the text causing several green dots to appear as shown in Figure 52.

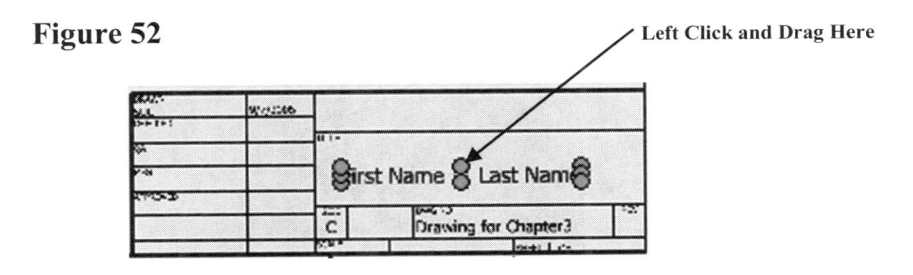

Figure 52

57. While the text is highlighted, left click (holding the left mouse button down) and drag the text to the desired location. After the text is in the desired location, release the left mouse button, move the cursor away from the text, and left click once.

207

Chapter 4: Advanced Detail Drawing Procedures

58. Move the cursor to the upper left portion of the screen and left click on the down arrow next to Drawing Annotation Panel. Left click on **Drawing Views Panel** as shown in Figure 53.

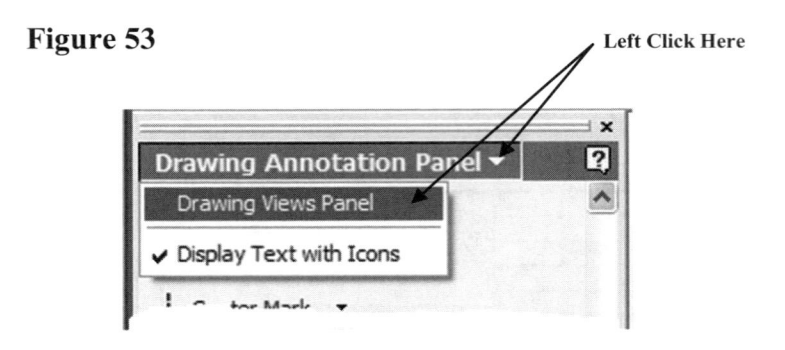

Figure 53

59. Your screen should look similar to Figure 54.

Figure 54

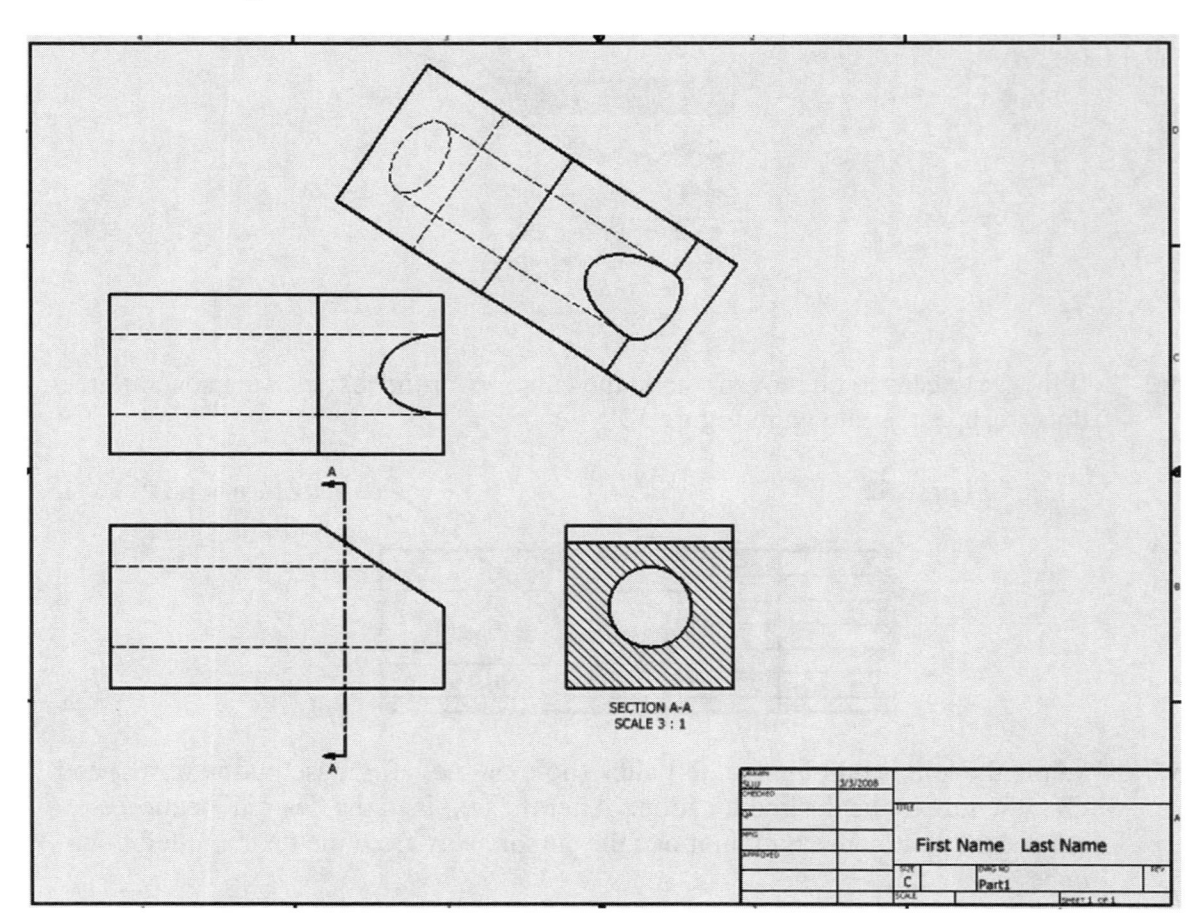

Chapter 4: Advanced Detail Drawing Procedures

60. Before starting a new sheet of detail drawings, make sure to first save the current sheet. **Caution: Once a new sheet has been created the old sheet is not retrievable unless it has been saved. If a new sheet is created before the old sheet was saved, left click on the Undo icon located at the top left portion of the screen as shown in Figure 55.**

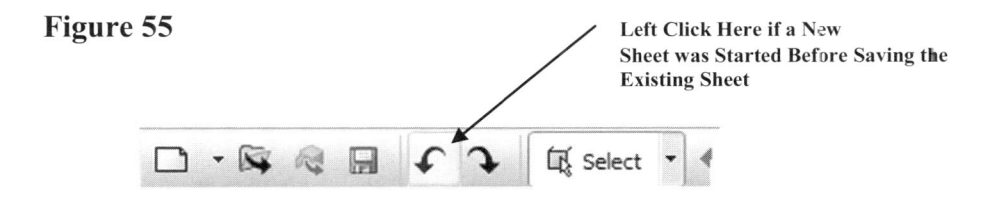

Figure 55

Left Click Here if a New Sheet was Started Before Saving the Existing Sheet

61. Move the cursor to the left middle portion of the screen and left click on **New Sheet** as shown in Figure 56.

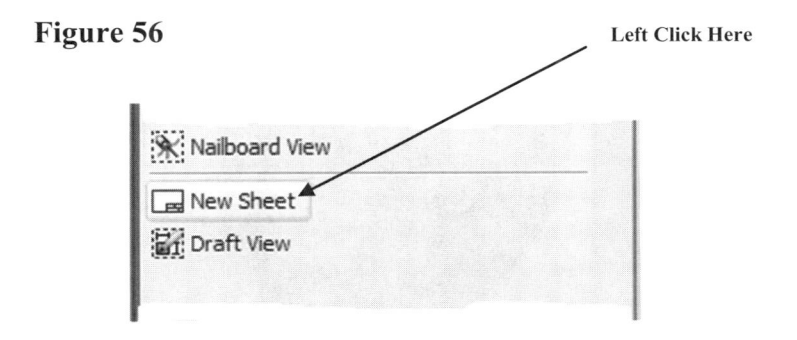

Figure 56

Left Click Here

62. This will begin a new sheet for more detail drawings if necessary.

209

Chapter 4: Advanced Detail Drawing Procedures

Drawing Activities

Create Section View Drawings for the following problems.

Problem 1

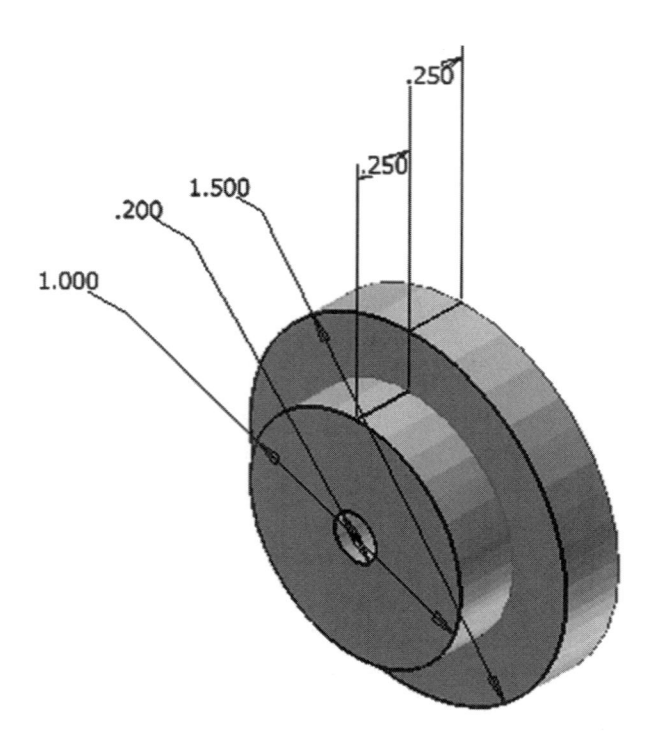

Problem 2

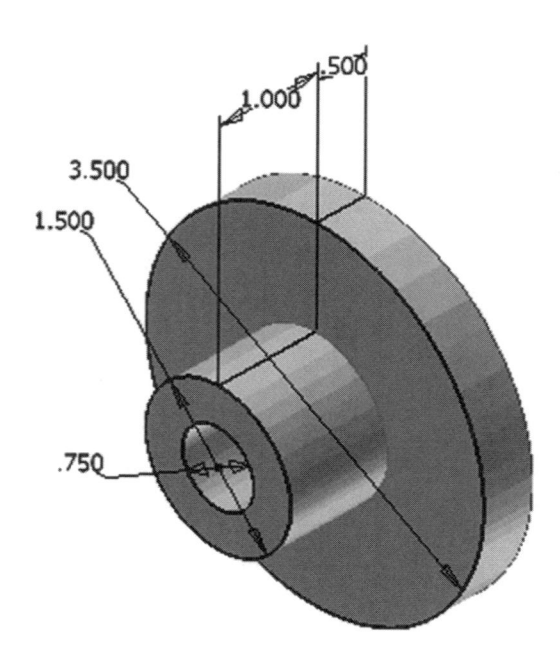

Chapter 4: Advanced Detail Drawing Procedures

Create Auxiliary View Drawings for the following problems.

Problem 3

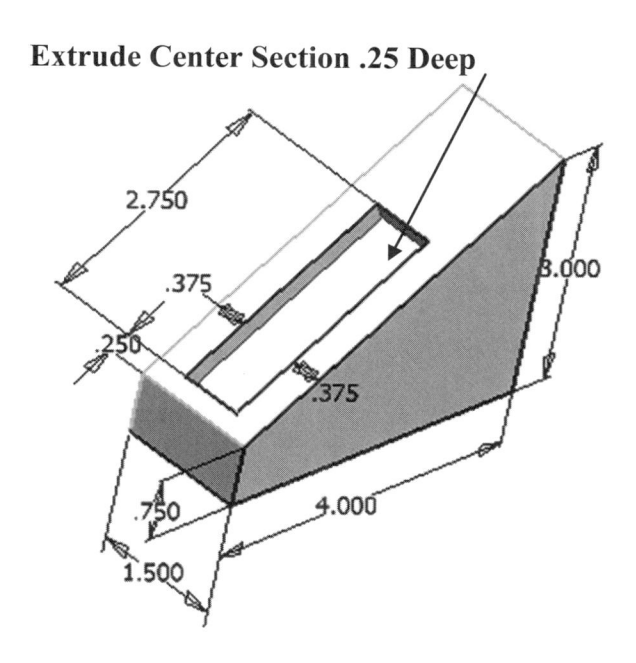

Extrude Center Section .25 Deep

Problem 4

211

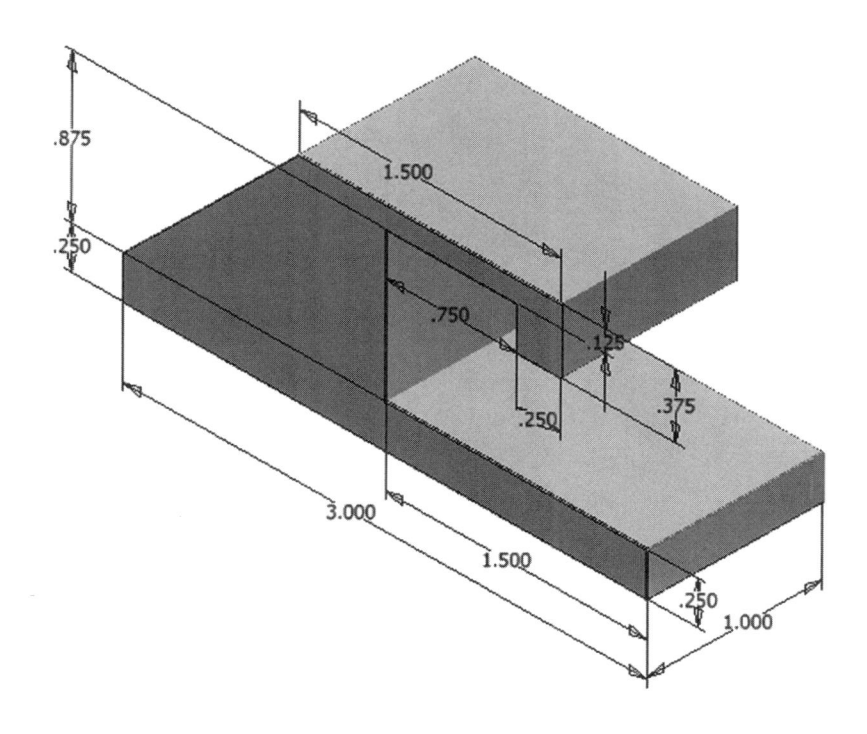

Chapter 4: Advanced Detail Drawing Procedures

Create Section View Drawings for the following problems.

Problem 5

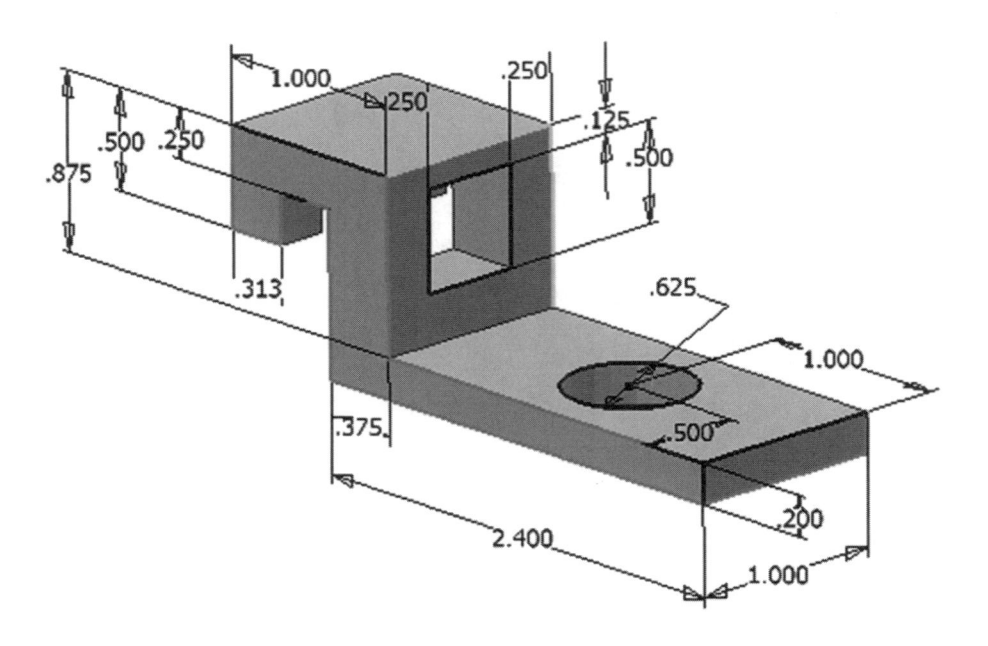

Problem 6

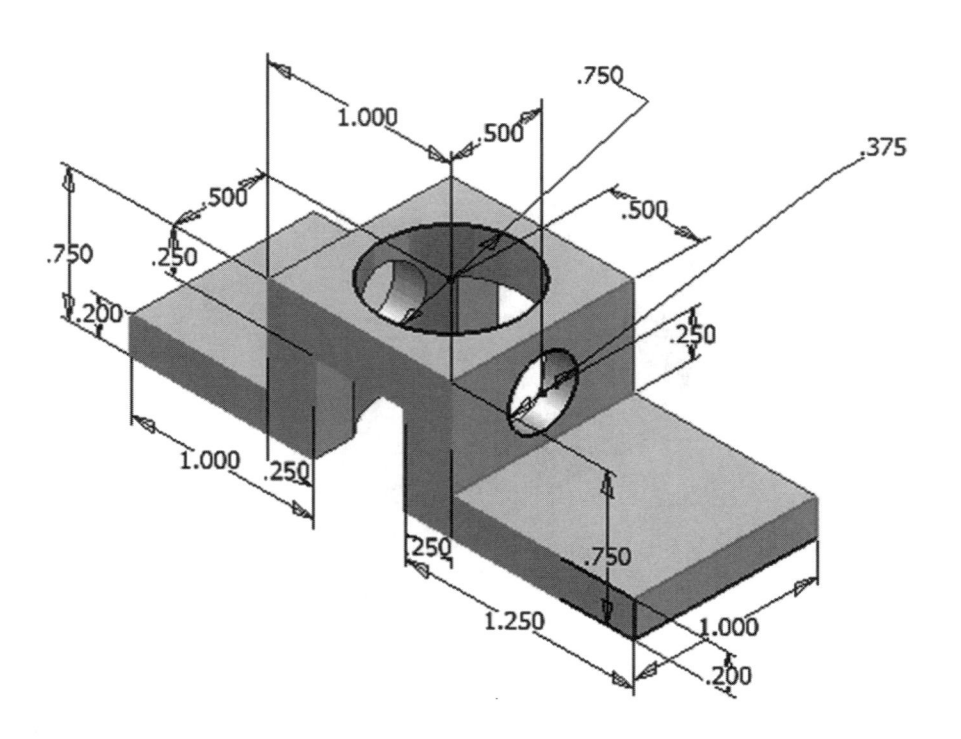

Chapter 4: Advanced Detail Drawing Procedures

Create Section View Drawings for the following problems.

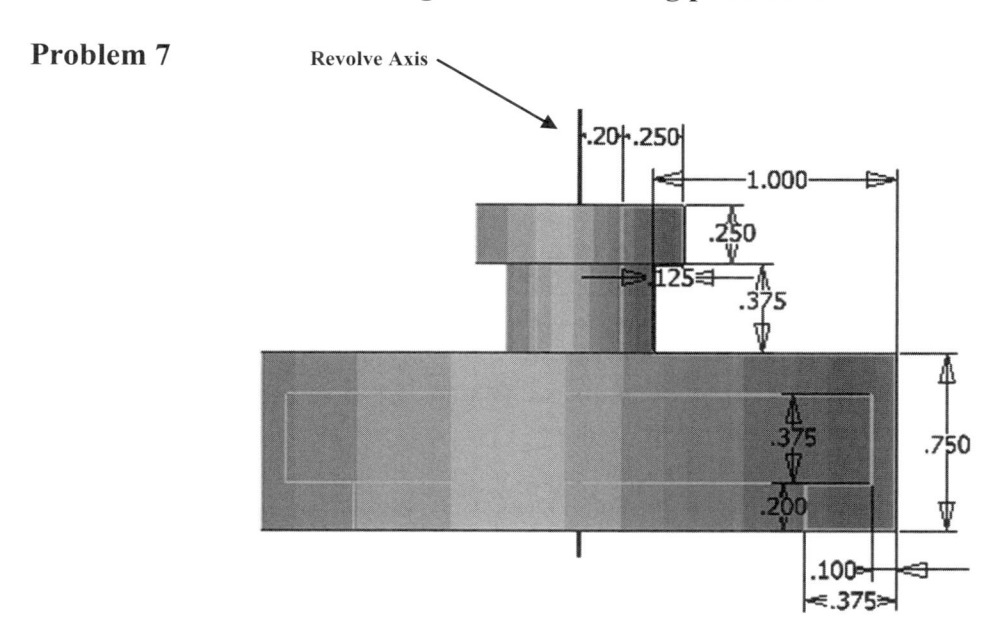

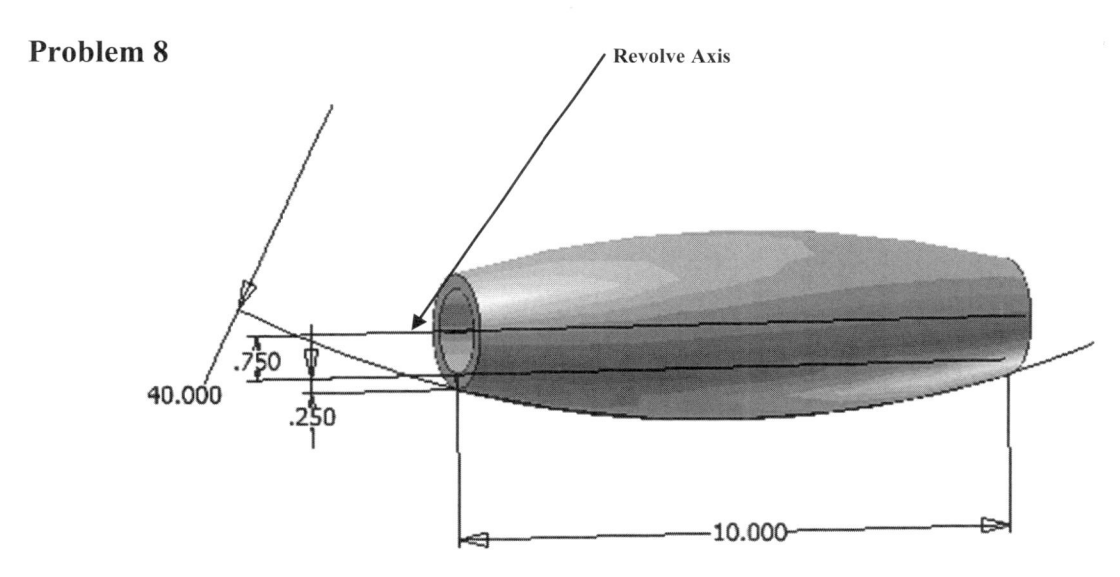

Problem 7

Chapter 5 Learning To Edit Existing Solid Models

Objectives:
- Design a simple part
- Learn to use the Circular Pattern Command
- Edit the part using the Sketch Panel
- Edit the part using the Extrude Command
- Edit the part using the Fillet Command

Chapter 5 includes instruction on how to design and edit the part shown below.

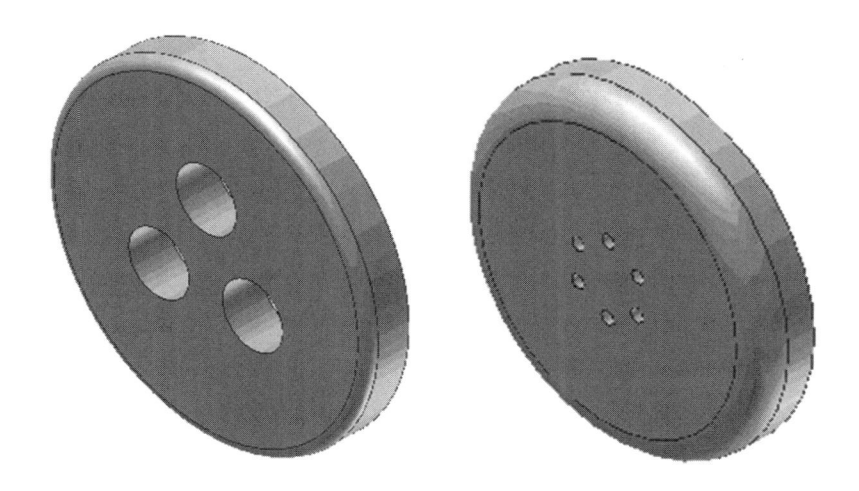

Chapter 5: Learning To Edit Existing Solid Models

1. Start Autodesk Inventor 2009 by referring to "Chapter 1 Getting Started".

2. After Autodesk Inventor 2009 is running, begin a new sketch.

3. Move the cursor to the upper left corner of the screen and left click on **Center Point Circle** as shown in Figure 1.

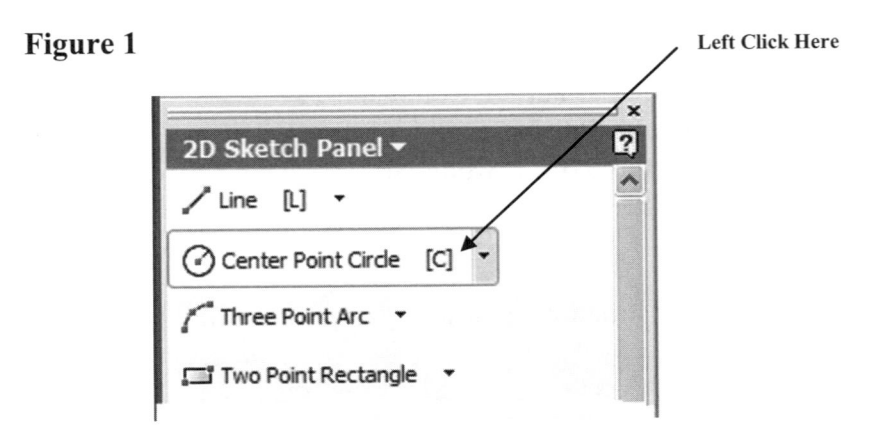

Figure 1

Left Click Here

4. Move the cursor to the center of the screen and left click once. This will be the center of the circle as shown in Figure 2.

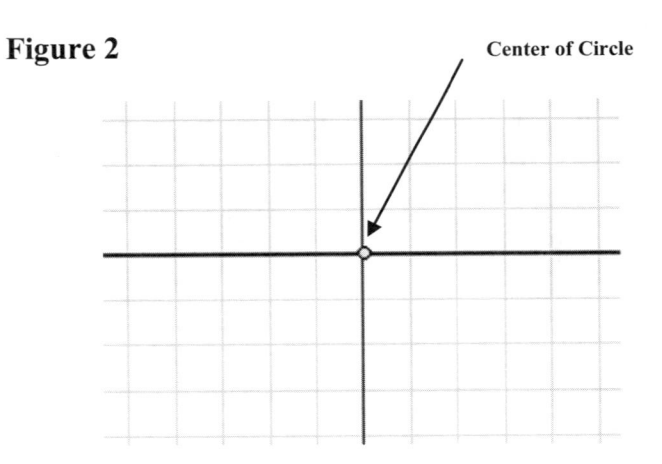

Figure 2

Center of Circle

216

Chapter 5: Learning To Edit Existing Solid Models

5. Move the cursor to the right and left click once as shown in Figure 3.

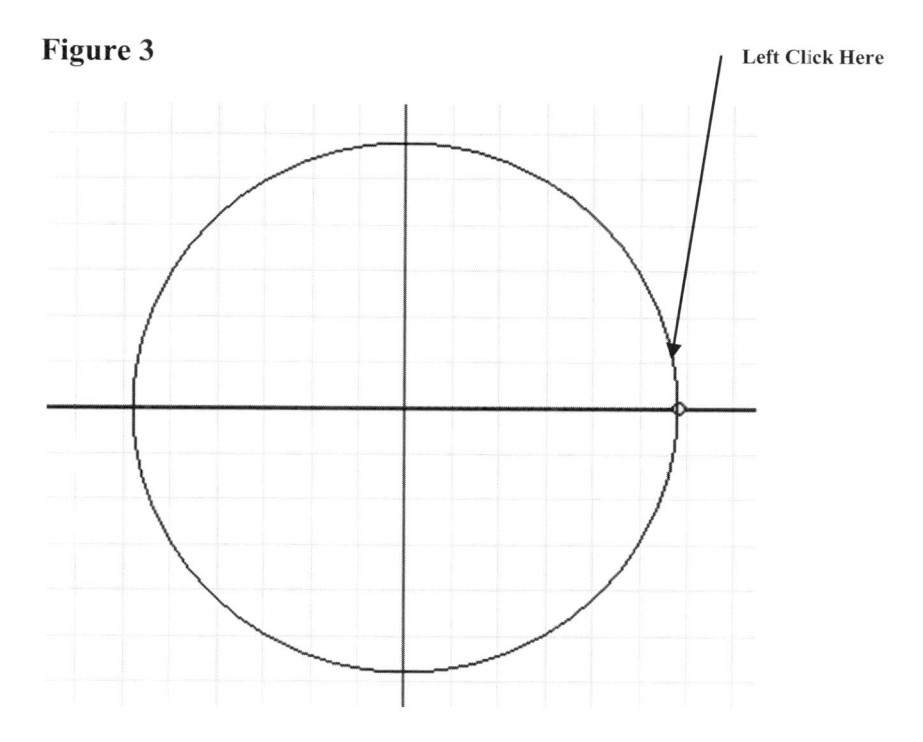

Figure 3

Left Click Here

6. Move the cursor to the middle left portion of the screen and left click on **General Dimension** as shown in Figure 4.

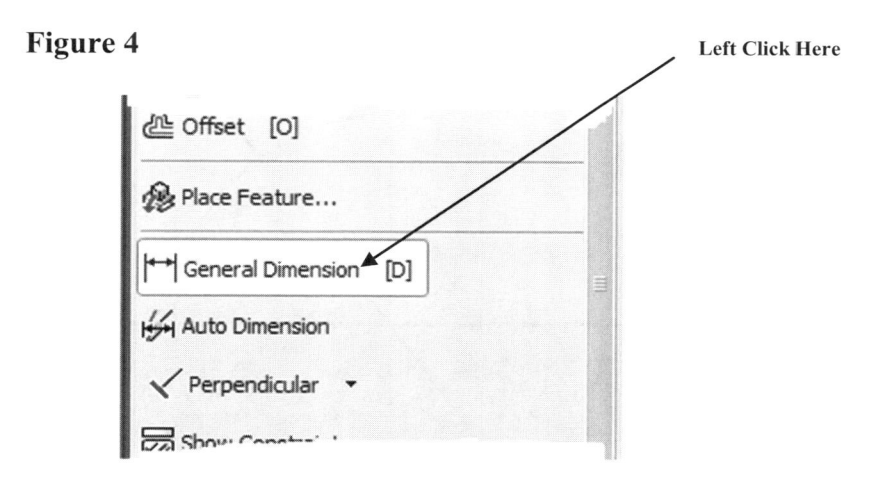

Figure 4

Left Click Here

217

Chapter 5: Learning To Edit Existing Solid Models

7. After selecting **General Dimension** move the cursor over the edge of the circle. The circle edge will turn red as shown in Figure 5. Left click once. The dimension will be attached to the cursor.

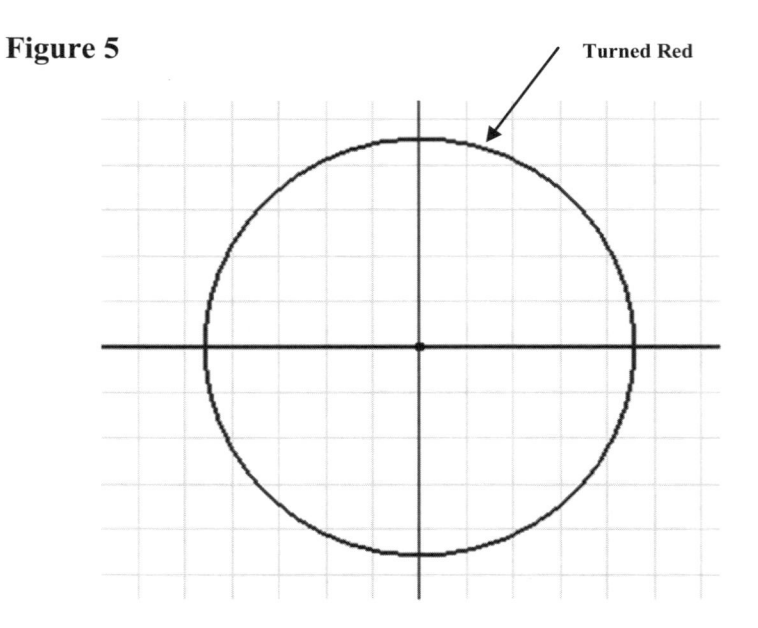

Figure 5

Turned Red

8. Move the cursor down. The actual dimension of the line will appear as shown in Figure 6.

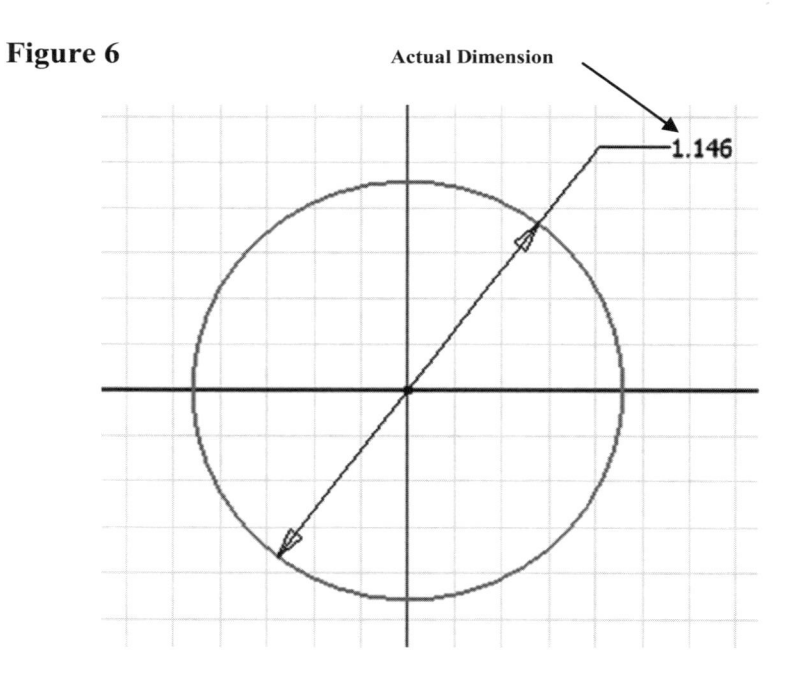

Figure 6

Actual Dimension

1.146

Chapter 5: Learning To Edit Existing Solid Models

9. Move the cursor to where the dimension will be placed and left click once. While the dimension is still in red, left click once. The Edit Dimension dialog box will appear as shown in Figure 7.

Figure 7

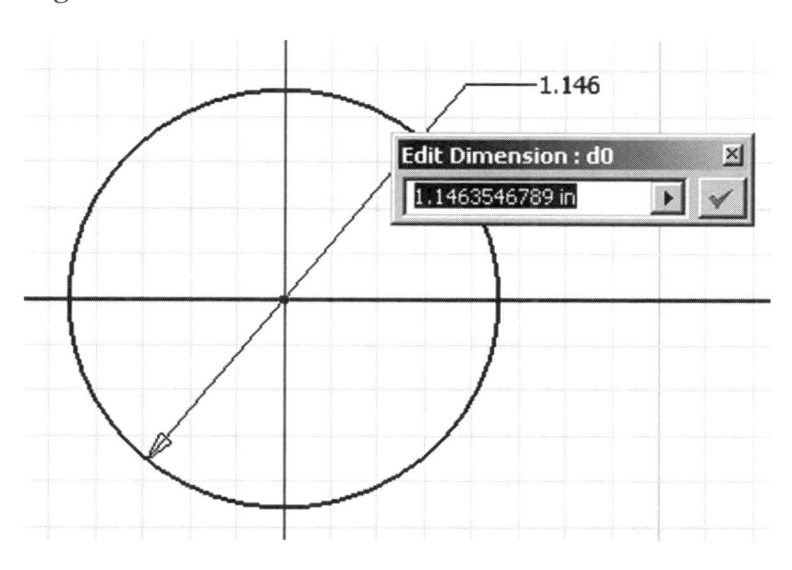

10. To edit the dimension, type **2.00** in the Edit Dimension dialog box (while the current dimension is highlighted) and press **Enter** on the keyboard.

11. The dimension of the circle will become 2.00 inches as shown in Figure 8.

Figure 8

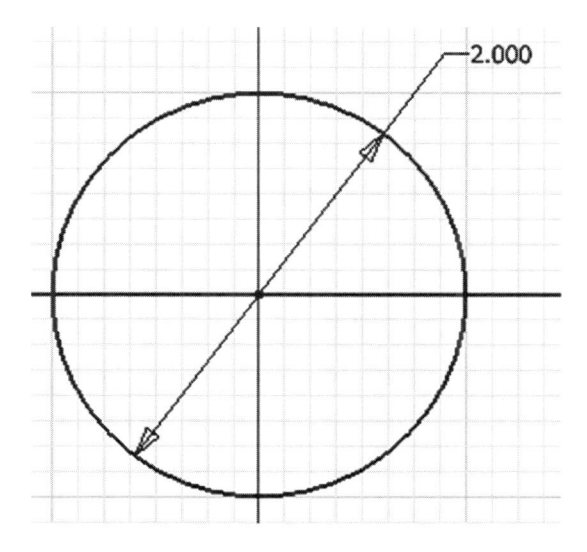

Chapter 5: Learning To Edit Existing Solid Models

12. To view the entire drawing it may be necessary to move the cursor to the middle portion of the screen and left click once on the "Zoom All" icon as shown in Figure 9.

Figure 9   Left Click Here

13. The drawing will "fill up" the entire screen. If the drawing is still too large, left click on the "Zoom" icon as shown in Figure 10. After selecting the Zoom icon, hold the left mouse button down and drag the cursor up and down to achieve the desired view of the sketch.

Figure 10   Left Click Here

14. After the sketch is complete it is time to extrude the sketch into a solid. Right click anywhere on the drawing. A pop up menu will appear. Left click on **Done [Esc]** as shown in Figure 11.

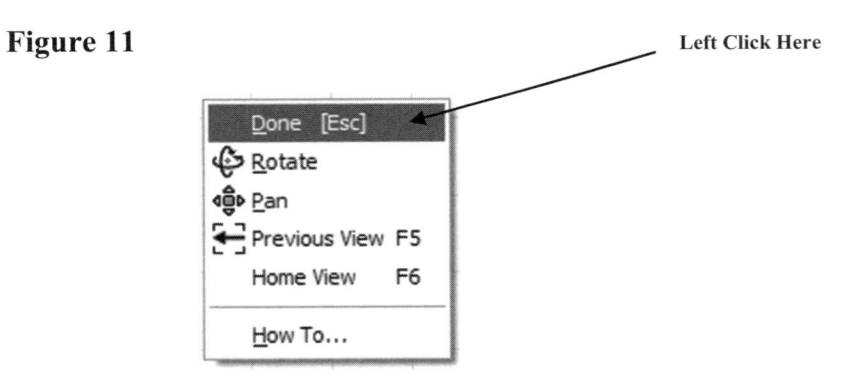

Figure 11   Left Click Here

220

Chapter 5: Learning To Edit Existing Solid Models

15. After you have verified that no commands are active, right click anywhere on the sketch. A pop up menu will appear. Left click on **Finish Sketch** as shown in Figure 12.

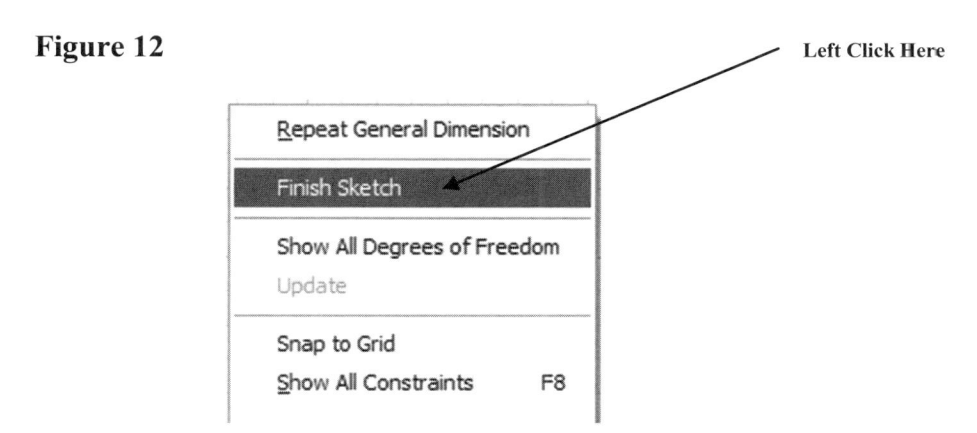

Figure 12

Left Click Here

Repeat General Dimension
Finish Sketch
Show All Degrees of Freedom
Update
Snap to Grid
Show All Constraints   F8

16. Inventor is now out of the Sketch Panel and into the Part Features Panel. Notice that the commands at the left of the screen are now different. To work in the Part Features Panel a sketch must be present and have no opens (non-connected lines). If there are any opens in the sketch an error message will appear. Your screen should look similar to Figure 13.

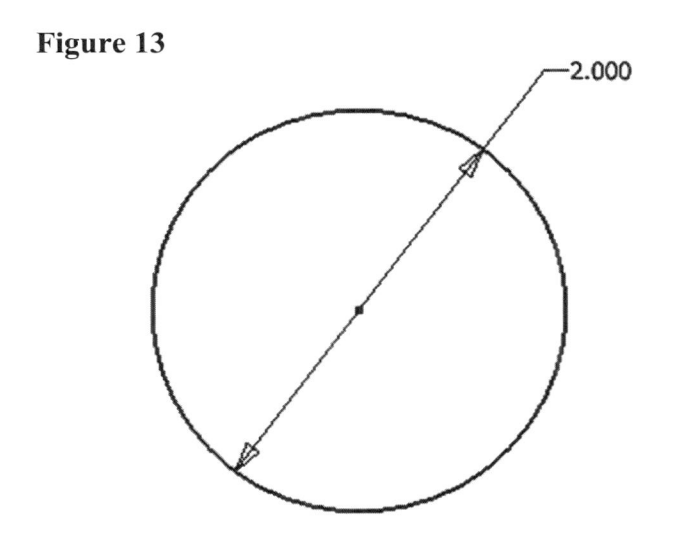

Figure 13

2.000

Chapter 5: Learning To Edit Existing Solid Models

17. Right click around the sketch. A pop up menu will appear. Left click on **Isometric/Home View** as shown in Figure 14.

Figure 14

Left Click Here

18. The view will become isometric as shown in Figure 15.

Figure 15

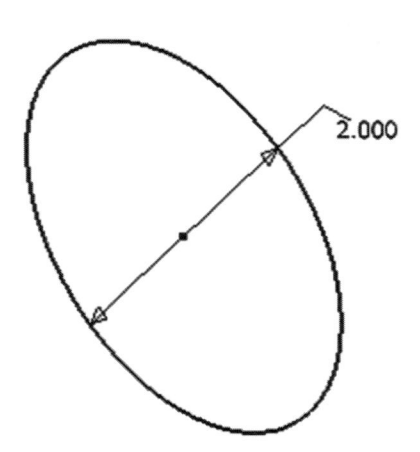

19. Move the cursor to the middle left portion of the screen and left click on **Extrude**. The Extrude dialog box will appear. Inventor also provides a preview of the extrusion. If Inventor gave you an error message there are opens (non-connected lines) somewhere on the sketch. Check each intersection for opens by using the **Extend** and **Trim** commands.

Chapter 5: Learning To Edit Existing Solid Models

20. Enter **.25** under Distance and left click on **OK** as shown in Figure 16.

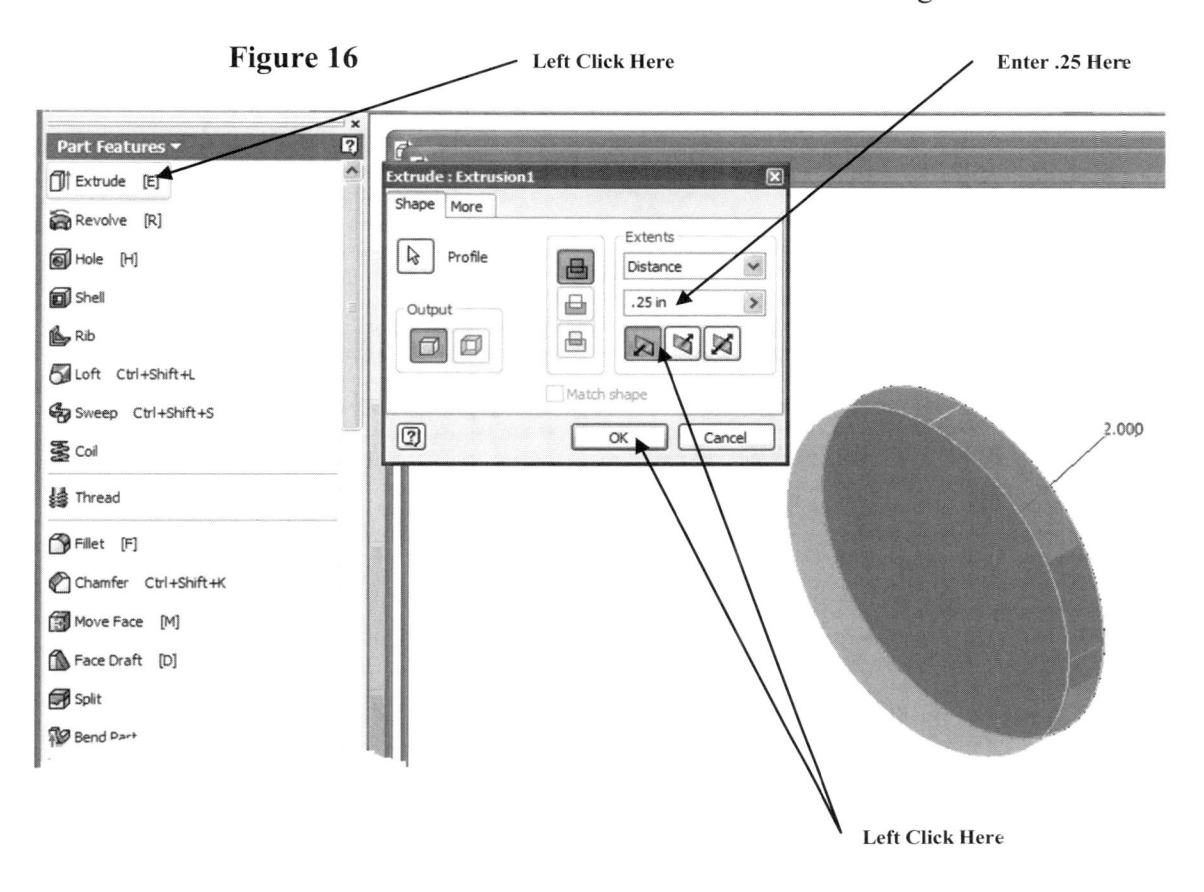

Figure 16

Chapter 5: Learning To Edit Existing Solid Models

21. Move the cursor to the front surface causing the edges of the surface to turn red and the surface to turn blue. After the surface appears blue, right click on the surface once. A pop up menu will appear. Left click on **New Sketch** as shown in Figure 17.

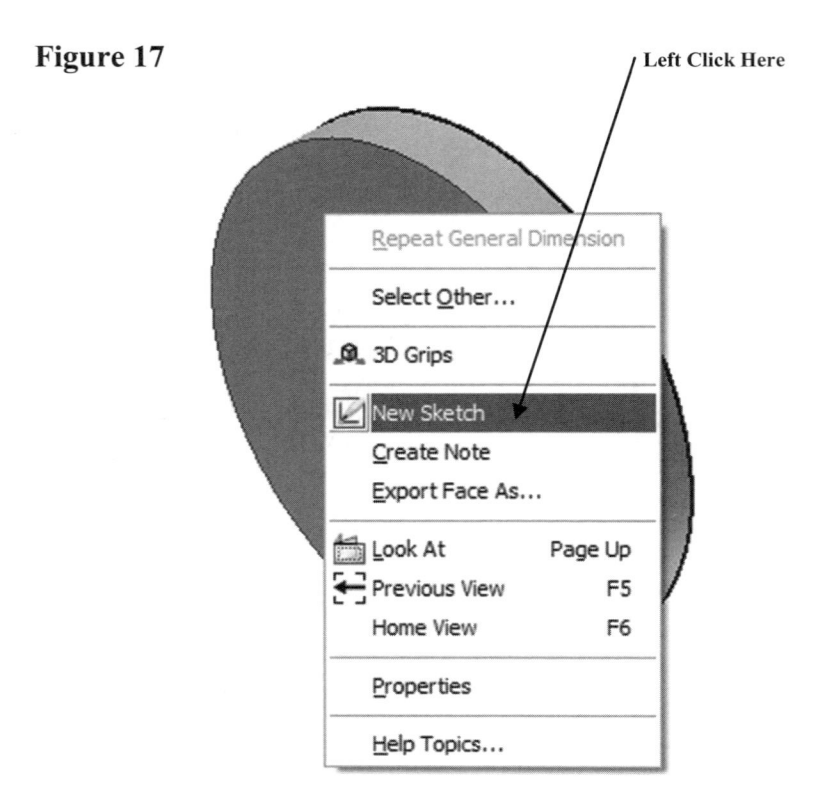

Figure 17

22. Inventor will start a new sketch on the selected surface as shown in Figure 18.

Figure 18

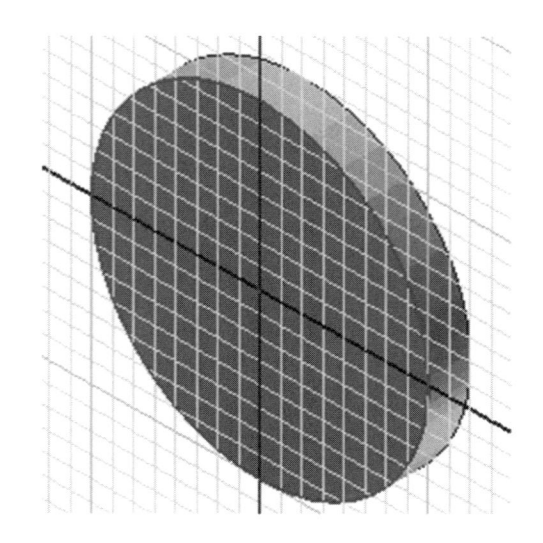

Chapter 5: Learning To Edit Existing Solid Models

23. Move the cursor to the upper middle portion of the screen and left click on the "Look At" icon as shown in Figure 19.

Figure 19

Left Click Here

24. Move the cursor to the front surface causing the edges to turn red and left click once as shown in Figure 20.

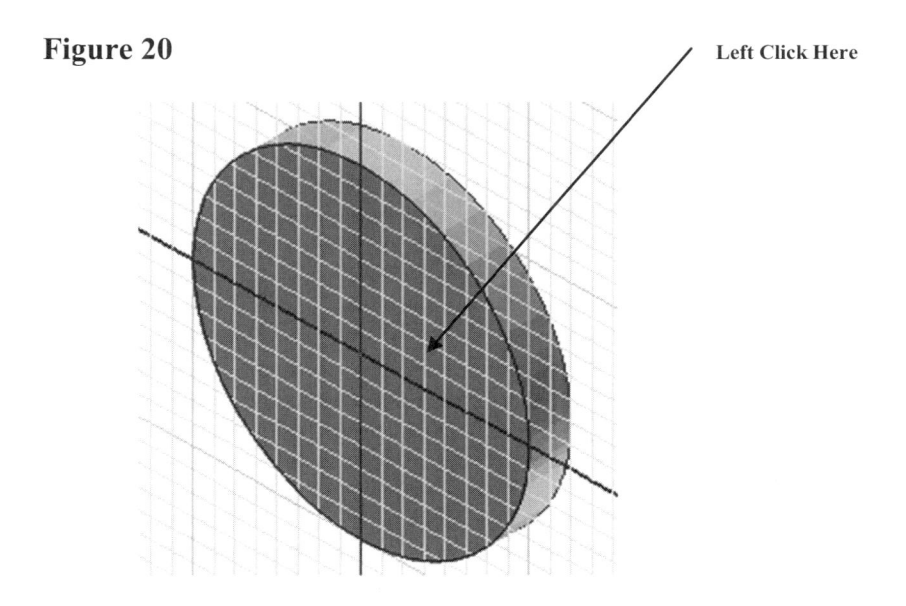

Figure 20

Left Click Here

225

Chapter 5: Learning To Edit Existing Solid Models

25. Inventor will now rotate the part providing a perpendicular view of the surface as shown in Figure 21.

Figure 21

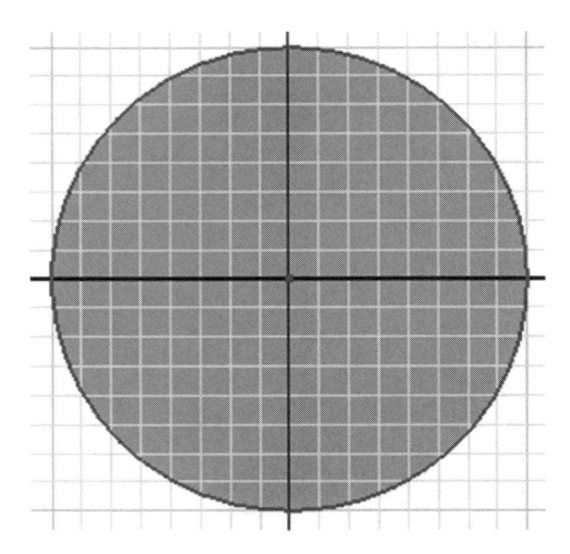

26. Move the cursor to the upper left corner of the screen and left click on **Center Point Circle** as shown in Figure 22.

Figure 22

Left Click Here

Chapter 5: Learning To Edit Existing Solid Models

27. Move the cursor to the center of the circle. After a green dot appears, move the cursor up staying directly above the center of the circle. Left click once as shown in Figure 23.

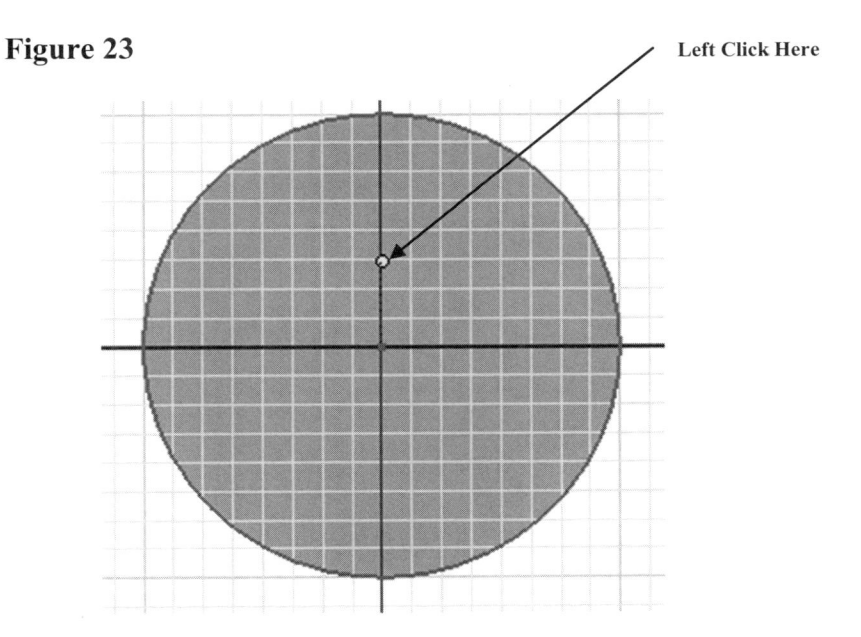

Figure 23   Left Click Here

28. Move the cursor out to the right to form a small circle. Left click as shown in Figure 24.

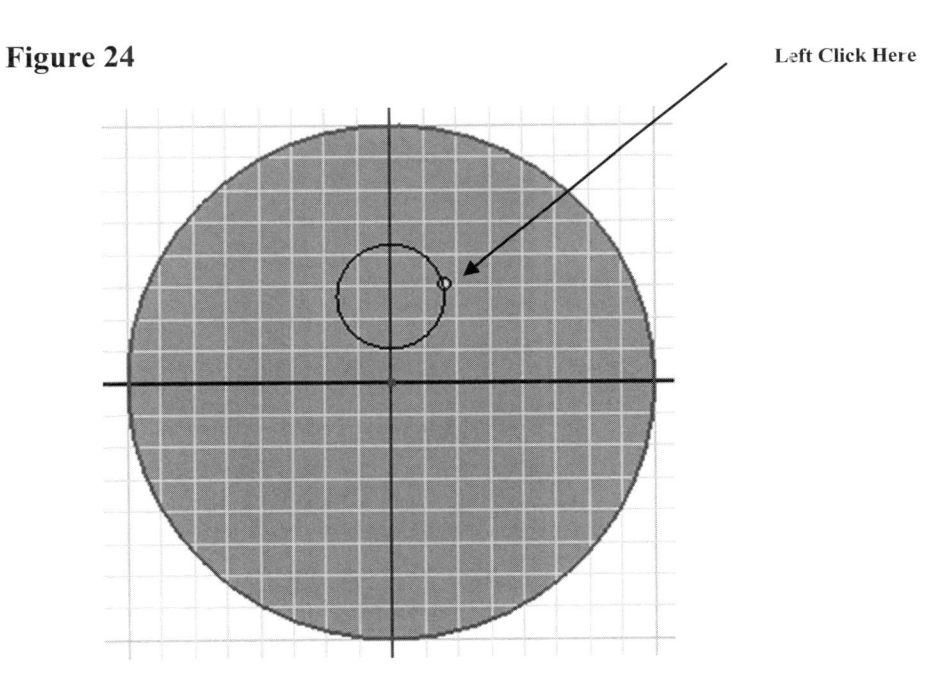

Figure 24   Left Click Here

Chapter 5: Learning To Edit Existing Solid Models

29. Move the cursor to the middle left portion of the screen and left click on **General Dimension** as shown in Figure 25.

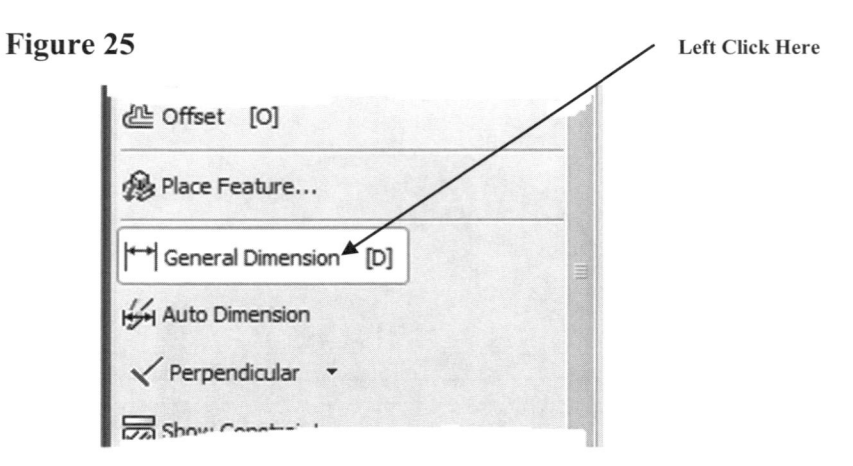

Figure 25 Left Click Here

30. After selecting **General Dimension** move the cursor over the edge (not center) of the circle until it turns red as shown in Figure 26. Select the line by left clicking once anywhere on the edge of the circle. The dimension will be attached to the cursor.

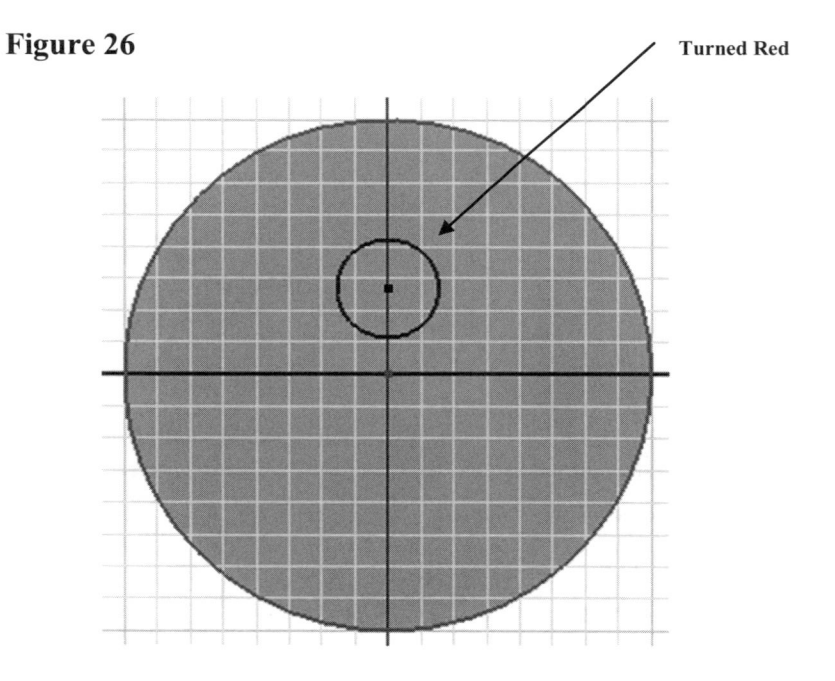

Figure 26 Turned Red

Chapter 5: Learning To Edit Existing Solid Models

31. Move the cursor around. The actual dimension of the line will appear as shown in Figure 27.

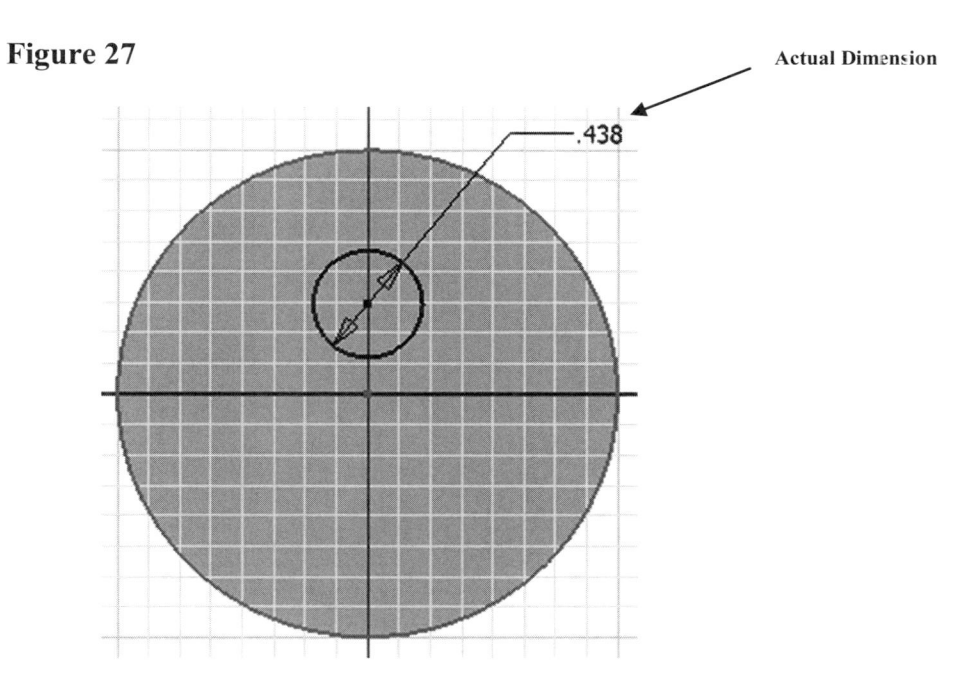

Figure 27

32. Move the cursor to where the dimension will be placed and left click once. While the dimension is still in red, left click once. The Edit Dimension dialog box will appear as shown in Figure 28.

Figure 28

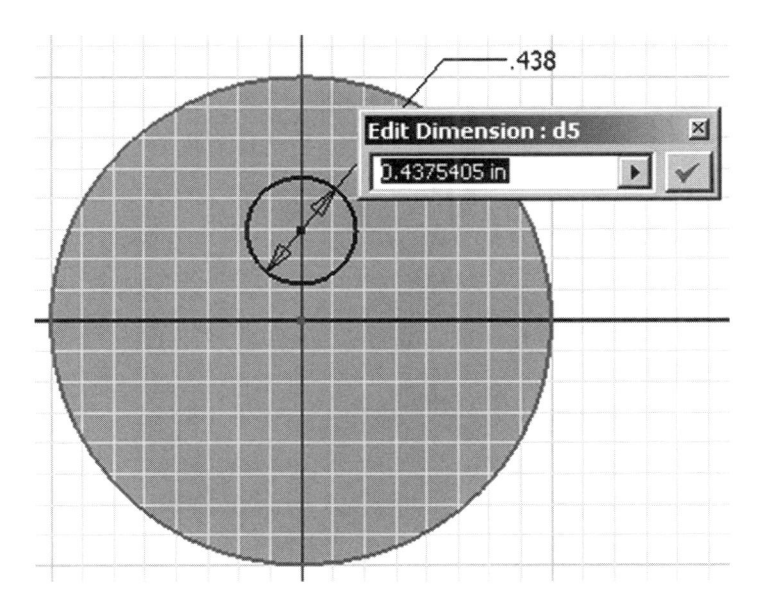

229

Chapter 5: Learning To Edit Existing Solid Models

33. To edit the dimension, type **.375** in the Edit Dimension dialog box (while the current dimension is highlighted) and press **Enter** on the keyboard.

34. The dimension of the circle will become .375 inches as shown in Figure 29. Use the Zoom icons to zoom out if necessary.

Figure 29

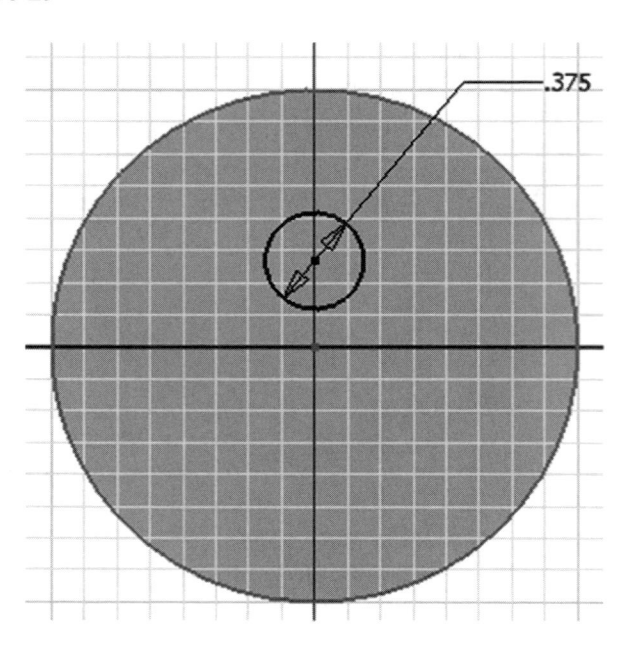

35. After the sketch is complete it is time to extrude the sketch into a solid. Right click anywhere on the drawing. A pop up menu will appear. Left click on **Done [Esc]** as shown in Figure 30.

Figure 30

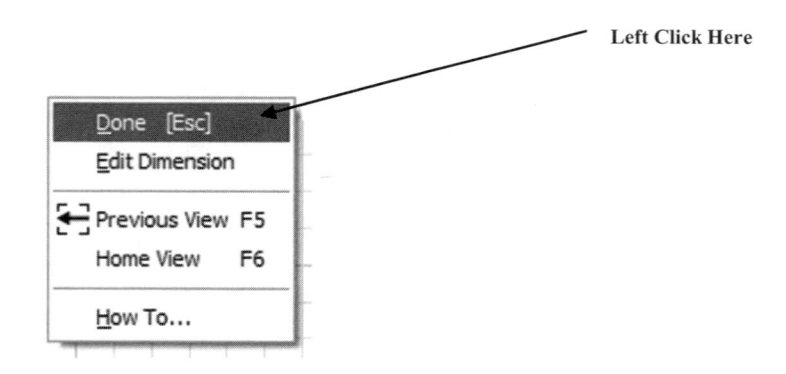

Chapter 5: Learning To Edit Existing Solid Models

36. After you have verified that no commands are active, right click anywhere on the sketch. A pop up menu will appear. Left click on **Finish Sketch** as shown in Figure 31.

Figure 31   **Left Click Here**

- Repeat Undo
- **Finish Sketch**
- Show All Degrees of Freedom
- Update
- Snap to Grid
- Show All Constraints   F8
- Constraint Visibility...
- Constraint Options...
- Create Line
- Crea...

37. Inventor is now out of the Sketch Panel and into the Part Features Panel. Notice that the commands at the left of the screen are now different. To work in the Part Features Panel a sketch must be present and have no opens (non-connected lines). If there are any opens in the sketch an error message will appear. Your screen should look similar to Figure 32.

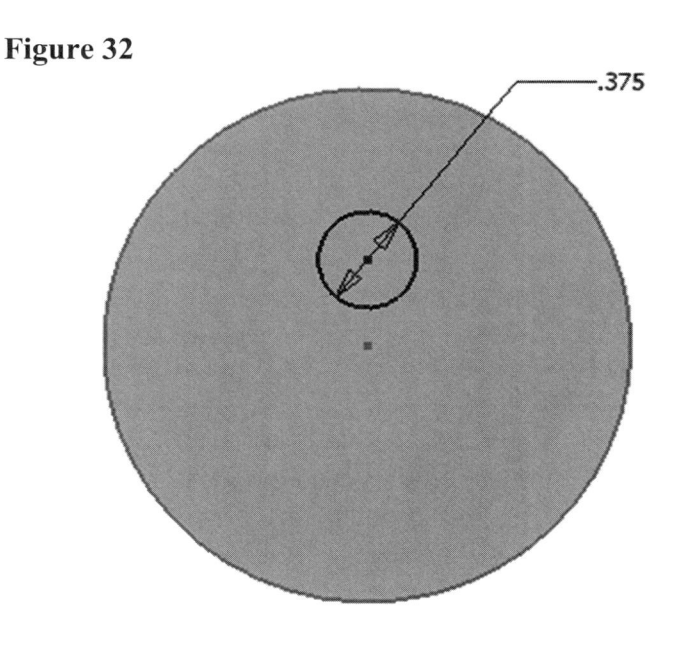

Figure 32

.375

231

Chapter 5: Learning To Edit Existing Solid Models

38. Right click around the sketch. A pop up menu will appear. Left click on **Isometric/Home View** as shown in Figure 33.

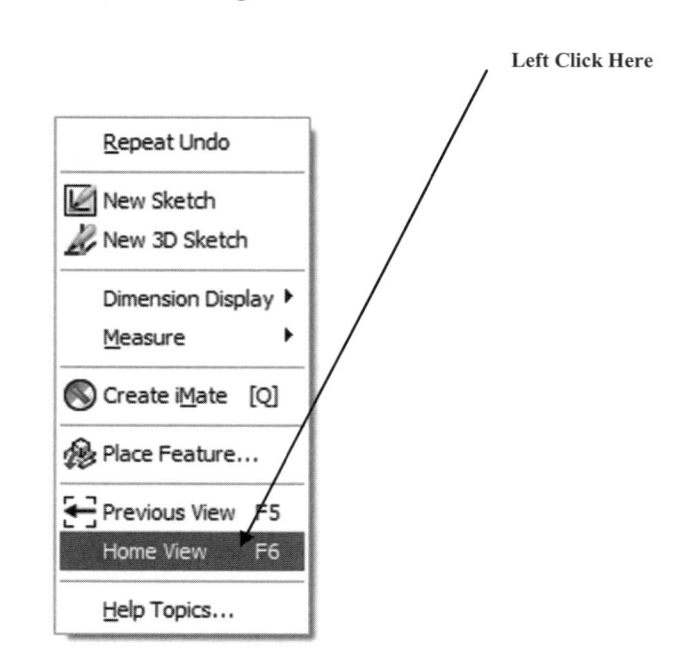

Figure 33

Left Click Here

39. The view will become isometric as shown in Figure 34.

Figure 34

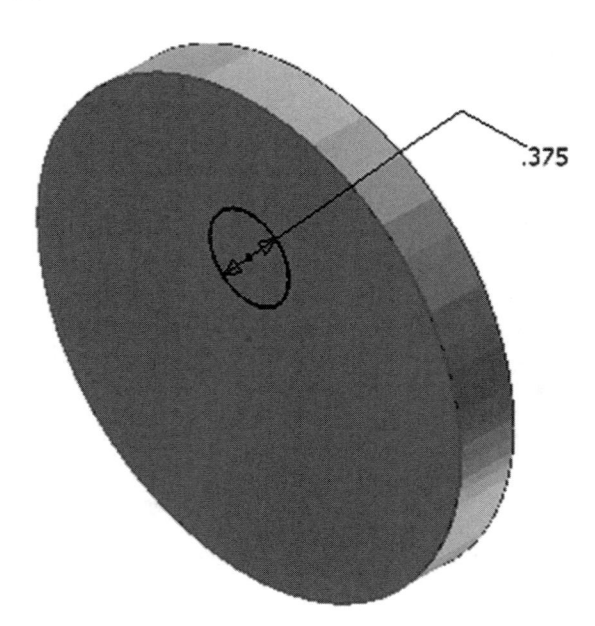

Chapter 5: Learning To Edit Existing Solid Models

40. Move the cursor to the middle left portion of the screen and left click on **Extrude**. The Extrude dialog box will appear. Inventor also provides a preview of the extrusion. If Inventor did not provide a preview of the extrusion move the cursor to the center of the circle causing it to turn red and left click once. If Inventor gave you an error message, there are opens (non-connected lines) somewhere on the sketch. Check each intersection for opens by using the **Extend** and **Trim** commands. Your screen should look similar to Figure 35.

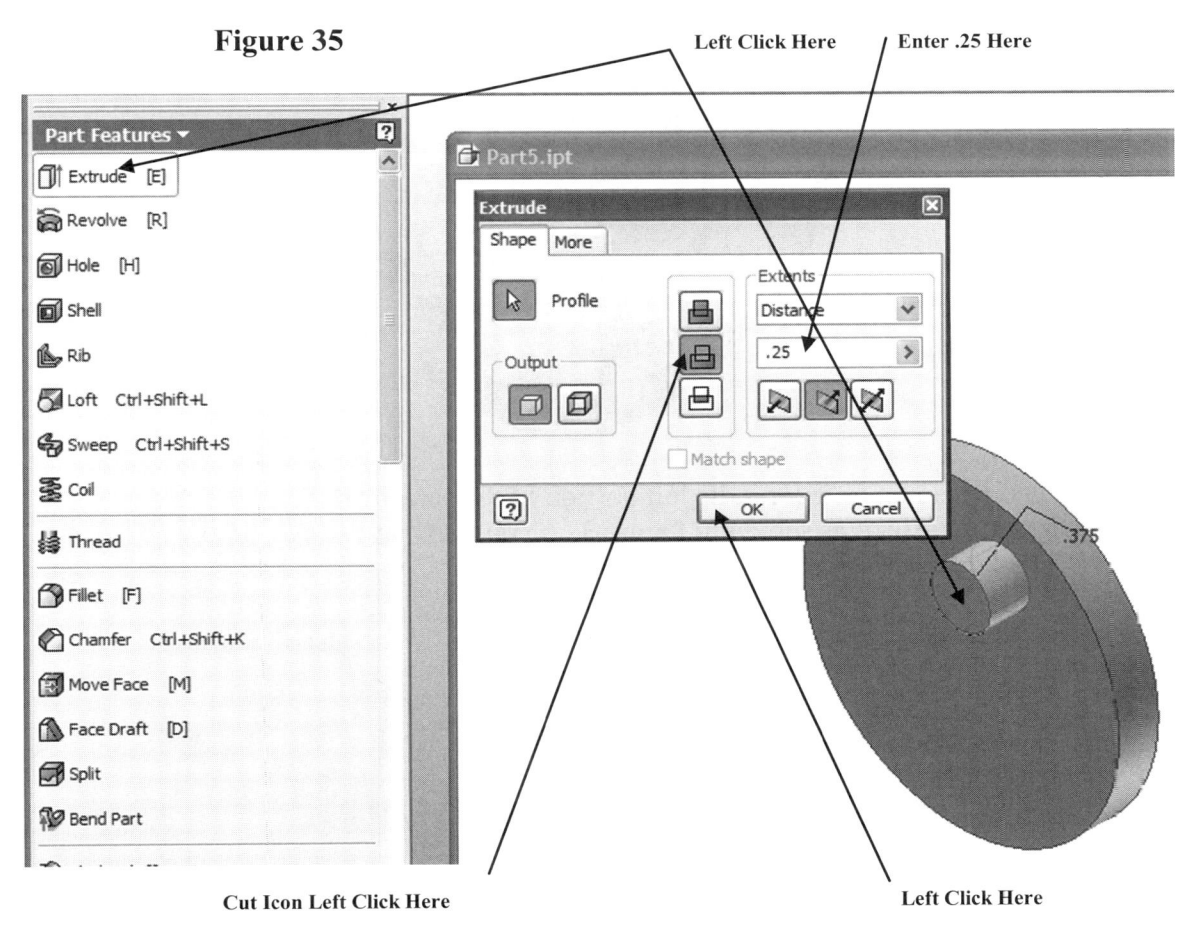

Figure 35

Cut Icon Left Click Here   Left Click Here

41. Enter **.25** under Distance. Left click on the "Cut" icon located in the middle of the dialog box as shown in Figure 35.

233

Chapter 5: Learning To Edit Existing Solid Models

42. Left click on **OK**. Your screen should look similar to Figure 36. You may have to use the zoom out command to view the entire part.

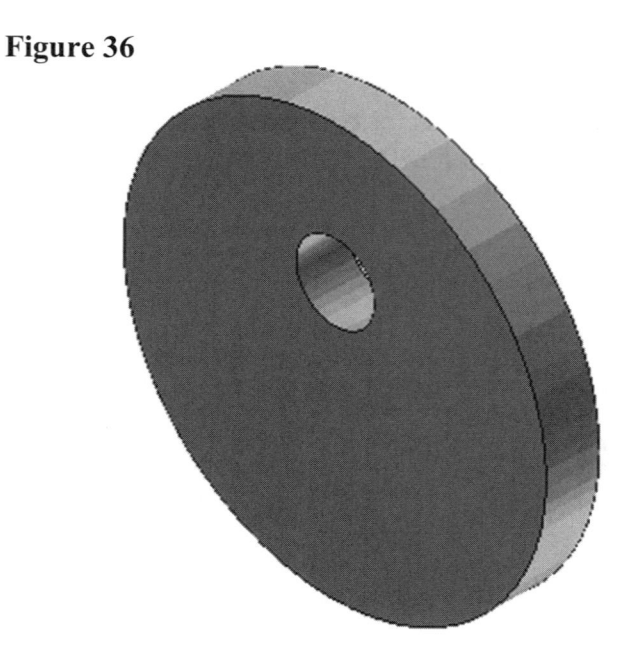

Figure 36

43. Move the cursor to the middle left portion of the screen and left click on **Circular Pattern** as shown in Figure 37. You may have to scroll down to locate it. Ensure the view is isometric as shown in Figure 36.

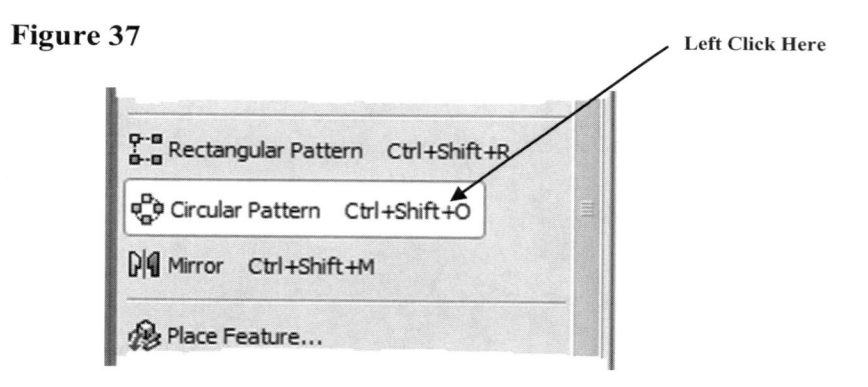

Figure 37

Left Click Here

Rectangular Pattern   Ctrl+Shift+R
Circular Pattern   Ctrl+Shift+O
Mirror   Ctrl+Shift+M
Place Feature...

Chapter 5: Learning To Edit Existing Solid Models

44. The Circular Pattern dialog box will appear as shown in Figure 38.

Figure 38

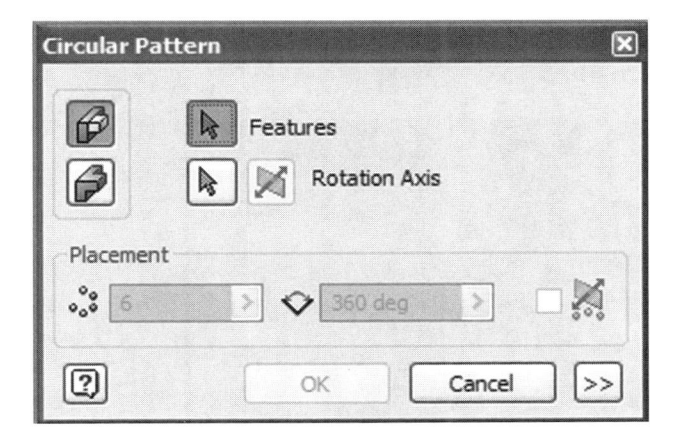

45. Move the cursor to the center of the circle (hole) causing the edges to become red dashed lines as shown in Figure 39.

Figure 39 Move Cursor Here

235

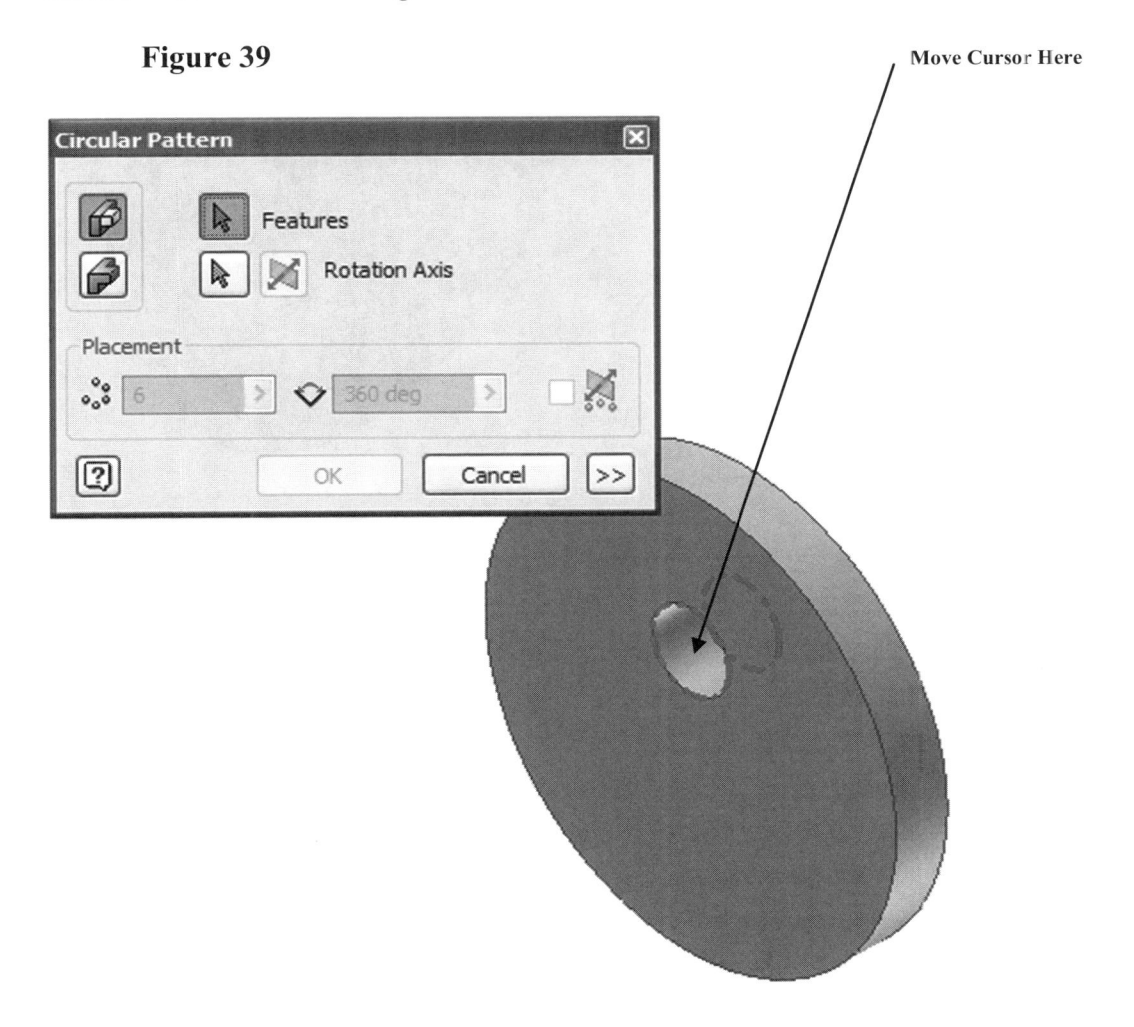

Chapter 5: Learning To Edit Existing Solid Models

46. Inventor will only find the circle (hole) if the view is isometric.

47. Left click inside the circle (hole). The edges of the circle (hole) will turn blue as shown in Figure 40.

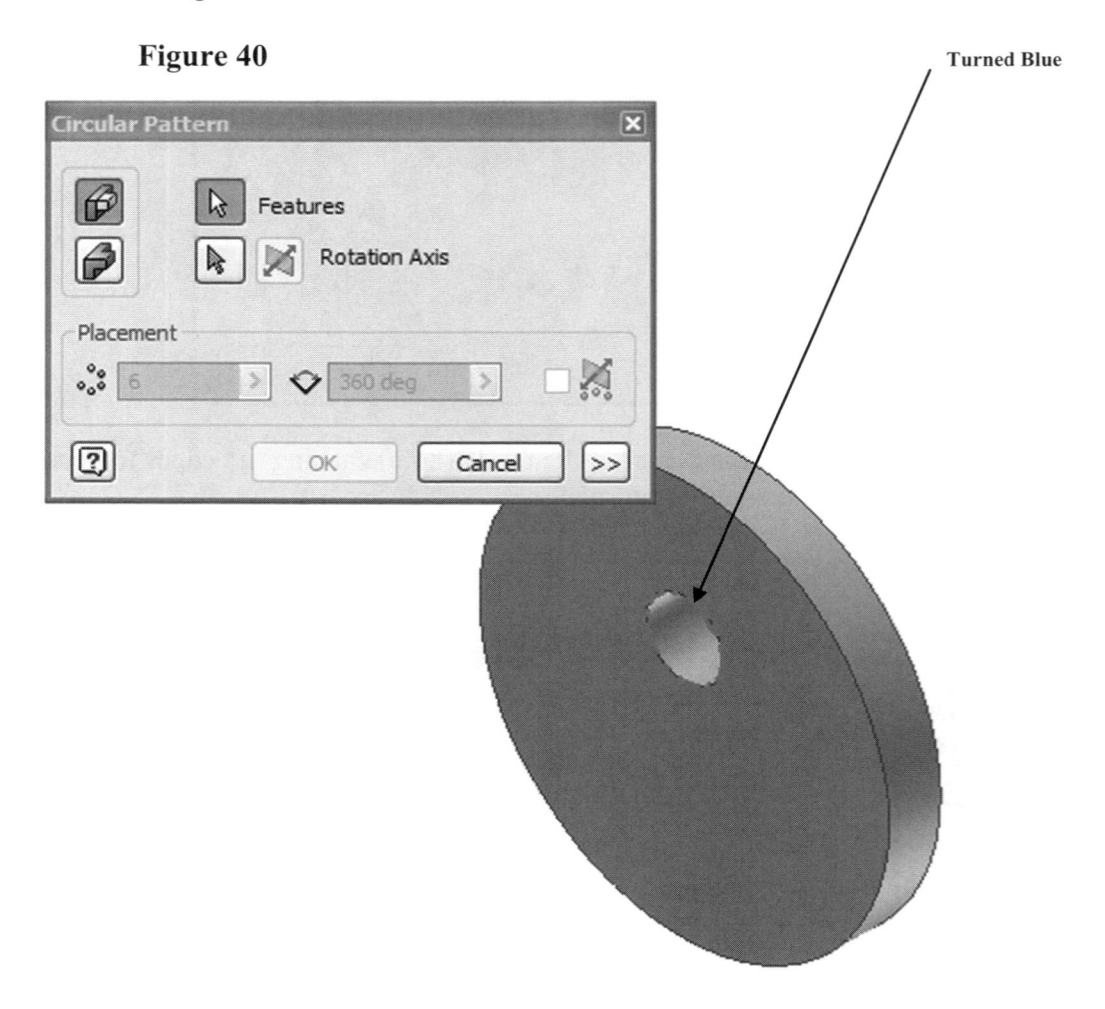

Figure 40

48. Left click on **Rotation Axis** located in the dialog box. Move the cursor over the outer edges of the part causing both edges to turn red and left click once as shown in Figure 41.

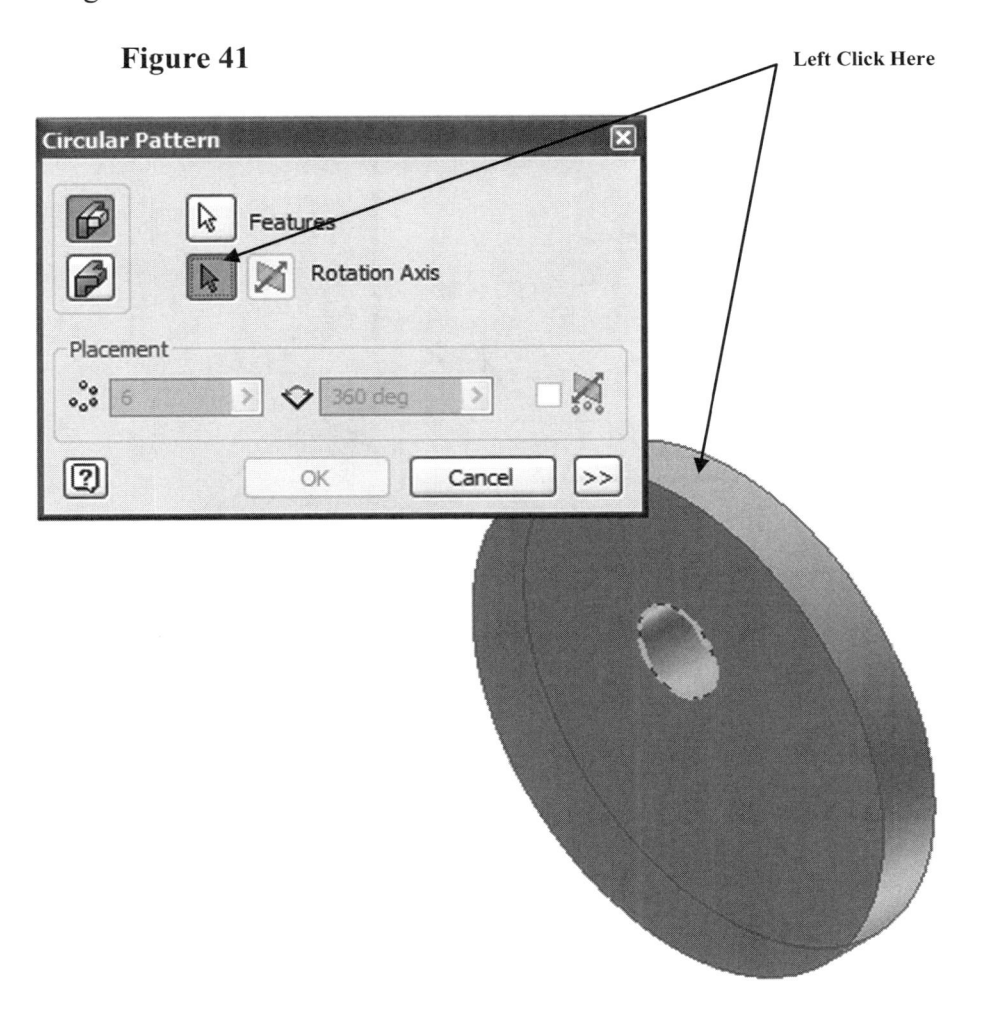

Figure 41

Chapter 5: Learning To Edit Existing Solid Models

49. Inventor will provide a preview of the anticipated circular pattern as shown in Figure 42.

Figure 42

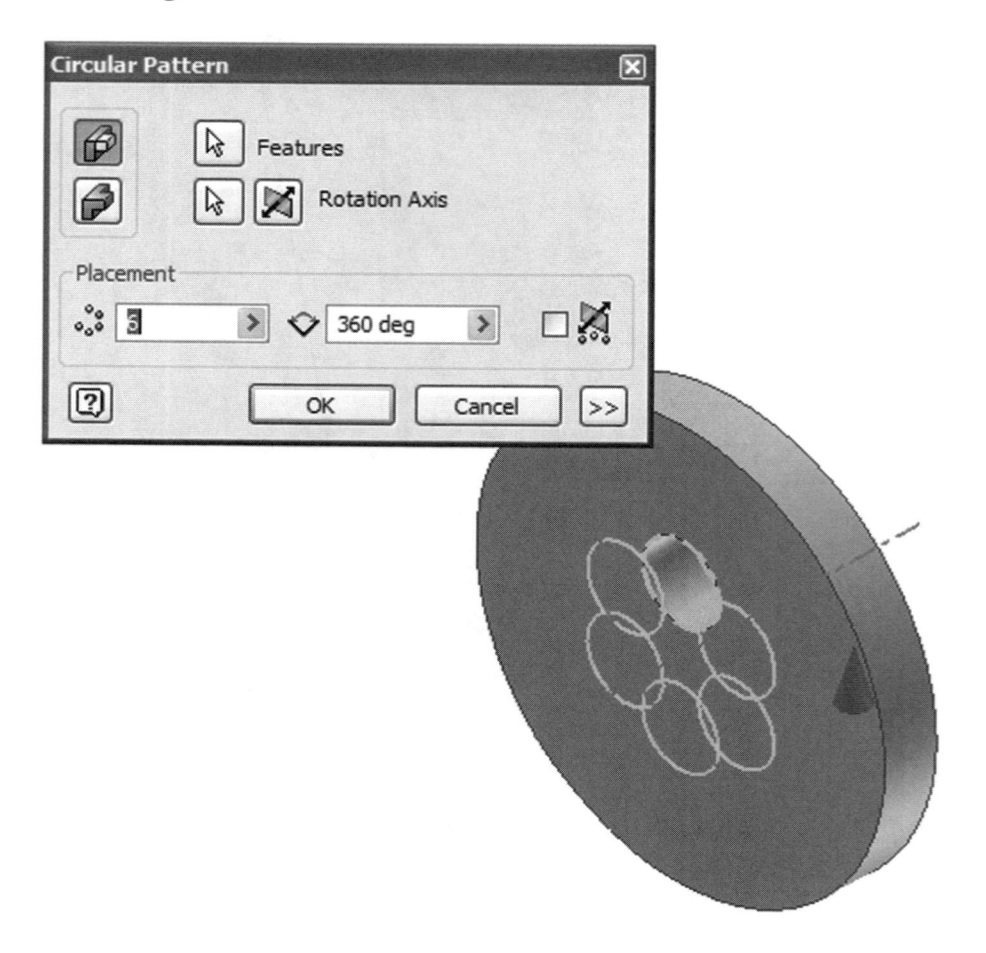

Chapter 5: Learning To Edit Existing Solid Models

50. Enter **3** under Placement (number of holes) and left click on **OK** as shown in Figure 43.

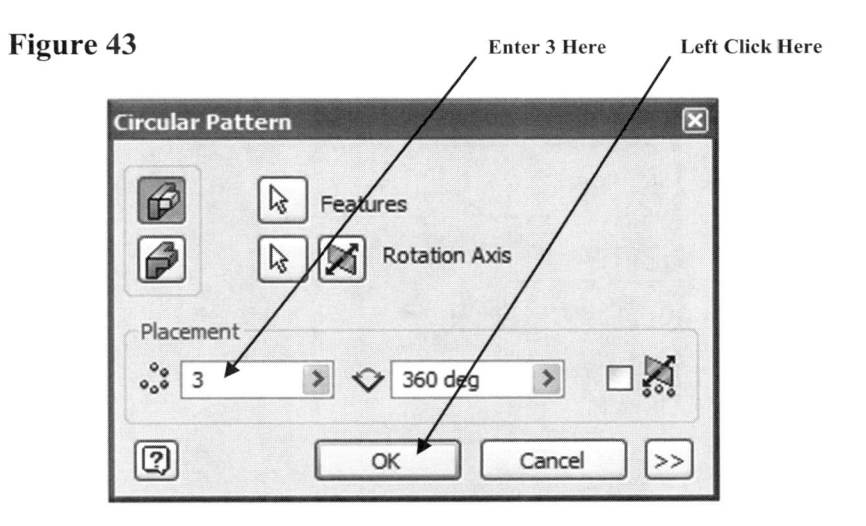

   Figure 43

51. Your screen should look similar to Figure 44.

   Figure 44

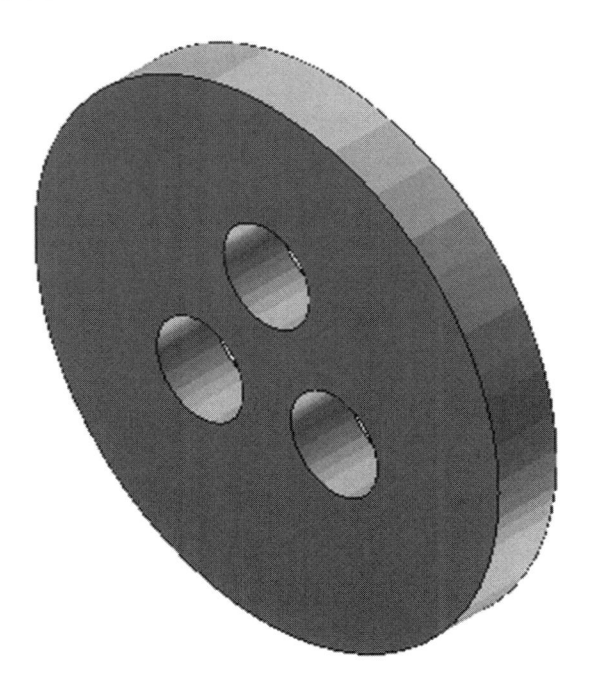

Chapter 5: Learning To Edit Existing Solid Models

52. Move the cursor over to the left middle portion of the screen and left click on **Fillet** as shown in Figure 45.

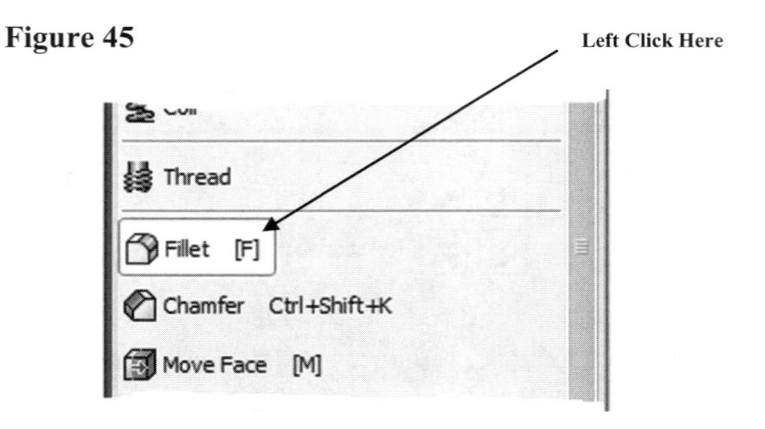

Figure 45

Left Click Here

53. The Fillet dialog box will appear. Highlight the numbers text under Radius by left clicking on the text (holding the left mouse button down). Drag the cursor across the text as shown in Figure 46.

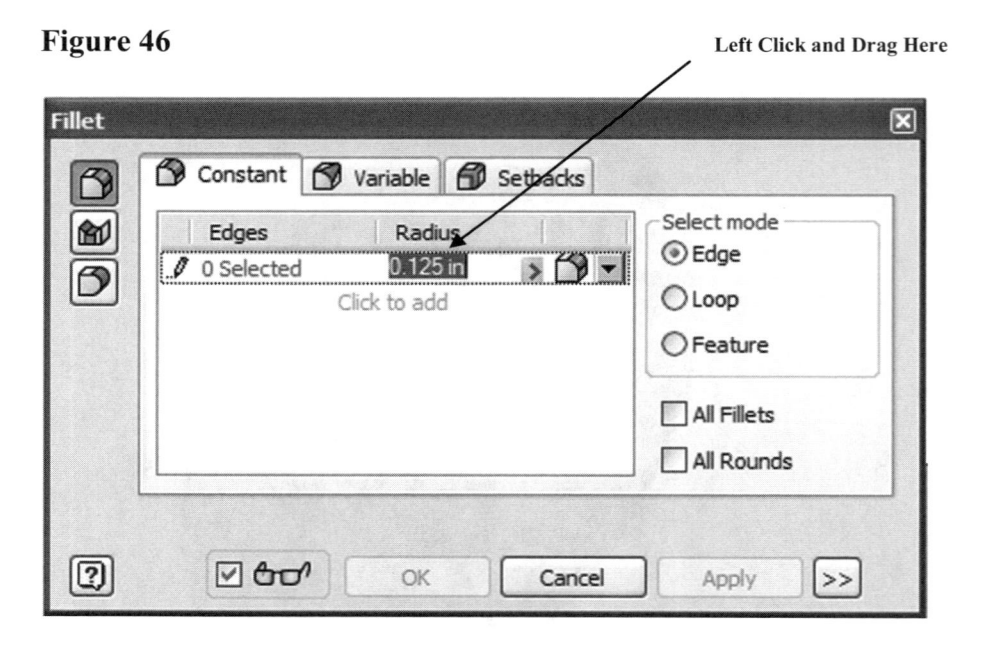

Figure 46

Left Click and Drag Here

240

Chapter 5: Learning To Edit Existing Solid Models

54. Enter **.0625** for the Radius and press **Enter** on the keyboard as shown in Figure 47.

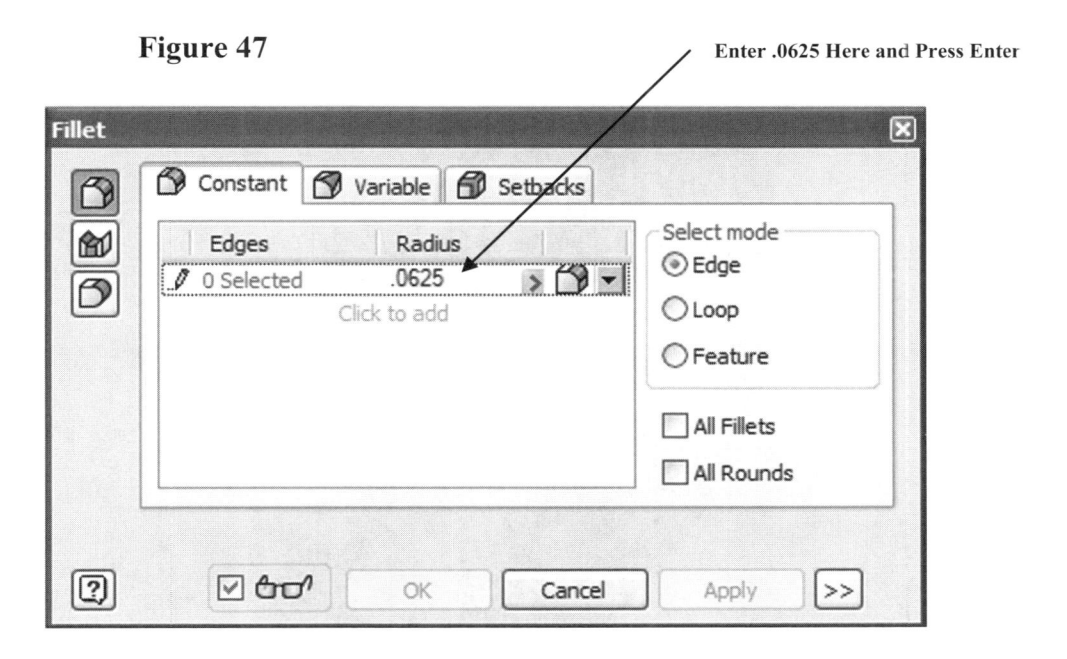

Figure 47

55. Move the cursor over the front edge of the part causing it to turn red and left click once. Inventor will provide a preview of the anticipated fillet as shown in Figure 48.

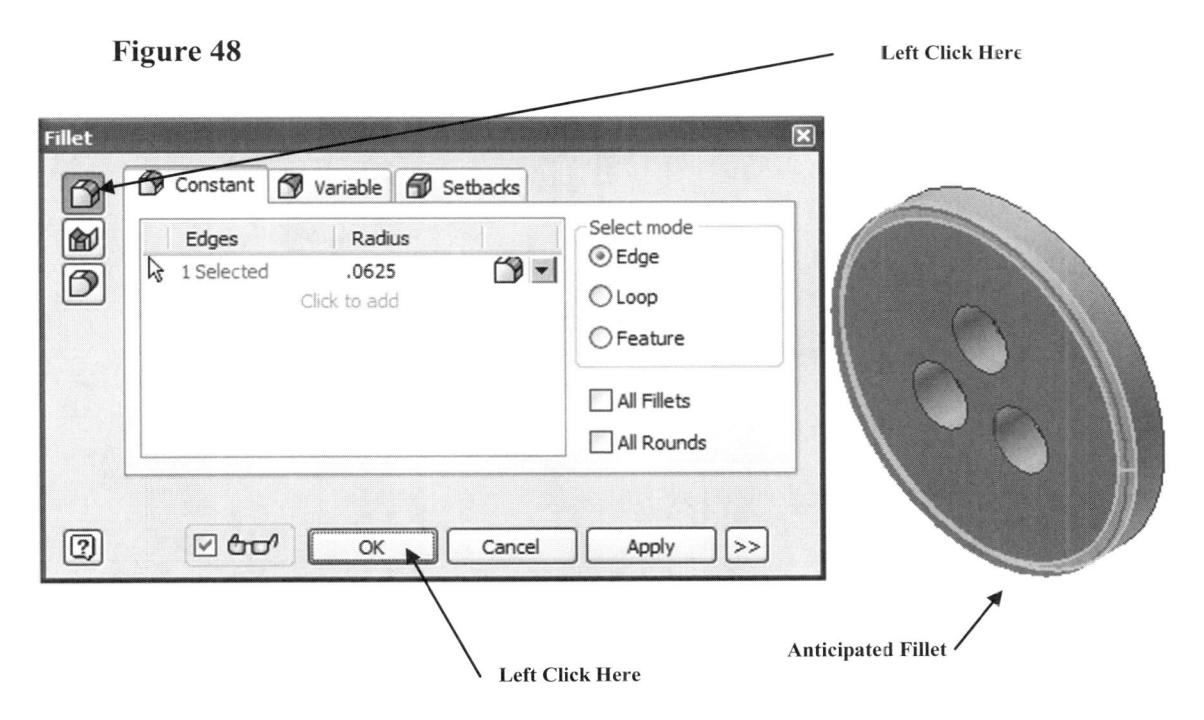

Figure 48

56. Left click on **OK** as shown in Figure 48.

Chapter 5: Learning To Edit Existing Solid Models

57. Your screen should look similar to Figure 49.

Figure 49

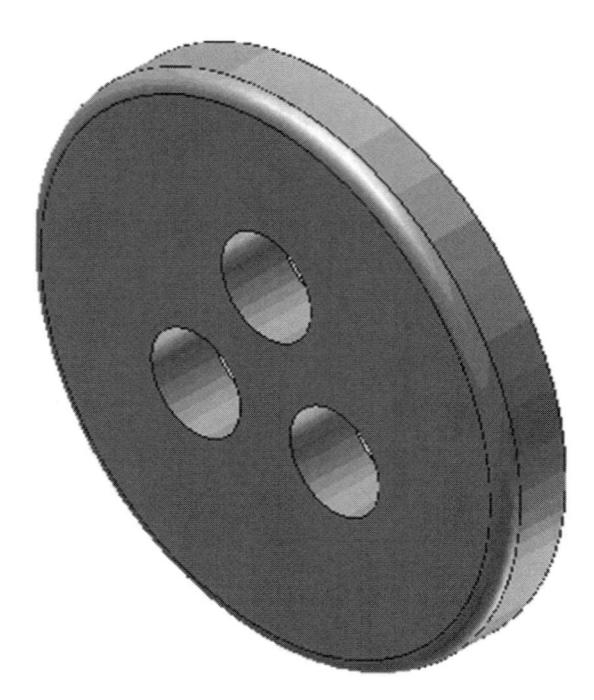

Chapter 5: Learning To Edit Existing Solid Models

58. If for some reason a change needs to be made to this part, it can be accomplished by editing either a sketch or a feature located in the Part Tree at the lower left corner of the screen as shown in Figure 50.

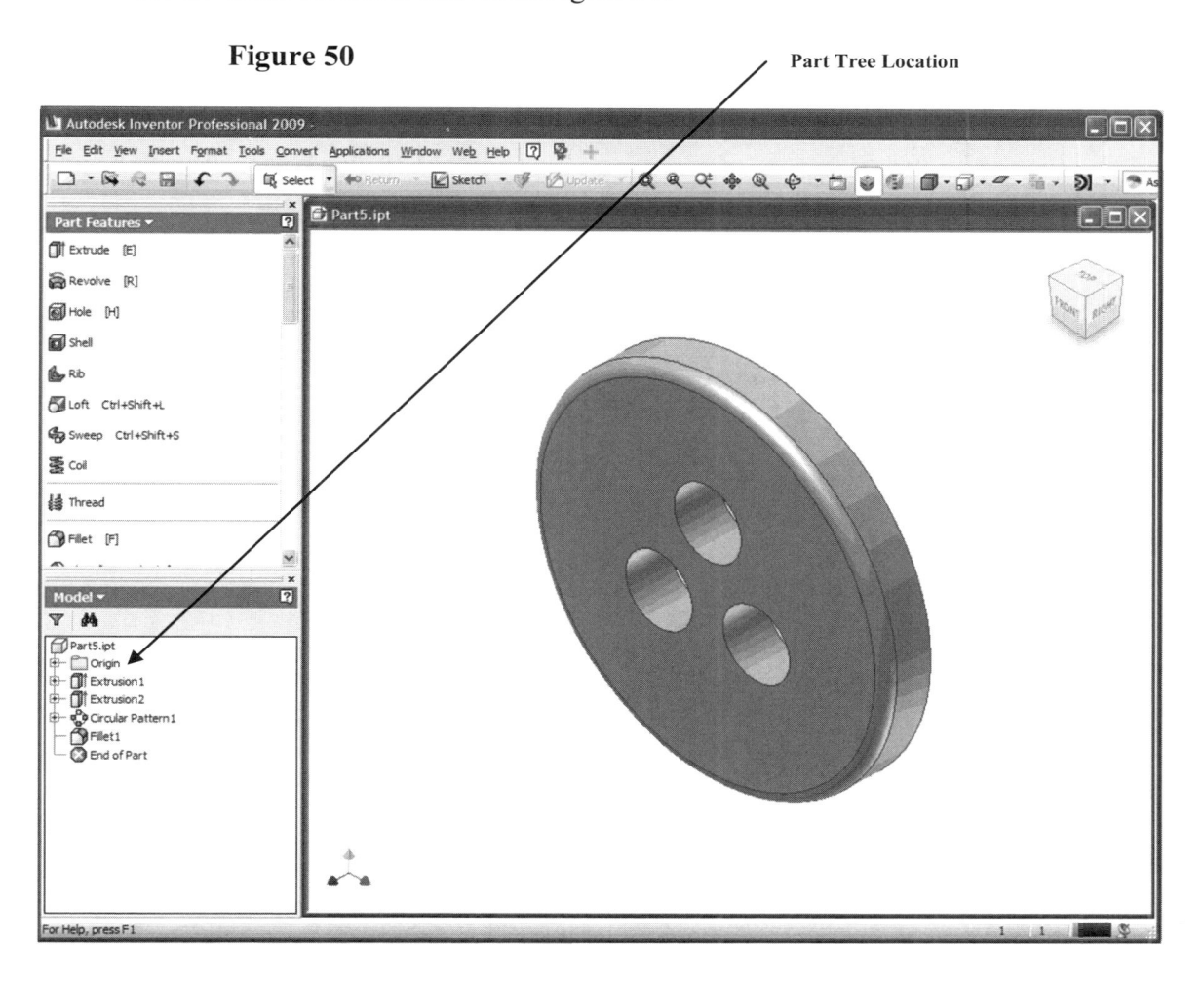

Figure 50

Chapter 5: Learning To Edit Existing Solid Models

59. A close-up of the Part Tree is shown in Figure 51. Left click on each of the "plus" signs in the part tree. The tree will expand showing more details for part construction. If the entire part tree is not visible, move the cursor to the border that separates the upper panel from the lower panel. Double arrows will appear. After the arrows appear, hold the left mouse button down to drag the border upward. More of the part tree will be exposed as shown in Figure 51.

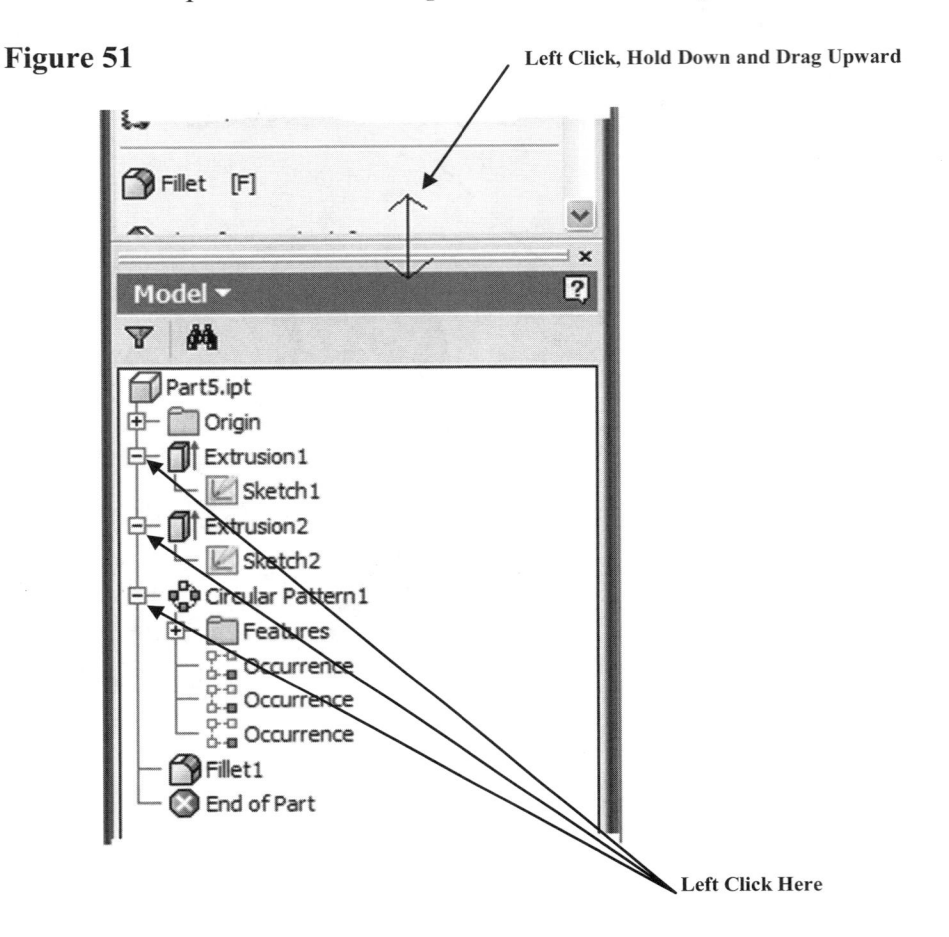

Figure 51

244

Chapter 5: Learning To Edit Existing Solid Models

60. If a change needs to be made to any portion of the part that was constructed using a Sketch1, the change can be made here.

61. Move the cursor over Sketch1. A red box will appear around the text "Sketch1" as shown in Figure 52.

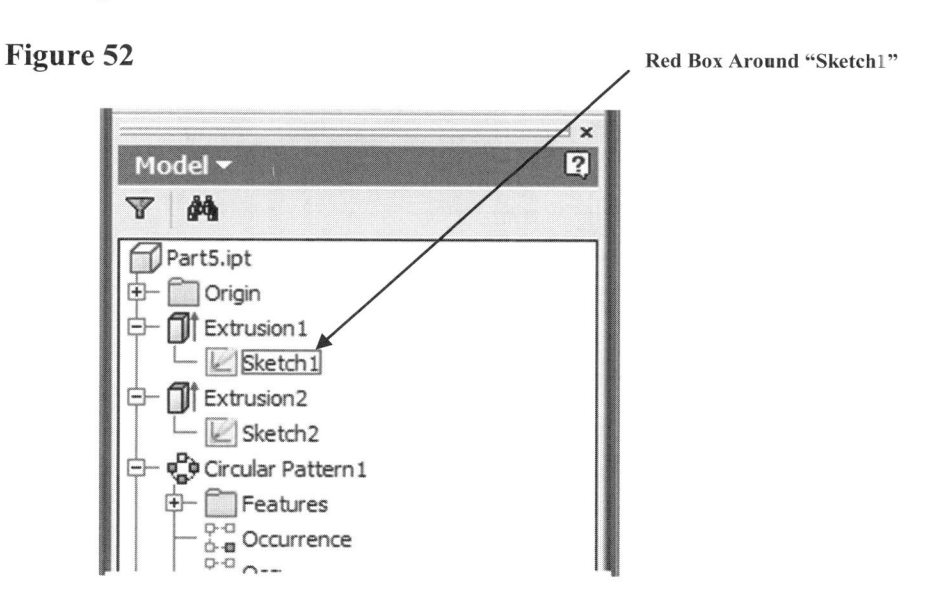

Figure 52

Red Box Around "Sketch1"

62. The original sketch will also appear as shown in Figure 53.

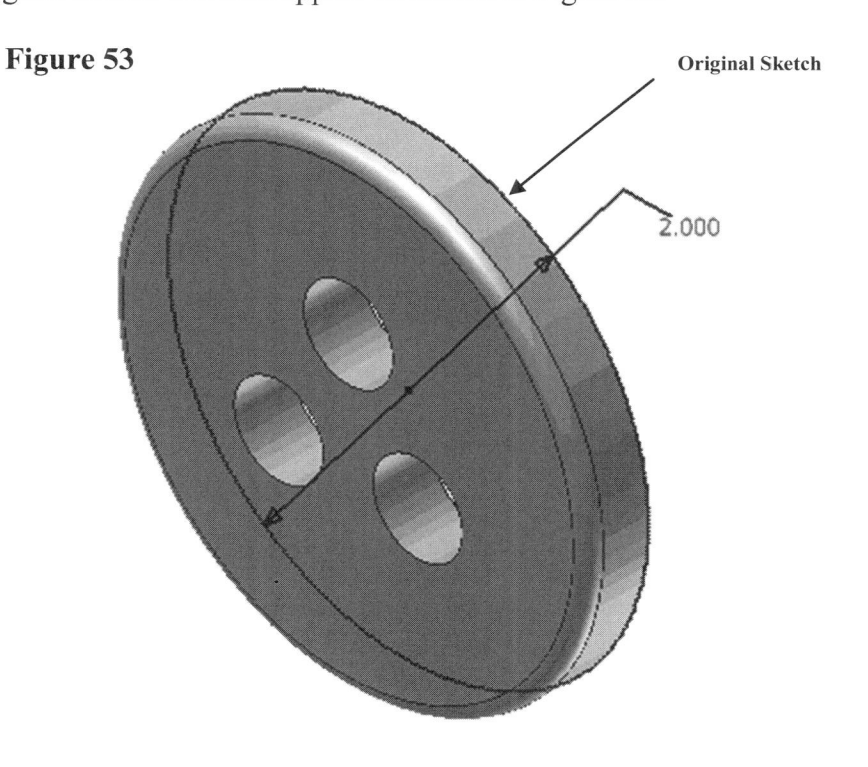

Figure 53

Original Sketch

2.000

245

Chapter 5: Learning To Edit Existing Solid Models

63. Right click on **Sketch1**. The text "Sketch1" will become highlighted. A pop up menu will appear. Left click on **Edit Sketch** as shown in Figure 54.

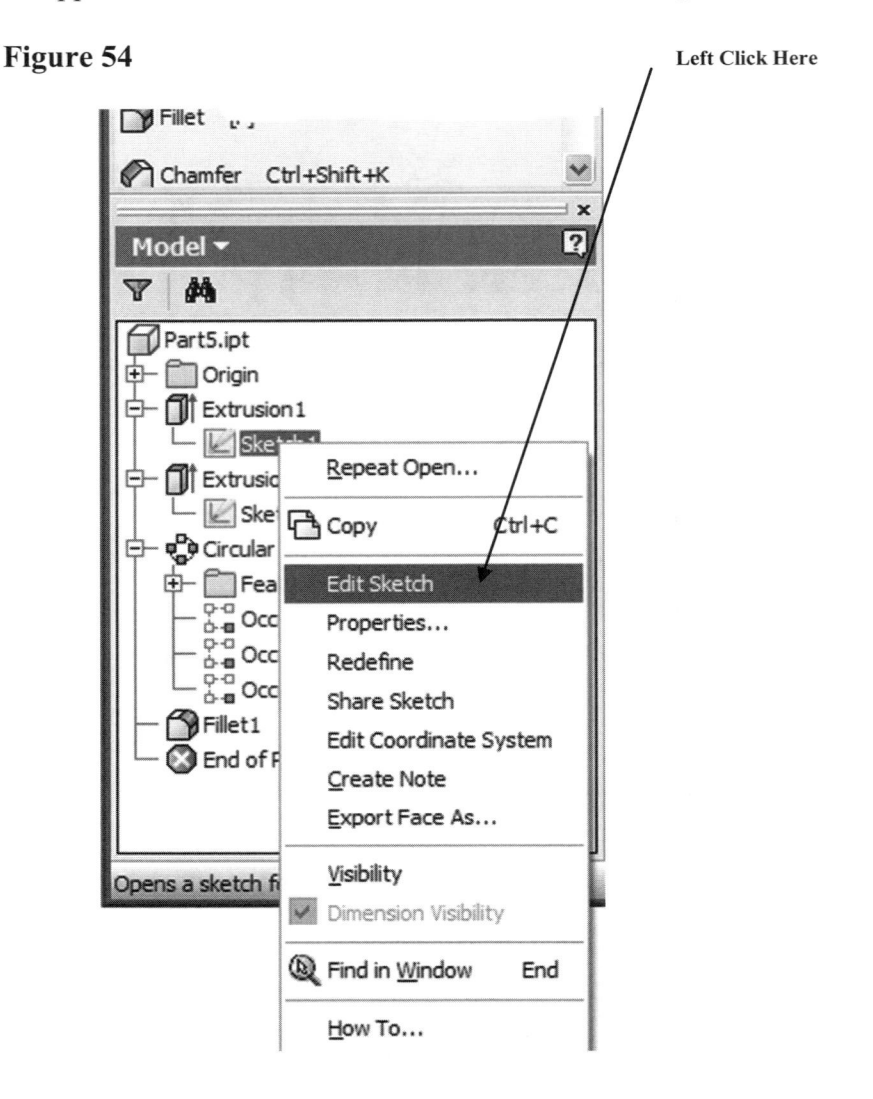

Figure 54

Chapter 5: Learning To Edit Existing Solid Models

64. The original sketch will appear as shown in Figure 55.

Figure 55

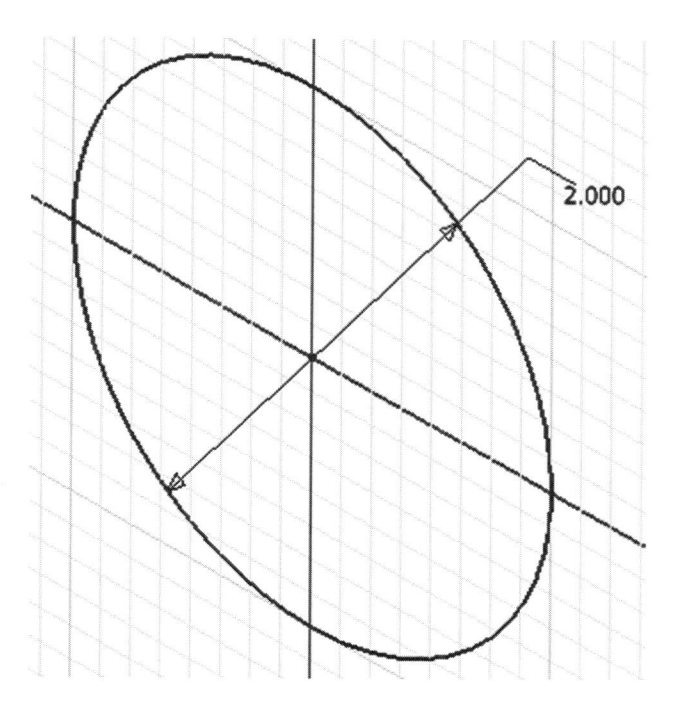

65. Move the cursor to the upper middle portion of the screen and left click on the "Look At" icon as shown in Figure 56.

Figure 56

247

Chapter 5: Learning To Edit Existing Solid Models

66. Move the cursor over to the part tree and left click on the "plus" sign to the left of Origin. The part tree will expand displaying all three work planes. Move the cursor over the text "XY Plane". A red box will appear around XY Plane and the sketch itself. After the red box appears, left click once on the **XY Plane** as shown in Figure 57.

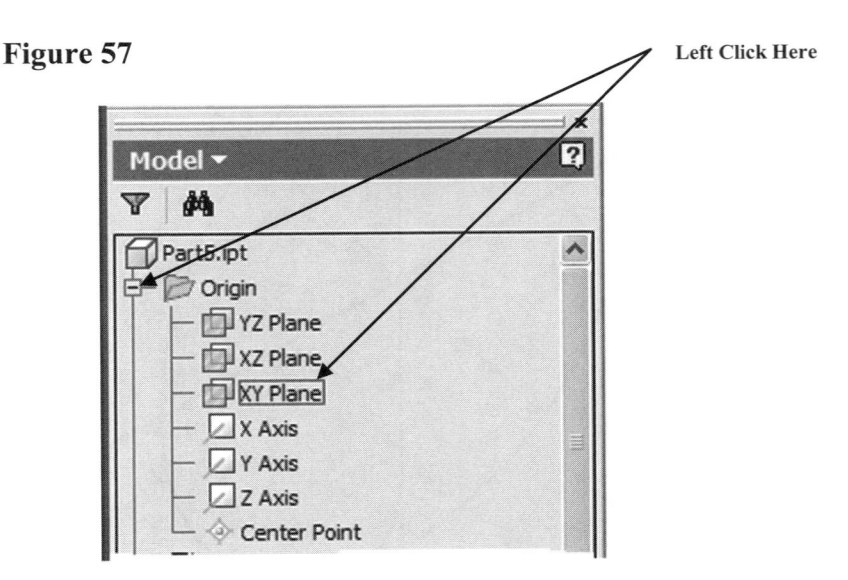

Figure 57

67. Inventor will provide a perpendicular view of the sketch similar to when the sketch was first constructed. Your screen should look similar to Figure 58.

Figure 58

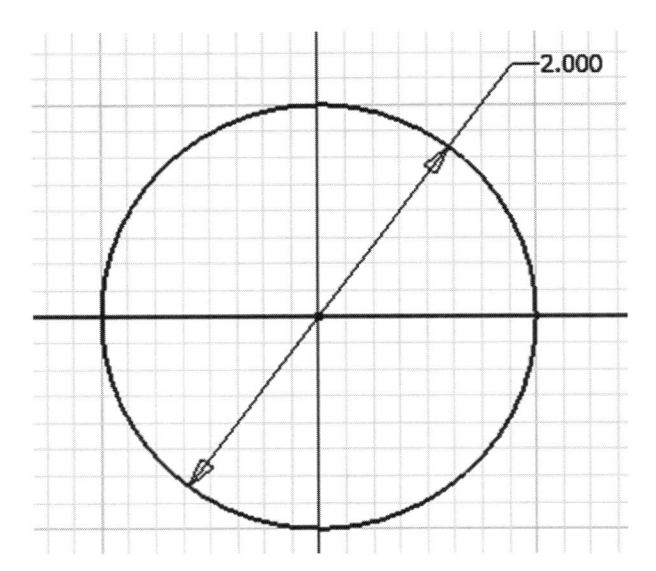

Chapter 5: Learning To Edit Existing Solid Models

68. Start by modifying the diameter of the part. First, double click on the overall dimension. The Edit Dimension dialog box will appear as shown in Figure 59.

Figure 59

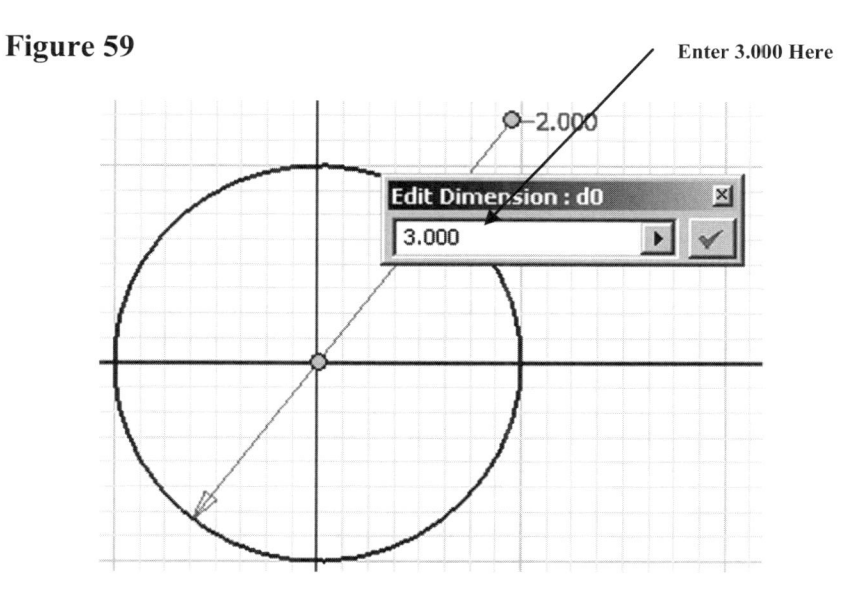

Enter **3.000** Here

69. Enter **3.000** as shown in Figure 59. Press **Enter** on the keyboard.

70. The diameter of the part will increase to 3.000 as shown in Figure 60.

Figure 60

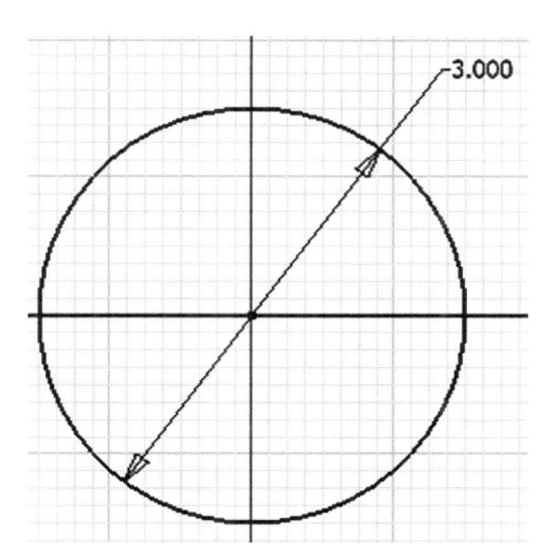

249

Chapter 5: Learning To Edit Existing Solid Models

71. Move the cursor to the upper middle portion of the screen and left click on **Update** as shown in Figure 61.

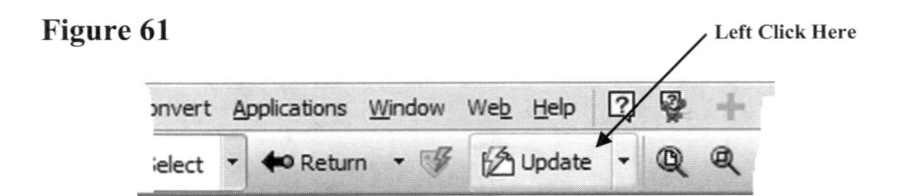

   Figure 61

72. Inventor will automatically update the part as shown in Figure 62. The part will be updated without the need to repeat any of the steps that created the original part.

   Figure 62

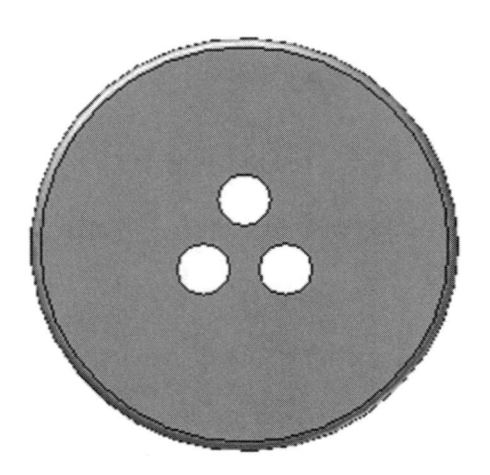

Chapter 5: Learning To Edit Existing Solid Models

73.   Move the cursor over the text "Extrusion1". A red box will appear around the text. After the red box appears, left click once on **Extrusion1** as shown in Figure 57.

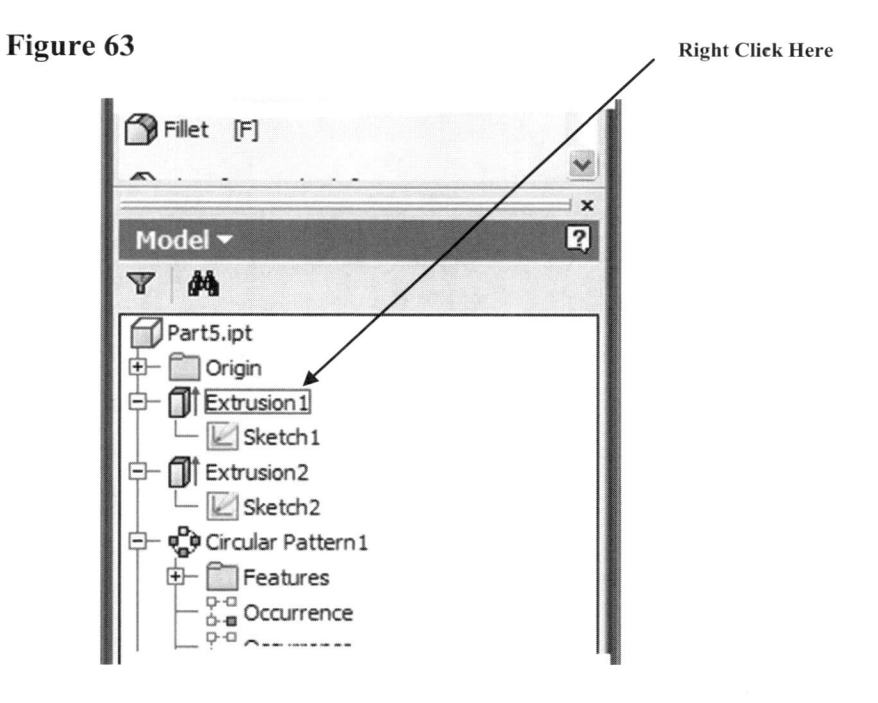

Figure 63

Right Click Here

Chapter 5: Learning To Edit Existing Solid Models

74. A pop up menu will appear. Left click on **Edit Feature** as shown in Figure 64.

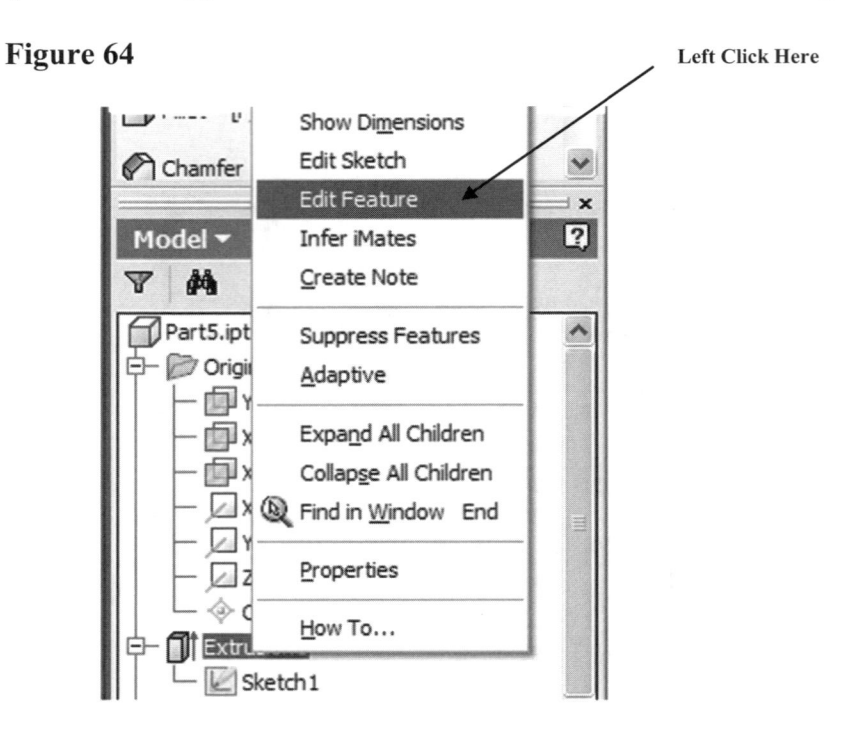

Figure 64

75. The Extrusion dialog box will appear. Enter **.500** for the extrusion distance and left click on **OK** as shown in Figure 65.

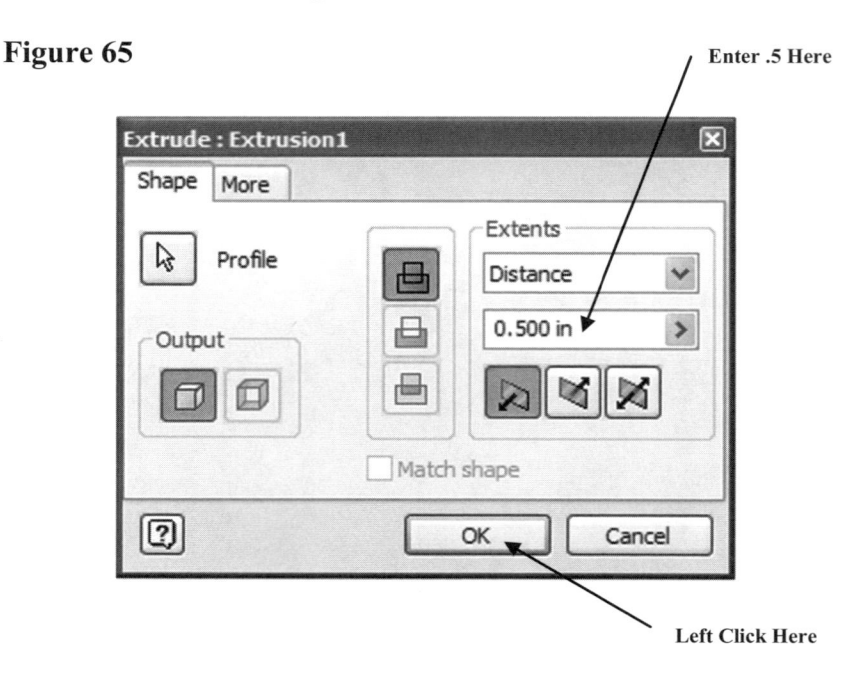

Figure 65

252

Chapter 5: Learning To Edit Existing Solid Models

76. Move the cursor to the upper middle portion of the screen and left click on **Update** as shown in Figure 66.

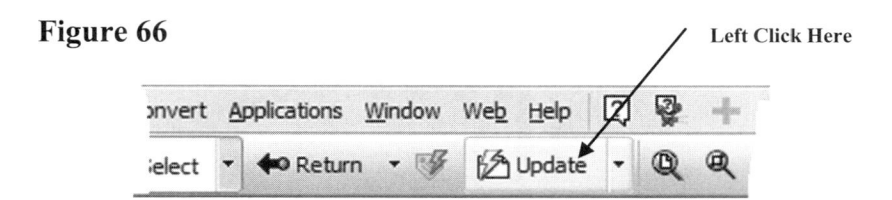

Figure 66

Left Click Here

77. Inventor will automatically update the part. Notice that the holes are no longer thru holes as shown in Figure 67.

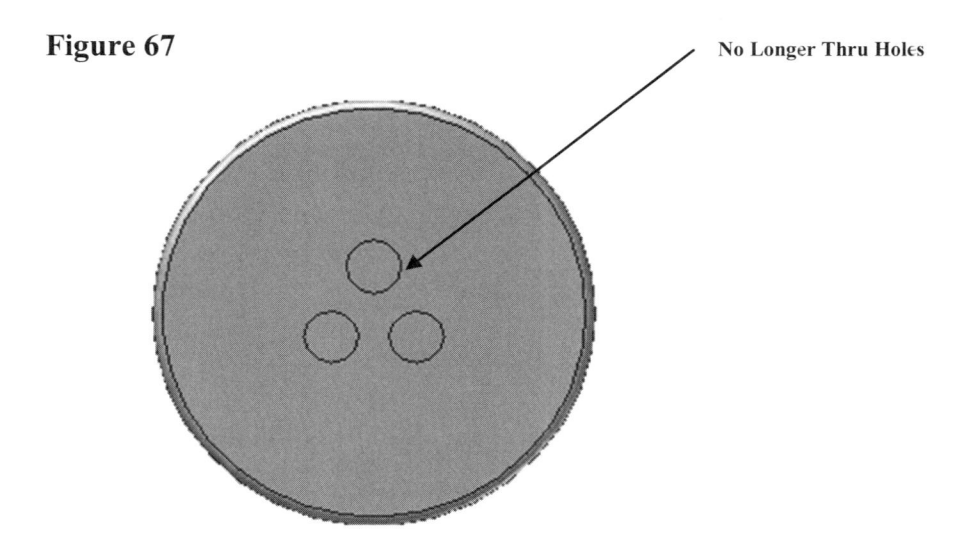

Figure 67

No Longer Thru Holes

Chapter 5: Learning To Edit Existing Solid Models

78. Right click anywhere on the screen. A pop up menu will appear. Left click on **Isometric/Home View** as shown in Figure 68.

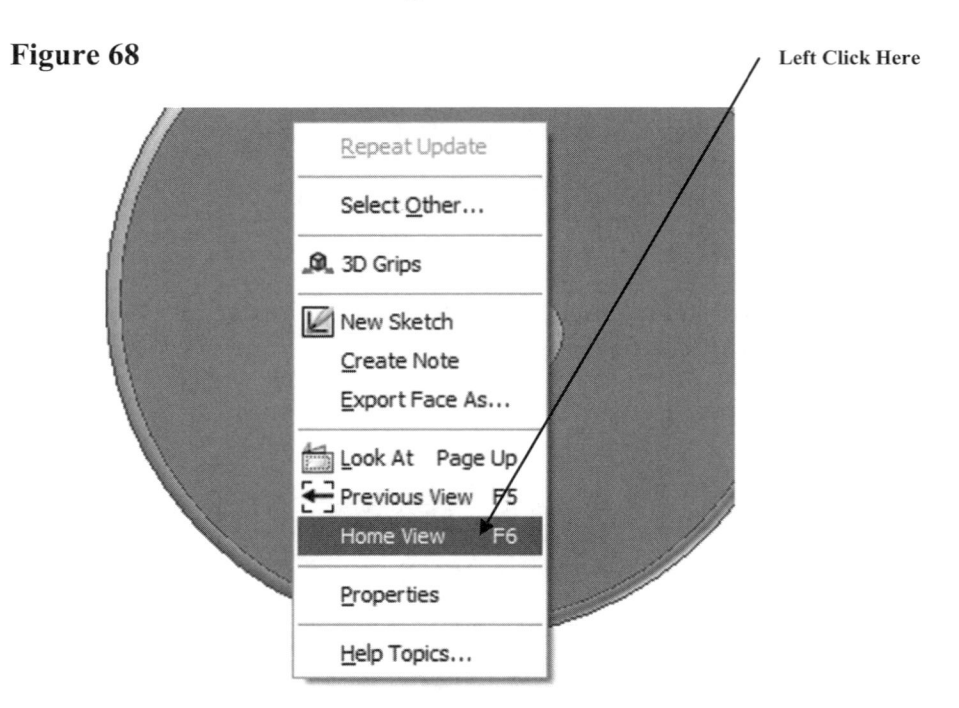

Figure 68

79. The part will now be viewed in Isometric. Your screen should look similar to Figure 69.

Figure 69

Chapter 5: Learning To Edit Existing Solid Models

80. Move the cursor over the text "Sketch2". A red box will appear around the text. After the red box appears, left click once on **Sketch2** as shown in Figure 57.

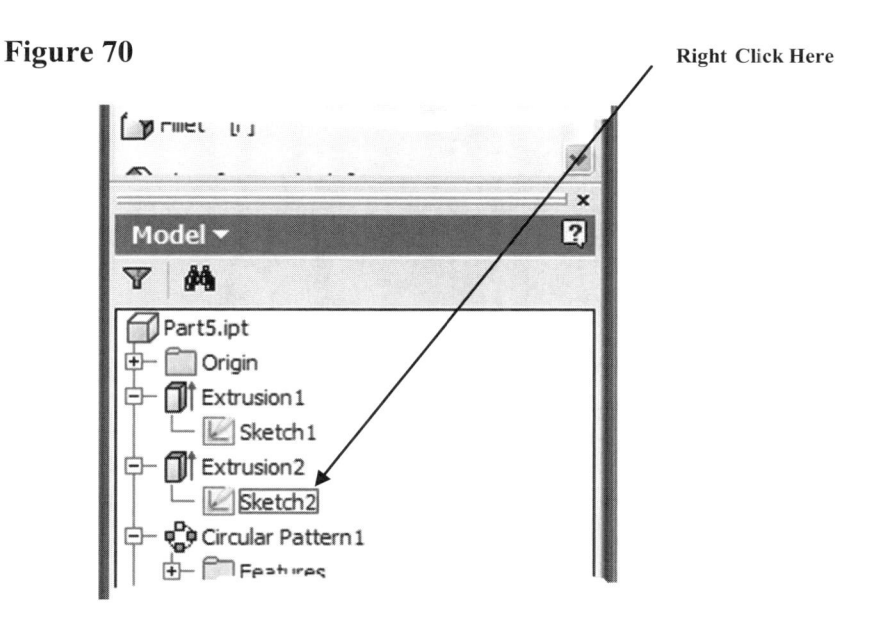

Figure 70

Right Click Here

81. A pop up menu will appear. Left click on **Edit Sketch** as shown in Figure 71.

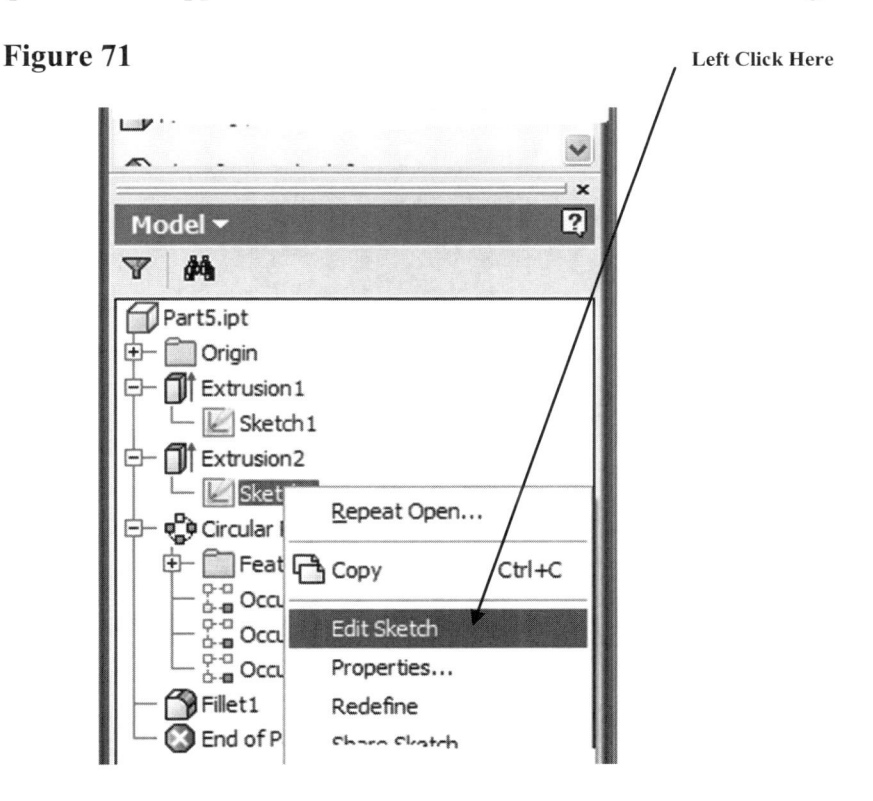

Figure 71

Left Click Here

255

Chapter 5: Learning To Edit Existing Solid Models

82. The original sketch will appear as shown in Figure 72.

Figure 72

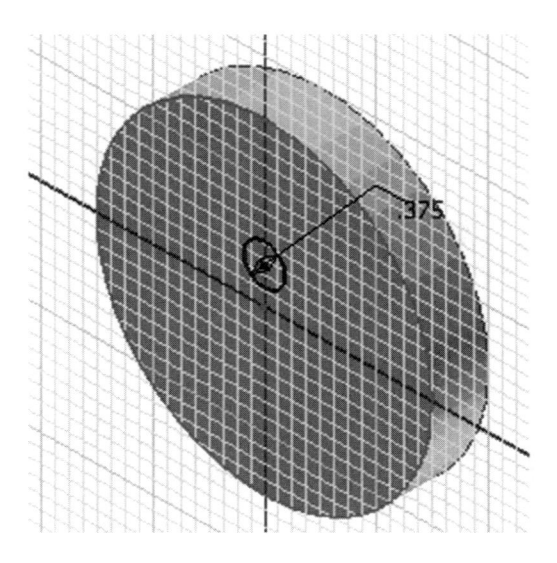

83. Modify the diameter of the holes by double clicking on the overall dimension. The Edit Dimension dialog box will appear as shown in Figure 73.

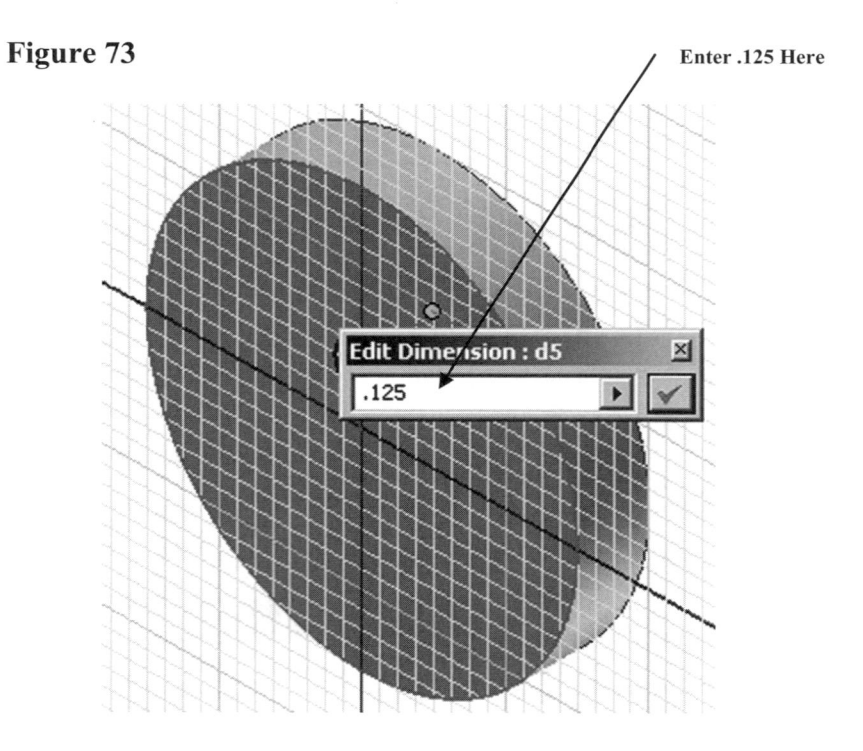

Figure 73

Enter .125 Here

84. Enter **.125** and press **Enter** on the keyboard as shown in Figure 73.

256

Chapter 5: Learning To Edit Existing Solid Models

85. The diameter of the holes will be reduced to .125 as shown in Figure 74.

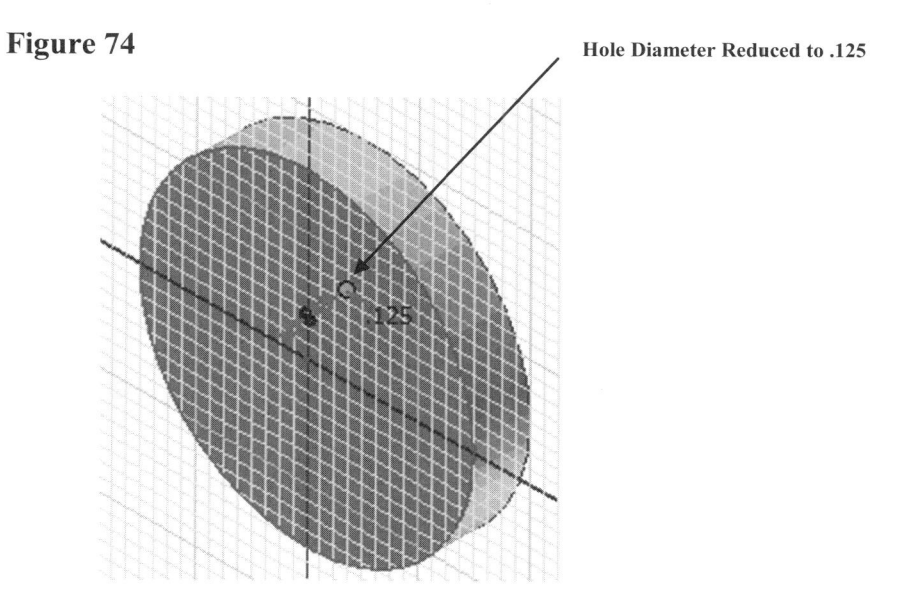

Figure 74   Hole Diameter Reduced to .125

86. Move the cursor to the upper middle portion of the screen and left click on **Update** as shown in Figure 75.

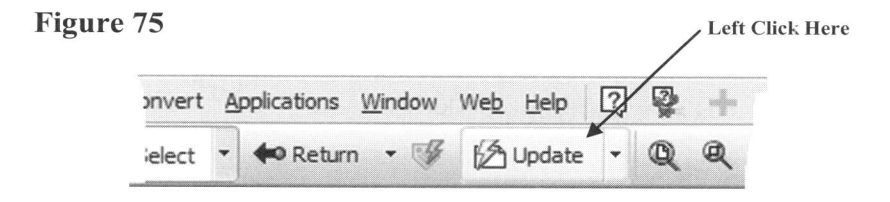

Figure 75   Left Click Here

87. Inventor will automatically update the part as shown in Figure 76.

Figure 76

Chapter 5: Learning To Edit Existing Solid Models

88. Move the cursor over the text "Extrusion2". A red box will appear around the text. After the red box appears, left click once on **Extrusion2** as shown in Figure 57.

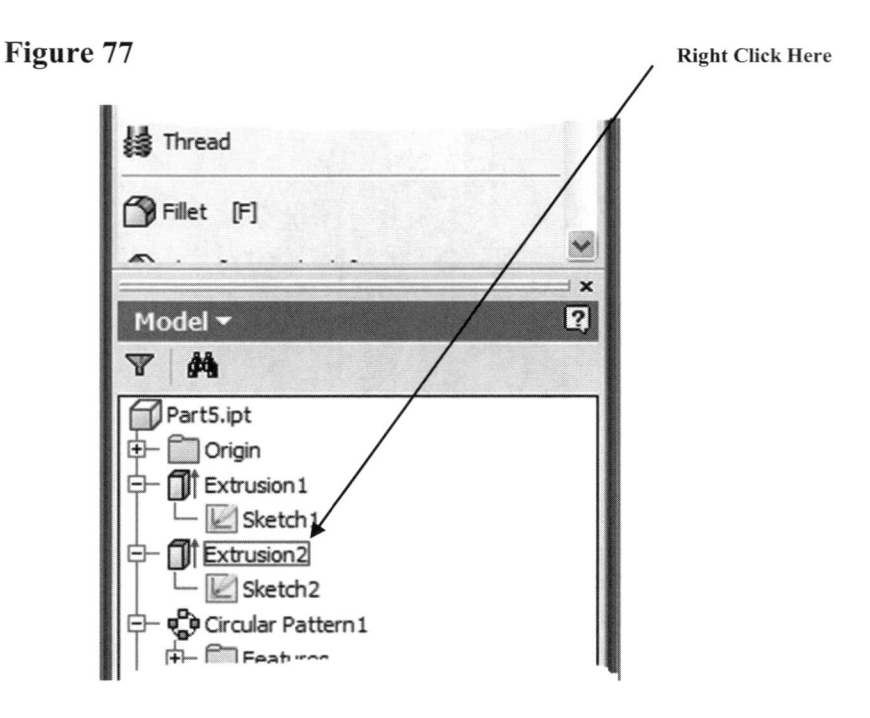

Figure 77

Right Click Here

89. Right click on **Extrusion2**. A pop up menu will appear. Left click on **Edit Feature** as shown in Figure 78.

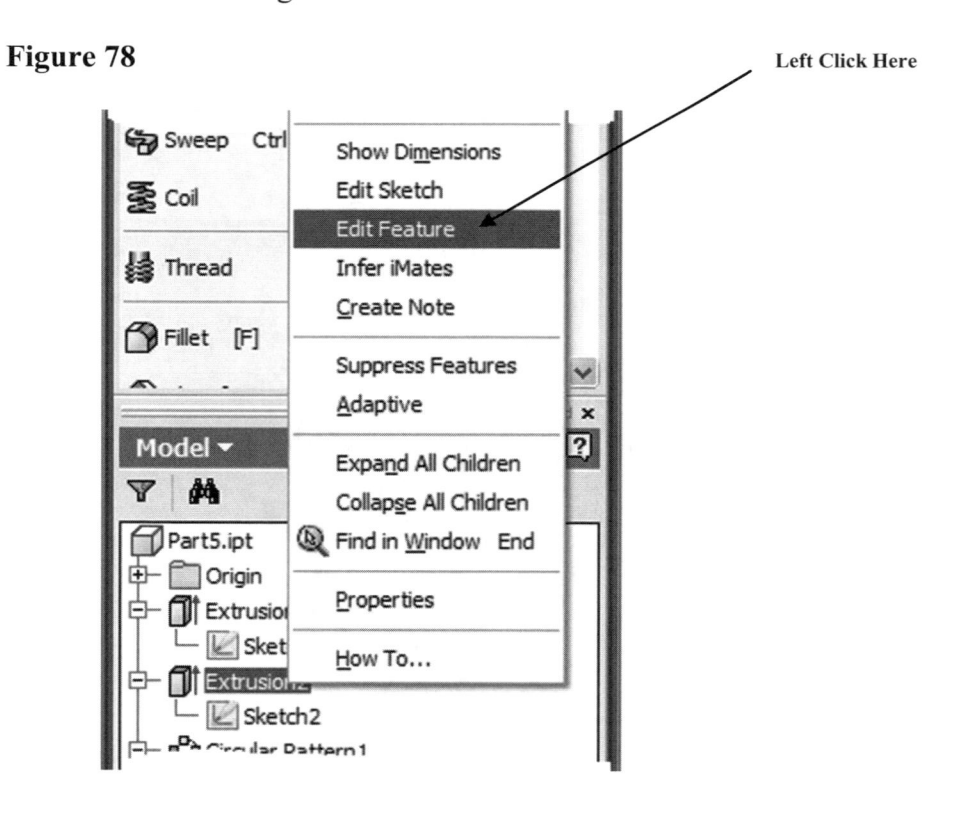

Figure 78

Left Click Here

258

Chapter 5: Learning To Edit Existing Solid Models

90. The Extrusion dialog box will appear. Enter **.5** for the extrusion distance and left click on **OK** as shown in Figure 79.

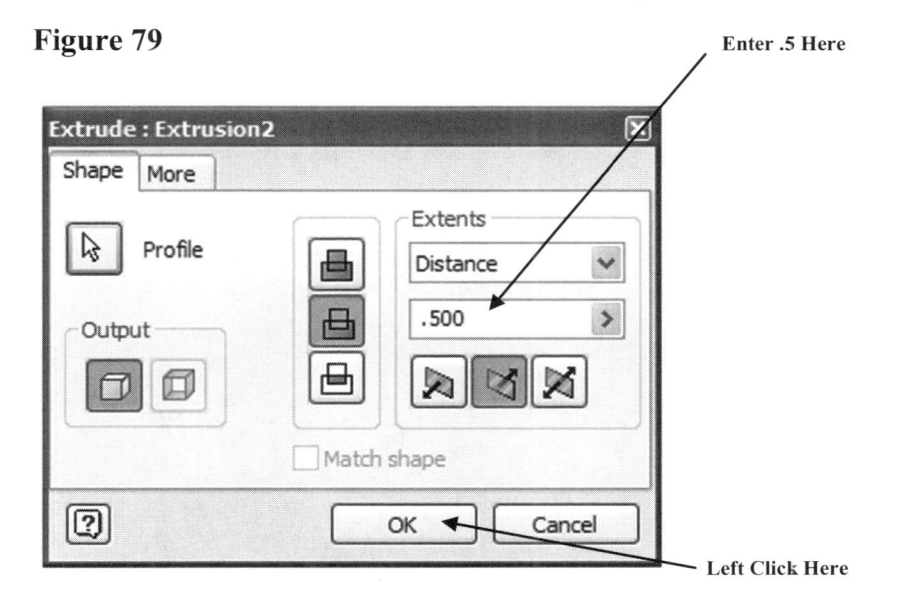

Figure 79

Enter .5 Here

Left Click Here

91. If the Update icon is visible, move the cursor to the upper middle portion of the screen and left click on **Update** as shown in Figure 80.

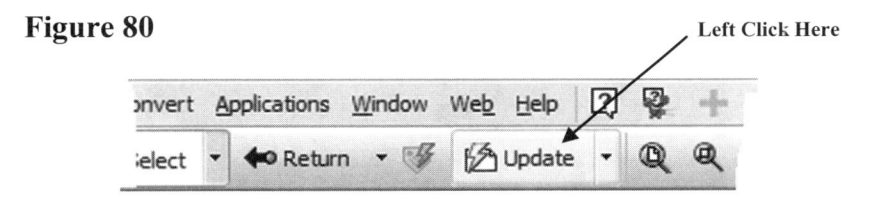

Figure 80

Left Click Here

92. Inventor will automatically update the part. Notice that the holes are now thru holes as shown in Figure 81.

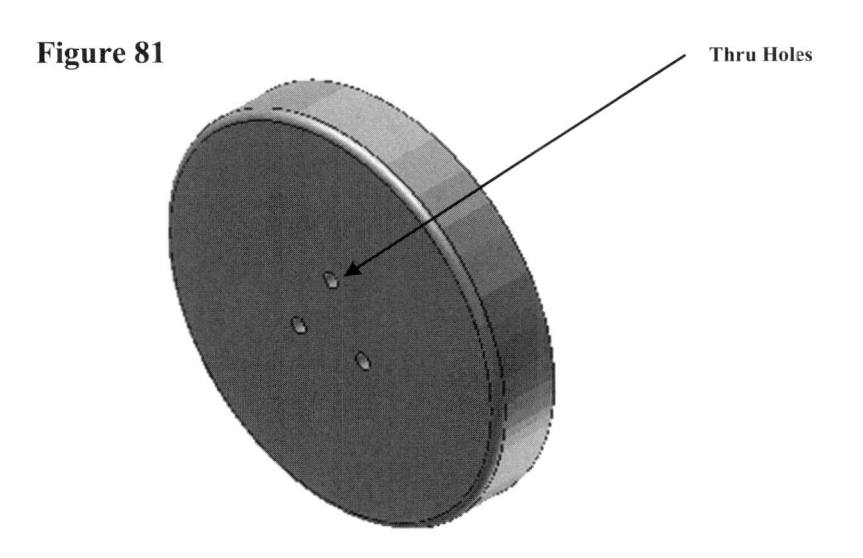

Figure 81

Thru Holes

Chapter 5: Learning To Edit Existing Solid Models

93. Move the cursor to the upper middle portion of the screen and left click on the "Rotate" icon as shown in Figure 82.

Figure 82   Left Click Here

94. A white circle will appear around the part. Left click (holding the left mouse button down) inside the white circle and drag the part around to verify the holes are actually thru holes as shown in Figure 83. Press the **Esc** key.

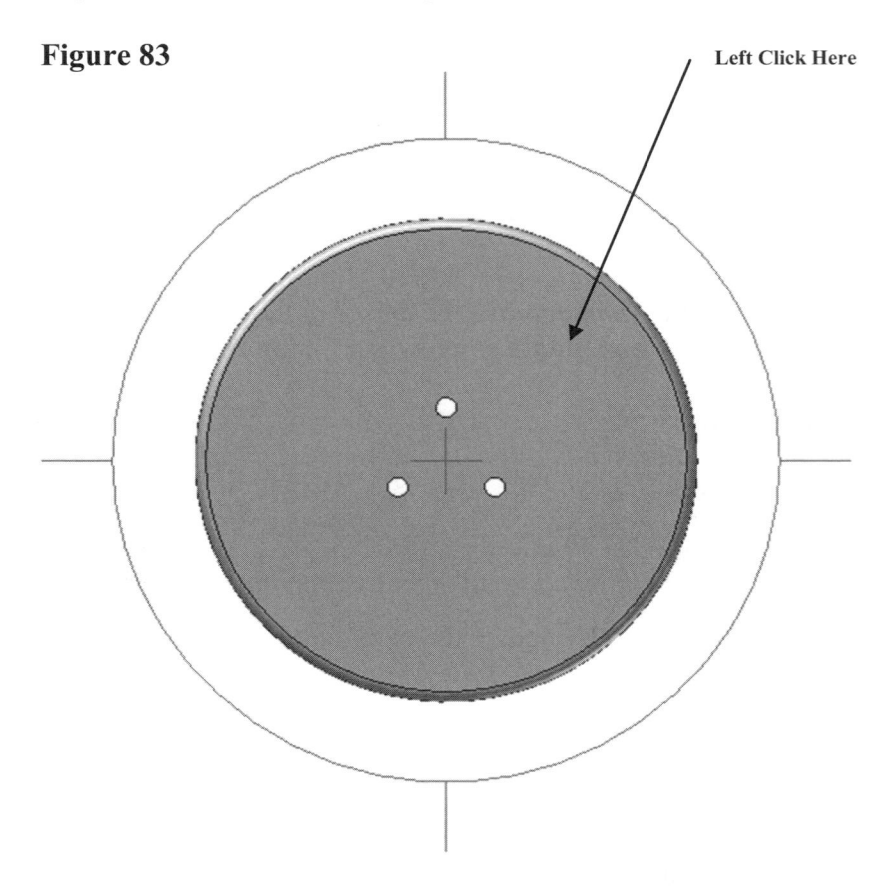

Figure 83   Left Click Here

260

Chapter 5: Learning To Edit Existing Solid Models

95. Move the cursor over the text "Circular Pattern1". A red box will appear around the text. After the red box appears, left click once on **Circular Pattern 1** as shown in Figure 57.

Figure 84   *Right Click Here*

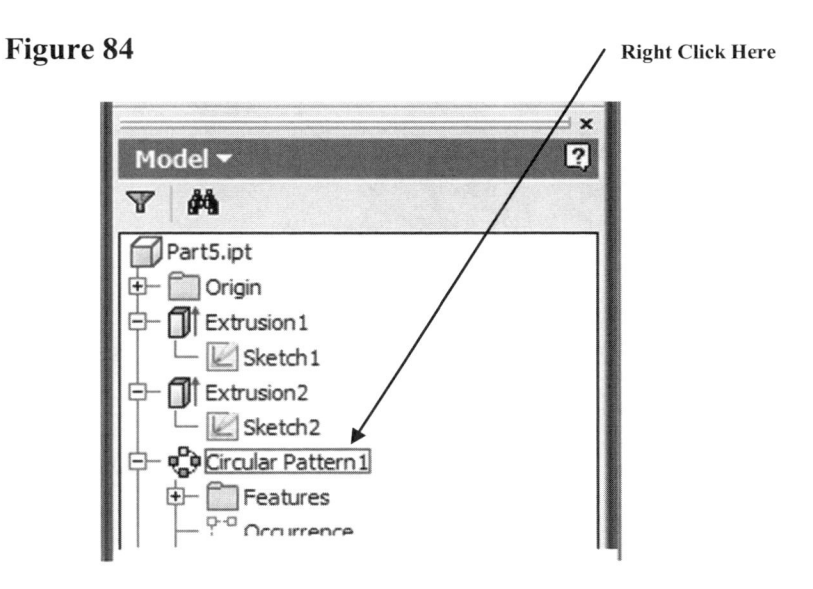

96. Right click on **Circular Pattern1**. A pop up menu will appear. Left click on **Edit Feature** as shown in Figure 85.

Figure 85   *Left Click Here*

261

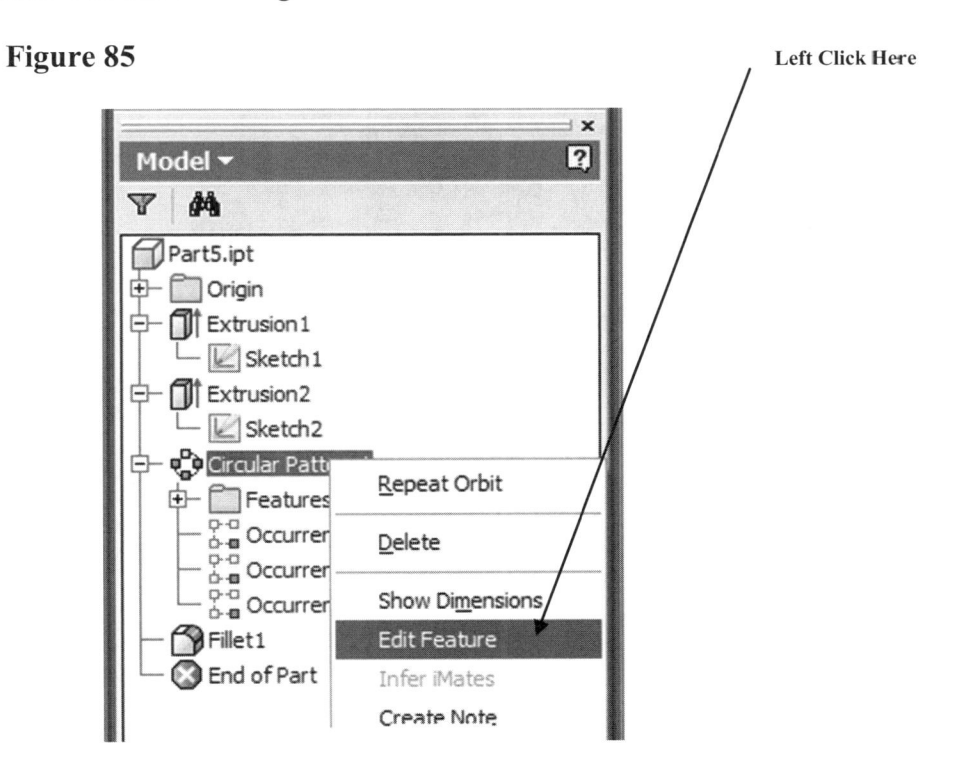

Chapter 5: Learning To Edit Existing Solid Models

97. The Circular Pattern dialog box will appear. Enter **6** under "Placement" as shown in Figure 86.

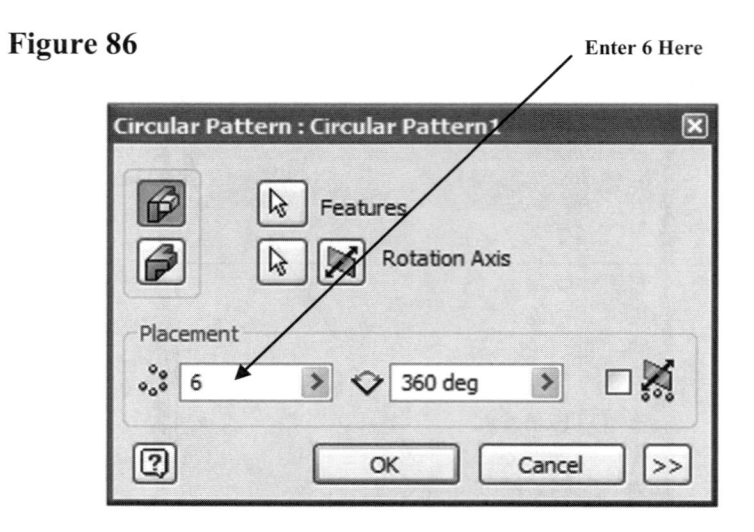

   Figure 86

98. Inventor will provide a preview as shown in Figure 87.

   Figure 87

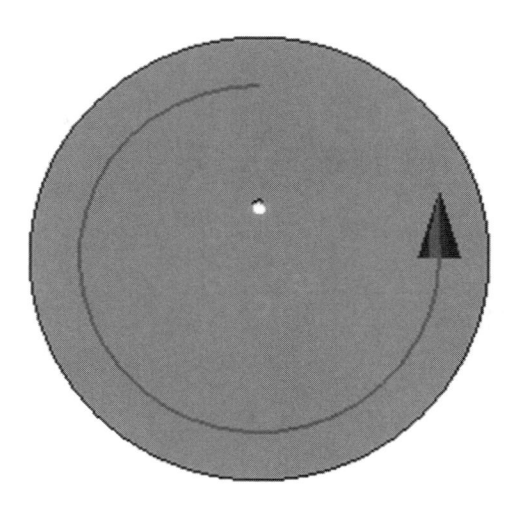

262

Chapter 5: Learning To Edit Existing Solid Models

99. Left click on **OK** in the Circular Pattern dialog box. Your screen should look similar to Figure 88.

Figure 88

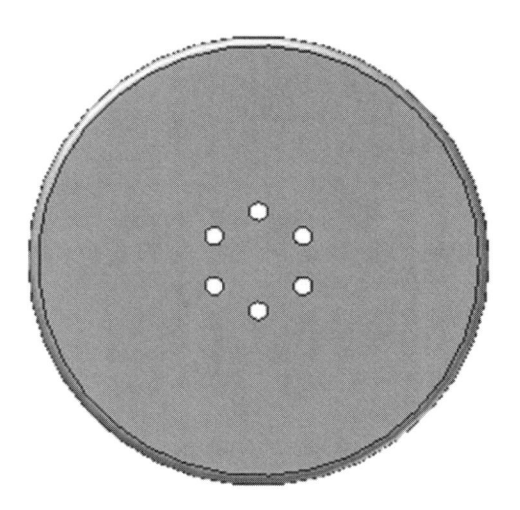

100. Right click anywhere around the drawing. A pop up menu will appear. Left click on **Home/Isometric View** as shown in Figure 89.

Figure 89   Left Click Here

263

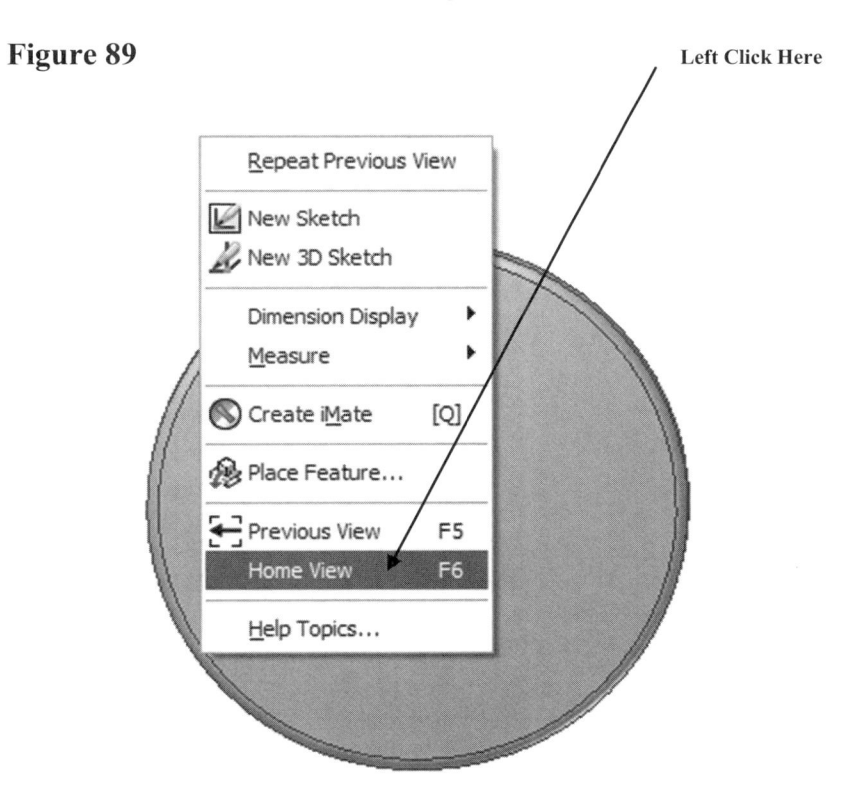

Chapter 5: Learning To Edit Existing Solid Models

101. The part will be shown in Isometric as shown in Figure 90.

Figure 90

102. Move the cursor over the text "Fillet1". A red box will appear around the text. After the red box appears, left click once on **Fillet1** as shown in Figure 57.

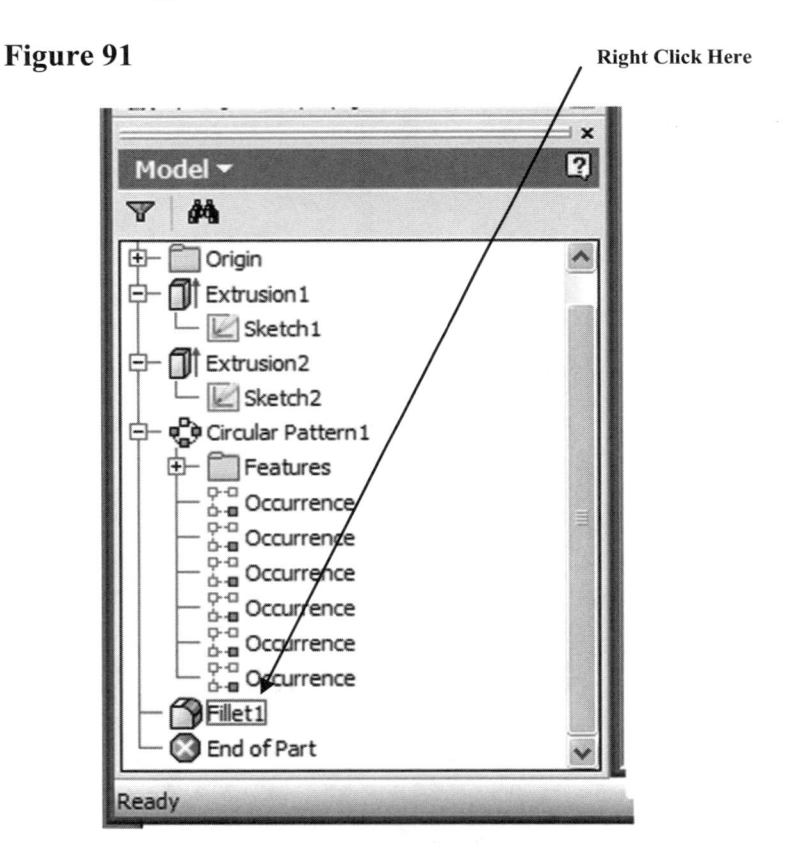

Figure 91   **Right Click Here**

264

Chapter 5: Learning To Edit Existing Solid Models

103. Right click on **Fillet1**. A pop up menu will appear. Left click on **Edit Feature** as shown in Figure 92.

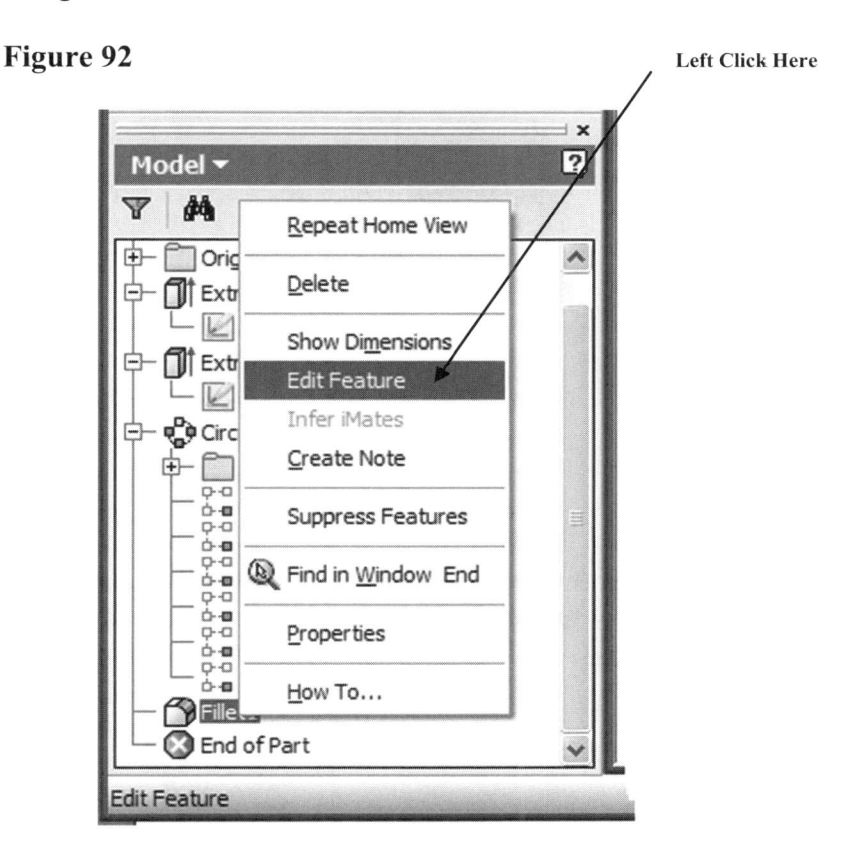

Figure 92

Left Click Here

104. The Fillet dialog box will appear. Enter **.250** for the Radius and left click on **OK** as shown in Figure 93.

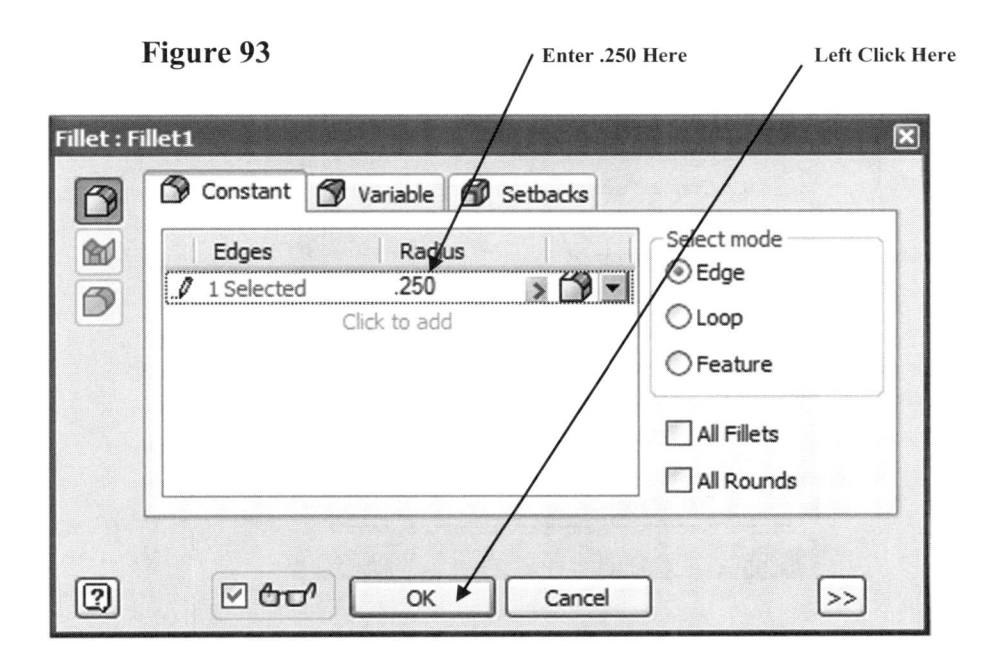

Figure 93

Enter .250 Here

Left Click Here

265

Chapter 5: Learning To Edit Existing Solid Models

105. Your screen should look similar to Figure 94.

Figure 94

106. Move the cursor over the second listed text "Occurrence". A red box will appear around the text. After the red box appears, left click once on **Occurrence** as shown in Figure 57.

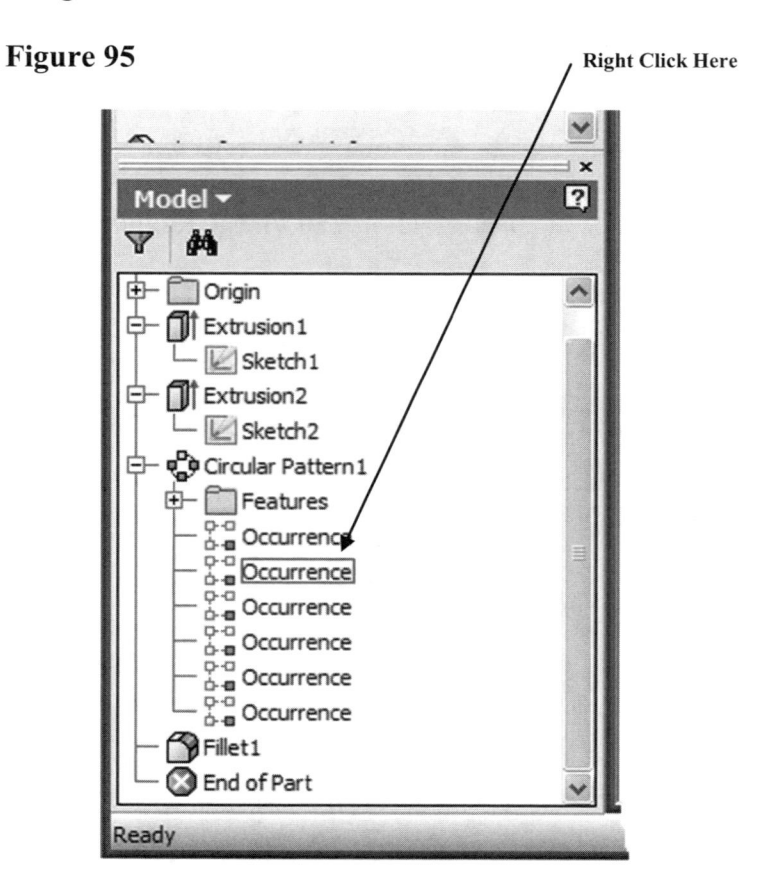

Figure 95

Right Click Here

266

Chapter 5: Learning To Edit Existing Solid Models

107. A pop up menu will appear. Left click on **Suppress** as shown in Figure 96. Inventor will suppress that particular occurrence while leaving all others active.

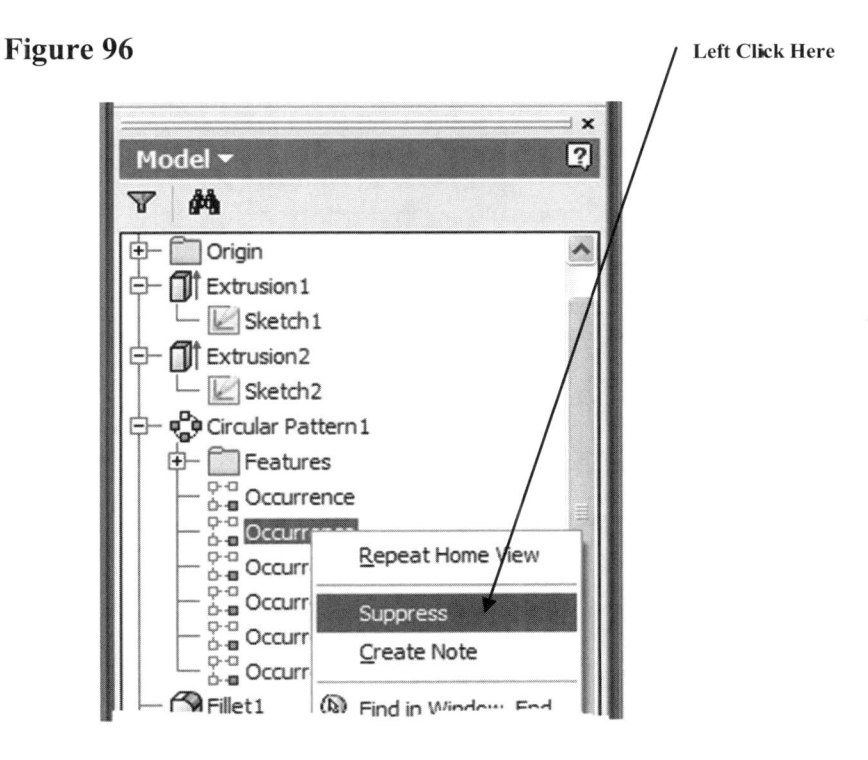

Figure 96

Left Click Here

108. Inventor will draw a line through and gray the text as shown in Figure 97. You will notice that the second hole created using the Circular Pattern command is not visible. Repeat the previous steps to un-suppress the occurrence.

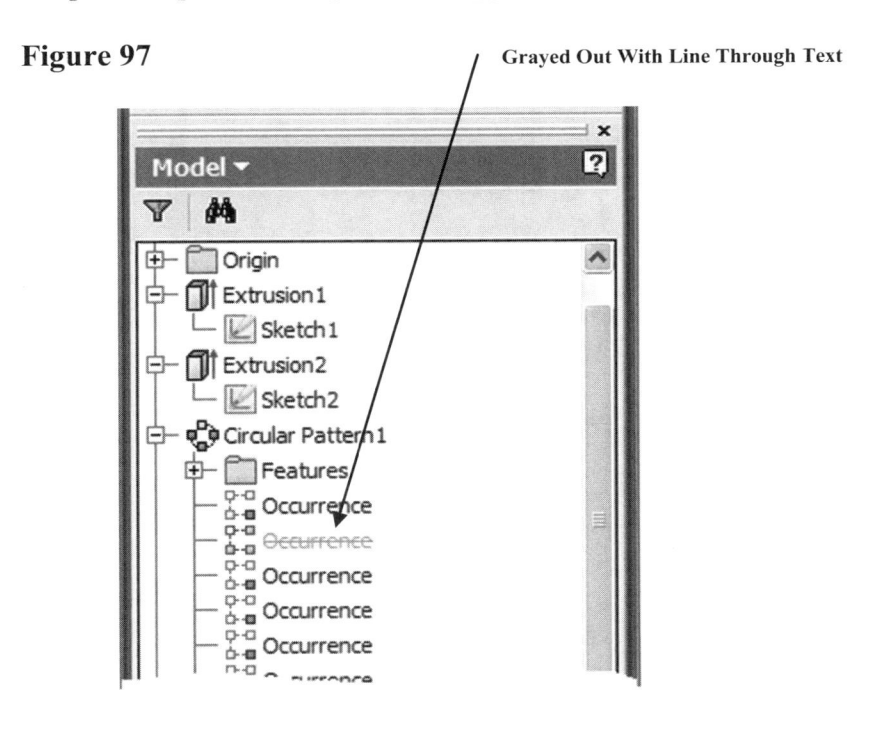

Figure 97

Grayed Out With Line Through Text

267

Chapter 5: Learning To Edit Existing Solid Models

109. The names of all branches in the part tree can also be edited. Move the cursor to the lower left portion of the screen where the part tree is located. Move the cursor over **Extrusion1** and left click once causing the text to become highlighted. After the text is highlighted, left click one time. The text may be edited as shown in Figure 98.

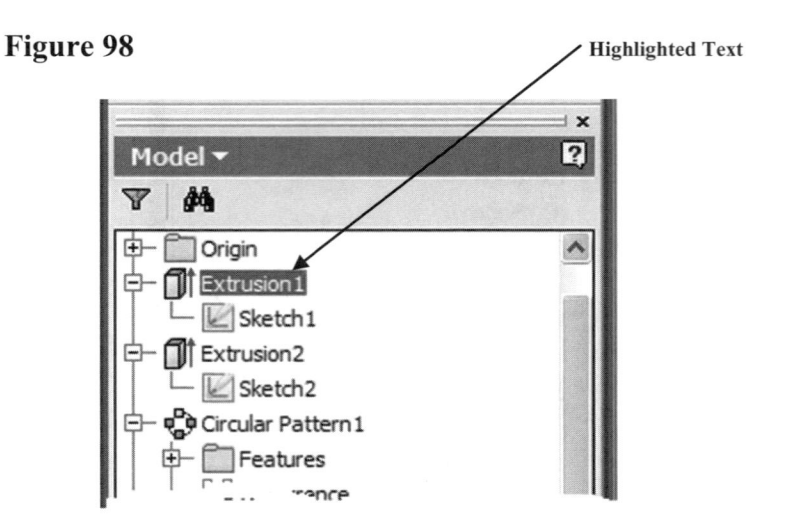

Figure 98 ⟶ Highlighted Text

110. Enter the text **Base Extrusion** as shown in Figure 99. Press **Enter** on the keyboard. Text for each individual operation can be edited if desired.

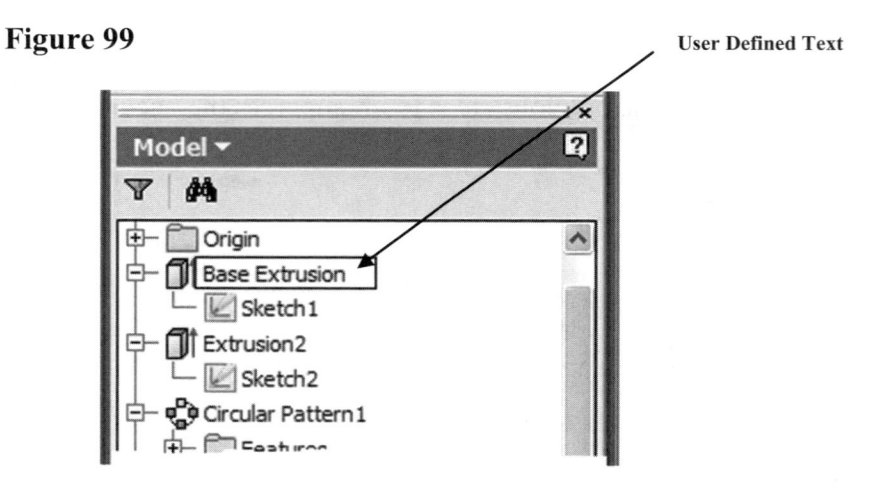

Figure 99 ⟶ User Defined Text

268

111. Notice that the final design looks significantly different than the original design. The part was redesigned by modifying the existing part as shown in Figure 100.

Figure 100

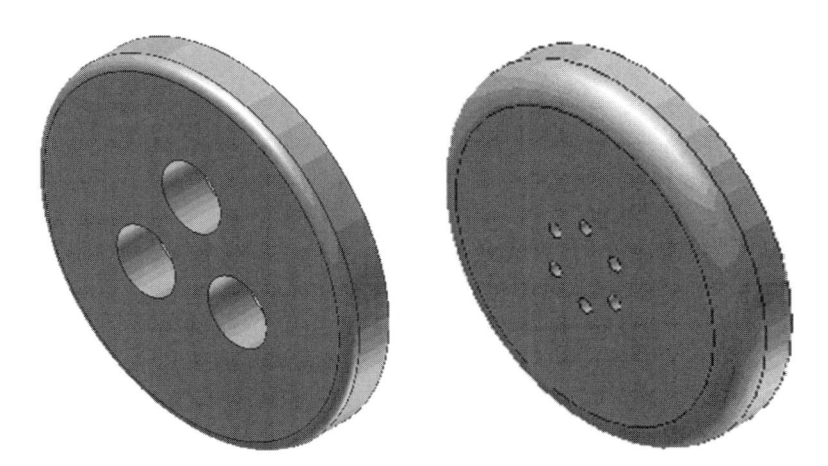

Chapter 5: Learning To Edit Existing Solid Models

Drawing Activities

Use these problems from Chapters 1 and 2 to create redesigned parts.

Problem 1

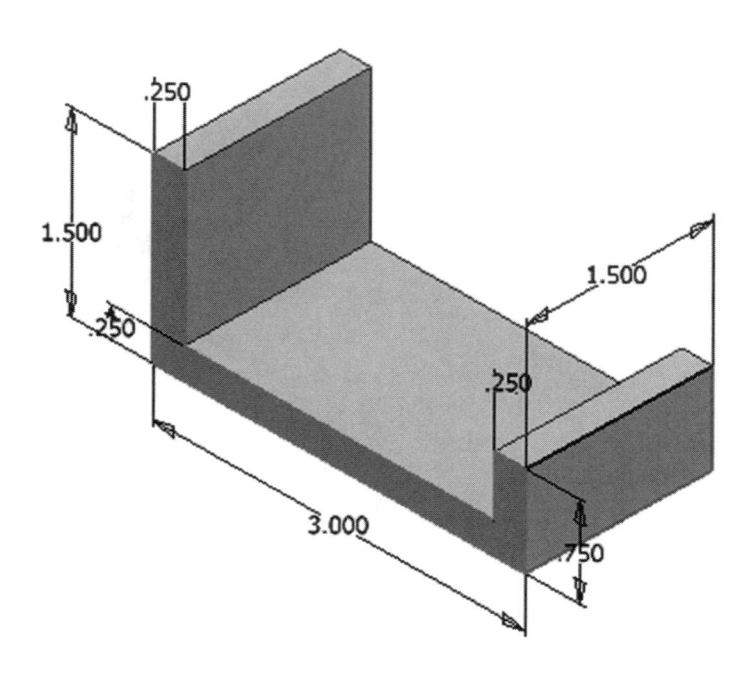

Problem 2

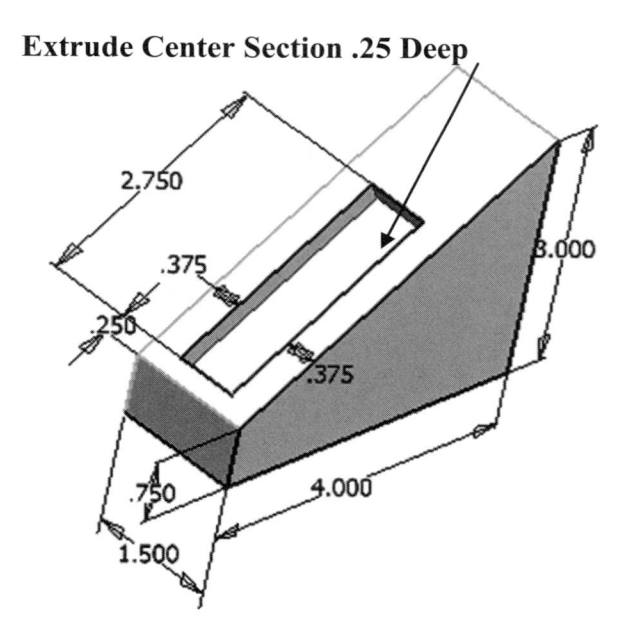

Extrude Center Section .25 Deep

Problem 3

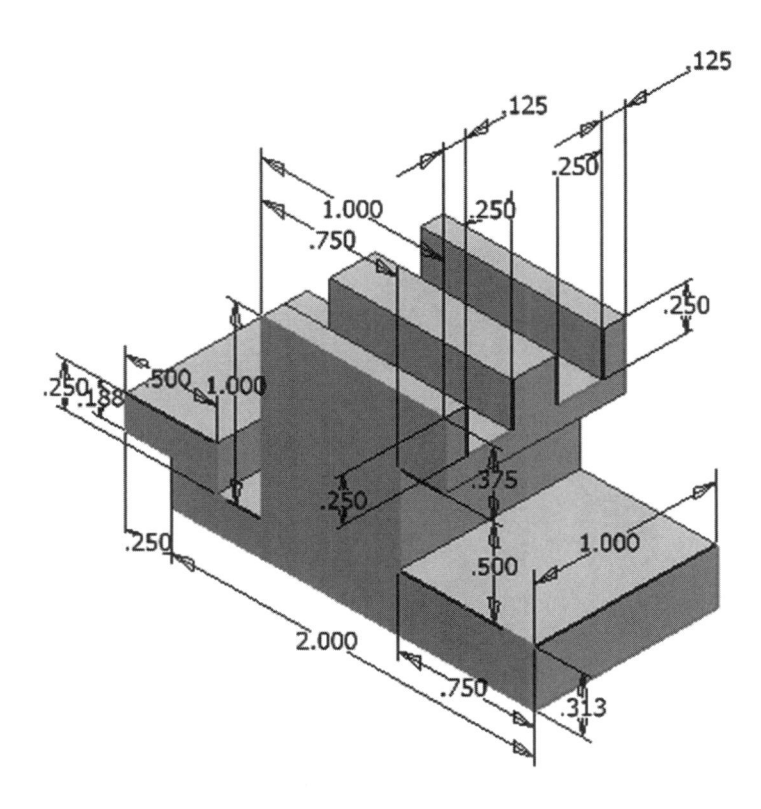

Problem 4

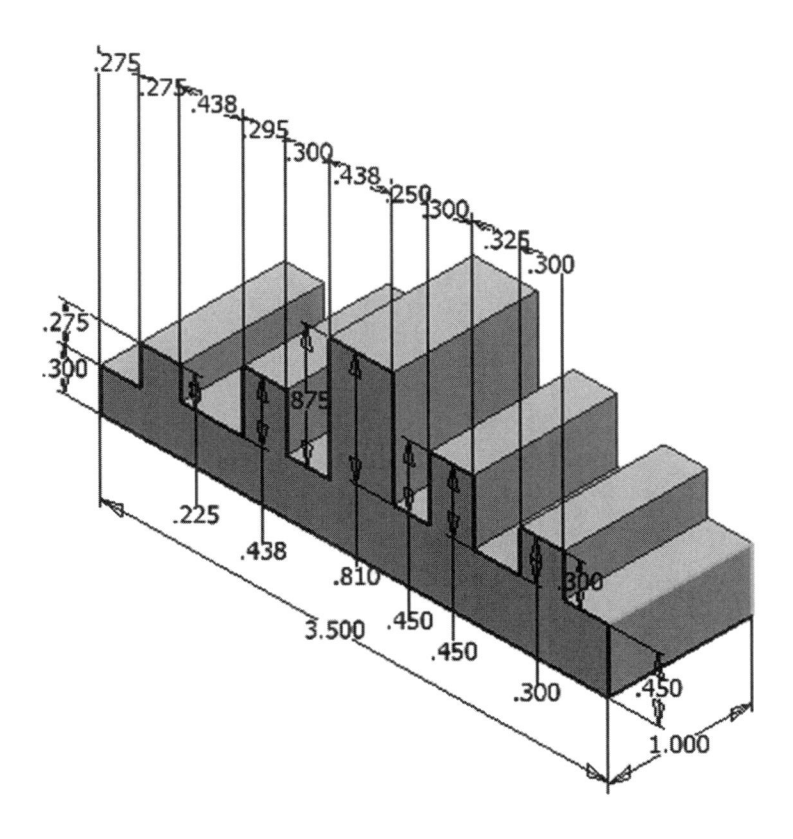

Chapter 5: Learning To Edit Existing Solid Models

Problem 5

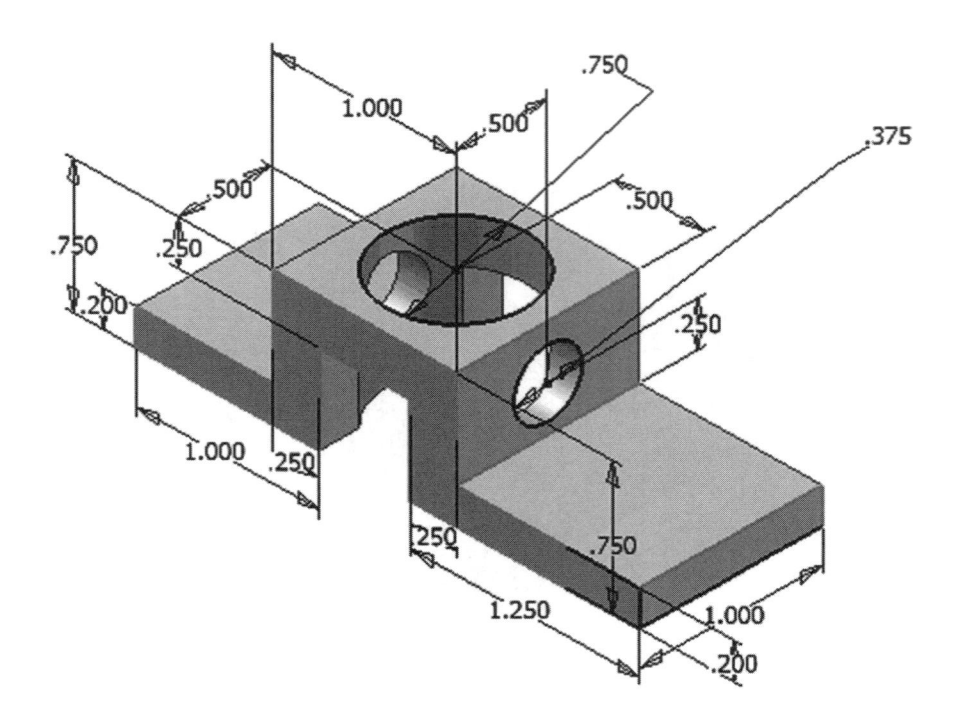

Problem 6

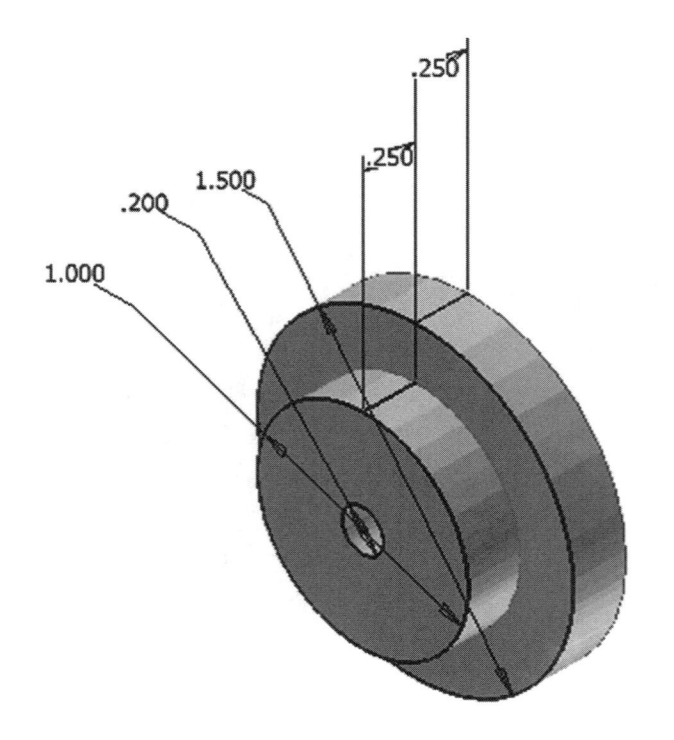

Chapter 5: Learning To Edit Existing Solid Models

Problem 7

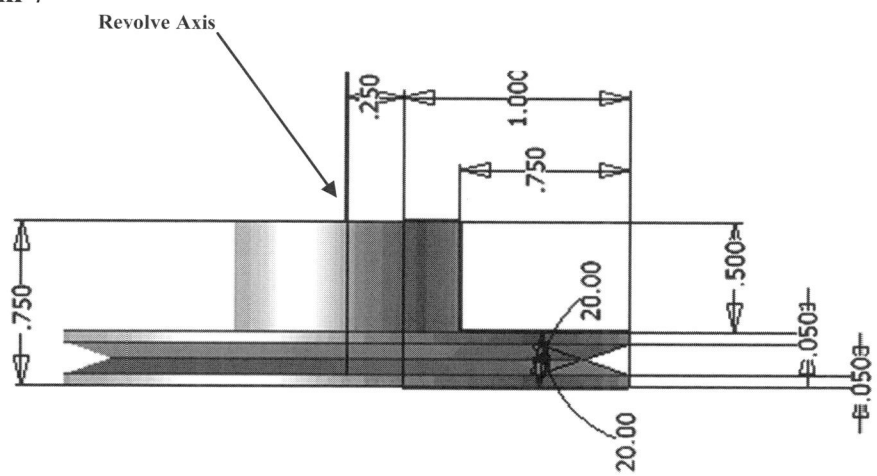

Revolve Axis

.250, 1.000, .750, .500, .050, .050, .750, 20.00, 20.00

Problem 8

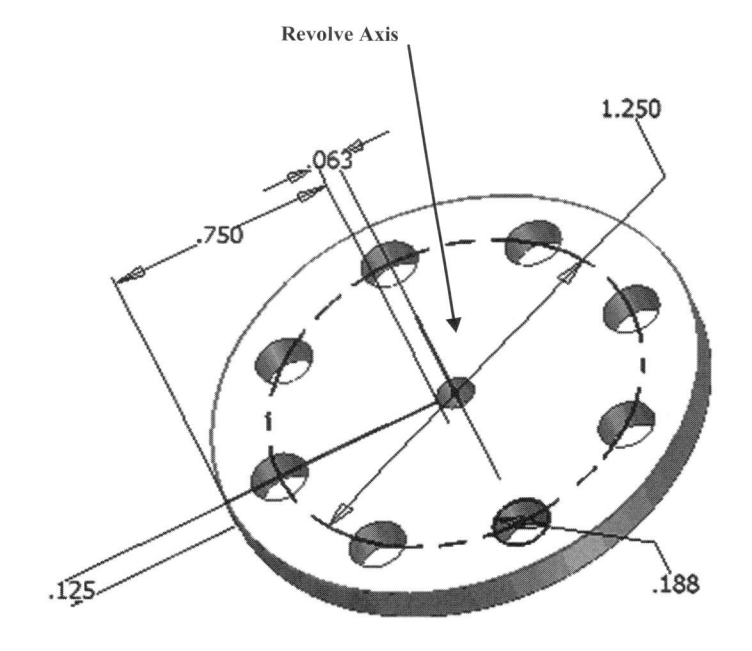

Revolve Axis

1.250, .063, .750, .125, .188

Chapter 6 Advanced Design Procedures

Objectives:
- Design multiple sketch parts
- Learn to use the X, Y, and Z Planes
- Learn to use the Wireframe viewing command
- Learn to project geometry to a new sketch
- Learn to use the Shell command

Chapter 6 includes instruction on how to design the parts shown below.

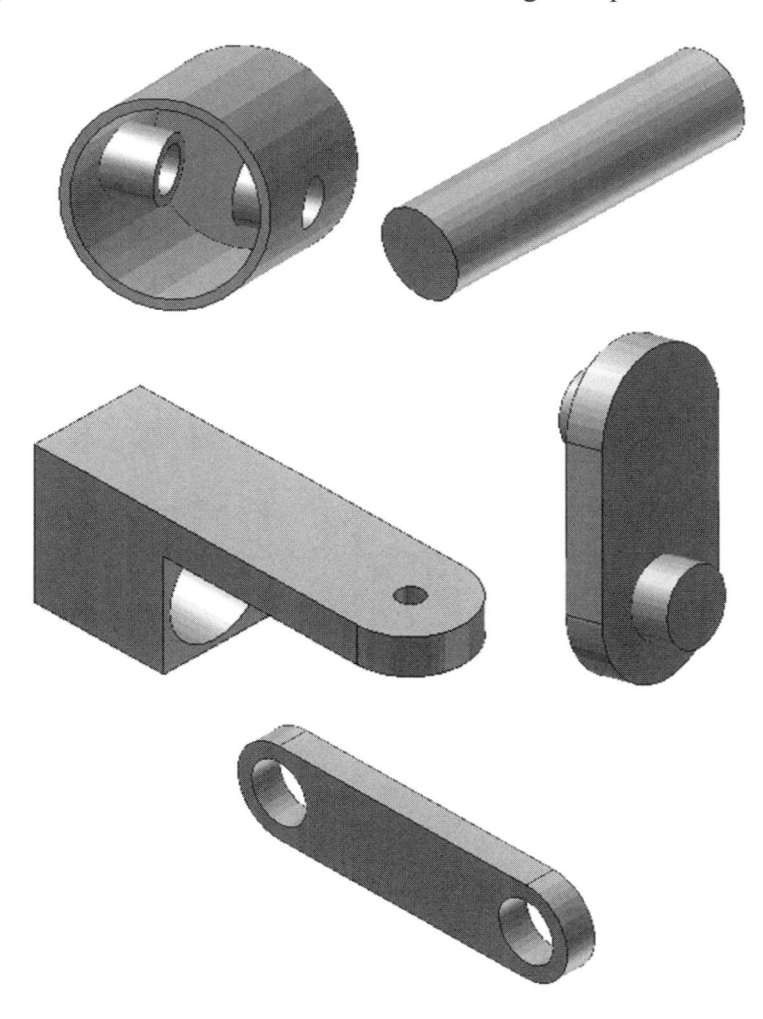

Chapter 6: Advanced Design Procedures

1. Start Autodesk Inventor 2009 by referring to "Chapter 1 Getting Started".

2. After Autodesk Inventor 2009 is running, begin a new sketch.

3. Move the cursor to the upper left corner of the screen and left click on **Center Point Circle** as shown in Figure 1.

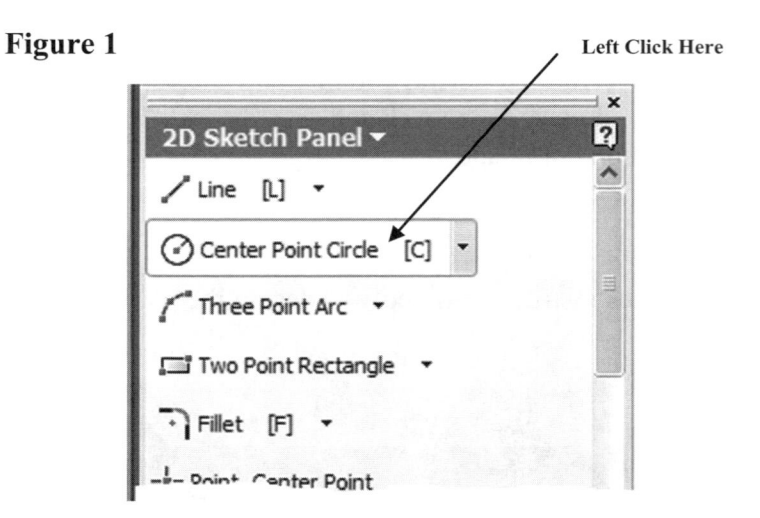

Figure 1

Left Click Here

4. Move the cursor to the center of the screen and left click once. This will be the center of the circle as shown in Figure 2.

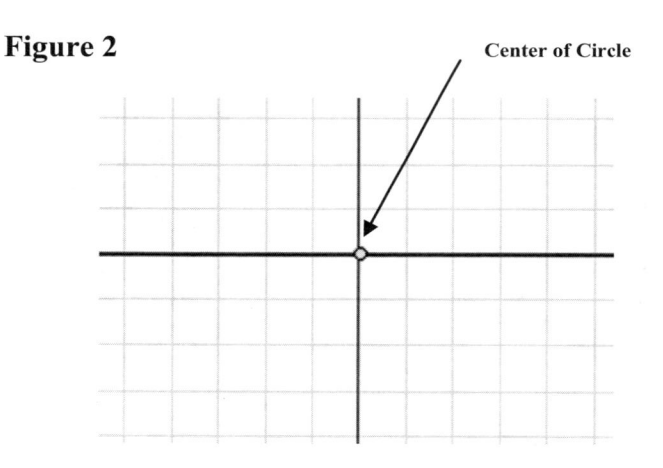

Figure 2

Center of Circle

276

5. Move the cursor to the right and left click once as shown in Figure 3.

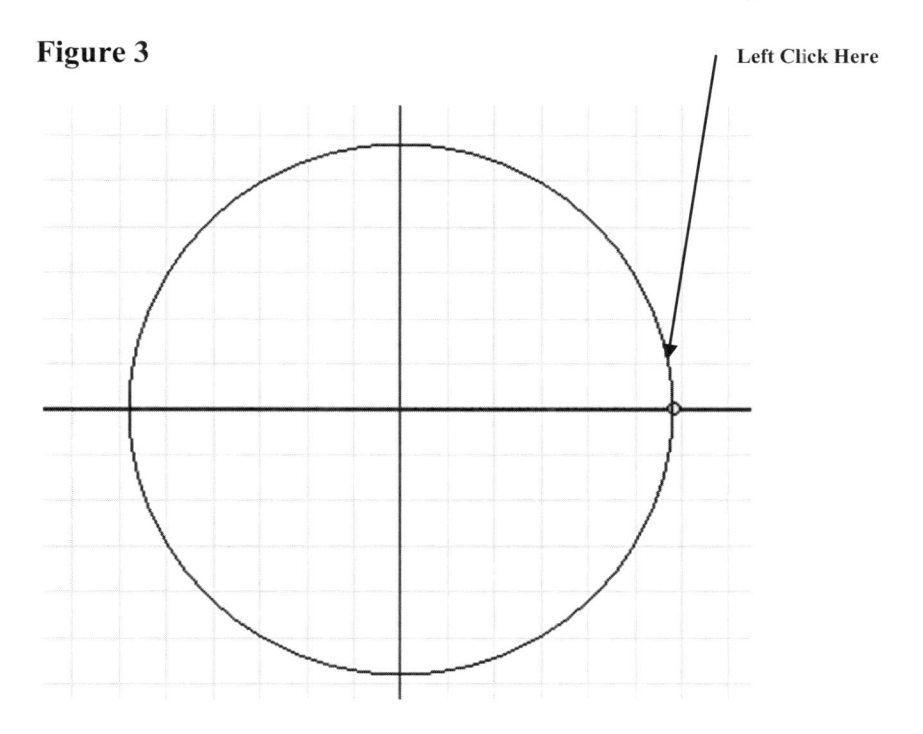

Figure 3

Left Click Here

6. Move the cursor to the middle left portion of the screen and left click on **General Dimension** as shown in Figure 4.

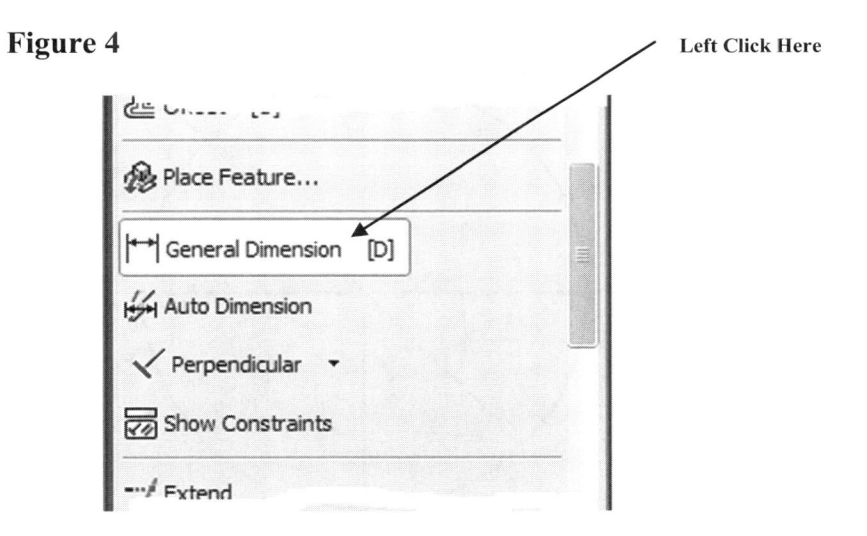

Figure 4

Left Click Here

Chapter 6: Advanced Design Procedures

7. After selecting **General Dimension** move the cursor over the edge of the circle. It will turn red. Left click once. The dimension will be attached to the cursor as shown in Figure 5.

Figure 5

Turned Red

8. Move the cursor down. The actual dimension of the line will appear as shown in Figure 6.

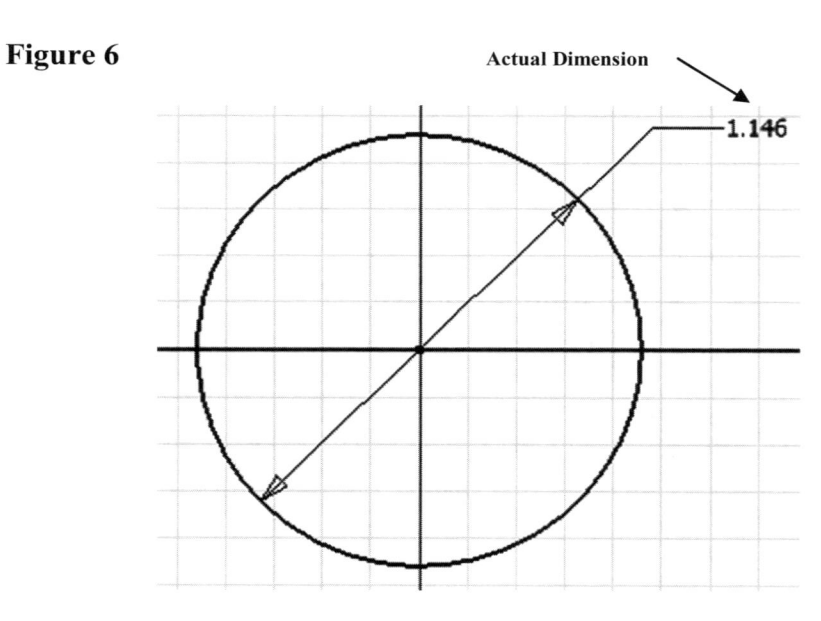

Figure 6

Actual Dimension

1.146

Chapter 6: Advanced Design Procedures

9. Move the cursor to where the dimension will be placed and left click once. While the dimension is still in red, left click once. The Edit Dimension dialog box will appear as shown in Figure 7.

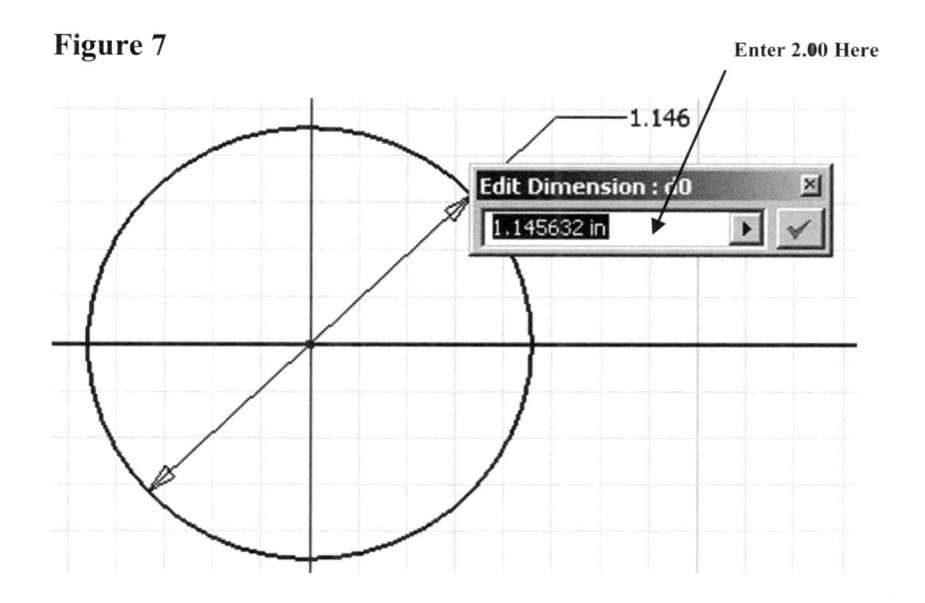

Figure 7

Enter 2.00 Here

10. To edit the dimension, type **2.00** in the Edit Dimension dialog box (while the current dimension is highlighted) and press **Enter** on the keyboard.

Chapter 6: Advanced Design Procedures

11. The dimension of the circle will become 2.00 inches as shown in Figure 8.

   Figure 8

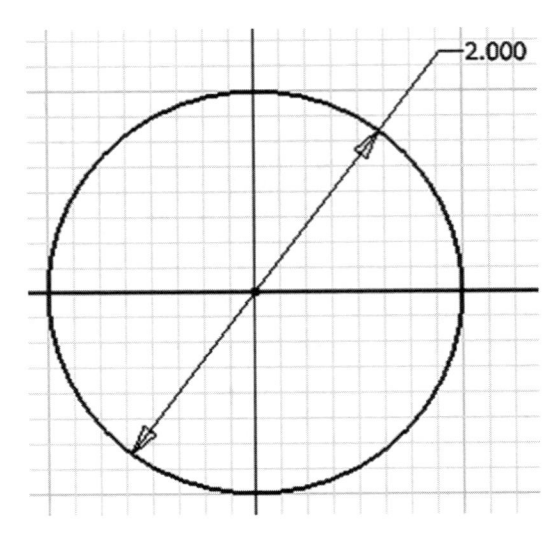

12. To view the entire drawing, it may be necessary to move the cursor to the middle portion of the screen and left click once on the "Zoom All" icon as shown in Figure 9.

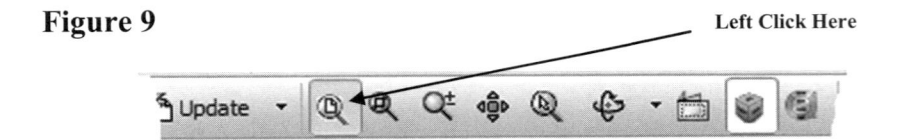

   Figure 9 Left Click Here

13. The drawing will "fill up" the entire screen. If the drawing is still too large, left click on the "Zoom" icon as shown in Figure 10. After selecting the Zoom icon, hold the left mouse button down and drag the cursor up and down to achieve the desired view of the sketch.

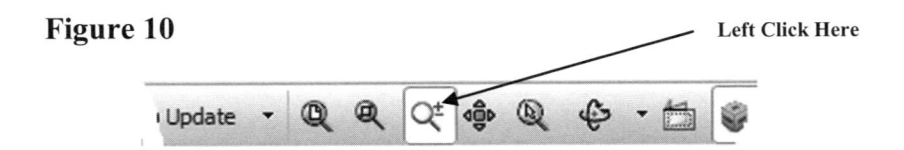

   Figure 10 Left Click Here

Chapter 6: Advanced Design Procedures

14. After the sketch is complete it is time to extrude the sketch into a solid. Right click anywhere on the drawing. A pop up menu will appear. Left click on **Done [Esc]** as shown in Figure 11.

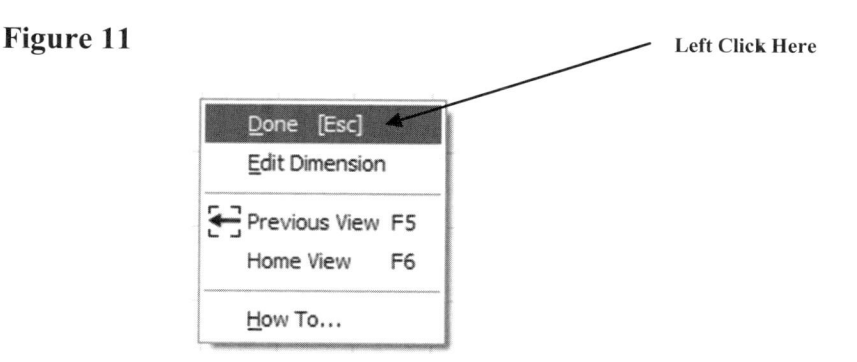

Figure 11

Left Click Here

15. After you have verified that no commands are active, right click anywhere on the sketch. A pop up menu will appear. Left click on **Finish Sketch** as shown in Figure 12.

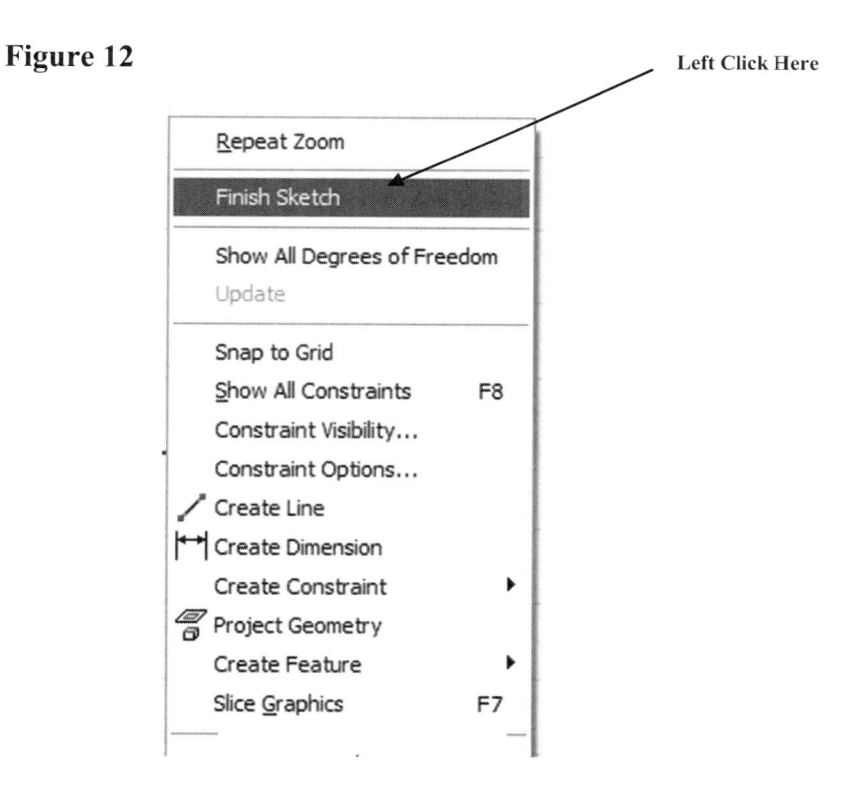

Figure 12

Left Click Here

281

Chapter 6: Advanced Design Procedures

16. Inventor is now out of the Sketch Panel and into the Part Features Panel. Notice that the commands at the left of the screen are now different. To work in the Part Features Panel a sketch must be present and have no opens (non-connected lines). If there are any opens in the sketch an error message will appear. Your screen should look similar to Figure 13.

Figure 13

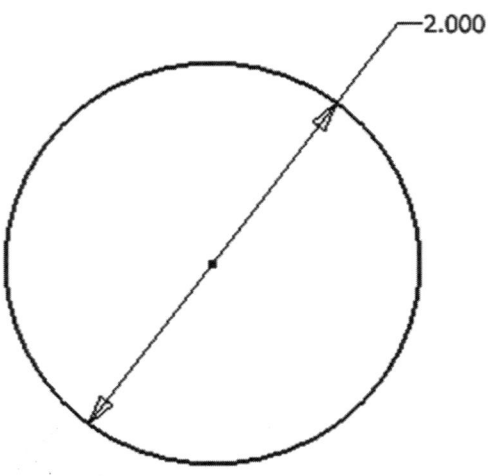

17. Right click around the sketch. A pop up menu will appear. Left click on **Isometric View** as shown in Figure 14.

Figure 14

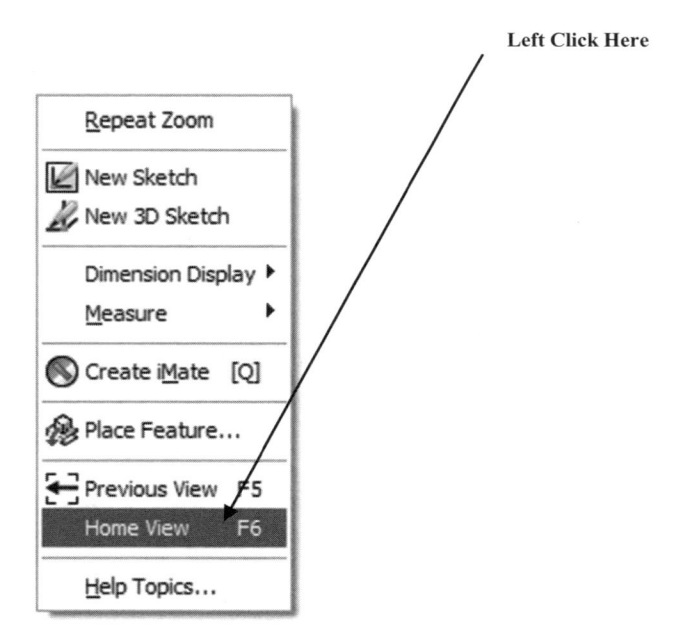

Left Click Here

282

18. The view will become isometric as shown in Figure 15.

Figure 15

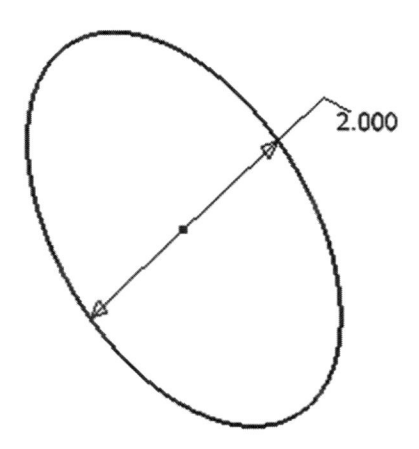

19. Move the cursor to the middle left portion of the screen and left click on **Extrude**. The Extrude dialog box will appear. Inventor also provides a preview of the extrusion. If Inventor gave you an error message there are opens (non-connected lines) somewhere on the sketch. Check each intersection for opens by using the **Extend** and **Trim** commands.

Chapter 6: Advanced Design Procedures

20. Enter **2.00** under Distance and left click on **OK** as shown in Figure 16.

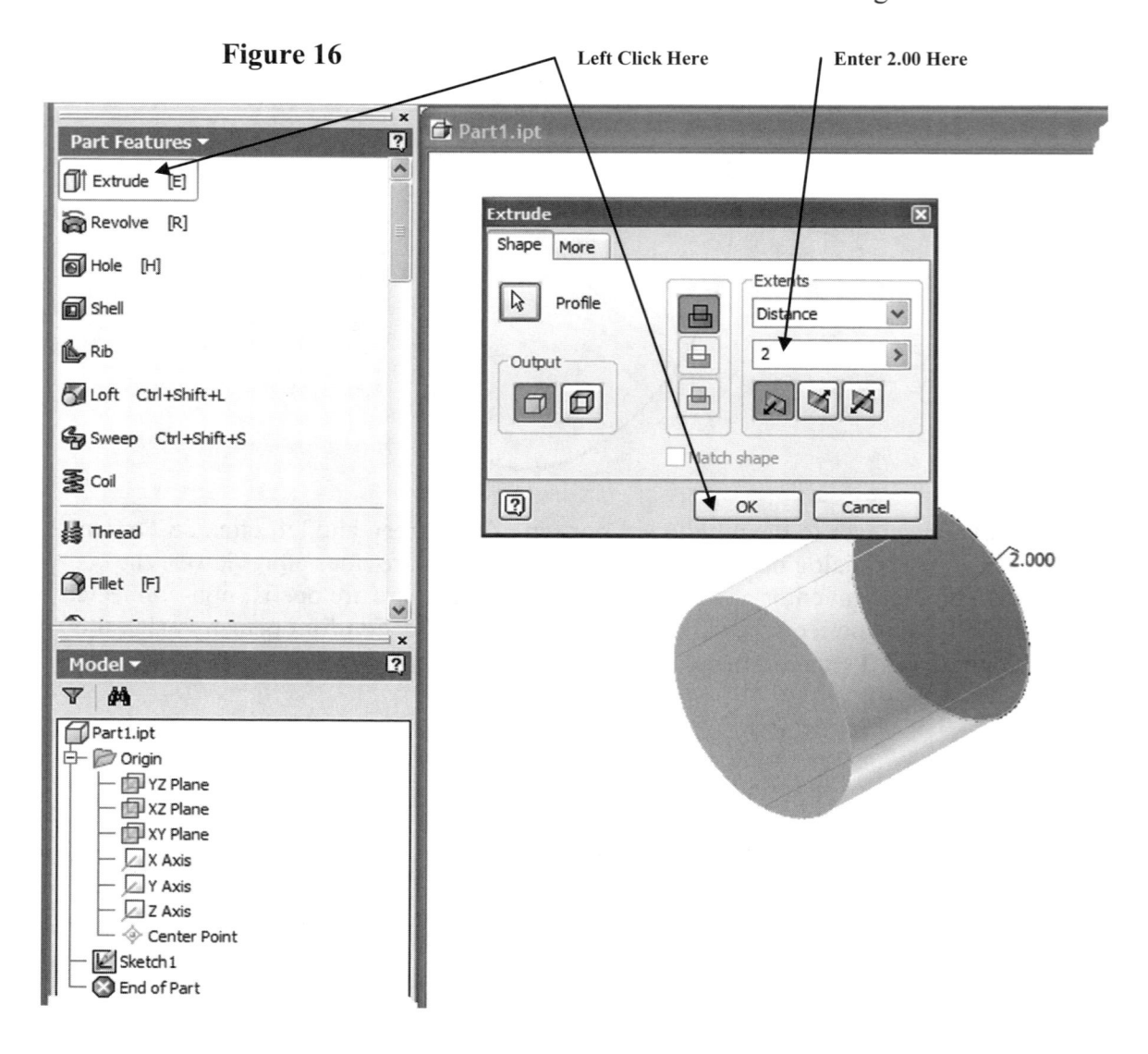

Figure 16

Chapter 6: Advanced Design Procedures

21. Your screen should look similar to Figure 17.

Figure 17

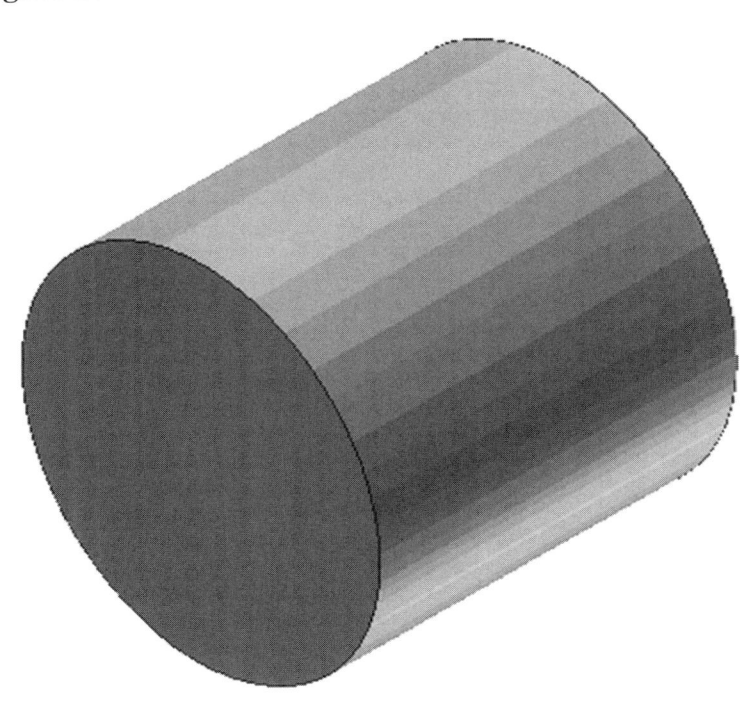

22. Move the cursor to the lower left portion of the screen and left click on the plus sign next to the text "Origin" as shown in Figure 18.

Figure 18 Left Click Here

Chapter 6: Advanced Design Procedures

23. The part tree will expand. Move the cursor over the text "YZ Plane" causing a red box to appear around the text as shown in Figure 19.

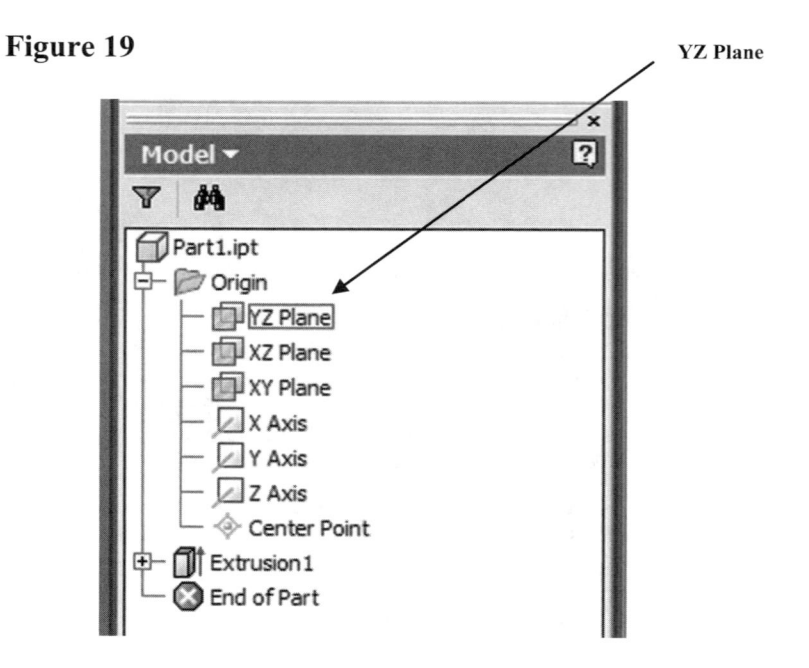

Figure 19

24. The YZ plane will become visible as shown in Figure 20.

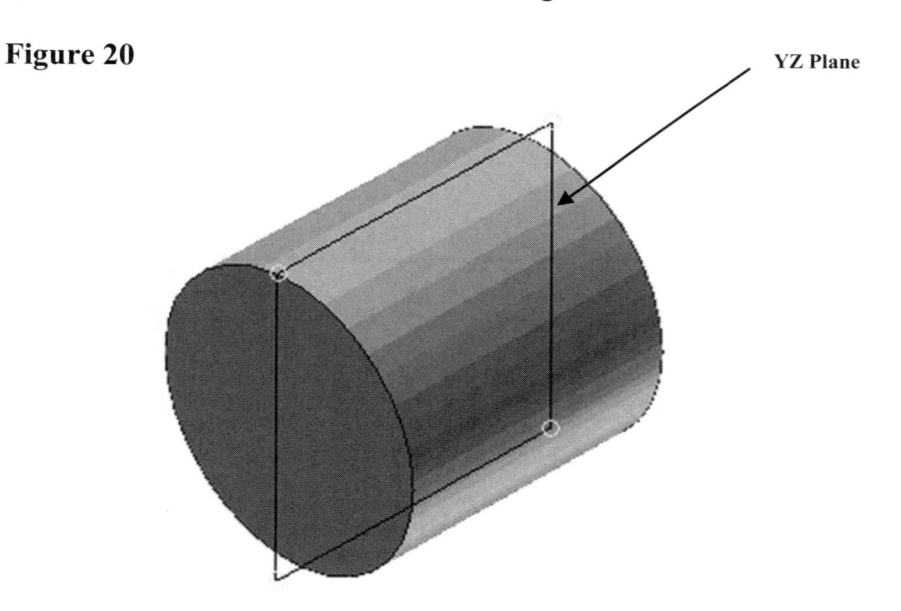

Figure 20

Chapter 6: Advanced Design Procedures

25. Right click on the text **YZ Plane**. A pop up menu will appear. Left click on **New Sketch** as shown in Figure 21.

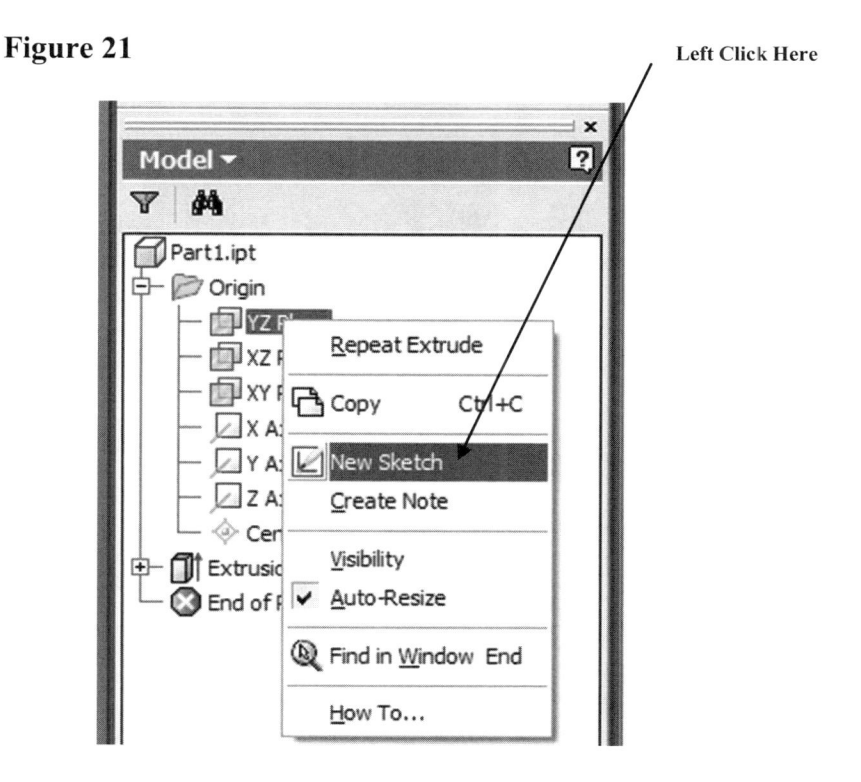

Figure 21

26. Your screen should look similar to Figure 22.

Figure 22

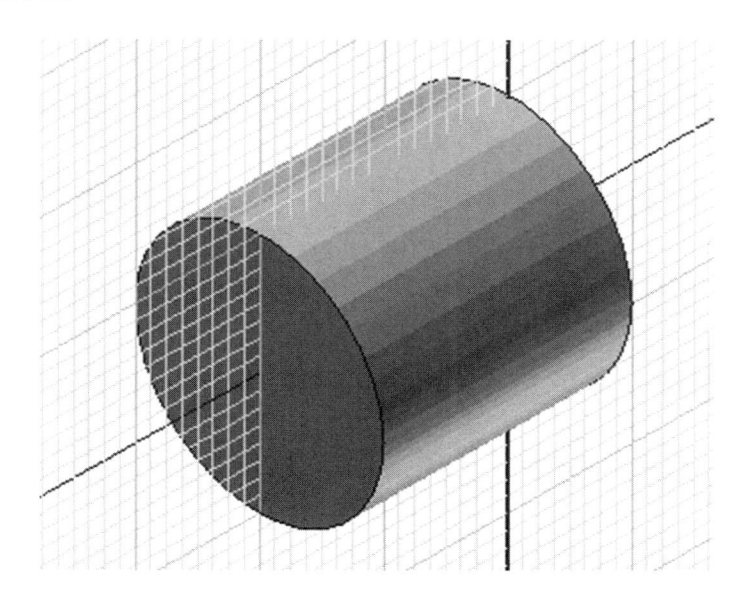

Chapter 6: Advanced Design Procedures

27. Move the cursor to the upper right portion of the screen and left click on the drop down arrow to the right of the "Shaded Display" icon. A drop down menu will appear. Left click on "Wireframe Display" as shown in Figure 23.

Figure 23

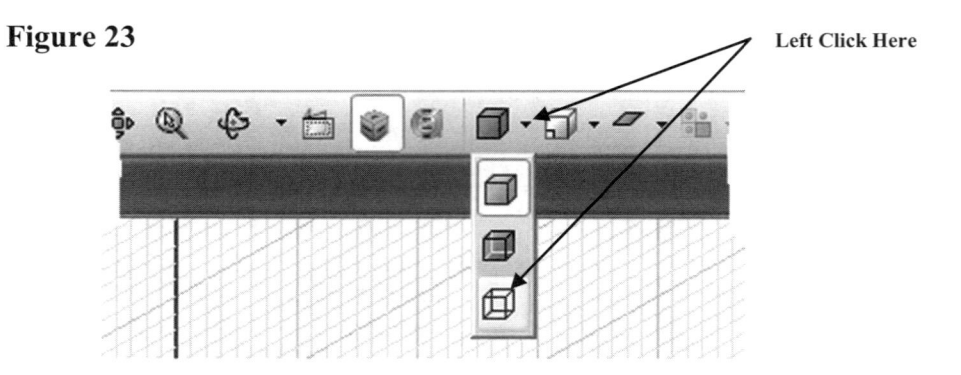

Left Click Here

28. Your screen should look similar to Figure 24.

Figure 24

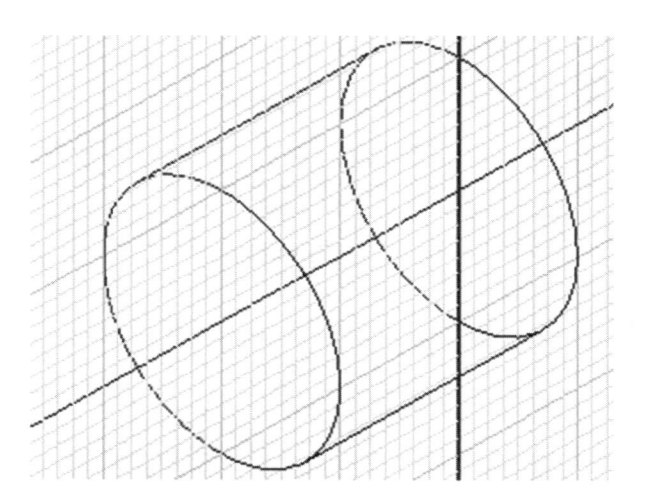

29. Move the cursor to the upper middle portion of the screen and left click on the "Look At" icon as shown in Figure 25.

Figure 25

Left Click Here

Chapter 6: Advanced Design Procedures

30. Move the cursor to the lower left portion of the screen and left click on the text **YZ Plane** in the part tree as shown in Figure 26.

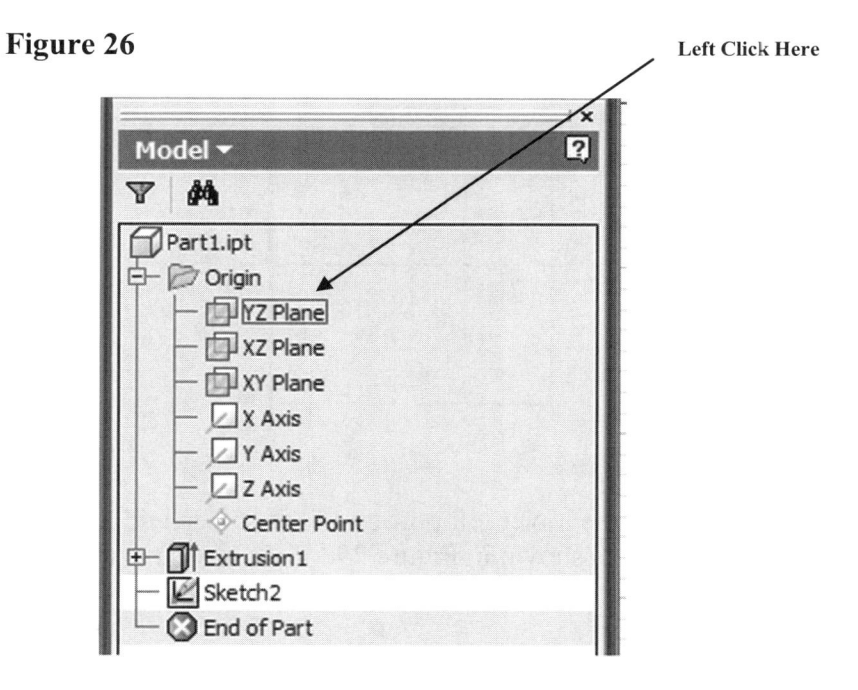

Figure 26

31. Notice the YZ plane becoming visible through the part as shown in Figure 27.

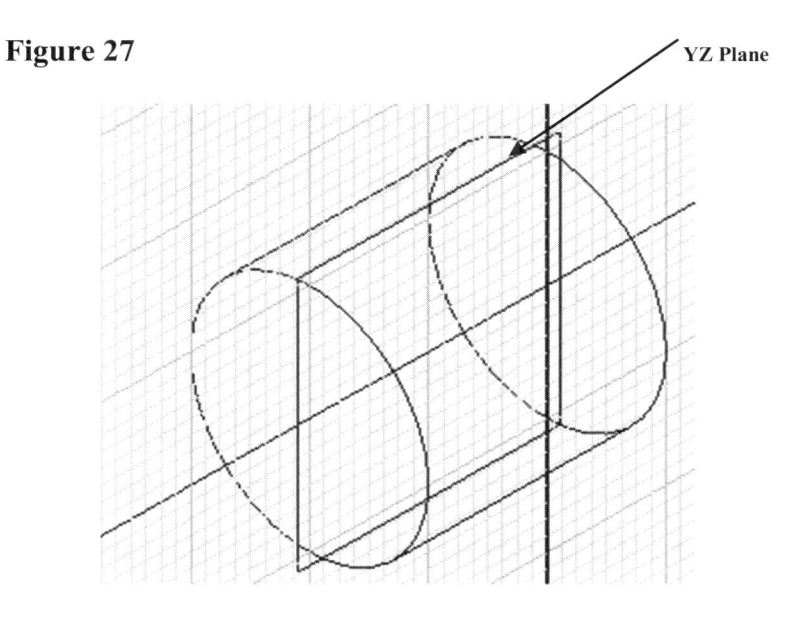

Figure 27

Chapter 6: Advanced Design Procedures

32. Inventor will rotate the YZ plane to provide a perpendicular view as shown in Figure 28.

   Figure 28

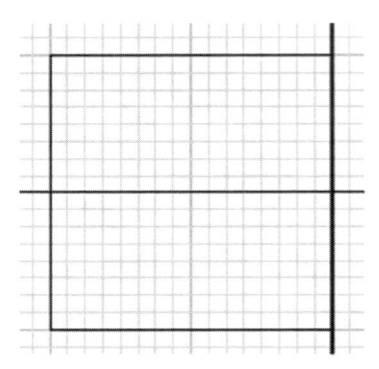

33. Move the cursor to the lower left portion of the screen and left click on **Project Geometry** as shown in Figure 29. You may have to scroll down.

   Figure 29

Chapter 6: Advanced Design Procedures

34. Move the cursor over and left click on each side of the part as shown in Figure 30.

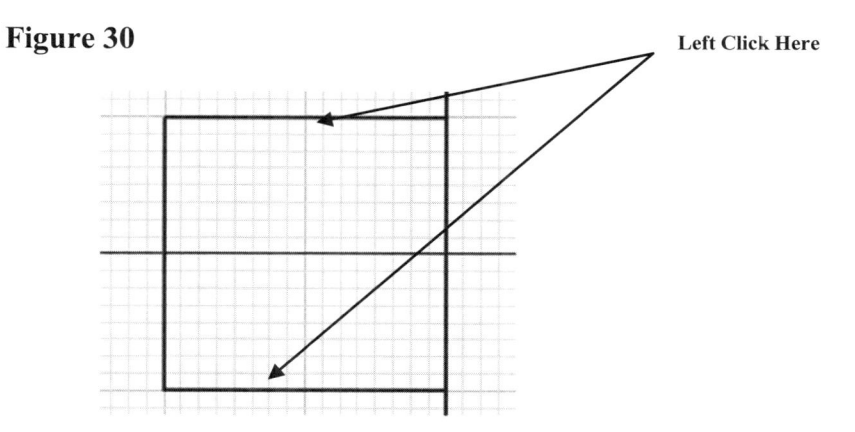

Figure 30   Left Click Here

35. Move the cursor to the upper left portion of the screen and left click on **Line** as shown in Figure 31.

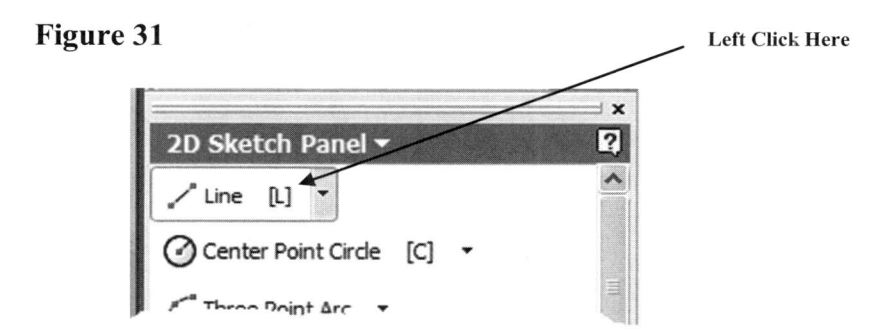

Figure 31   Left Click Here

36. Move the cursor to the midpoint of the upper line causing a green dot to appear and left click once as shown in Figure 32.

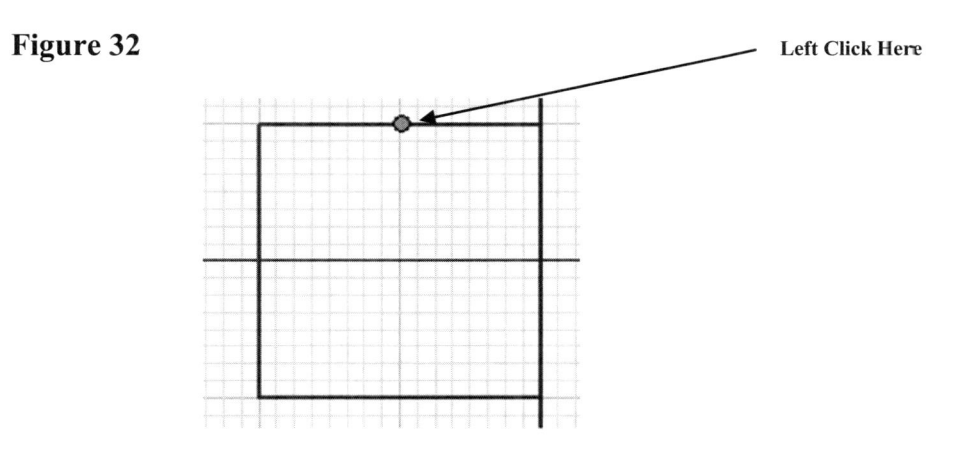

Figure 32   Left Click Here

291

Chapter 6: Advanced Design Procedures

37. Move the cursor down to the lower line causing a green dot to appear and left click as shown in Figure 33.

Figure 33

Left Click Here

38. Your screen should look similar to Figure 34.

Figure 34

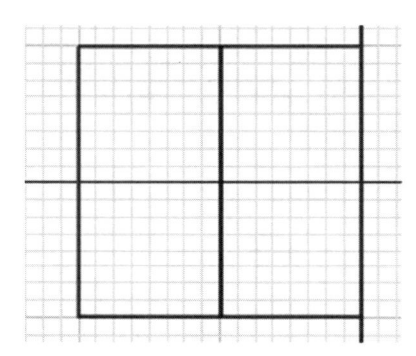

39. Move the cursor to the upper left corner of the screen and left click on **Center Point Circle** as shown in Figure 35.

Figure 35

Left Click Here

Chapter 6: Advanced Design Procedures

40. Move the cursor to the midpoint of the center line causing a green dot to appear and left click as shown in Figure 36.

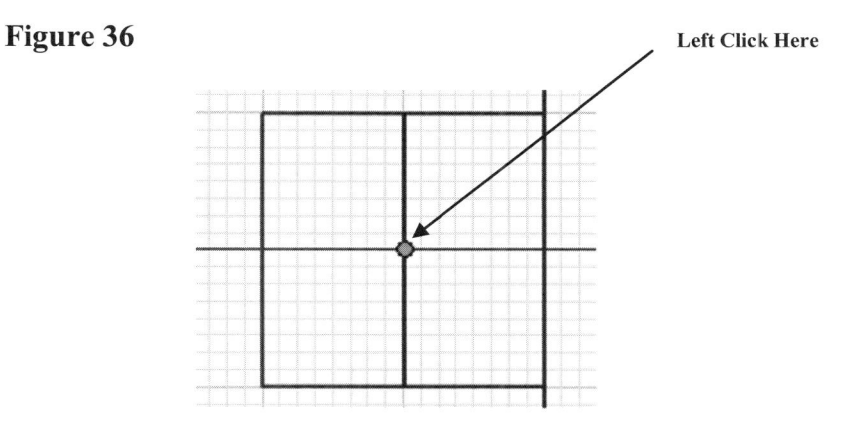

Figure 36

Left Click Here

41. Move the cursor out to the side and left click as shown in Figure 37.

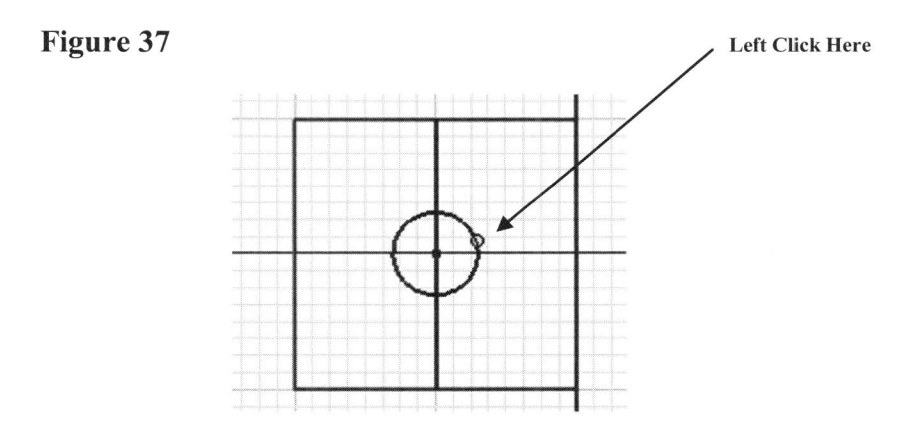

Figure 37

Left Click Here

42. Move the cursor to the middle left portion of the screen and left click on **General Dimension** as shown in Figure 38.

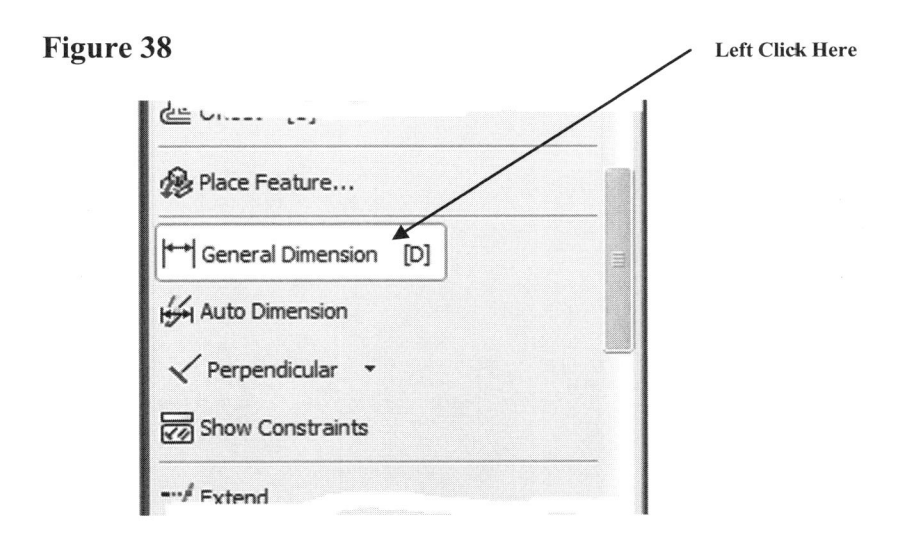

Figure 38

Left Click Here

293

Chapter 6: Advanced Design Procedures

43. After selecting **General Dimension** move the cursor over the edge (not center) of the circle until it turns red as shown in Figure 39. Select the line by left clicking once anywhere on the edge of the circle. The dimension will be attached to the cursor.

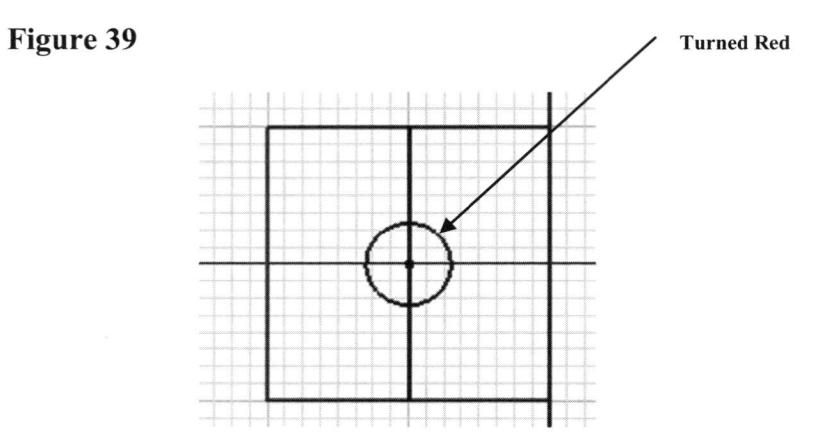

Figure 39   Turned Red

44. Move the cursor around. The actual dimension of the line will appear as shown in Figure 40.

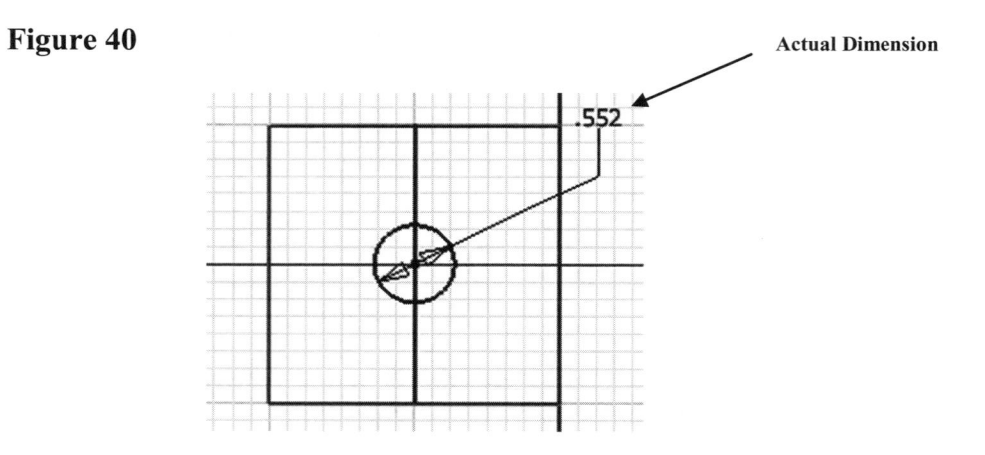

Figure 40   Actual Dimension

Chapter 6: Advanced Design Procedures

45. Move the cursor to where the dimension will be placed and left click once. While the dimension is still in red, left click once. The Edit Dimension dialog box will appear as shown in Figure 41.

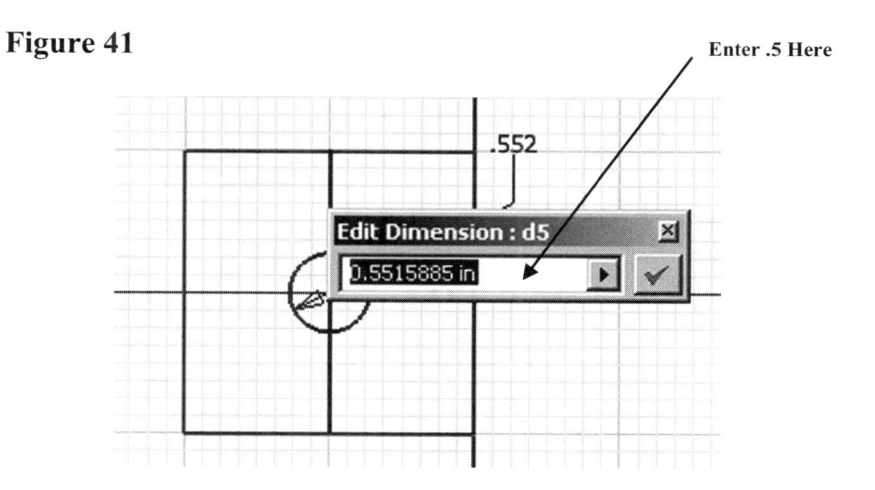

Figure 41

46. To edit the dimension, type **.5** in the Edit Dimension dialog box (while the current dimension is highlighted) and press **Enter** on the keyboard.

47. Your screen should look similar to Figure 42.

Figure 42

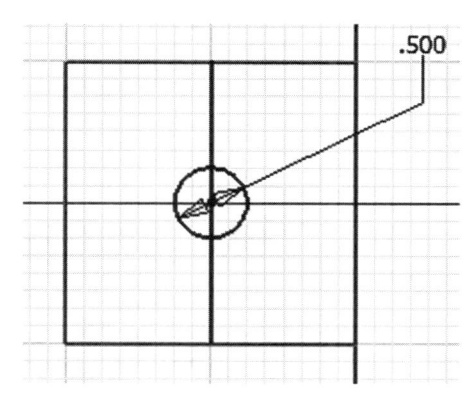

295

Chapter 6: Advanced Design Procedures

48. Right click anywhere around the drawing. A pop up menu will appear. Left click on **Done [Esc]** as shown in Figure 43.

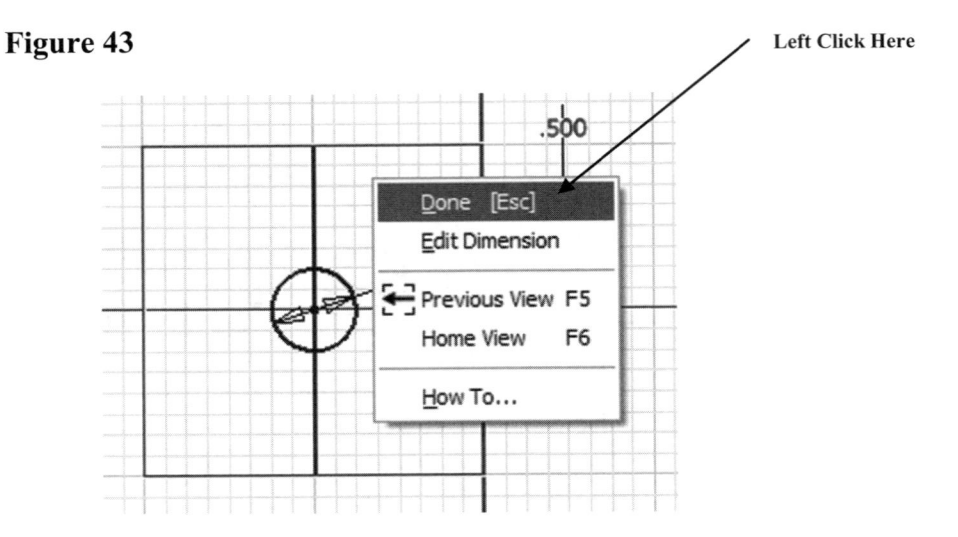

Figure 43

Left Click Here

49. Move the cursor over the center line causing it to turn red. Right click on the line. A pop up menu will appear. Left click on **Delete** as shown in Figure 44.

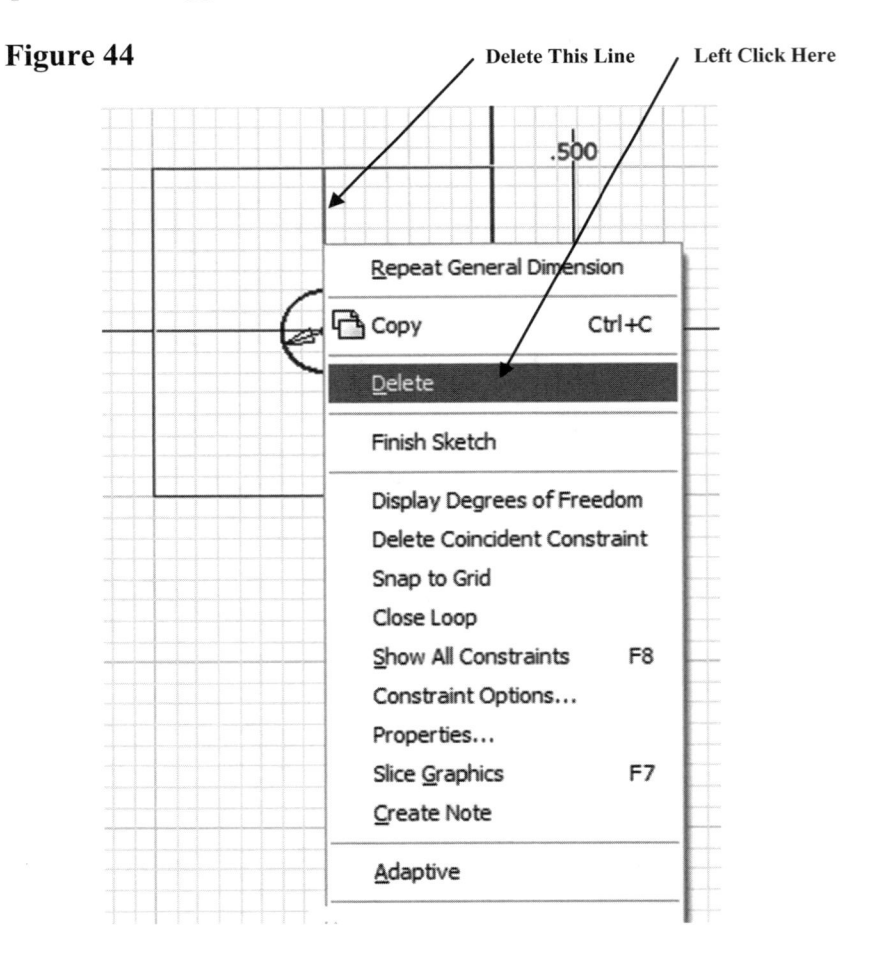

Figure 44

Delete This Line

Left Click Here

296

Chapter 6: Advanced Design Procedures

50. Repeat the same steps to delete each of the three lines that were projected on to the YZ plane. Your screen should look similar to Figure 45.

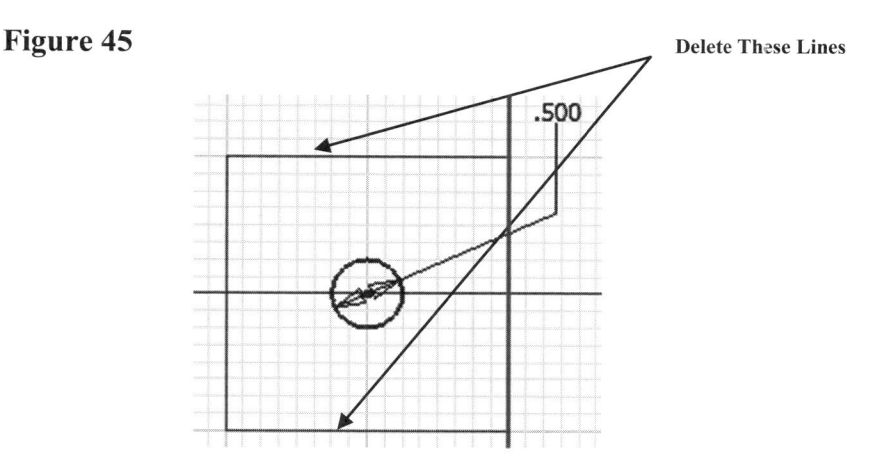

Figure 45

51. After you have verified that no commands are active, right click anywhere on the sketch. A pop up menu will appear. Left click on **Finish Sketch** as shown in Figure 46.

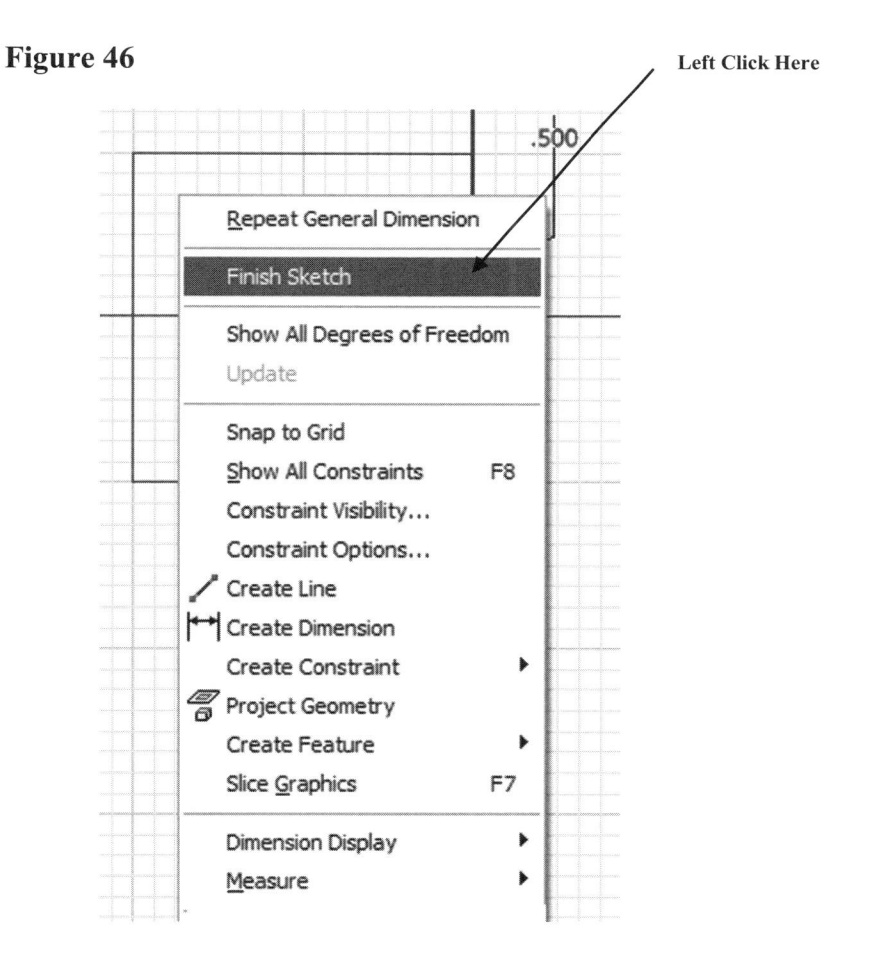

Figure 46

Chapter 6: Advanced Design Procedures

52. Right click around the sketch. A pop up menu will appear. Left click on **Isometric/Home View** as shown in Figure 47.

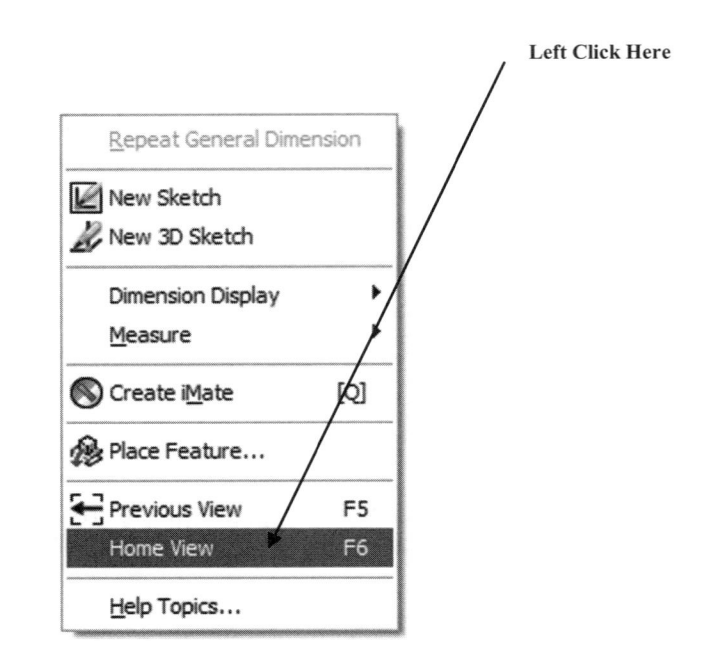

Figure 47

Left Click Here

53. Your screen should look similar to Figure 48.

Figure 48

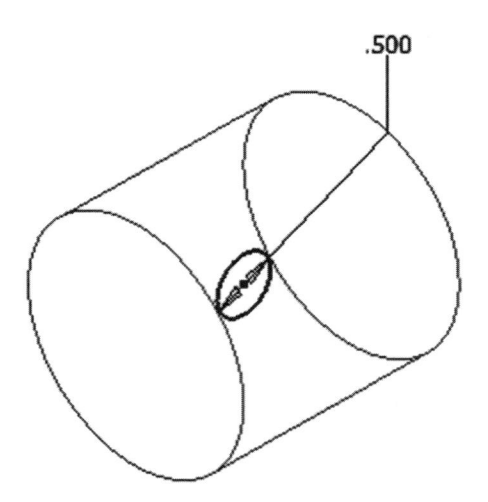

298

Chapter 6: Advanced Design Procedures

54. Move the cursor to the upper left portion of the screen and left click on **Extrude**. The Extrude dialog box will appear. Move the cursor inside the small circle causing it to turn red and left click once as shown in Figure 49.

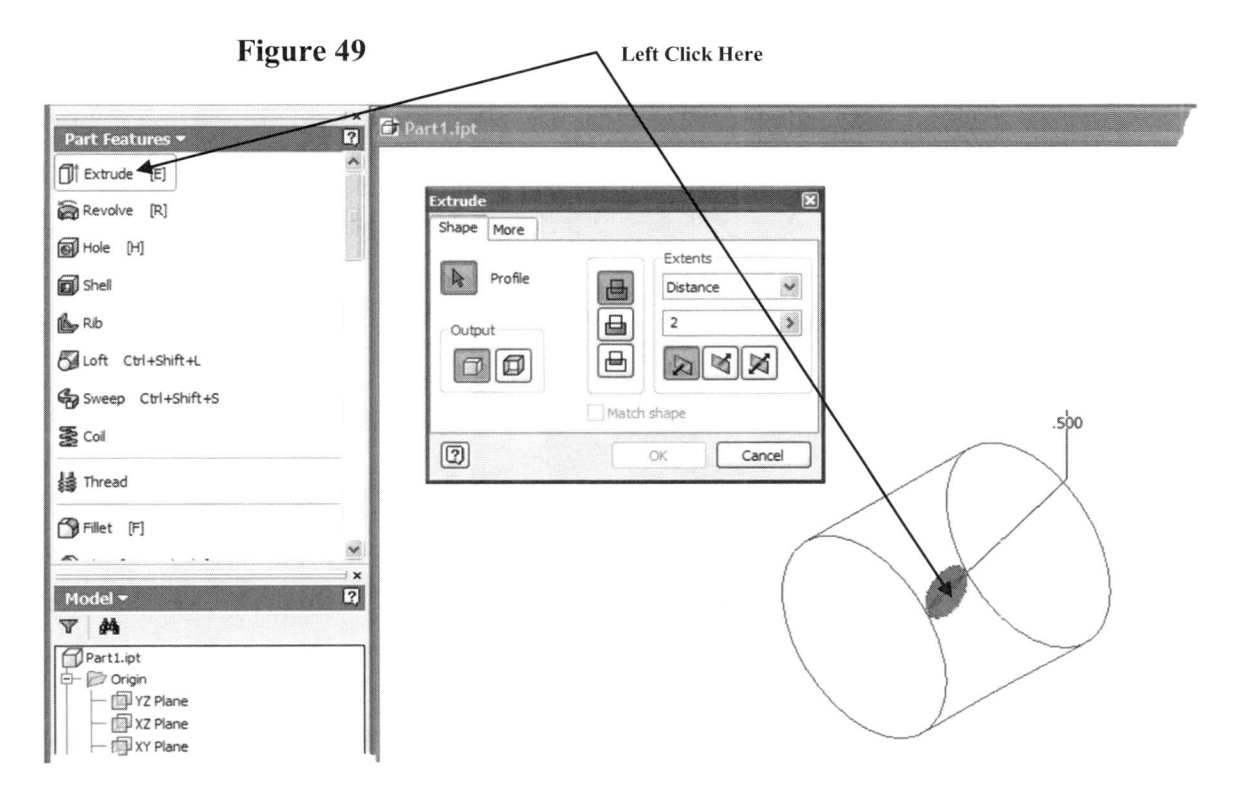

Figure 49

Chapter 6: Advanced Design Procedures

55. Left click on the "Cut" icon. Enter **2.00** for the distance. Left click on the "Bi-directional" icon. Inventor will provide a preview of the extrusion as shown in Figure 50.

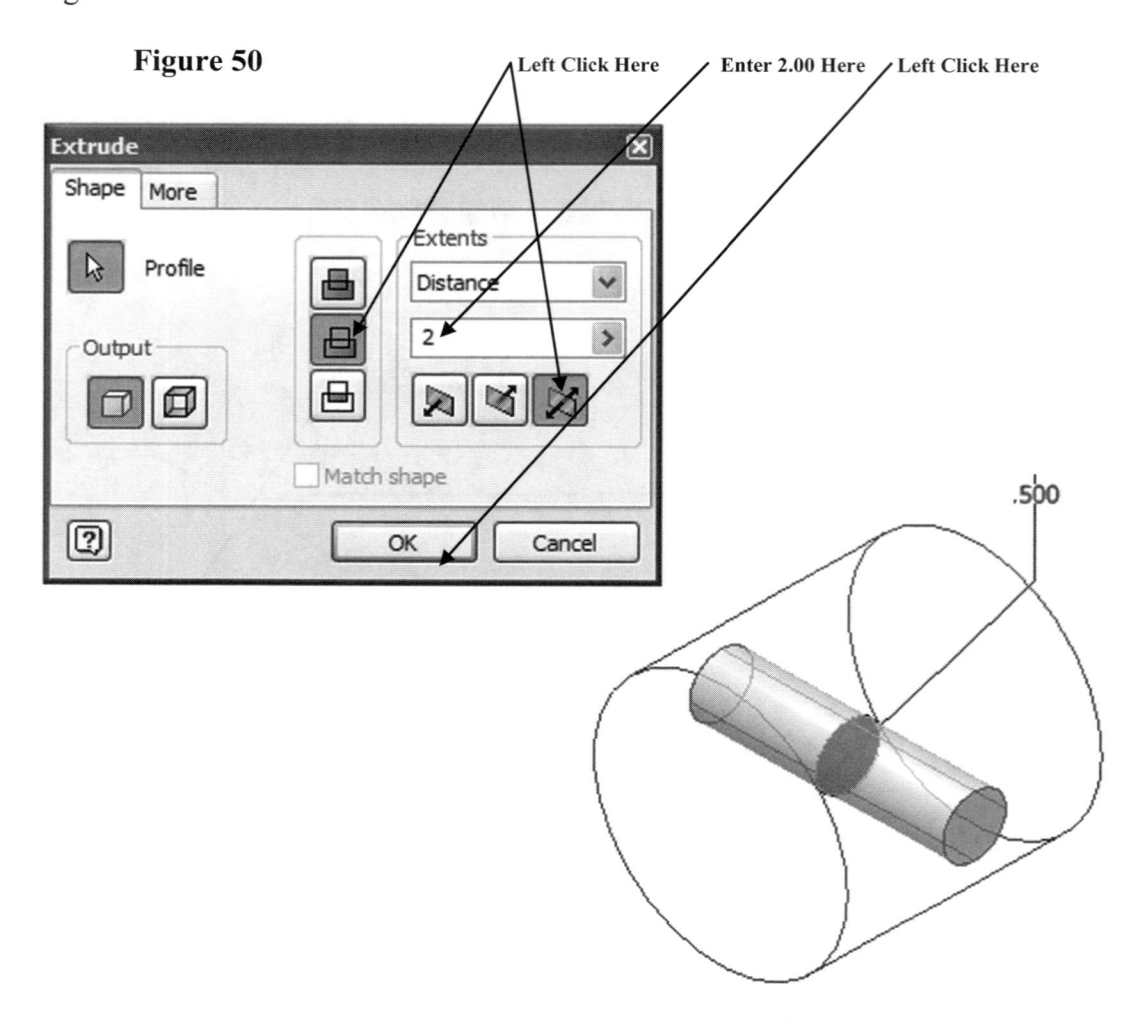

Figure 50

56. Left click on **OK** as shown in Figure 50.

300

Chapter 6: Advanced Design Procedures

57. Your screen should look similar to Figure 51.

Figure 51

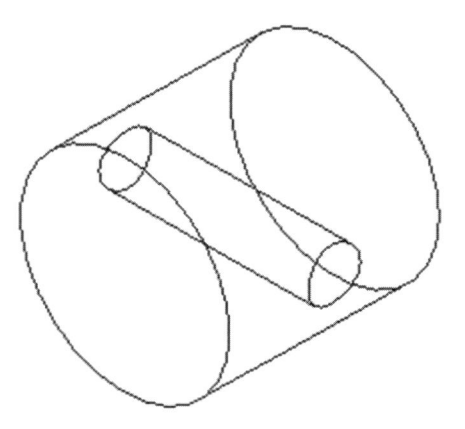

58. Move the cursor to the upper right portion of the screen and left click on the drop down arrow to the right of "Wireframe Display". Left click on "Shaded Display" as shown in Figure 52.

Figure 52

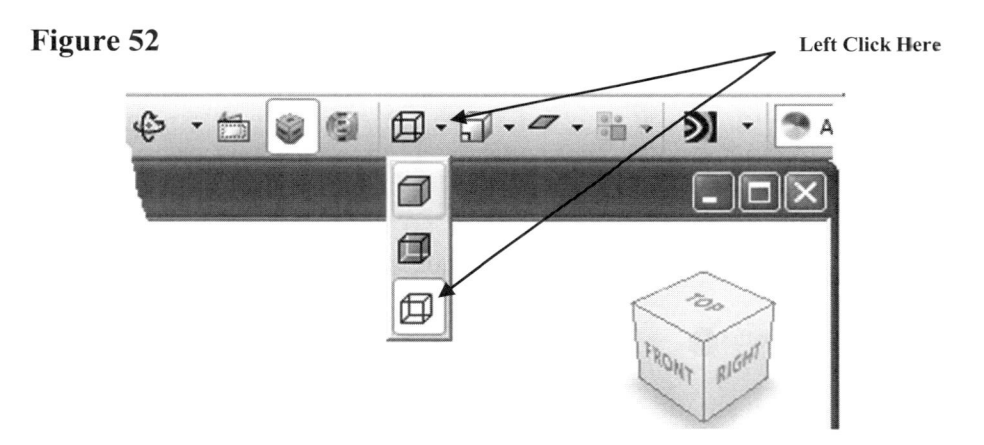

Left Click Here

59. Your screen should look similar to Figure 53.

Figure 53

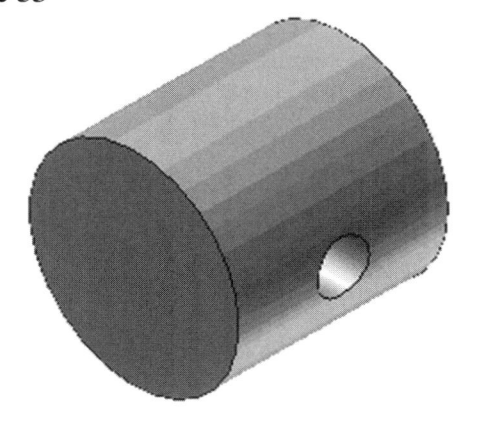

301

Chapter 6: Advanced Design Procedures

60. Move the cursor to the upper left portion of the screen and left click on **Shell**. The Shell dialog box will appear as shown in Figure 54.

Figure 54

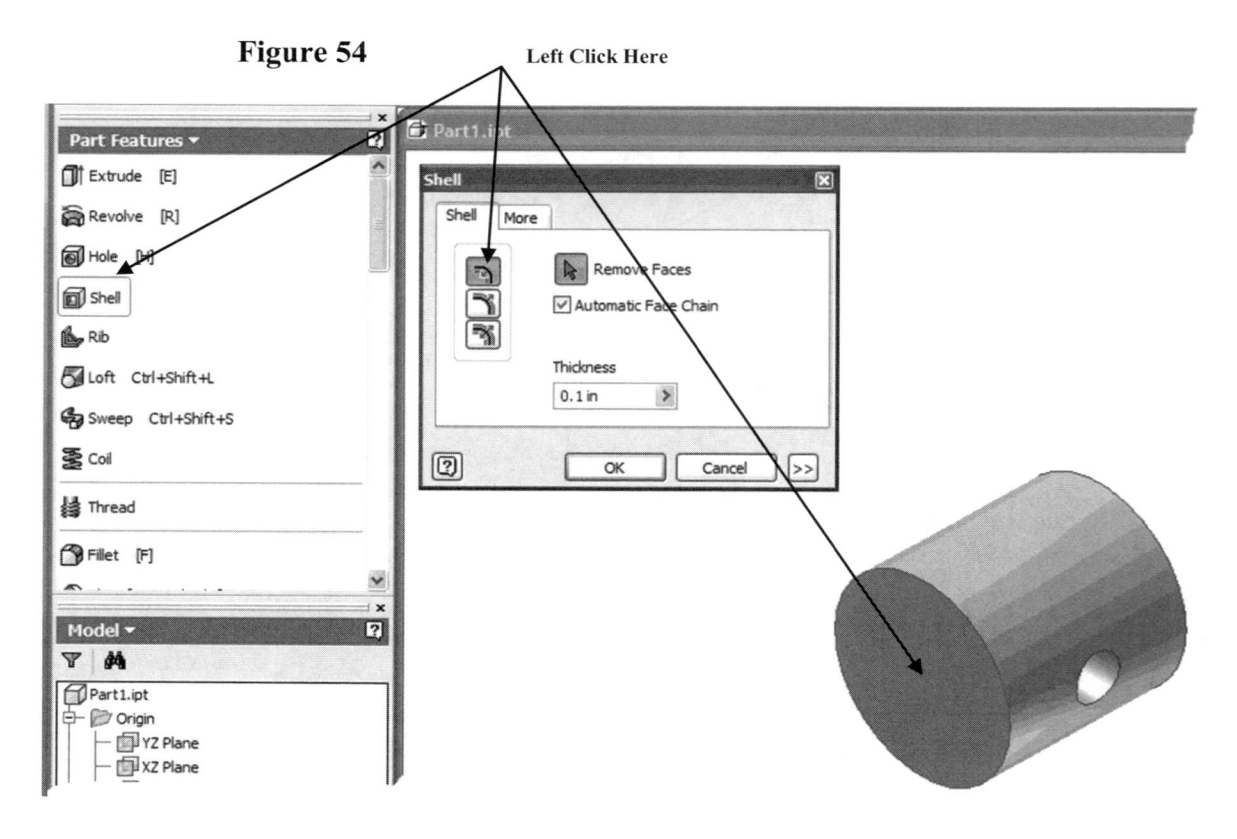

61. Left click on the lower surface of the part as shown in Figure 54.

62. Left click on **OK**.

63. Your screen should look similar to Figure 55.

Figure 55

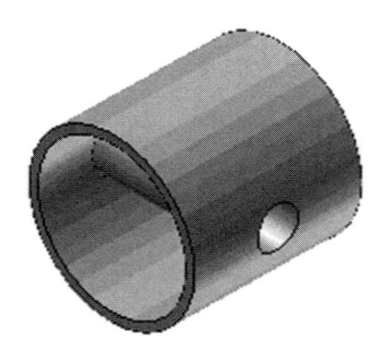

Chapter 6: Advanced Design Procedures

64. Move the cursor to the upper middle portion of the screen and left click on the "Look At" icon as shown in Figure 56.

Figure 56

Left Click Here

65. Move the cursor to the lower surface of the part causing the inside and outside edges to turn red and left click as shown in Figure 57.

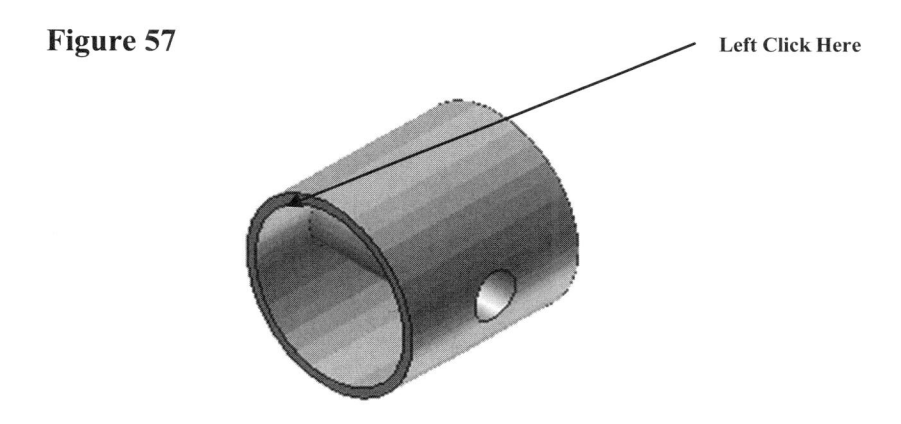

Figure 57

Left Click Here

66. After both edges turn red, left click once. Inventor will rotate the part providing a perpendicular view of the inside as shown in Figure 58.

Figure 58

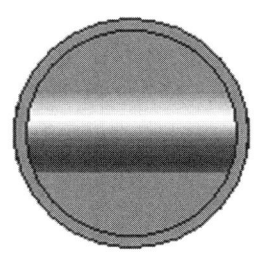

303

Chapter 6: Advanced Design Procedures

67. Move the cursor over the same surface causing both the inside and outside lines to turn red. You may have to zoom in for Inventor to find both lines at the same time. Both lines must be red at the same time. After both lines are red at the same time, right click on the surface as shown in Figure 59. The surface will turn blue.

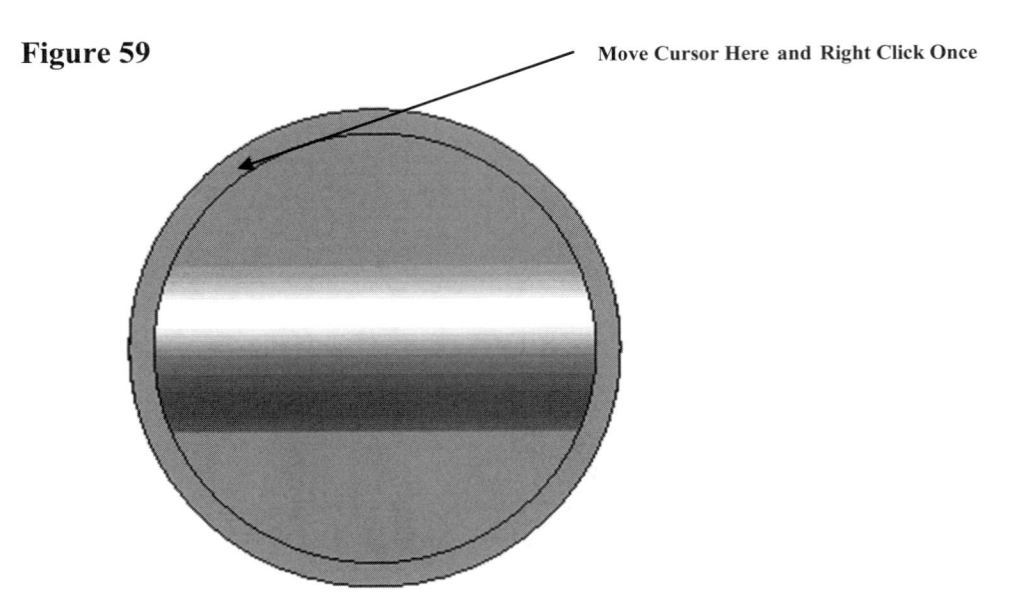

Figure 59 — Move Cursor Here and Right Click Once

68. A pop up menu will appear. Left click on **New Sketch** as shown in Figure 60.

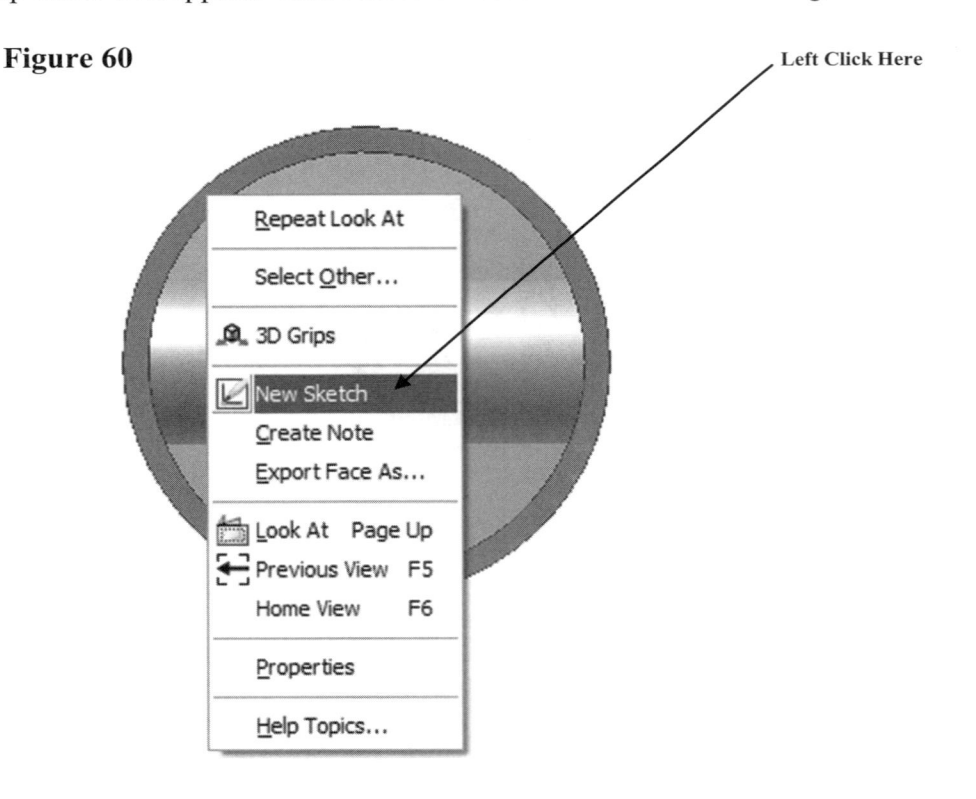

Figure 60 — Left Click Here

304

69. Inventor will start a new sketch on the selected surface. Your screen should look similar to Figure 61.

Figure 61

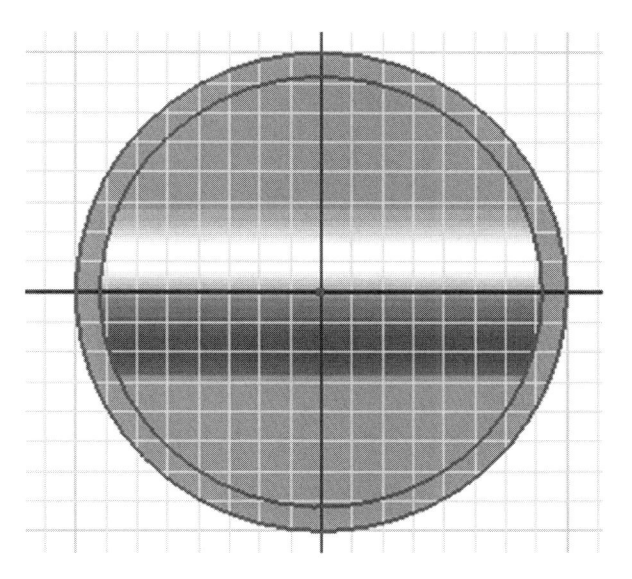

70. Move the cursor to the upper left portion of the screen and left click on **Line** as shown in Figure 62.

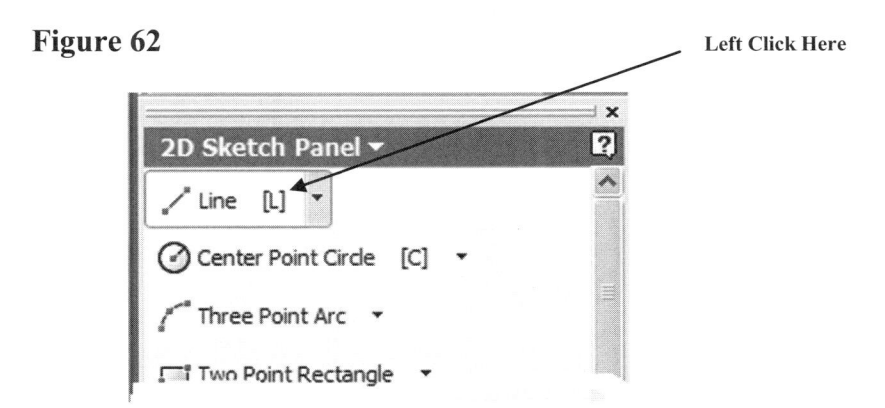

Figure 62 Left Click Here

Chapter 6: Advanced Design Procedures

71. Move the cursor to the center of the part causing a green dot to appear and left click as shown in Figure 63.

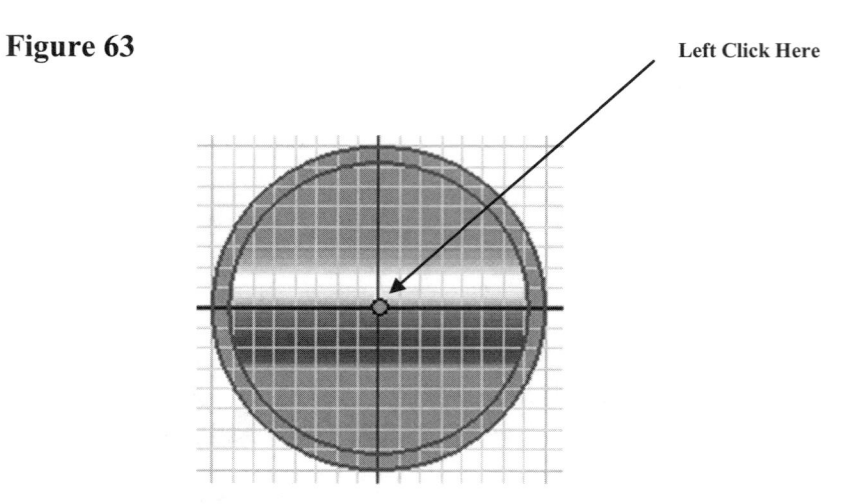

Figure 63

Left Click Here

72. Move the cursor upward and left click as shown in Figure 64.

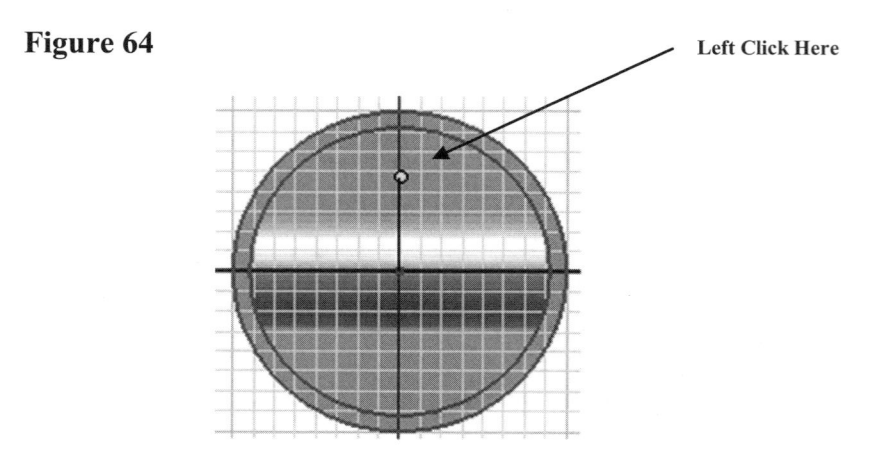

Figure 64

Left Click Here

Chapter 6: Advanced Design Procedures

73. Right click anywhere around the drawing. A pop up menu will appear. Left click on **Done [Esc]** as shown in Figure 65.

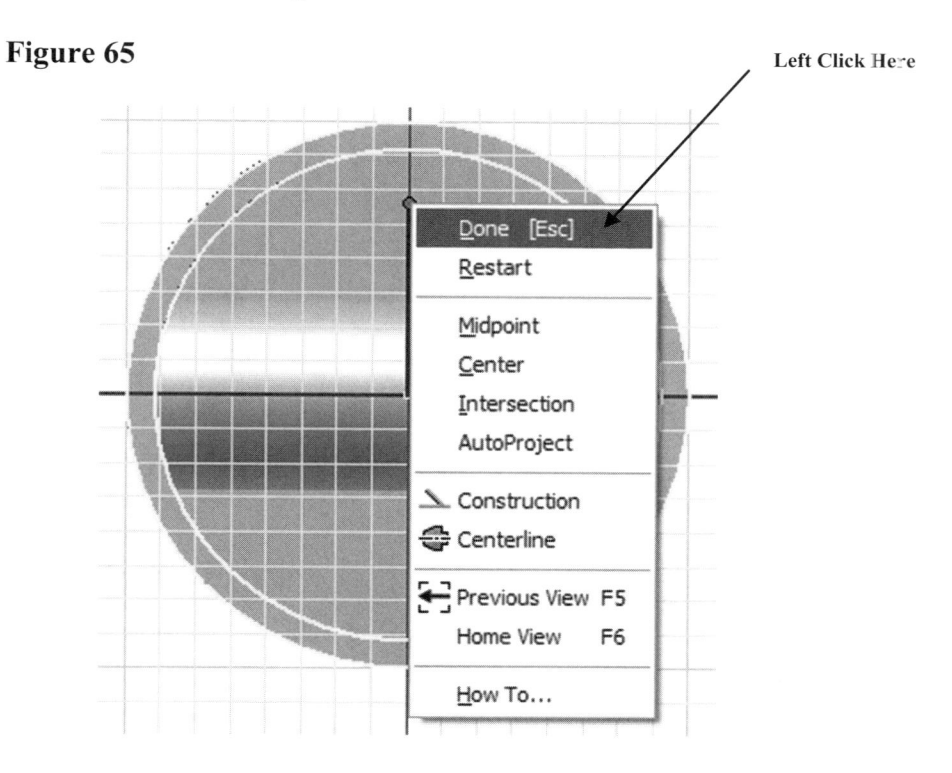

   Figure 65

74. Move the cursor to the upper left portion of the screen and left click on **Line** as shown in Figure 66.

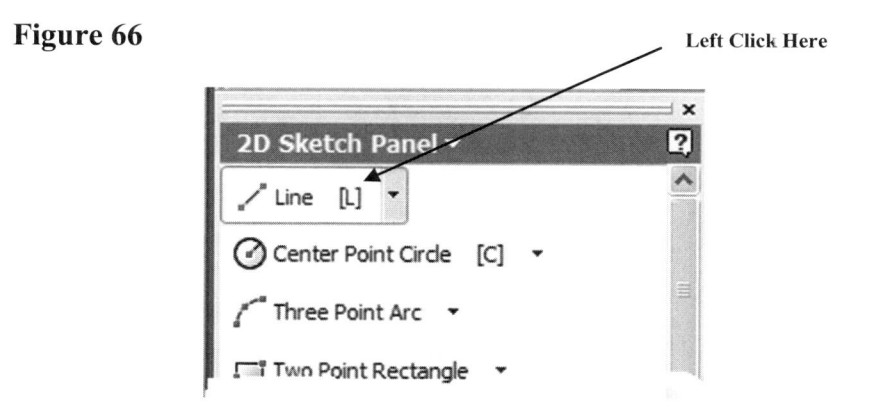

   Figure 66

307

Chapter 6: Advanced Design Procedures

75. Move the cursor to the center of the part causing a green dot to appear and left click as shown in Figure 67.

Figure 67

Left Click Here

76. Move the cursor to the left and left click as shown in Figure 68.

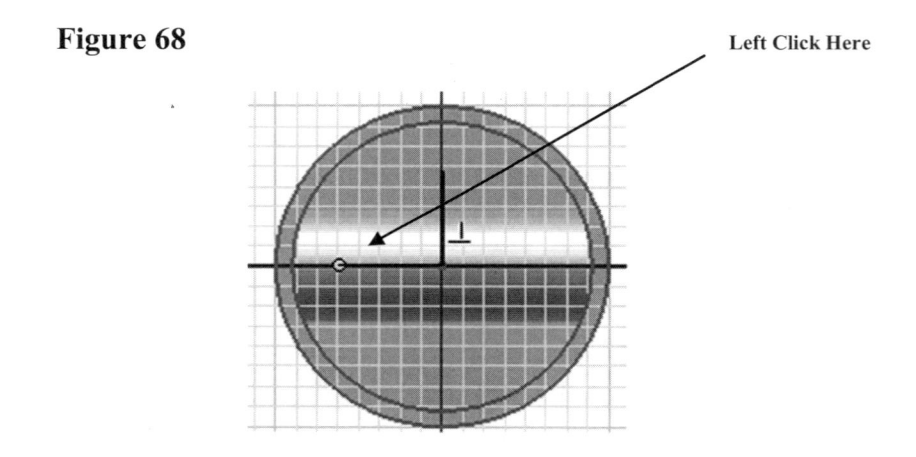

Figure 68

Left Click Here

Chapter 6: Advanced Design Procedures

77. Right click anywhere around the drawing. A pop up menu will appear. Left click on **Done [Esc]** as shown in Figure 69.

Figure 69

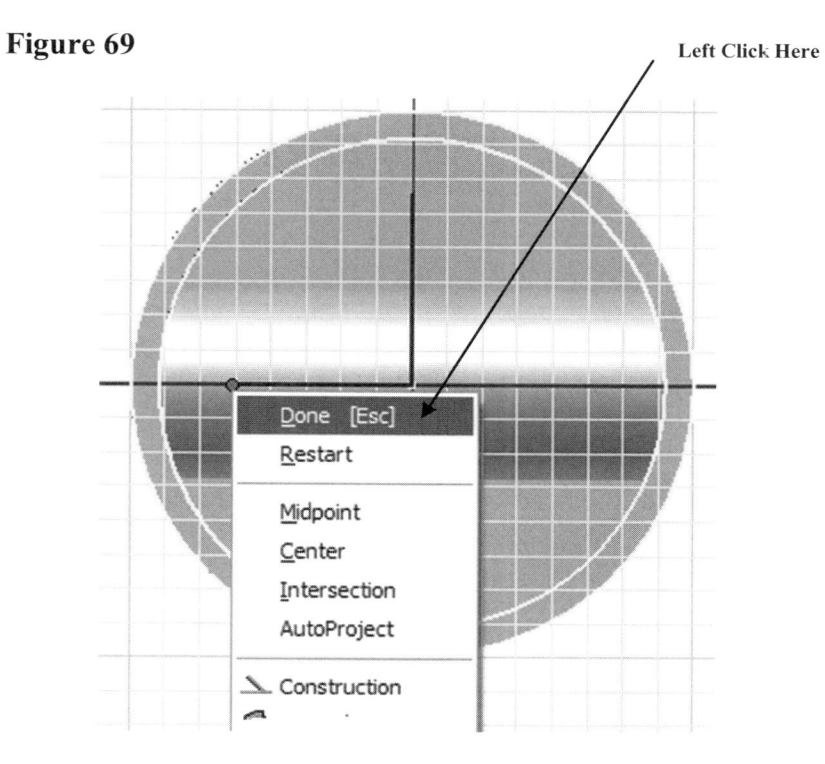

78. Your screen should look similar to Figure 70.

Figure 70

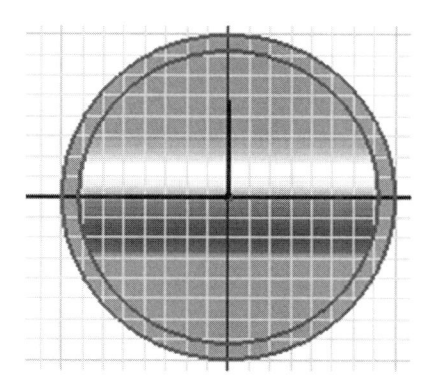

Chapter 6: Advanced Design Procedures

79. Move the cursor to the upper left portion of the screen and left click on **Line** as shown in Figure 71.

Figure 71

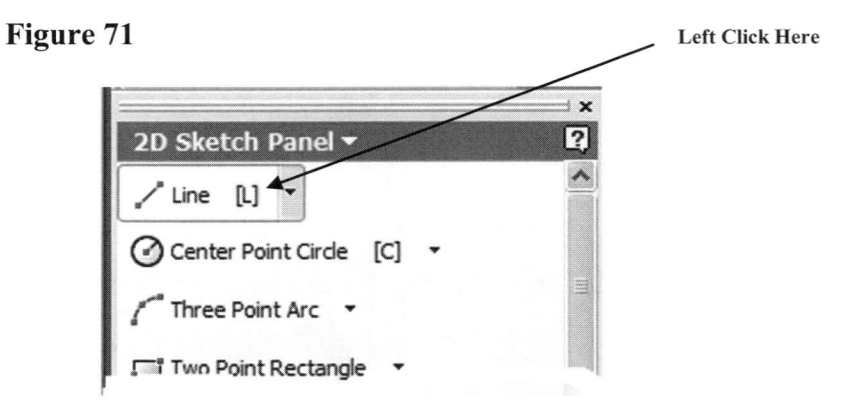

80. Move the cursor to the position shown in Figure 72 and left click once.

Figure 72

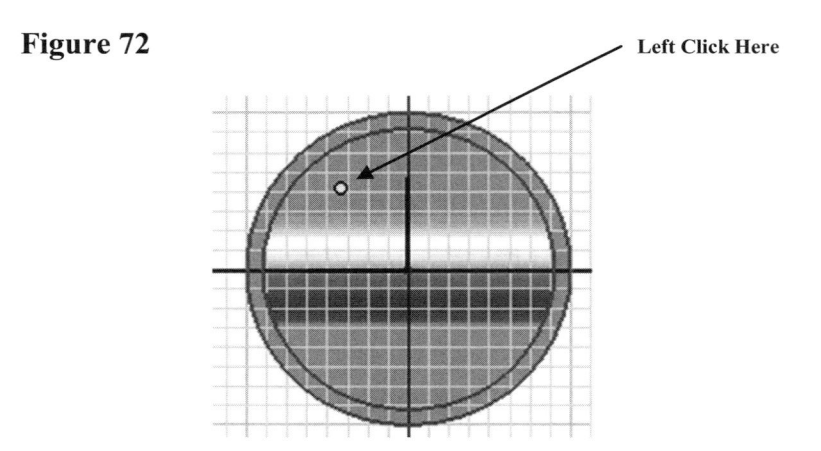

81. Move the cursor downward and left click as shown in Figure 73.

Figure 73

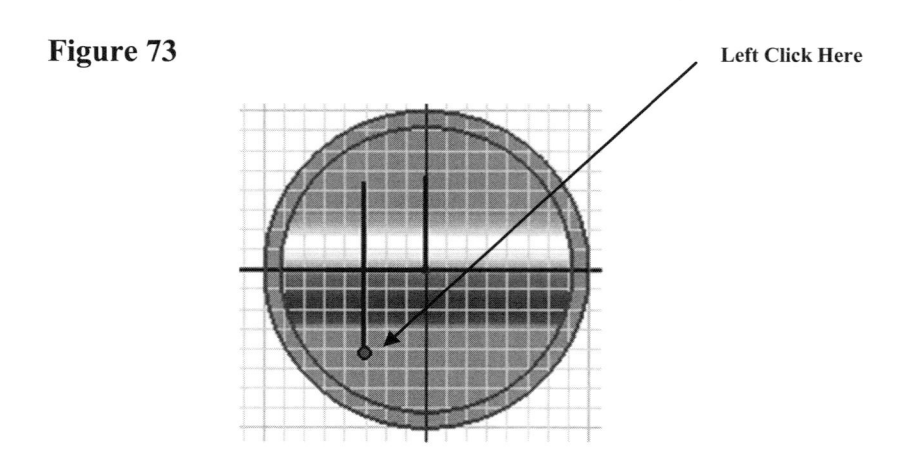

310

Chapter 6: Advanced Design Procedures

82. Move the cursor to the right and left click as shown in Figure 74.

Figure 74

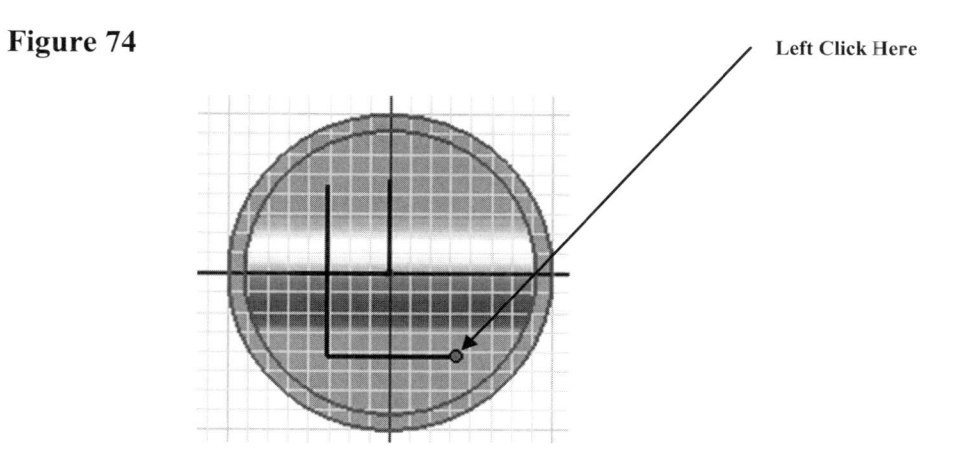

Left Click Here

83. Move the cursor upward and left click. Ensure that the dots appear from the original starting point as shown in Figure 75.

Figure 75

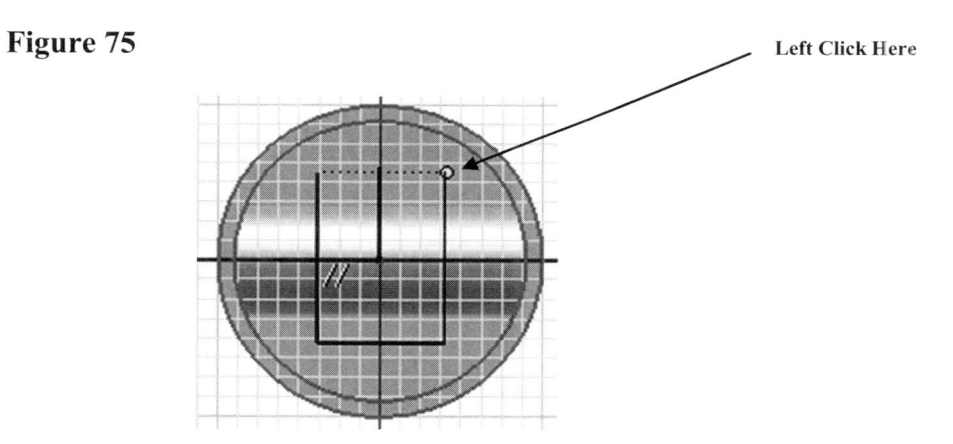

Left Click Here

311

Chapter 6: Advanced Design Procedures

84. Move the cursor to the left and left click as shown in Figure 76.

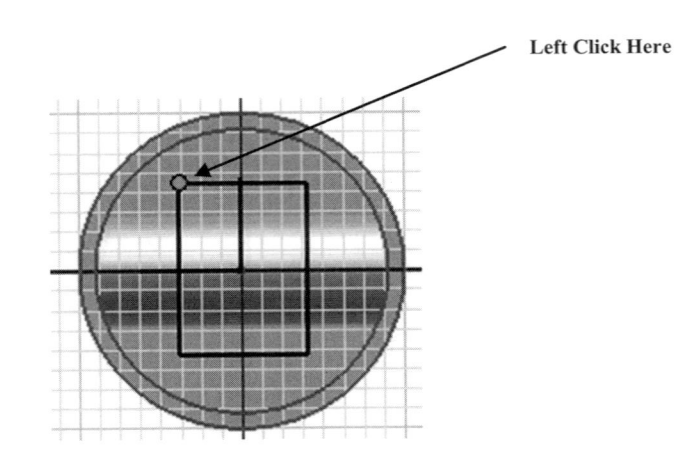

Figure 76   Left Click Here

85. Right click anywhere around the drawing. A pop up menu will appear. Left click on **Done [Esc]** as shown in Figure 77.

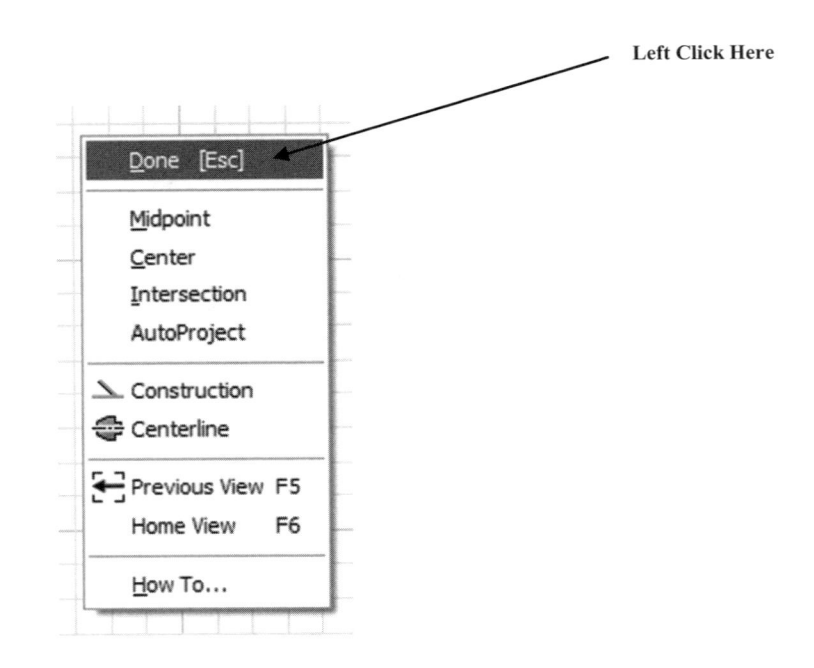

Figure 77   Left Click Here

312

86. Your screen should look similar to Figure 78.

Figure 78

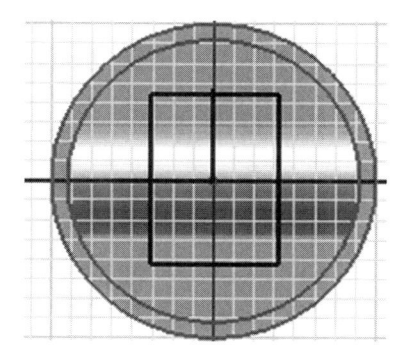

87. Move the cursor to the middle left portion of the screen and left click on **General Dimension** as shown in Figure 79.

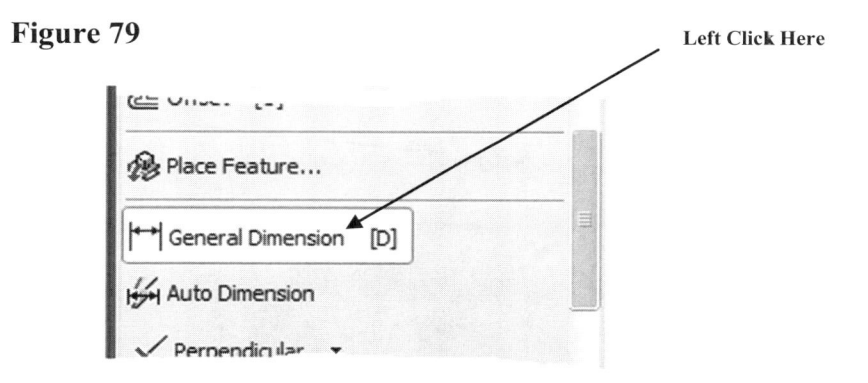

Figure 79

Left Click Here

88. After selecting **General Dimension** move the cursor over the vertical line coming out of the center of the part. The line will turn red. Select the line by left clicking anywhere on the line as shown in Figure 80.

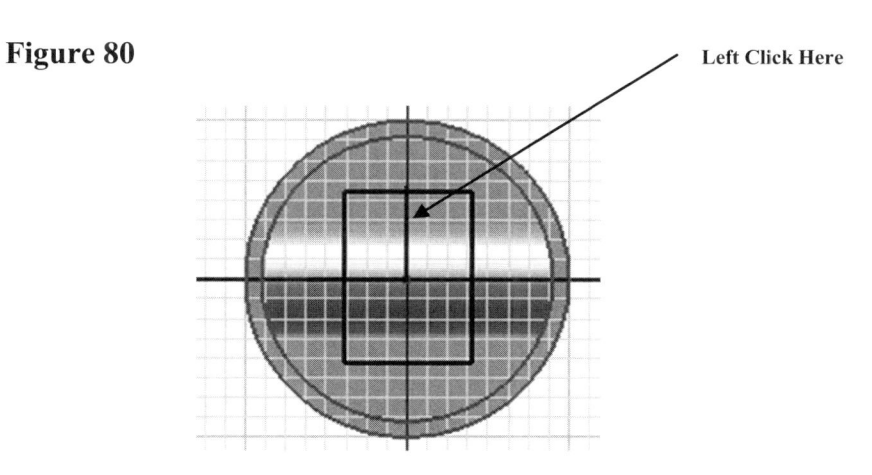

Figure 80

Left Click Here

313

Chapter 6: Advanced Design Procedures

89. Move the cursor to the far left line causing it to turn red and left click once as shown in Figure 81.

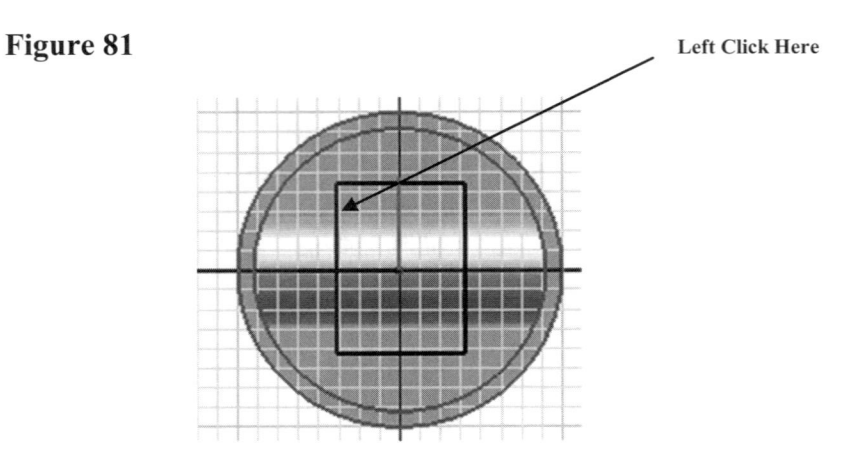

Figure 81   Left Click Here

90. Move the cursor upward. The actual dimension of the line will appear as shown in Figure 82.

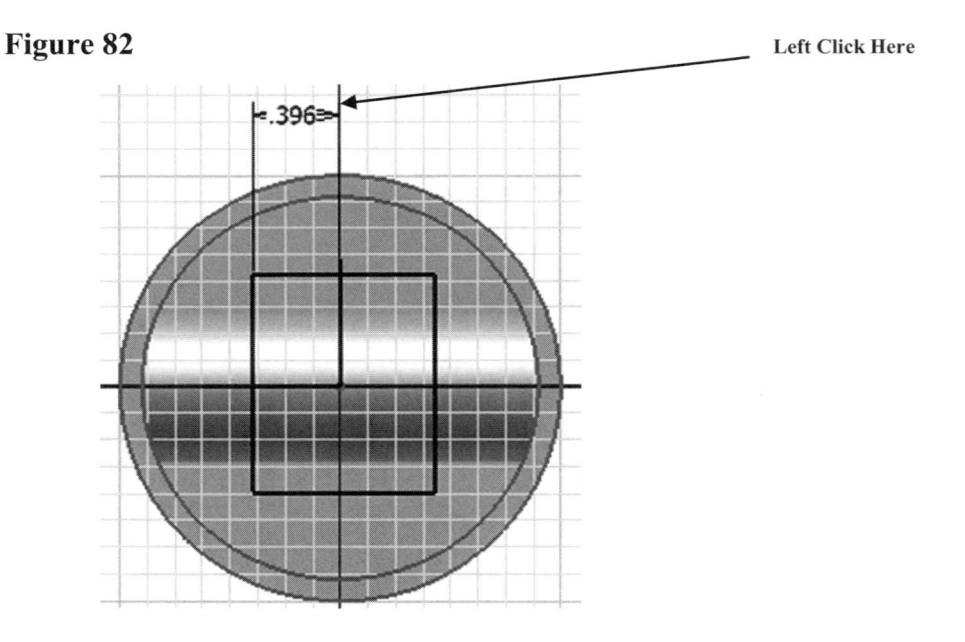

Figure 82   Left Click Here

.396

Chapter 6: Advanced Design Procedures

91. The dimension is attached to the cursor. Move the cursor up and down to verify it is attached. Move the cursor to where the dimension will be placed and left click once. While the dimension is still in red, left click once. The Edit Dimension dialog box will appear as shown in Figure 83.

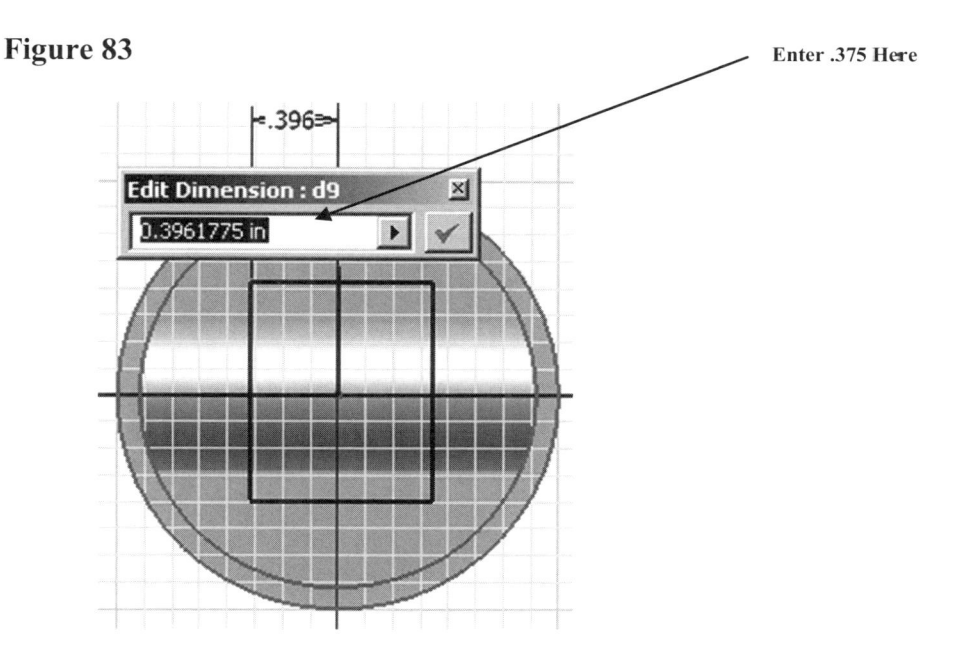

Figure 83

Enter .375 Here

92. To edit the dimension, type **.375** in the Edit Dimension dialog box (while the current dimension is highlighted) press **Enter** on the keyboard.

93. The dimension of the line will become .375 inches as shown in Figure 84.

Figure 84

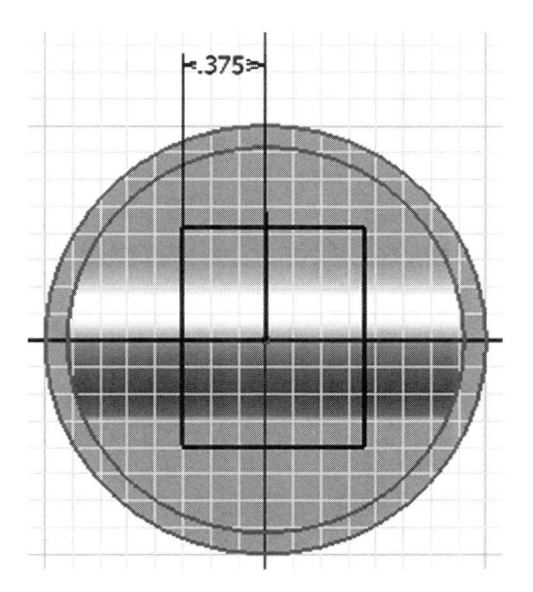

Chapter 6: Advanced Design Procedures

94. Move the cursor to the middle left portion of the screen and left click on **General Dimension** as shown in Figure 85.

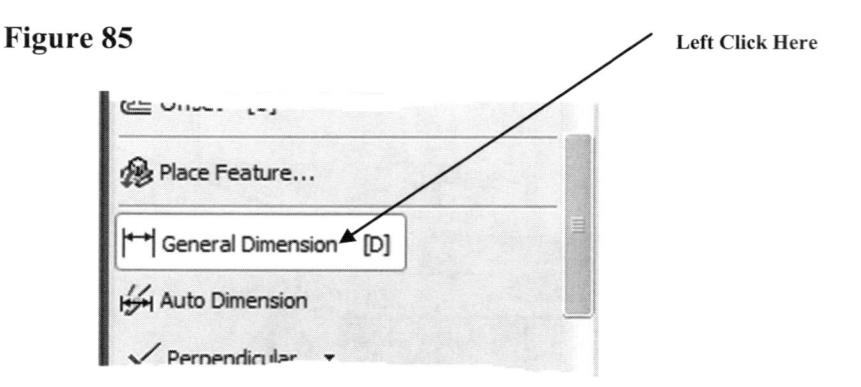

Figure 85   Left Click Here

95. After selecting **General Dimension** move the cursor over the horizontal line coming out of the center of the part until it turns red. Select the line by left clicking anywhere on the line as shown in Figure 86.

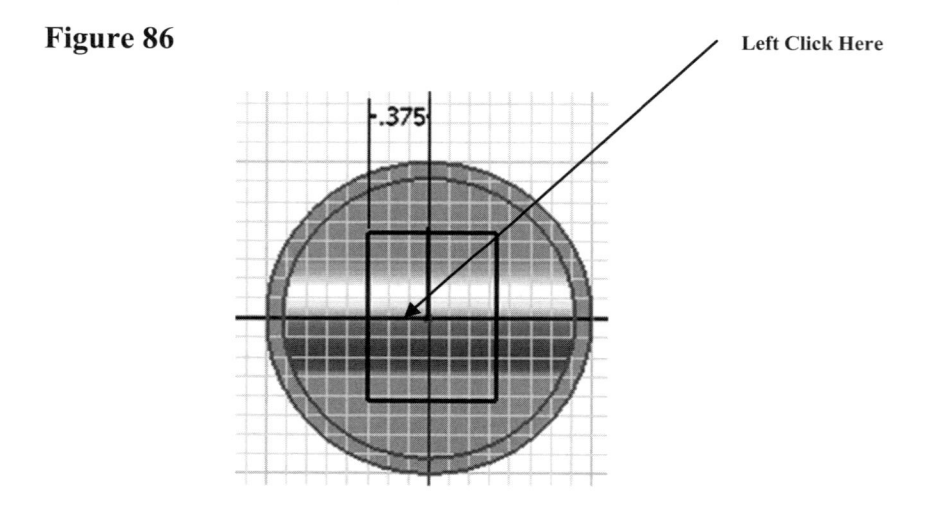

Figure 86   Left Click Here

Chapter 6: Advanced Design Procedures

96. Move the cursor to the upper line causing it to turn red and left click once as shown in Figure 87.

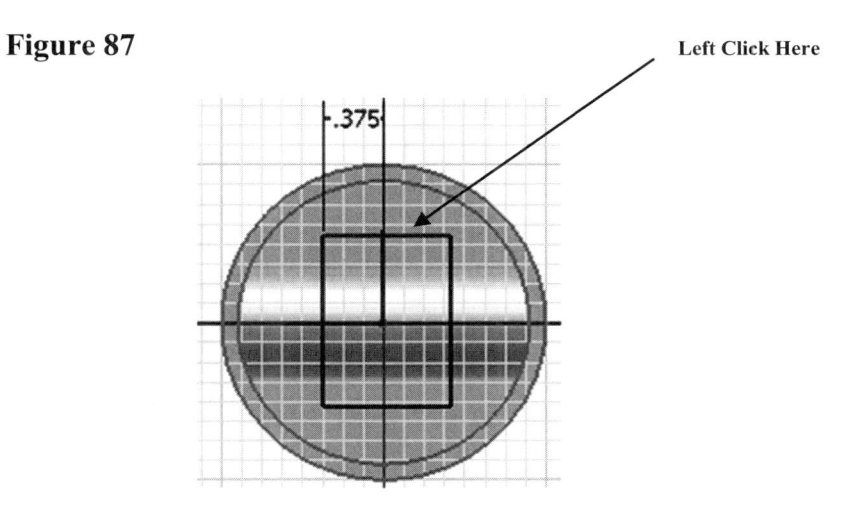

Figure 87

Left Click Here

97. Move the cursor out to the side. The actual dimension of the line will appear as shown in Figure 88.

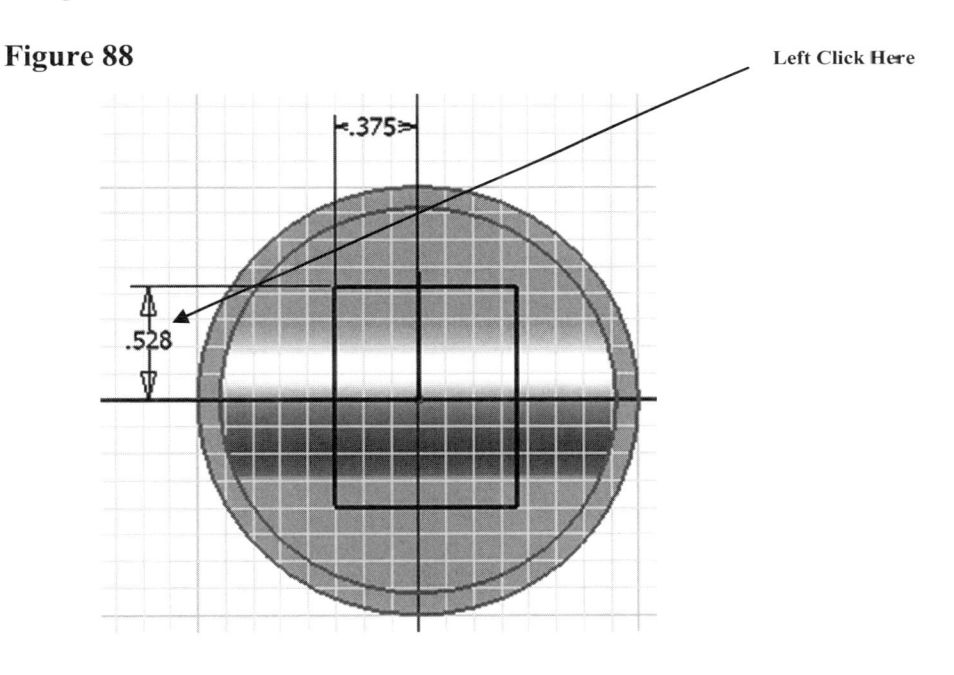

Figure 88

Left Click Here

317

Chapter 6: Advanced Design Procedures

98. The dimension is attached to the cursor. Move the cursor back and forth to verify it is attached. Move the cursor to where the dimension will be placed and left click once. While the dimension is still in red, left click once. The Edit Dimension dialog box will appear as shown in Figure 89.

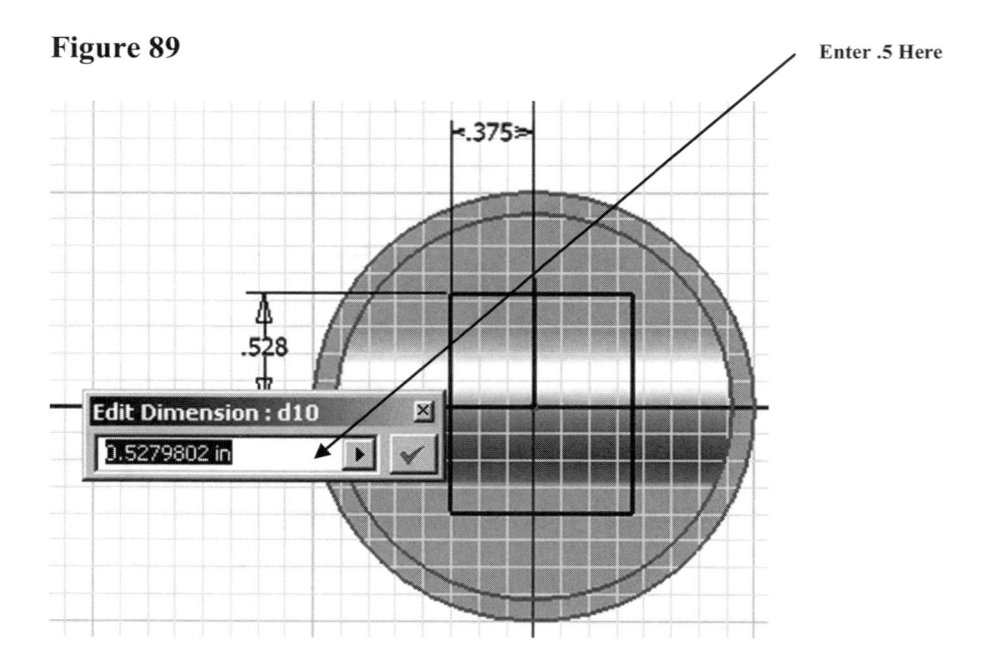

Figure 89

Enter .5 Here

99. To edit the dimension, type **.5** in the Edit Dimension dialog box (while the current dimension is highlighted) and press **Enter** on the keyboard.

100. The dimension of the line will become .500 inches as shown in Figure 90.

Figure 90

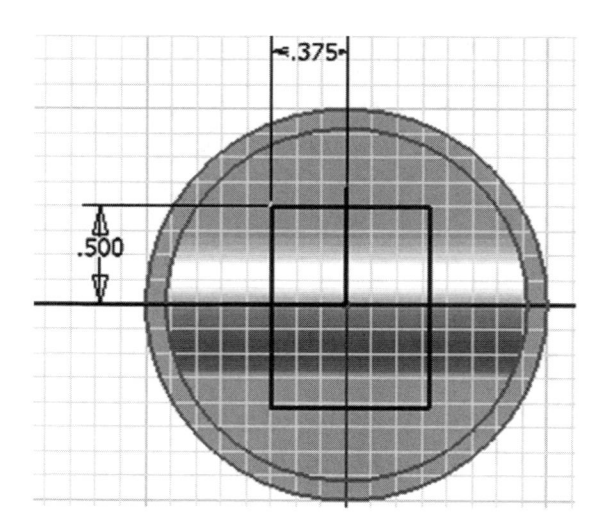

101. Move the cursor to the middle left portion of the screen and left click on **General Dimension** as shown in Figure 91.

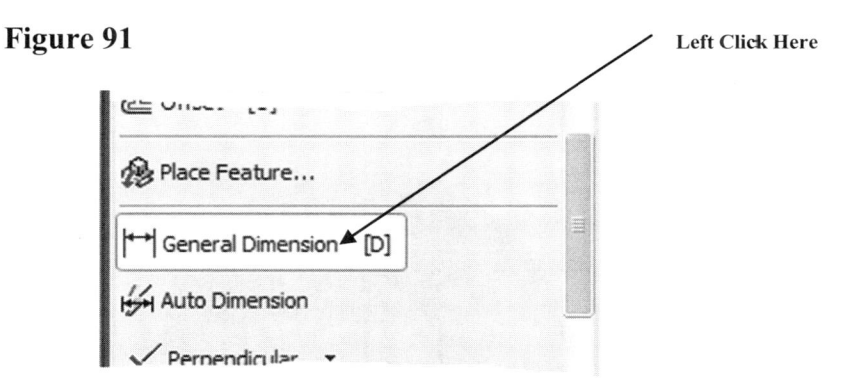

Figure 91

102. After selecting **General Dimension** move the cursor over the horizontal line coming out of the center of the part until it turns red. Select the line by left clicking anywhere on the line as shown in Figure 92.

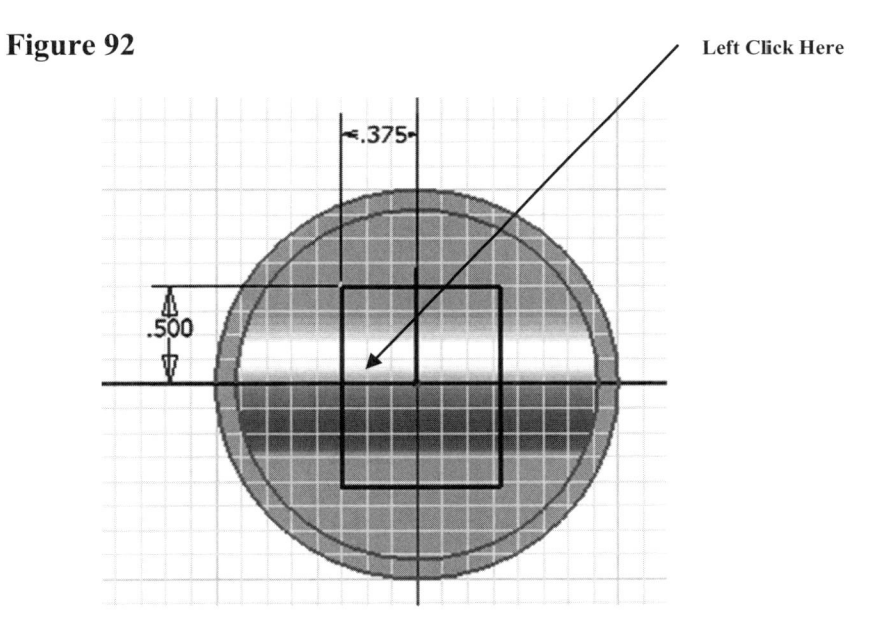

Figure 92

319

Chapter 6: Advanced Design Procedures

103. Move the cursor to the lower line causing it to turn red and left click once as shown in Figure 93.

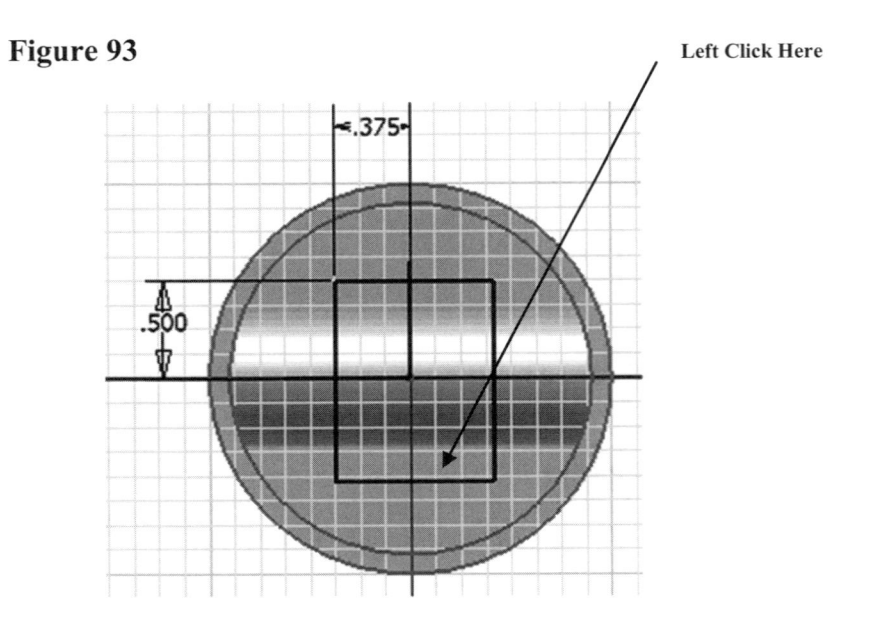

Figure 93 Left Click Here

104. Move the cursor out to the side. The actual dimension of the line will appear as shown in Figure 94.

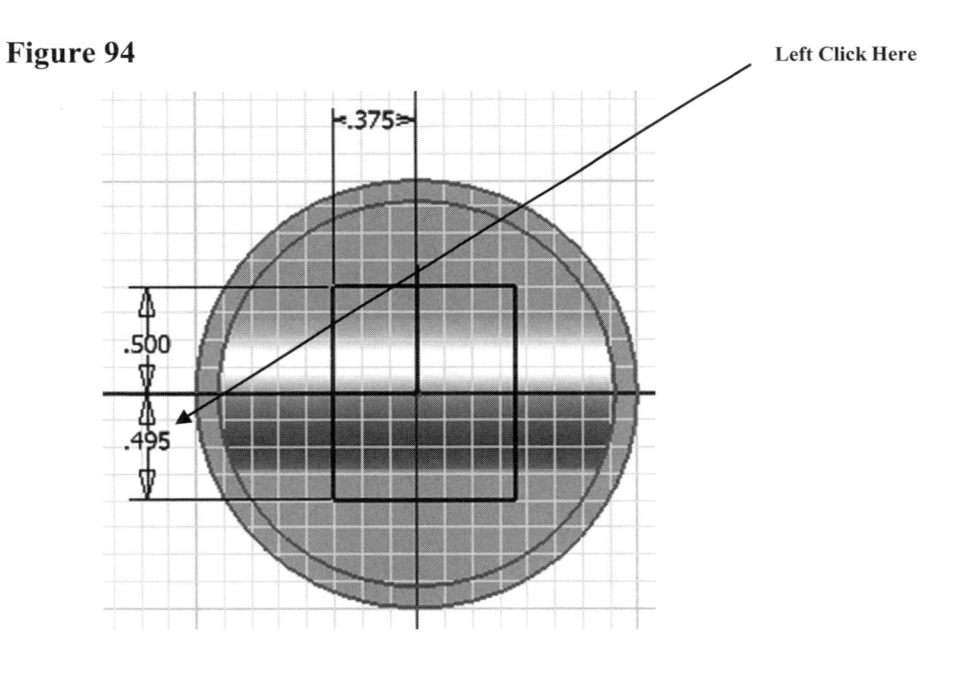

Figure 94 Left Click Here

Chapter 6: Advanced Design Procedures

105. The dimension is attached to the cursor. Move the cursor back and forth to verify it is attached. Move the cursor to where the dimension will be placed and left click once. While the dimension is still in red, left click once. The Edit Dimension dialog box will appear as shown in Figure 95.

Figure 95

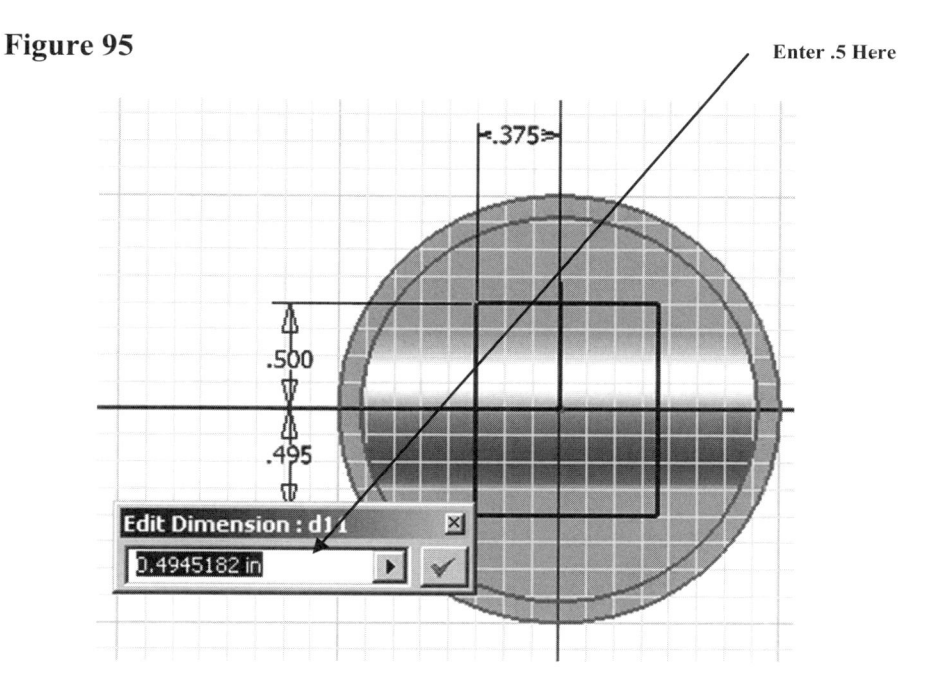

Enter .5 Here

106. To edit the dimension, type **.5** in the Edit Dimension dialog box (while the current dimension is highlighted) and press **Enter** on the keyboard.

107. The dimension of the line will become .5 inches as shown in Figure 96.

Figure 96

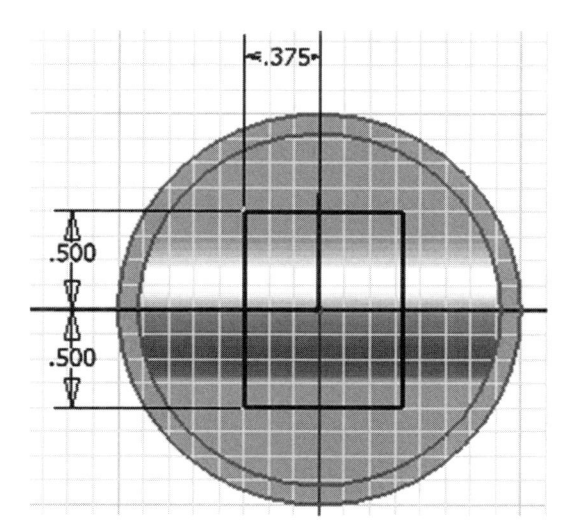

321

Chapter 6: Advanced Design Procedures

108. Move the cursor to the middle left portion of the screen and left click on **General Dimension** as shown in Figure 97.

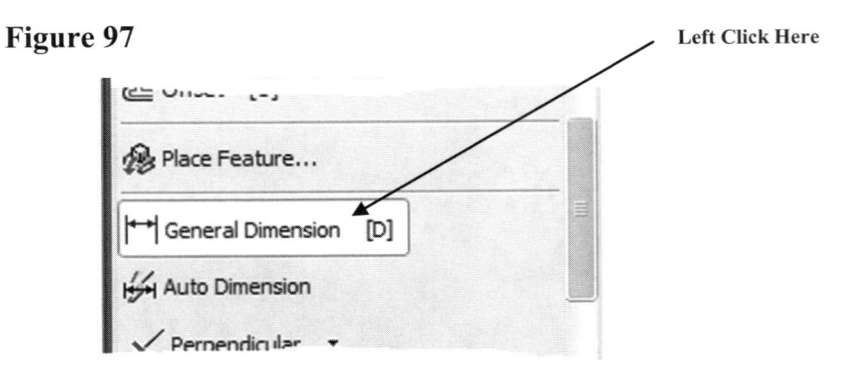

Figure 97 Left Click Here

109. After selecting **General Dimension** move the cursor over the vertical line coming out of the center of the part. The line will turn red. Select the line by left clicking anywhere on the line as shown in Figure 98.

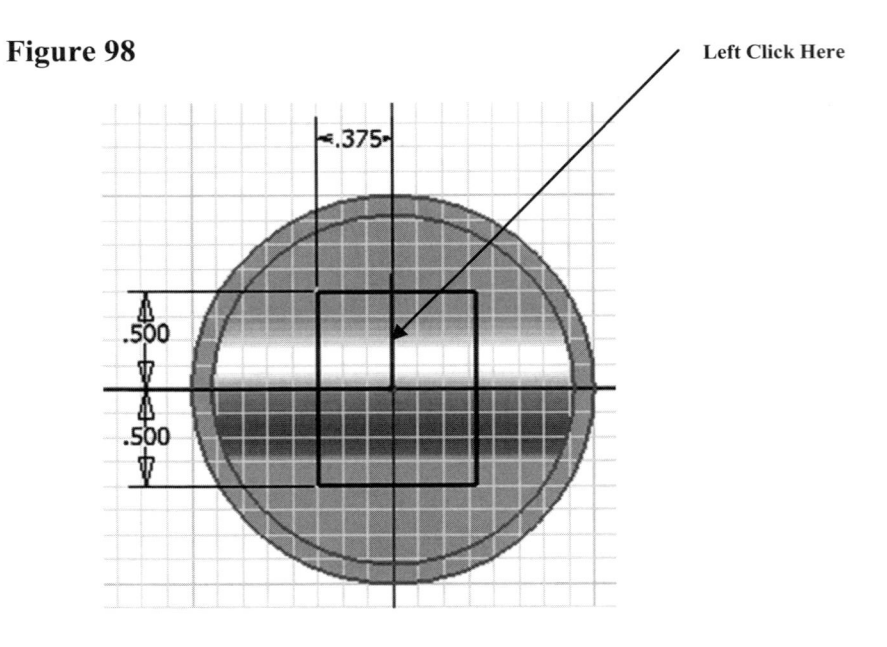

Figure 98 Left Click Here

Chapter 6: Advanced Design Procedures

110. Move the cursor to the line on the right side causing it to turn red and left click once as shown in Figure 99.

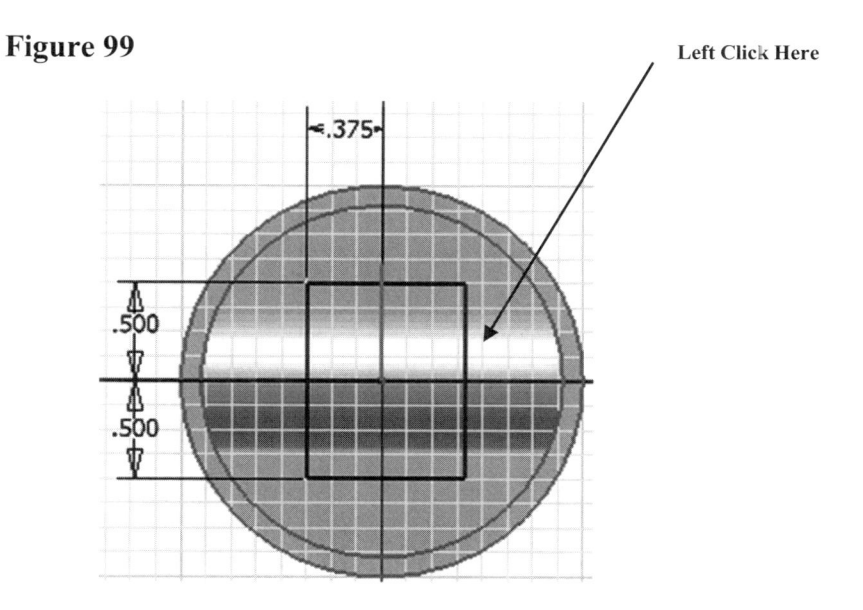

Figure 99

Left Click Here

111. Move the cursor out to the side. The actual dimension of the line will appear as shown in Figure 100.

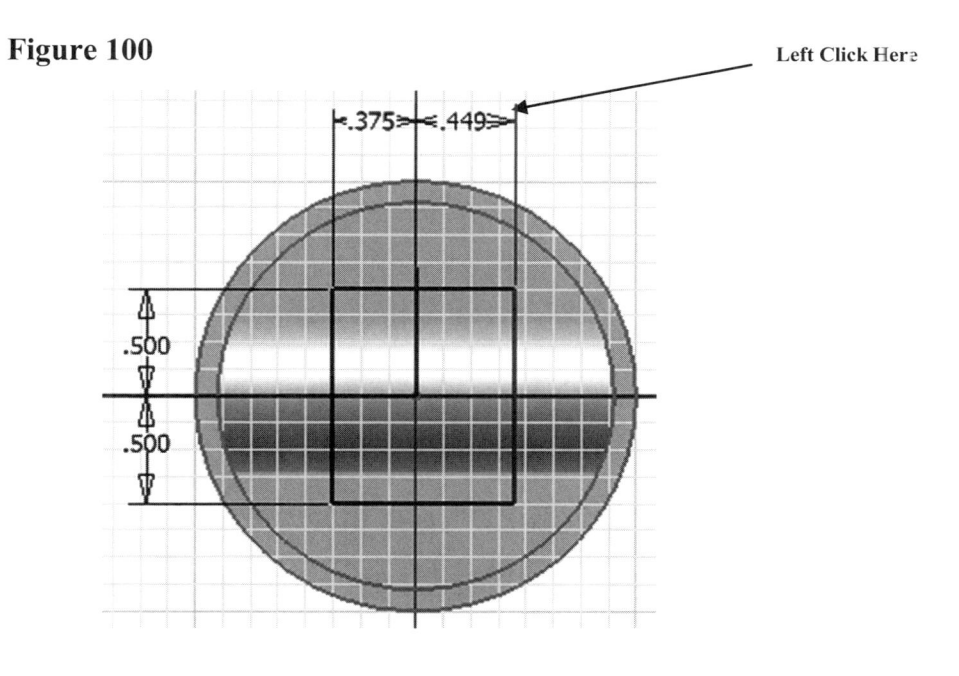

Figure 100

Left Click Here

Chapter 6: Advanced Design Procedures

112. The dimension is attached to the cursor. Move the cursor back and forth to verify it is attached. Move the cursor to where the dimension will be placed and left click once. While the dimension is still in red, left click once. The Edit Dimension dialog box will appear as shown in Figure 101.

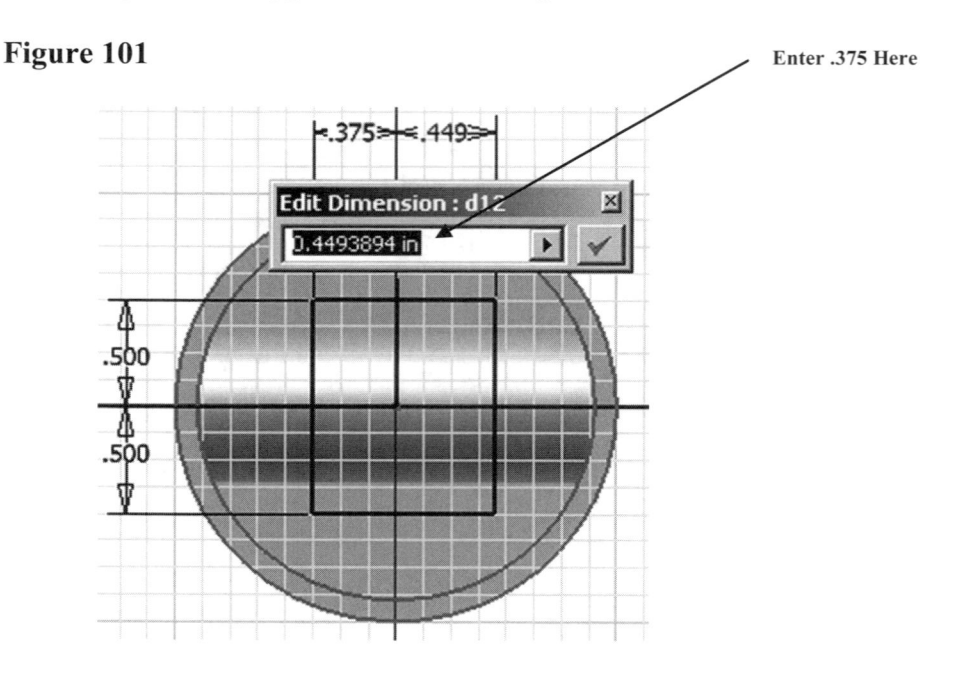

Figure 101

Enter .375 Here

113. To edit the dimension, type **.375** in the Edit Dimension dialog box (while the current dimension is highlighted) and press **Enter** on the keyboard.

114. The dimension of the line will become .375 inches as shown in Figure 102.

Figure 102

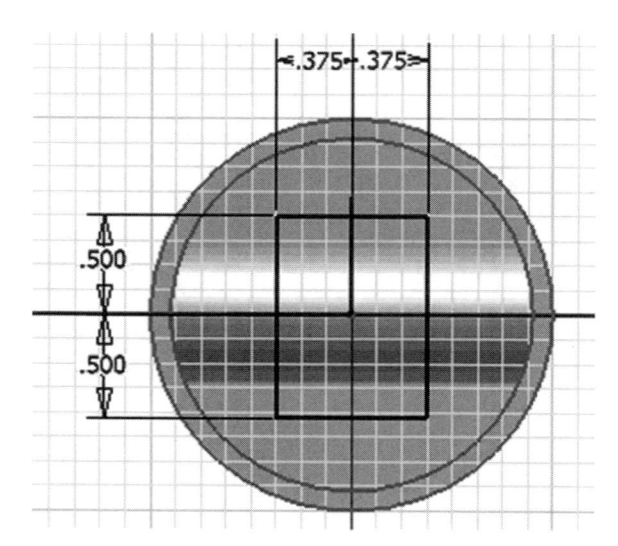

Chapter 6: Advanced Design Procedures

115. Right click anywhere around the drawing. A pop up menu will appear. Left click on **Done [Esc]** as shown in Figure 103.

Figure 103

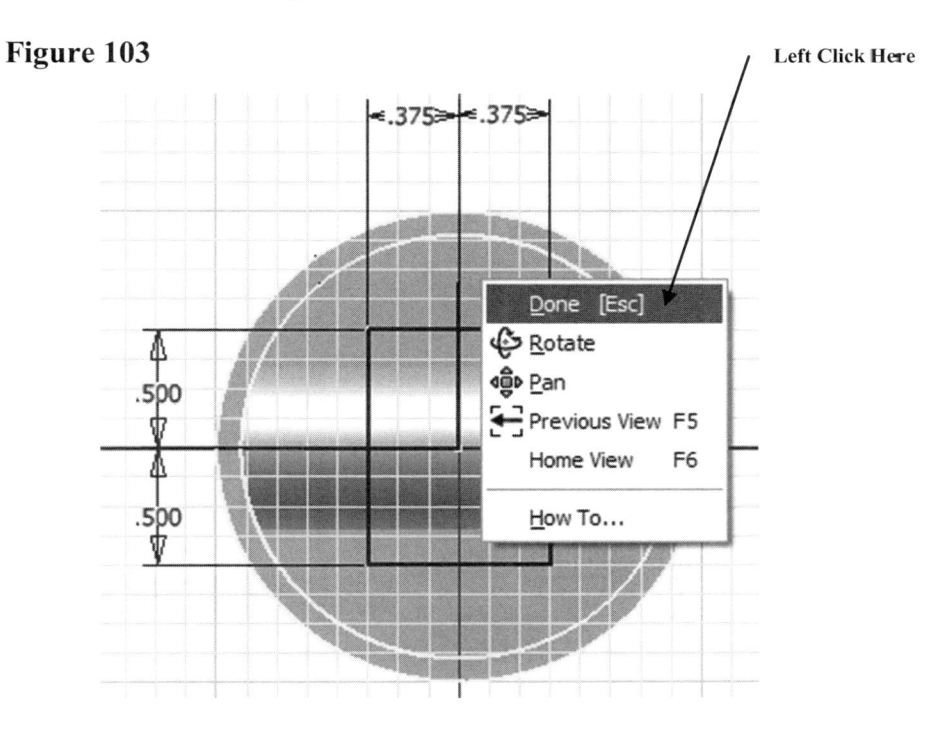

Left Click Here

116. Move the cursor over the vertical line coming out of the center of the part. The line will turn red as shown in Figure 104.

Figure 104

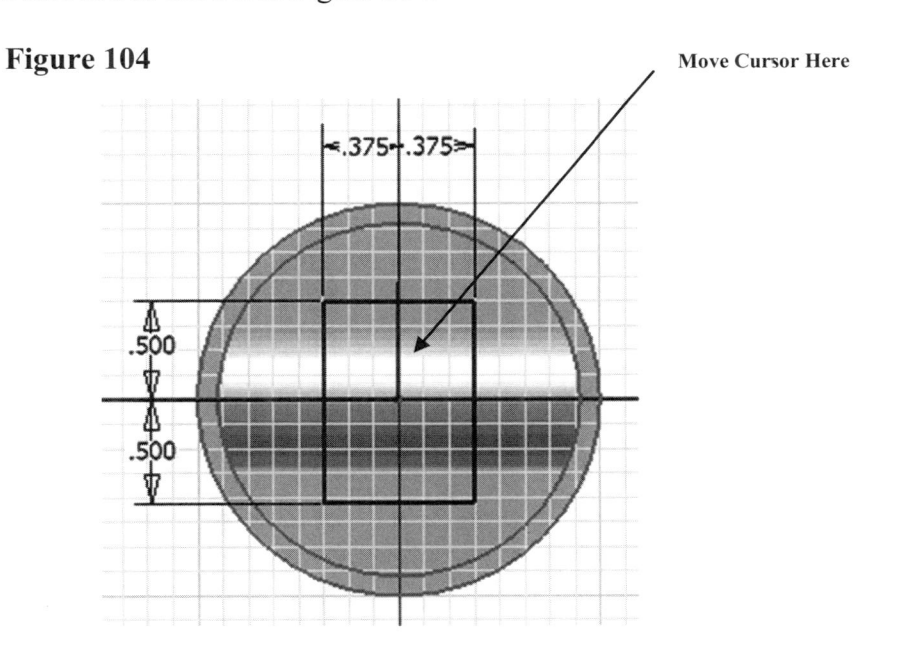

Move Cursor Here

325

Chapter 6: Advanced Design Procedures

117. After the line has turned red, right click once. A pop up menu will appear. Left click on **Delete** as shown in Figure 105.

Figure 105

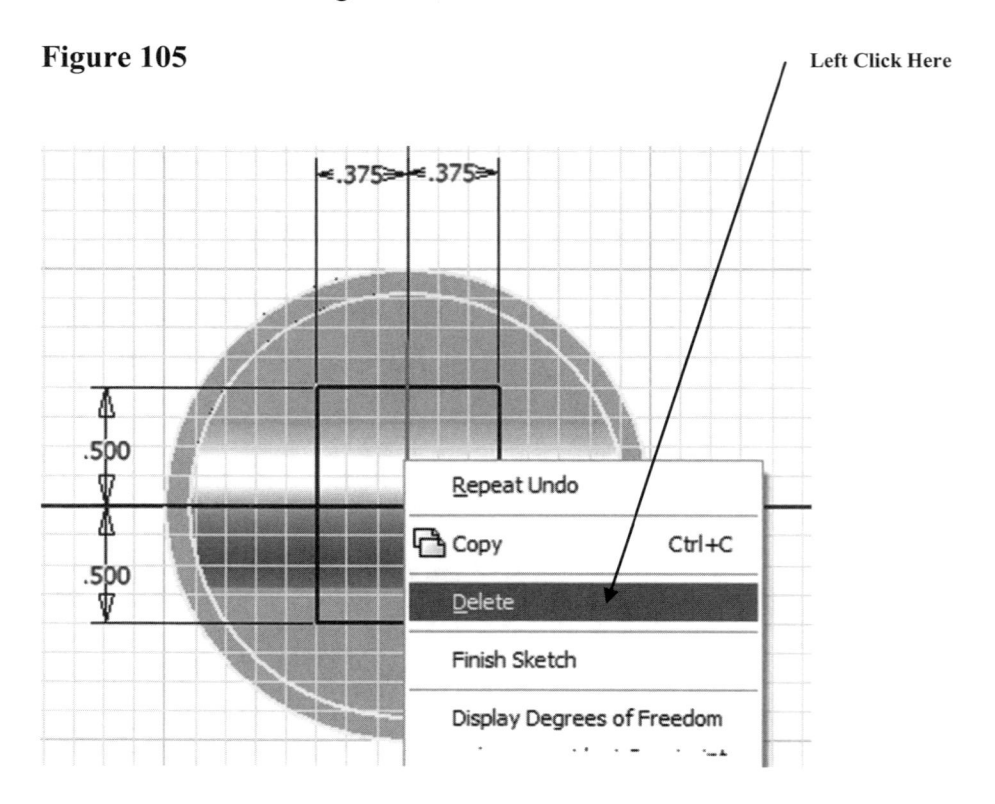

Left Click Here

118. Use the same steps to delete the horizontal line coming out of the center of the part as shown in Figure 106. Do not be concerned if the dimensions disappear.

Figure 106

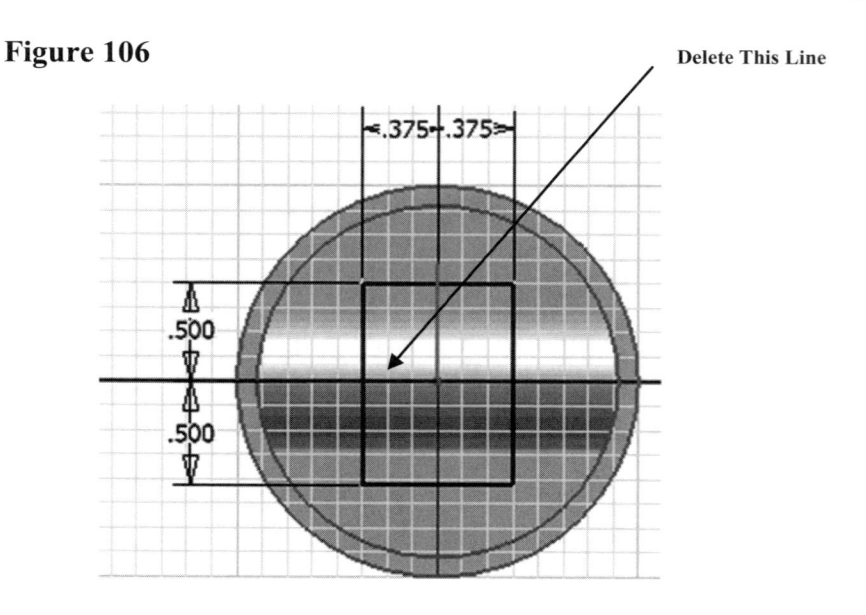

Delete This Line

Chapter 6: Advanced Design Procedures

119. Right click anywhere around the drawing. A pop up menu will appear. Left click on **Finish Sketch** as shown in Figure 107.

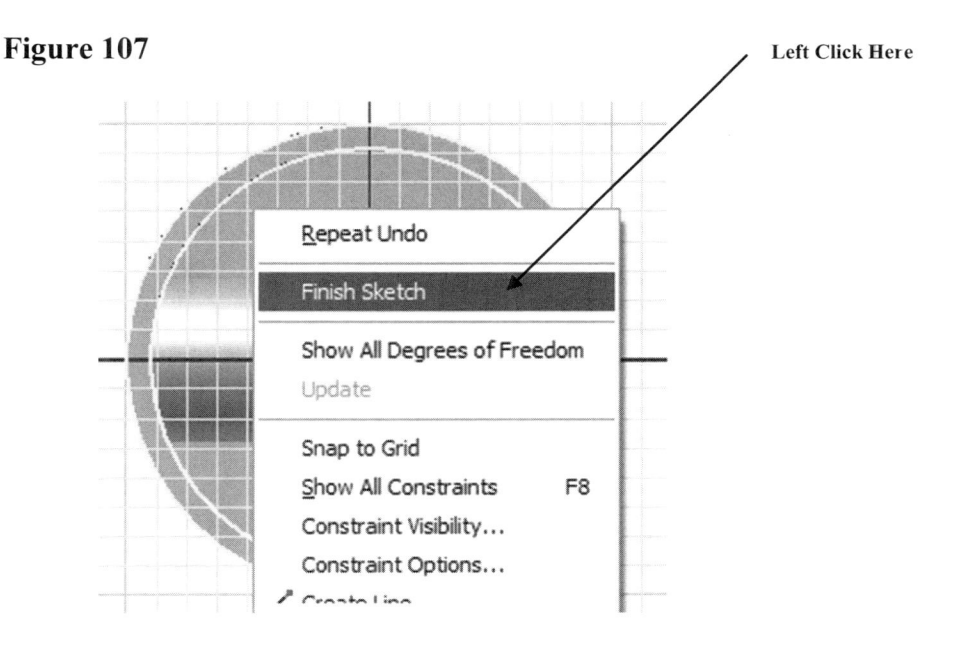

Figure 107

Left Click Here

120. Right click anywhere around the drawing. A pop up menu will appear. Left click on **Home/Isometric View** as shown in Figure 108.

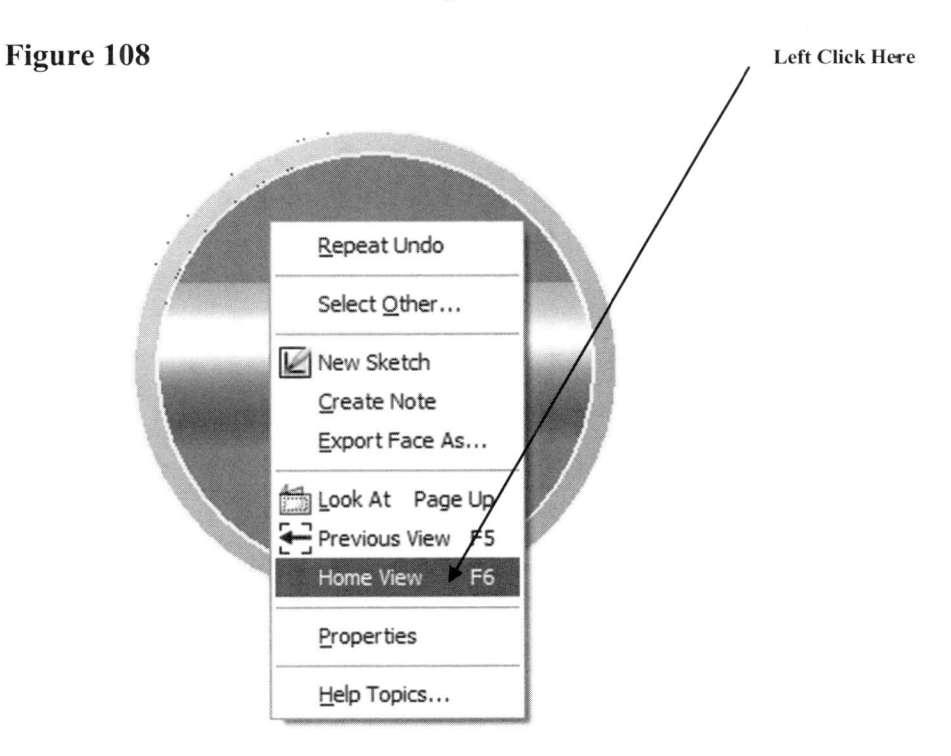

Figure 108

Left Click Here

327

Chapter 6: Advanced Design Procedures

121. Your screen should look similar to Figure 109.

Figure 109

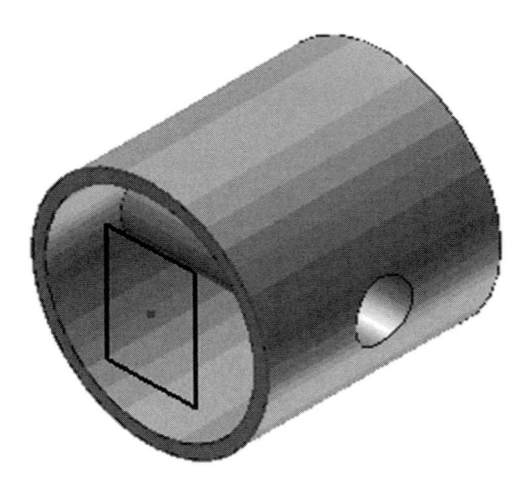

122. Move the cursor to the middle left portion of the screen and left click on **Extrude**. The Extrude dialog box will appear. Left click on the square located inside the piston area. If the square does not turn red, left click on the **Profile** icon then left on click the square again. Your screen should look similar to Figure 110.

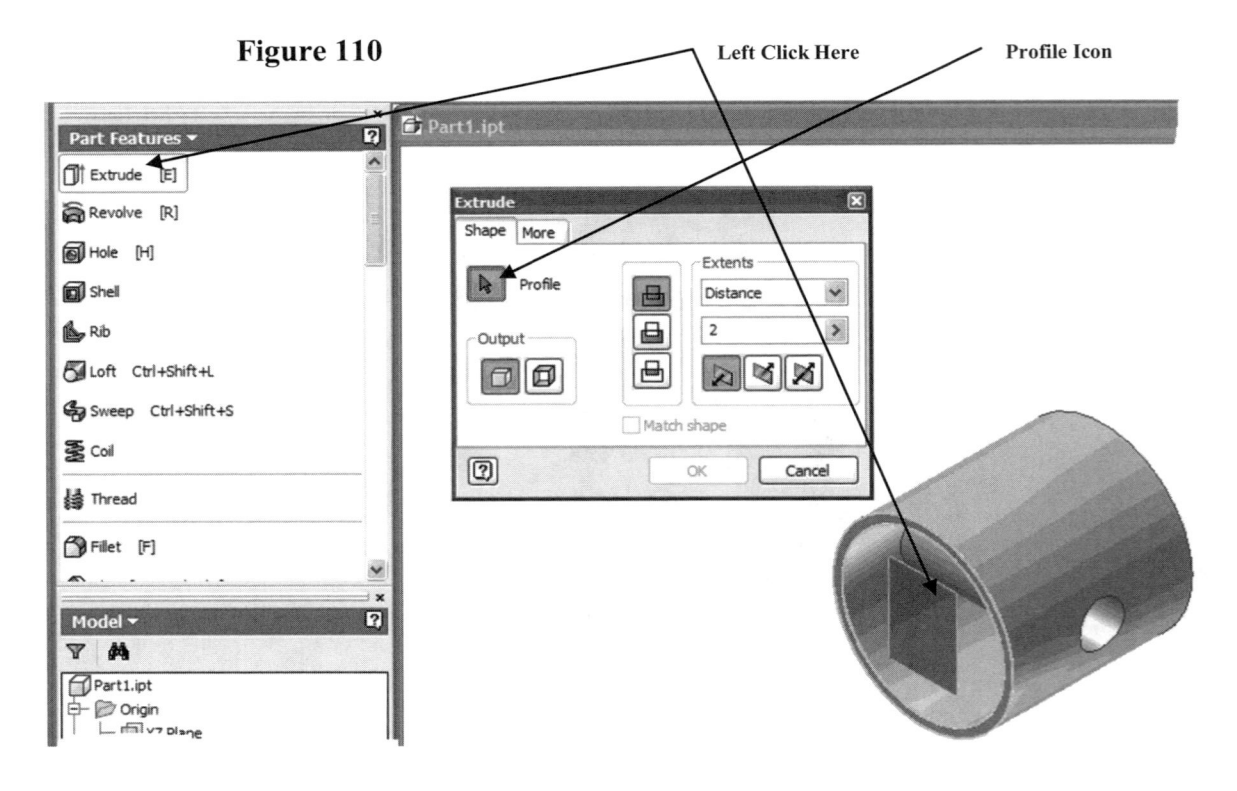

Figure 110   Left Click Here   Profile Icon

328

Chapter 6: Advanced Design Procedures

123. Left click on the "Cut" icon and on the "Extrude Back" icon as shown in Figure 111.

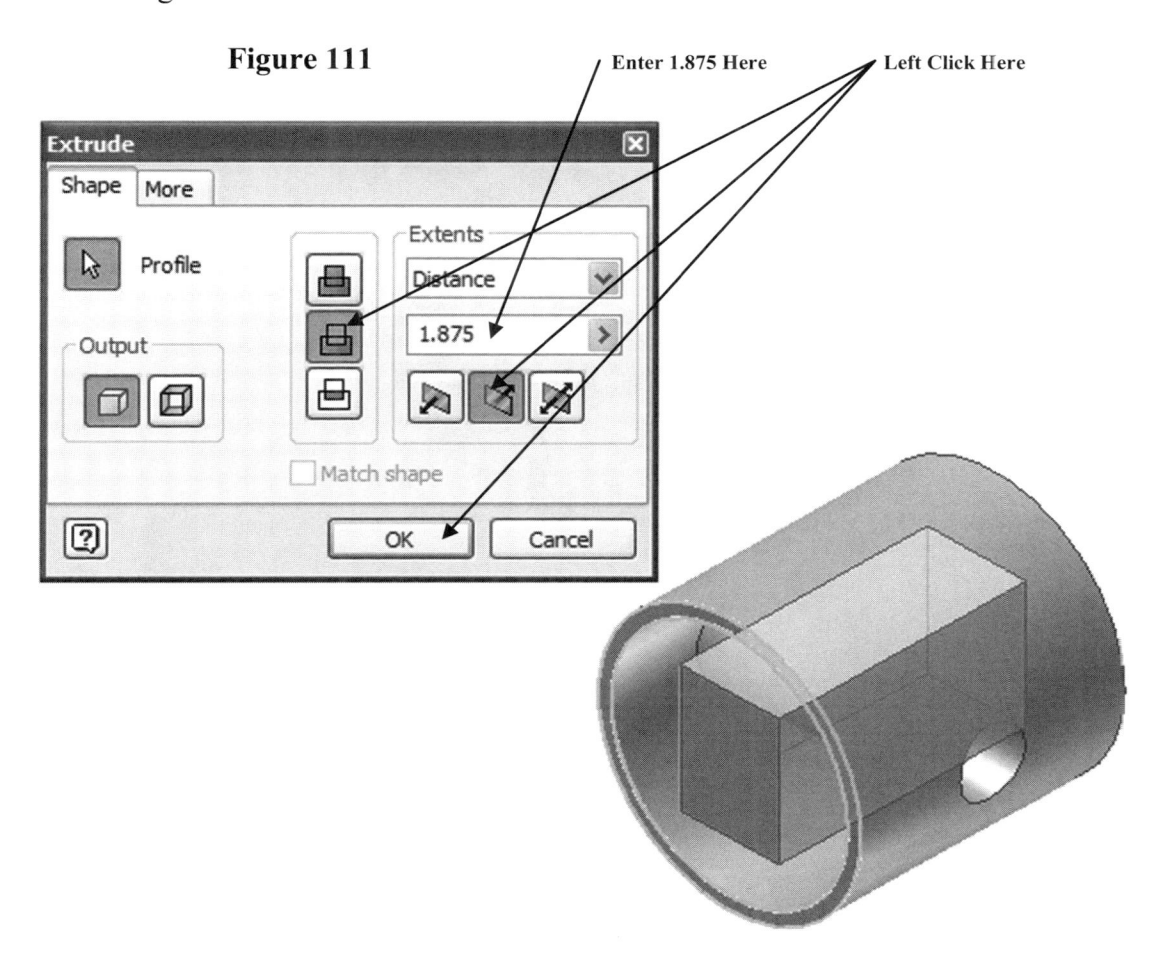

Figure 111

Chapter 6: Advanced Design Procedures

124. Highlight the text located under Distance and enter **1.875**. Left click on **OK**. Inventor will create a hole from the sketch as shown in Figure 112. Use the "Rotate" command to roll the part around to view the inside.

Figure 112

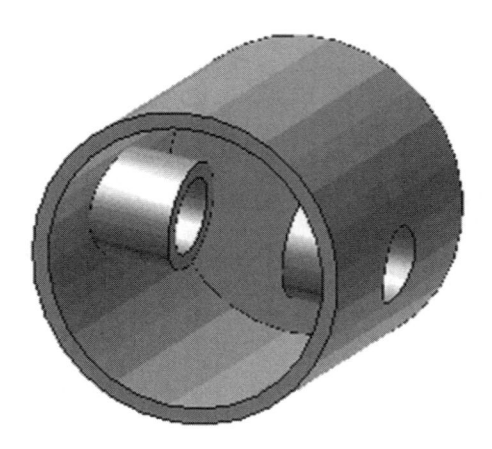

125. Save the part as Piston1.ipt where it can be easily retrieved later.

126. Begin a new drawing as described in Chapter 1.

127. Draw a circle in the center of the grid as shown in Figure 113.

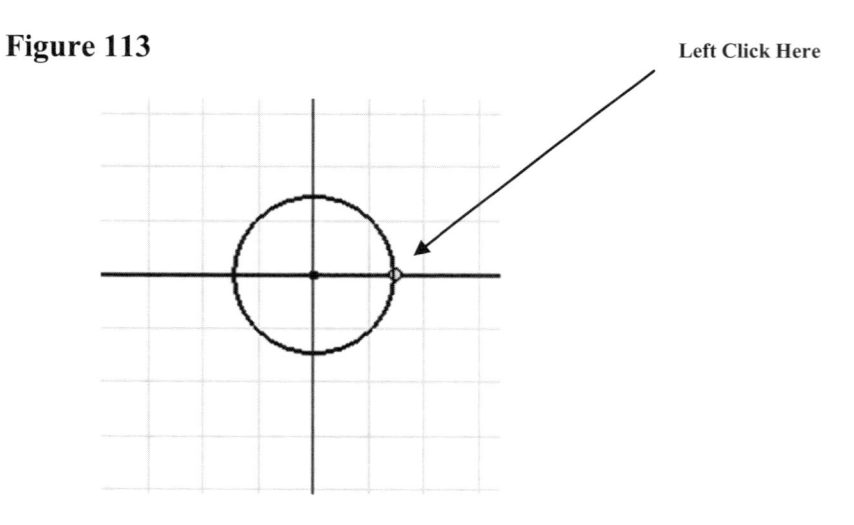

Figure 113

Left Click Here

330

Chapter 6: Advanced Design Procedures

128. Use the **General Dimension** command to dimension the circle to **.5** inches as shown in Figure 114.

   Figure 114

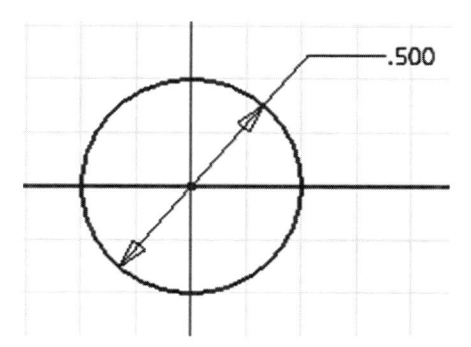

129. Exit the Sketch Panel and Extrude the circle to a length of **1.875** inches as shown in Figure 115.

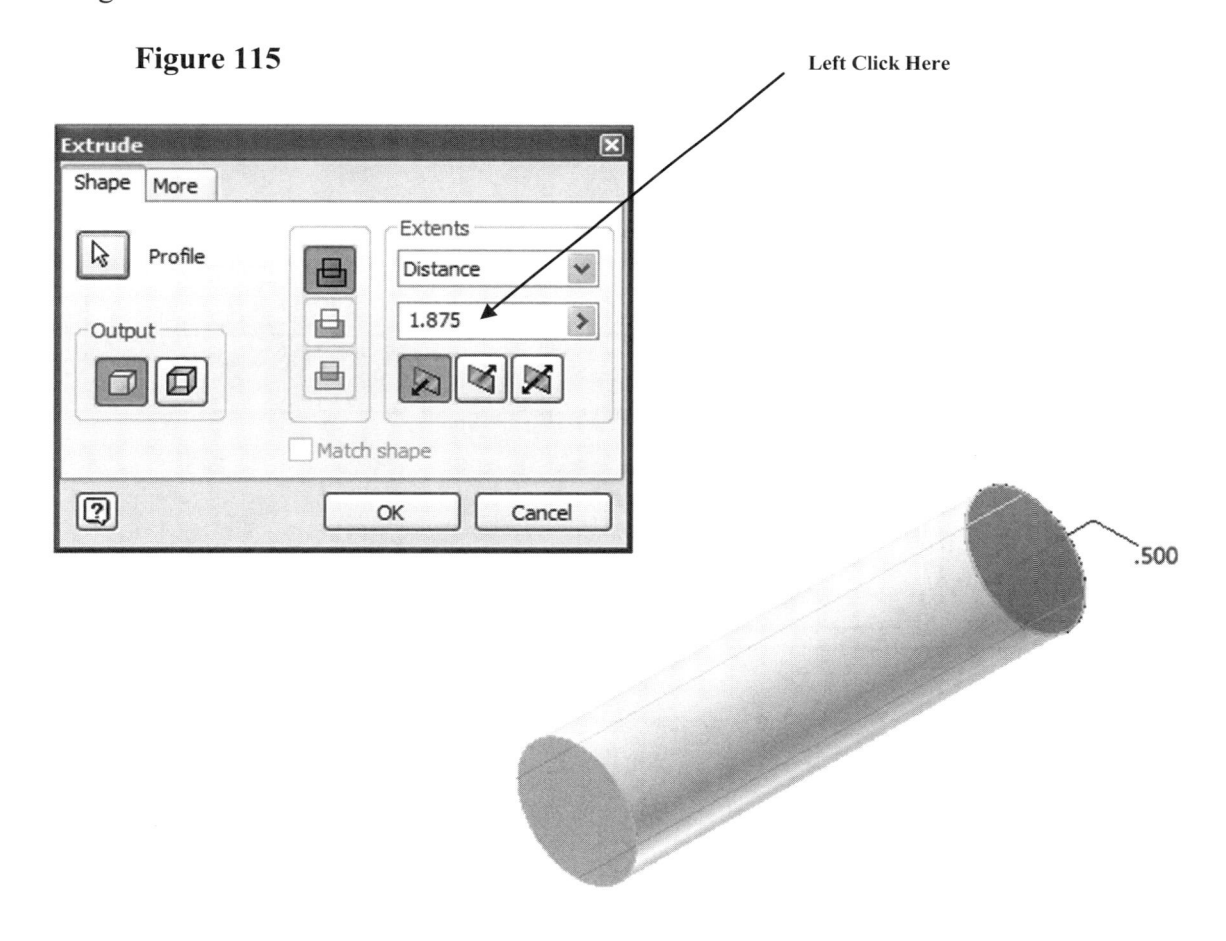

   Figure 115

130. Left click on **OK** as shown in Figure 115.

331

Chapter 6: Advanced Design Procedures

131. Your screen should look similar to Figure 116.

Figure 116

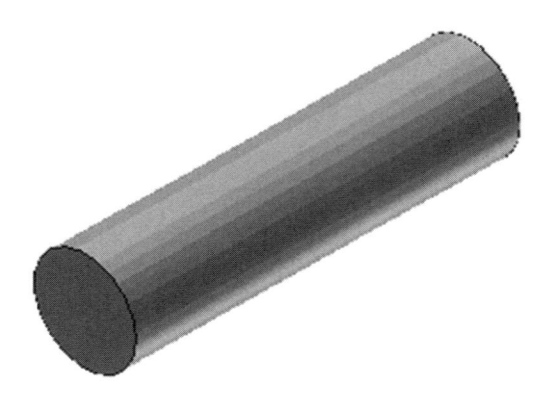

132. Save the part as Wristpin1.ipt where it can be easily retrieved later.

133. Begin a new sketch as described in Chapter 1.

134. Complete the sketch shown in Figure 117.

Figure 117

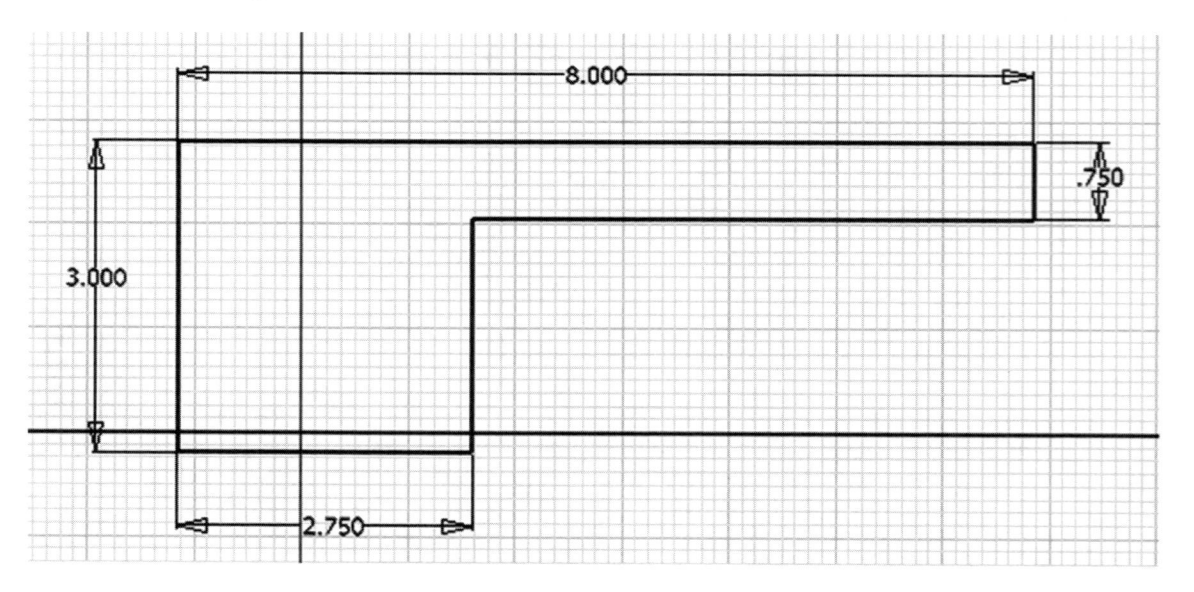

Chapter 6: Advanced Design Procedures

135. Right click anywhere around the drawing. A pop up menu will appear. Left click on **Done [Esc]** as shown in Figure 118.

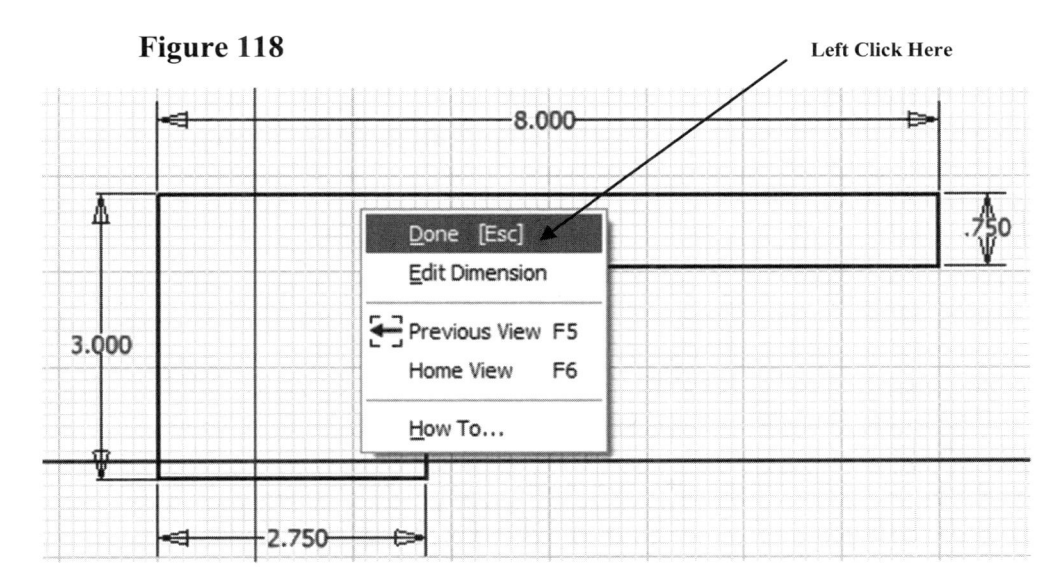

Figure 118

136. Right click anywhere around the drawing. A pop up menu will appear. Left click on **Finish Sketch** as shown in Figure 119.

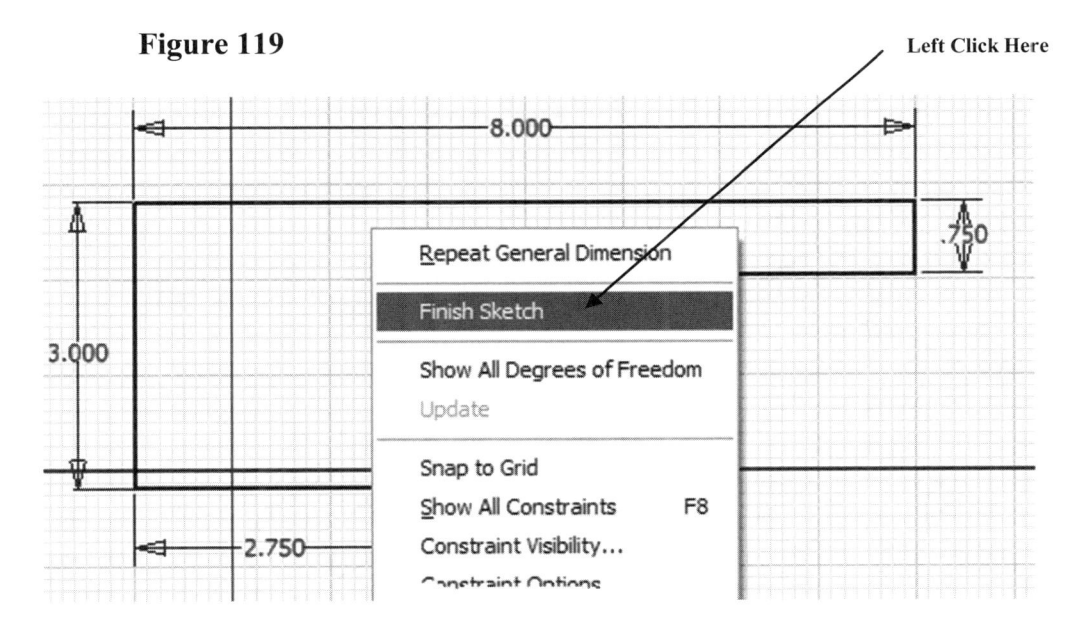

Figure 119

Chapter 6: Advanced Design Procedures

137. Right click anywhere around the drawing. A pop up menu will appear. Left click on **Isometric View** as shown in Figure 120.

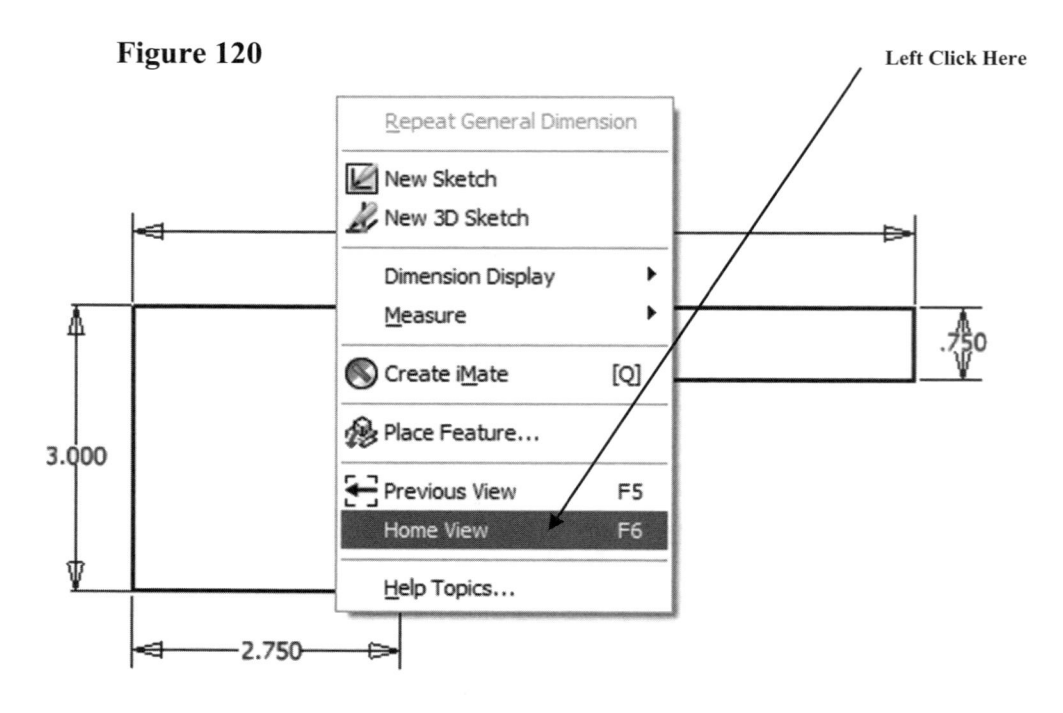

Figure 120

138. Inventor will provide an isometric view as shown in Figure 121.

Figure 121

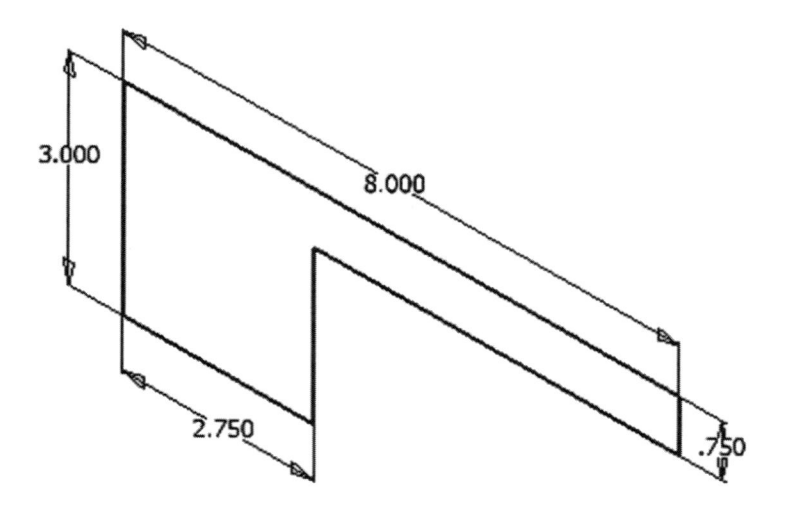

139. Extrude the sketch to a distance of **2.25** inches. Your screen should look similar to what is shown in Figure 122.

Figure 122

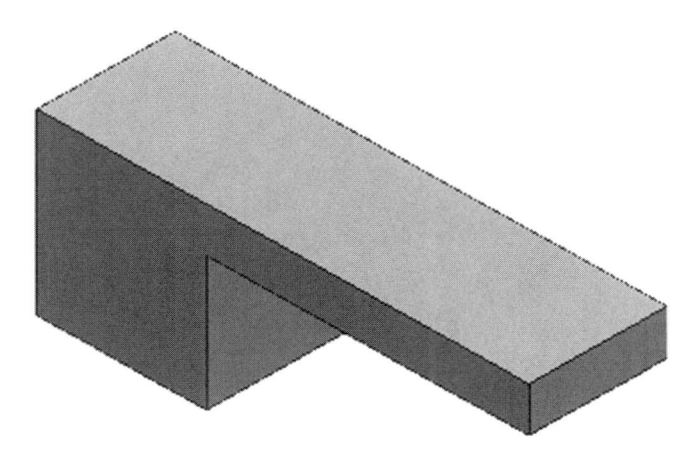

140. Use the Fillet command to create **1.125** inch fillets on the front portion of the part as shown in Figure 123.

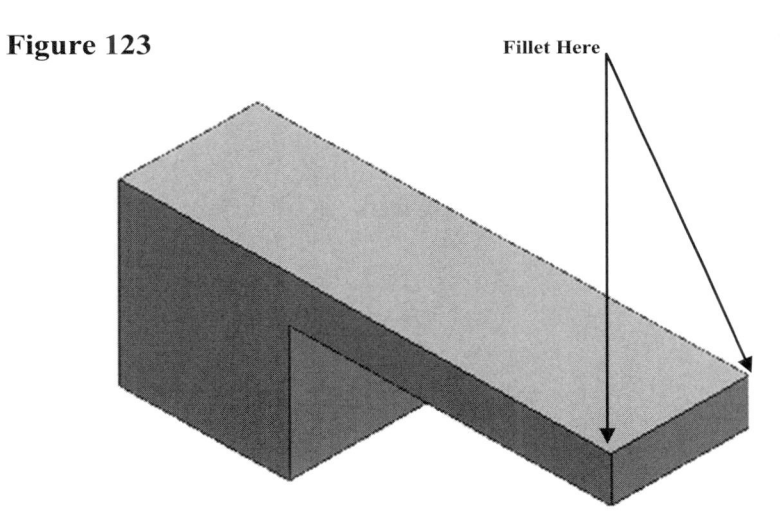

Figure 123

Fillet Here

Chapter 6: Advanced Design Procedures

141. Your screen should look similar to Figure 124.

Figure 124

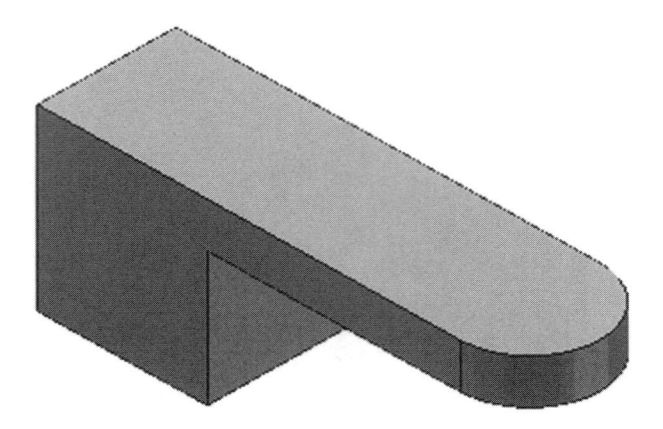

142. Move the cursor to the upper middle portion of the screen and left click on the "Look At" icon as shown in Figure 125.

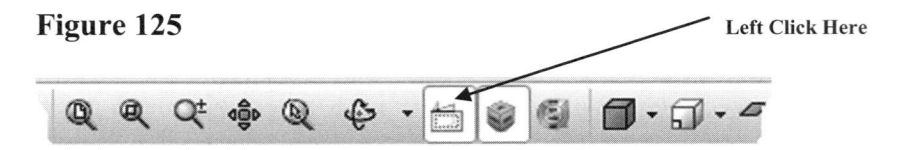

Figure 125

Left Click Here

143. Move the cursor to the surface shown in Figure 126 causing it to turn red. Left click once.

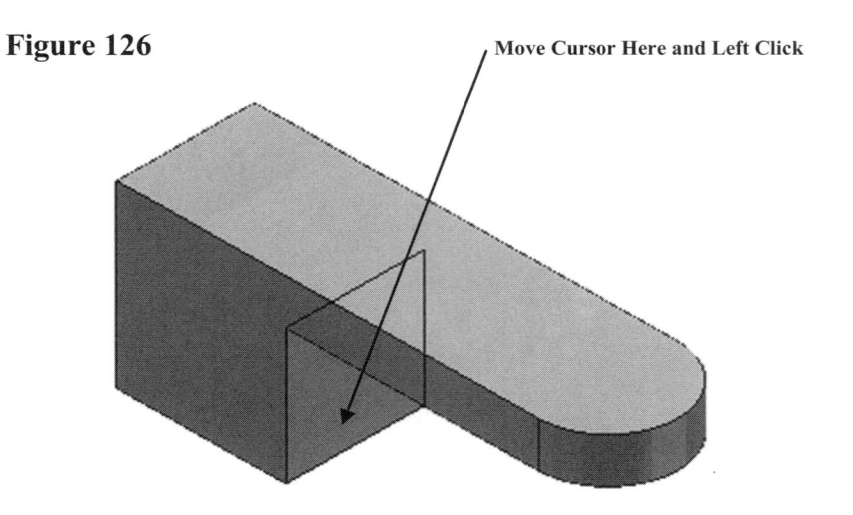

Figure 126

Move Cursor Here and Left Click

Chapter 6: Advanced Design Procedures

144. Inventor will provide a perpendicular view of the surface as shown in Figure 127.

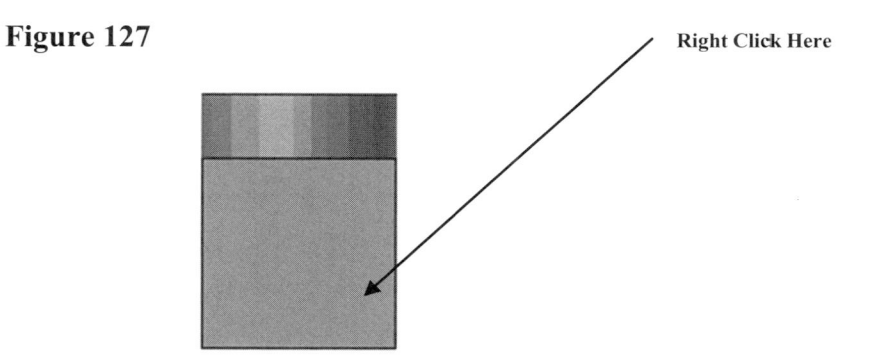

Figure 127

Right Click Here

145. Move the cursor to the surface shown in Figure 127 causing the edges of the surface to turn red and right click once. A pop up menu will appear. Left click on **New Sketch** as shown in Figure 128.

Figure 128

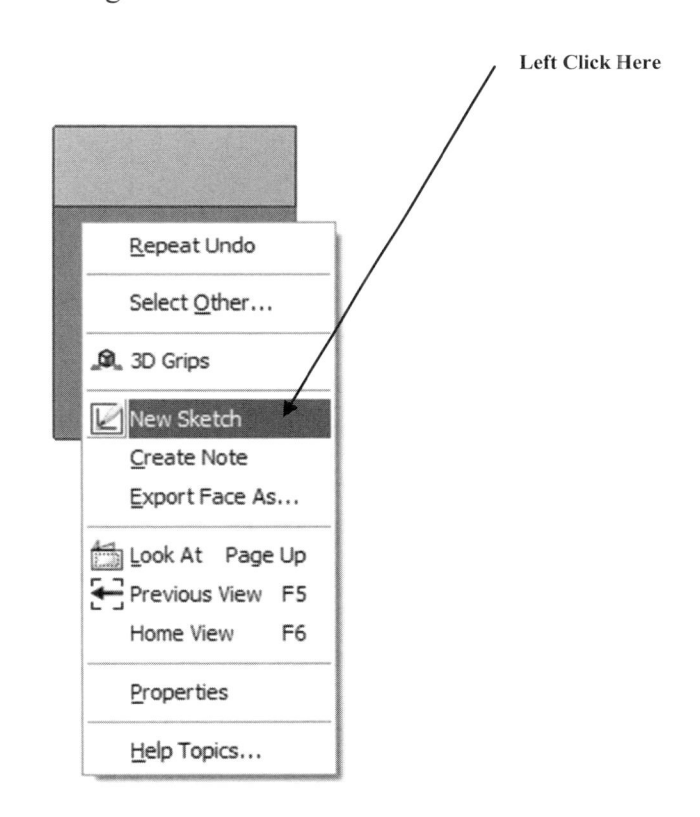

Left Click Here

337

Chapter 6: Advanced Design Procedures

146. Inventor will begin a new sketch on the selected surface. Your screen should look similar to Figure 129.

Figure 129

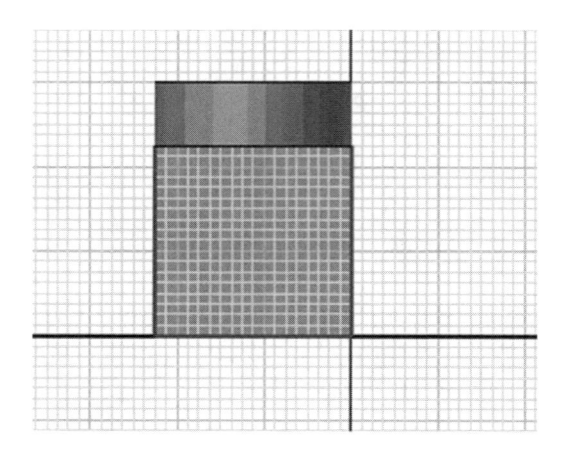

147. Create a sketch on the selected surface as shown in Figure 130.

Figure 130

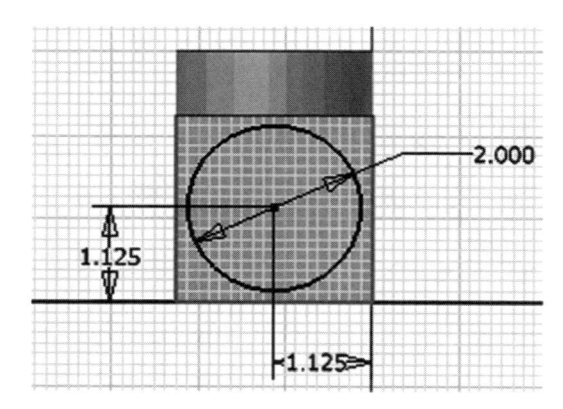

Chapter 6: Advanced Design Procedures

148. Right click anywhere around the drawing. A pop up menu will appear. Left click on **Done [Esc]** as shown in Figure 131.

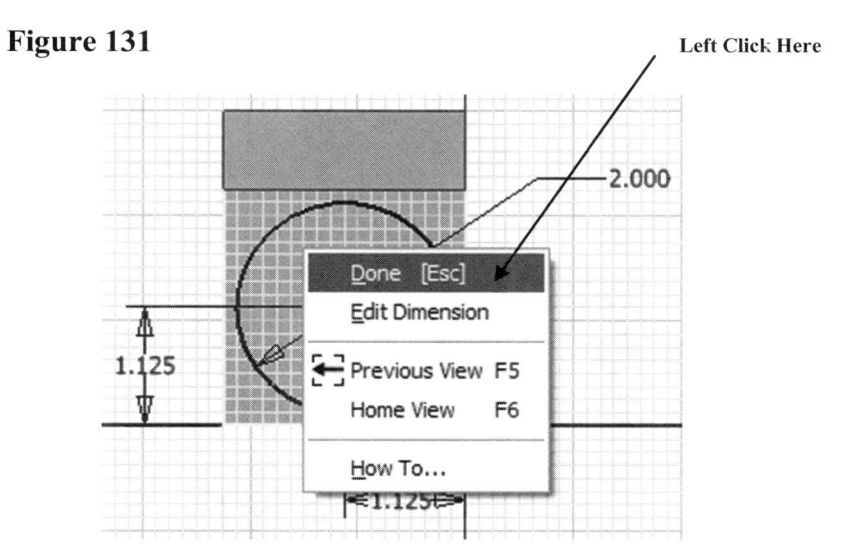

Figure 131

149. Right click anywhere around the drawing. A pop up menu will appear. Left click on **Finish Sketch** as shown in Figure 132.

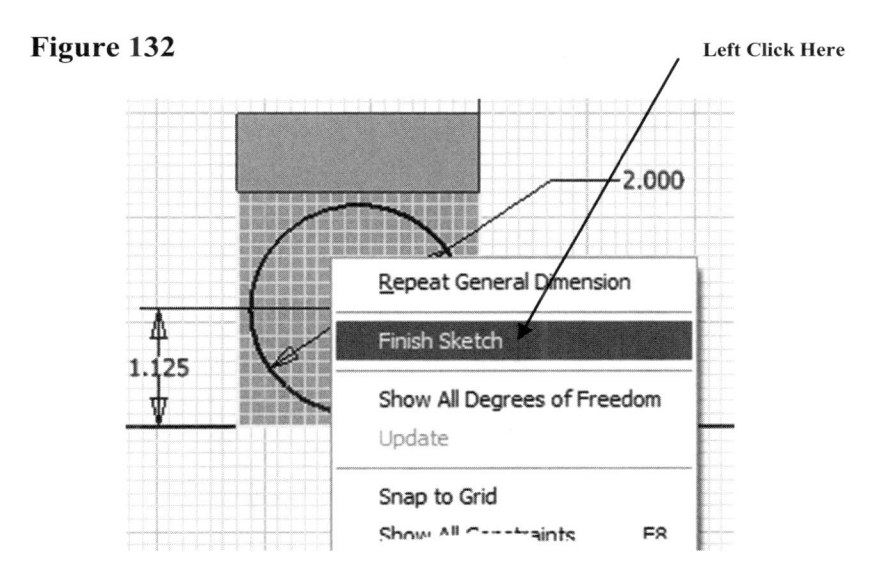

Figure 132

Chapter 6: Advanced Design Procedures

150. Right click anywhere around the drawing. A pop up menu will appear. Left click on **Isometric/Home View** as shown in Figure 133.

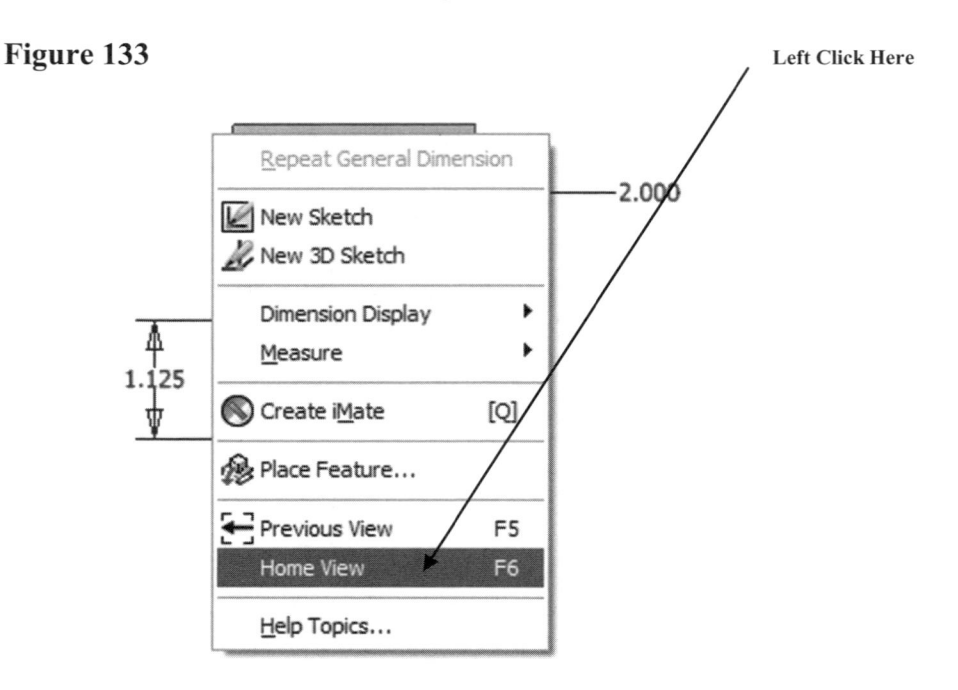

Figure 133

Left Click Here

151. Inventor will provide an isometric view as shown in Figure 134.

Figure 134

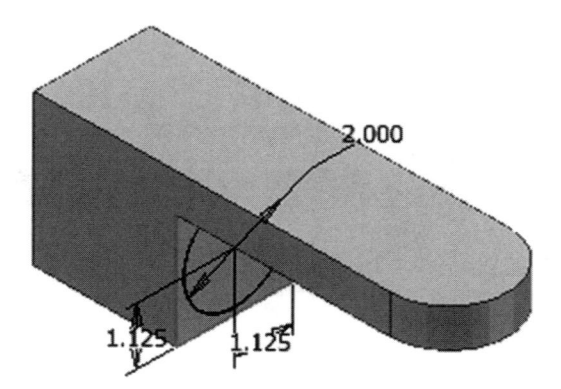

Chapter 6: Advanced Design Procedures

152. Use the Extrude command to extrude or cut out the circle that was just completed. Your screen should look similar to Figure 135.

Figure 135

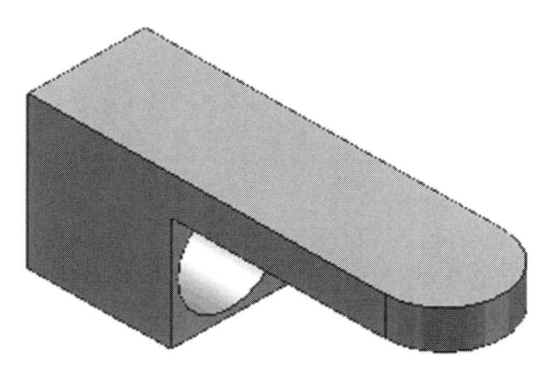

153. Move the cursor to the upper middle portion of the screen and left click on the "Look At" icon as shown in Figure 136.

Figure 136 Left Click Here

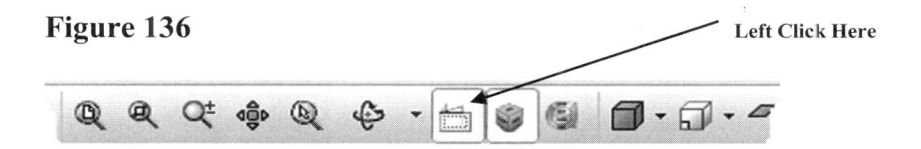

154. Left click on the surface shown in Figure 137.

Figure 137 Left Click Here

341

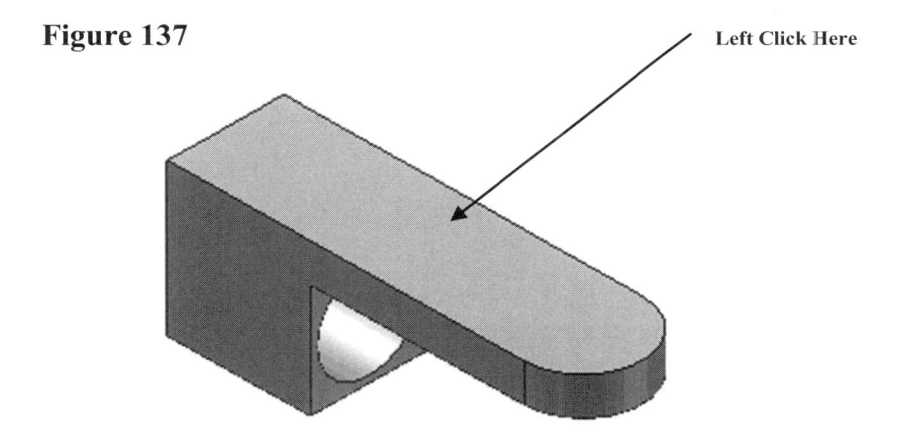

Chapter 6: Advanced Design Procedures

155. Inventor will provide a perpendicular view as shown in Figure 138.

Figure 138

156. Move the cursor to the surface shown in Figure 139 causing the edges of the surface to turn red. Right click once. A pop up menu will appear. Left click on **New Sketch** as shown in Figure 139.

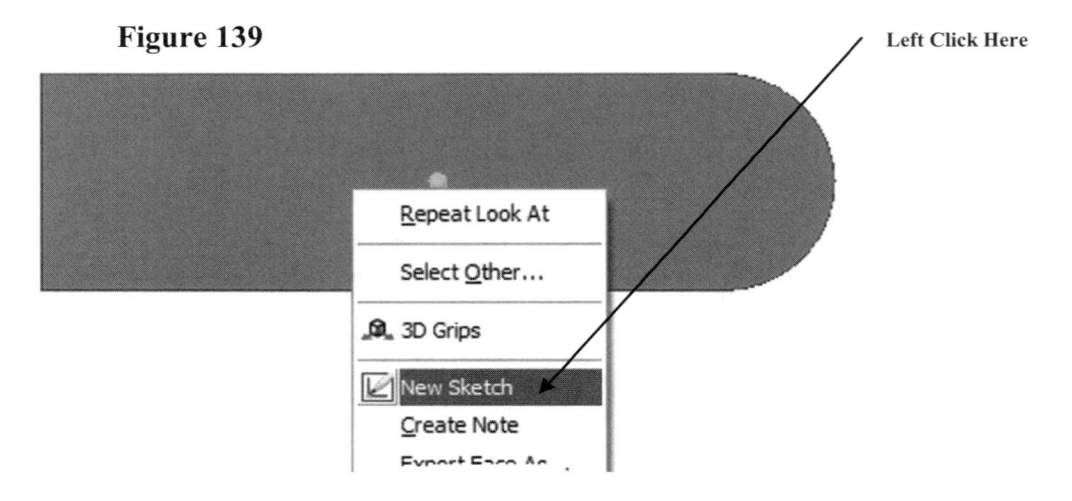

Figure 139

Left Click Here

157. Your screen should look similar to Figure 140.

Figure 140

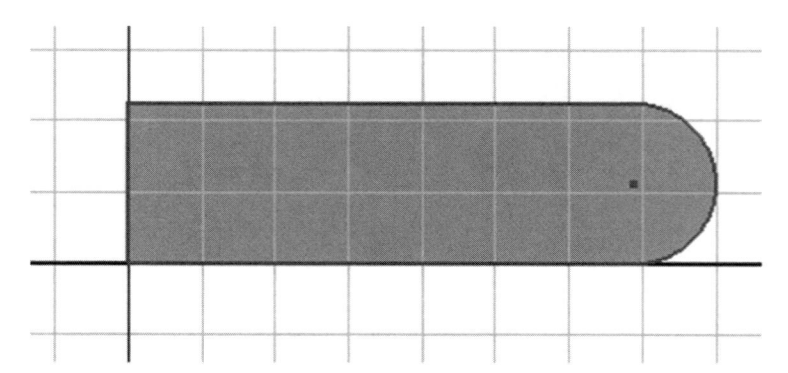

342

Chapter 6: Advanced Design Procedures

158. Draw a sketch as shown in Figure 141.

Figure 141

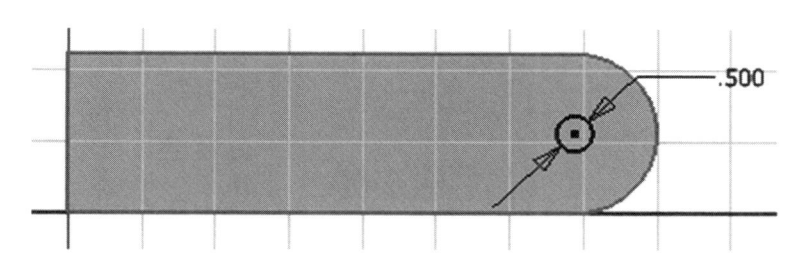

159. Right click anywhere around the drawing. A pop up menu will appear. Left click on **Done [Esc]** as shown in Figure 142.

Figure 142

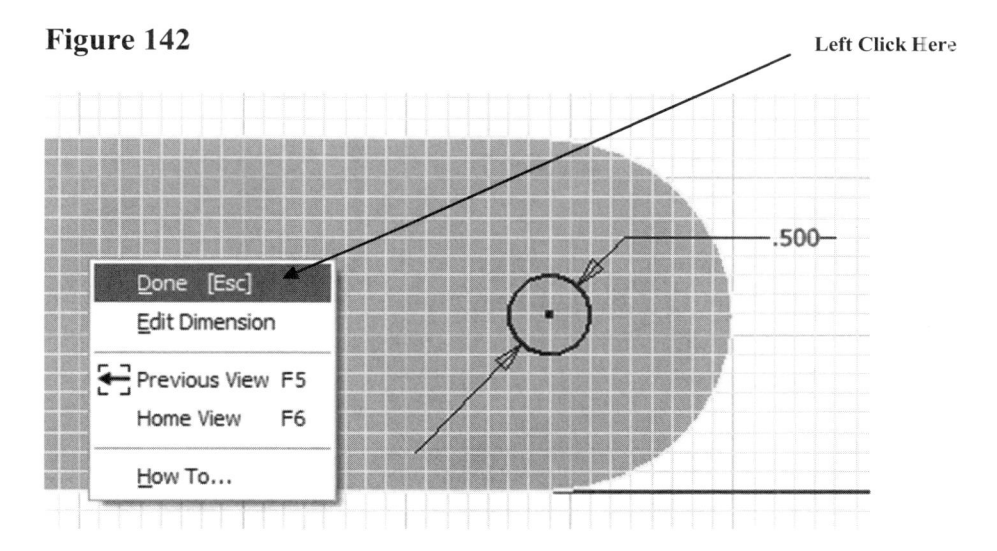

343

Chapter 6: Advanced Design Procedures

160. Right click anywhere around the drawing. A pop up menu will appear. Left click on **Finish Sketch** as shown in Figure 143.

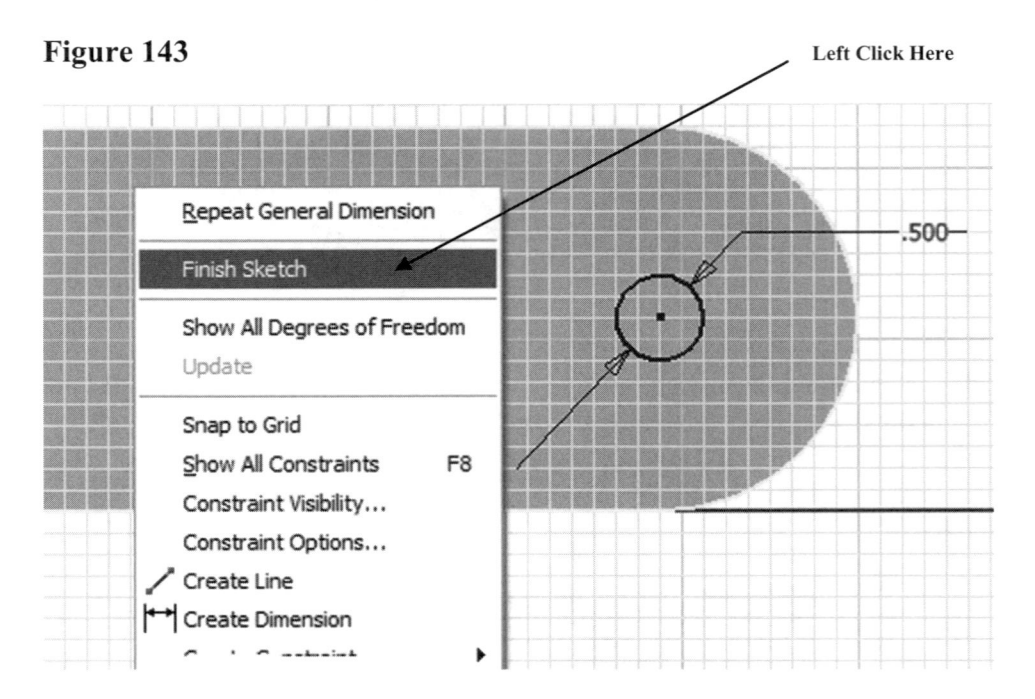

   Figure 143

161. Your screen should look similar to Figure 144.

   Figure 144

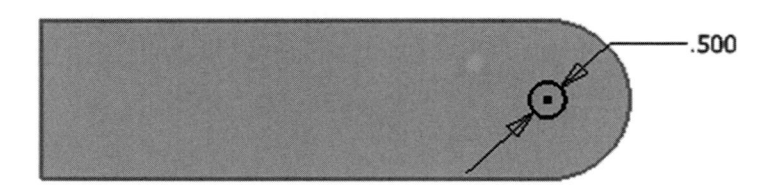

162. Use the Extrude command to extrude or cut out the circle that was just completed. Your screen should look similar to Figure 145.

   Figure 145

163. Right click anywhere around the drawing. A pop up menu will appear. Left click on **Isometric/Home View** as shown in Figure 146.

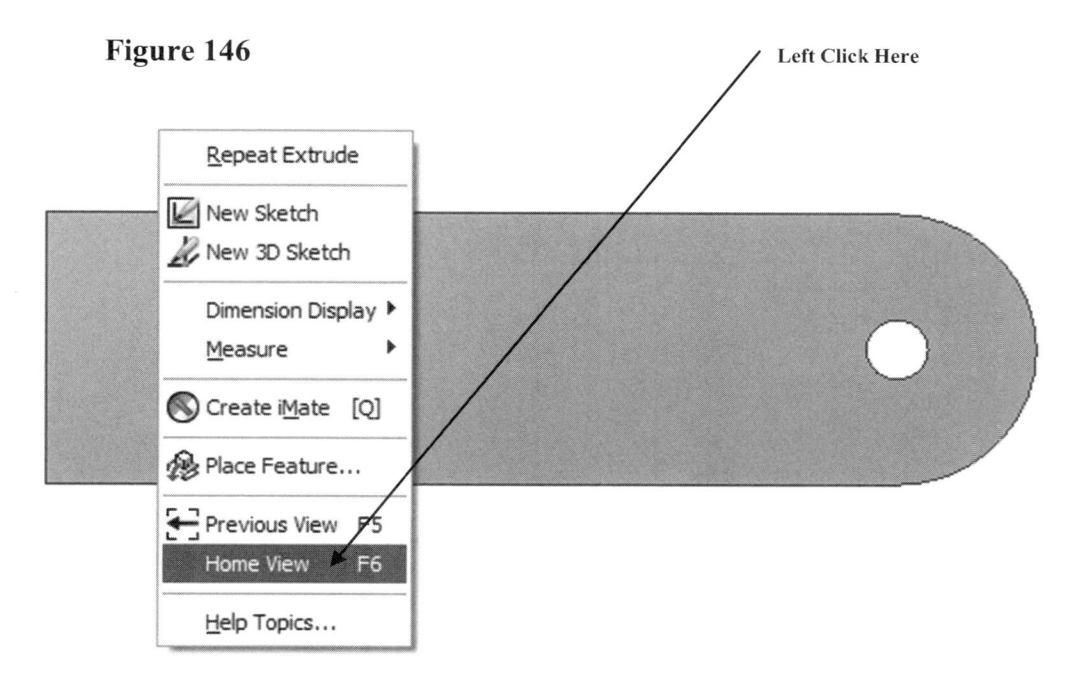

Figure 146

Left Click Here

164. Your screen should look similar to Figure 147.

Figure 147

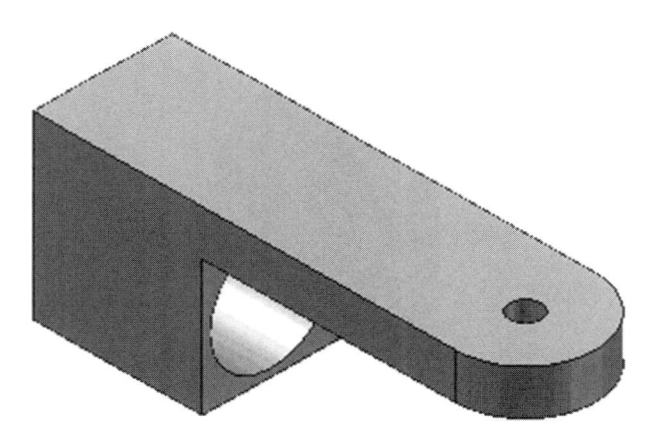

165. Save the part as Pistoncase1.ipt where it can be easily retrieved later.

166. Begin a new drawing as described in Chapter 1.

Chapter 6: Advanced Design Procedures

167. Complete the sketch shown in Figure 148.

Figure 148

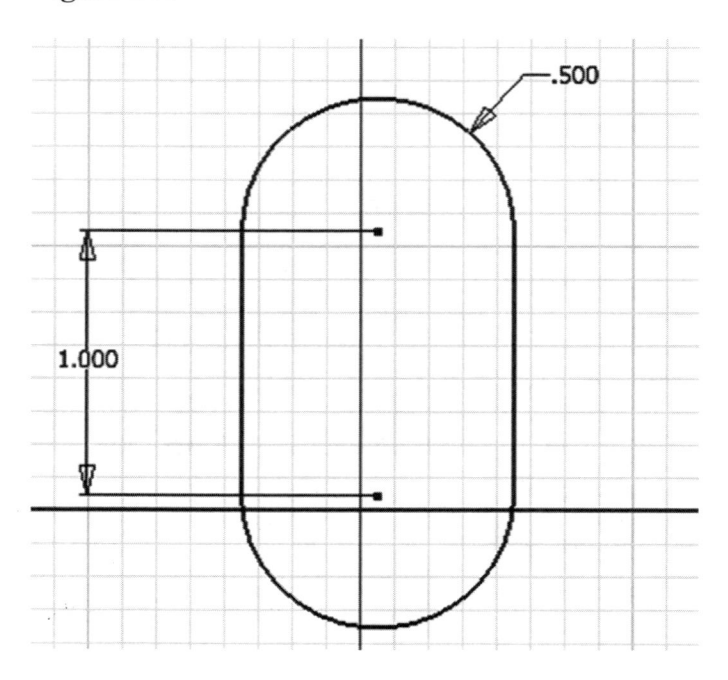

168. Extrude the sketch into a solid with a thickness of **.25** as shown in Figure 149.

Figure 149

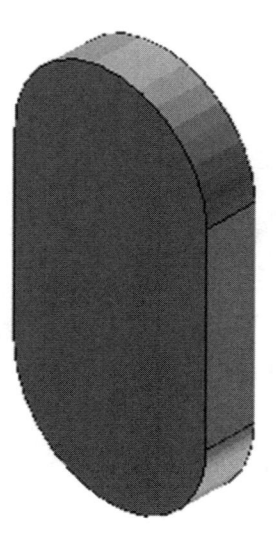

169. Complete the following sketch. Use the center of the outside fillet radius as the center of the circle as shown in Figure 150.

Figure 150

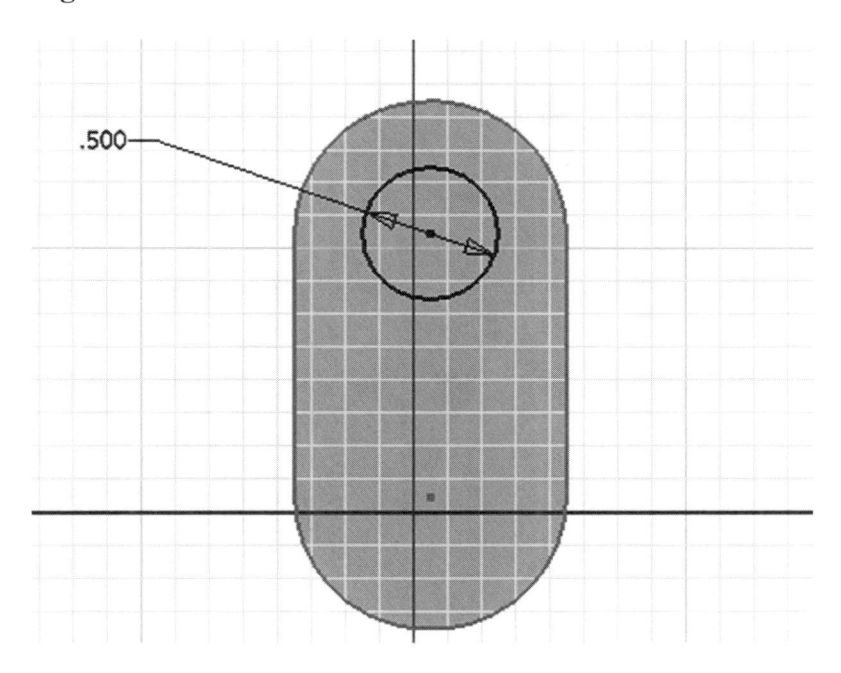

170. Extrude the sketch into a solid with a thickness of **.25** as shown in Figure 151.

Figure 151

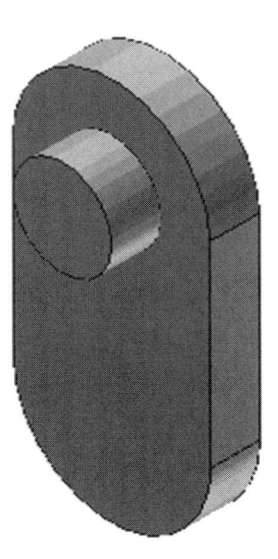

Chapter 6: Advanced Design Procedures

171. Use the "Rotate" command and roll the part around to gain access to the opposite side as shown in Figure 152.

Figure 152

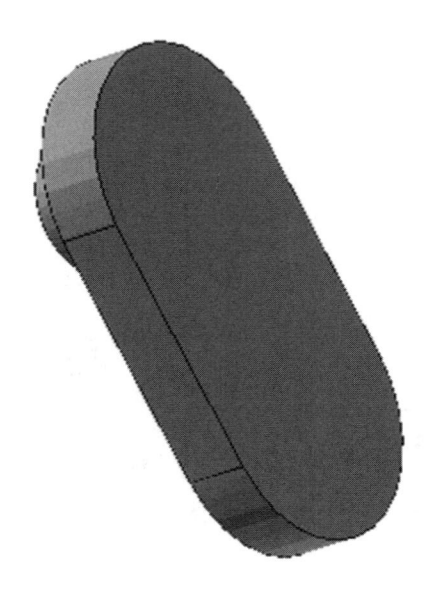

172. Begin a new sketch on the opposite side as shown in Figure 153.

Figure 153

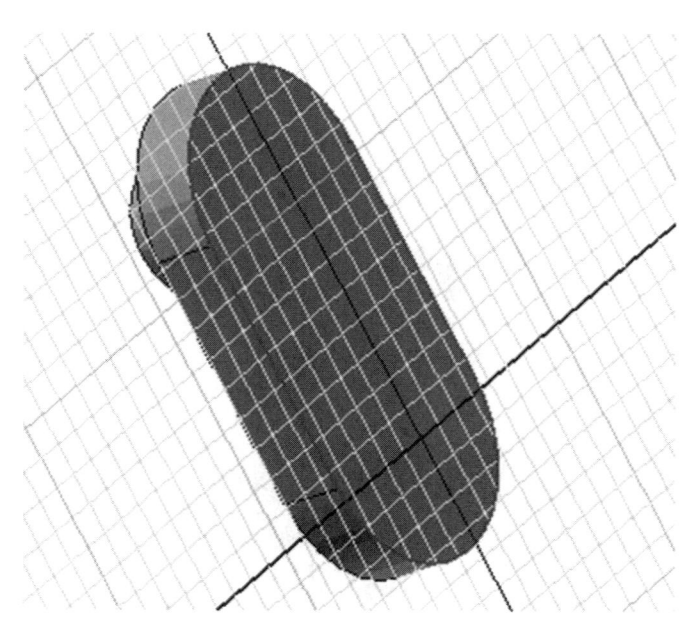

Chapter 6: Advanced Design Procedures

173. Use the "Look At" command to gain a perpendicular view as shown in Figure 154.

Figure 154

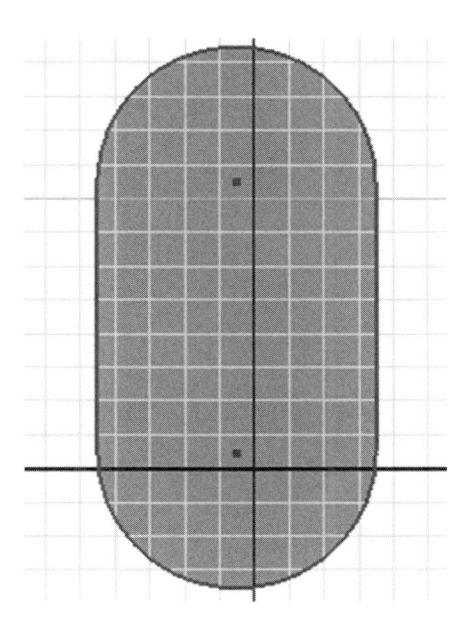

174. Complete the following sketch as shown in Figure 155.

Figure 155

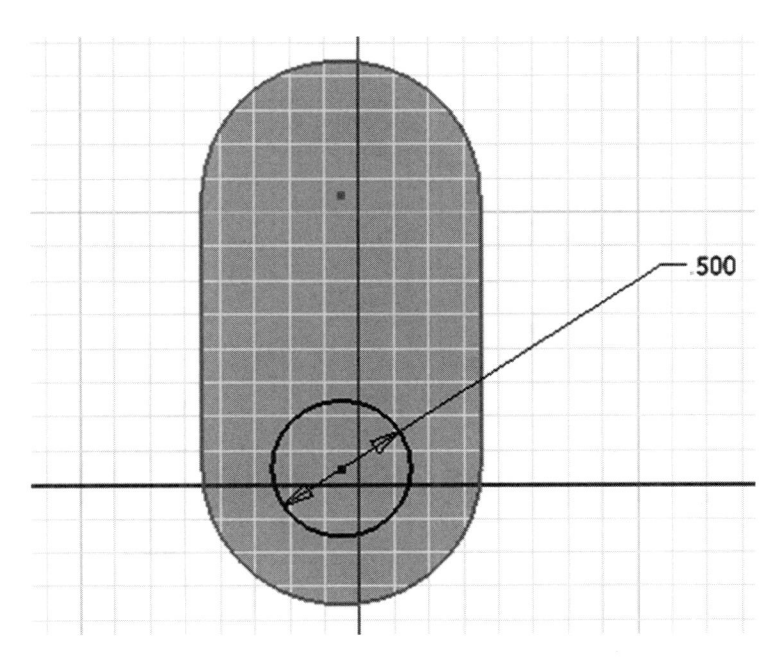

Chapter 6: Advanced Design Procedures

175. Extrude the sketch into a solid with a thickness of **.25** as shown in Figure 156.

Figure 156

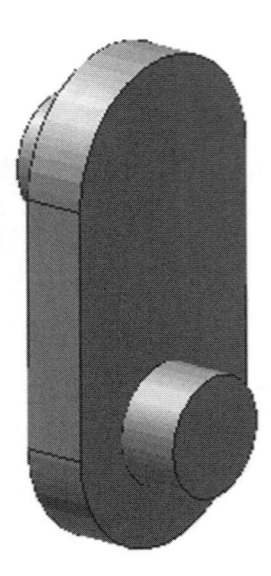

176. Save the part as Crankshaft1.ipt where it can be easily retrieved later.

177. Begin a new drawing as described in Chapter 1.

178. Complete the sketch shown. Extrude the sketch into a solid with a thickness of **.25** as shown in Figure 157.

Figure 157

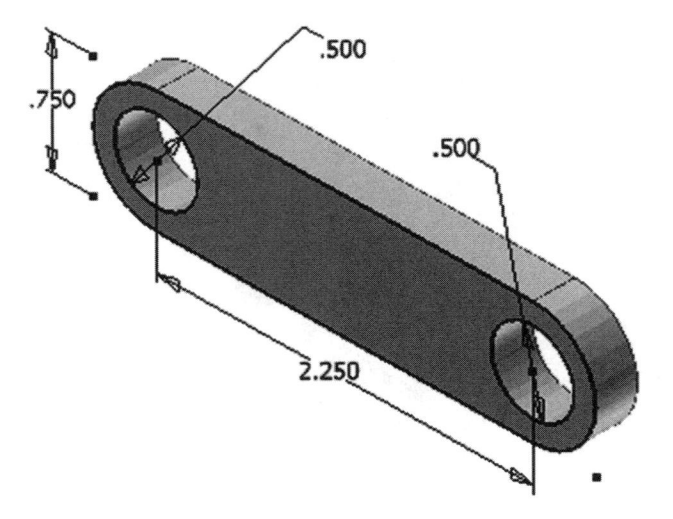

179. Save the part as Conrod1.ipt where it can be easily retrieved later.

180. All of these parts will be used in the next chapter.

350

Chapter 7 Introduction to Assembly View Procedures

Objectives:
- Learn to import existing solid models into the Assembly Panel
- Learn to constrain all parts in the Assembly Panel
- Learn to edit/modify parts while in the Assembly Panel
- Learn to assign colors to different parts in the Assembly Panel
- Learn to animate/simulate motion
- Learn to create an .avi or .wmv file while in the Assembly Panel

Chapter 7 includes instruction on how to construct the assembly shown below.

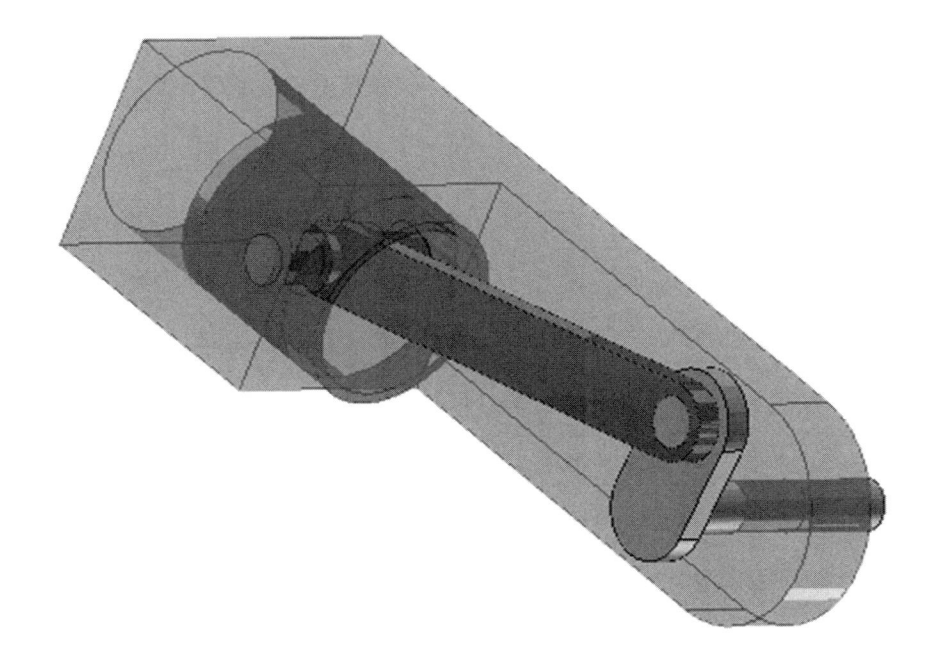

Chapter 7: Introduction to Assembly View Procedures

1. Start Inventor 2009 by referring to "Chapter 1 Getting Started".

2. After Autodesk Inventor 2009 is running, begin an Assembly Drawing. First, move the cursor to the upper left corner of the screen and left click on **New**. The New File dialog box will appear. Left click on the **English** tab. Left click on **Standard (in).iam** as shown in Figure 1.

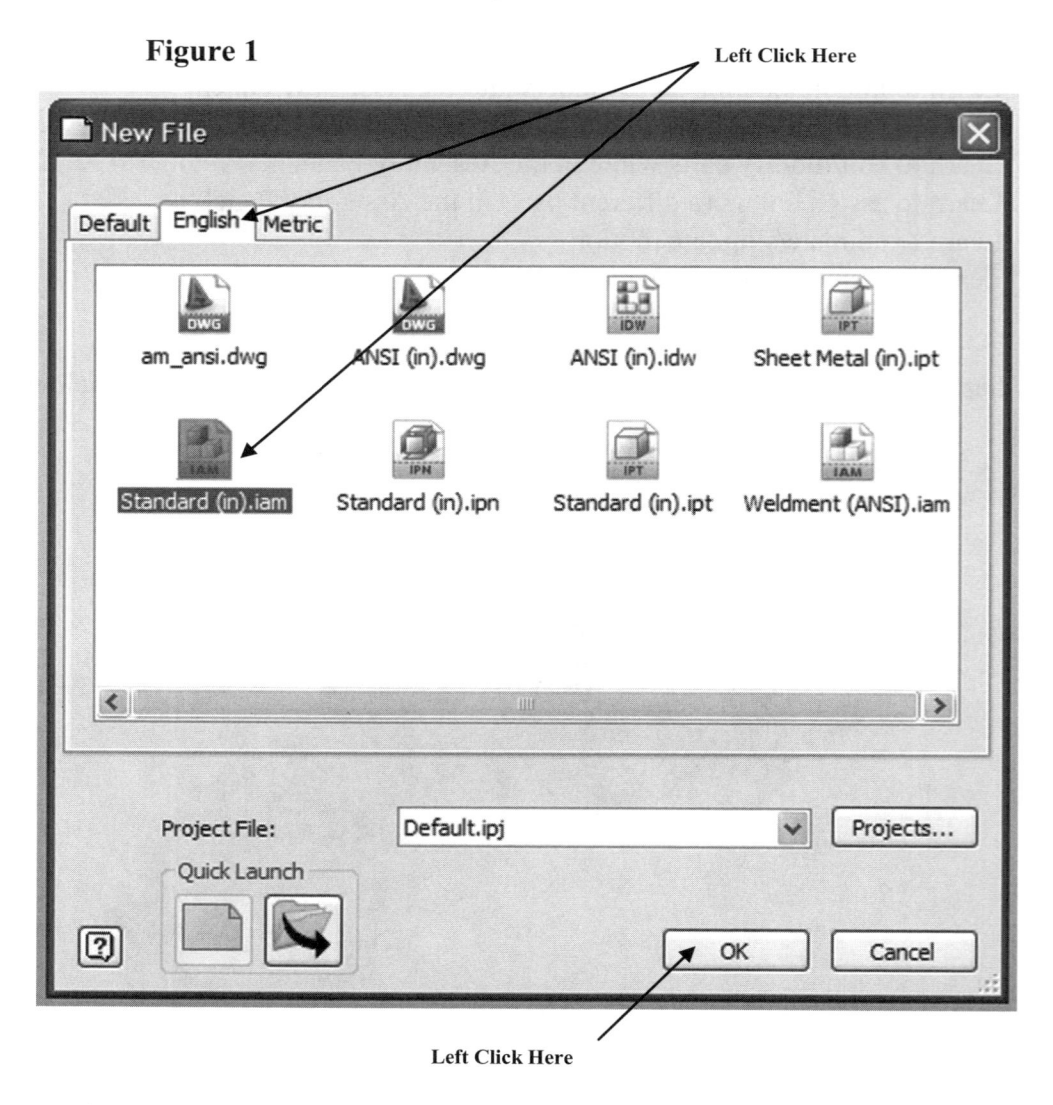

Figure 1

3. Left click on **OK**.

Chapter 7: Introduction to Assembly View Procedures

4. The Assembly Panel will open. Your screen should look similar to Figure 2.

   Figure 2

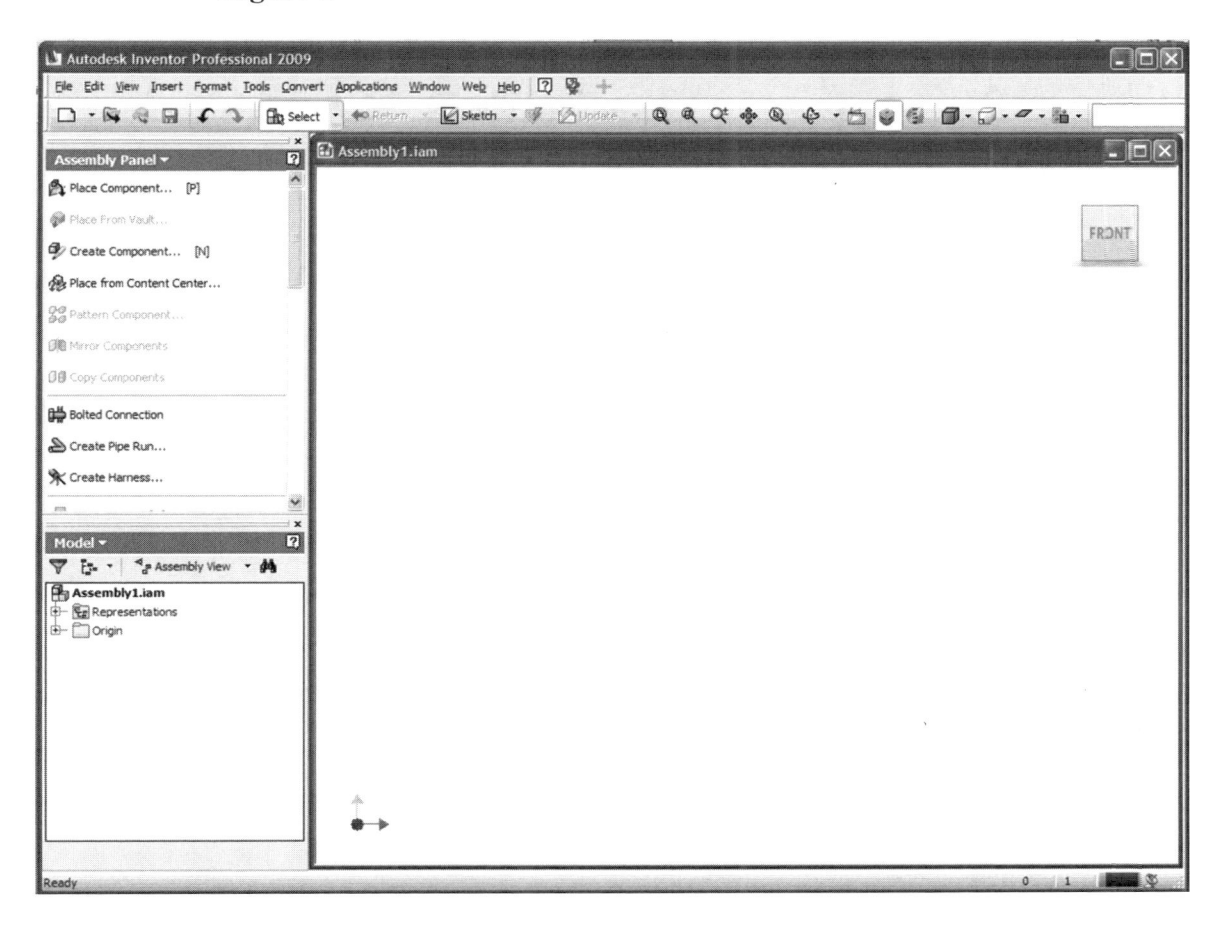

5. Move the cursor to the middle left portion of the screen and left click on **Place Component** as shown in Figure 3.

   Figure 3   Left Click Here

353

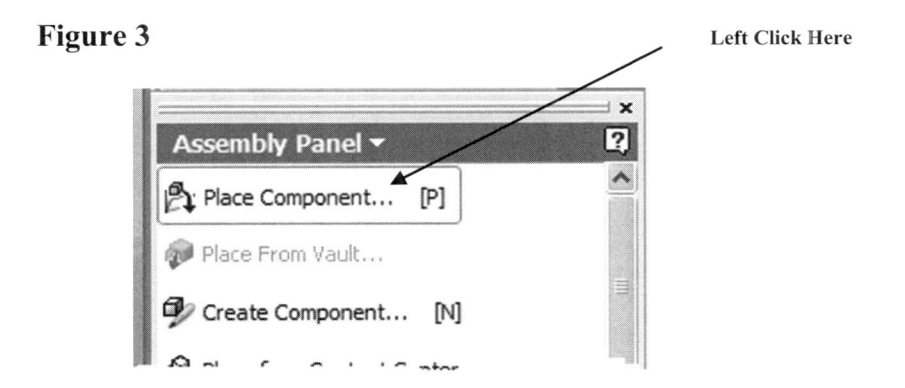

Chapter 7: Introduction to Assembly View Procedures

6.   The Place Component dialog box will appear. Locate the Pistoncase1.ipt file and left click on **Open** as shown in Figure 4.

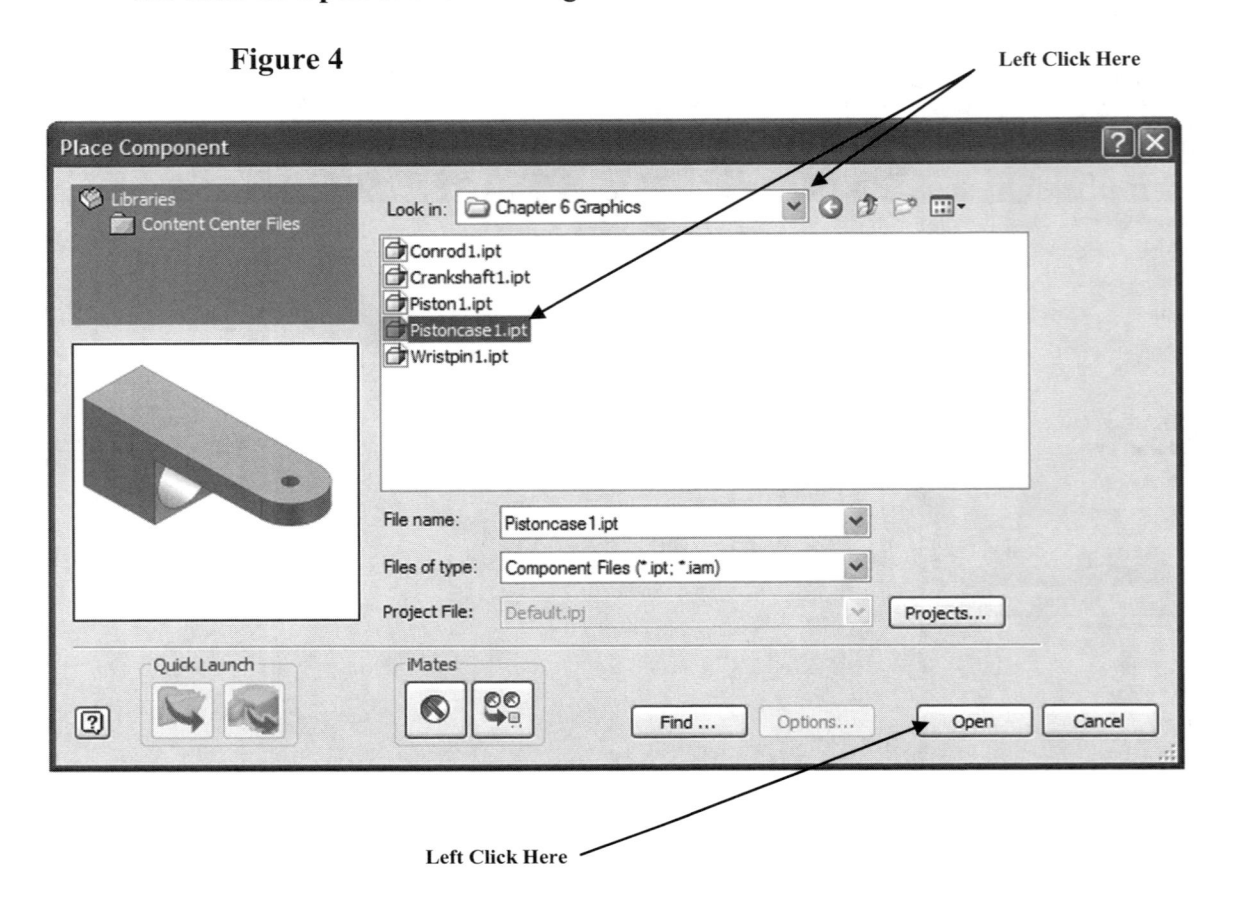

Figure 4

Left Click Here

Left Click Here

Chapter 7: Introduction to Assembly View Procedures

7. Inventor will place one piston case in the drawing space while another piston case will be attached to the cursor as shown in Figure 5.

   Figure 5

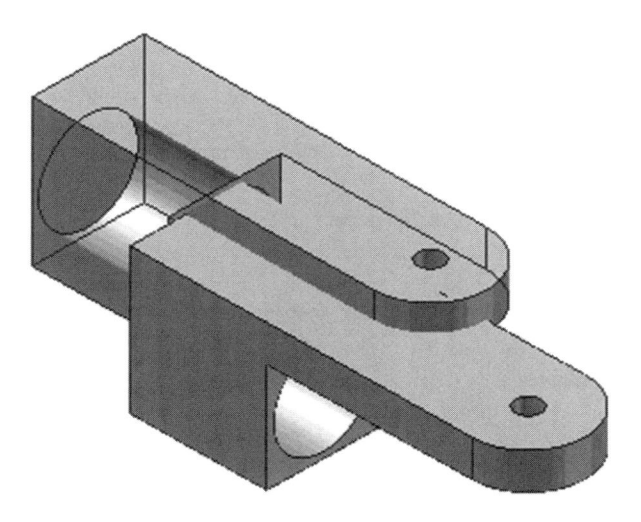

8. Do **NOT** left click. Left clicking would cause Inventor to place two piston cases in the Assembly area. Press the **Esc** key on the keyboard. Your screen should look similar to Figure 6.

   Figure 6

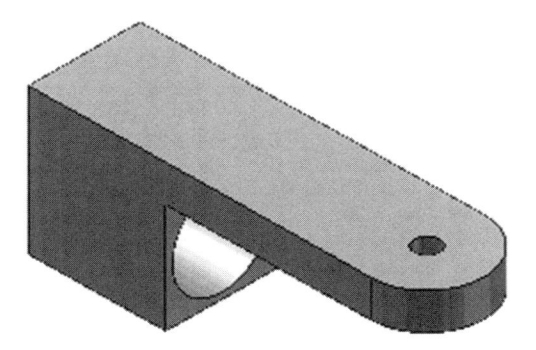

355

Chapter 7: Introduction to Assembly View Procedures

9. Move the cursor to the middle left portion of the screen and left click on **Place Component** as shown in Figure 7.

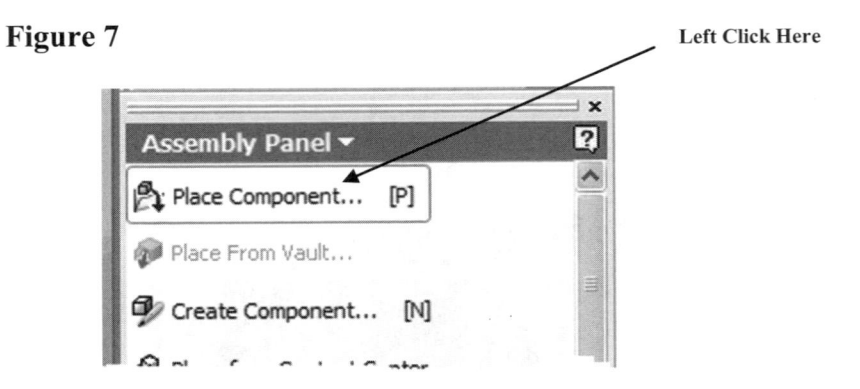

Figure 7

10. The Place Component dialog box will appear. Locate the Piston1.ipt file and left click on **Open** as shown in Figure 8.

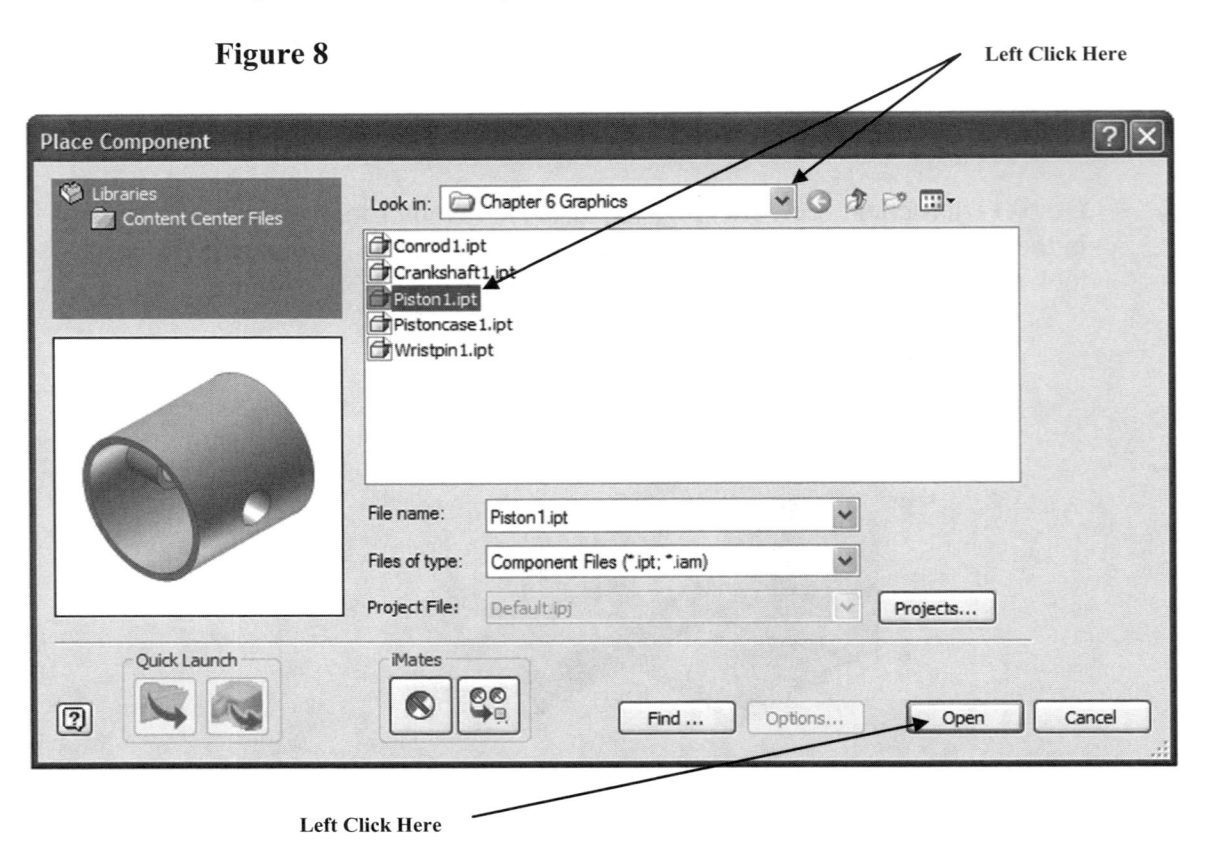

Figure 8

Chapter 7: Introduction to Assembly View Procedures

11. The piston will be attached to the cursor. Place the piston anywhere near the piston case and left click once. Another piston will be attached to the cursor in case another will be used. In this drawing there is no need to import the same part multiple times. Press the **Esc** button on the keyboard once. Your screen should look similar to Figure 9.

Figure 9

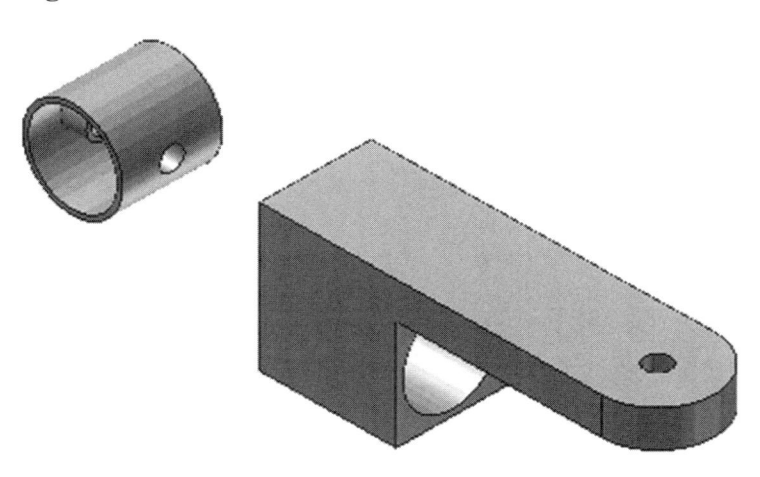

12. Move the cursor to the middle left portion of the screen and left click on **Place Component** as shown in Figure 10.

Figure 10 Left Click Here

357

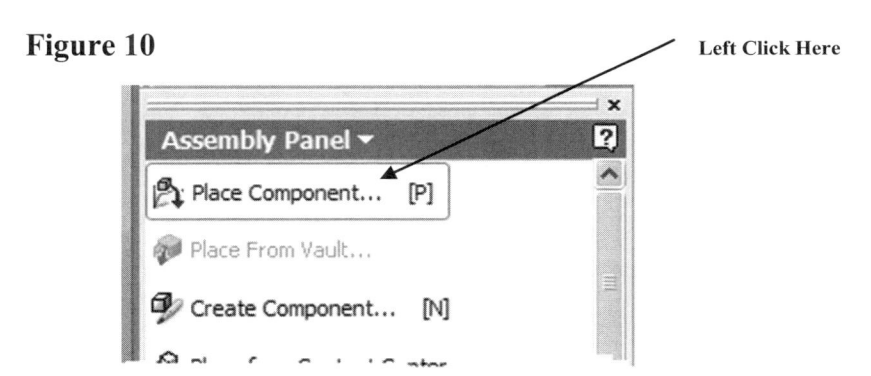

Chapter 7: Introduction to Assembly View Procedures

13. The Place Component dialog box will appear. Locate the Conrod1.ipt file and left click on **Open** as shown in Figure 11.

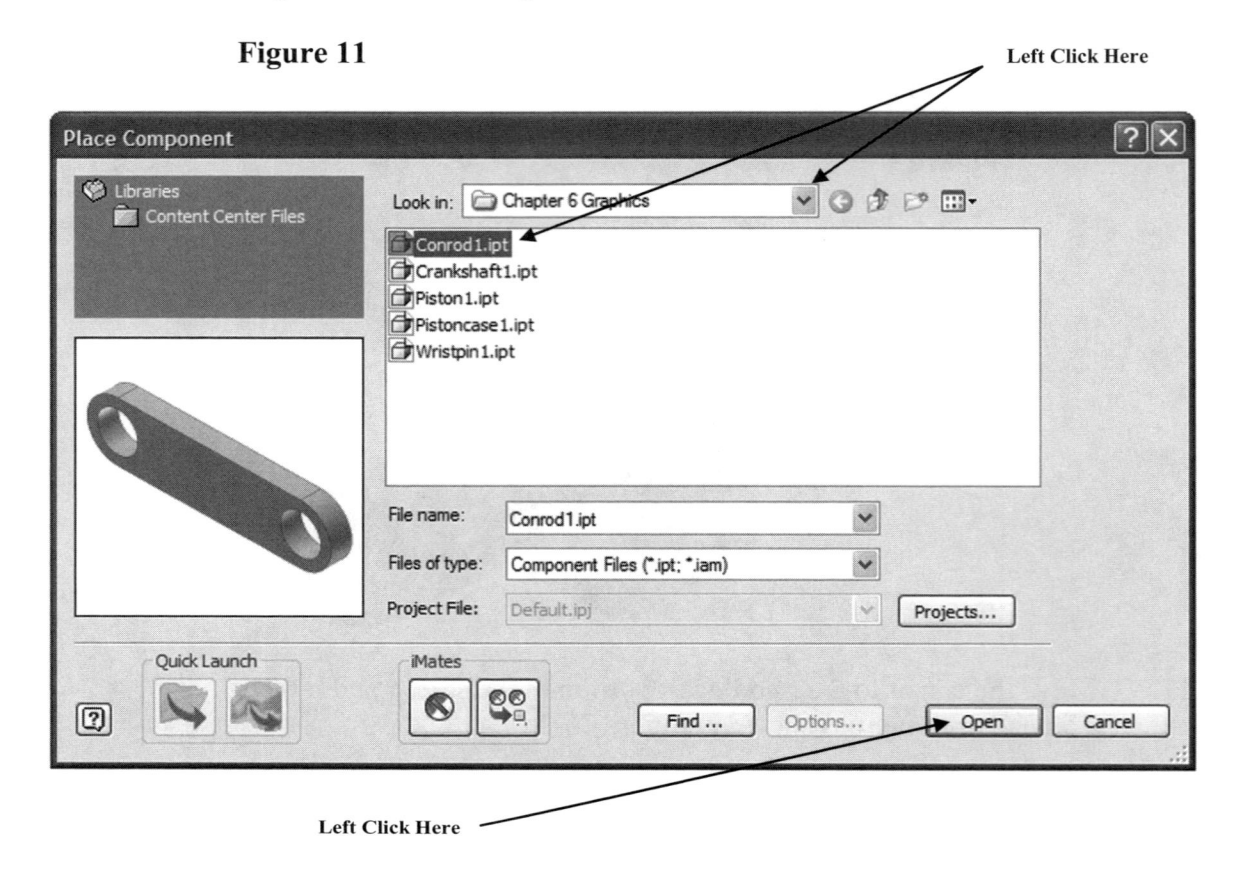

Figure 11

Chapter 7: Introduction to Assembly View Procedures

14. The connecting rod will be attached to the cursor. Place the connecting rod anywhere near the piston case and left click once. Press the **Esc** button on the keyboard once. Your screen should look similar to Figure 12.

Figure 12

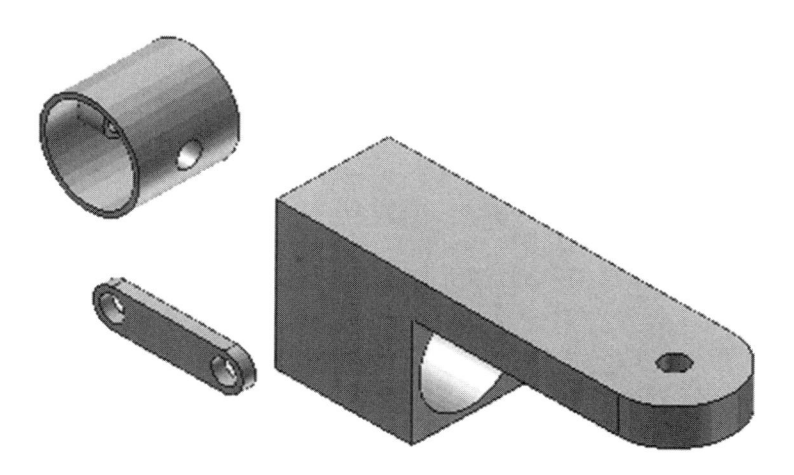

15. Move the cursor to the middle left portion of the screen and left click on **Place Component** as shown in Figure 13.

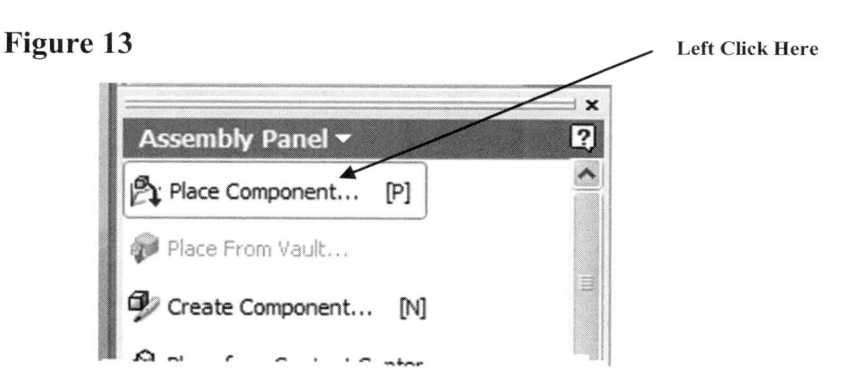

Figure 13

Left Click Here

359

Chapter 7: Introduction to Assembly View Procedures

16. The Place Component dialog box will appear. Locate the Crankshaft1.ipt file and left click on **Open** as shown in Figure 14.

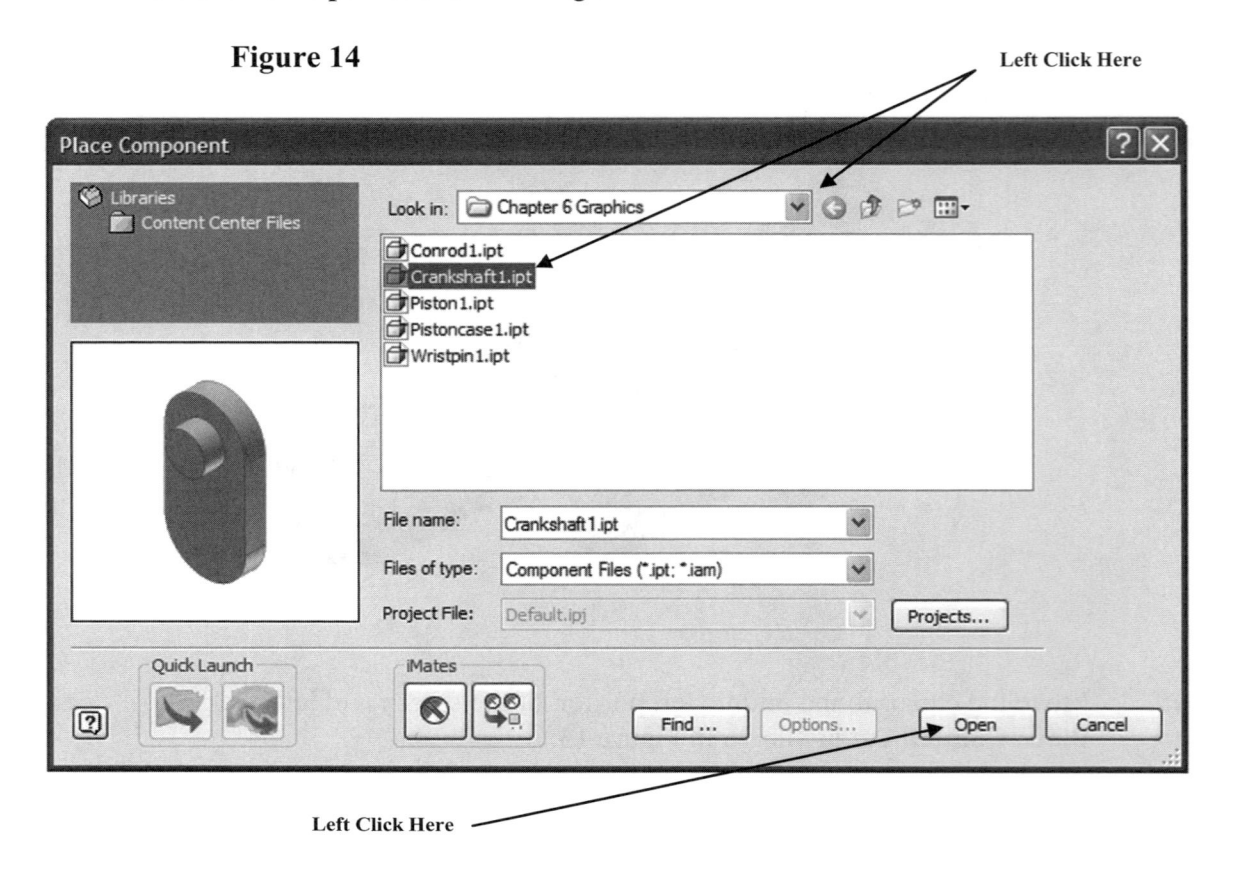

Figure 14

Chapter 7: Introduction to Assembly View Procedures

17. The crankshaft will be attached to the cursor. Place the crankshaft anywhere near the piston case and left click once. Press the **Esc** button on the keyboard once. Your screen should look similar to Figure 15.

Figure 15

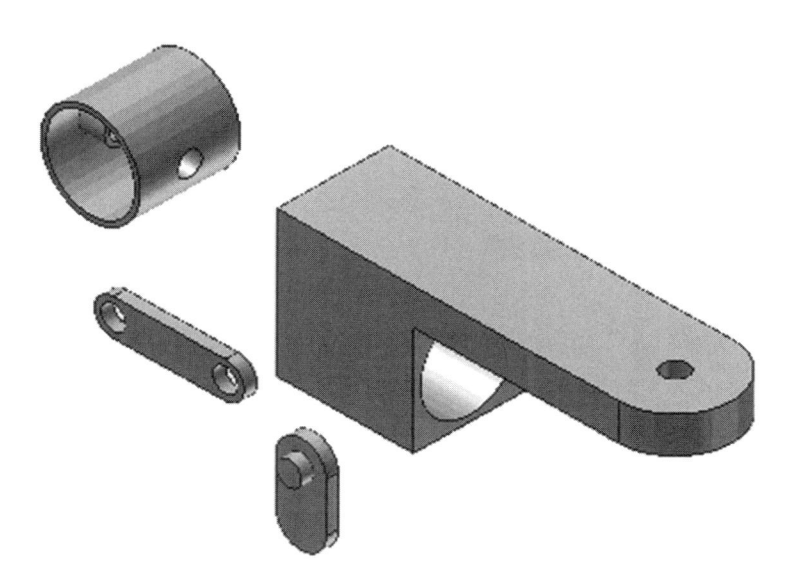

18. Move the cursor to the middle left portion of the screen and left click on **Place Component** as shown in Figure 16.

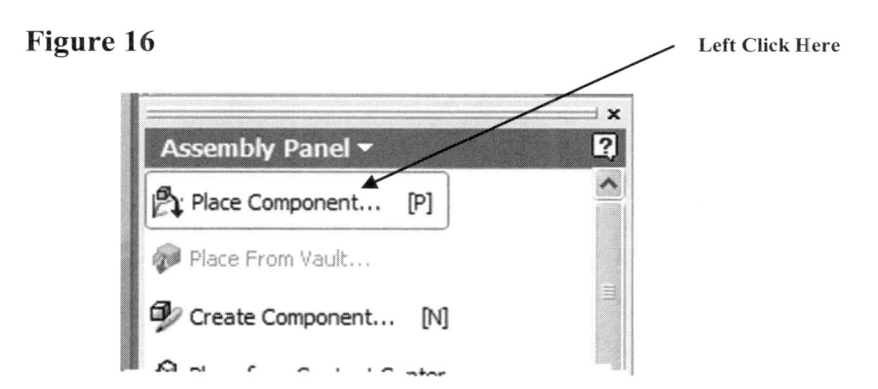

Figure 16

Left Click Here

Chapter 7: Introduction to Assembly View Procedures

19. The Place Component dialog box will appear. Locate the wristpin1.ipt file and left click on **Open** as shown in Figure 17.

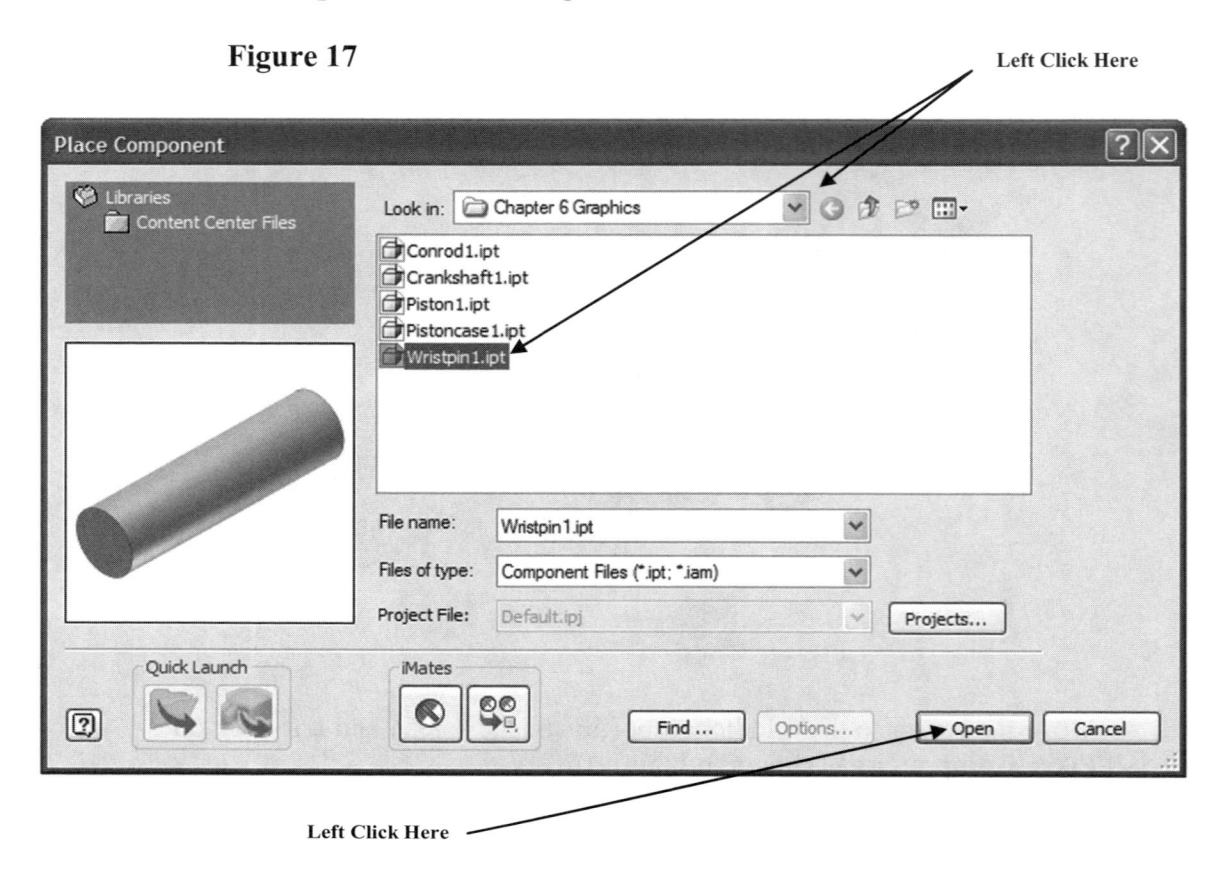

Figure 17

Chapter 7: Introduction to Assembly View Procedures

20. The wristpin will be attached to the cursor. Place the wristpin anywhere near the piston case and left click once. Press the **Esc** button on the keyboard once. Your screen should look similar to Figure 18.

Figure 18

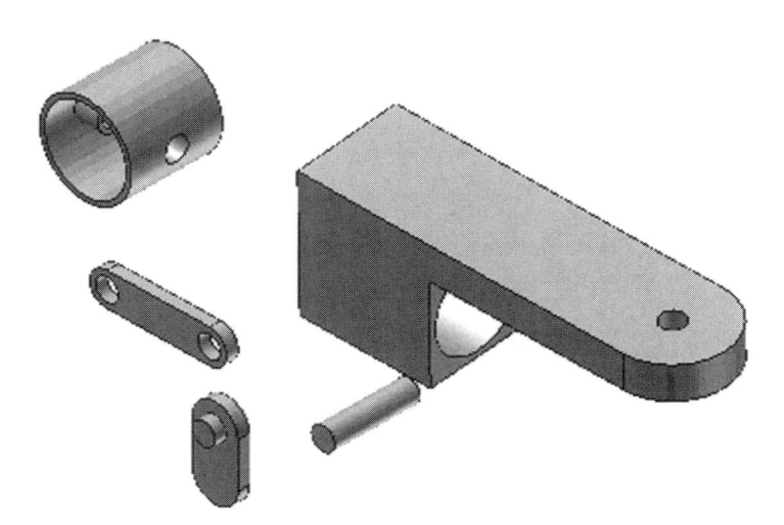

Chapter 7: Introduction to Assembly View Procedures

21. Move the cursor to the lower left portion of the screen in the part tree. Notice the picture of a push pin that appears next to the piston case text in the branch of the part tree. Move the cursor over the words **Pistoncase:1** and left click once. The text will turn blue. Right click once. A pop up menu will appear. Left click on **Grounded** as shown in Figure 19. Inventor will "unground" the case allowing it to be moved using the rotate component command as shown in Figure 20. **The first part placed into any assembly is automatically grounded**.

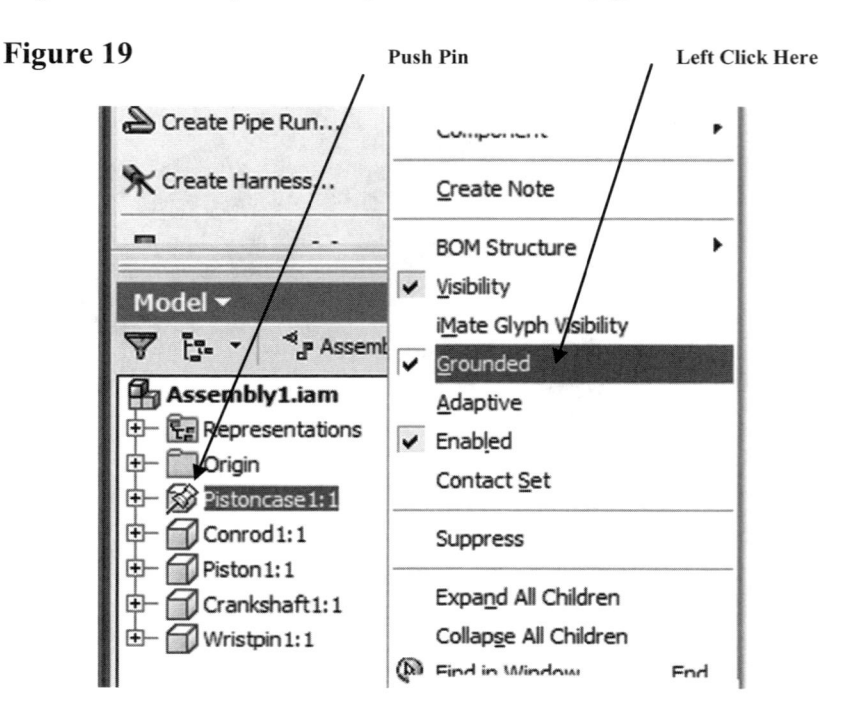

Figure 19

22. Move the cursor to the left middle portion of the screen and left click on **Rotate Component** as shown in Figure 20.

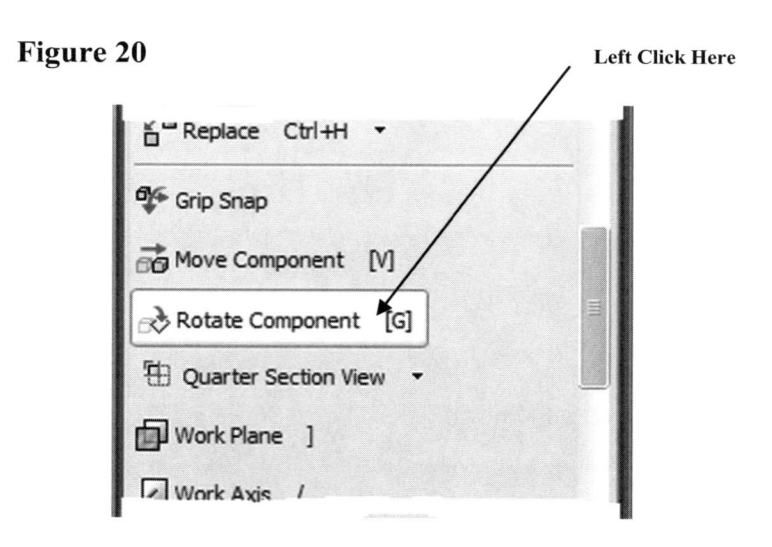

Figure 20

364

23. Move the cursor to the piston case and left click once. A white circle will appear around the piston case. Rotate the piston case upward as shown in Figure 21.

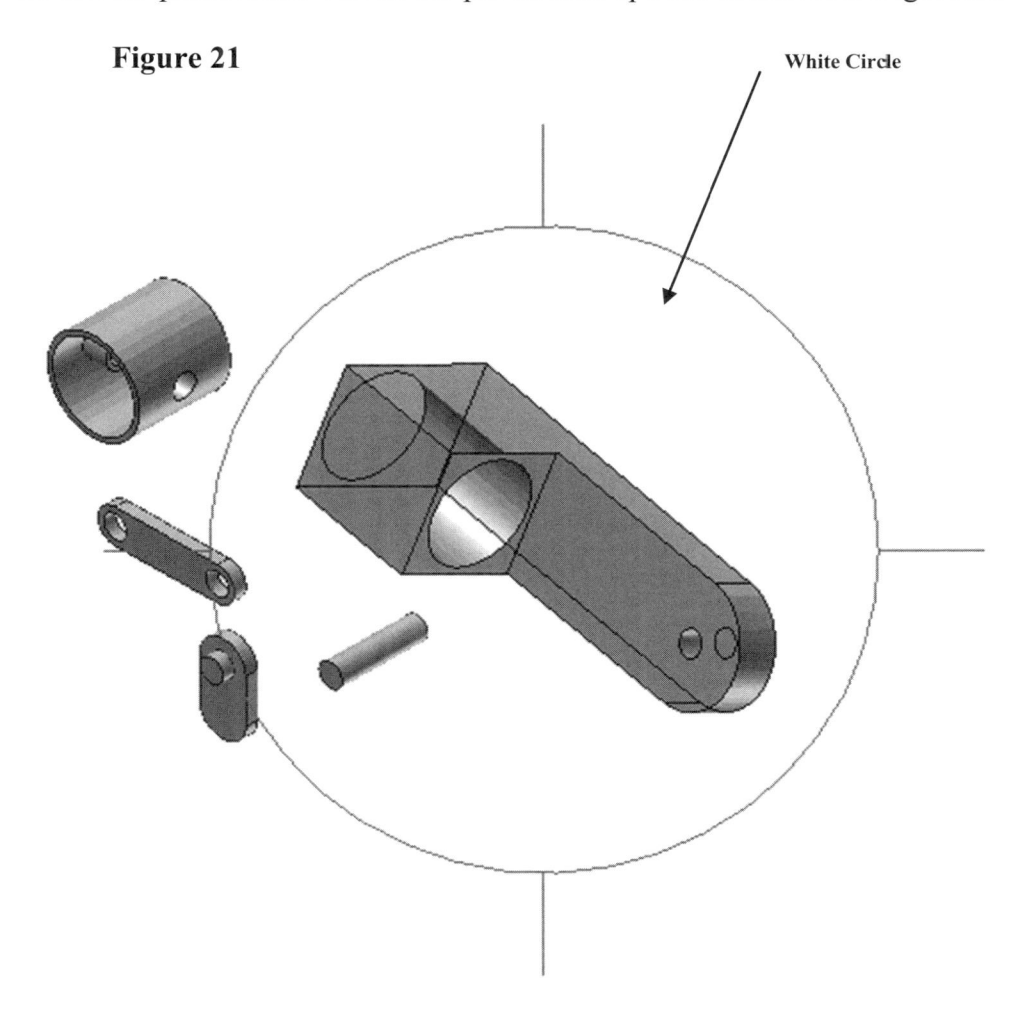

Figure 21

White Circle

24. Your screen should look similar to Figure 21.

Chapter 7: Introduction to Assembly View Procedures

25. After the piston case is rotated as shown in Figure 22, right click once. A pop up menu will appear. Left click on **Done** as shown in Figure 22.

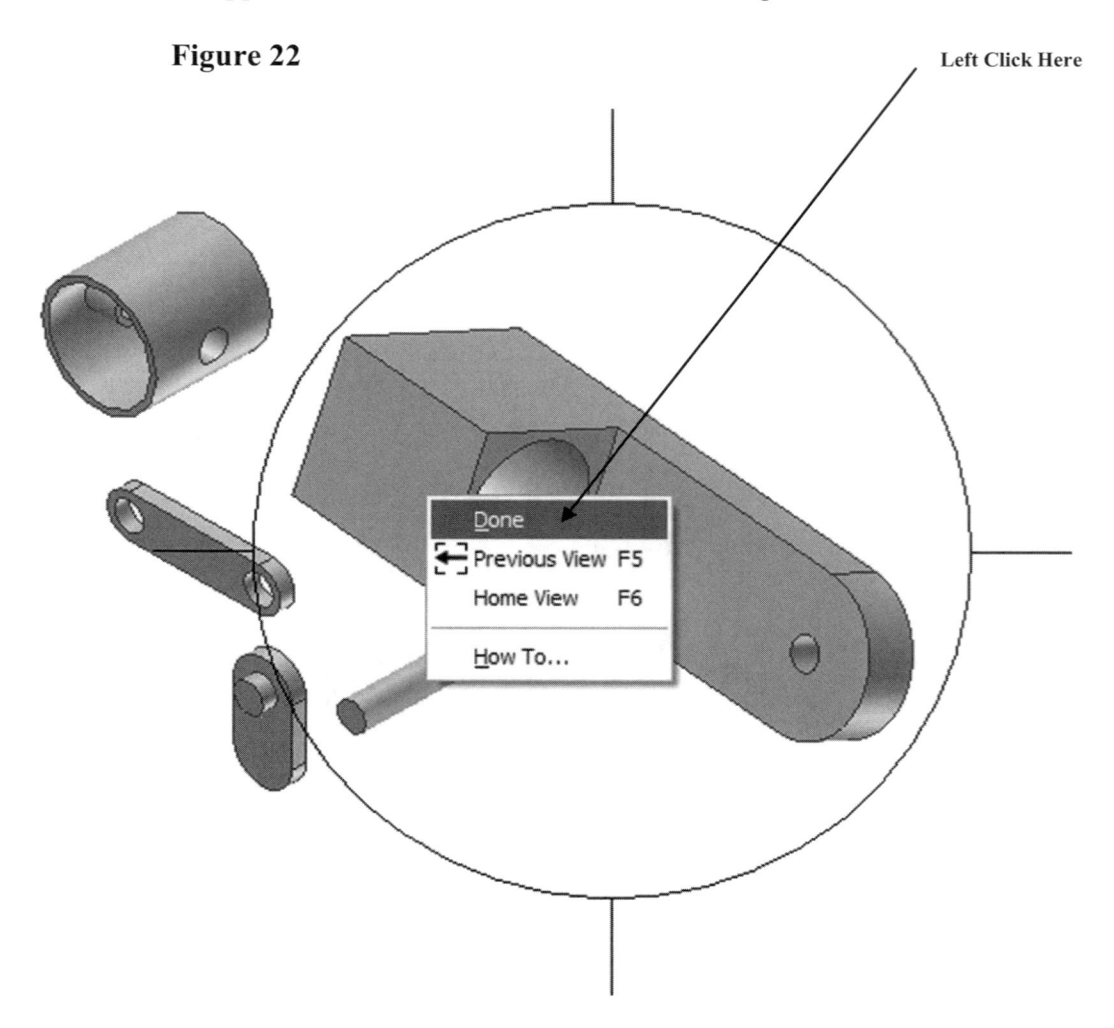

Figure 22

Left Click Here

Chapter 7: Introduction to Assembly View Procedures

26. Move the cursor to the lower left portion of the screen in the part tree. Notice the picture of the push pin that appeared next to the piston case text is gone. This means the piston case is NOT grounded. Move the cursor over the words **Pistoncase1:1** and left click once. The text will turn blue. Right click once. A pop up menu will appear. Left click on **Grounded** as shown in Figure 23. Inventor will "ground" the case preventing it from being moved while the rest of the assembly is constructed. **Caution: Only ground the Piston Case.**

Figure 23

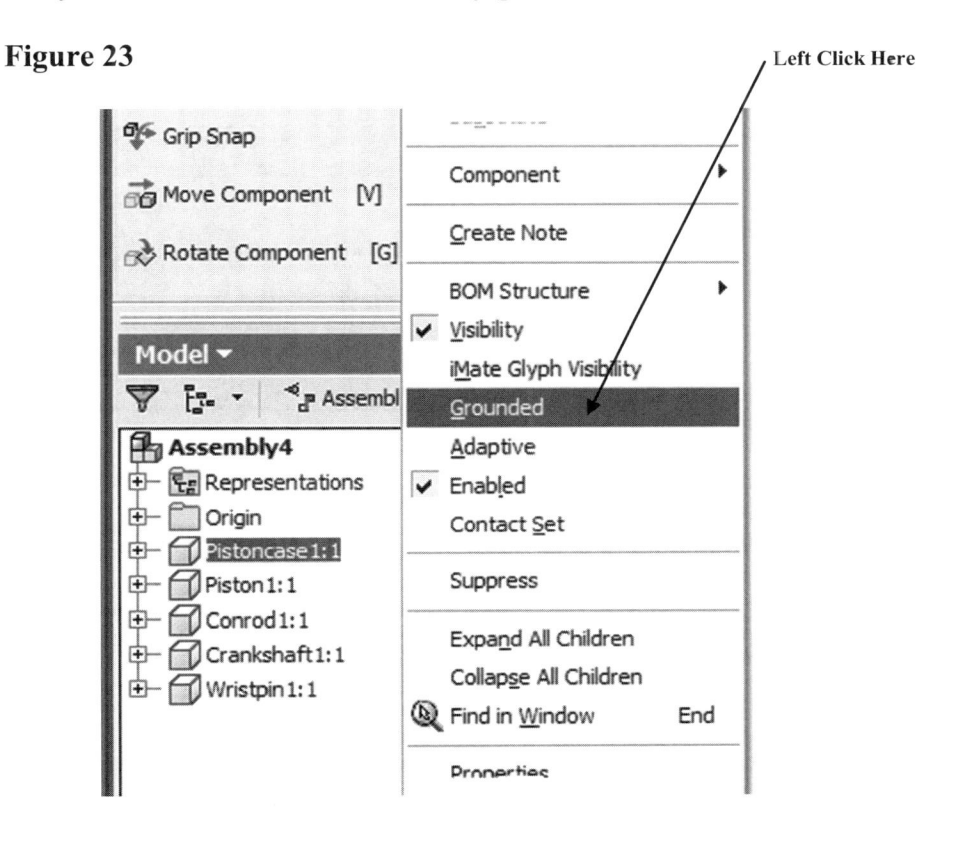

Chapter 7: Introduction to Assembly View Procedures

27. Move the cursor to the middle left portion of the screen and left click on **Constraint**. The Place Constraint dialog box will appear as shown in Figure 24.

Figure 24 — Left Click Here

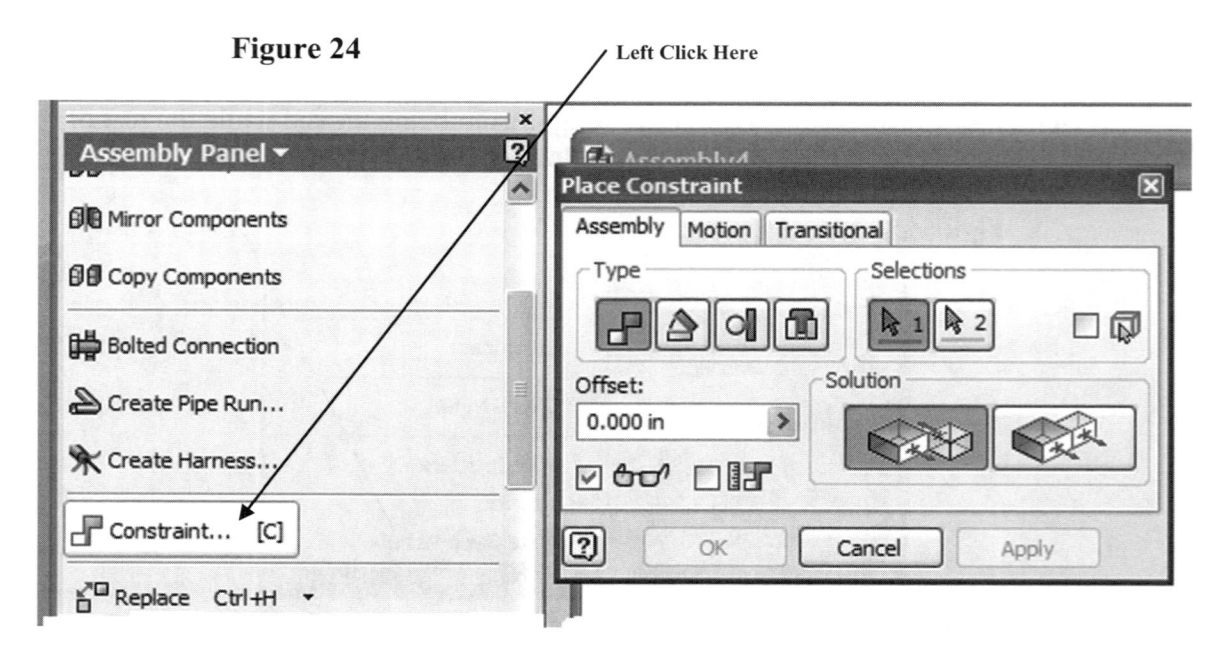

28. Move the cursor over the piston until a red center line appears as shown in Figure 25. Left click once.

Figure 25 — Center Line

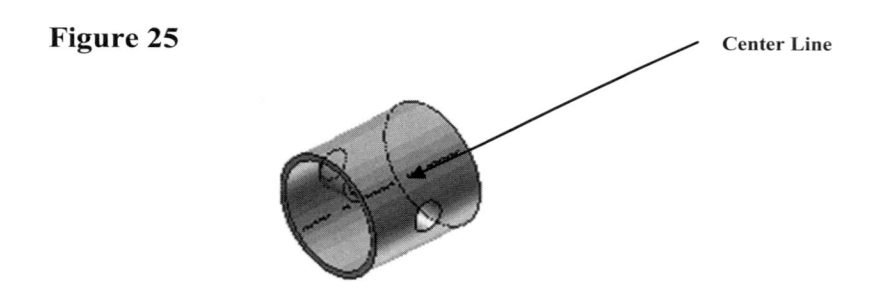

Chapter 7: Introduction to Assembly View Procedures

29. Move the cursor over the piston case until a red center line appears as shown in Figure 26. Left click once.

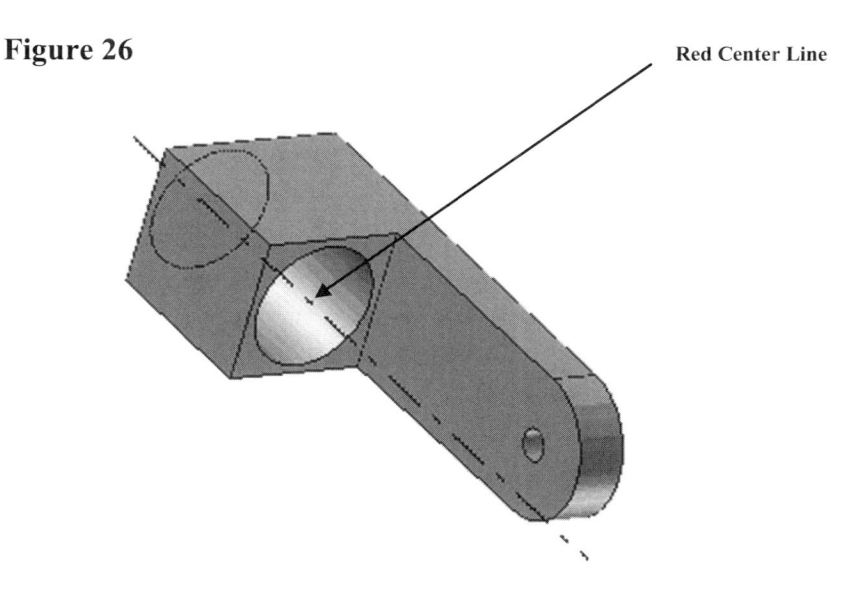

Figure 26

Red Center Line

30. Inventor will align the centers of the piston and the piston case. Your screen should look similar to Figure 27.

Figure 27

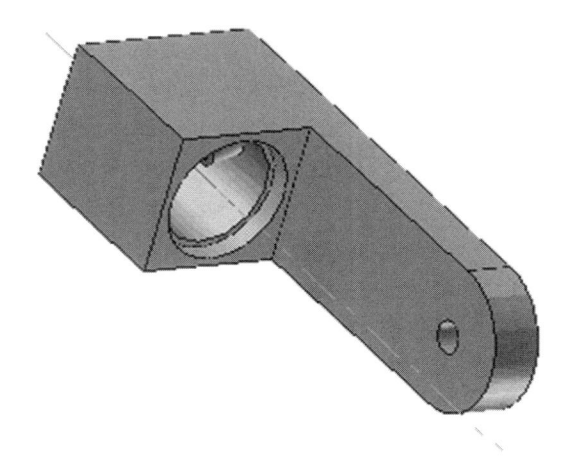

31. If Inventor installed the piston upside down, click on the "Undo" icon. Use the Rotate Component command to rotate the piston so that Inventor has to rotate it less than 180 degrees to install it.

Chapter 7: Introduction to Assembly View Procedures

32. Left click on **OK** as shown in Figure 28.

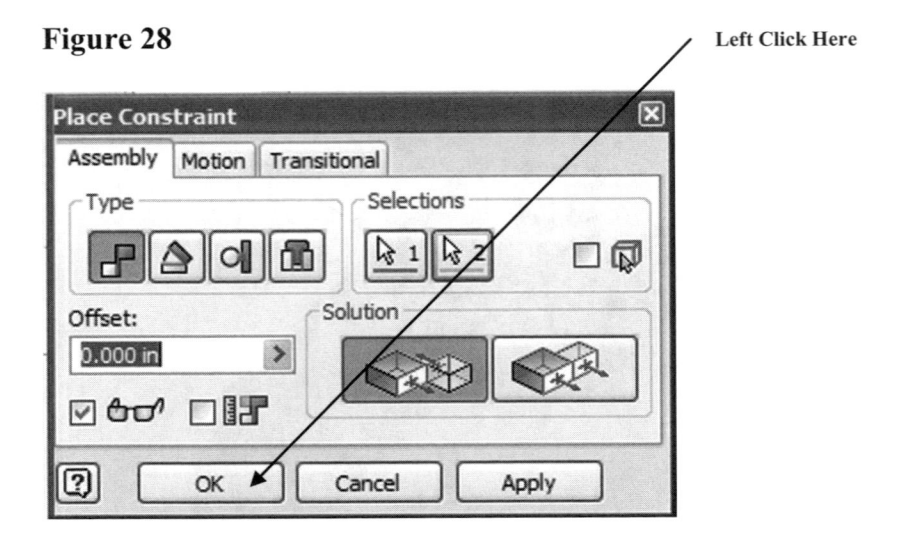

Figure 28

Left Click Here

33. Your screen should look similar to Figure 29.

Figure 29

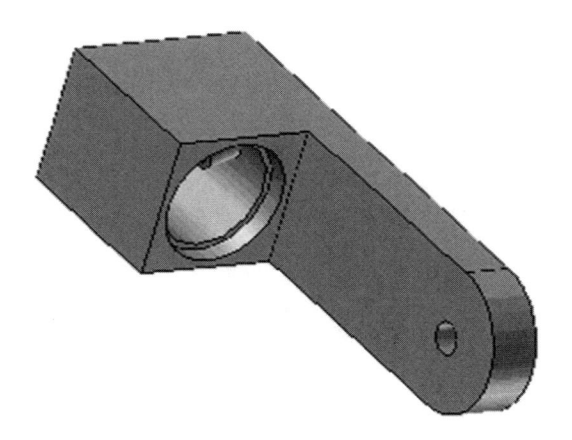

370

Chapter 7: Introduction to Assembly View Procedures

34. Move the cursor to the lower left portion of the piston. Left click (holding the left mouse button down) and slide the piston down out below the bore as shown in Figure 30.

Figure 30

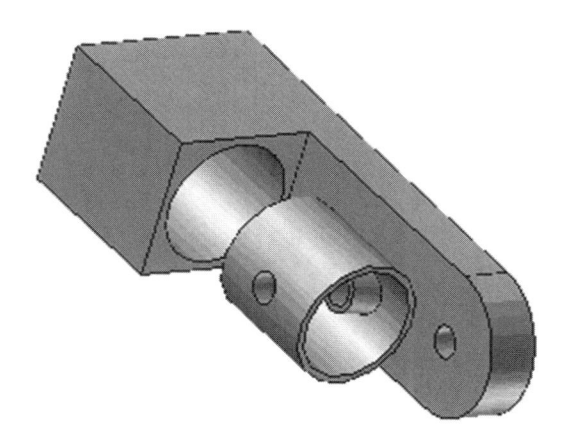

35. Move the cursor to the middle left portion of the screen and left click on **Constraint**. The Place Constraint dialog box will appear as shown in Figure 31.

Figure 31

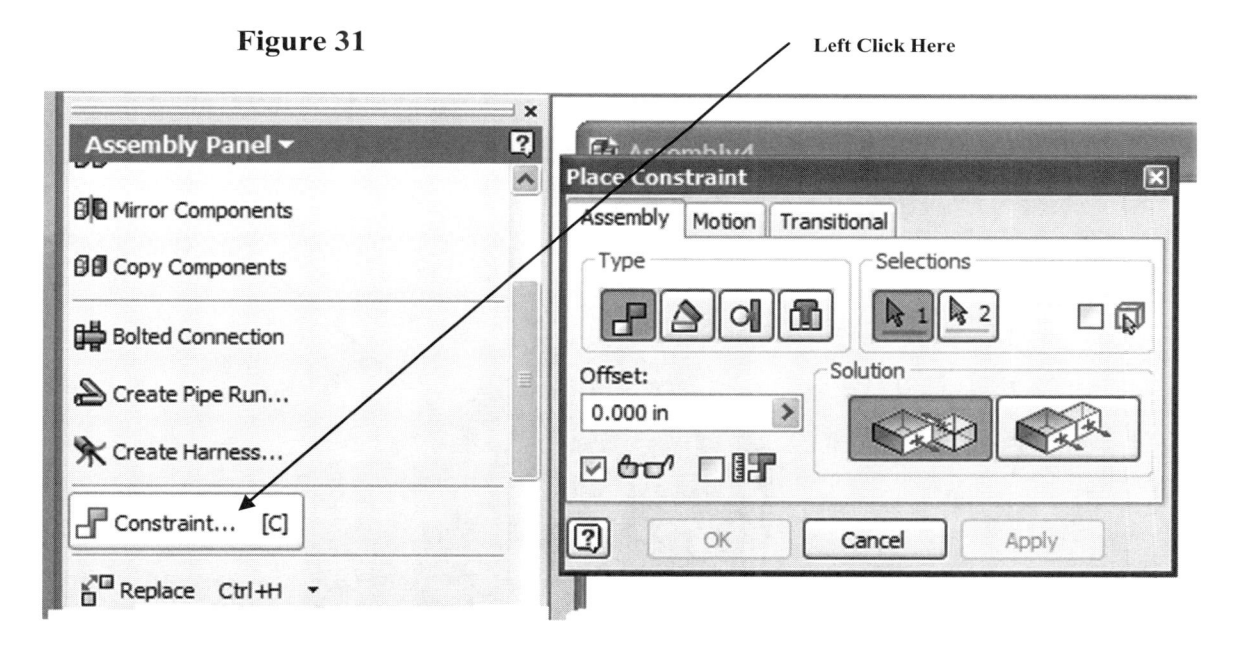

371

Chapter 7: Introduction to Assembly View Procedures

36. Move the cursor to the wristpin hole on the piston. A red center line will appear. Left click once as shown in Figure 32.

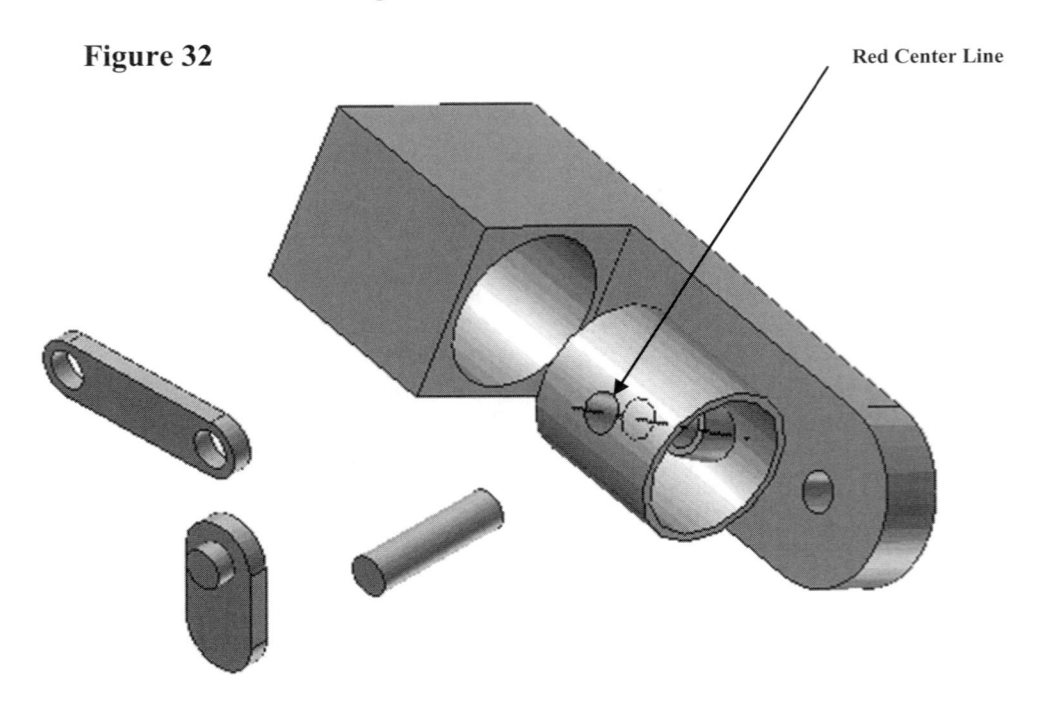

Figure 32   Red Center Line

37. Move the cursor to the upper portion of the connecting rod. A red center line will appear. Left click once as shown in Figure 33. You may have to zoom in to accomplish this.

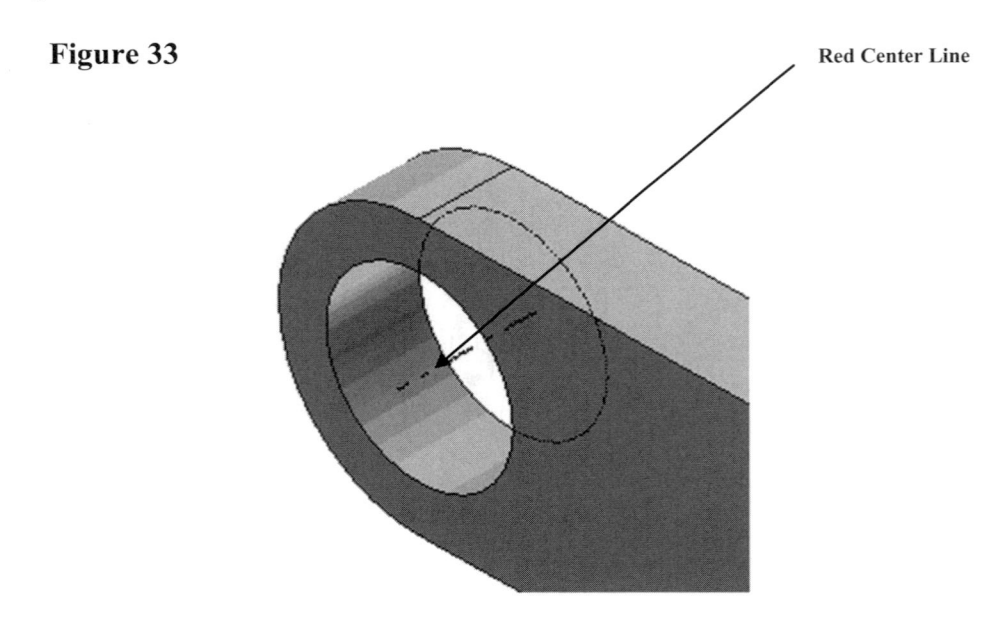

Figure 33   Red Center Line

Chapter 7: Introduction to Assembly View Procedures

38. Left click on **OK** as shown in Figure 34.

Figure 34

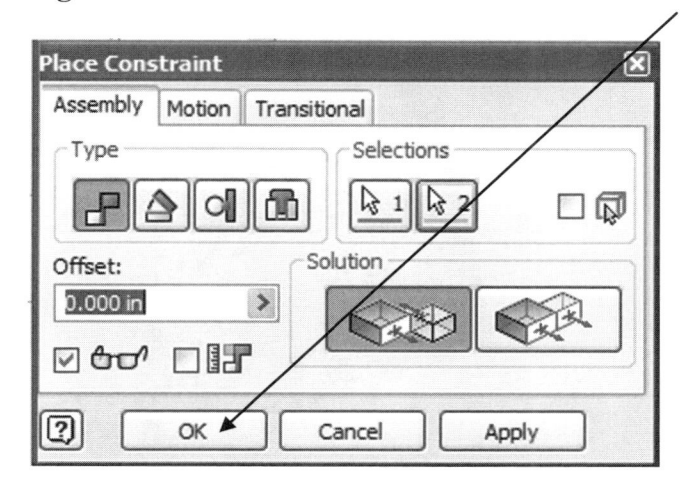

Left Click Here

39. Your screen should look similar to Figure 35.

Figure 35

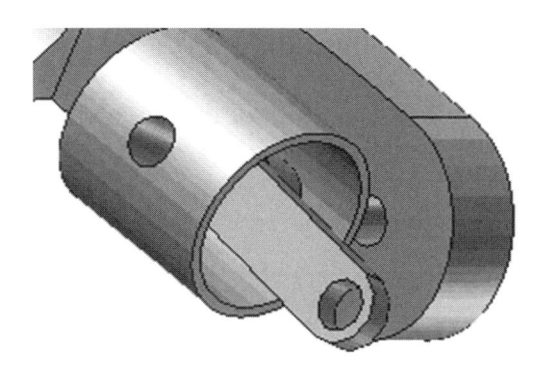

373

Chapter 7: Introduction to Assembly View Procedures

40. Use the Rotate command to rotate the entire assembly to gain access to the underside of the piston as shown in Figure 36.

Figure 36

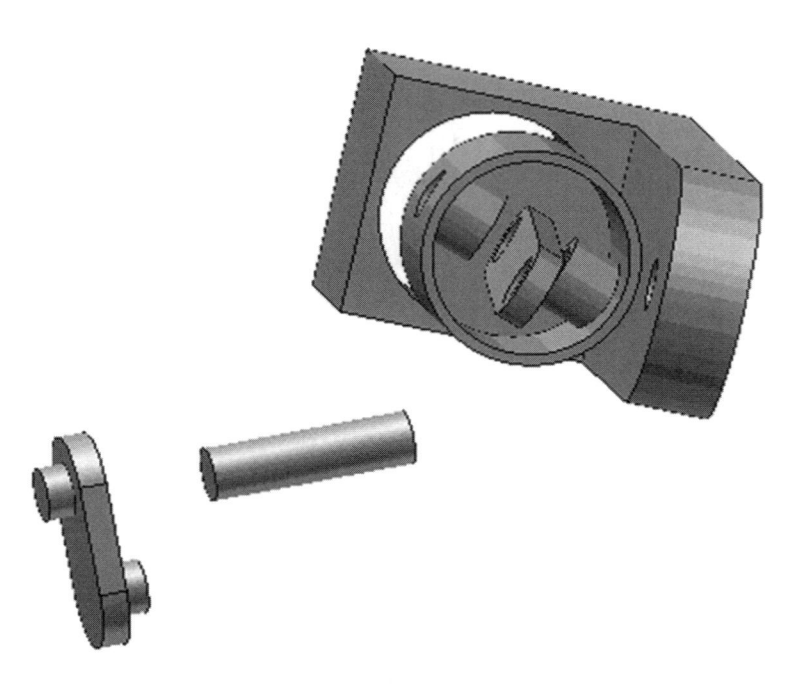

41. Move the cursor to the middle left portion of the screen and left click on **Constraint**. The Place Constraint dialog box will appear as shown in Figure 37.

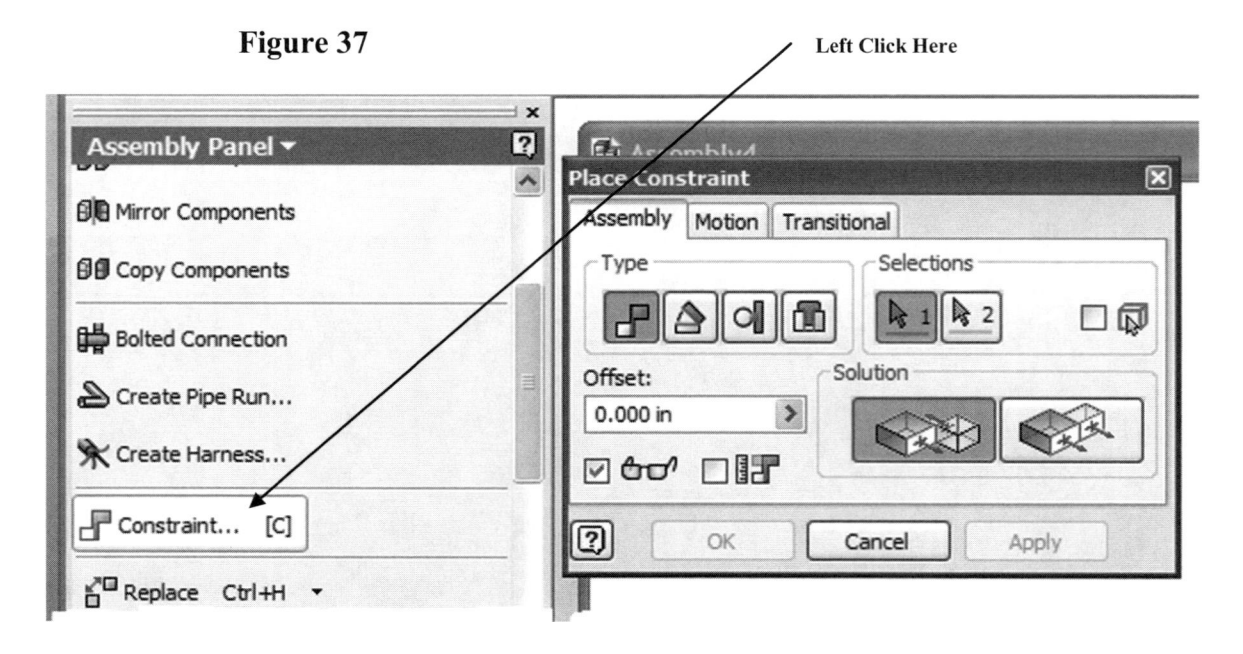

Figure 37   Left Click Here

Chapter 7: Introduction to Assembly View Procedures

42. Move the cursor to the left side of the connecting rod causing a red arrow to appear. Left click as shown in Figure 38. You may have to zoom in so that Inventor will find the proper surface.

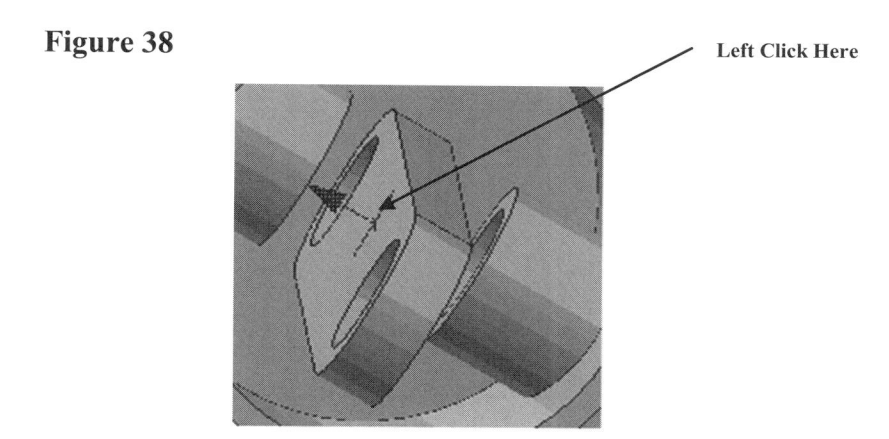

Figure 38

Left Click Here

43. Use the Rotate command to turn the piston in order to gain access to the surface opposite the previously selected surface. Hit the **ESC** key once or right click and select **Done** to get out of the Rotate command. Left click on the surface opposite the previously selected surface as shown in Figure 39.

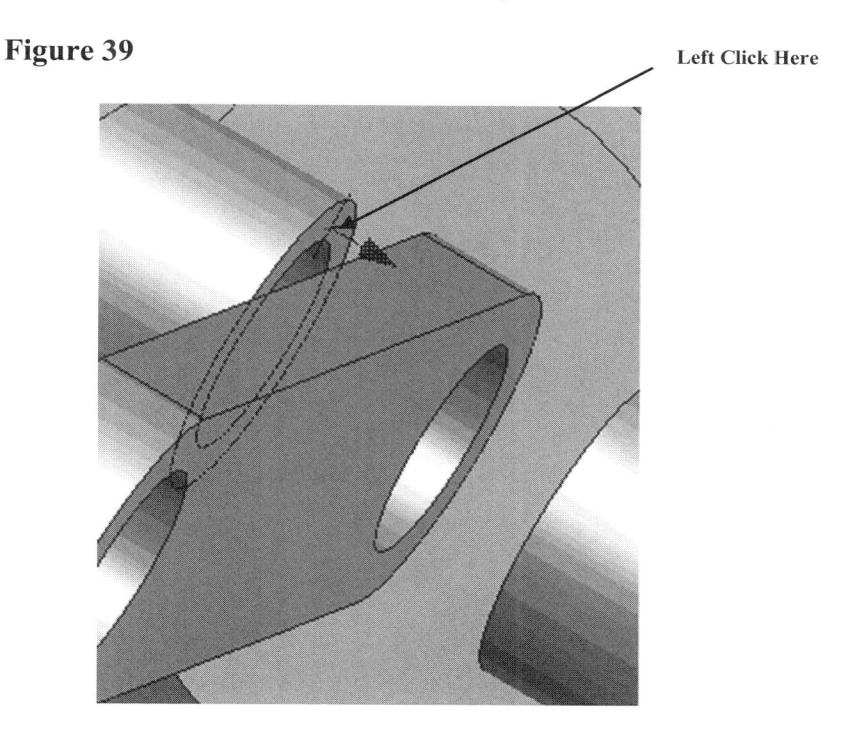

Figure 39

Left Click Here

Chapter 7: Introduction to Assembly View Procedures

44. Enter **.250** for the offset as shown in Figure 40.

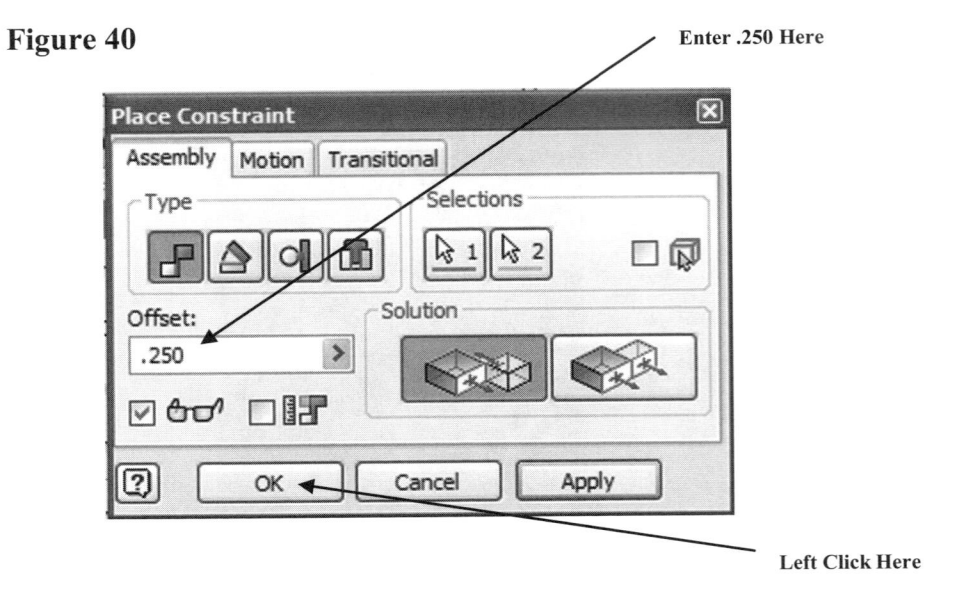

Figure 40

Enter .250 Here

Left Click Here

45. Left click on **OK**.

46. The connecting rod should be centered in the piston. Your screen should look similar to Figure 41.

Figure 41

Chapter 7: Introduction to Assembly View Procedures

47. Right click anywhere around (not on) the drawing. A pop up menu will appear. Left click on **Isometric/Home View** as shown in Figure 42.

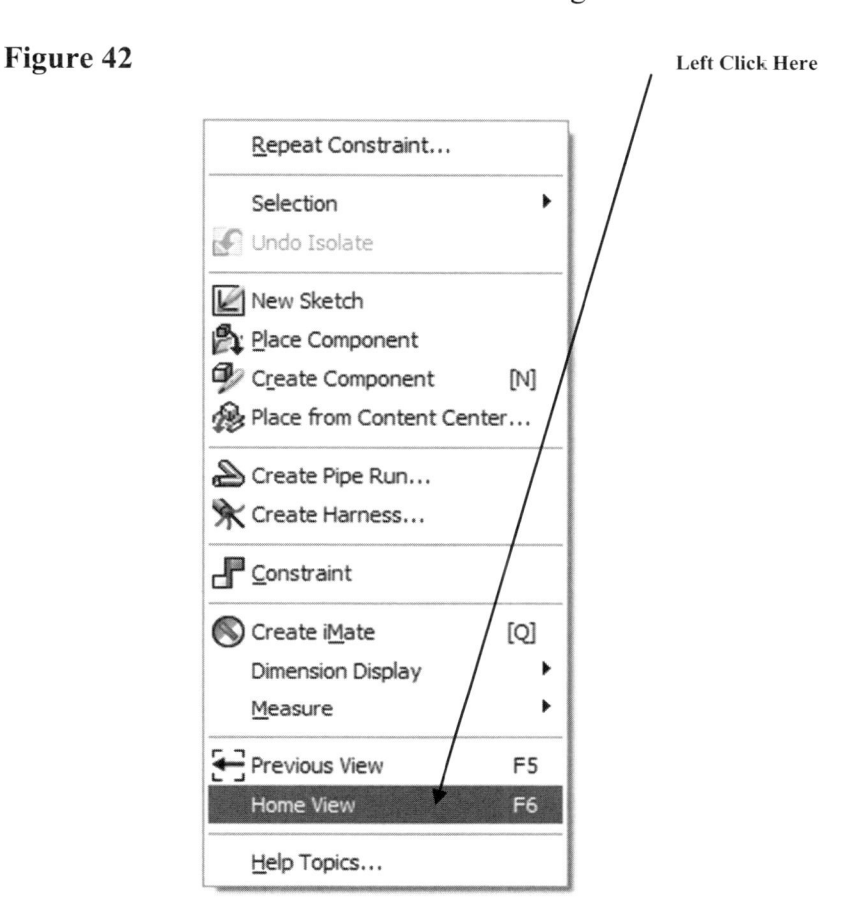

Figure 42

48. Inventor will provide an isometric view of the assembly as shown in Figure 43.

Figure 43

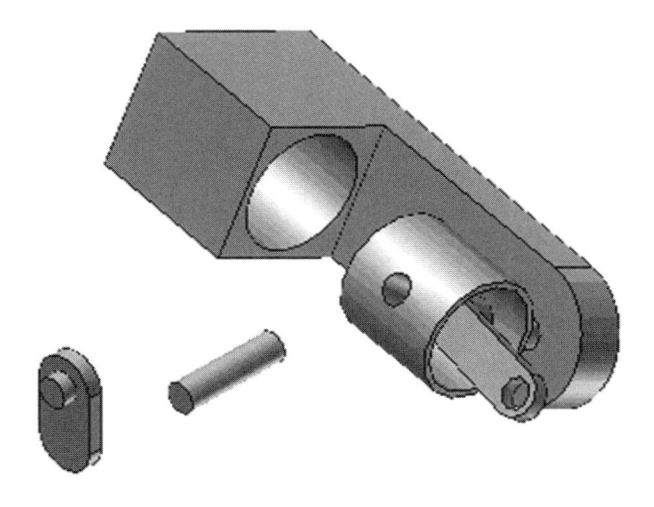

377

Chapter 7: Introduction to Assembly View Procedures

49. Move the cursor to the middle left portion of the screen and left click on **Constraint**. The Place Constraint dialog box will appear as shown in Figure 44.

Figure 44

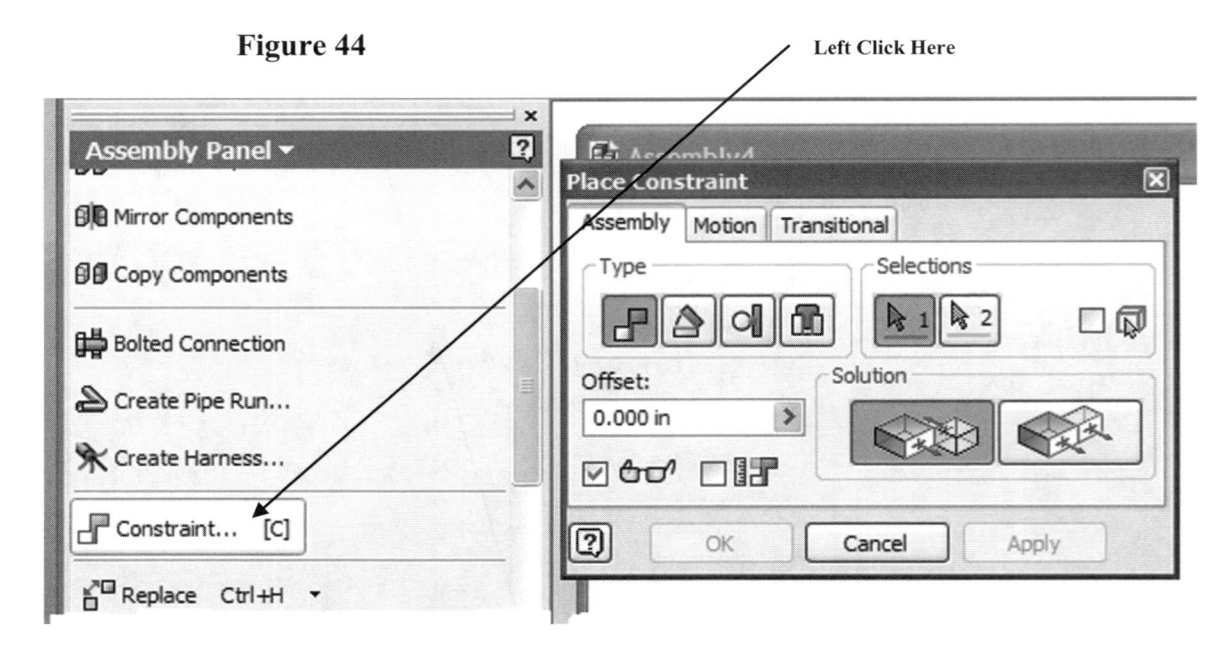

50. Move the cursor to the wrist pin causing a red center line to appear. After a red center line appears, left click once as shown in Figure 45.

Figure 45

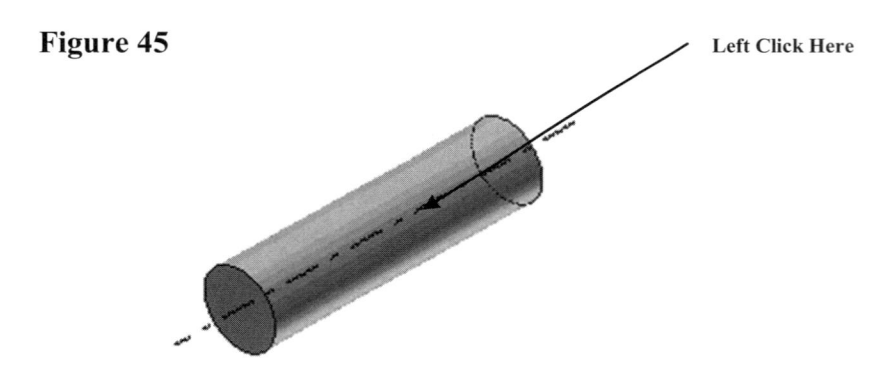

Chapter 7: Introduction to Assembly View Procedures

51. Move the cursor to the piston causing a red center line to appear. After a red center line appears, left click once as shown in Figure 46.

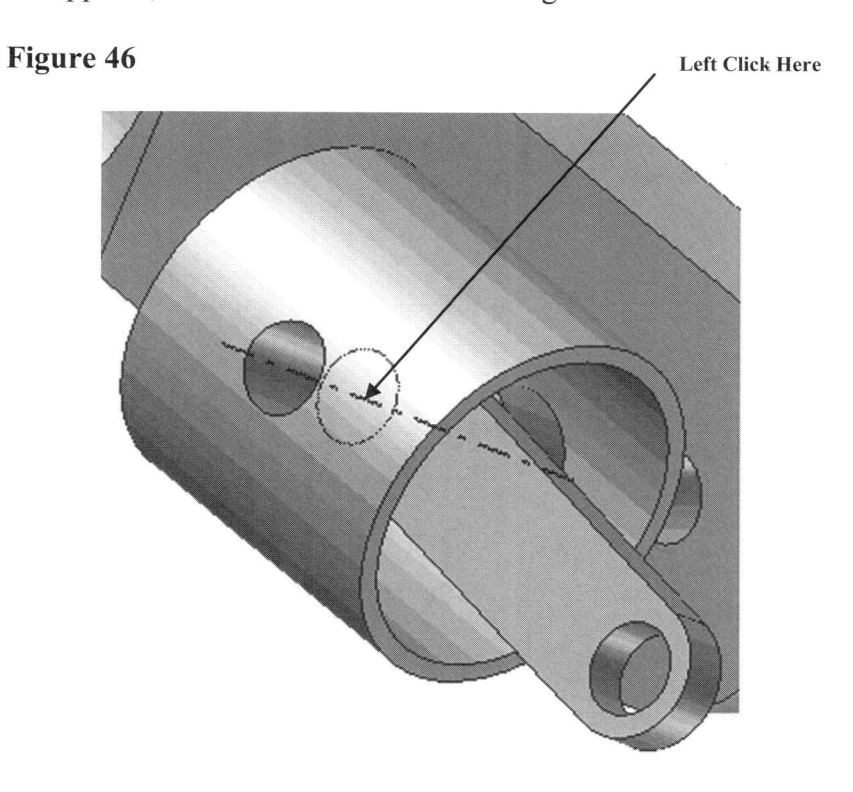

Figure 46

Left Click Here

52. Left click on **OK** as shown in Figure 47.

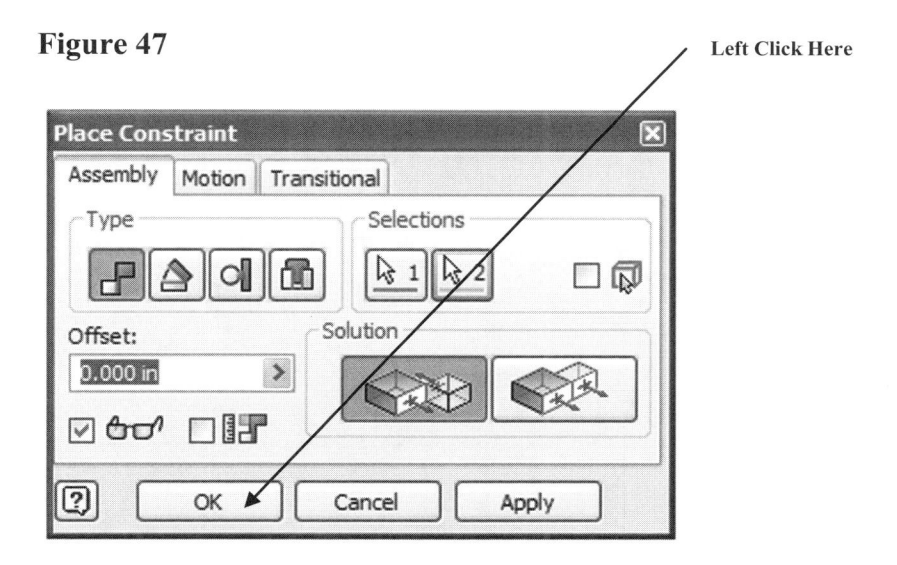

Figure 47

Left Click Here

379

Chapter 7: Introduction to Assembly View Procedures

53. Move the cursor to the middle left portion of the screen and left click on **Constraint**. The Place Constraint dialog box will appear as shown in Figure 48.

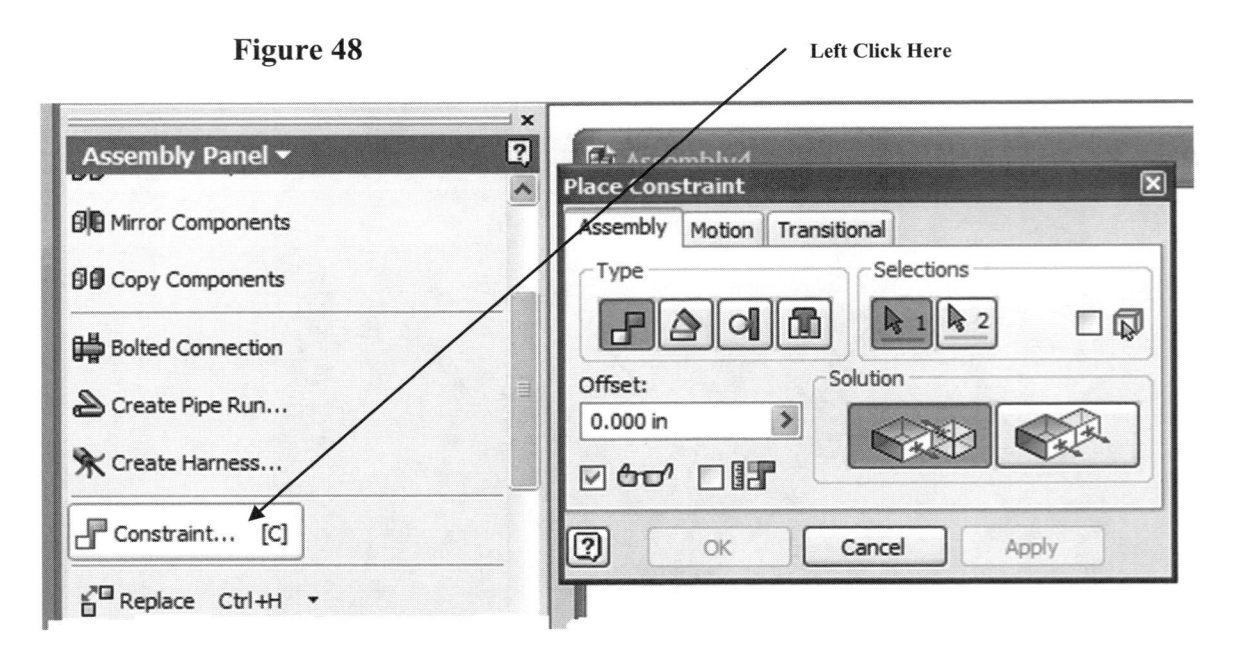

Figure 48

Left Click Here

54. Left click on the "Flush" icon as shown in Figure 49.

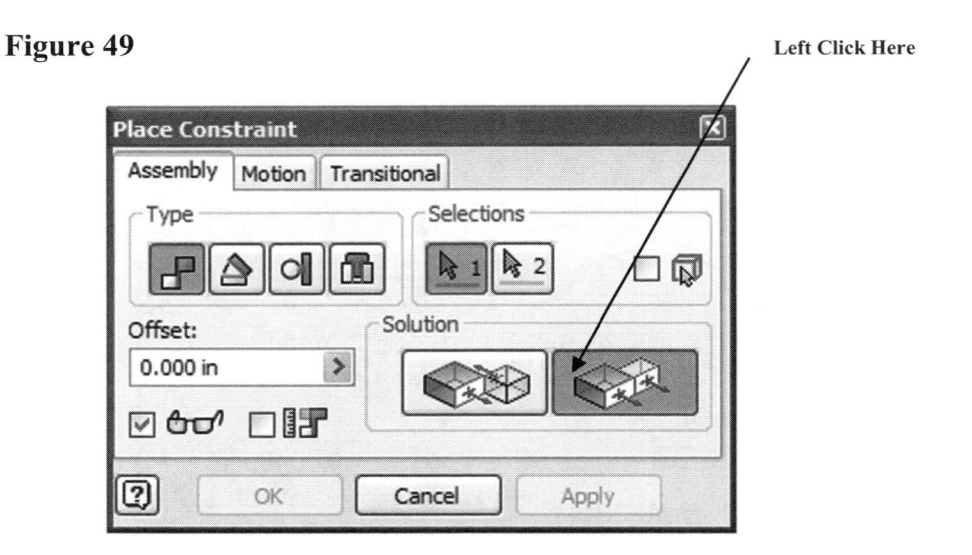

Figure 49

Left Click Here

380

Chapter 7: Introduction to Assembly View Procedures

55. Move the cursor to the side of the wrist pin causing a red arrow to appear. After a red arrow appears, left click once as shown in Figure 50.

Figure 50

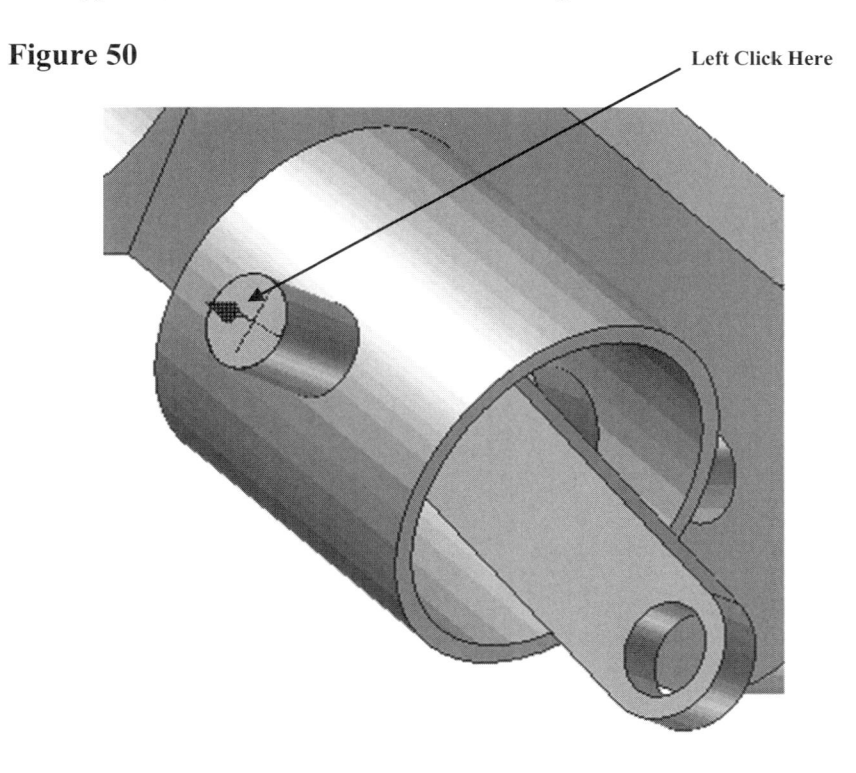

Left Click Here

Chapter 7: Introduction to Assembly View Procedures

56. Move the cursor to the side of the connecting rod causing a red arrow to appear. After a red arrow appears, left click once as shown in Figure 51.

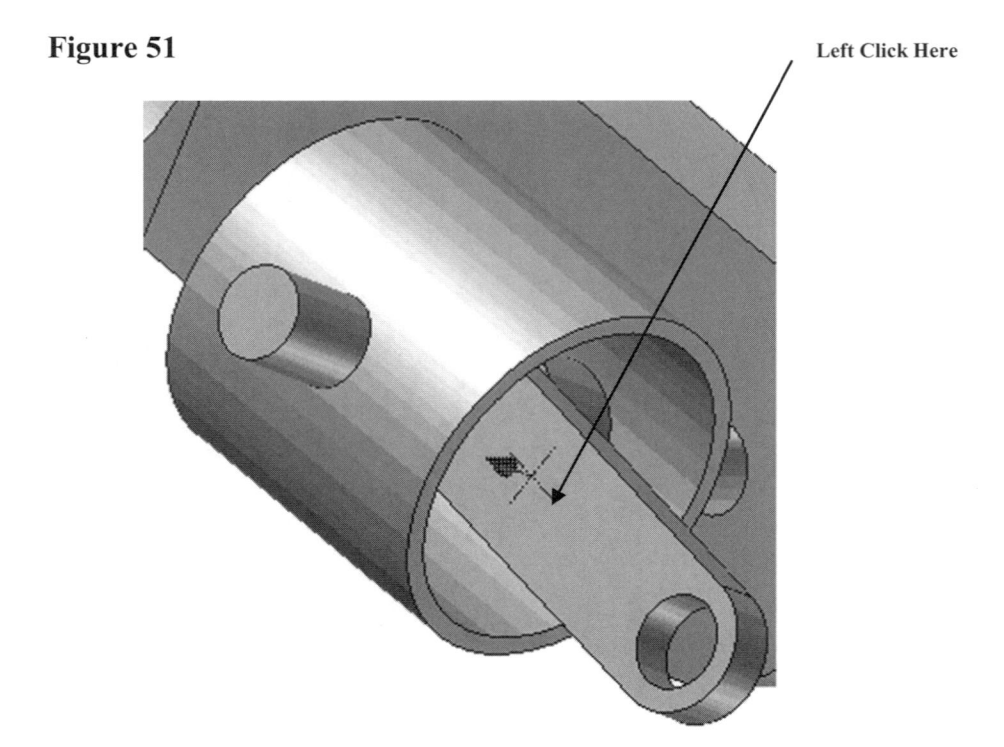

Figure 51

Left Click Here

Chapter 7: Introduction to Assembly View Procedures

57. Enter **-.7825** under Offset. Left click on **OK** as shown in Figure 52.

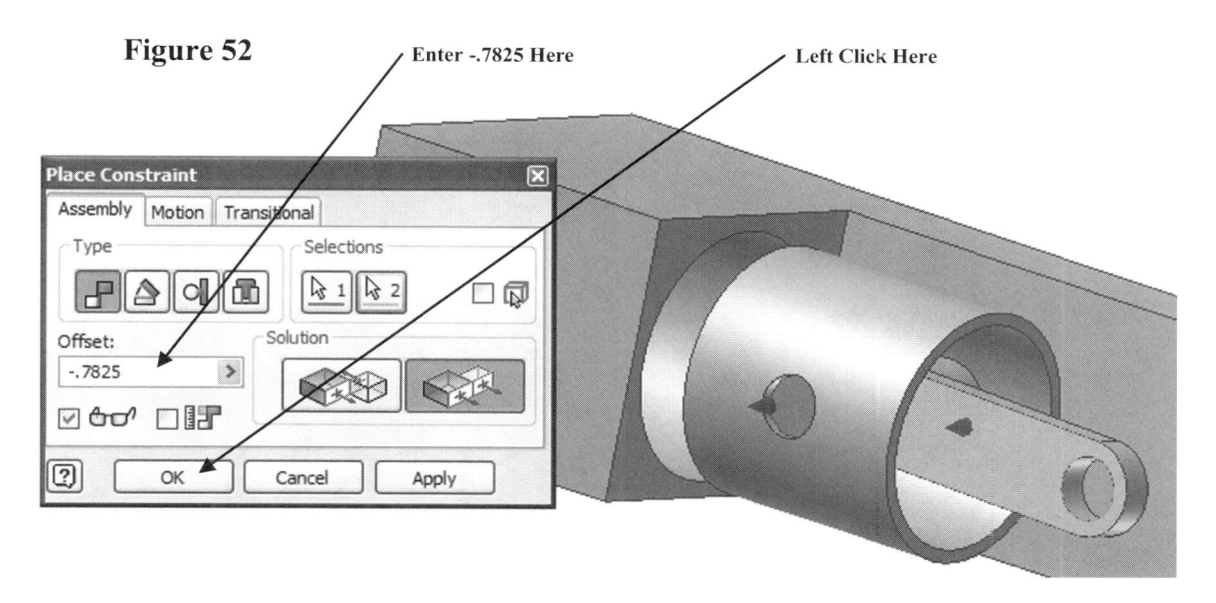

Figure 52

58. Your screen should look similar to Figure 53.

Figure 53

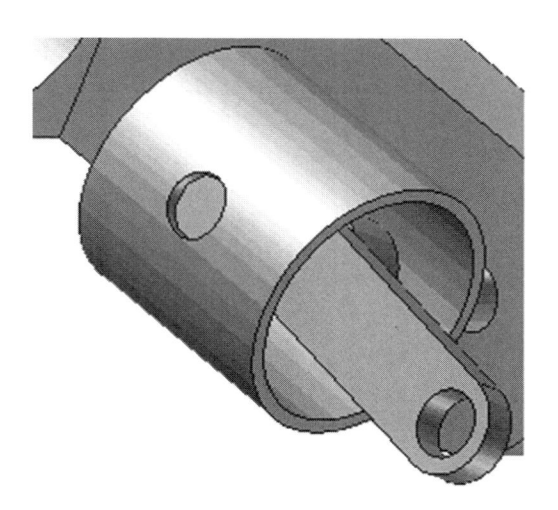

383

Chapter 7: Introduction to Assembly View Procedures

59. Move the cursor to the middle left portion of the screen and left click on **Constraint**. The Place Constraint dialog box will appear as shown in Figure 54.

Figure 54

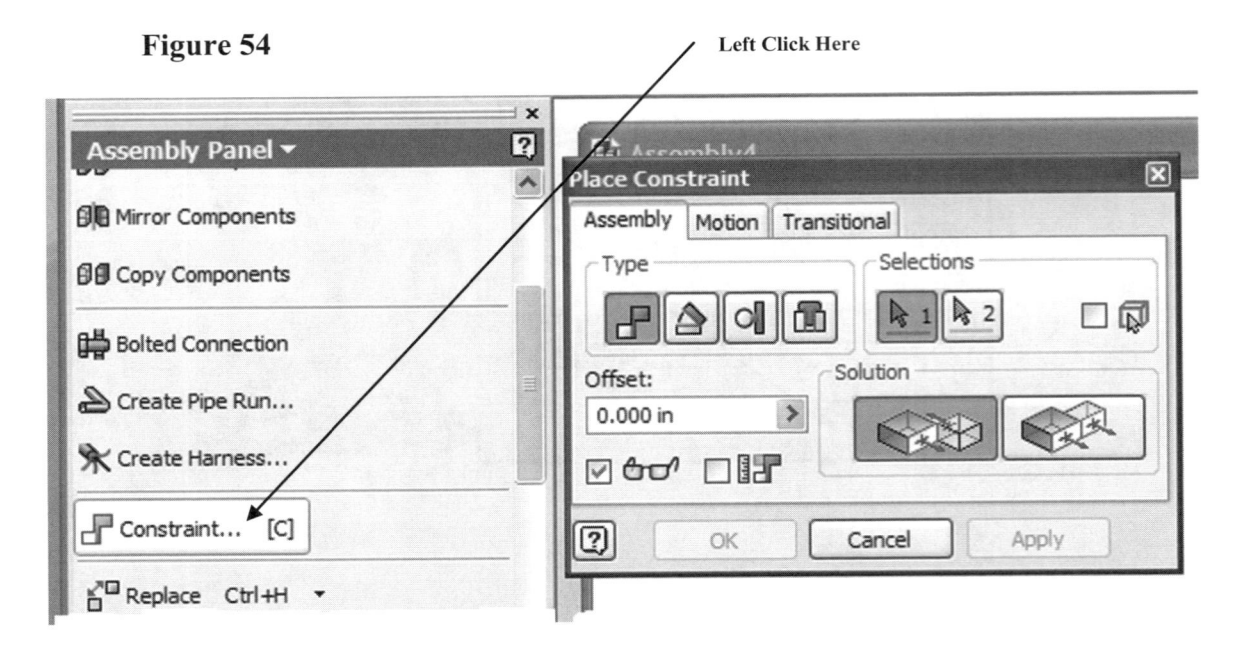

Left Click Here

60. Move the cursor to the crankshaft pin causing a red center line to appear. After a red center line appears, left click once as shown in Figure 55. The crankshaft pin will be secured to the connecting rod.

Figure 55

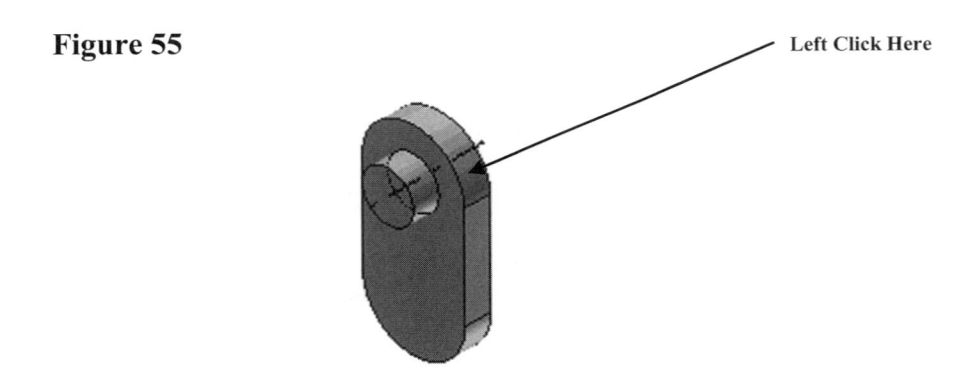

Left Click Here

384

Chapter 7: Introduction to Assembly View Procedures

61. Move the cursor to the connecting rod end, which will be secured to the crankshaft. Make the red center line appear. After the red center line appears, left click once as shown in Figure 56.

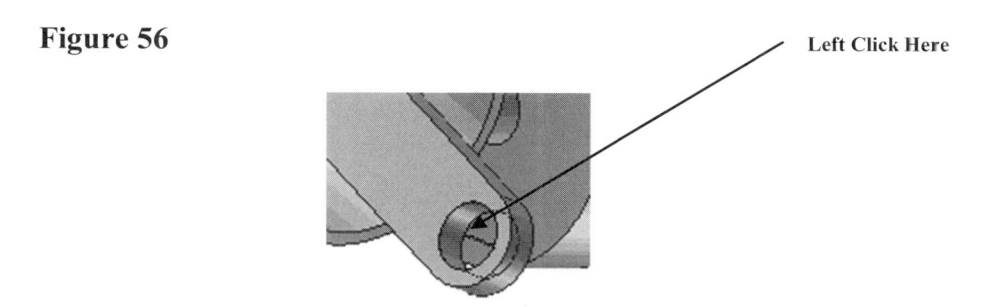

Figure 56

Left Click Here

62. Inventor will place the connecting rod and crankshaft together as shown in Figure 57.

Figure 57

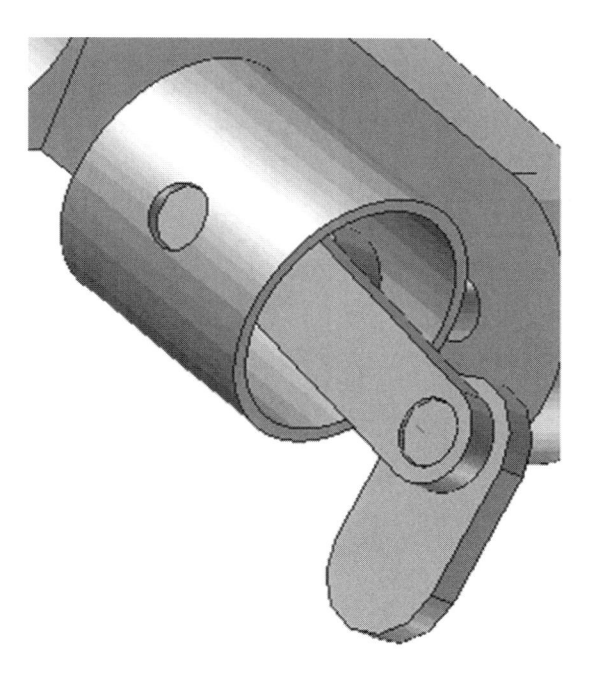

Chapter 7: Introduction to Assembly View Procedures

63. Left click on **OK** as shown in Figure 58.

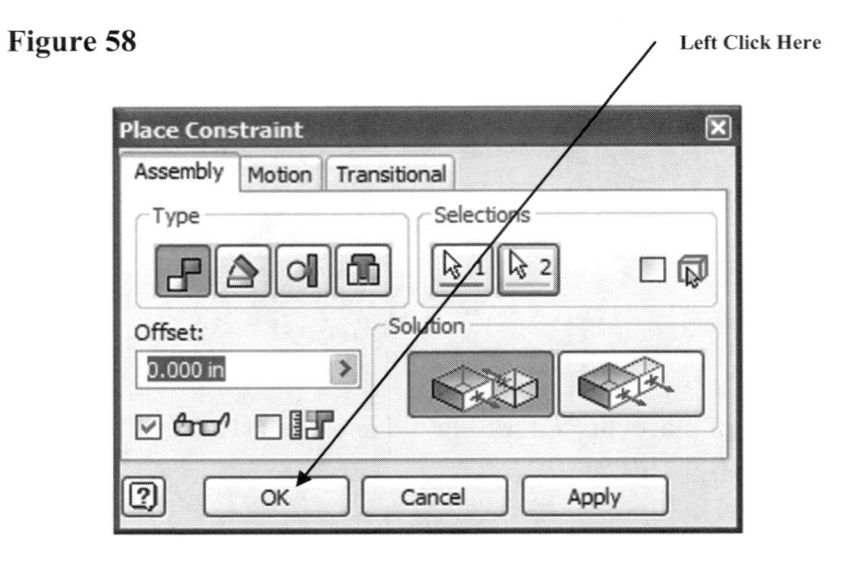

Figure 58

64. Move the cursor over the piston. Left click (holding the left mouse button down) and drag the piston upward toward the bottom of the bore as shown in Figure 59.

Figure 59

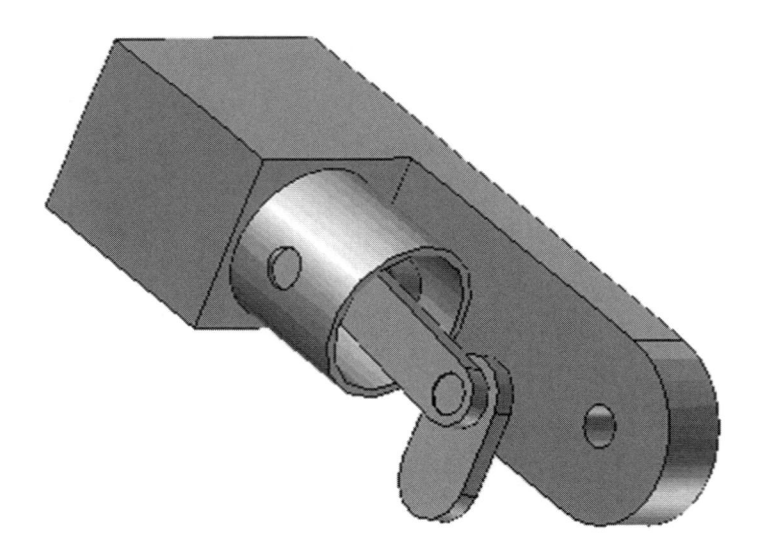

Chapter 7: Introduction to Assembly View Procedures

65. Use the Rotate command and roll the assembly around to gain access to the opposite side as shown in Figure 60.

Figure 60

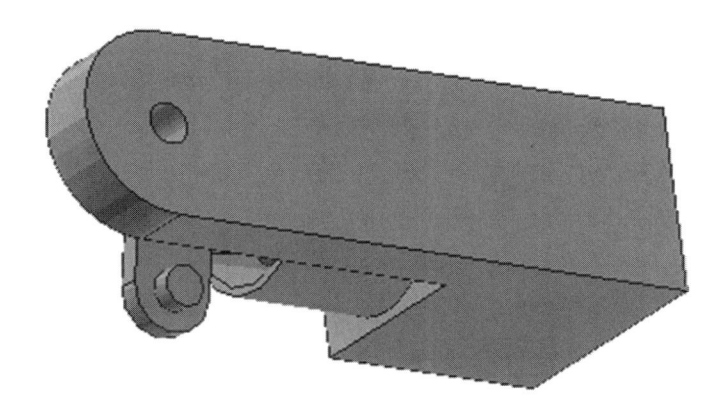

66. Move the cursor to the middle left portion of the screen and left click on **Constraint**. The Place Constraint dialog box will appear as shown in Figure 61.

Figure 61

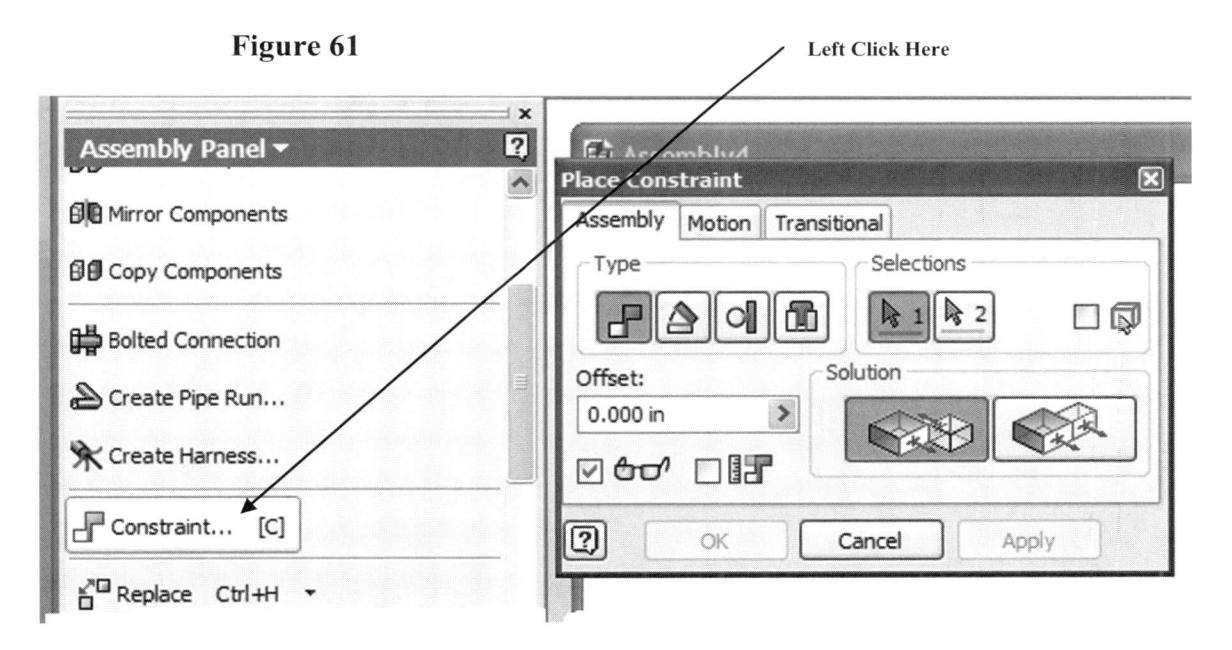

387

Chapter 7: Introduction to Assembly View Procedures

67. Move the cursor to the crankshaft pin, which will be secured in the piston case causing a red center line appear. After the red center line appears, left click once as shown in Figure 62.

Figure 62

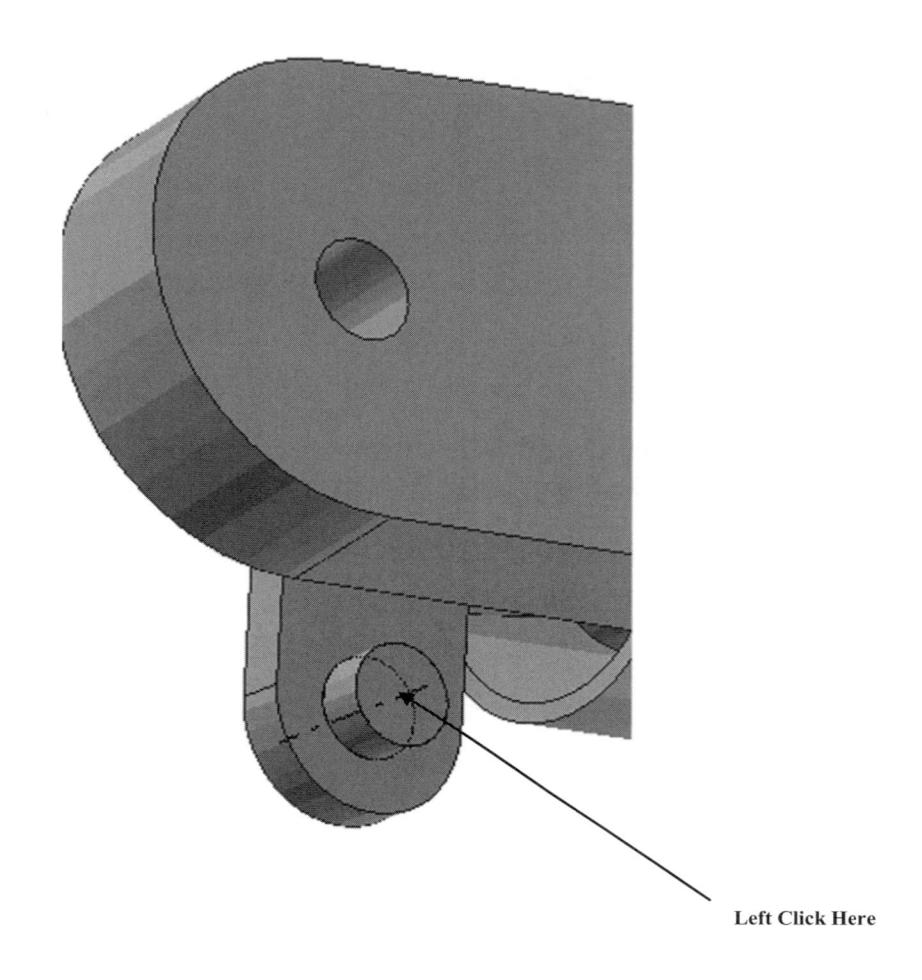

Left Click Here

Chapter 7: Introduction to Assembly View Procedures

68. Move the cursor to the piston case hole that will secure the crankshaft causing a red center line appear. After the red center line appears, left click once as shown in Figure 63.

Figure 63   Left Click Here

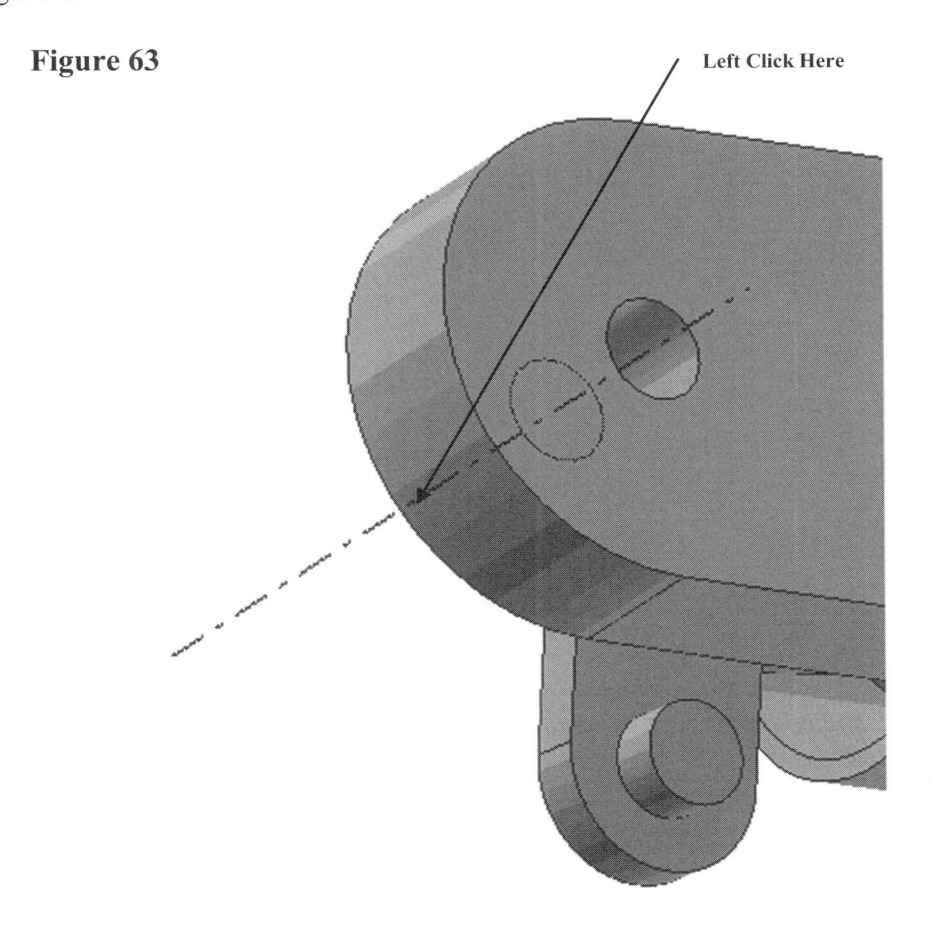

Chapter 7: Introduction to Assembly View Procedures

69. Inventor will place the crankshaft pin into the piston case as shown in Figure 64.

Figure 64

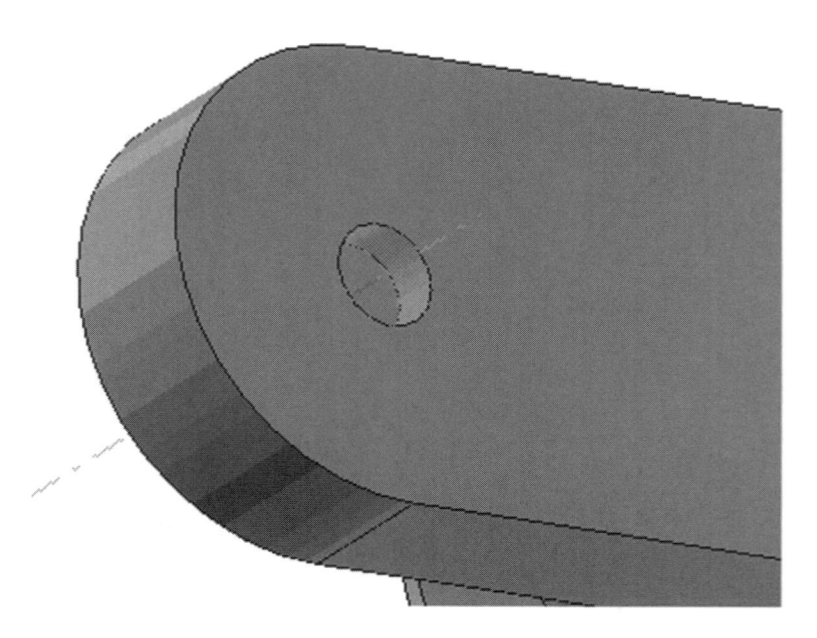

70. Left click on **OK** as shown in Figure 65.

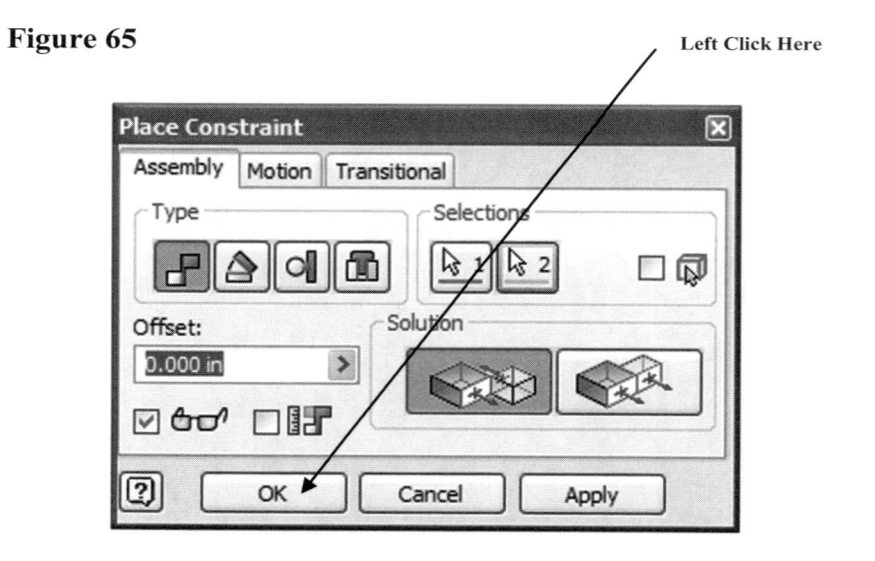

Figure 65

Chapter 7: Introduction to Assembly View Procedures

71. Your screen should look similar to Figure 66.

Figure 66

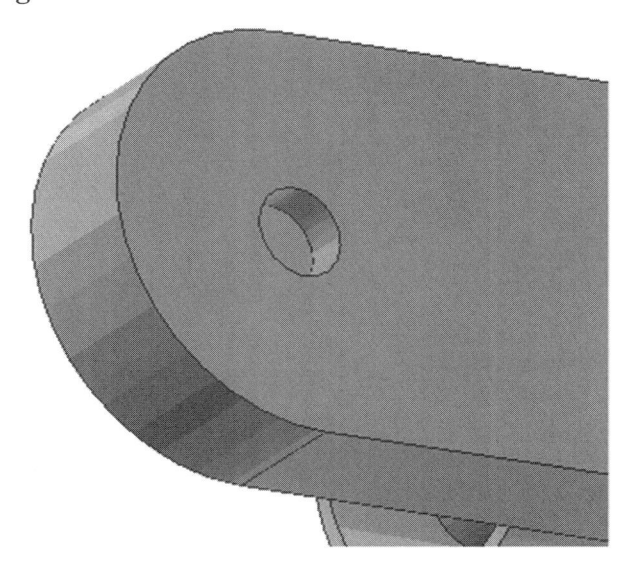

72. Right click anywhere around the drawing. A pop up menu will appear. Left click on **Home/Isometric View** as shown in Figure 67.

Figure 67

Left Click Here

391

Chapter 7: Introduction to Assembly View Procedures

73. Your screen should look similar to Figure 68.

Figure 68

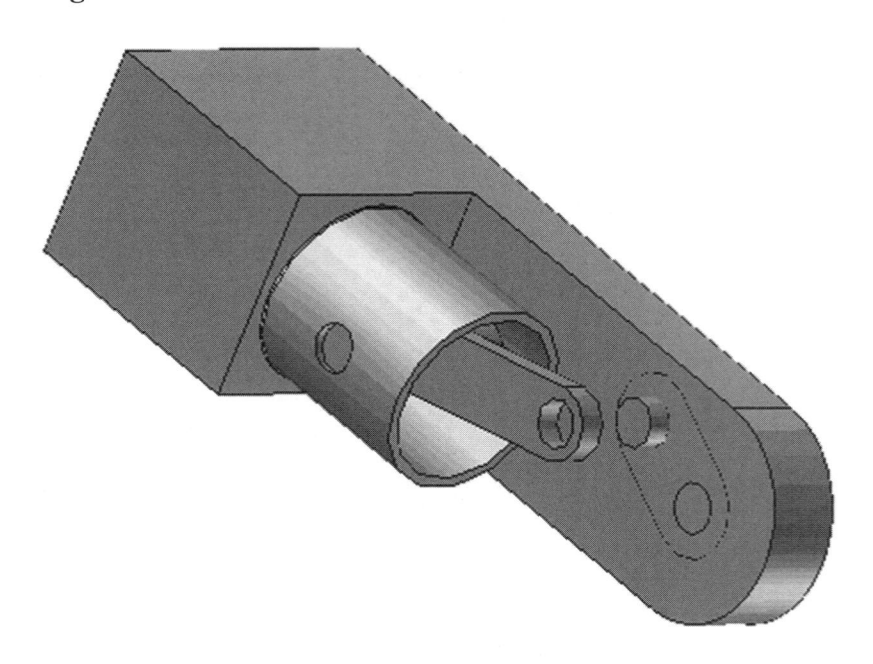

74. Move the cursor to the middle left portion of the screen and left click on **Constraint**. The Place Constraint dialog box will appear as shown in Figure 69.

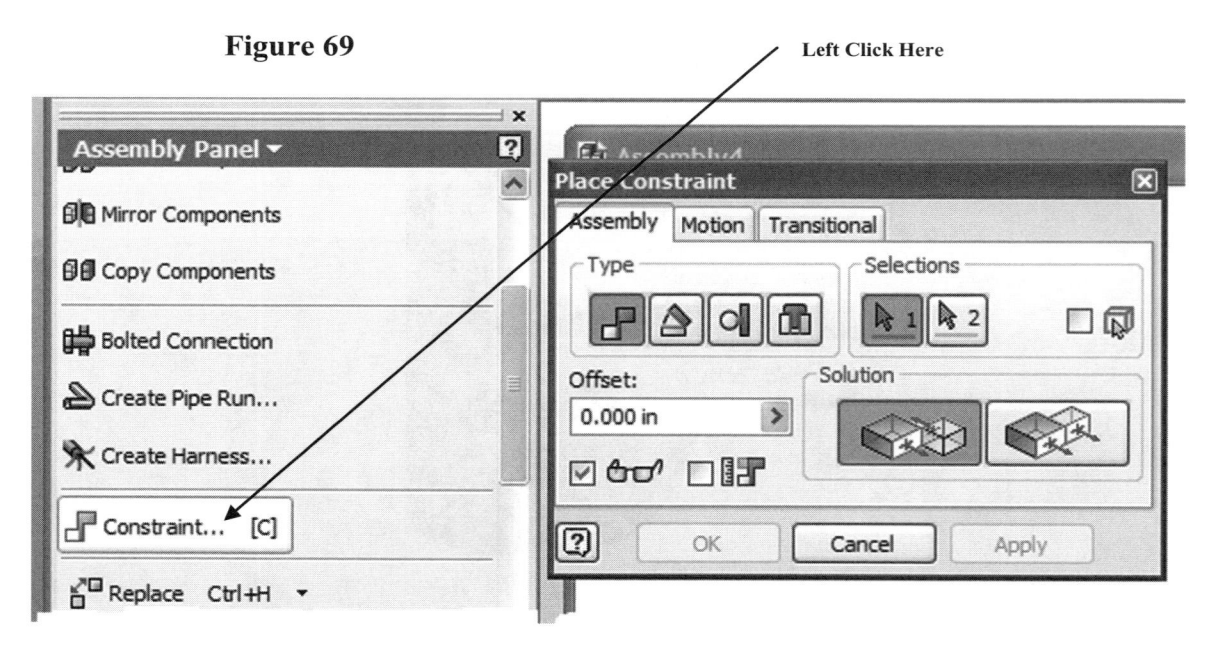

Figure 69

Chapter 7: Introduction to Assembly View Procedures

75. Left click on the "Flush" icon as shown in Figure 70.

Figure 70

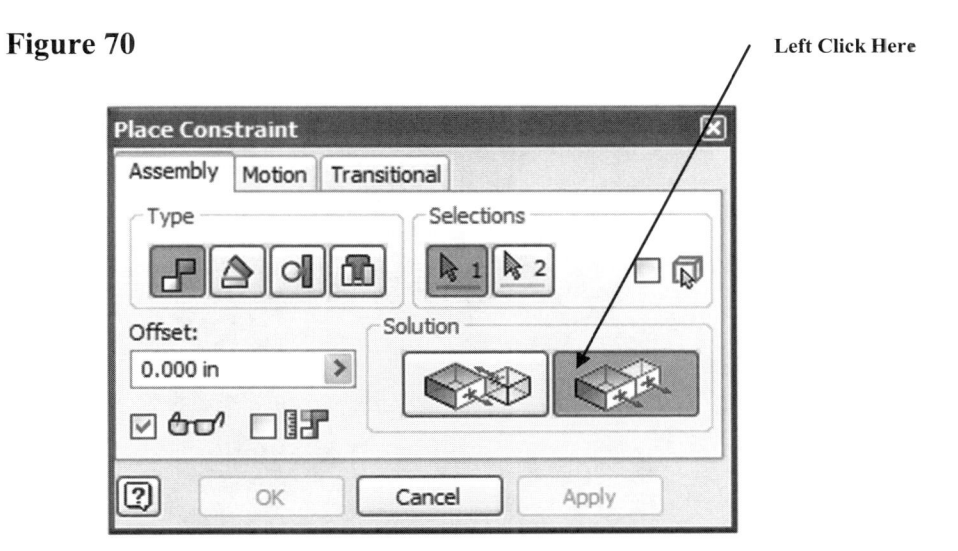

Left Click Here

76. Move the cursor to the left side of the connecting rod causing a red arrow to appear. After a red arrow appears, left click once as shown in Figure 71.

Figure 71

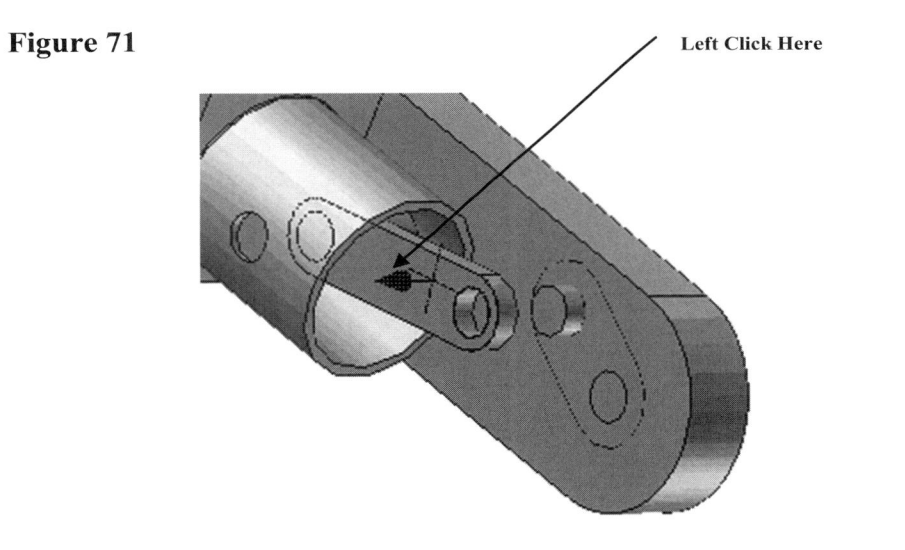

Left Click Here

Chapter 7: Introduction to Assembly View Procedures

77. Move the cursor to the crankshaft connecting rod pin causing the red arrow to appear. After a red arrow appears, left click once as shown in Figure 72.

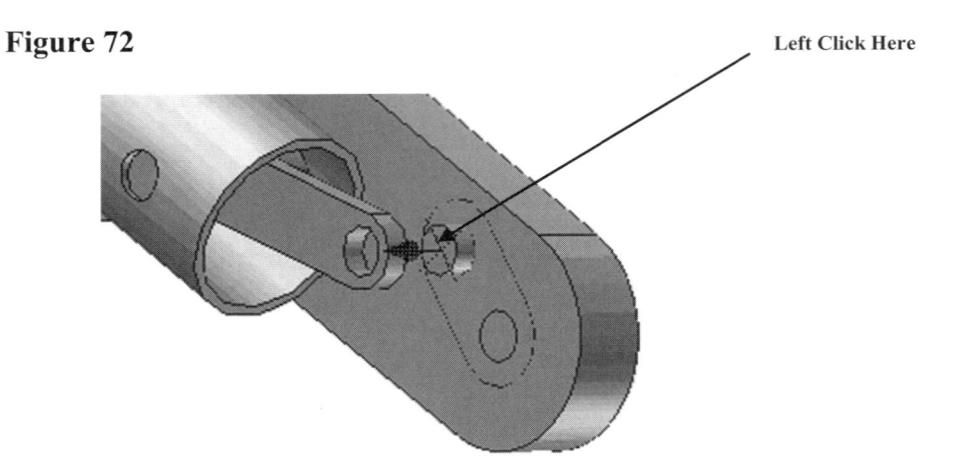

Figure 72

Left Click Here

78. Inventor will place the connecting rod flush with the crankshaft connecting rod pin as shown in Figure 73.

Figure 73

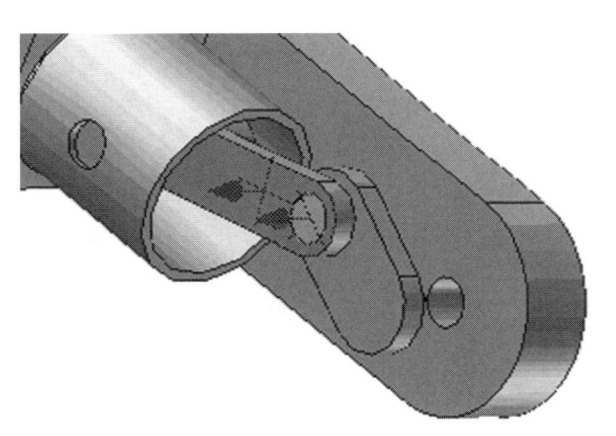

Chapter 7: Introduction to Assembly View Procedures

79. Left click on **OK** as shown in Figure 74.

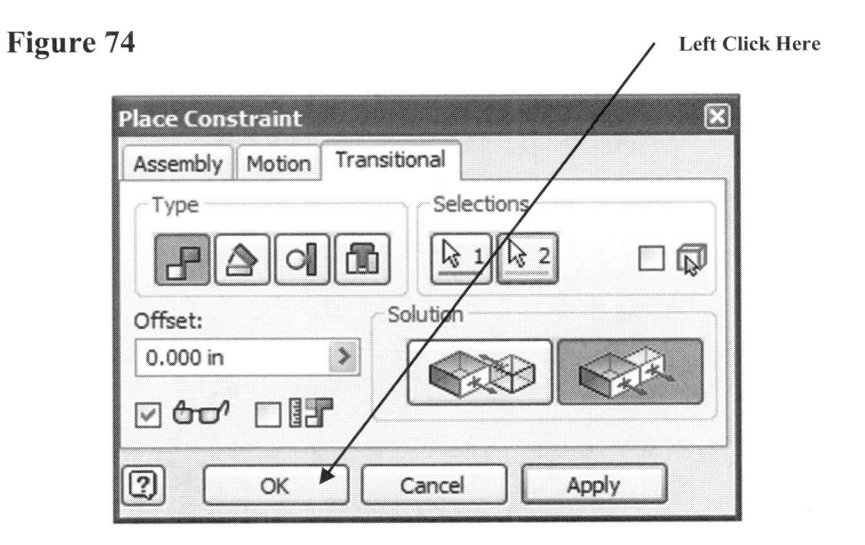

Figure 74

80. Your screen should look similar to Figure 75.

Figure 75

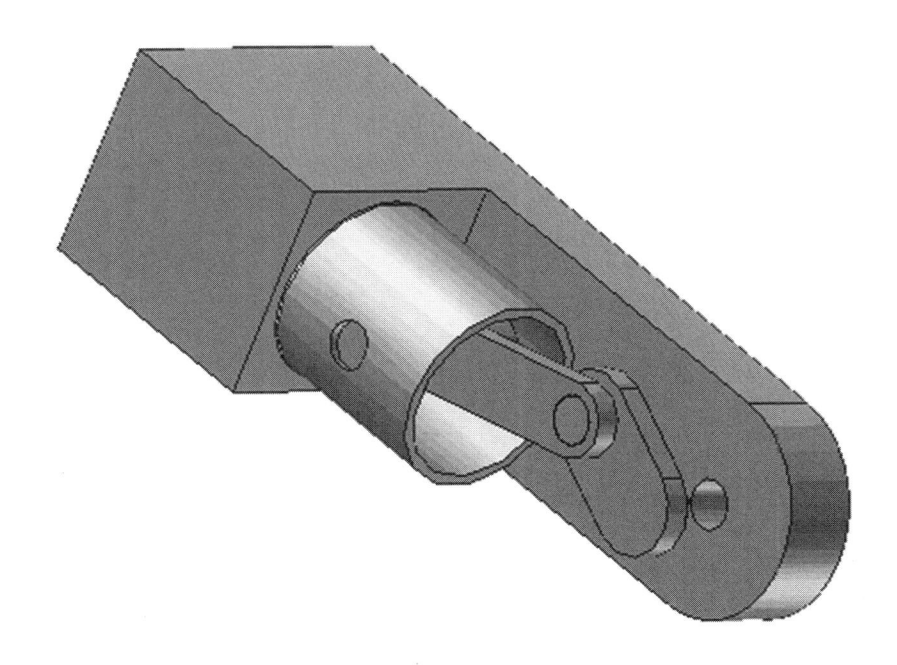

Chapter 7: Introduction to Assembly View Procedures

81. The length of the connecting rod must be modified. Move the cursor over the connecting rod causing the edges to turn red as shown in Figure 76.

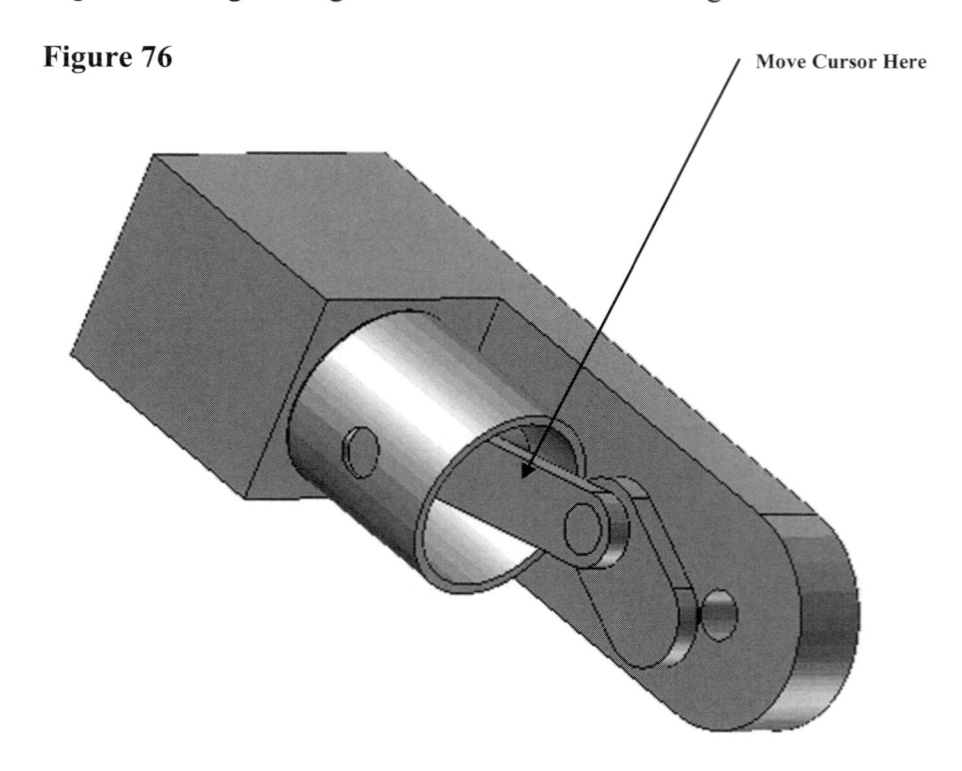

Figure 76

82. Double click (left click) on the connecting rod. All other parts will become grayed as shown in Figure 77.

Figure 77

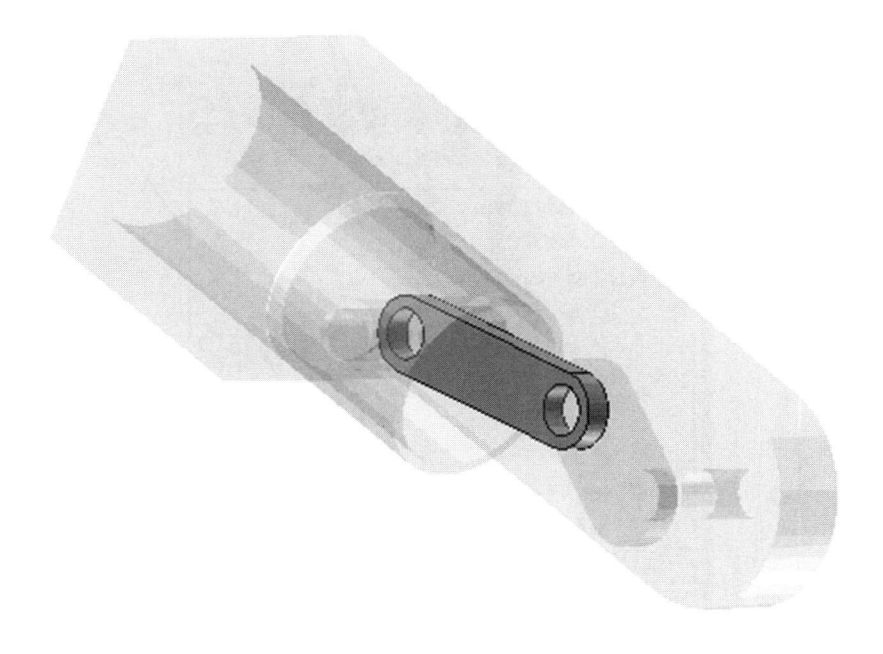

Chapter 7: Introduction to Assembly View Procedures

83. Notice that the part tree at the lower left of the screen has changed. All of the branches related to all other parts are grayed (inactive). The branches that illustrate the connecting rod are white (active) as shown in Figure 78.

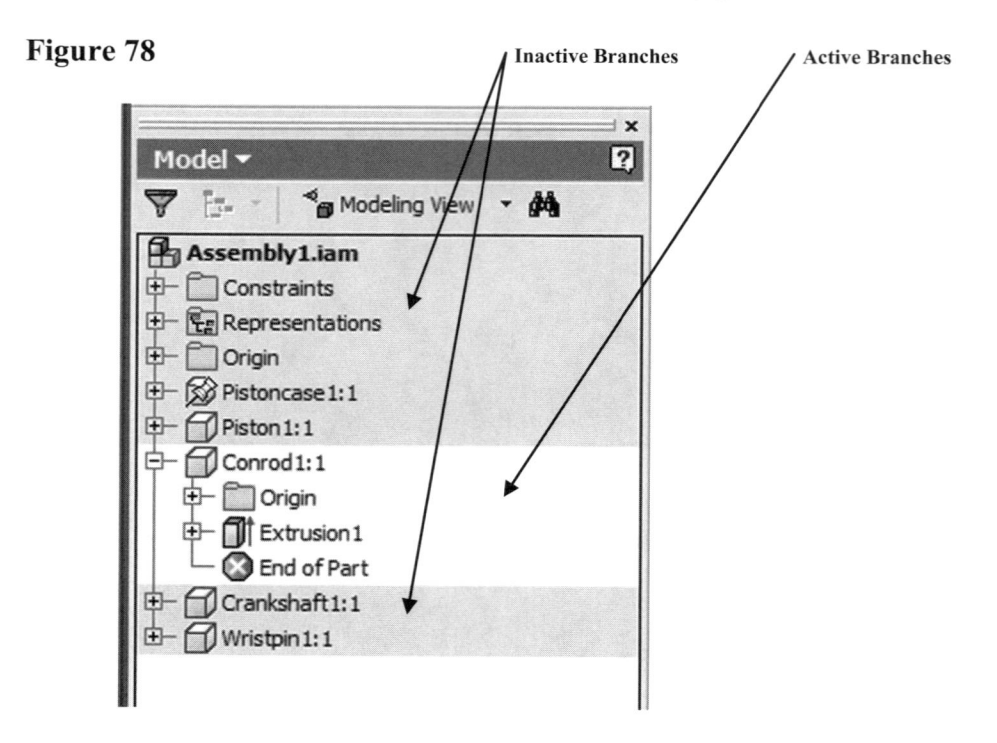

Figure 78

Inactive Branches

Active Branches

Chapter 7: Introduction to Assembly View Procedures

84. Left click on the "Plus" sign next to the text "Extrusion1" as shown in Figure 79.

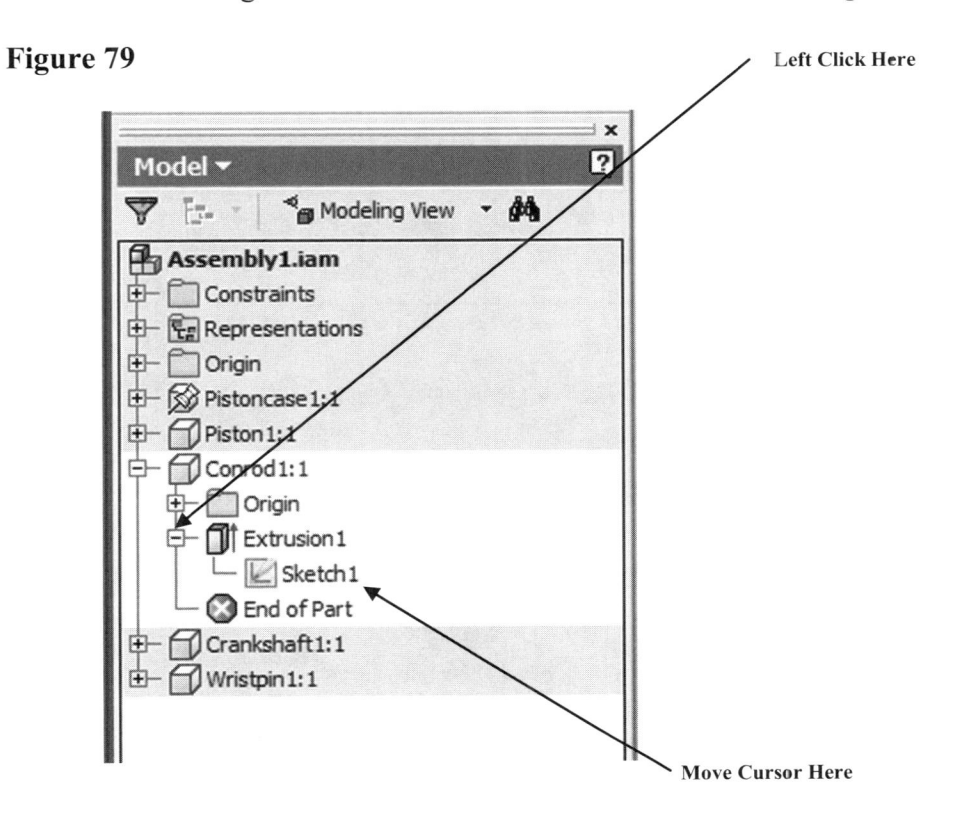

Figure 79

85. Move the cursor over the text "Sketch1" causing a red box to appear around the text. Notice at the same time the sketch will appear in red on the connecting rod as shown in Figure 80.

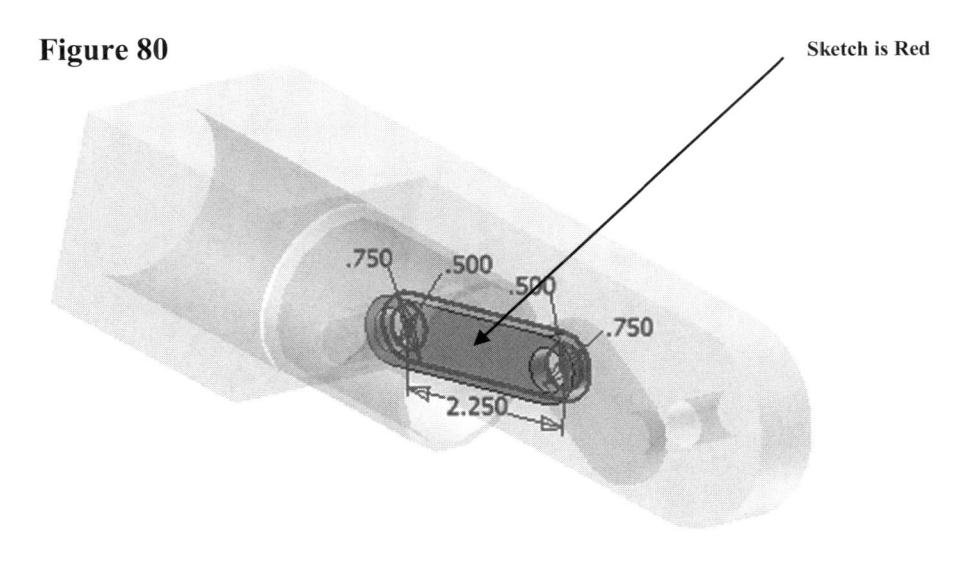

Figure 80

Chapter 7: Introduction to Assembly View Procedures

86. Right click on **Sketch1** while the red box is visible around the text. A pop up menu will appear. Left click on **Edit Sketch** as shown in Figure 81.

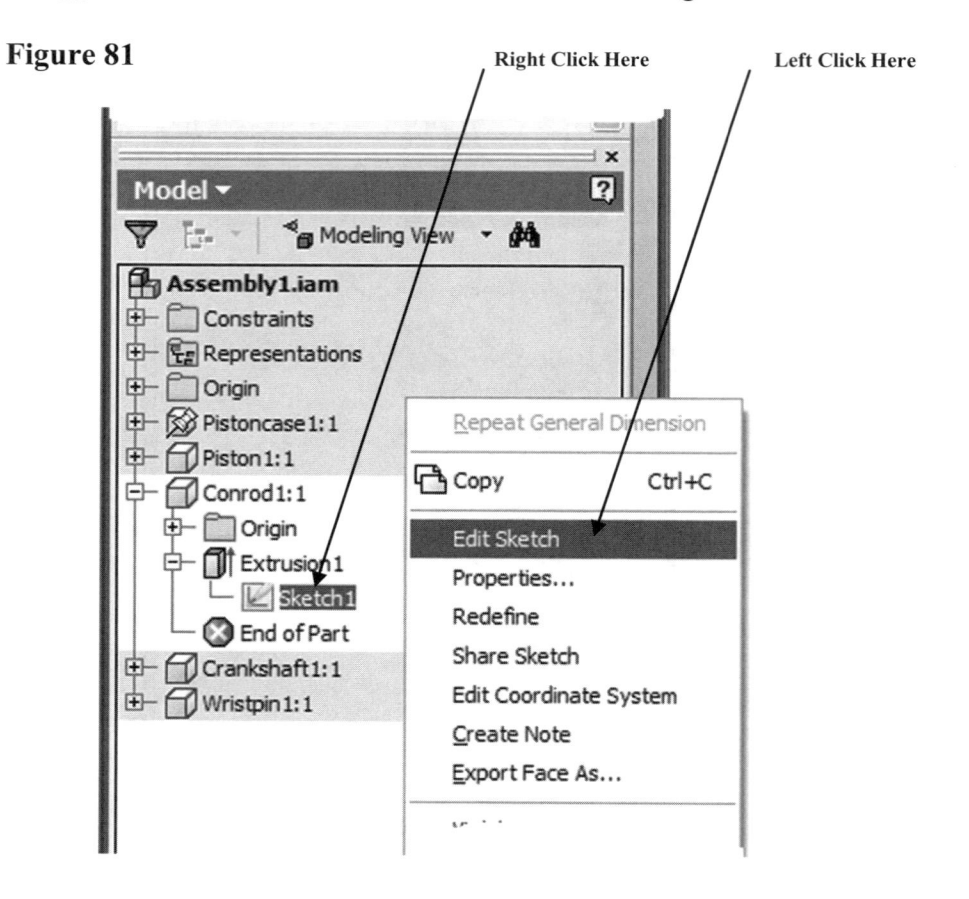

Figure 81

Chapter 7: Introduction to Assembly View Procedures

87. Your screen should look similar to Figure 82.

Figure 82

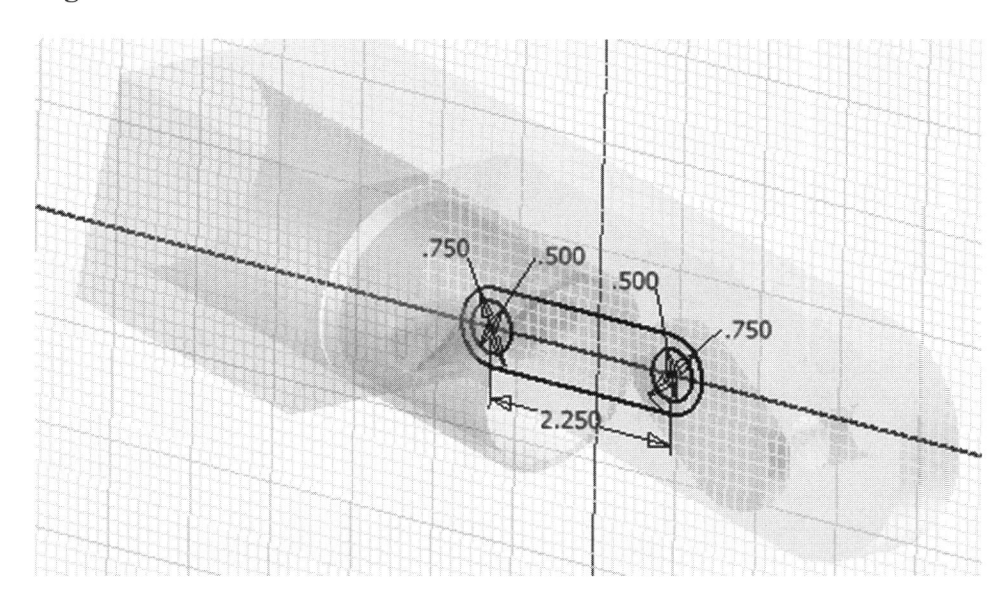

88. Move the cursor over the 2.25 dimension. After it turns red, double click the left mouse button. The Edit Dimension dialog box will appear as shown in Figure 83.

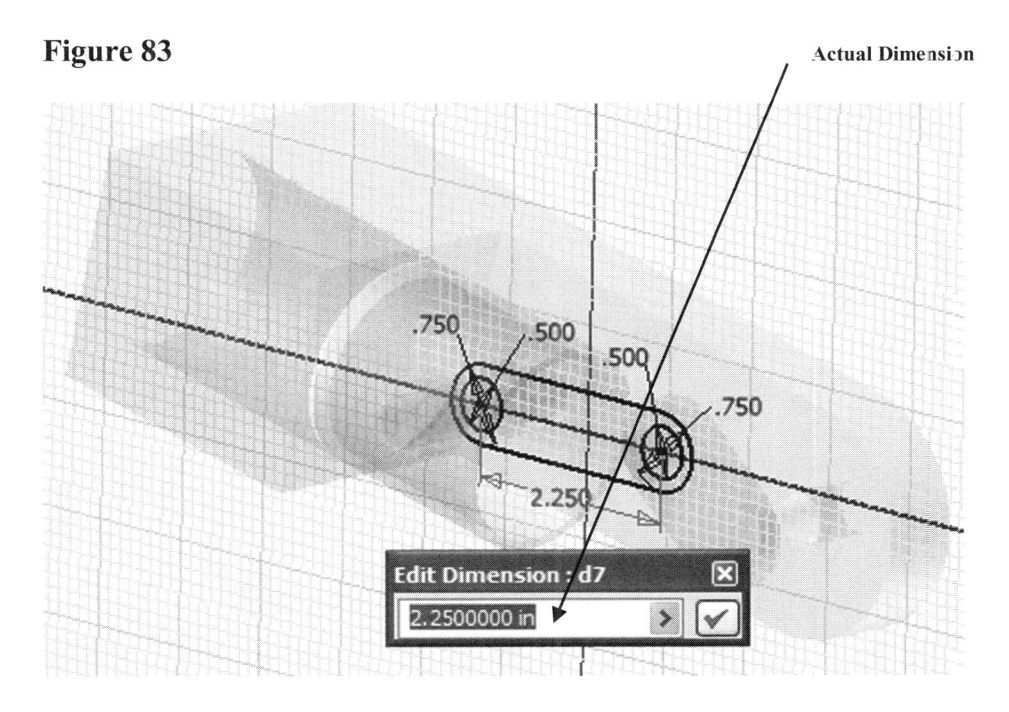

Figure 83

Actual Dimension

401

Chapter 7: Introduction to Assembly View Procedures

89. While the text is still highlighted, enter **4.75** as shown in Figure 84 and press **Enter** on the keyboard.

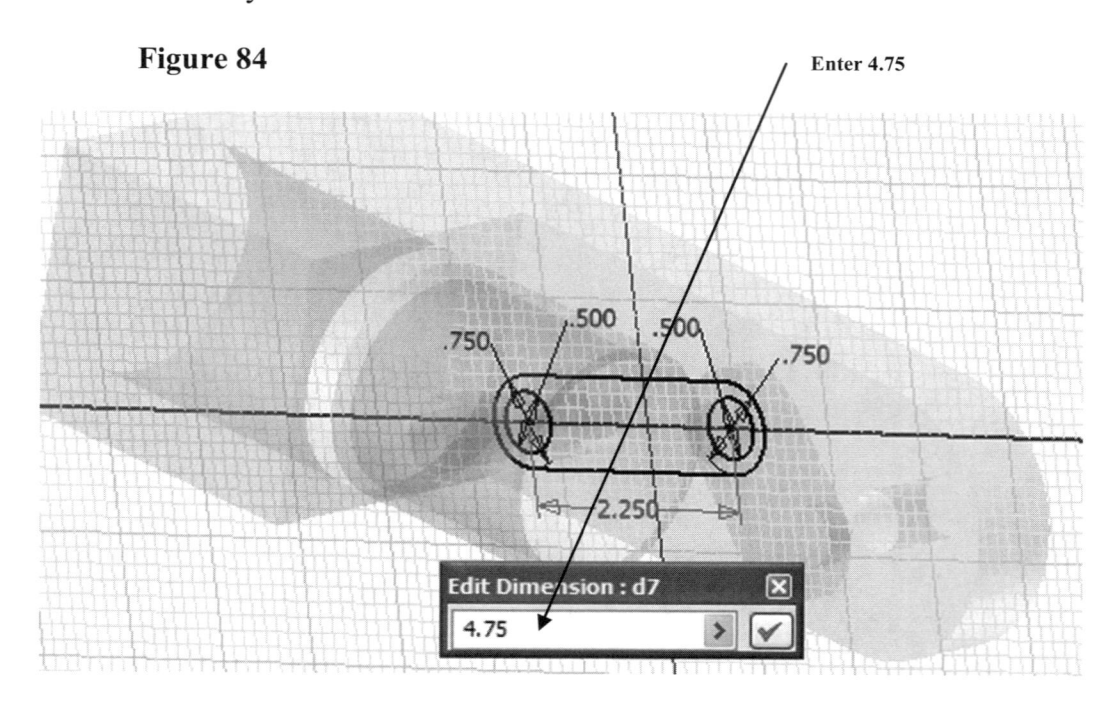

Figure 84

402

Chapter 7: Introduction to Assembly View Procedures

90. The length of the connecting rod will become 4.75 inches as shown in Figure 85.

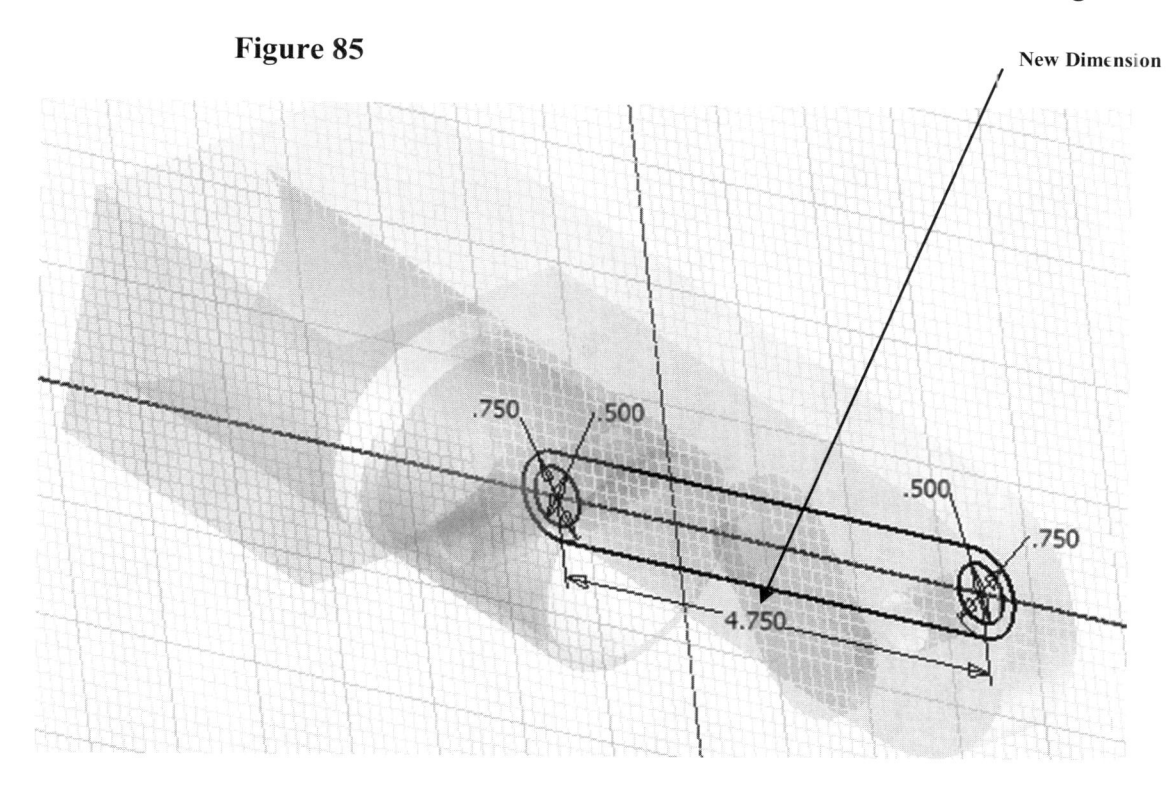

Figure 85

91. Move the cursor to the upper middle portion of the screen and left click on **Update** as shown in Figure 86.

Figure 86

Chapter 7: Introduction to Assembly View Procedures

92. Inventor will update the change made to the sketch in the Part Features Panel as shown in Figure 87.

Figure 87

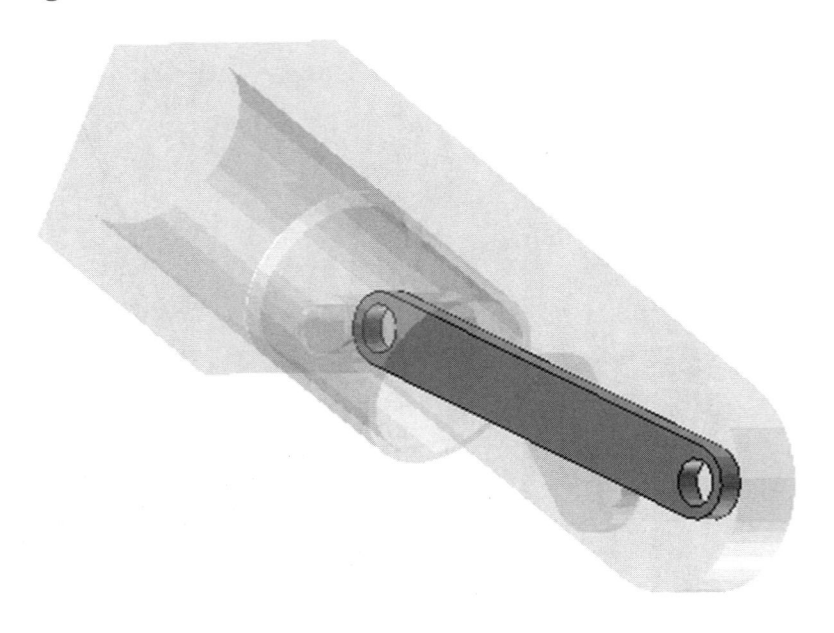

93. Move the cursor to the upper middle portion of the screen and left click on **Return** as shown in Figure 88.

Figure 88

Left Click Here

Chapter 7: Introduction to Assembly View Procedures

94. Inventor will return to the Assembly Panel displaying the changes made to the connecting rod. Your screen should look similar to Figure 89.

Figure 89

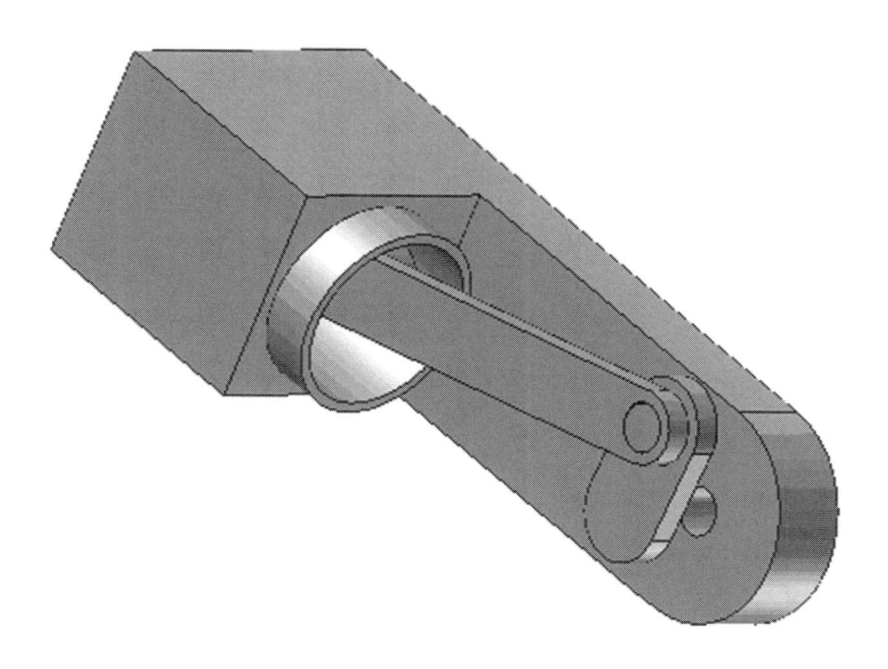

95. The length of the crankshaft pin also must be modified. Move the cursor over the crankshaft as shown in Figure 90. The edges will turn red.

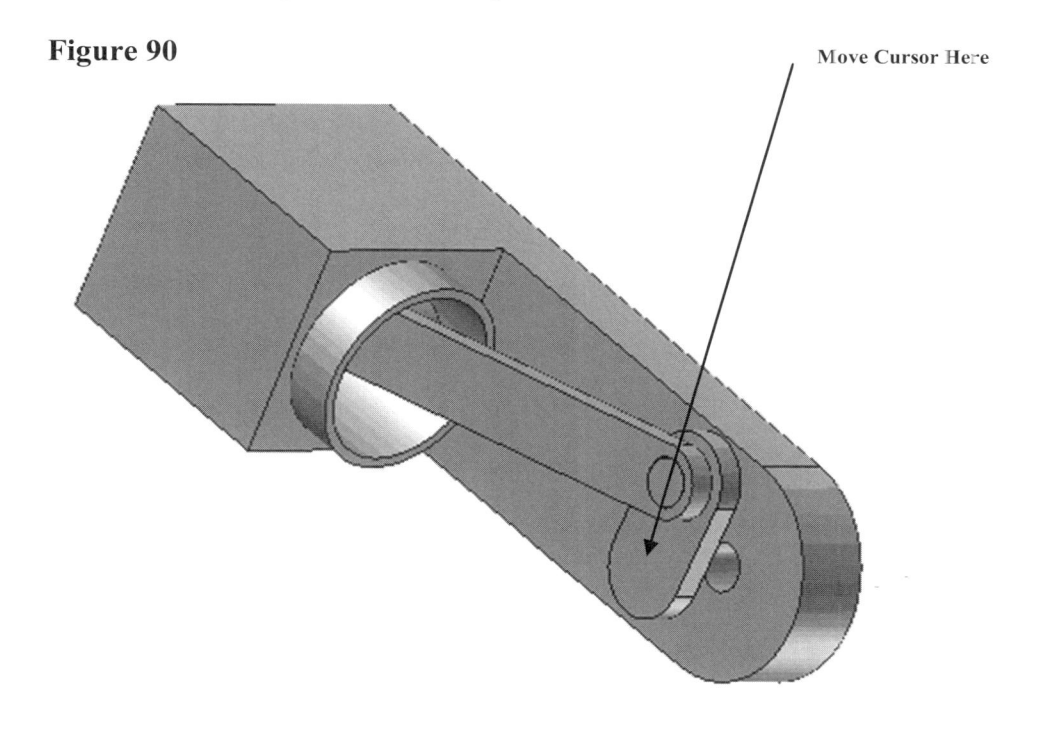

Figure 90

Move Cursor Here

Chapter 7: Introduction to Assembly View Procedures

96. Double click (left click) on the crankshaft. All other parts will become grayed as shown in Figure 91.

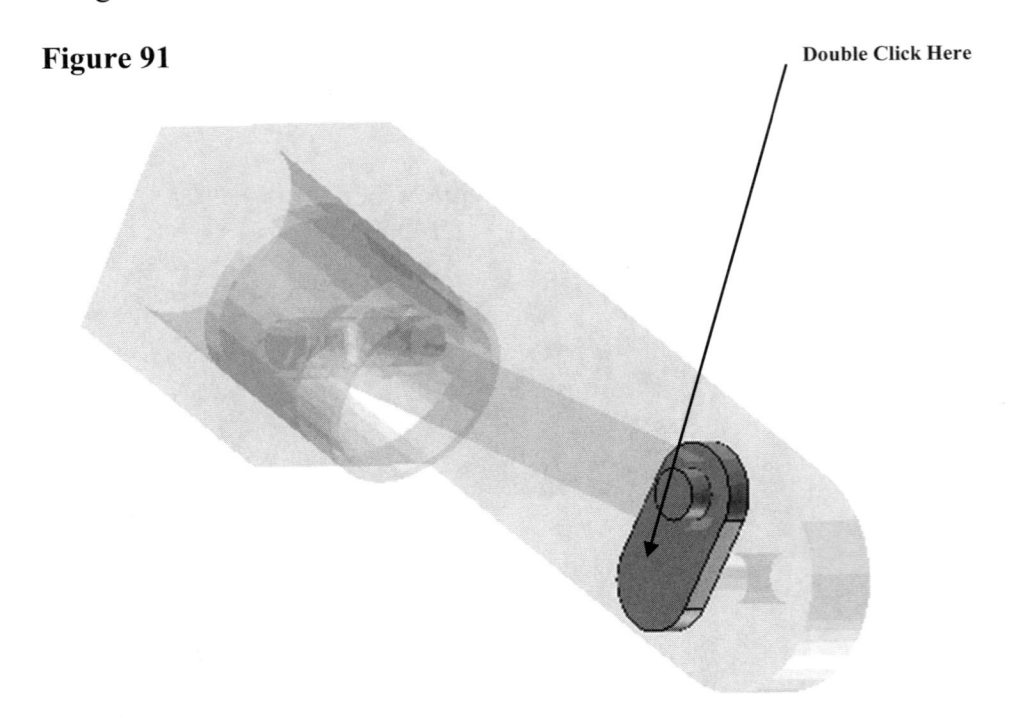

Figure 91

Double Click Here

Chapter 7: Introduction to Assembly View Procedures

97. Notice that the part tree at the lower left of the screen has changed. All of the branches related to all other parts are grayed (inactive). The branches that illustrate the crankshaft are white (active) as shown in Figure 92.

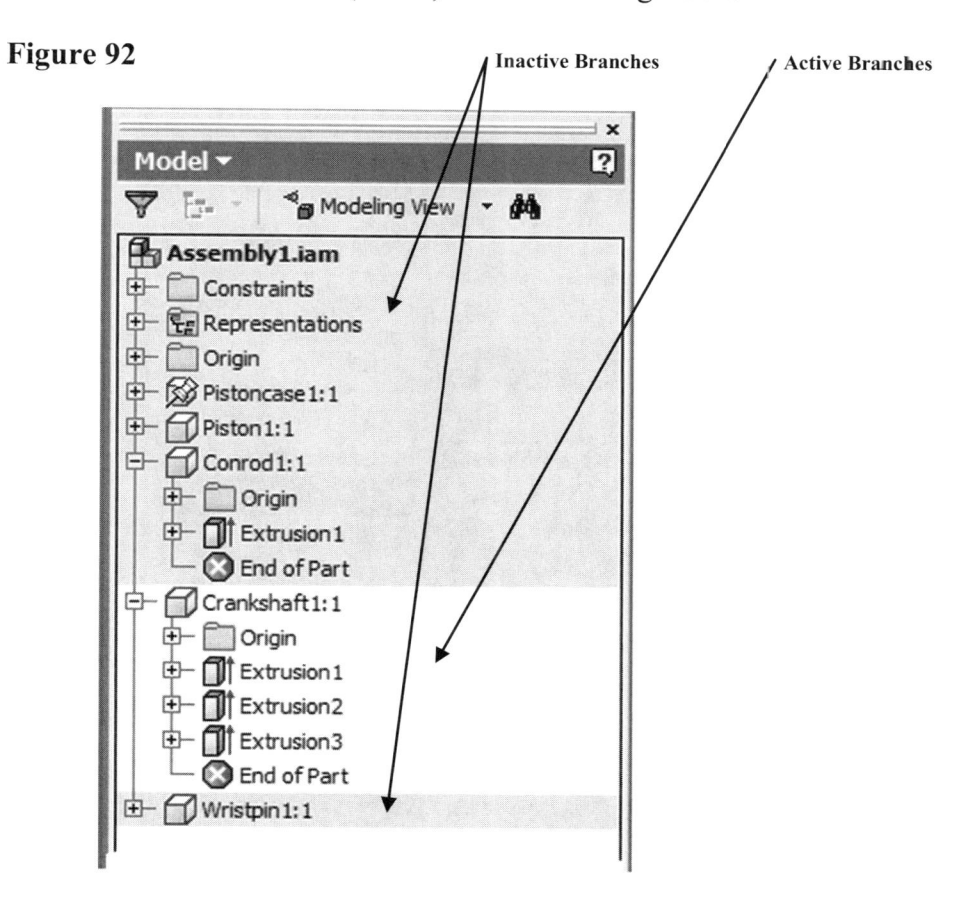

Figure 92

Chapter 7: Introduction to Assembly View Procedures

98. Right click on **Extrusion3**. A pop up menu will appear. Left click on **Edit Feature** as shown in Figure 93.

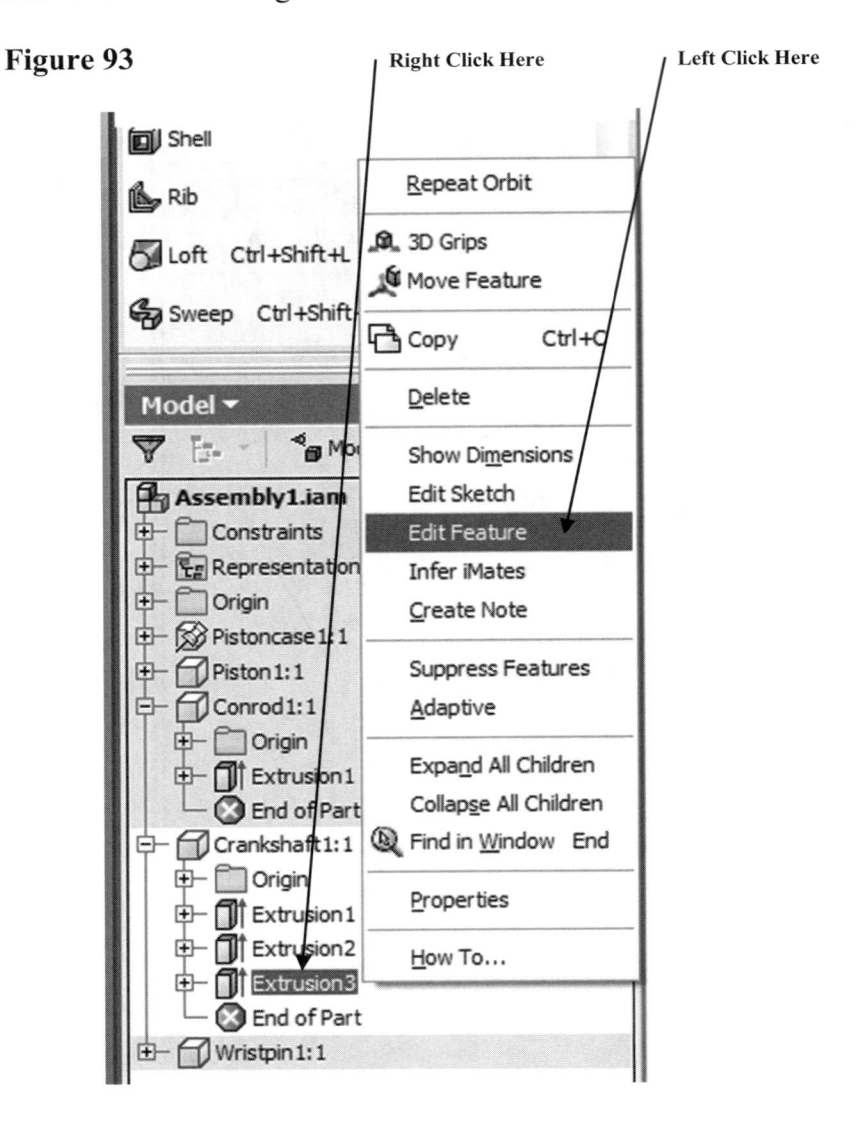

Figure 93

Chapter 7: Introduction to Assembly View Procedures

99. The Extrude dialog box will appear. Enter **2.00** for the extrusion distance and left click on **OK** as shown in Figure 94.

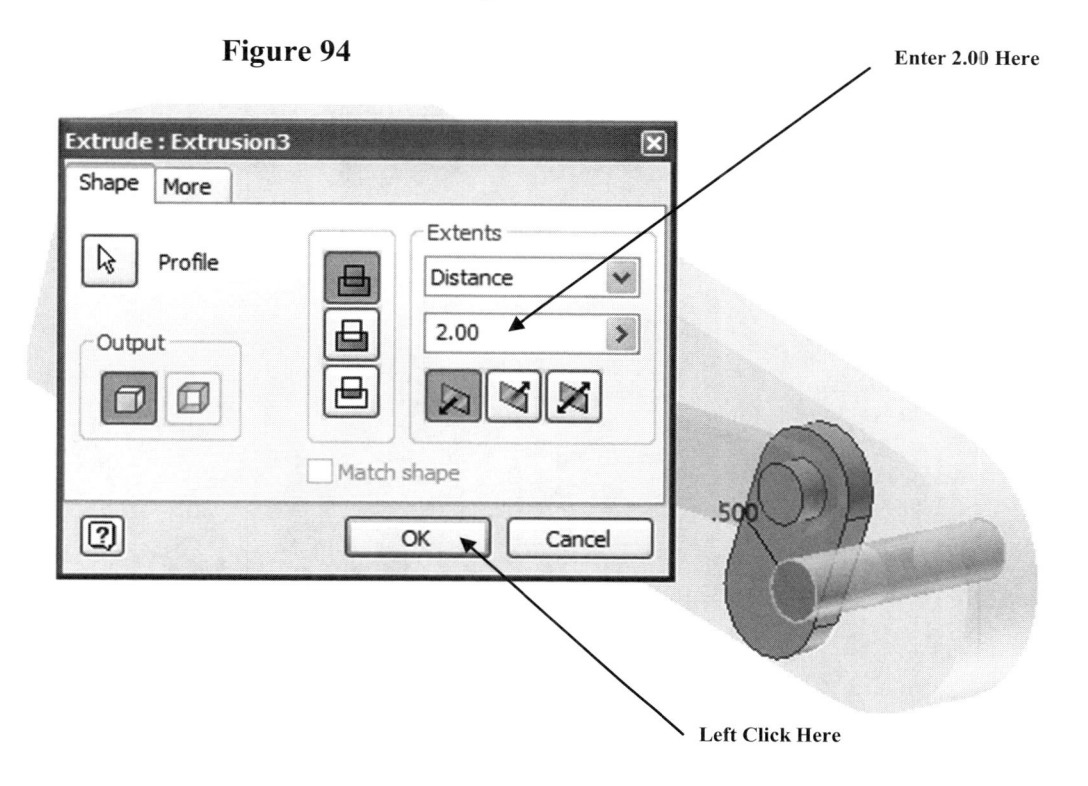

Figure 94

Chapter 7: Introduction to Assembly View Procedures

100. Inventor will update the change made to the sketch in the Part Features Panel as shown in Figure 95.

Figure 95

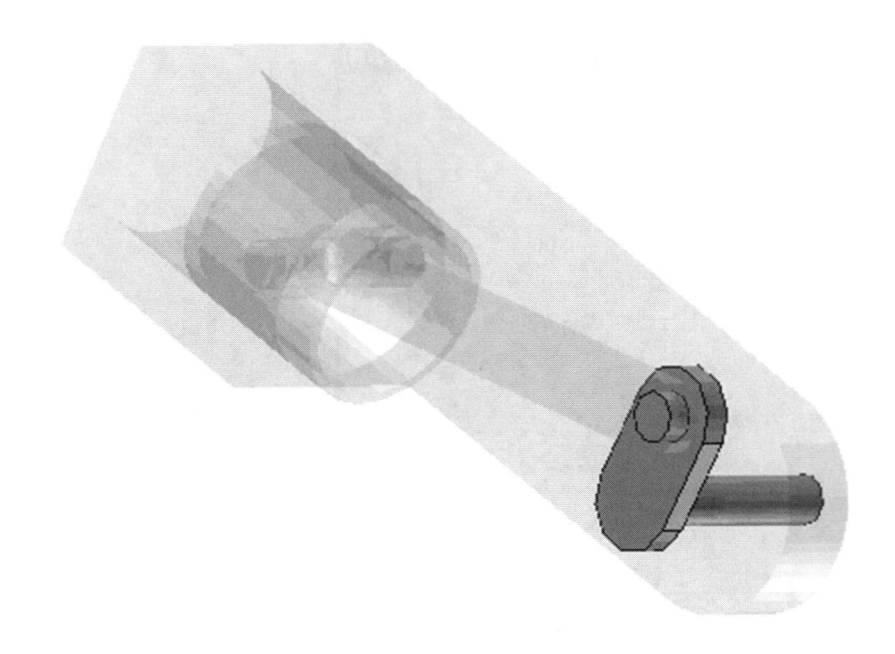

101. Move the cursor to the upper middle portion of the screen and left click on **Update** as shown in Figure 96.

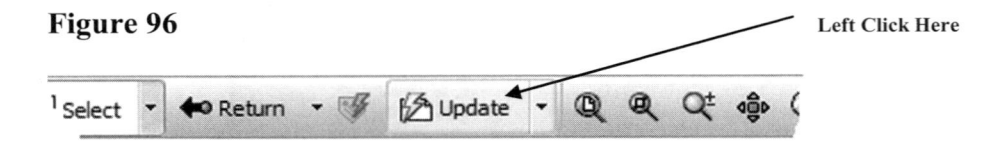

Figure 96 — Left Click Here

102. Move the cursor to the upper middle portion of the screen and left click on **Return** as shown in Figure 97.

Figure 97 — Left Click Here

Chapter 7: Introduction to Assembly View Procedures

103. Inventor will return to the Assembly Panel displaying the changes made to the crankshaft. Your screen should look similar to Figure 98.

Figure 98

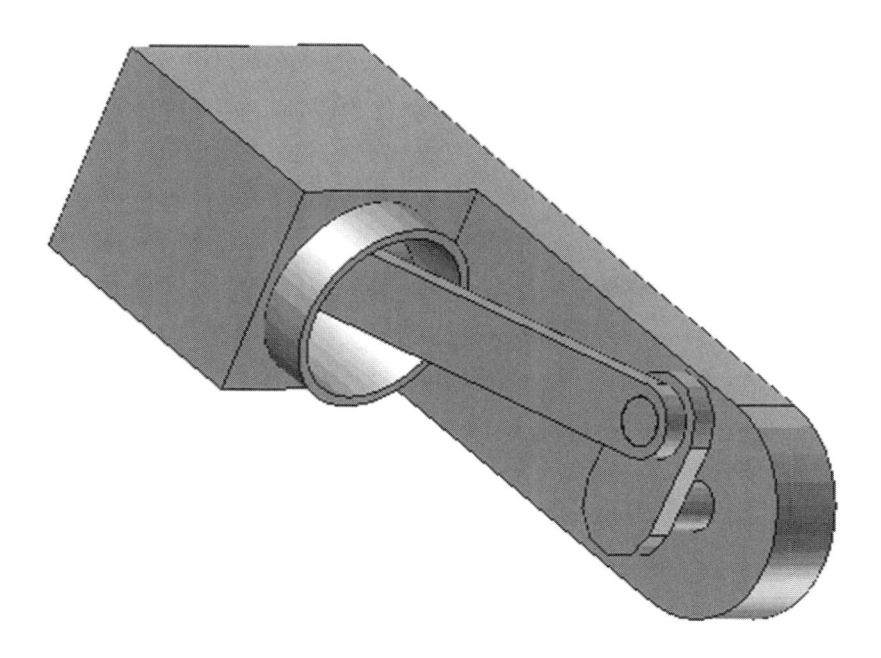

Chapter 7: Introduction to Assembly View Procedures

104. Move the cursor to any portion of the piston case. After the edges turn red, left click as shown in Figure 99.

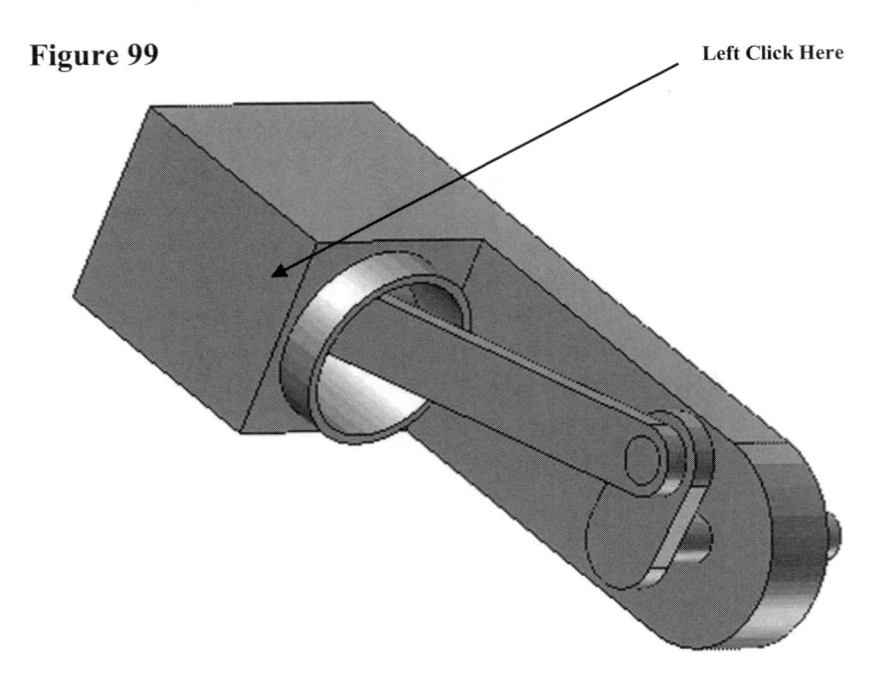

Figure 99

Left Click Here

105. Move the cursor to the upper right portion of the screen and left click on the drop down arrow next to the text "As Material". A drop down menu will appear. Scroll down to **Green (Clear/Polished)** and left click as shown in Figure 100.

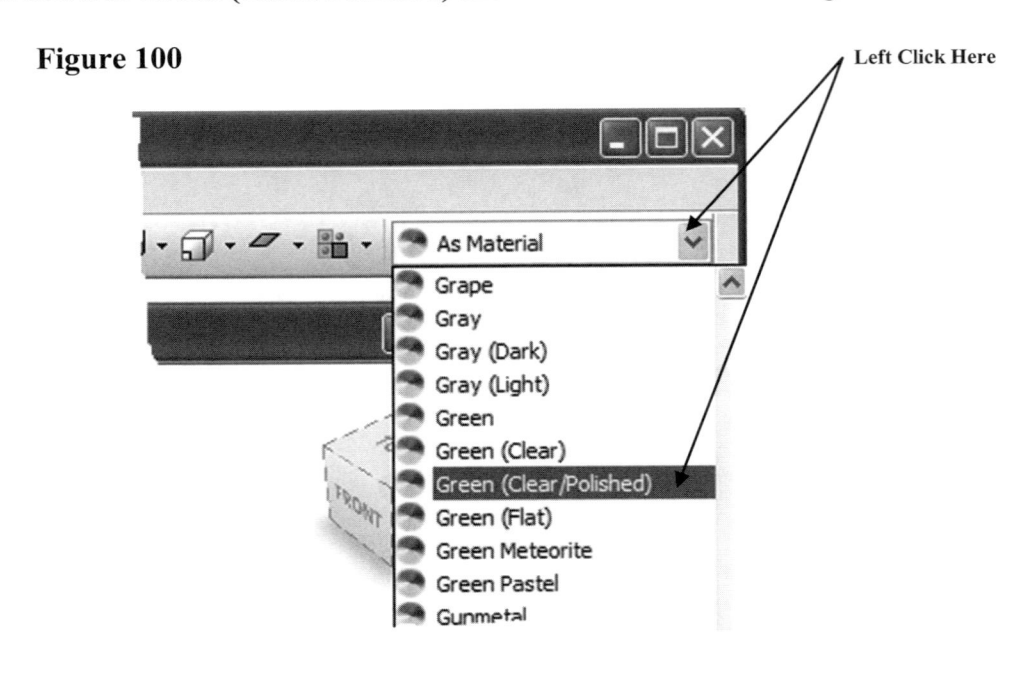

Figure 100

Left Click Here

412

Chapter 7: Introduction to Assembly View Procedures

106. Inventor will change the color of the piston case to clear polished green as shown in Figure 101.

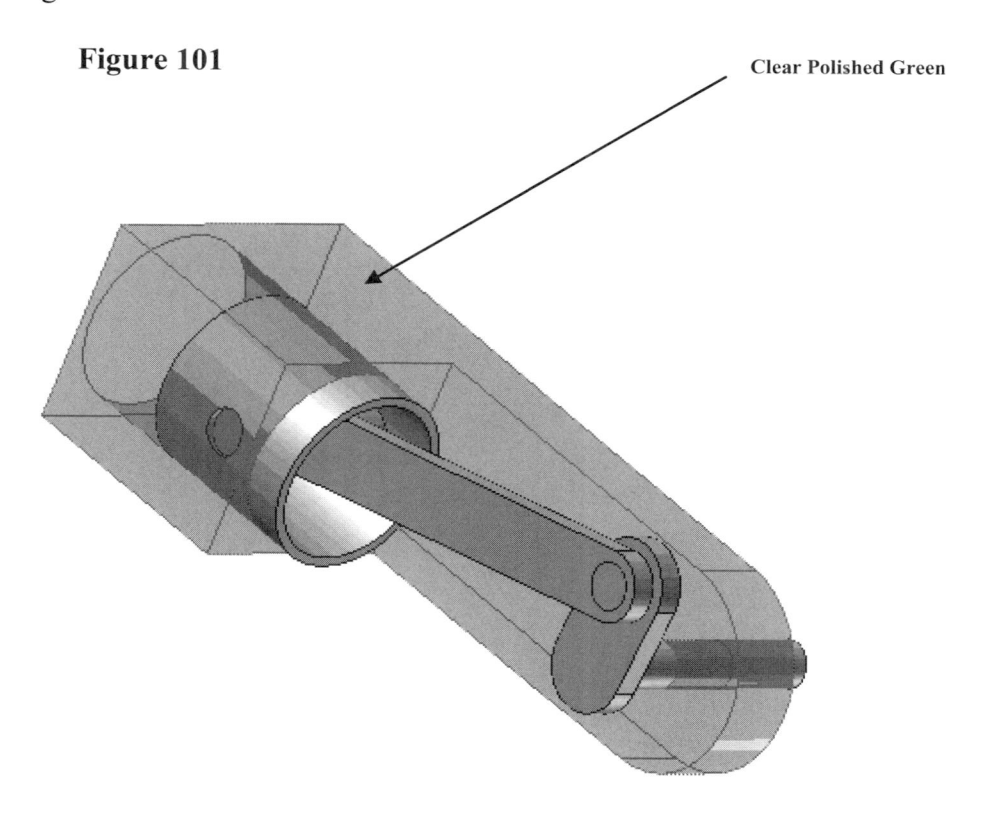

Figure 101

Clear Polished Green

Chapter 7: Introduction to Assembly View Procedures

107. Move the cursor to any portion of the piston causing the edges to turn red. Left click as shown in Figure 102.

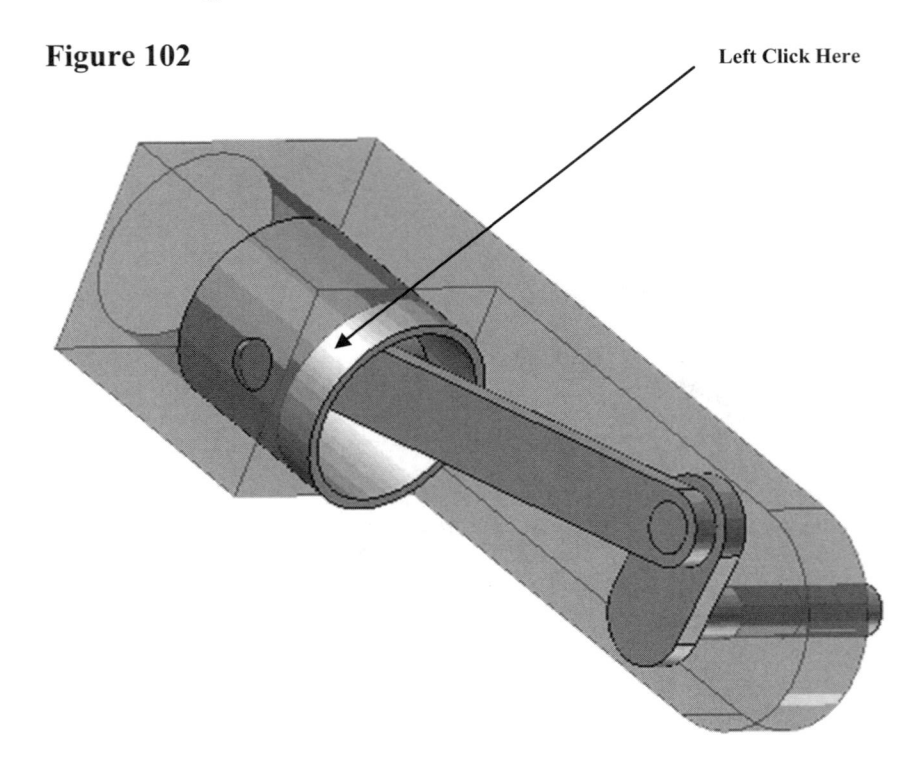

Figure 102 Left Click Here

108. Move the cursor to the upper right portion of the screen and left click on the drop down arrow next to the text "Green (Clear/Polished)". A drop down menu will appear. Scroll down to **Blue (Clear/Polished)** and left click as shown in Figure 103.

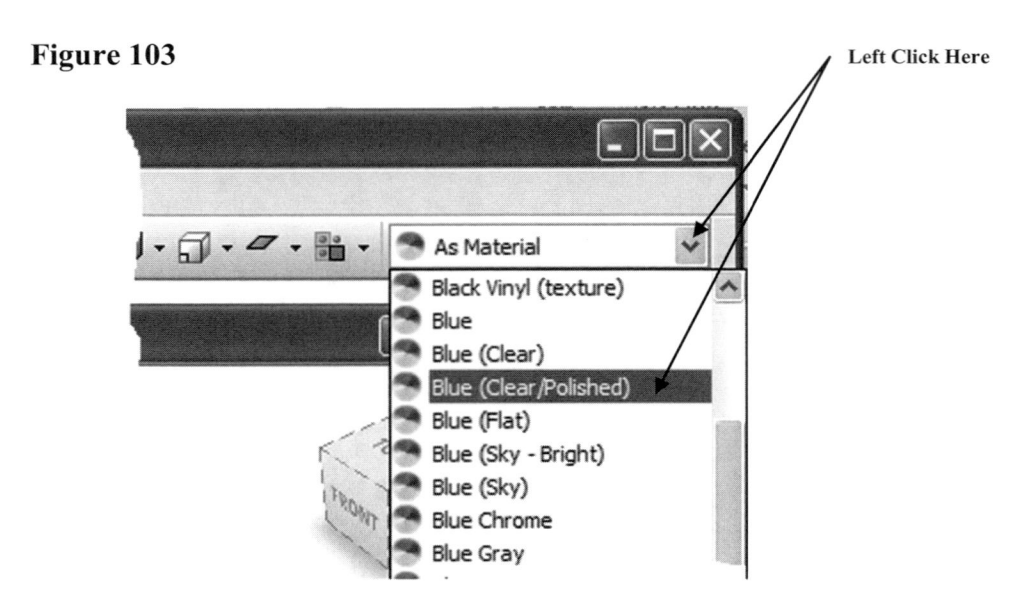

Figure 103 Left Click Here

109. Inventor will change the color of the piston to clear polished blue as shown in Figure 104.

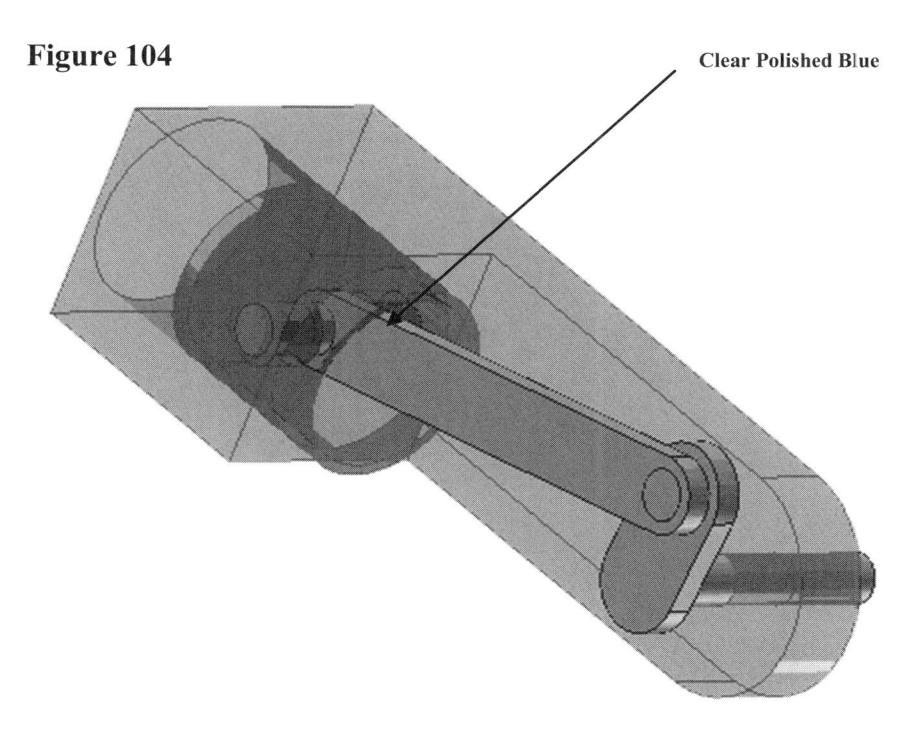

Figure 104

Clear Polished Blue

Chapter 7: Introduction to Assembly View Procedures

110. Using the same procedure, change the connecting rod color to **Copper (New/Polished)** as shown in Figure 105.

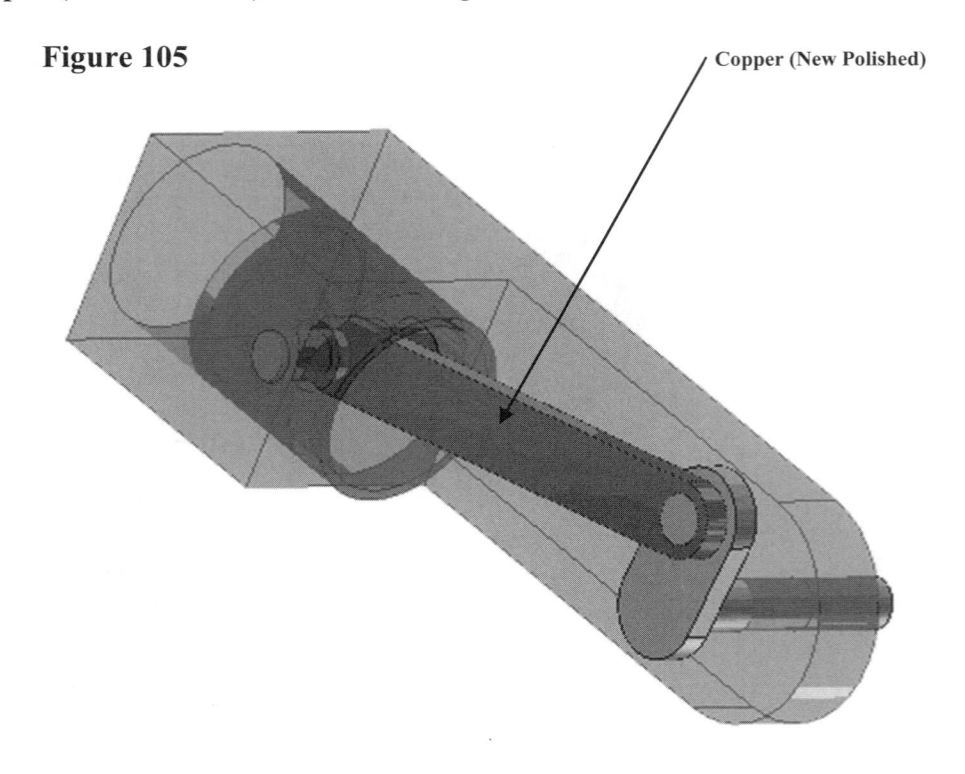

Figure 105

Copper (New Polished)

Chapter 7: Introduction to Assembly View Procedures

111. Move the cursor to the face of the connecting rod causing the edges to turn red. After the edges turn red, left click (holding the left mouse button down) and drag the cursor in a circle causing the crankshaft to turn. Rotate the crankshaft upward to the position shown in Figure 106.

Figure 106

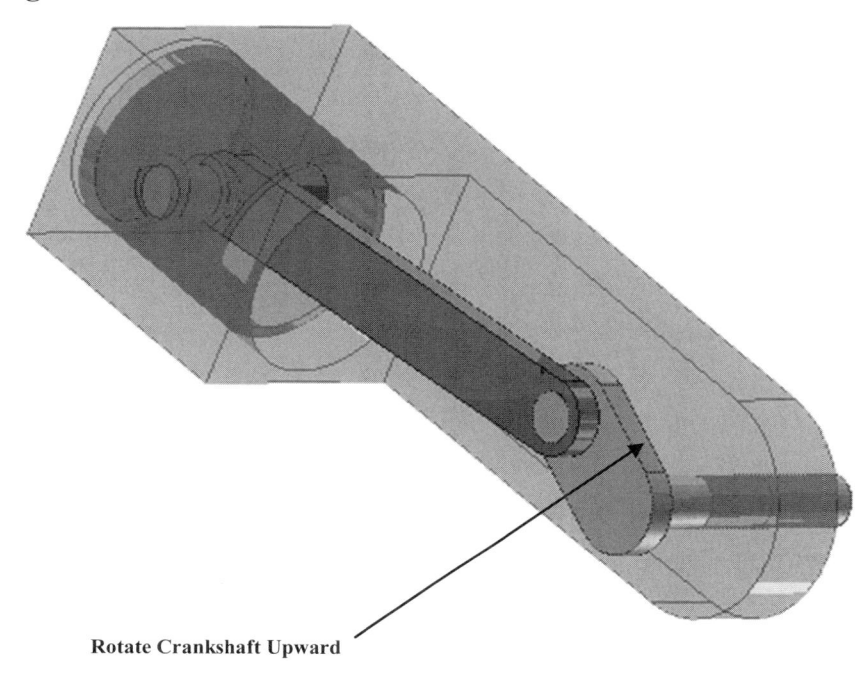

Rotate Crankshaft Upward

Chapter 7: Introduction to Assembly View Procedures

112. Move the cursor to the middle left portion of the screen and left click on **Constraint.** The Place Constraint dialog box will appear. Left click on the "Angle Constraint" icon as shown in Figure 107.

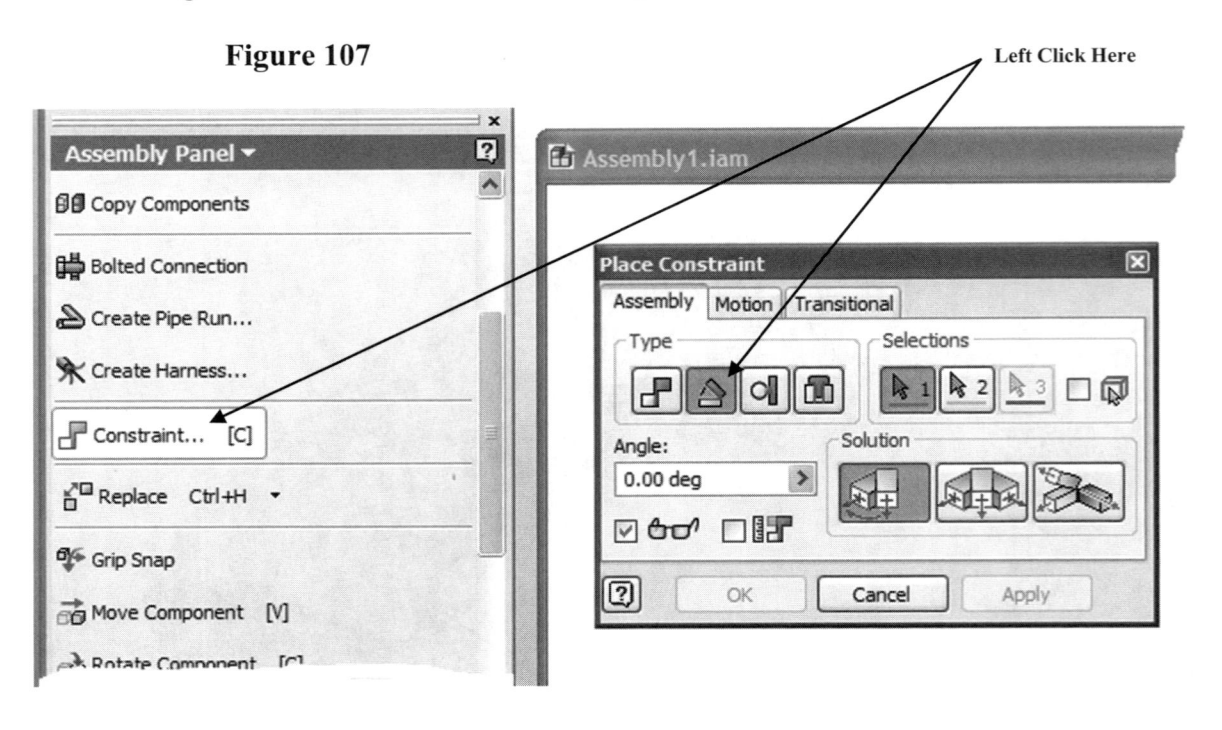

Figure 107

Chapter 7: Introduction to Assembly View Procedures

113. Move the cursor to the top portion of the crankshaft causing a red arrow to appear. Left click as shown in Figure 108. You may have to zoom in to select the surface.

Figure 108

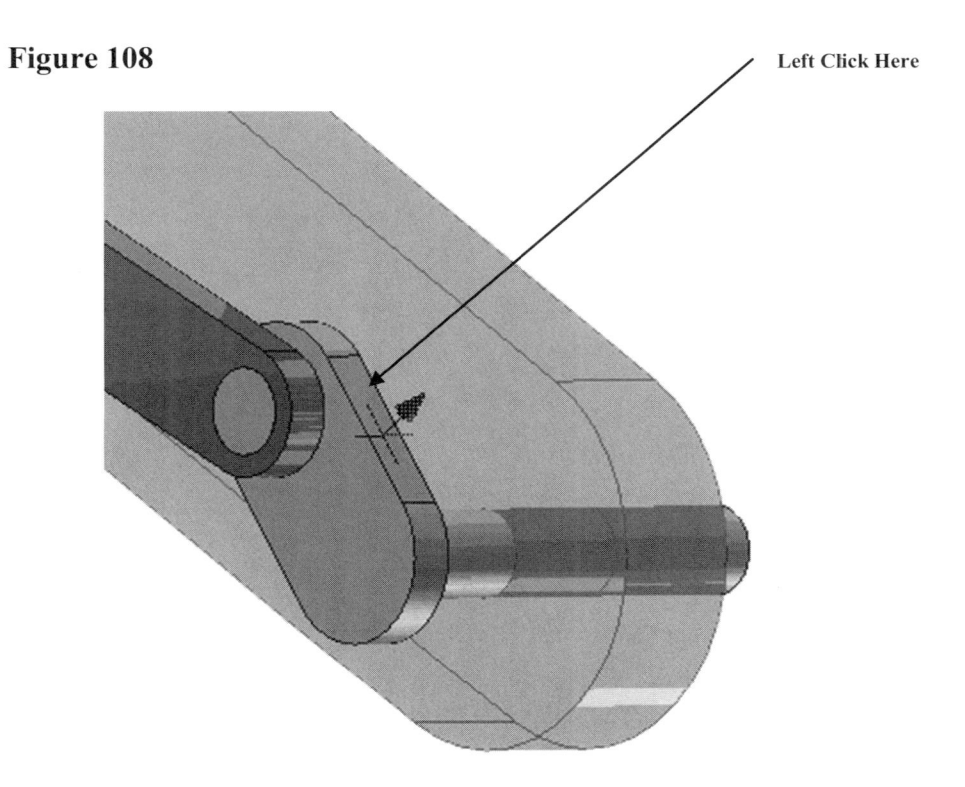

Left Click Here

Chapter 7: Introduction to Assembly View Procedures

114. Move the cursor to the side of the piston case causing a red arrow to appear. Left click once as shown in Figure 109.

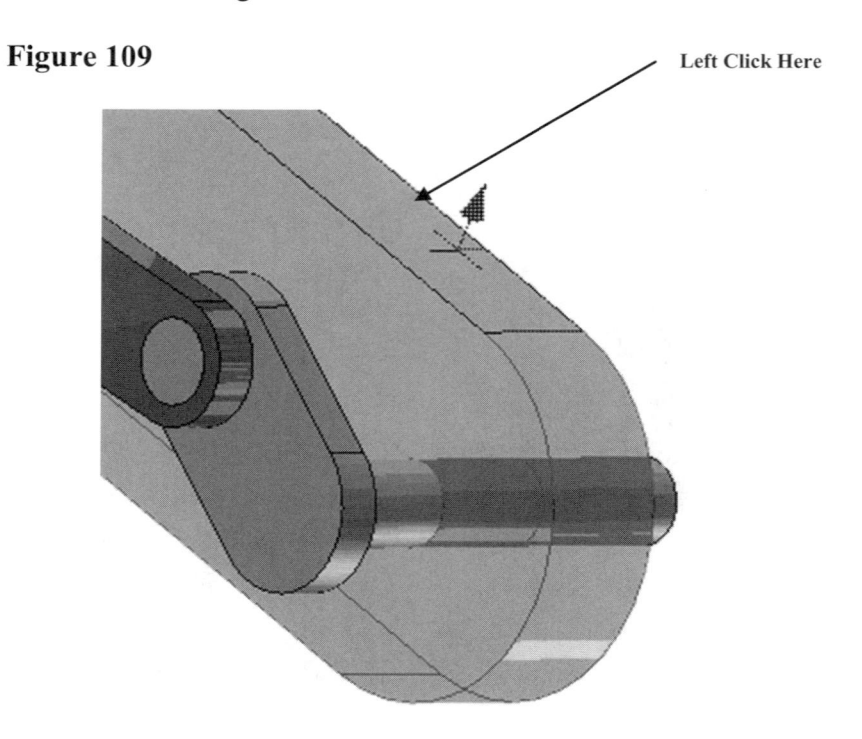

Figure 109

Left Click Here

Chapter 7: Introduction to Assembly View Procedures

115. Inventor will rotate the crankshaft so that it is parallel (0 degrees) to the side of the piston case. If 20 or 30 degrees were entered in the Angle box, Inventor would rotate the crankshaft to a position 20 or 30 degrees from the side of the piston case. When 0 is entered into the Angle box, Inventor will rotate the crankshaft parallel to the piston case side as shown in Figure 110.

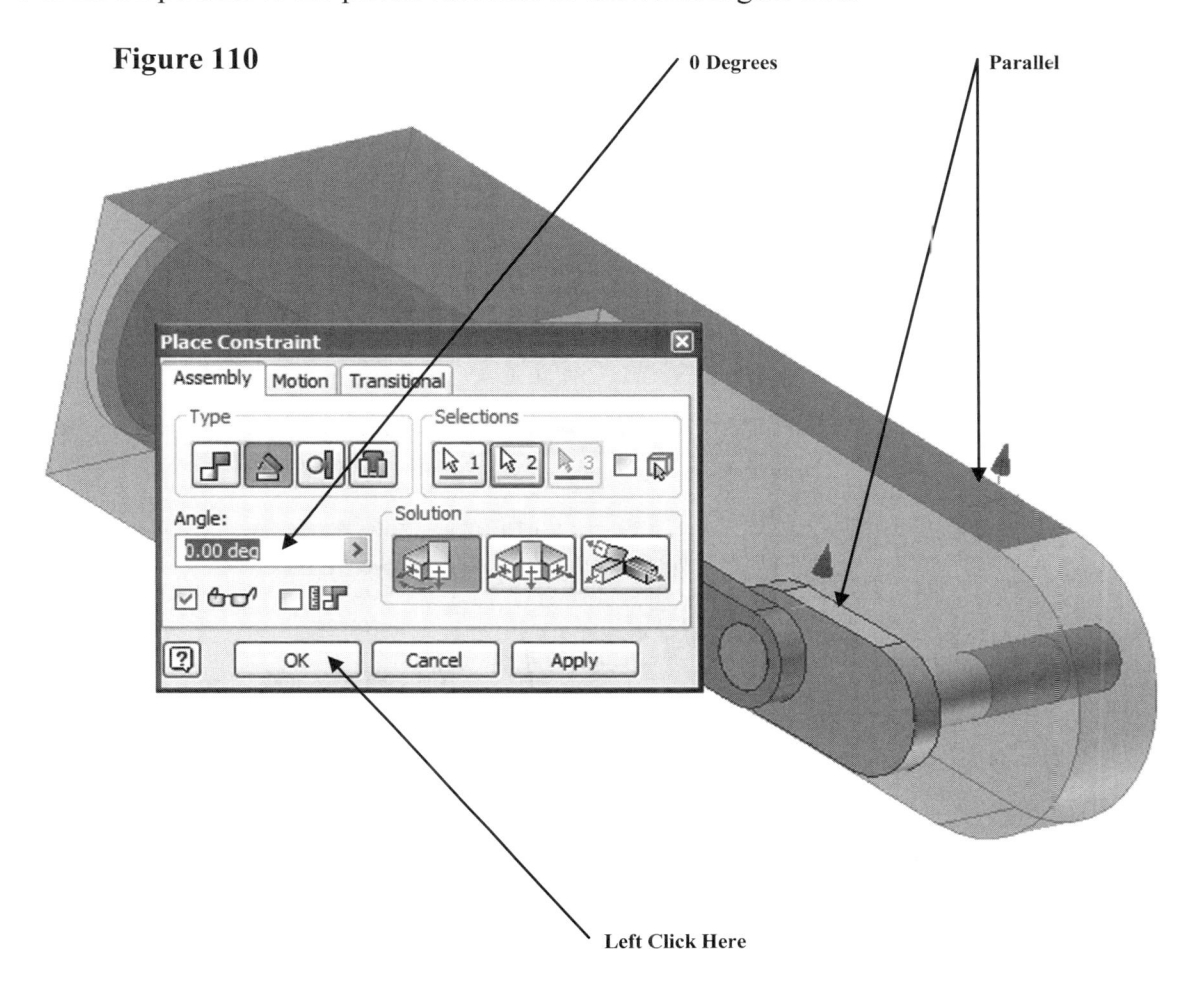

Figure 110

116. Left click on **OK** as shown in Figure 110.

Chapter 7: Introduction to Assembly View Procedures

117. Move the cursor to the lower left portion of the screen to the part tree. Scroll down to **Angle:1** and right click once. A pop up menu will appear. Left click on **Drive Constraint** as shown in Figure 111.

Figure 111

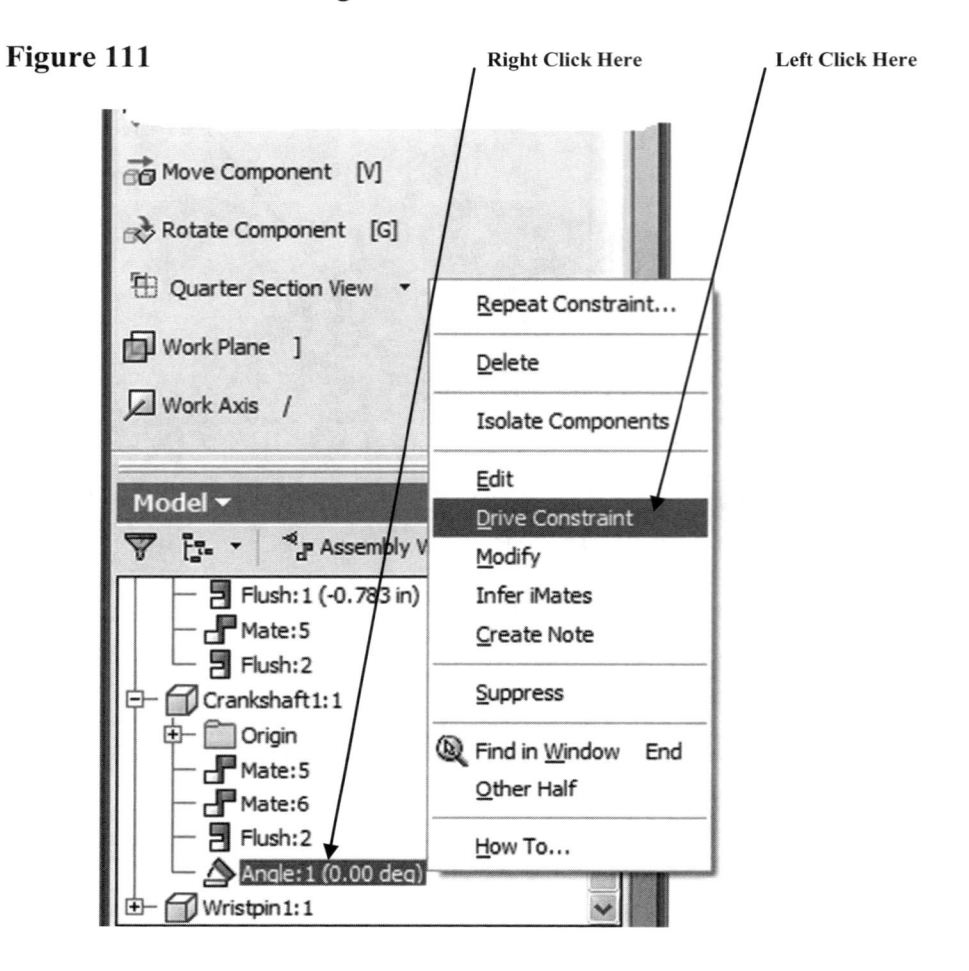

118. The Drive Constraint dialog box will appear. Enter **0** degrees under "Start". Enter **360000** degrees under "End". Left click on the double arrows at the far right lower corner of the dialog box as shown in Figure 112.

Figure 112

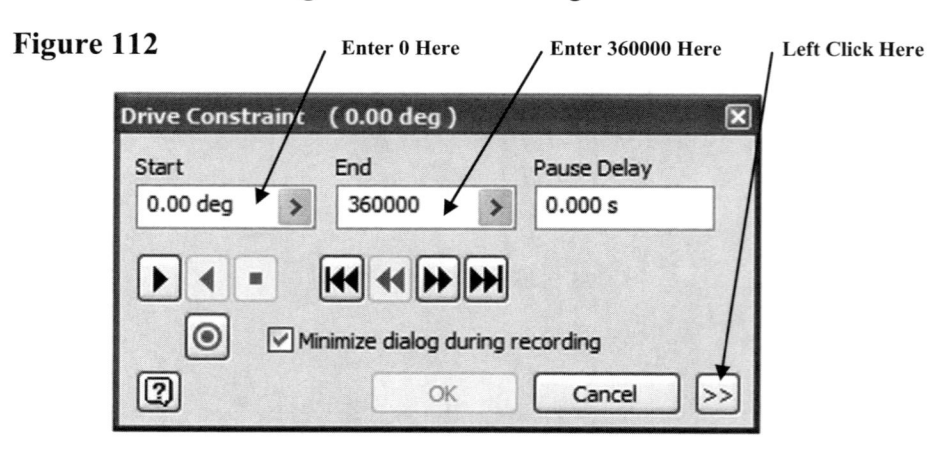

Chapter 7: Introduction to Assembly View Procedures

119. The Drive Constraint dialog box will expand, providing more options. Enter **10** for number of degrees as shown in Figure 113.

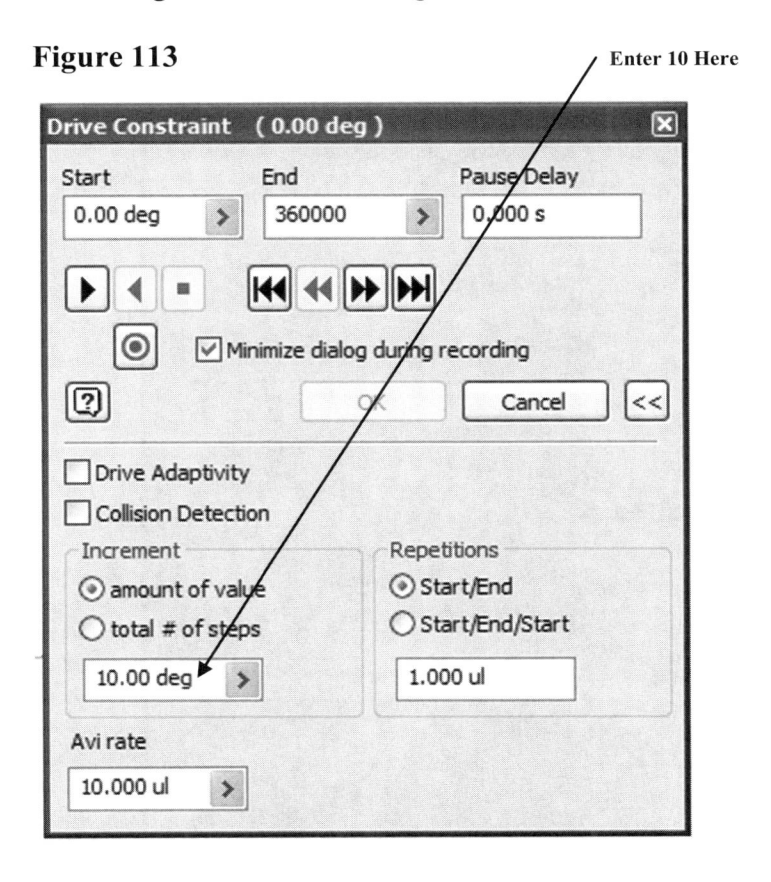

Figure 113

Enter 10 Here

423

Chapter 7: Introduction to Assembly View Procedures

120. Use the Zoom option to zoom out. Use the Pan option to move the assembly off to the side. Left click on the "Play" icon as shown in Figure 114.

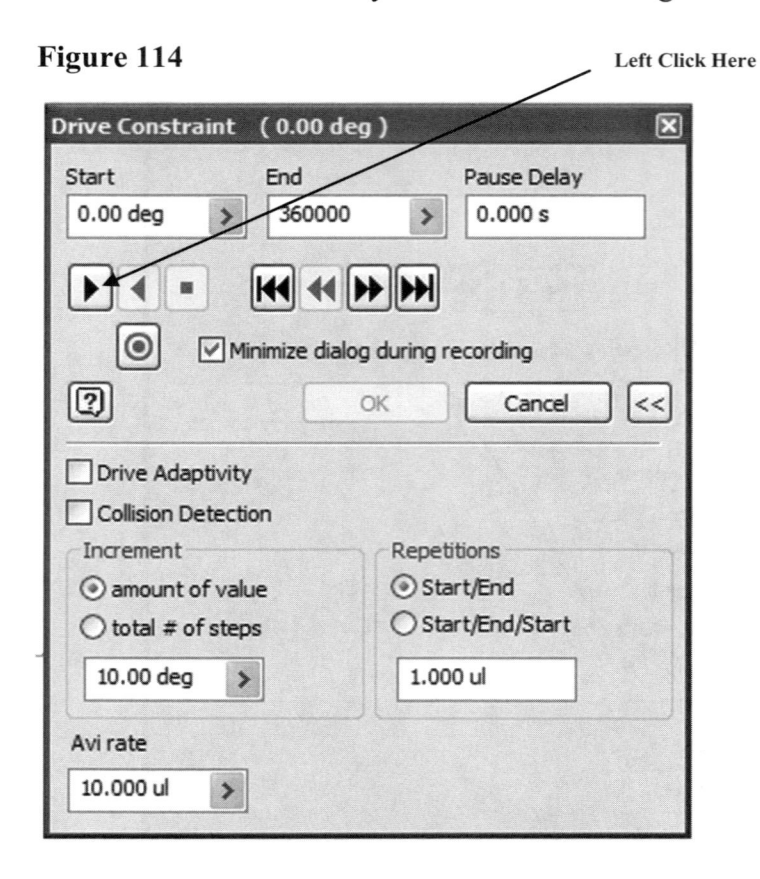

Figure 114

121. Inventor will animate the part causing the crankshaft to rotate.

424

Chapter 7: Introduction to Assembly View Procedures

122. Left click on the "Stop" icon. The animation will stop. Left click on the "Minimize" icon. The Drive Constraint dialog box will get smaller. Left click on the "Rewind" icon. This will rewind the animation back to 0 degrees as shown in Figure 115.

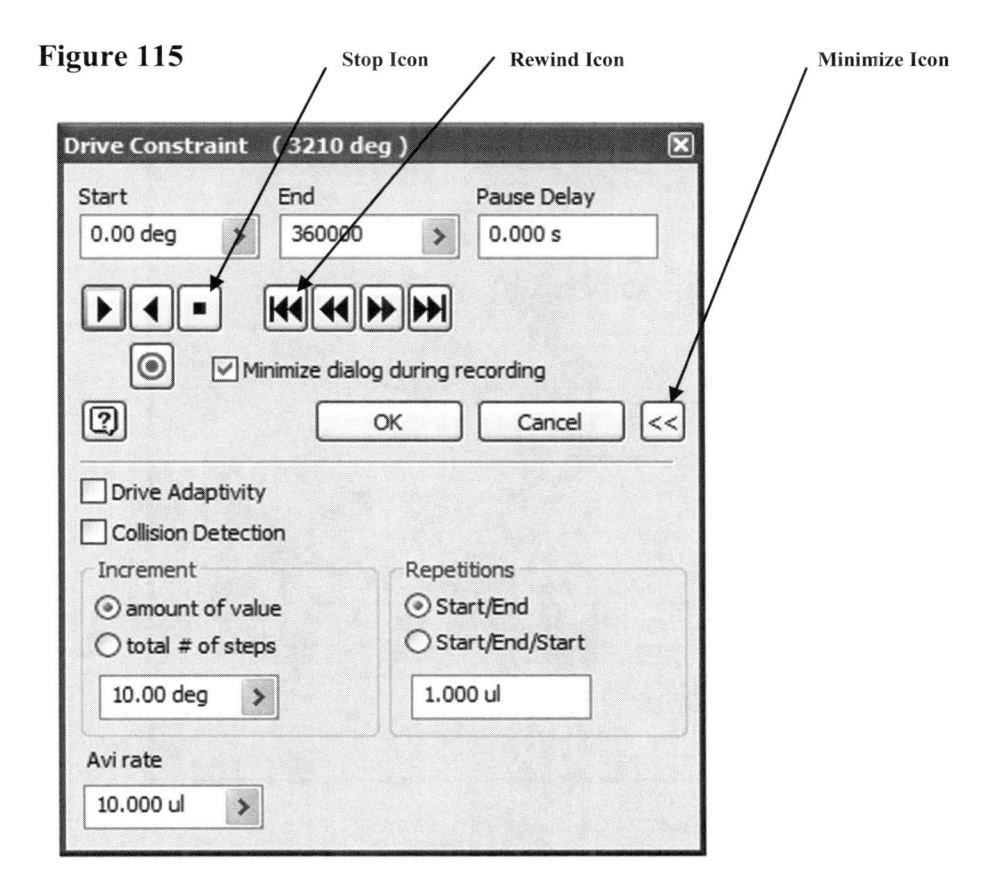

Figure 115

Chapter 7: Introduction to Assembly View Procedures

123. Left click on the "Play" icon and immediately left click on the "Record" icon as shown in Figure 116.

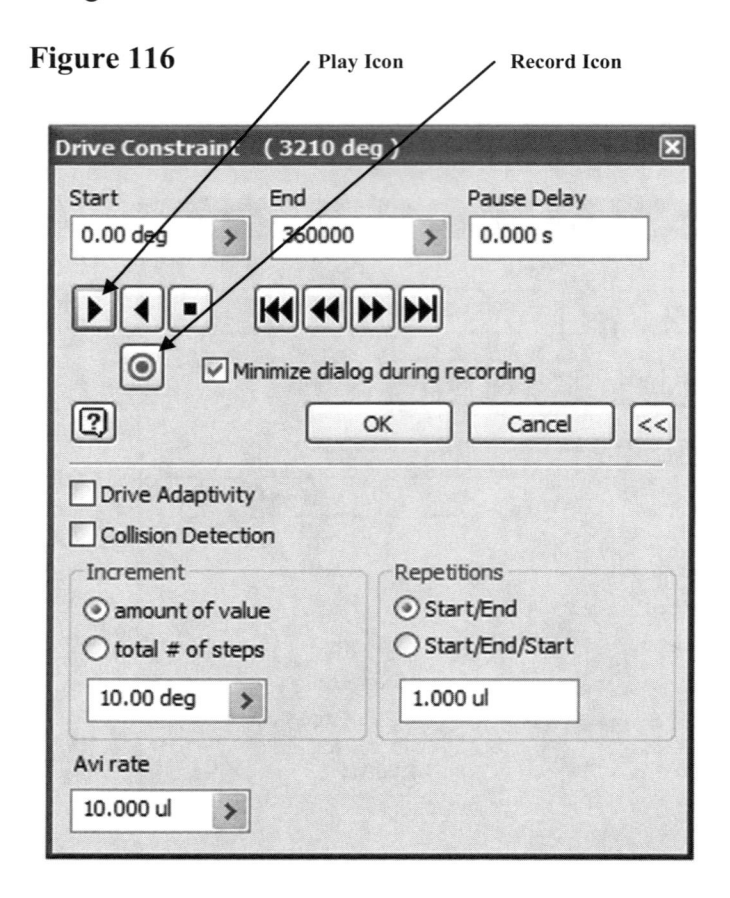

Figure 116 — Play Icon — Record Icon

124. The Save As dialog box will appear. Save the file where it can be easily retrieved later and left click on **OK**.

Chapter 7: Introduction to Assembly View Procedures

125. The ASF Export Properties dialog box will appear. Left click on **OK** as shown in Figure 117.

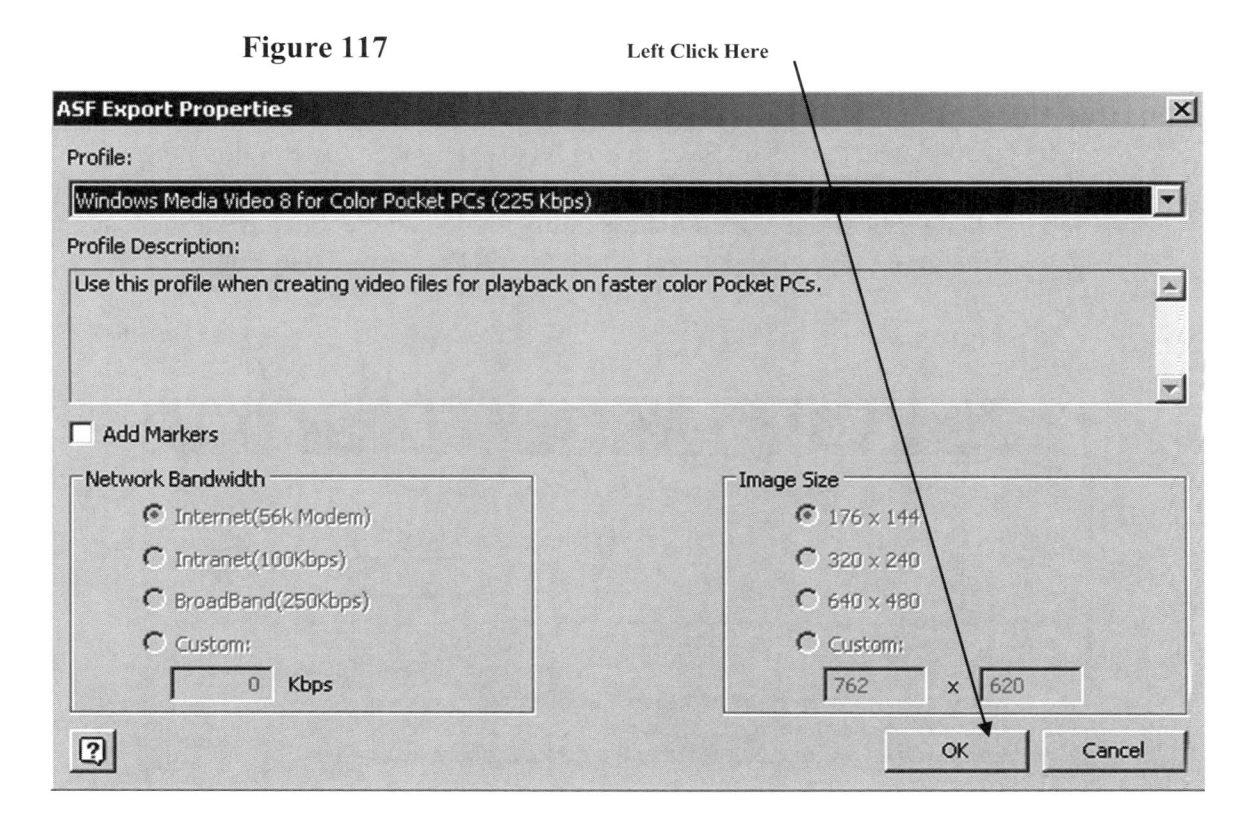

Figure 117 Left Click Here

126. While Inventor is recording the simulation, the Drive Constraint dialog box will minimize in the lower left corner of the screen. The speed of the animation will decrease during the recording time. Allow Inventor to record for approximately 15-30 seconds. Inventor is in the process of creating an .wmv file that can be viewed in Windows Media Player. After about 30 seconds left click on the Close symbol in the upper right corner of the dialog box as shown in Figure 118. The Drive Constraint dialog box will close and the recording will be complete.

Figure 118 Left Click Here

Chapter 7: Introduction to Assembly View Procedures

127. Go to the location where the file was saved and double click on it.

128. Windows Media Player or Real Player will play the file. The file can also be opened in either Windows Media Player or Real Player.

129. Save the Inventor file (.iam) as Chapter 7 Assembly1.iam where it can be easily retrieved at a later time. The Save dialog box will appear. The dialog box will ask if you want to save the assembly itself along with any changes that were made to individual parts that make up the assembly. You can elect to save or not save changes made to individual parts. Left click on **OK** as shown in Figure 119.

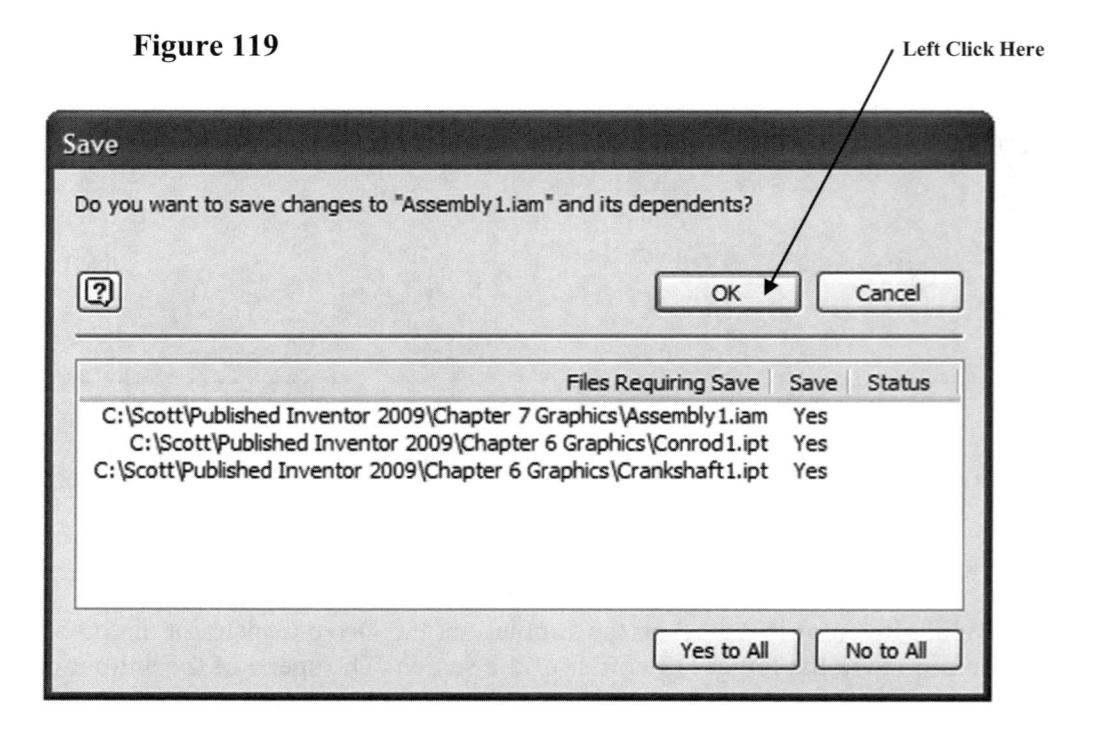

Figure 119

Chapter 8 Introduction to the Presentation Panel

Objectives:
- Learn to import existing solid models into the Presentation Panel
- Learn to design parts trails in the Presentation Panel

Chapter 8 includes instruction on how to design the presentation shown below.

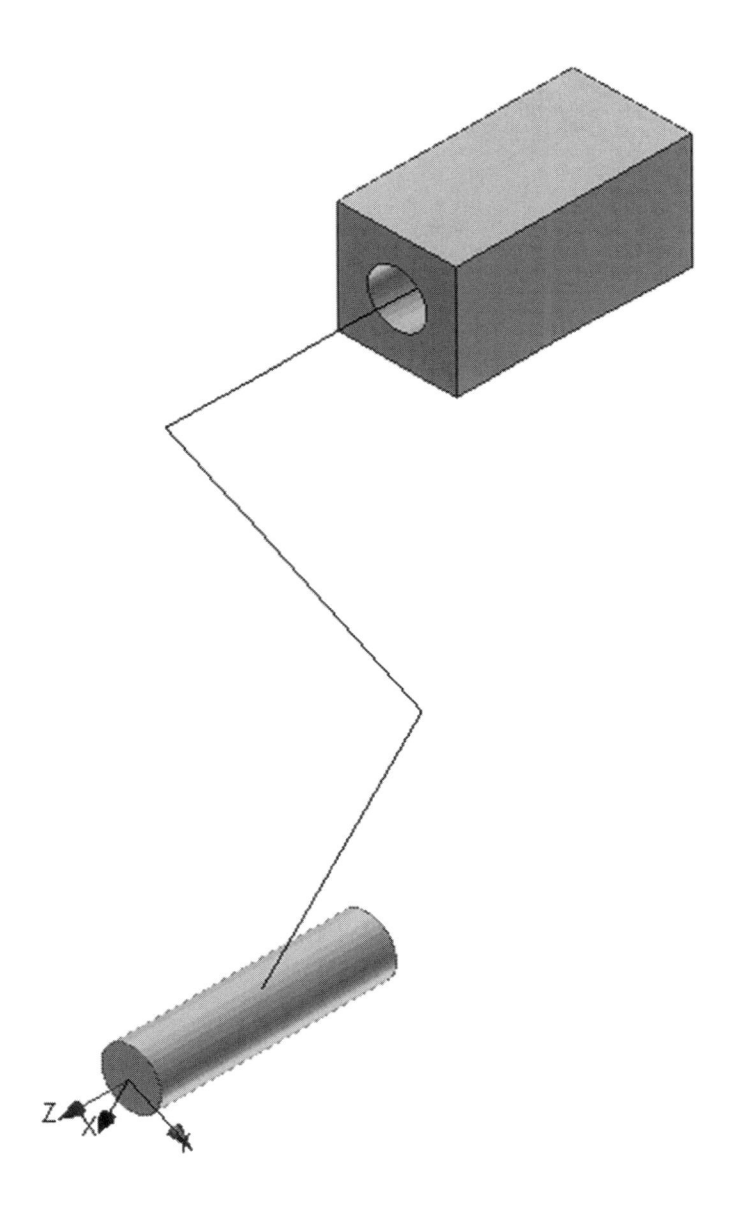

Chapter 8: Introduction to the Presentation Panel

1. Start Inventor by referring to "Chapter 1 Getting Started".

2. After Inventor is running, begin by creating the parts shown in Figure 1.

Figure 1

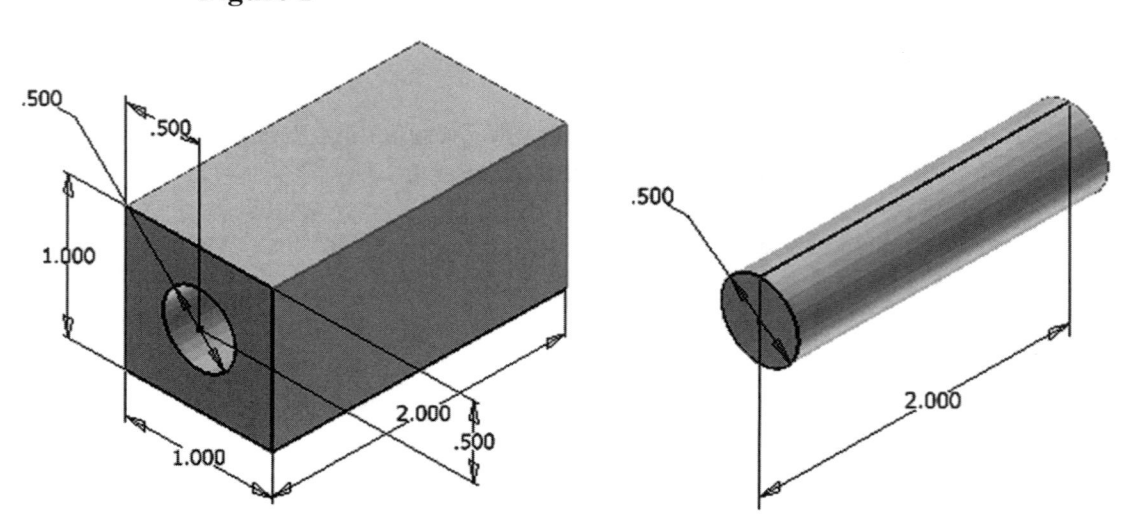

Left Click Here

3. Save the block as Chapter 8 Part1.ipt. and save the pin as Chapter 8 Part2.ipt where they can easily be retrieved at a later time. Close both files.

4. Move the cursor to the upper left portion of the screen and left click on the "New" icon as shown in Figure 2.

Figure 2

Left Click Here

5. The New File dialog box will appear. Select the **English** tab and **Standard (in).iam** and left click on **OK** as shown in Figure 3.

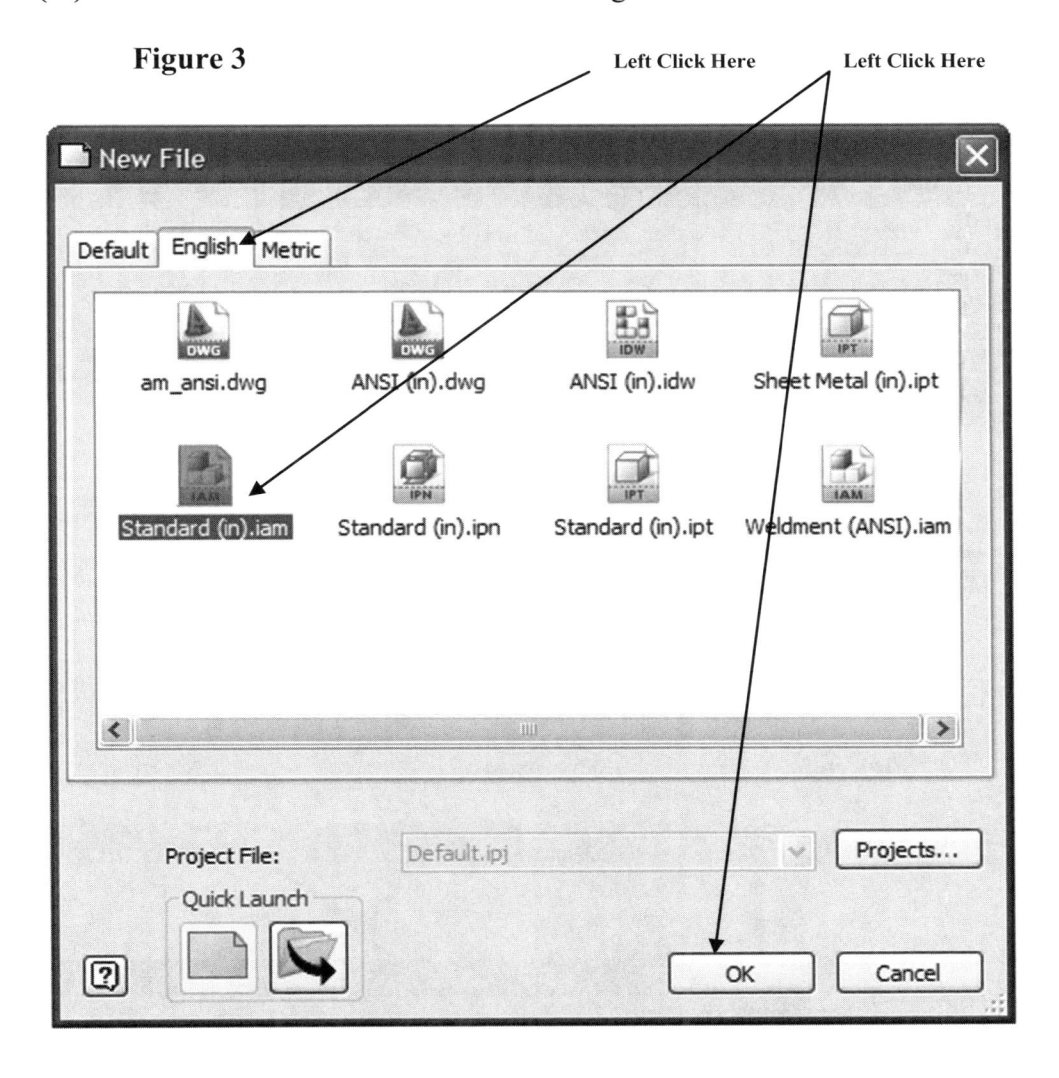

Figure 3

6. The Assembly Panel will open.

Chapter 8: Introduction to the Presentation Panel

7. Your screen should look similar to Figure 4. If the Assembly Panel tools are not visible, left click on the drop down arrow to the right. A drop down menu will appear. Left click on **Assembly Panel** as shown in Figure 4.

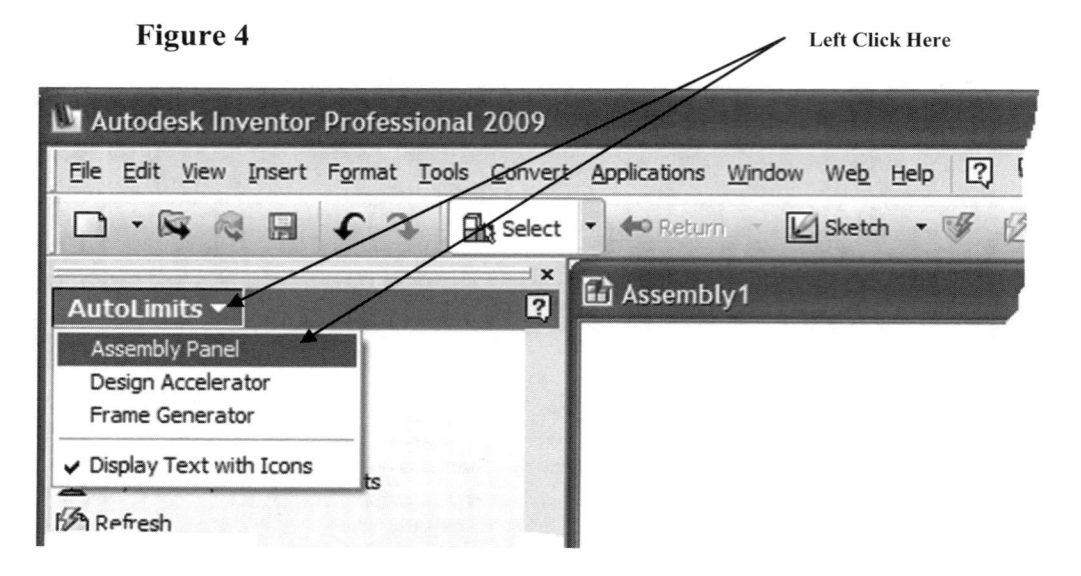

Figure 4

8. Move the cursor to the upper left portion of the screen and left click on **Place Component** as shown in Figure 5.

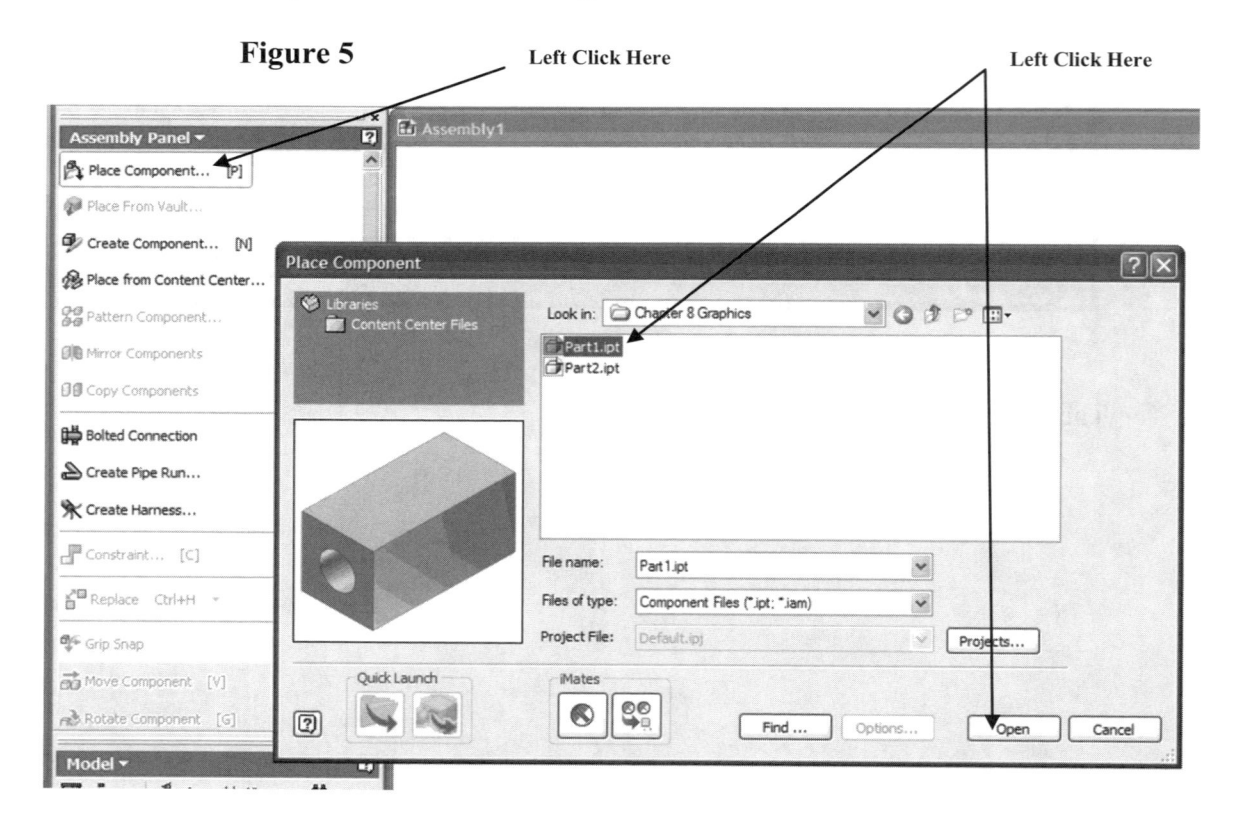

Figure 5

432

9. The Open dialog box will appear. Left click on **Chapter 8 Part1.ipt**. Left click on **Open** as shown in Figure 5.

10. The block will appear attached to the cursor. Do NOT left click. Press **Esc** on the keyboard. Your screen should look similar to Figure 6.

   Figure 6

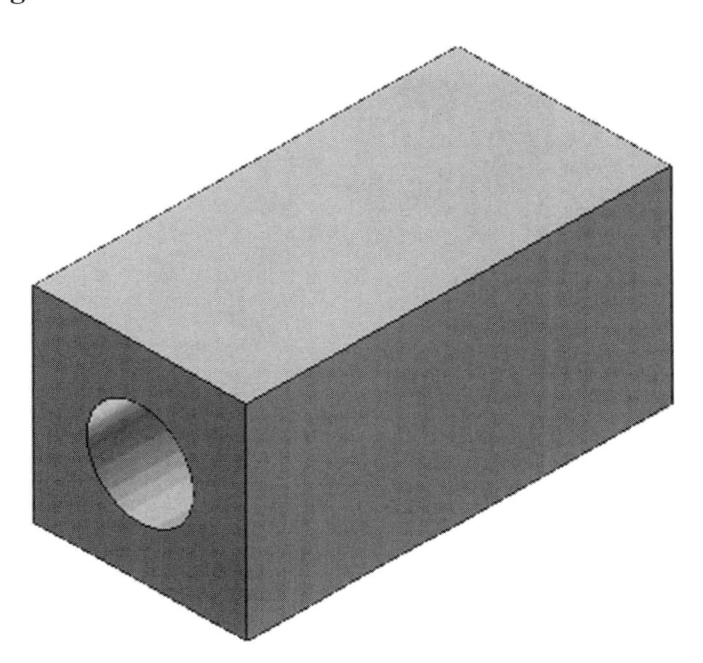

Chapter 8: Introduction to the Presentation Panel

11. Move the cursor to the upper left portion of the screen and left click on **Place Component** as shown in Figure 7.

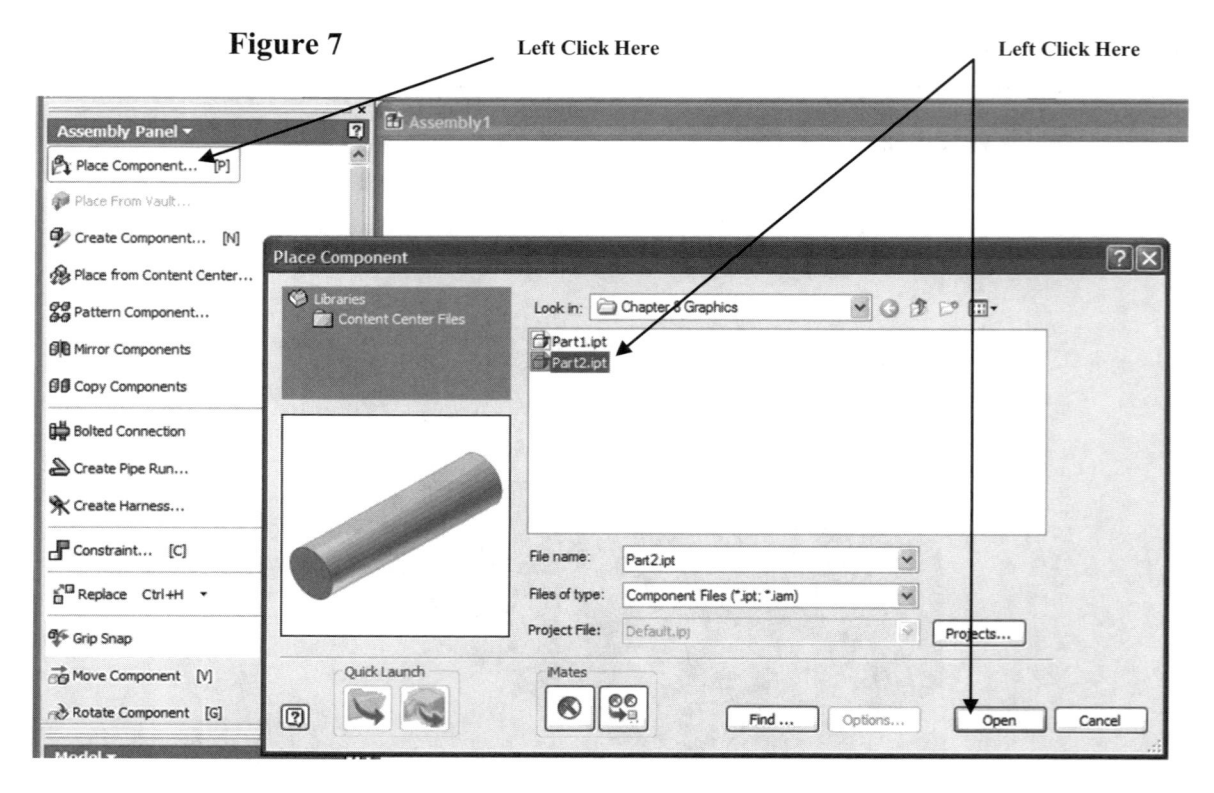

Figure 7

Left Click Here

12. The Place Component dialog box will appear. Left click on **Chapter 8 Part2.ipt**. Left click on **Open** as shown in Figure 7.

434

13. The pin will appear attached to the cursor. Place the pin near the block and left click once. Press **Esc** on the keyboard. Your screen should look similar to Figure 8.

   Figure 8

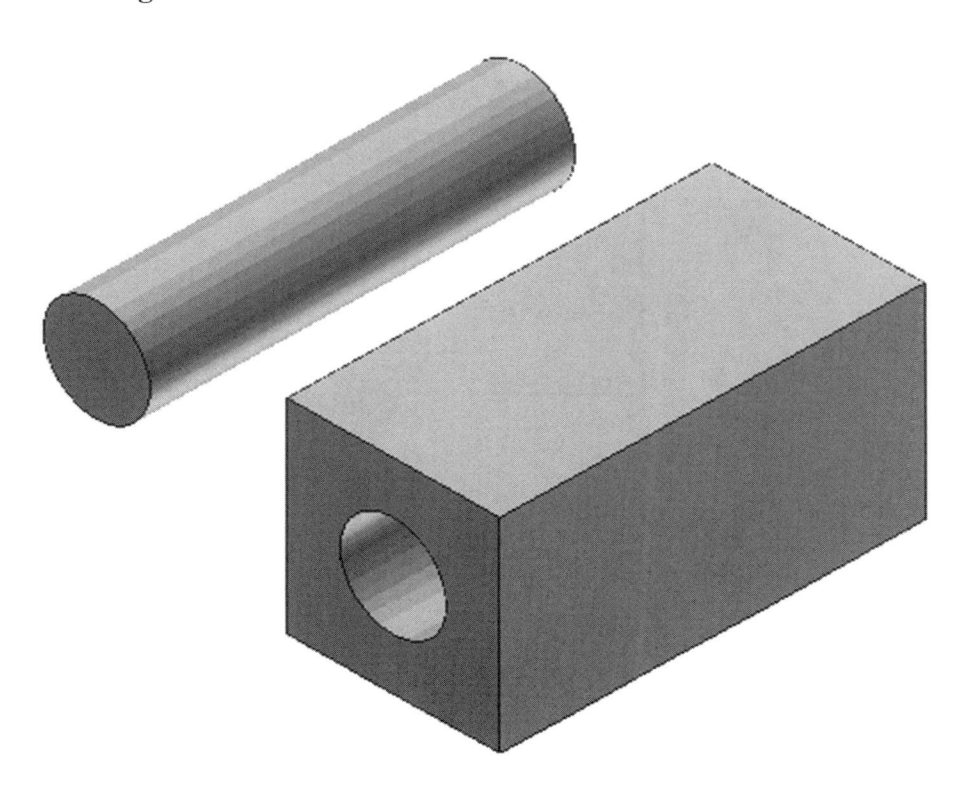

Chapter 8: Introduction to the Presentation Panel

14. Move the cursor to the middle left portion of the screen and left click on **Constraint** as shown in Figure 9.

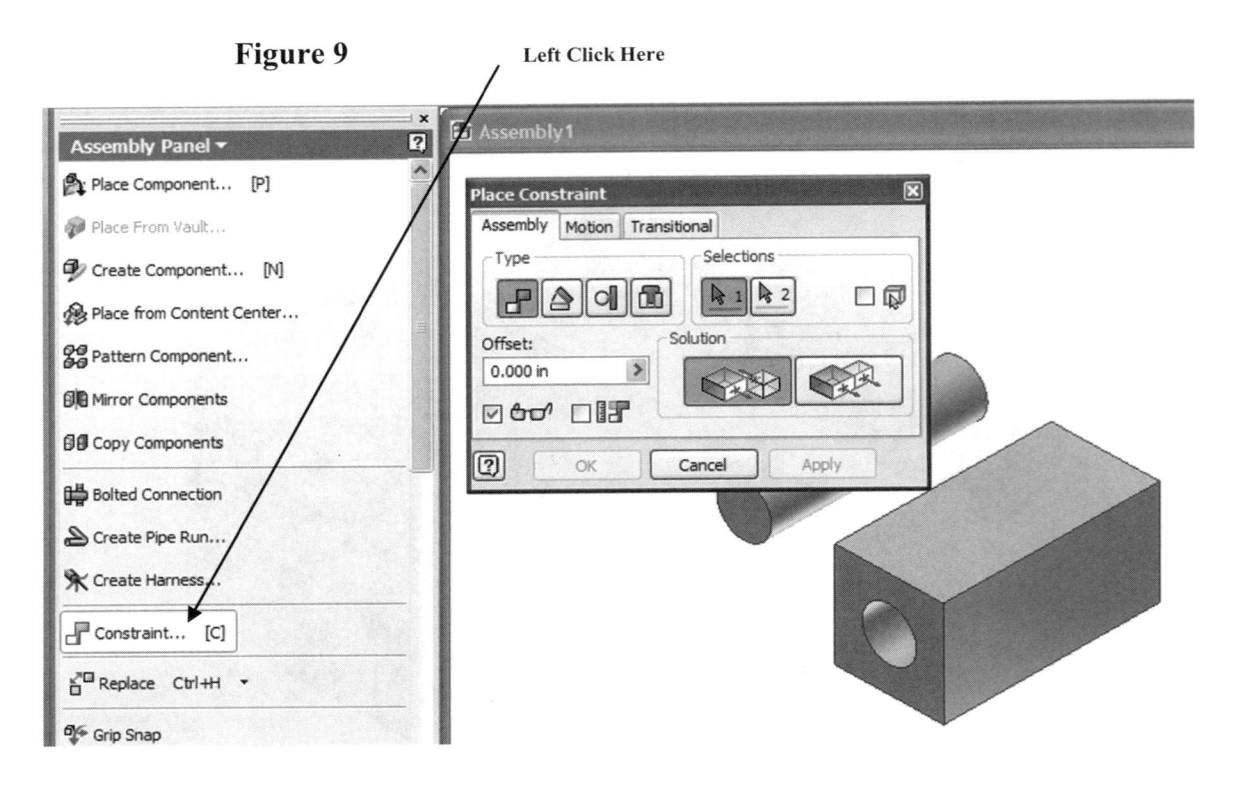

Figure 9   Left Click Here

15. The Place Constraint dialog box will appear as shown in Figure 9.

Chapter 8: Introduction to the Presentation Panel

16. Move the cursor over the hole in the block. A red dashed center line will appear. Left click once as shown in Figure 10.

Figure 10

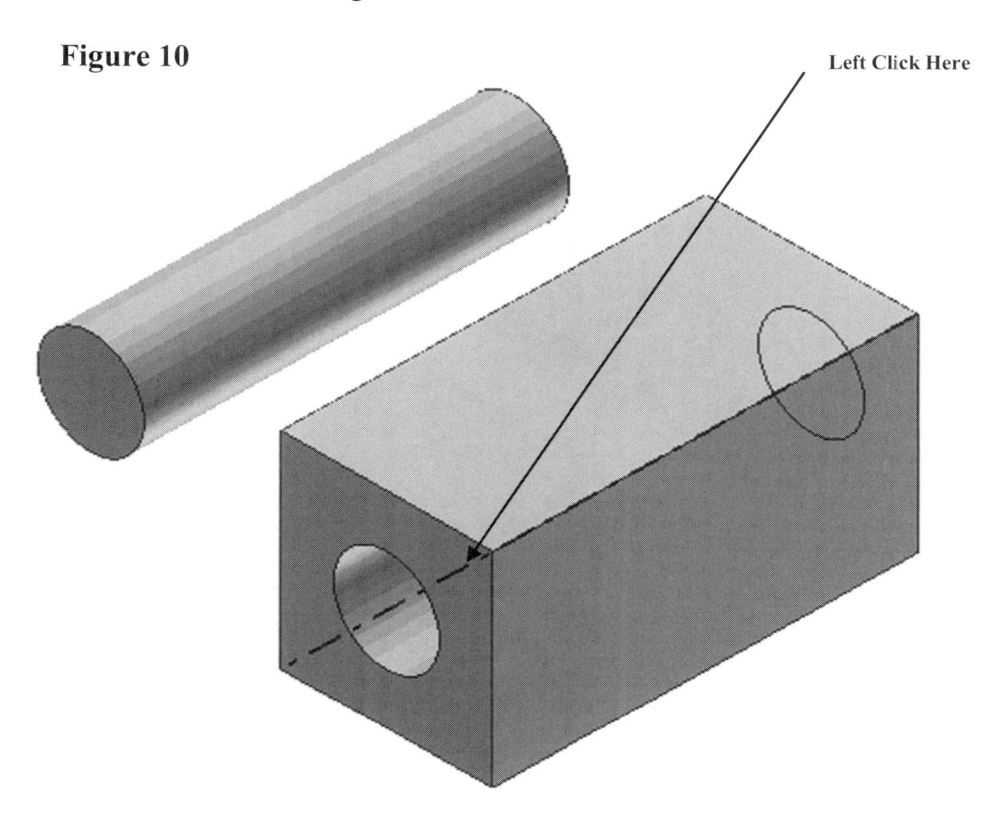

Left Click Here

Chapter 8: Introduction to the Presentation Panel

17. Move the cursor over the pin. A red dashed center line will appear. Left click once as shown in Figure 11.

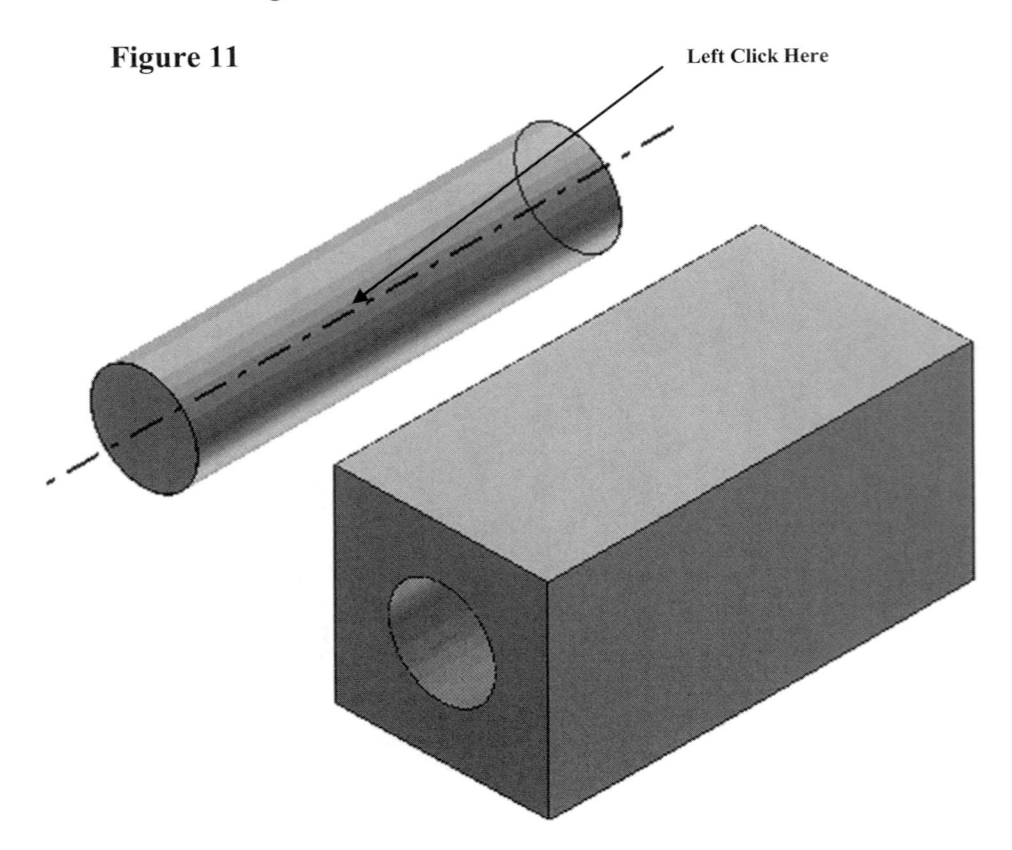

Figure 11

Left Click Here

Chapter 8: Introduction to the Presentation Panel

18. Inventor will insert the pin into the block. Your screen should look similar to Figure 12.

Figure 12

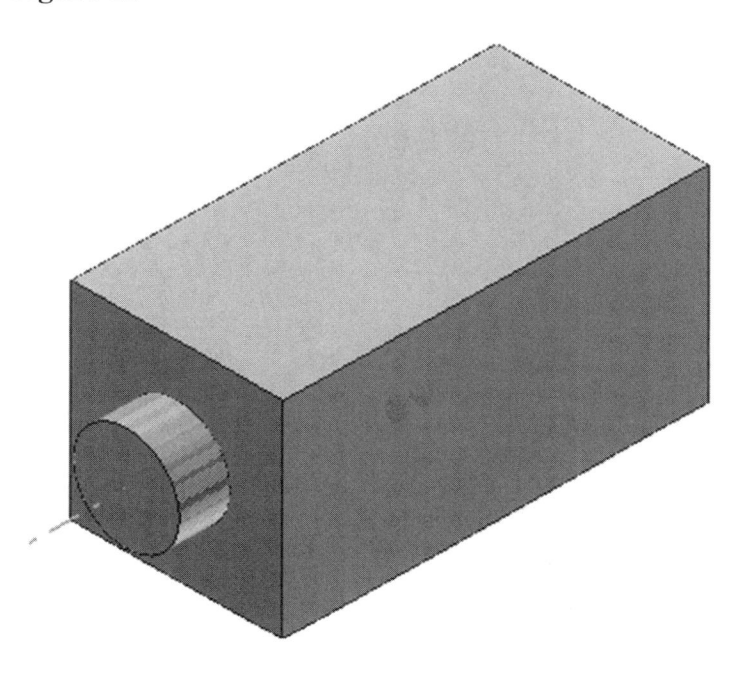

19. Typically a surface constraint would be added to prevent the pin from sliding back and forth in the block. However, this assembly will be used in the Presentation Panel. A surface constraint will not be added because the pin must slide in and out of the block.

Chapter 8: Introduction to the Presentation Panel

20. Move the cursor to the center of the pin. Left click (holding down the left mouse button) and slide the pin flush with the outside of the block as shown in Figure 13.

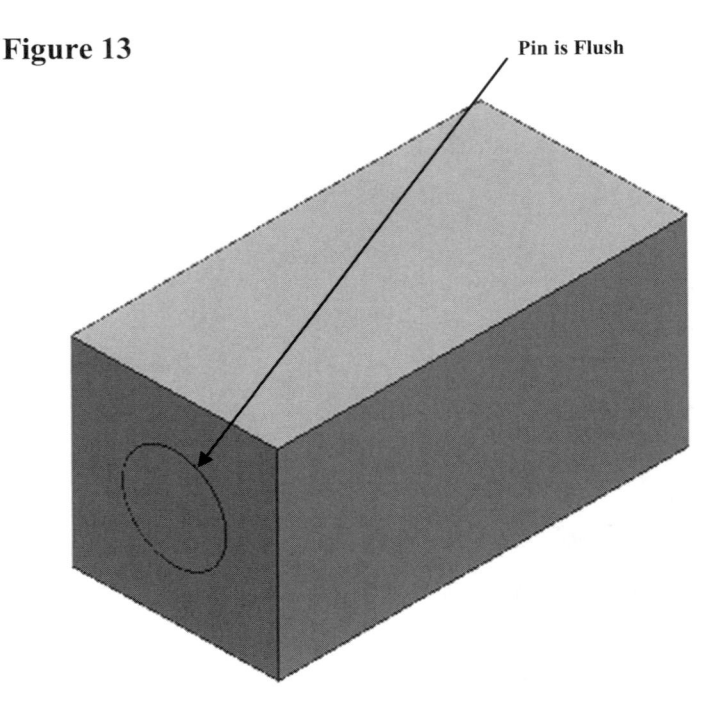

Figure 13   Pin is Flush

21. Save the parts as Chapter 8 Assembly1.iam where it can be easily retrieved later. Leave the file open at this time.

22. Move the cursor to the upper left portion of the screen and left click on the "New" icon as shown in Figure 14.

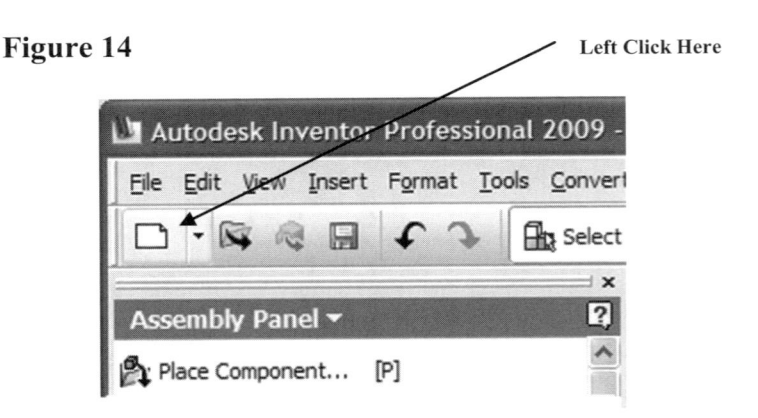

Figure 14   Left Click Here

440

Chapter 8: Introduction to the Presentation Panel

23. The New File dialog box will appear. Select the **English** tab and **Standard (in).ipn**. Left click on **OK** as shown in Figure 15.

Figure 15

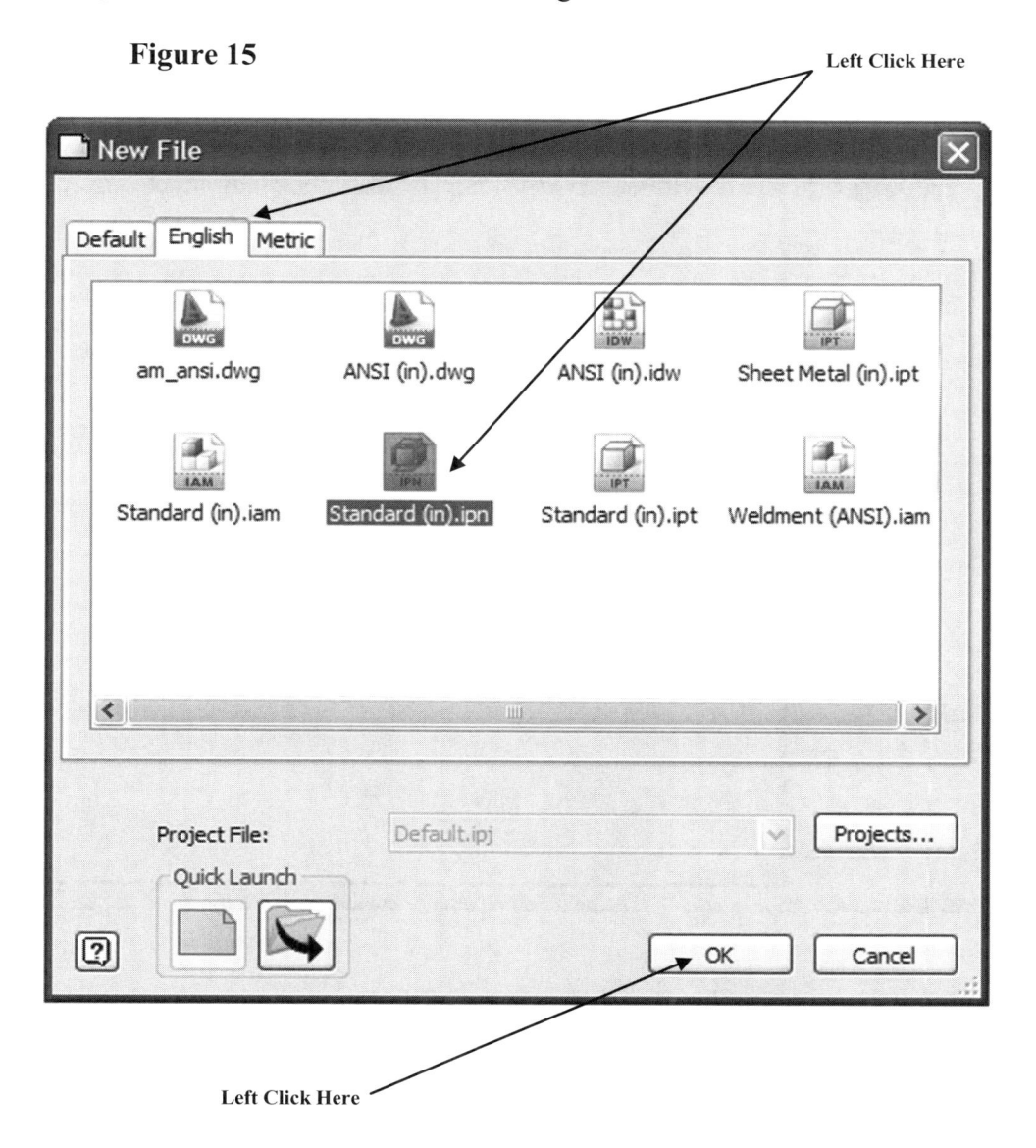

Chapter 8: Introduction to the Presentation Panel

24. The Presentation Panel will open as shown in Figure 16.

Figure 16

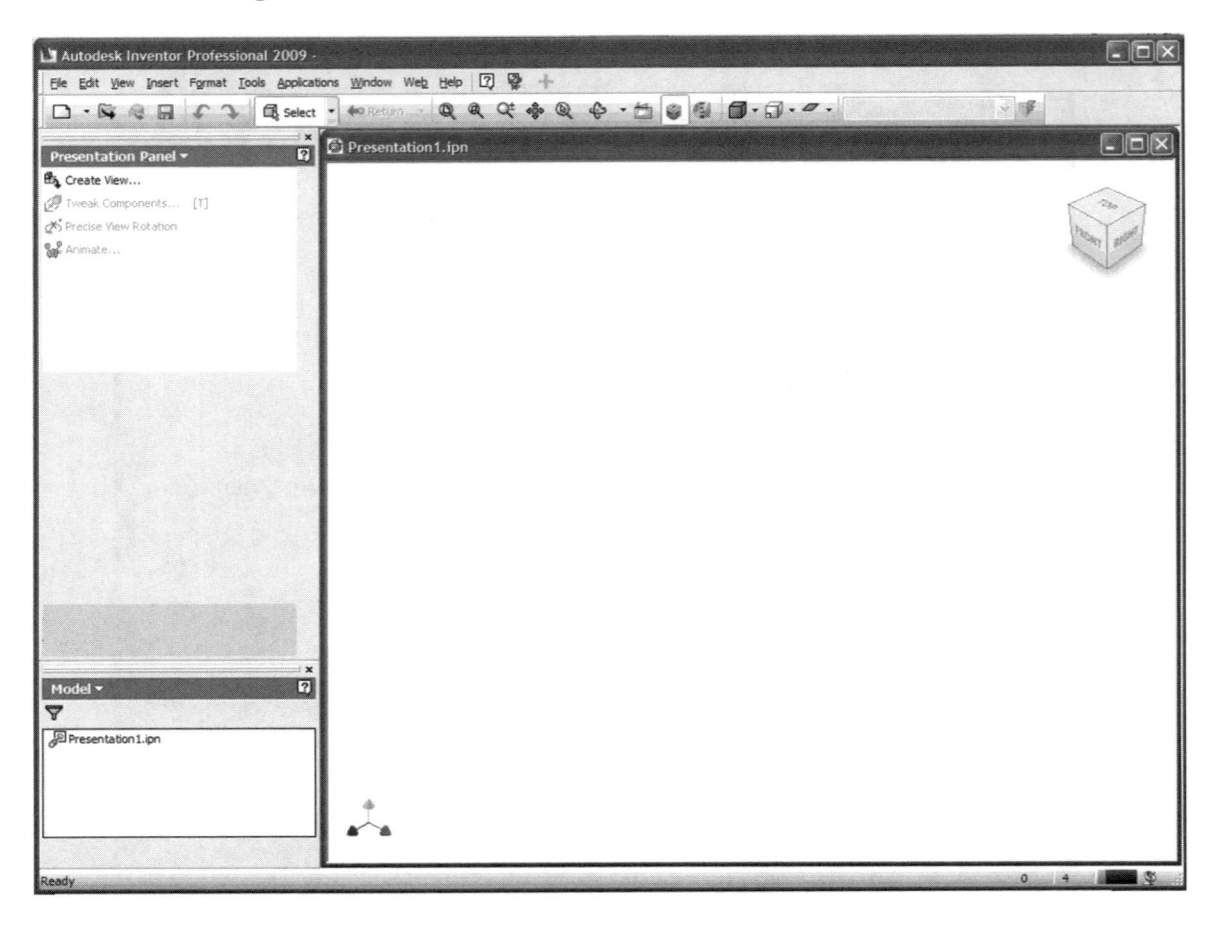

25. Move the cursor to the upper left portion of the screen and left click on **Create View** as shown in Figure 17.

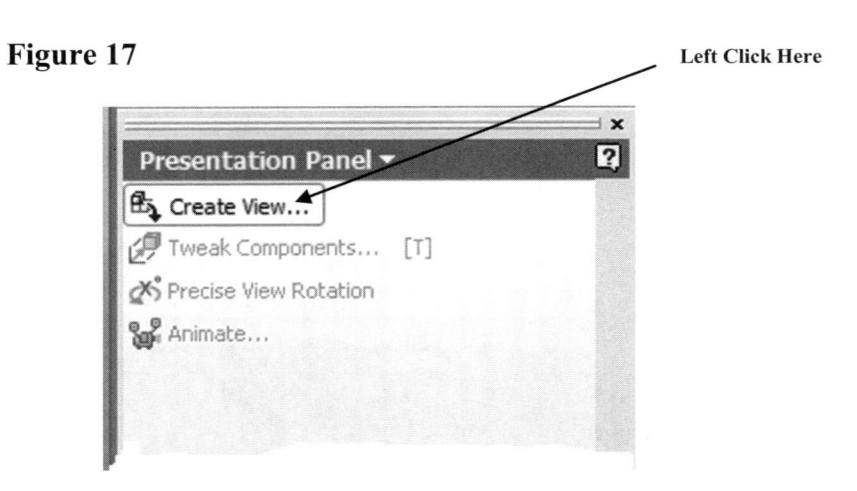

Figure 17 Left Click Here

442

Chapter 8: Introduction to the Presentation Panel

26. The Select Assembly dialog box will appear. If the current assembly file does not appear as shown it will need to be located. Left click on the "Explore" icon located at the upper right portion of the dialog box. Left click on **OK** as shown in Figure 18. If an error message appears, left click on OK.

Figure 18

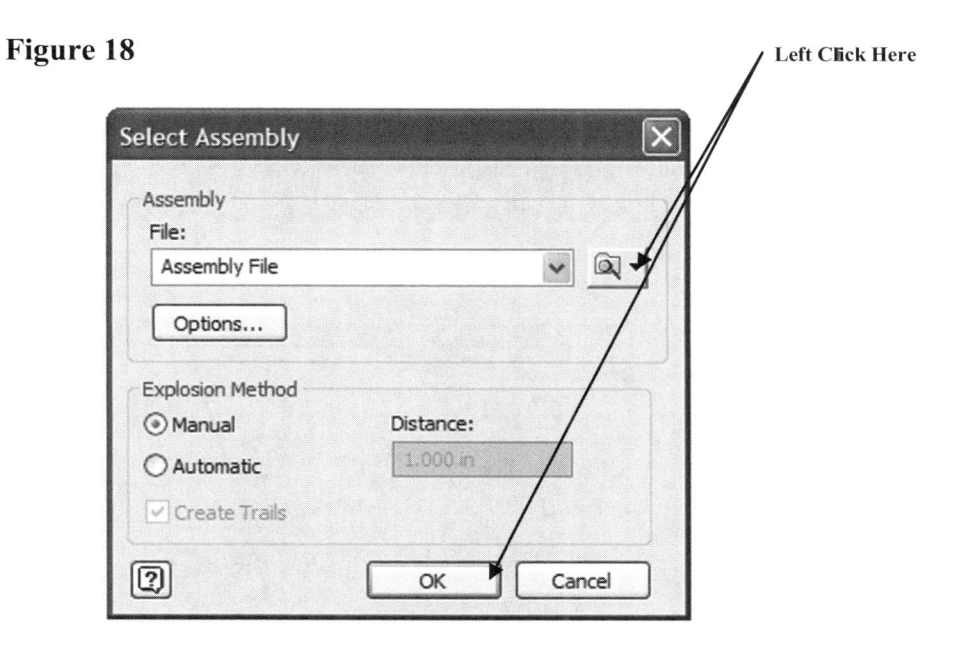

27. The Open dialog box will appear. Left click on **Chapter 8 Assmebly1.iam**. Left click on **Open** as shown in Figure 19.

Figure 19

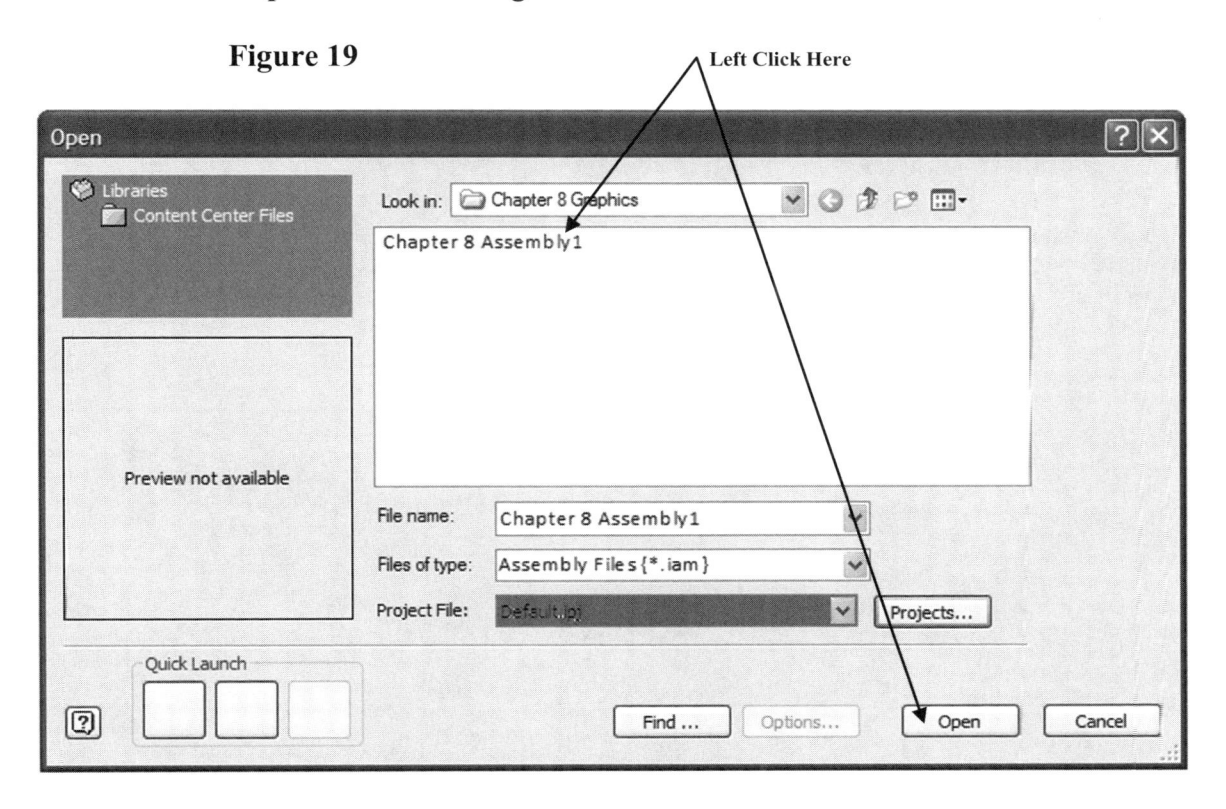

443

Chapter 8: Introduction to the Presentation Panel

28. *The Presentation Panel will only read assembly drawings.* Assembly drawings are imported into the Presentation Panel in order to create an .ipn file (Inventor Presentation).

29. The Select Assembly dialog box will open. Left click on **OK** as shown in Figure 20.

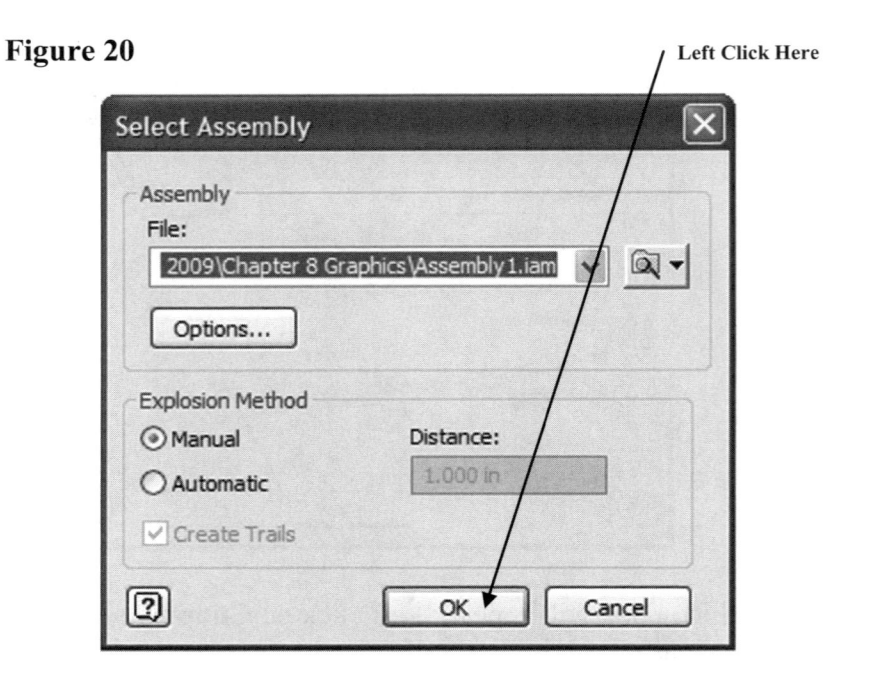

Figure 20

Left Click Here

444

Chapter 8: Introduction to the Presentation Panel

30. Your screen should look similar to Figure 21.

Figure 21

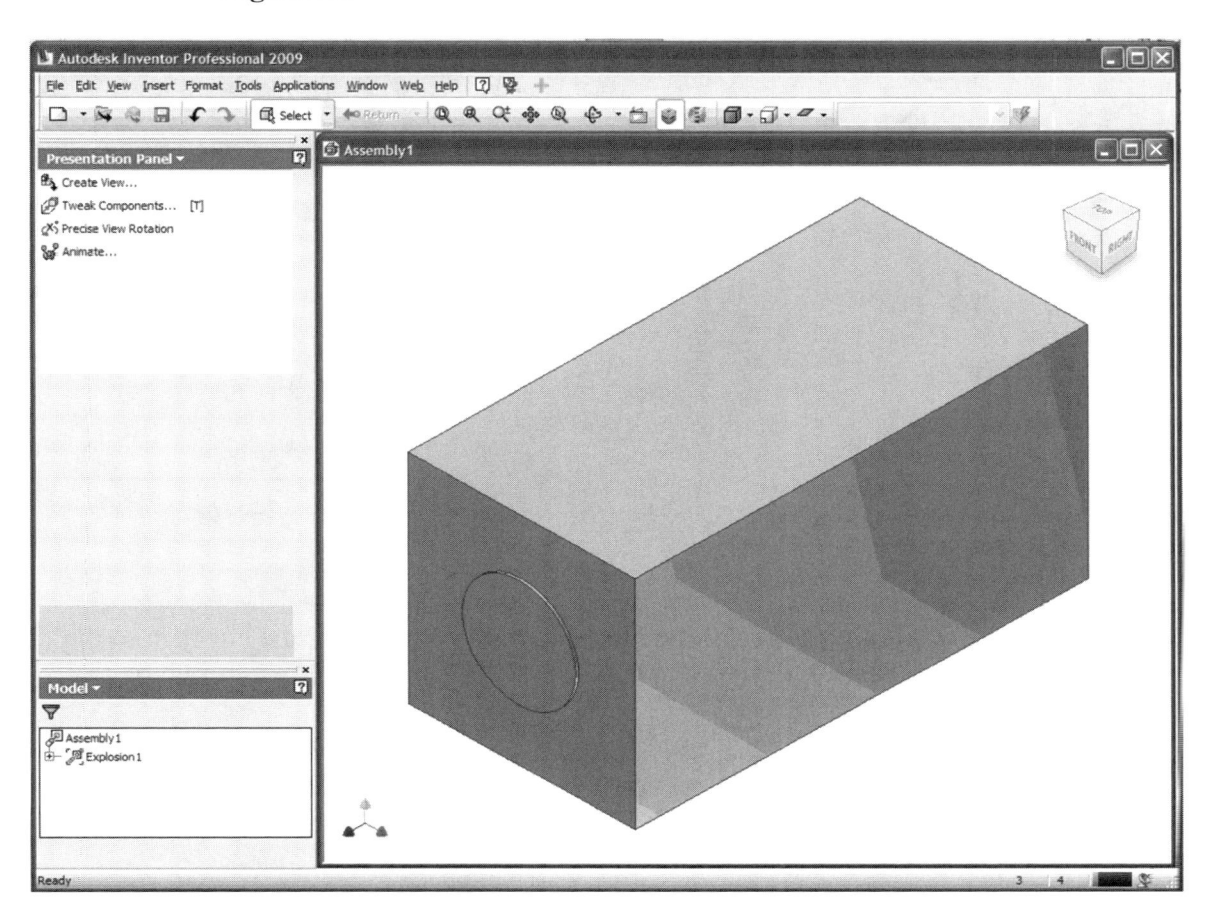

Chapter 8: Introduction to the Presentation Panel

31. Move the cursor to the upper left portion of the screen and left click on **Tweak Components**. Left click on the "Z" icon as shown in Figure 22.

Figure 22

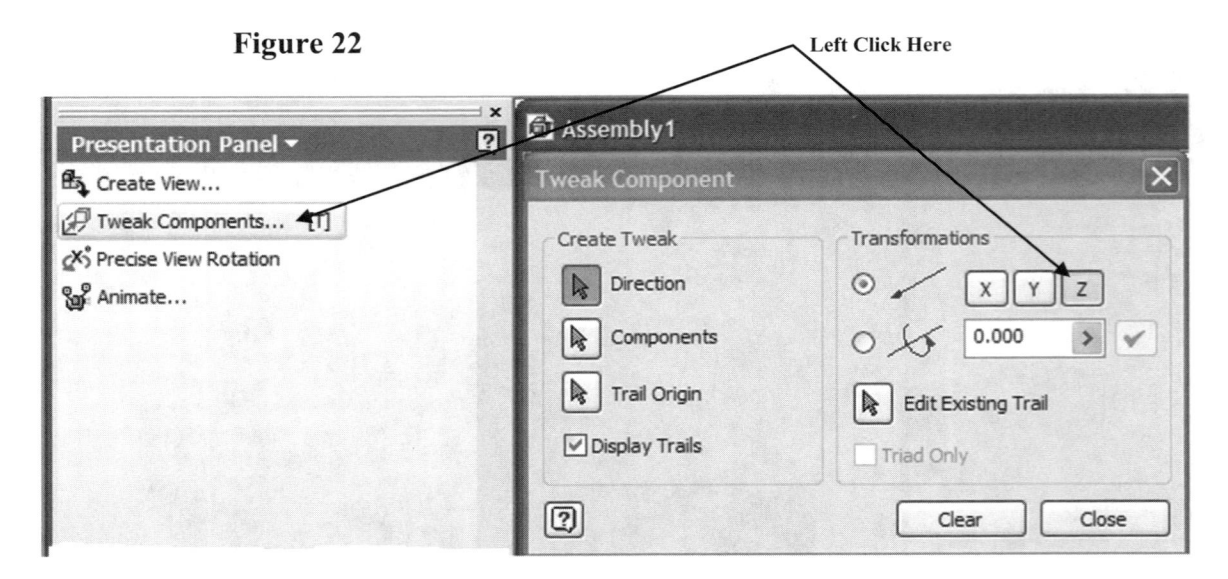

32. Move the cursor to the face of the pin. An origin symbol will be attached to the cursor. After the origin symbol appears, left click once as shown in Figure 23.

Figure 23

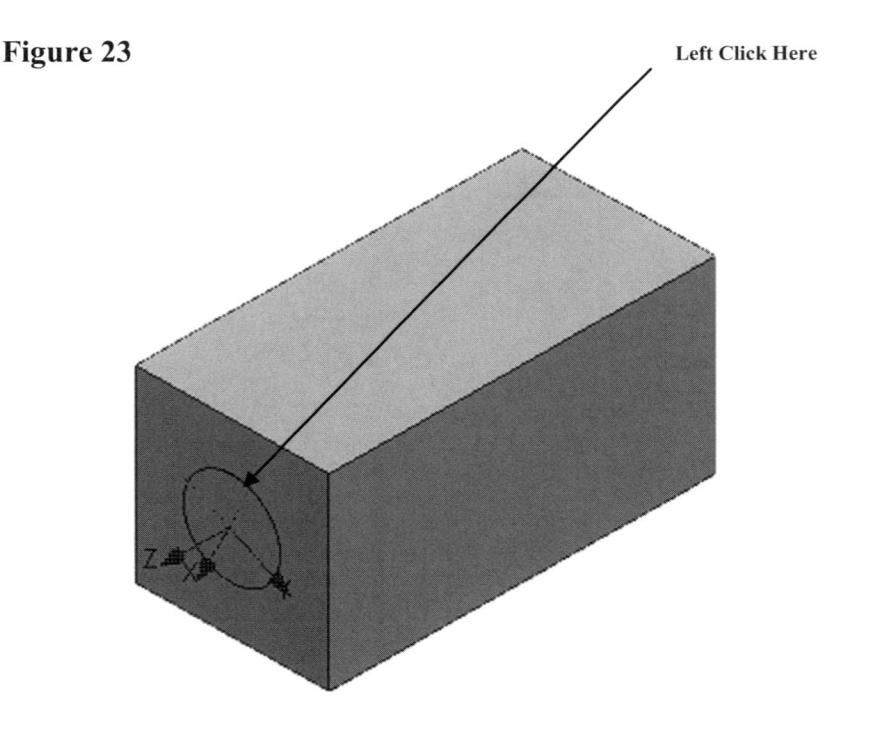

33. Move the cursor to the face of the pin. Left click (holding the left mouse button down) and drag the pin out of the block towards the lower left portion of the screen as shown in Figure 24. Notice the blue line coming out of the hole in the block. This is the "trail" that the pin will follow. This is the "Z" axis.

Figure 24

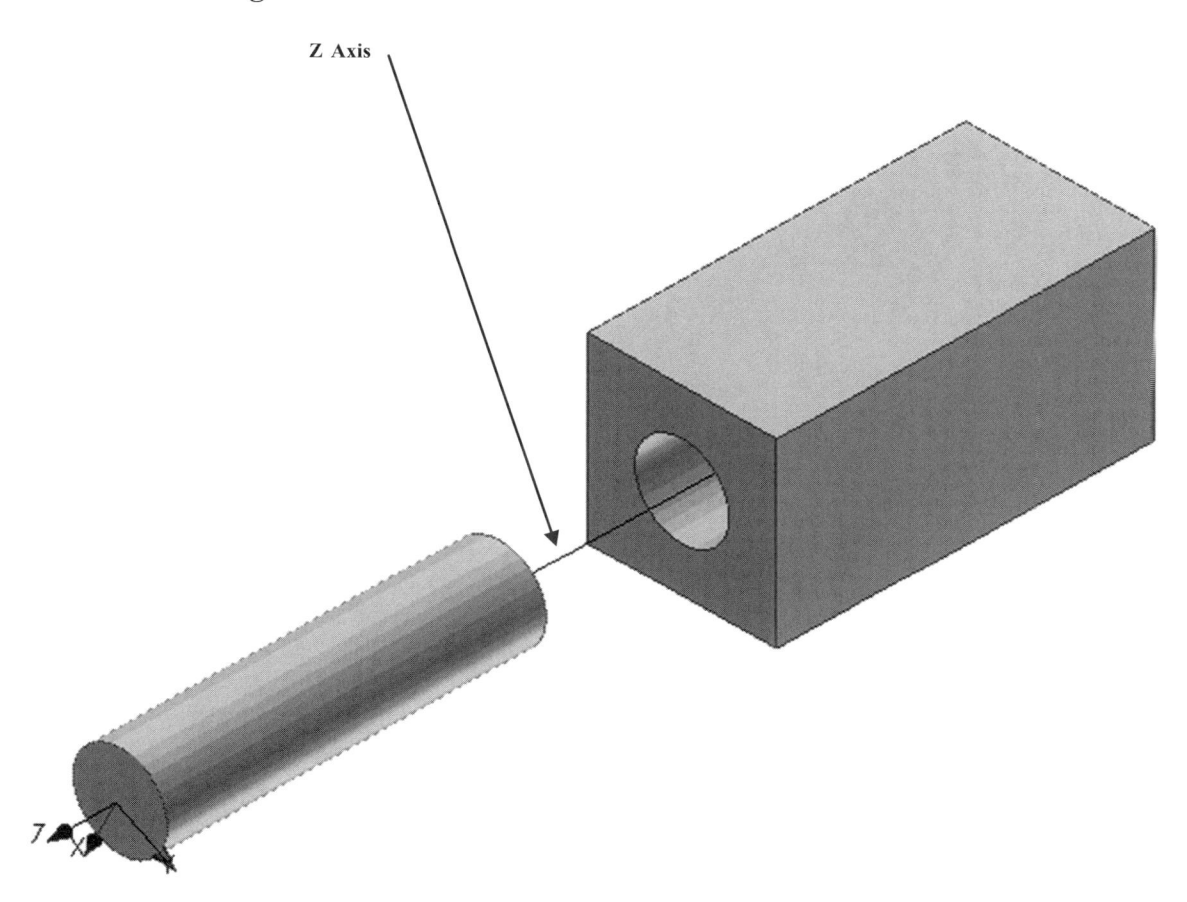

Chapter 8: Introduction to the Presentation Panel

34. Enter **3.000** for the distance that appears below the X, Y and Z icons. This is the distance the pin has traveled on the Z axis. The text can be highlighted so users can enter any numerical distance. Move the cursor to the Tweak Component dialog box and left click on **Y** as shown in Figure 25.

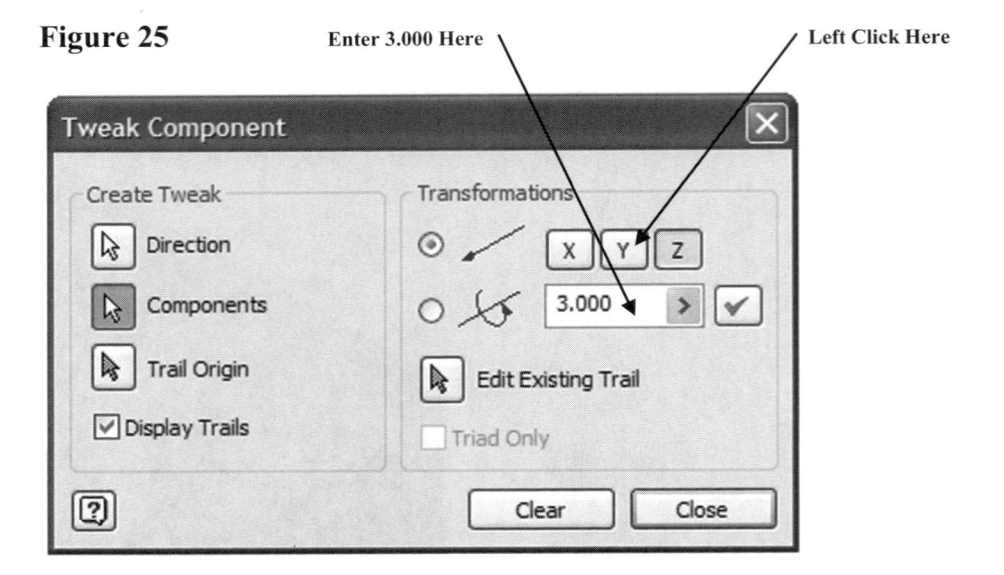

Figure 25

35. Move the cursor to the center of the pin. Left click (holding the left mouse button down) and drag the pin from the end of the "Z" trail towards the lower right portion of the screen as shown in Figure 26. Notice the direction change of the blue line. This is the "trail" that the pin will follow. This is the "Y" axis.

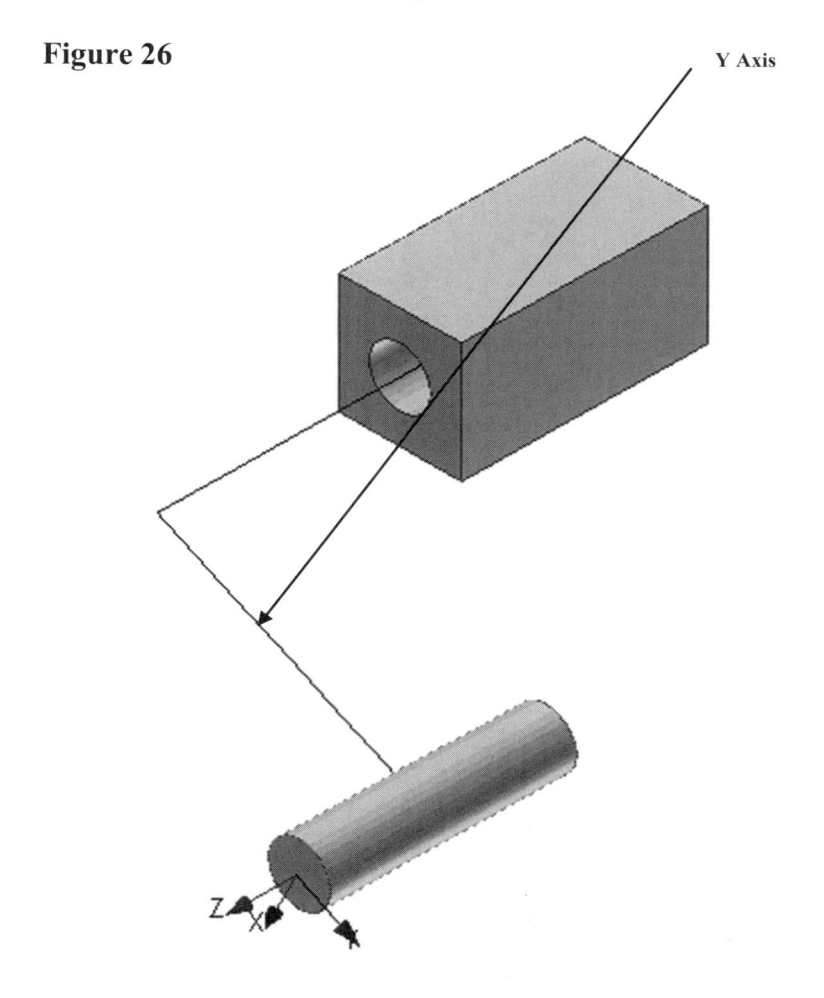

Figure 26

Chapter 8: Introduction to the Presentation Panel

36. Enter **-3.000** for the distance. Move the cursor to the Tweak Component dialog box and left click on **X** as shown in Figure 27.

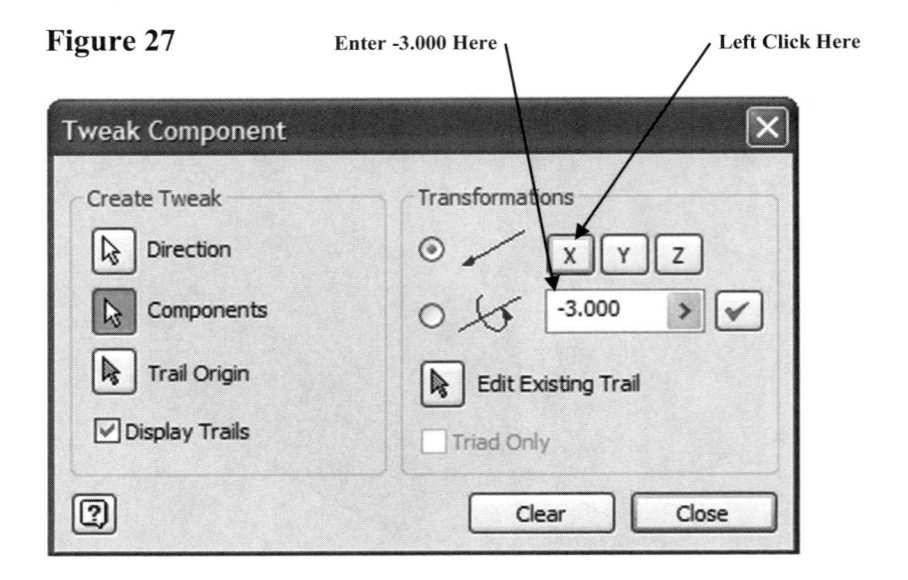

Figure 27 Enter -3.000 Here   Left Click Here

37. Move the cursor to the center of the pin. Left click (holding the left mouse button down) and drag the pin from the end of the "Y" trail towards the lower left portion of the screen as shown in Figure 28. Notice the direction change of the blue line. This is the "trail" that the pin will follow. This is the "X" axis.

Figure 28

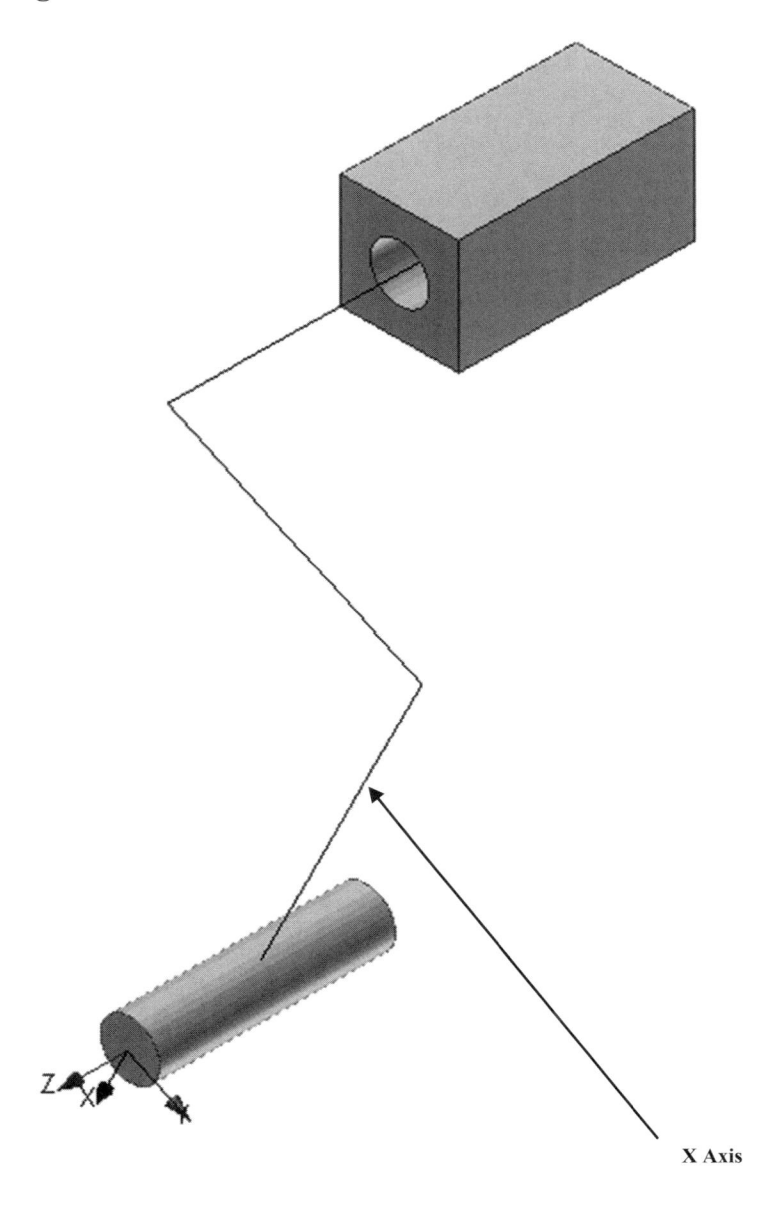

X Axis

Chapter 8: Introduction to the Presentation Panel

38. Enter **-2.000** for the Distance. Left click on **Clear** and then **Close** as shown in Figure 29.

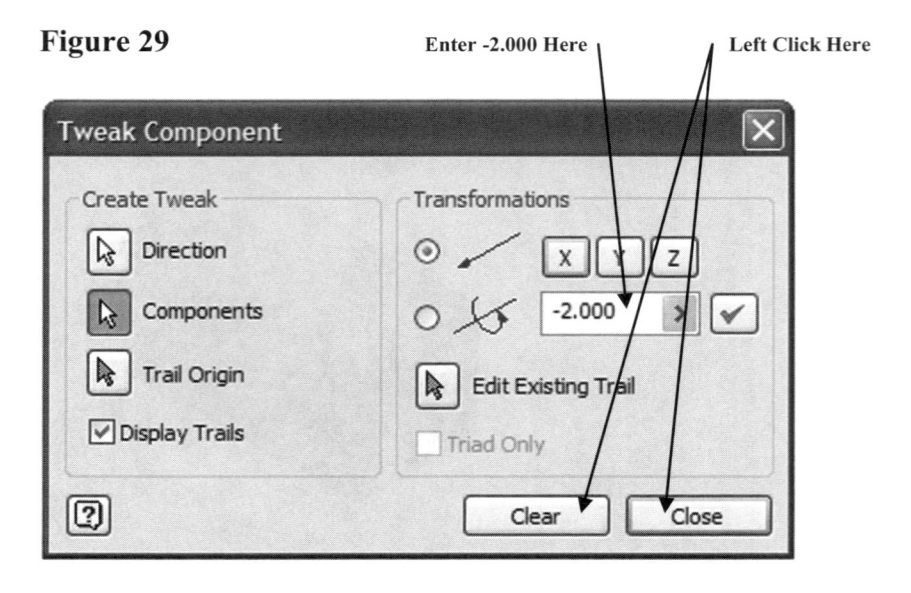

Figure 29

Enter -2.000 Here

Left Click Here

Left Click Here

39. The Tweak Component dialog box will close.

40. Move the cursor to the upper left portion of the screen and left click on **Animate**. The Animation dialog box will appear. Left click on "Play" as shown in Figure 30.

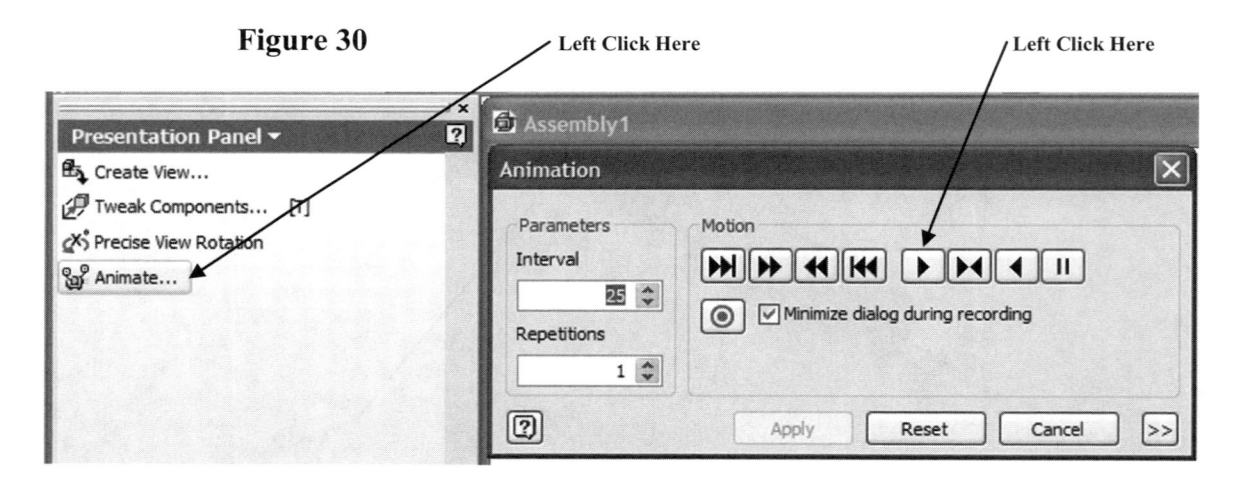

Figure 30

Left Click Here

Left Click Here

452

41. Inventor will animate the parts. The pin should follow the part trail back to the hole in the block. Your screen should look similar to Figure 31.

Figure 31

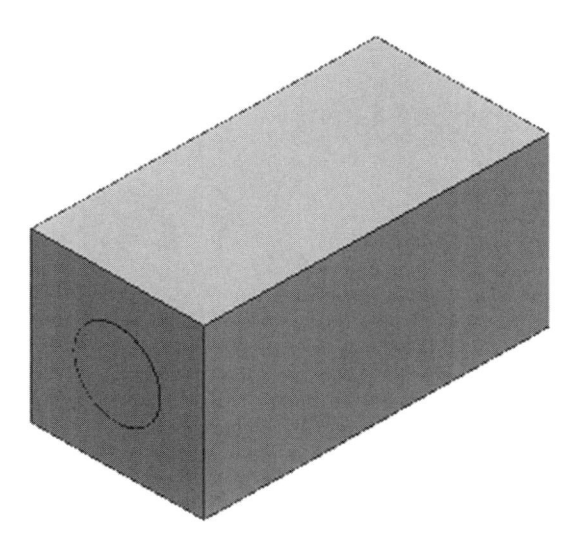

Chapter 8: Introduction to the Presentation Panel

42. Create the parts shown in Figure 32 and use them to design your own presentation.

Figure 32

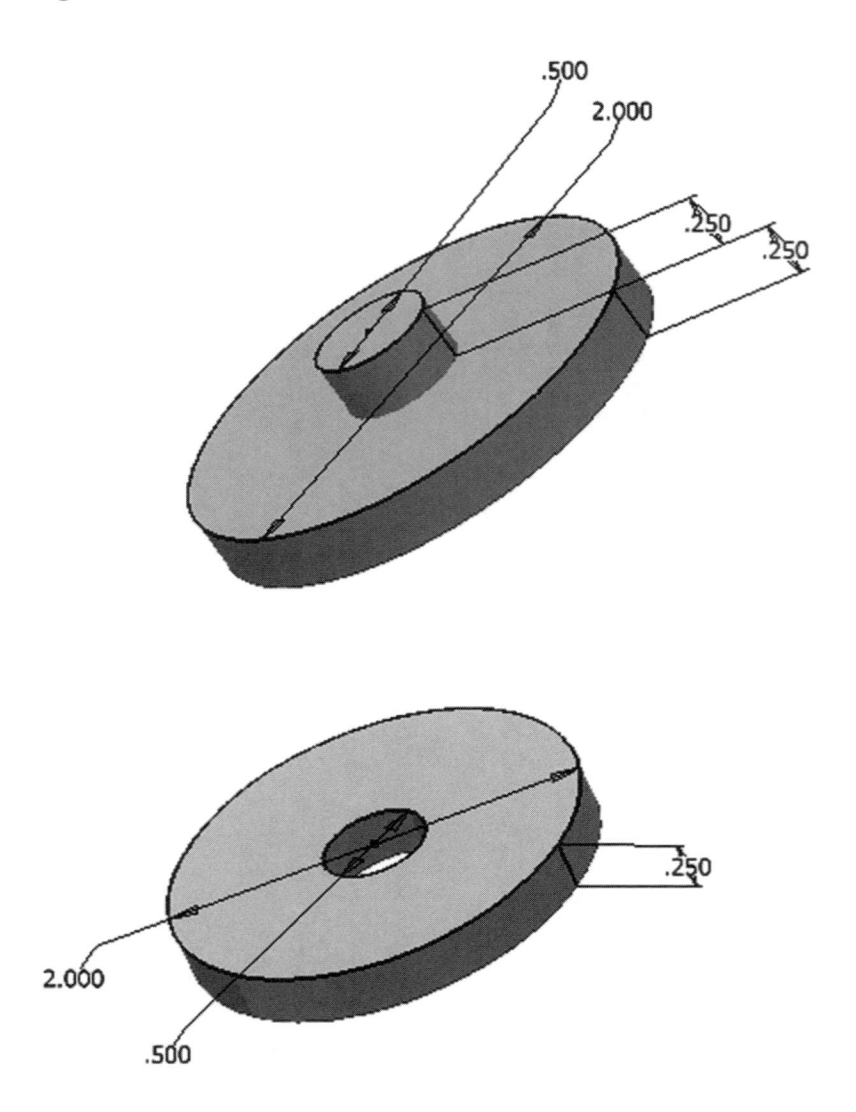

Chapter 9 Introduction to Advanced Commands

Objectives:
- Learn to use the Sweep command
- Learn to use the Loft command
- Learn to use the Work Plane command
- Learn to use the Coil command

Chapter 9 includes instruction on how to design the parts shown below.

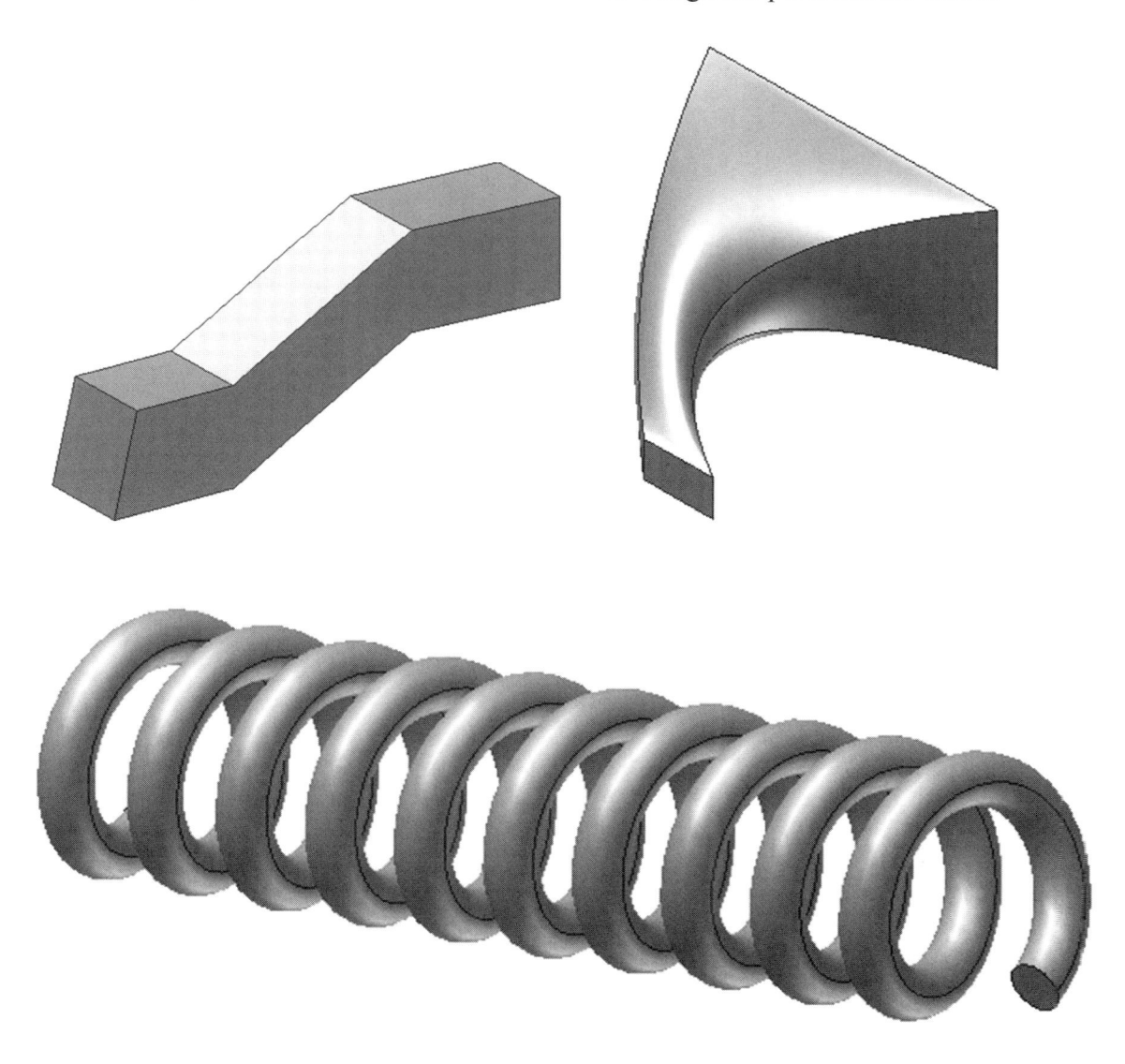

Chapter 9: Introduction to Advanced Commands

1. Start Inventor by referring to "Chapter 1 Getting Started".

2. After Inventor is running, begin a New Sketch.

3. Move the cursor to the upper left portion of the screen and left click on **Line** as shown in Figure 1.

Figure 1

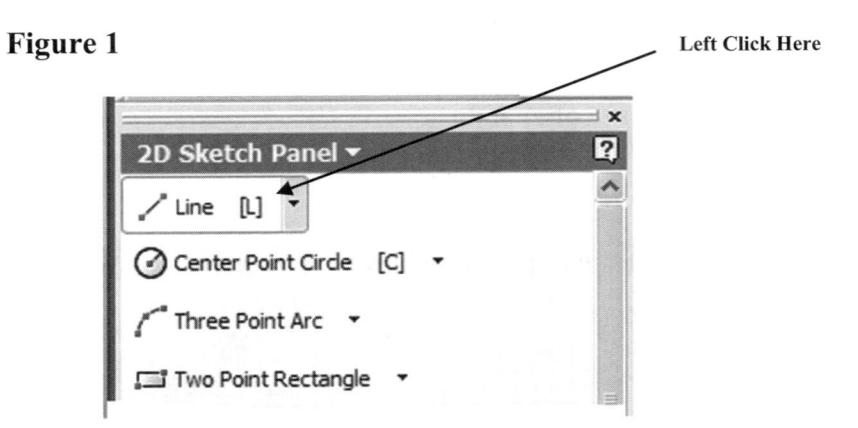

Left Click Here

4. Move the cursor to the center of the screen and left click once. Ensure that the yellow dot appears on the intersection of the darkened grid lines as shown in Figure 2.

Figure 2

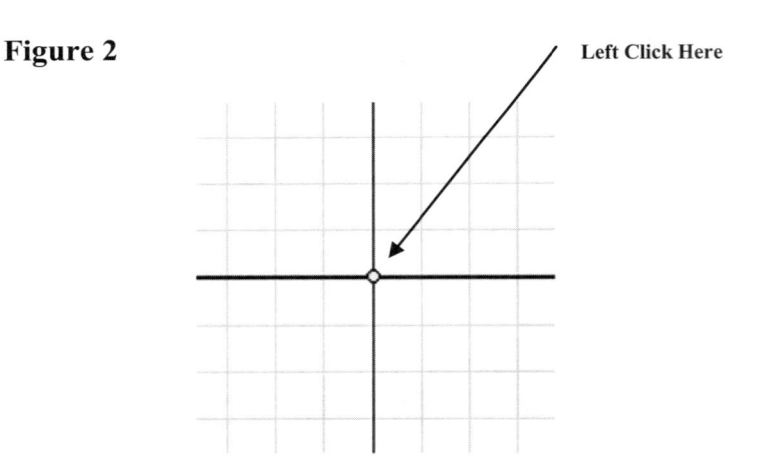

Left Click Here

456

Chapter 9: Introduction to Advanced Commands

5. Move the cursor to the left portion of the screen and left click once as shown in Figure 3. Right click anywhere on the screen. A pop up menu will appear. Left click on **Done**.

Figure 3

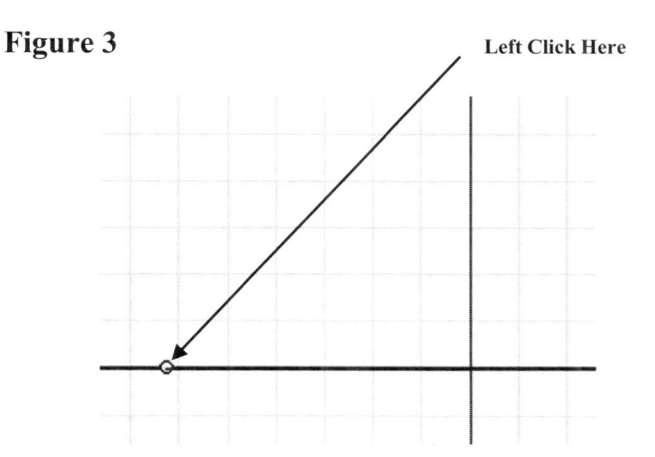

Left Click Here

6. Move the cursor to the upper left portion of the screen and left click on **Two Point Rectangle** as shown in Figure 4.

Figure 4

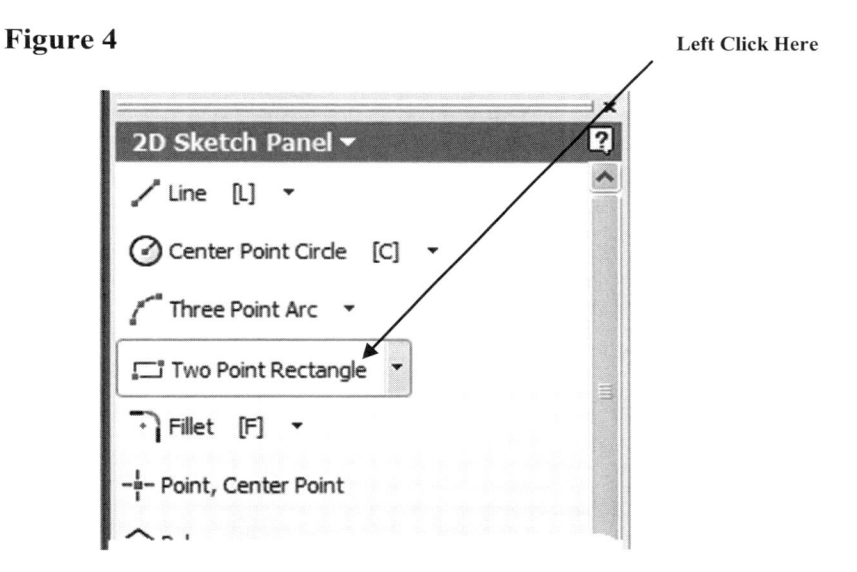

Left Click Here

457

Chapter 9: Introduction to Advanced Commands

7. Move the cursor to the center of the grid and left click once as shown in Figure 5. Move the cursor to the upper right portion of the screen and left click once. Complete the sketch shown in Figure 5. After the sketch has been dimensioned, delete the horizontal line that was drawn first. Right click anywhere on the screen. A pop up menu will appear. Left click on **Done [Esc]**.

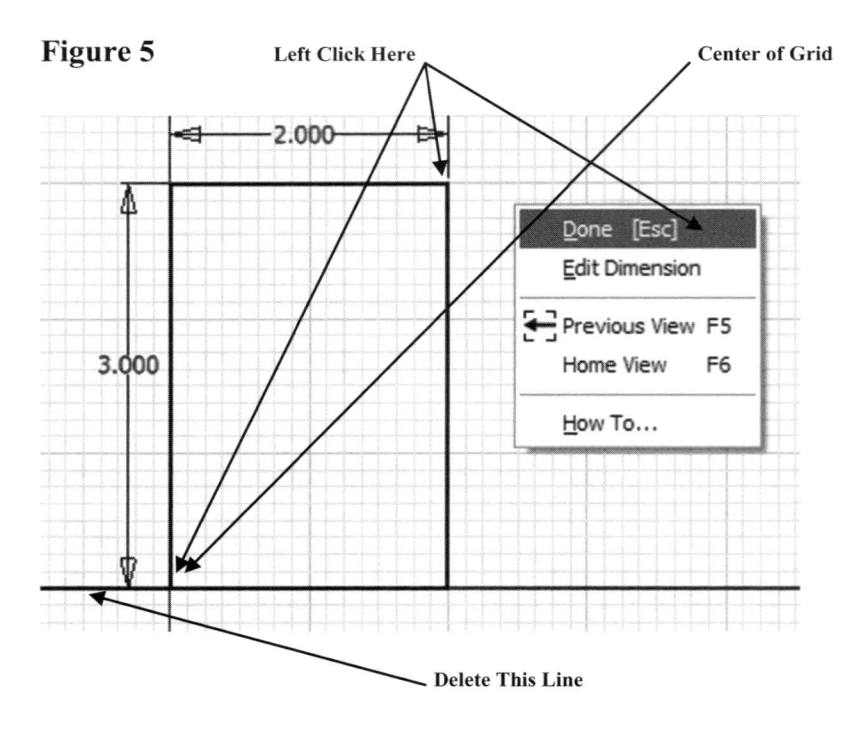

Figure 5

Chapter 9: Introduction to Advanced Commands

8. Right click anywhere on the screen. A pop up menu will appear. Left click **Finish Sketch** as shown in Figure 6.

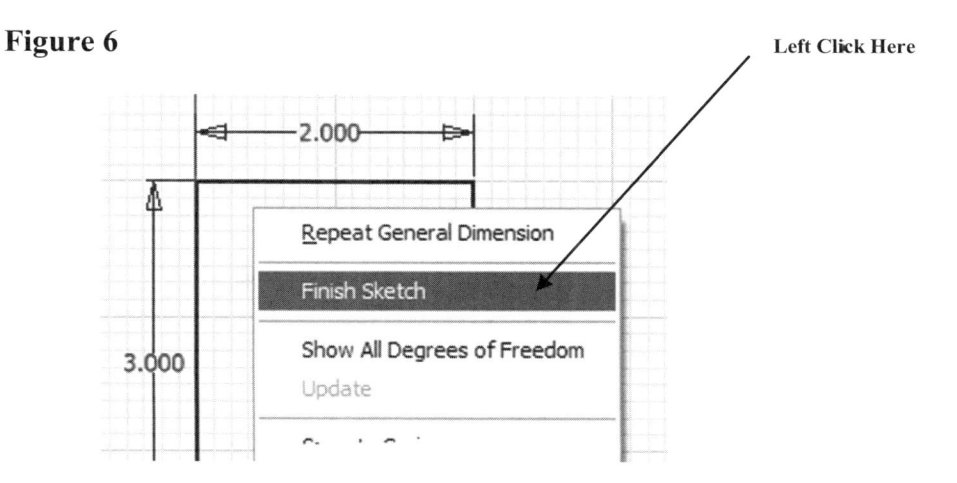

Figure 6

9. Right click anywhere on the screen. A pop up menu will appear. Left click on **Isometric/Home View** as shown in Figure 7.

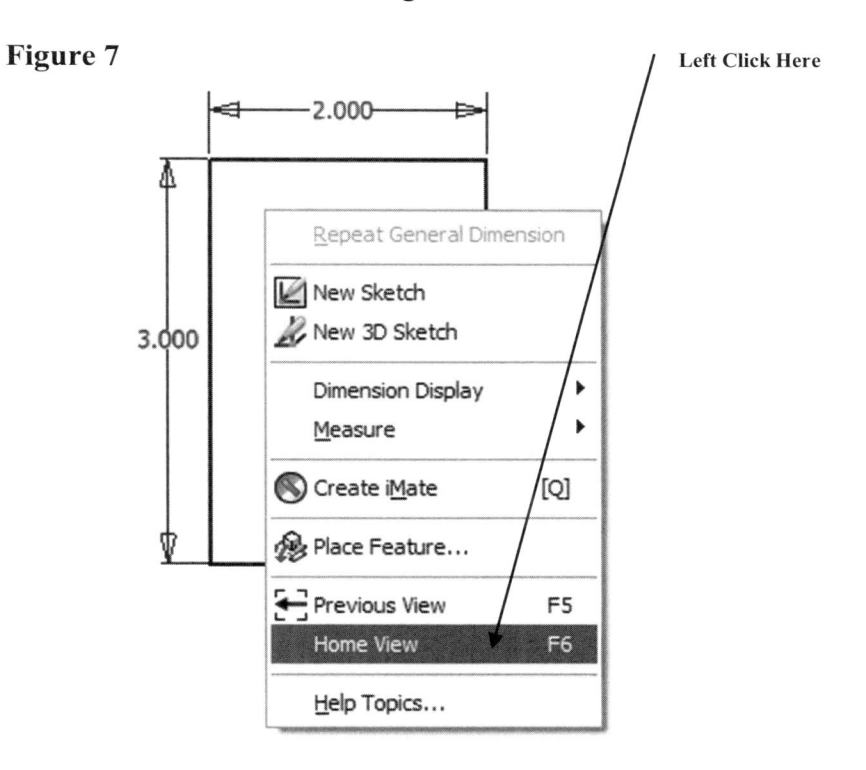

Figure 7

459

Chapter 9: Introduction to Advanced Commands

10. Your screen should look similar to Figure 8.

Figure 8

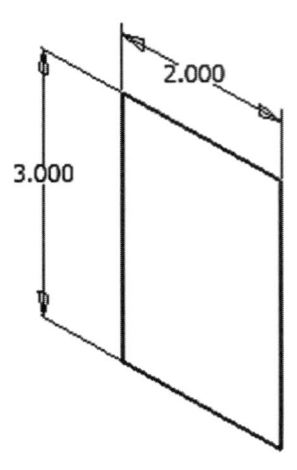

11. Move the cursor over the text "YZ Plane" causing a red box to appear. Right click once. A pop up menu will appear. Left click on **New Sketch** as shown in Figure 9.

Figure 9

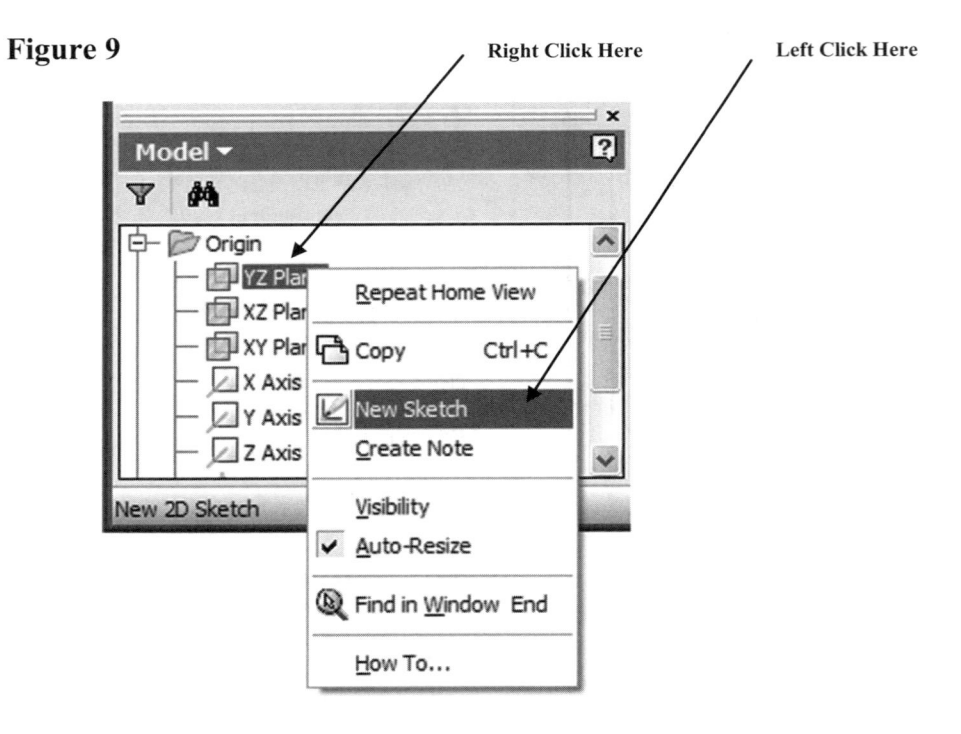

Right Click Here   Left Click Here

460

Chapter 9: Introduction to Advanced Commands

12. Your screen should look similar to Figure 10.

Figure 10

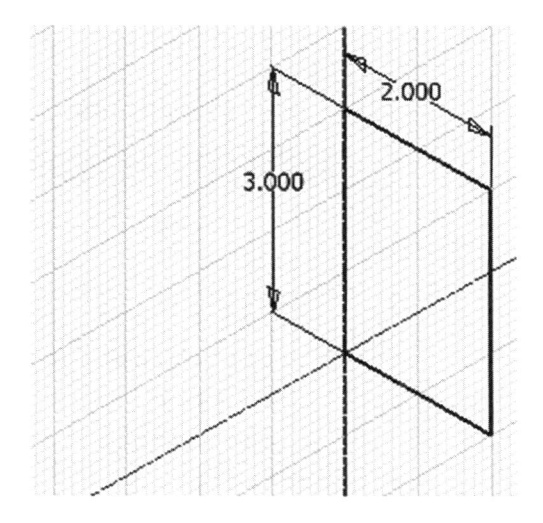

13. Complete the following sketch. The angle of the lines can be estimated. The sketch lines must intersect with the corner of the 2 inch by 3 inch box as shown in Figure 11. Remember to use the **Aligned** dimension function (while the dimension is attached to the cursor right click causing a pop up menu to appear then left click on **Aligned**). Press the **Esc** key on the keyboard after completing the dimensioning.

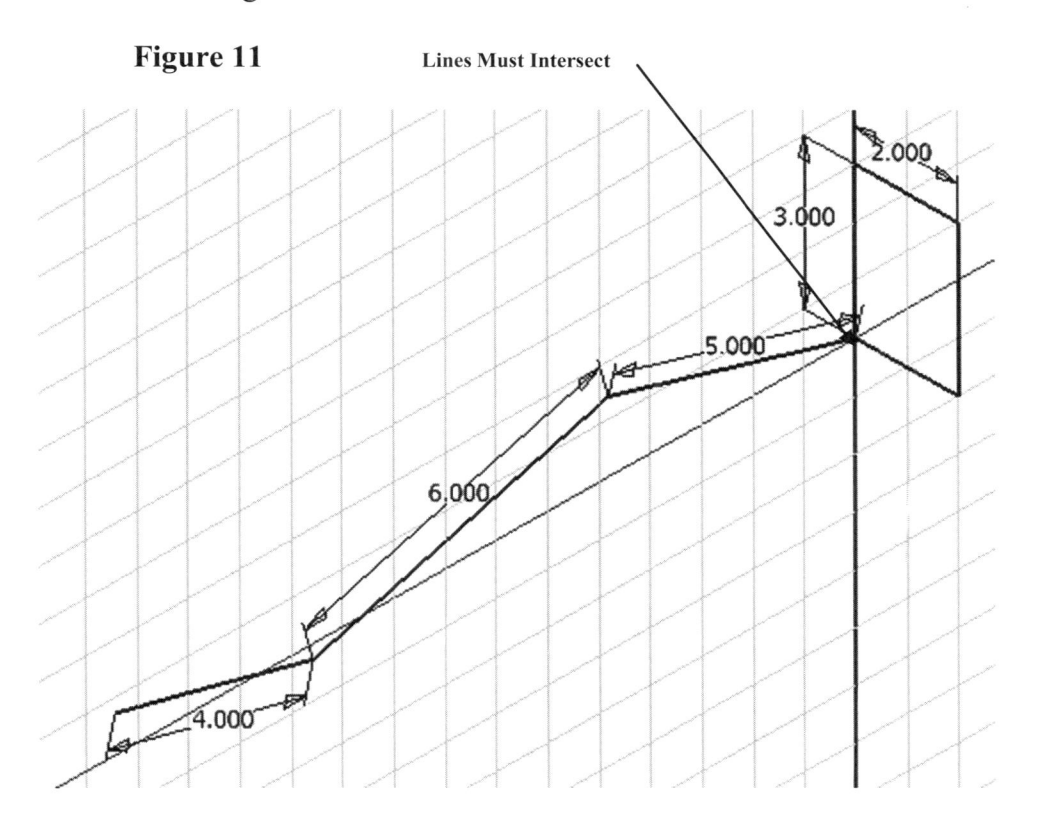

Figure 11   Lines Must Intersect

461

Chapter 9: Introduction to Advanced Commands

14. Right click anywhere on the screen. A pop up menu will appear. Left click on **Finish Sketch** as shown in Figure 12.

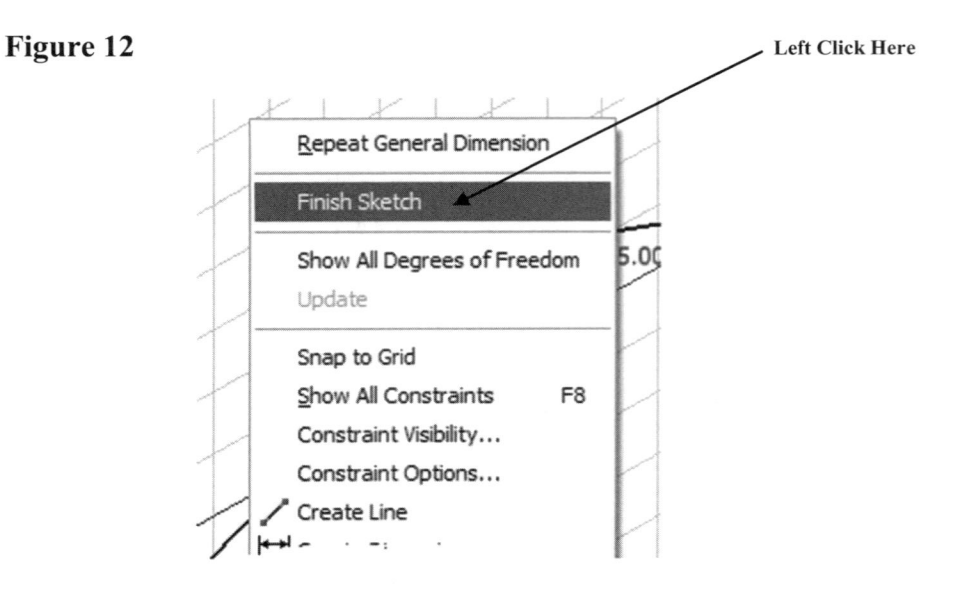

Figure 12

15. Your screen should look similar to Figure 13.

Figure 13

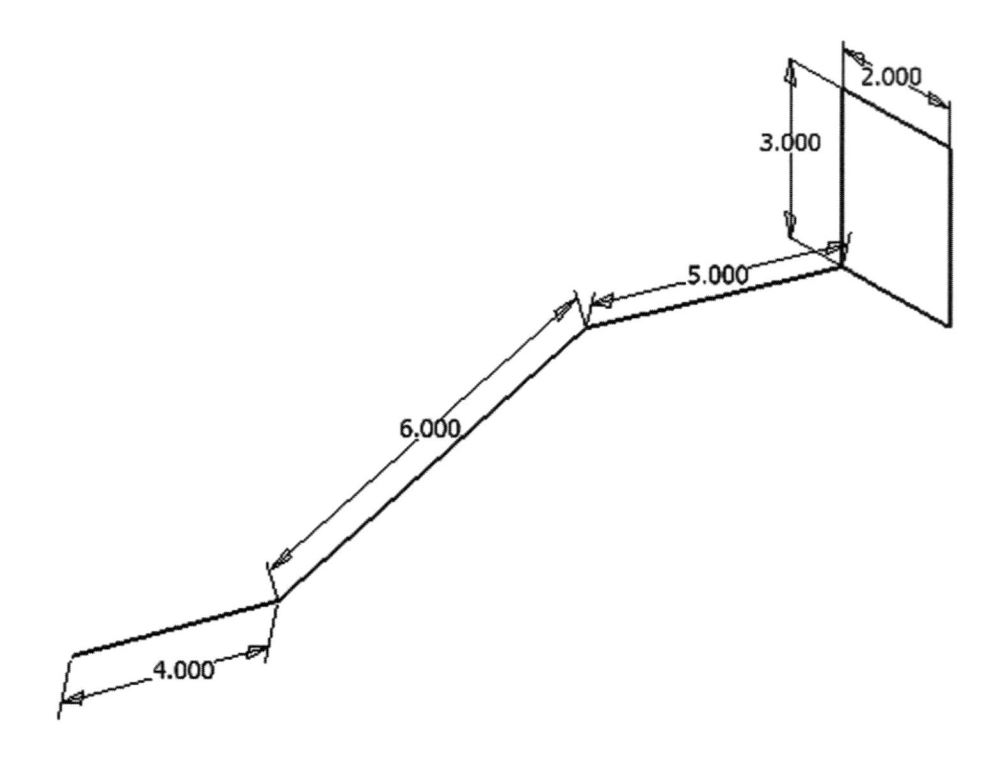

Chapter 9: Introduction to Advanced Commands

16. Move the cursor to the upper left portion of the screen and left click on **Sweep**. Move the cursor over the sweep line causing it to turn red and left click once as shown in Figure 14.

Figure 14

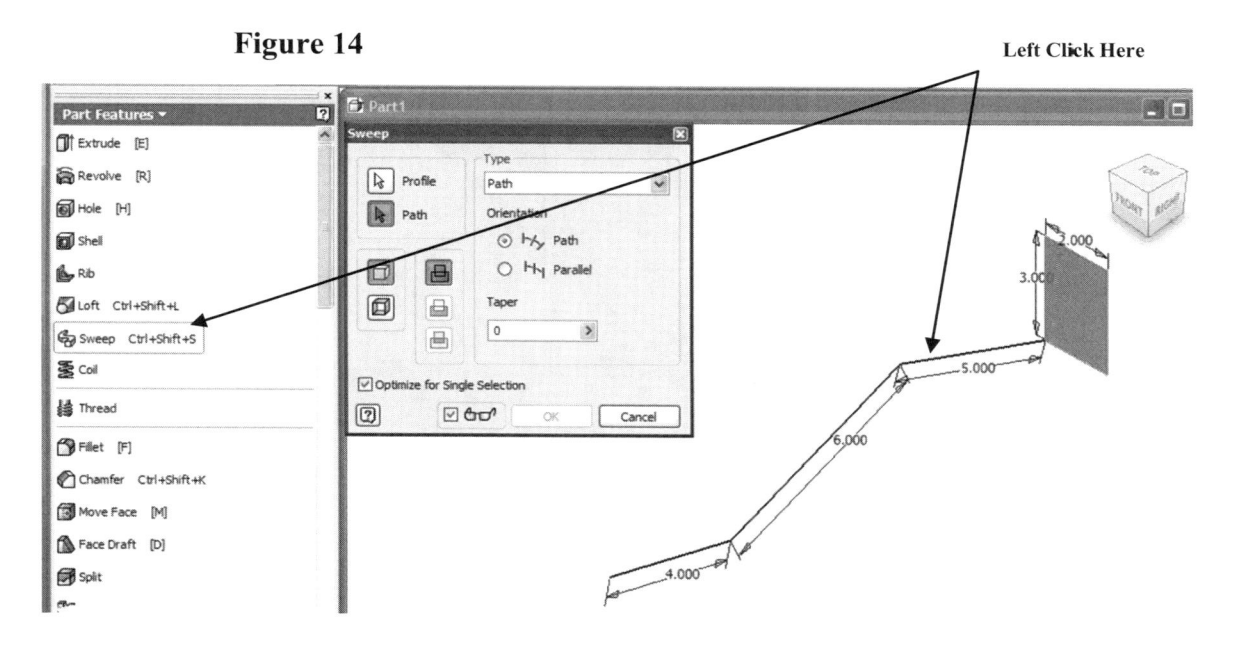

Chapter 9: Introduction to Advanced Commands

17. A preview of the sweep will appear as shown in Figure 15.

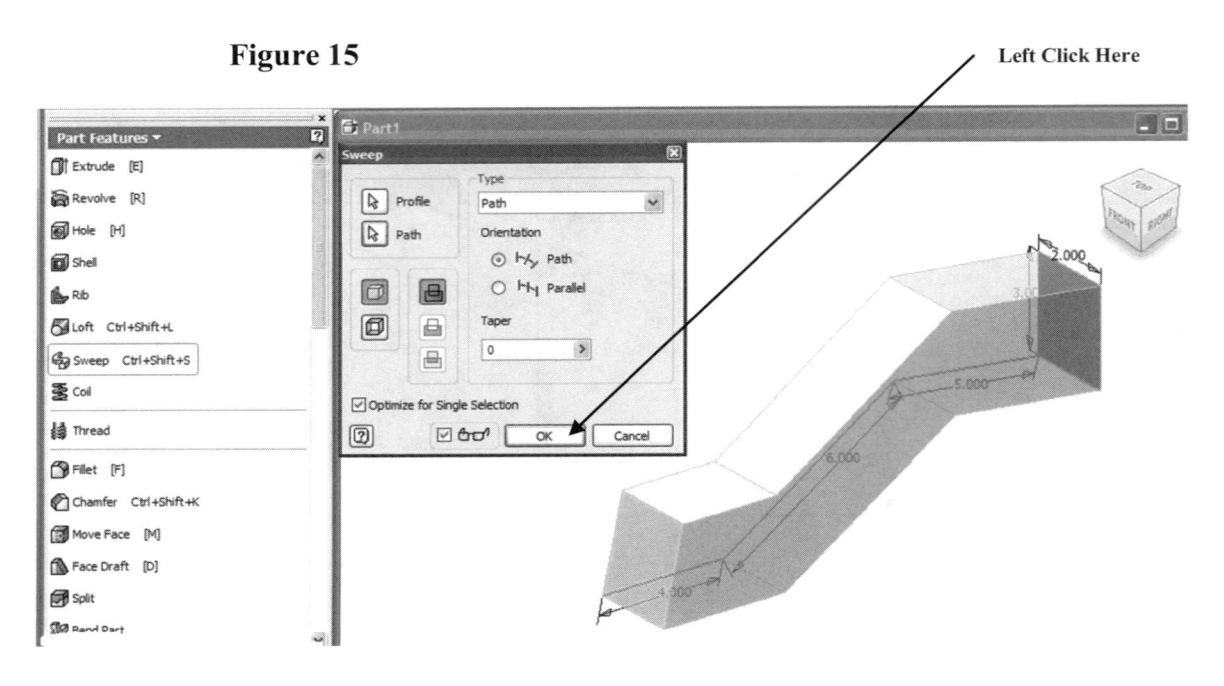

Figure 15

18. Left click on **OK** as shown in Figure 15.

19. Your screen should look similar to Figure 16.

Figure 16

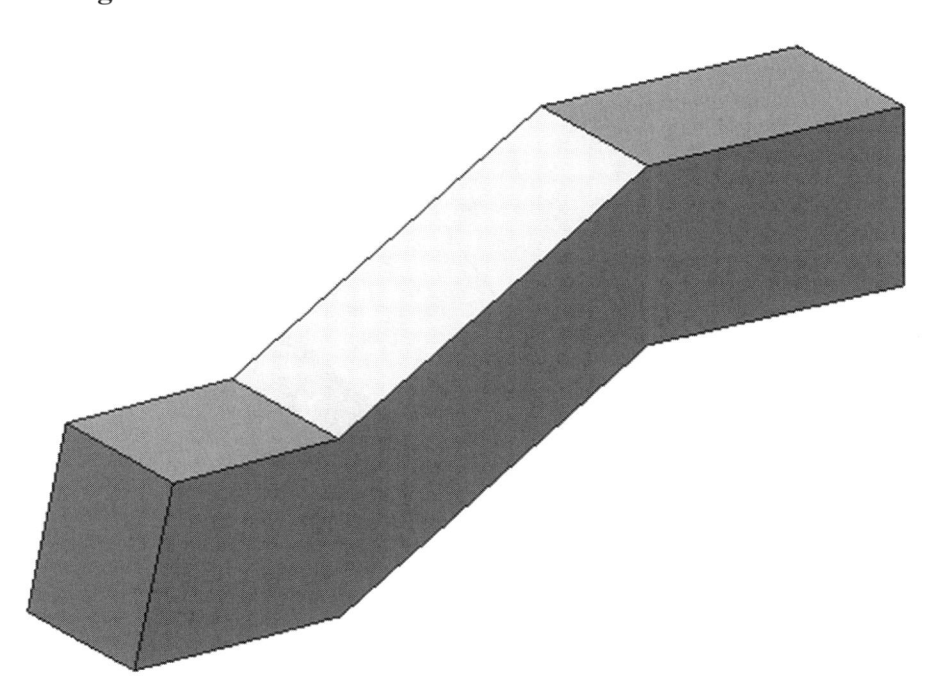

20. Move the cursor to the upper left portion of the screen and left click on **Shell** as shown in Figure 17.

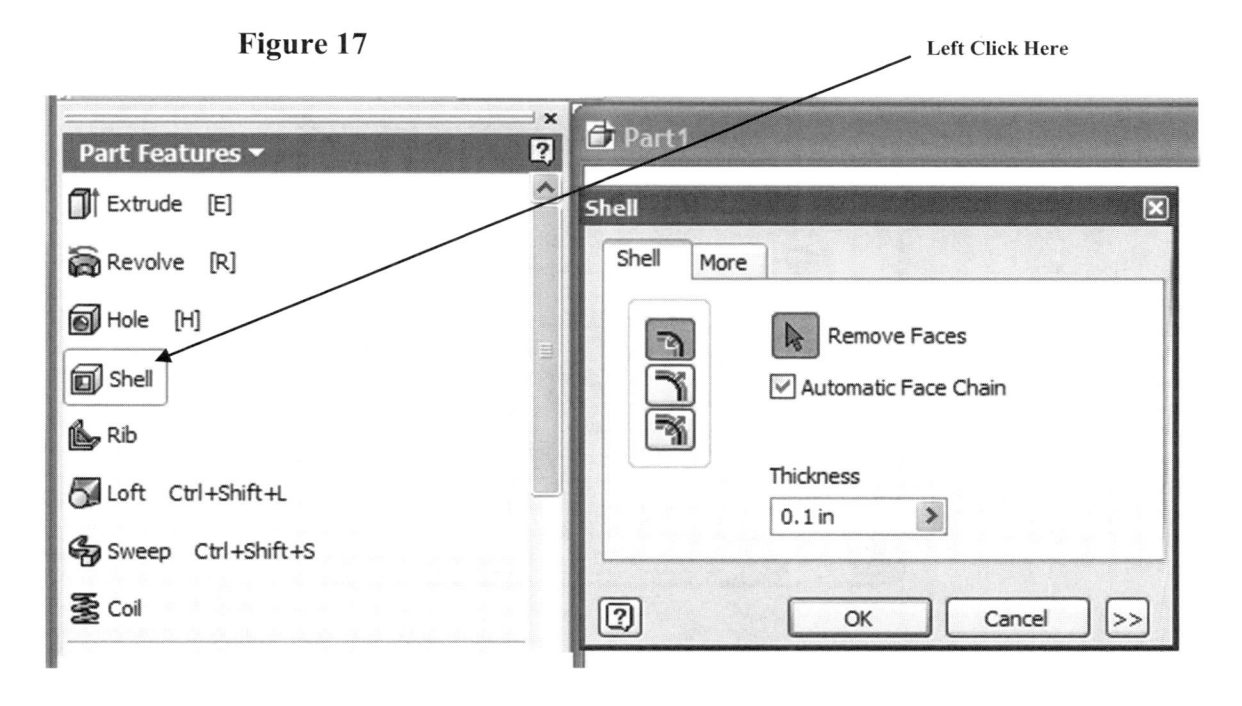

Figure 17

Chapter 9: Introduction to Advanced Commands

21. Move the cursor to the left side face and left click once. Using the **Rotate** command, rotate the part around to gain access to the right side face and left click once as shown in Figure 18.

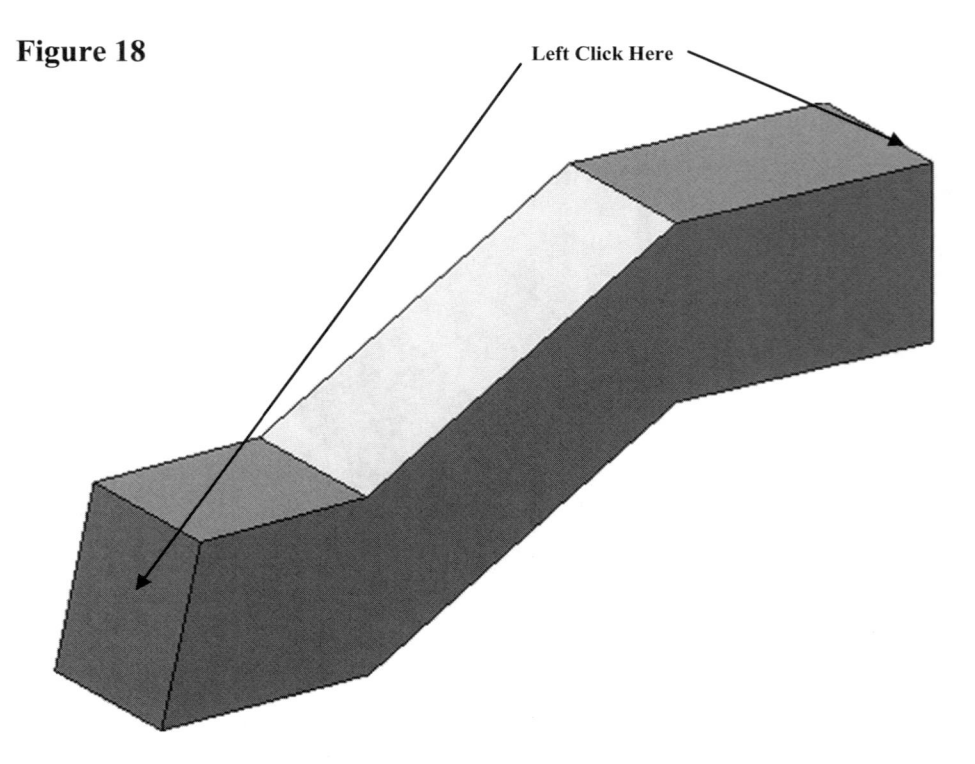

Figure 18

Left Click Here

22. Left click on **OK** as shown in Figure 19.

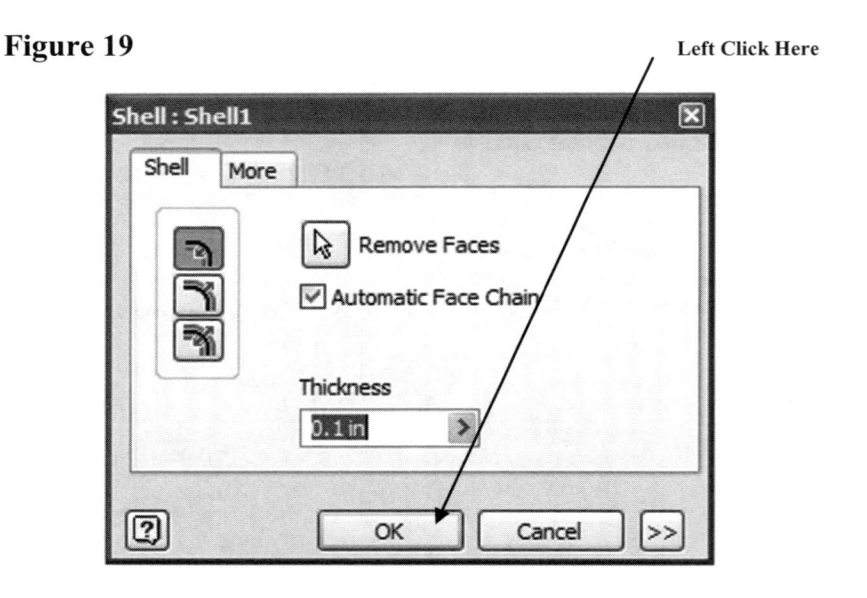

Figure 19

Left Click Here

466

Chapter 9: Introduction to Advanced Commands

23. Use the Rotate command to access the ends of the model. The model should be open on both ends similar to a piece of rectangular tubing. Your screen should look similar to Figure 20.

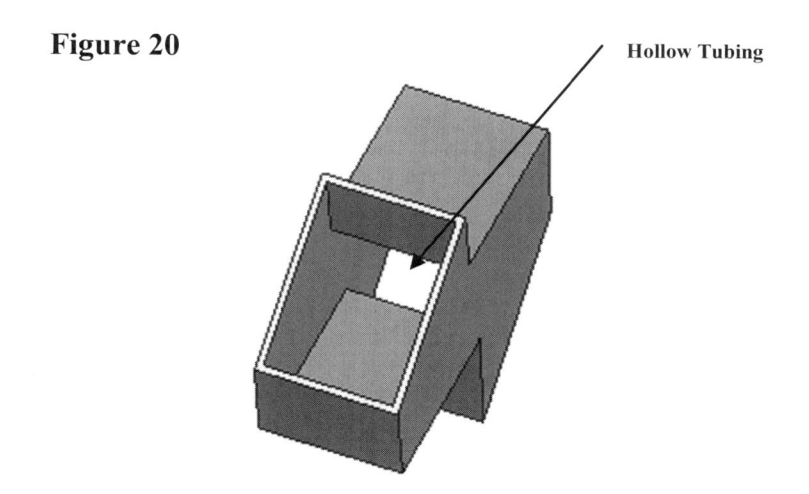

Figure 20

Hollow Tubing

24. Begin a new drawing as shown in Figure 21.

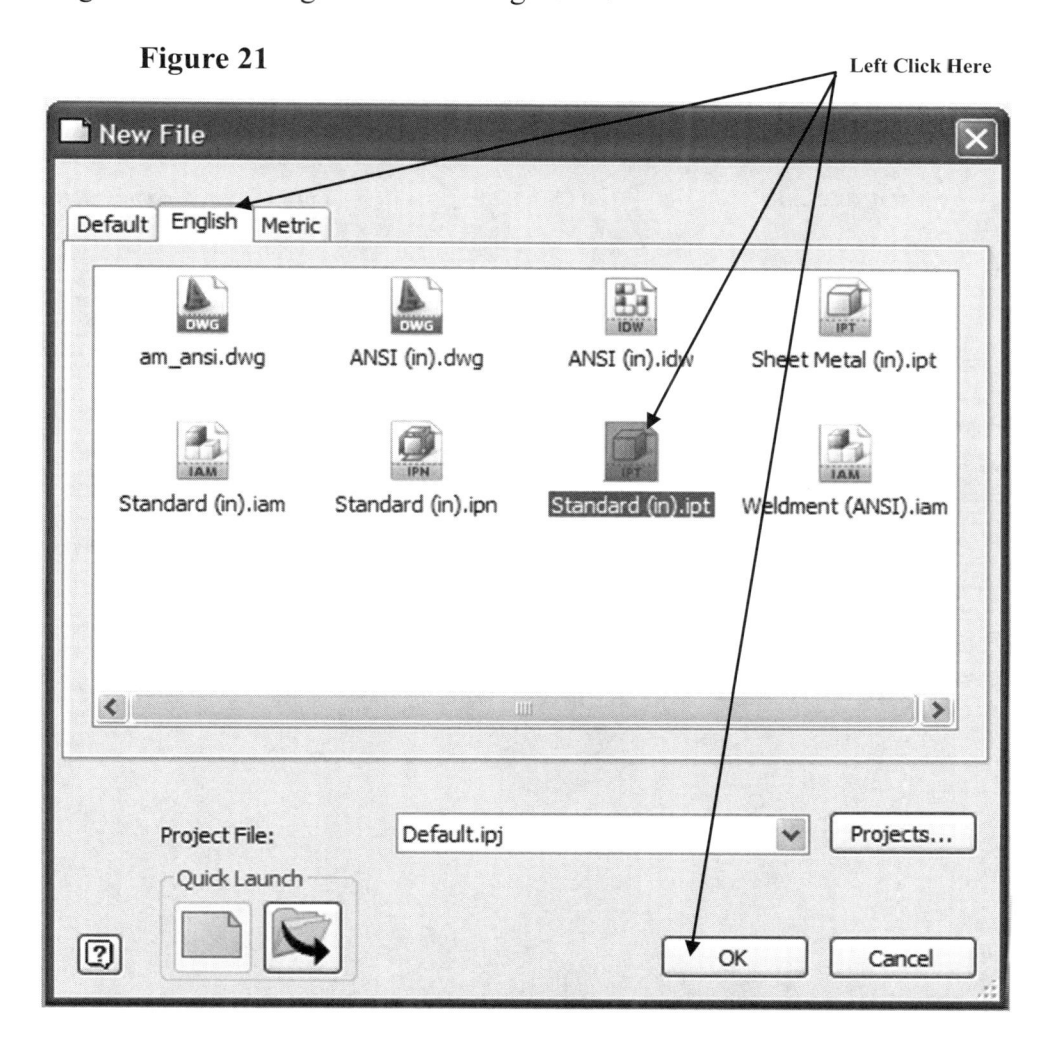

Figure 21

Left Click Here

Chapter 9: Introduction to Advanced Commands

25. Complete the sketch as shown in Figure 22. Right click anywhere on the screen. A pop up menu will appear. Left click on **Done [Esc]** as shown in Figure 22.

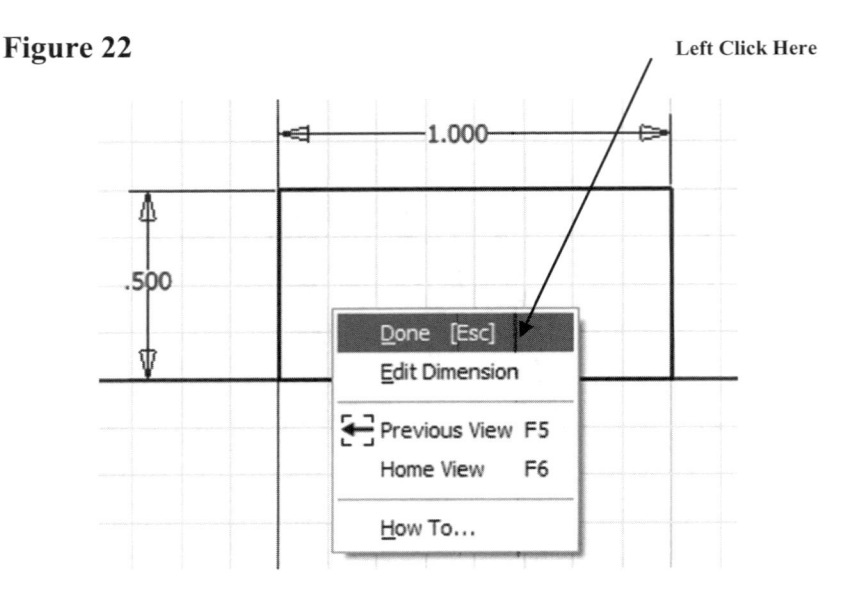

Figure 22

26. Right click anywhere on the screen. A pop up menu will appear. Left click on **Finish Sketch** as shown in Figure 23.

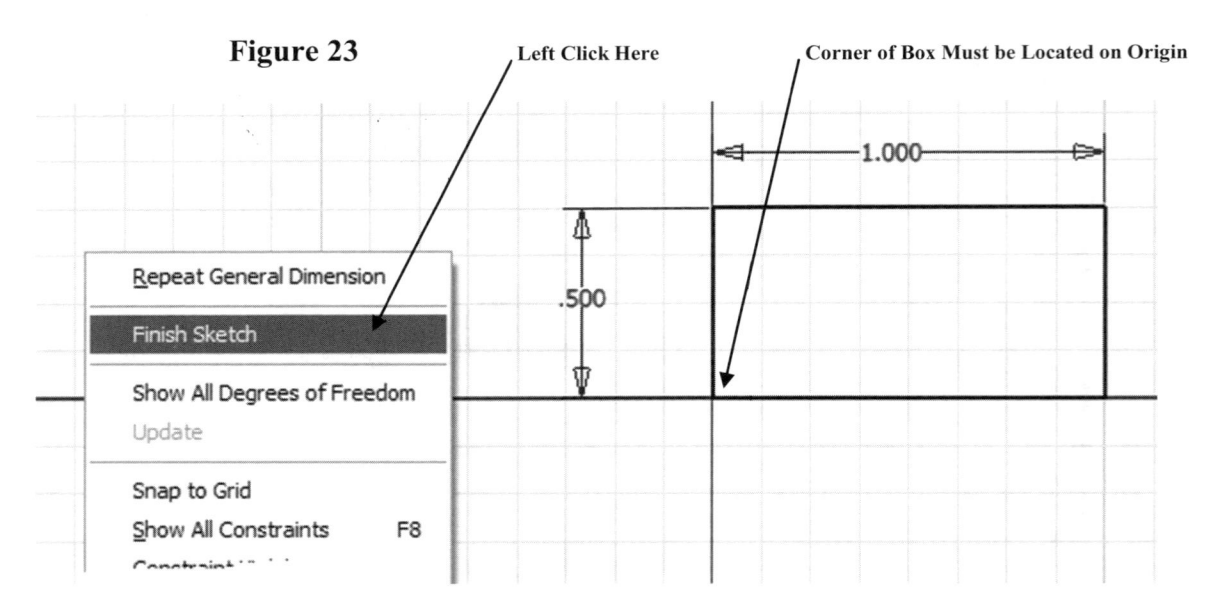

Figure 23

Chapter 9: Introduction to Advanced Commands

27. Right click anywhere on the screen. A pop up menu will appear. Left click on **Isometric/Home View** as shown in Figure 24.

Figure 24

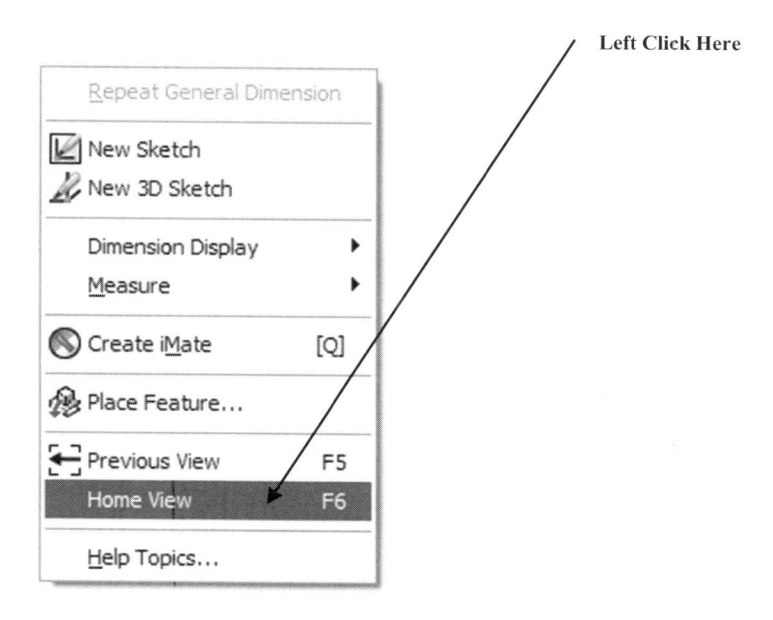

Left Click Here

28. Your screen should look similar to Figure 25.

Figure 25

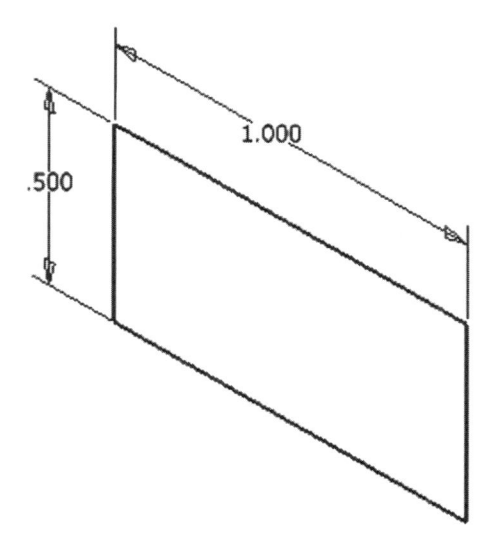

Chapter 9: Introduction to Advanced Commands

29. Left click on the "plus" sign to the left of the text "Origin". The part tree will expand as shown in Figure 26.

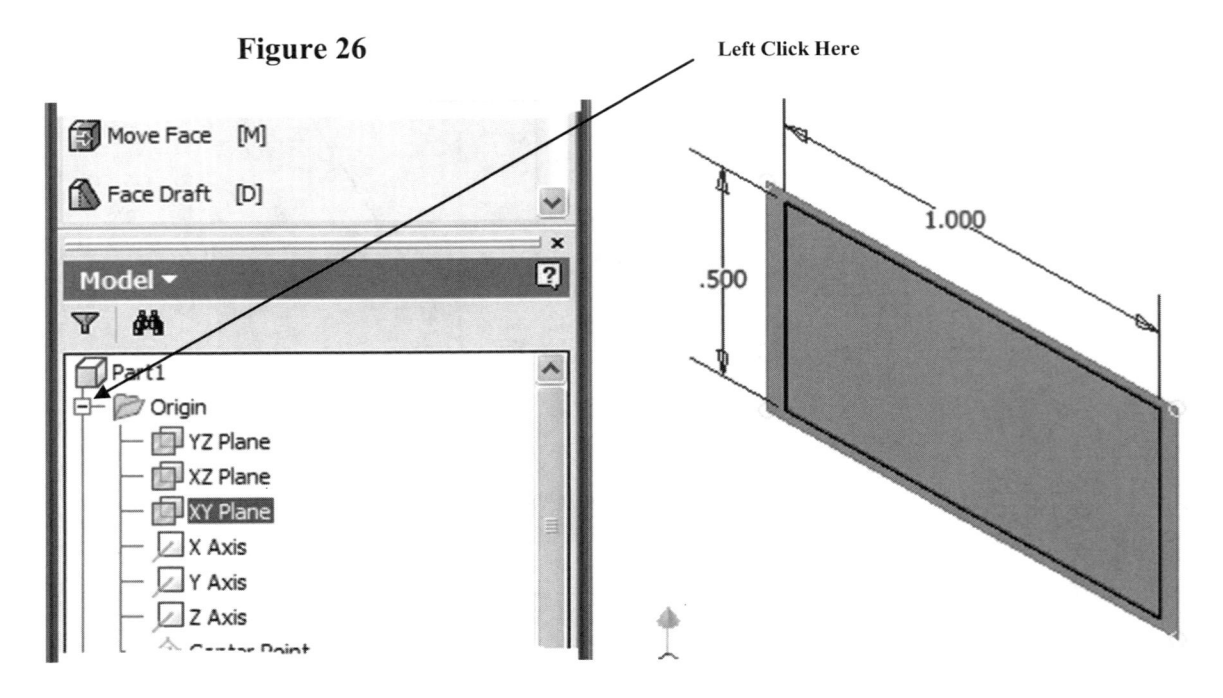

Figure 26

30. Move the cursor to the middle left portion of the screen and left click on **Work Plane** as shown in Figure 27. If this text is not visible, scroll down.

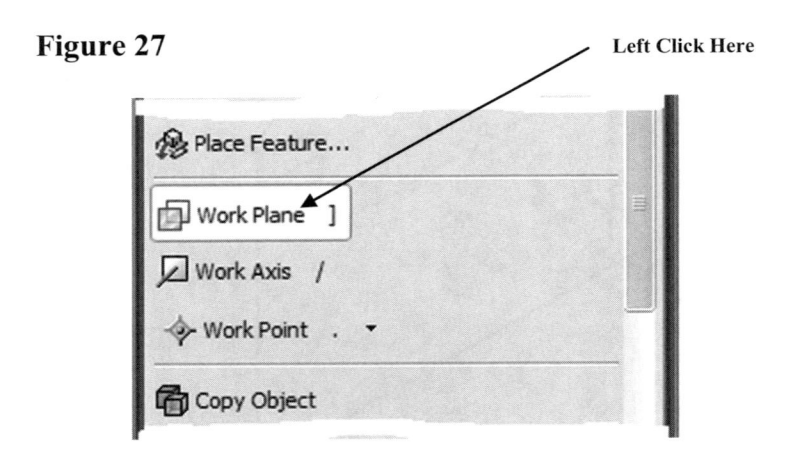

Figure 27

470

Chapter 9: Introduction to Advanced Commands

31. Left click on **XY Plane** in the part tree. The "XY Plane" text will become highlighted as shown in Figure 28.

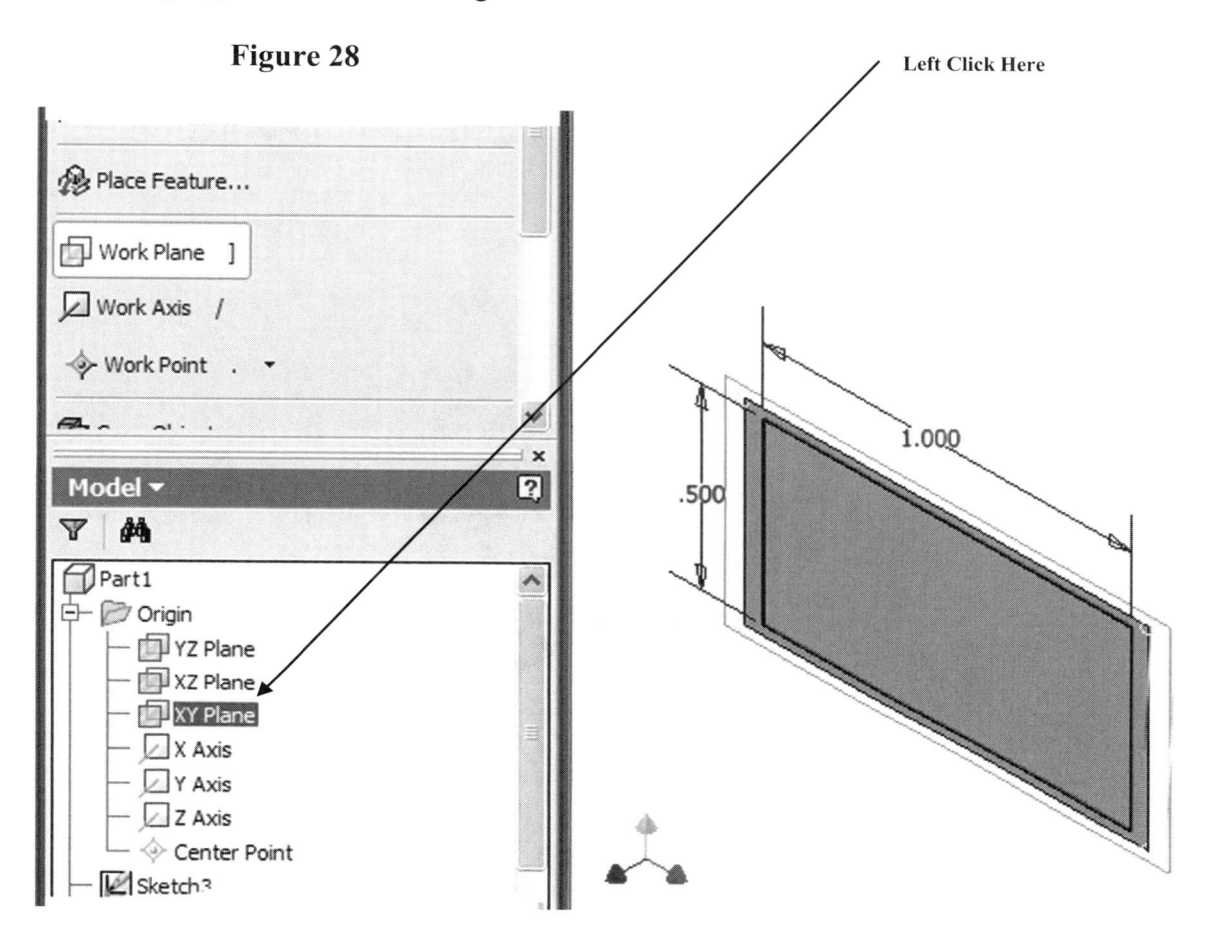

Figure 28

Chapter 9: Introduction to Advanced Commands

32. Move the cursor to the center of the sketch and left click (holding the left mouse button down) dragging the cursor to the lower left portion of the screen. The Offset dialog box will appear. Enter **.500** as shown in Figure 29 and press the **Enter** key on the keyboard.

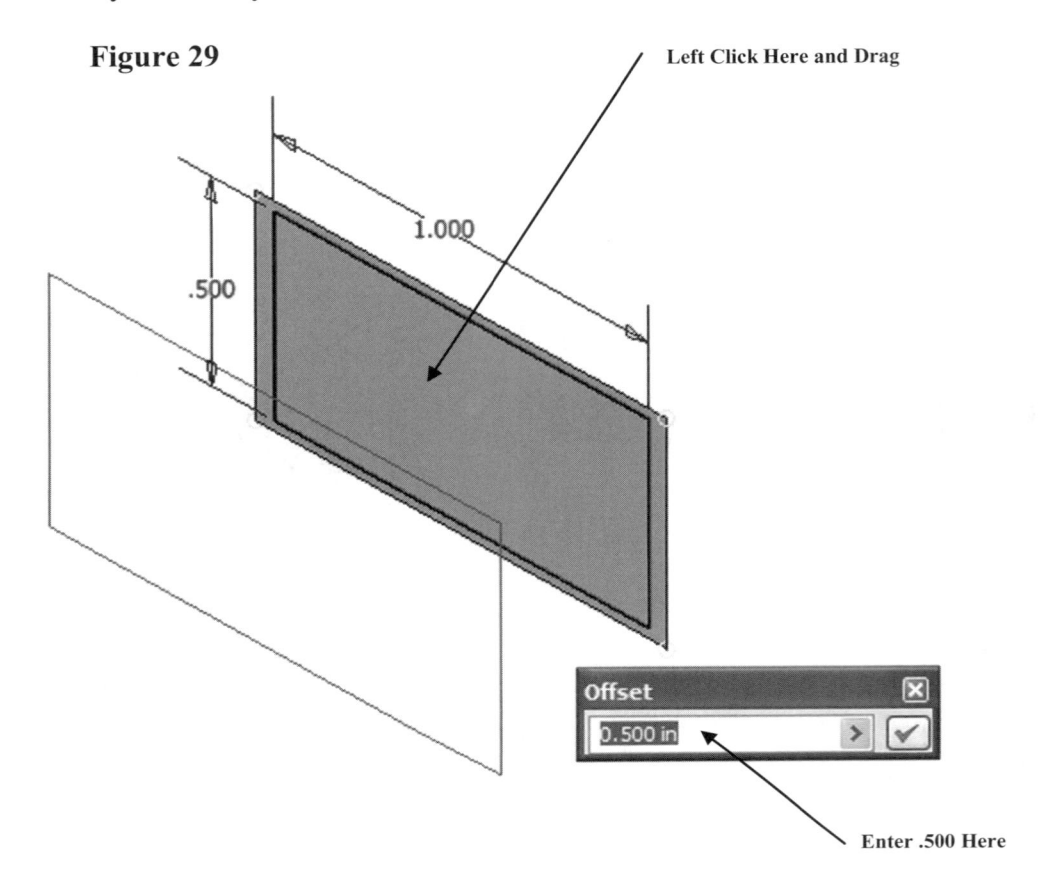

Figure 29

Left Click Here and Drag

Enter .500 Here

Chapter 9: Introduction to Advanced Commands

33. Your screen should look similar to Figure 30.

Figure 30

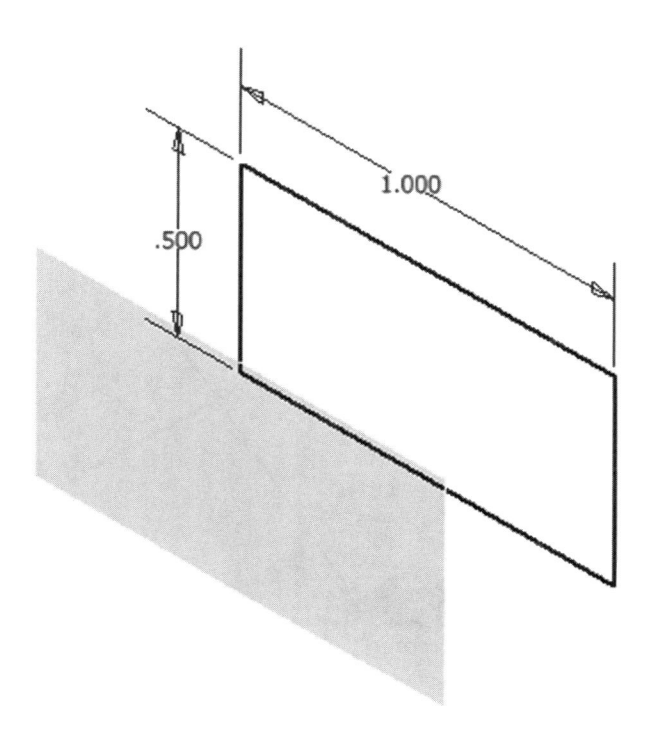

Chapter 9: Introduction to Advanced Commands

34. Move the cursor to the edge of the newly created plane causing the edges to turn red. Small circles will also appear at each corner. After the edges of the plane are highlighted (red), right click once. A pop up menu will appear. Left click on **New Sketch** as shown in Figure 31.

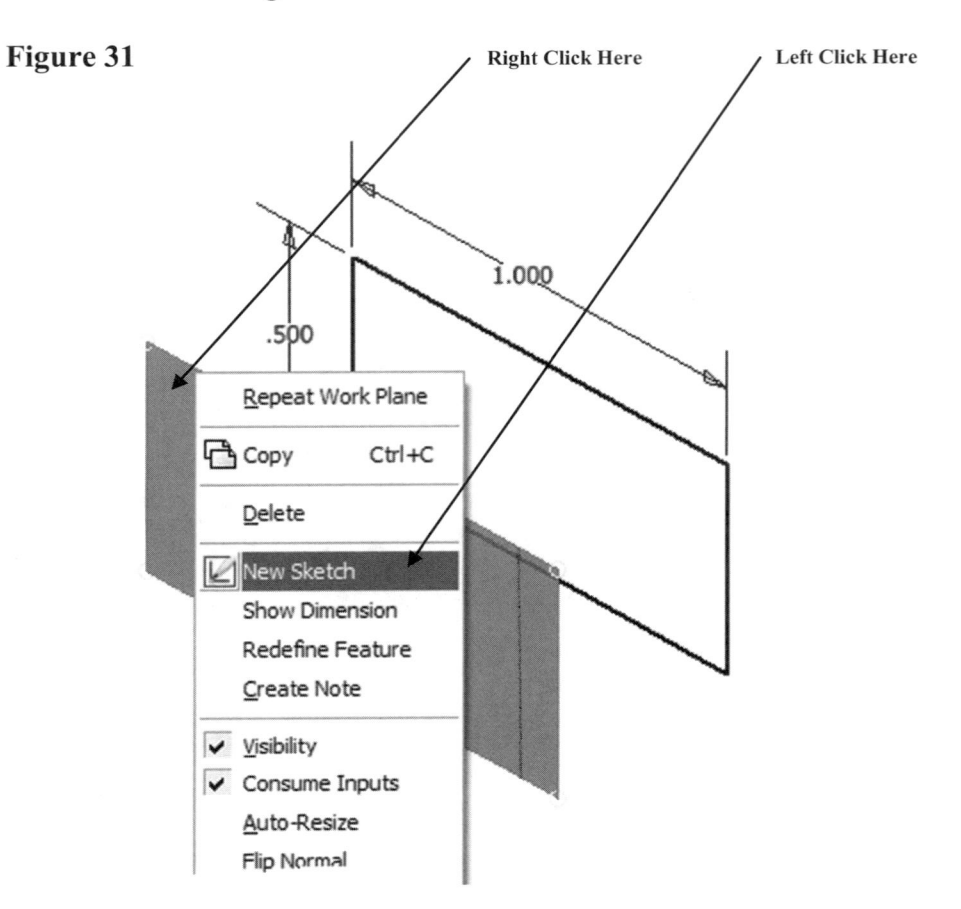

Figure 31

Right Click Here

Left Click Here

Repeat Work Plane
Copy   Ctrl+C
Delete
New Sketch
Show Dimension
Redefine Feature
Create Note
✓ Visibility
✓ Consume Inputs
Auto-Resize
Flip Normal

Chapter 9: Introduction to Advanced Commands

35. Your screen should look similar to Figure 32.

Figure 32

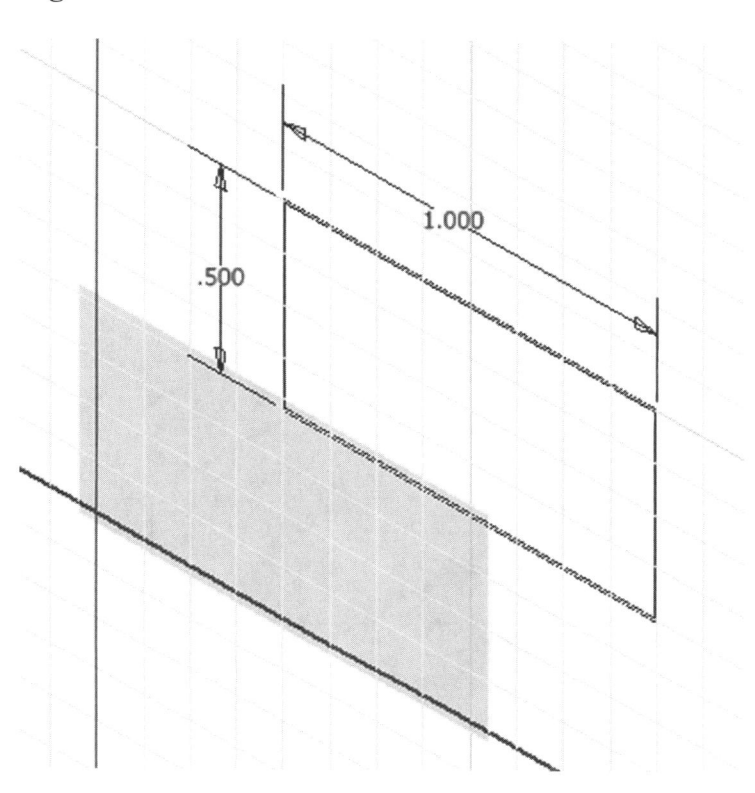

Chapter 9: Introduction to Advanced Commands

36. Complete the sketch shown in Figure 33. Estimate the location of the circle and exit the Sketch Panel.

Figure 33

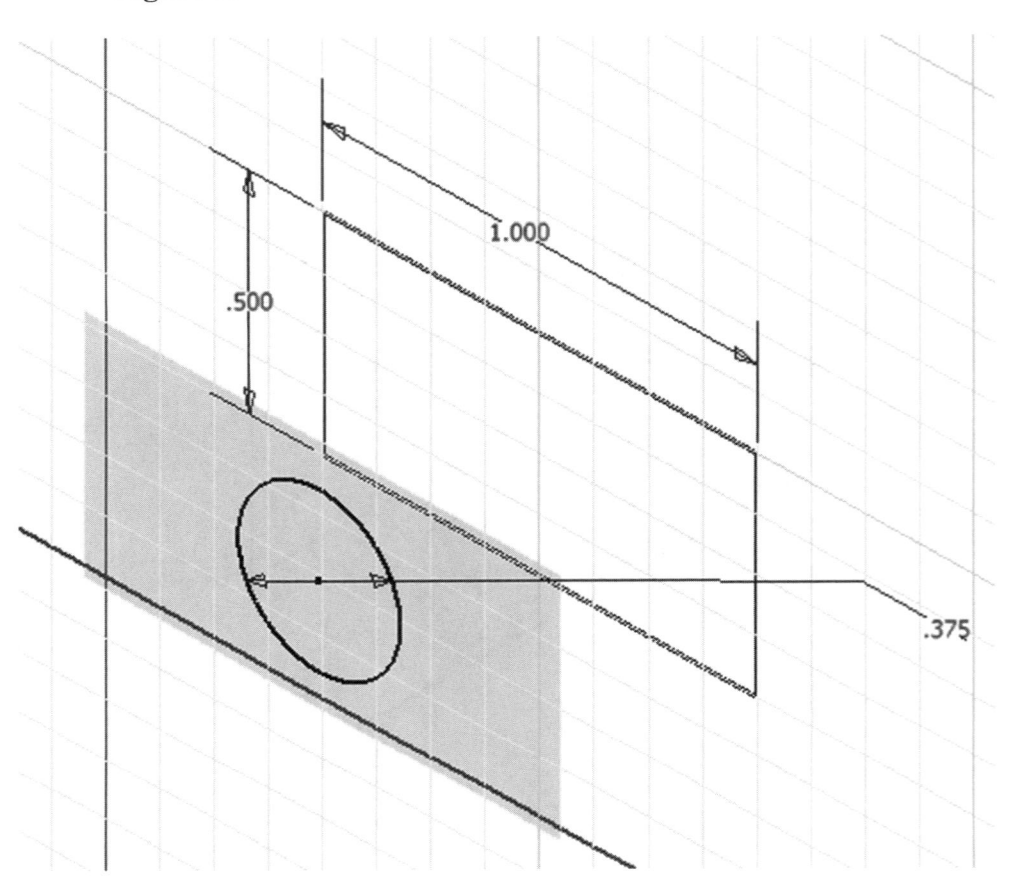

Chapter 9: Introduction to Advanced Commands

37. Your screen should look similar to Figure 34.

Figure 34

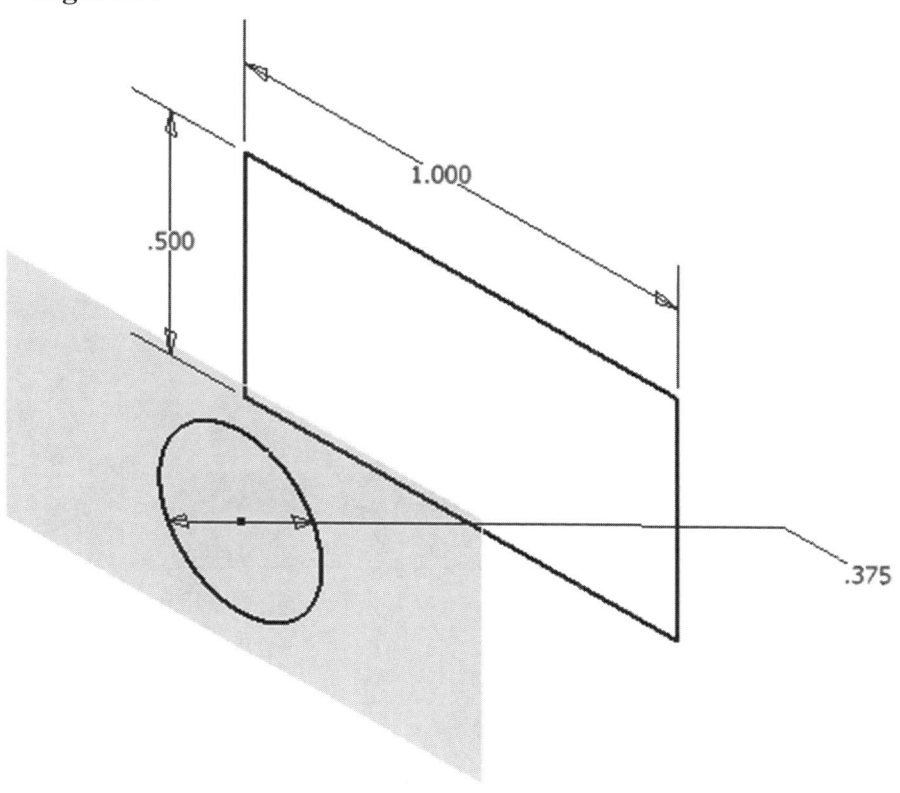

38. Move the cursor to the middle left portion of the screen and left click on **Work Plane** as shown in Figure 35.

Figure 35   Left Click Here

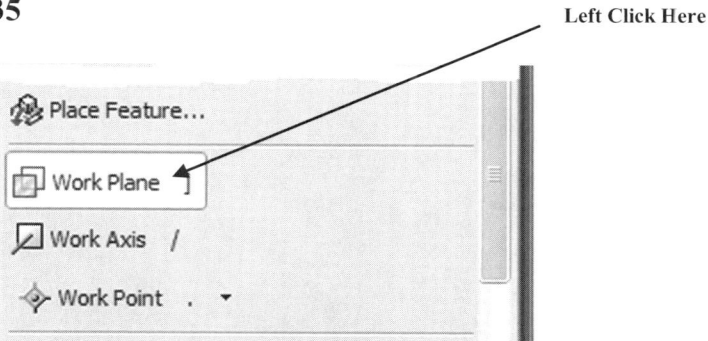

Chapter 9: Introduction to Advanced Commands

39. Left click on **XY Plane** in the part tree. The "XY Plane" text will become highlighted as shown in Figure 36.

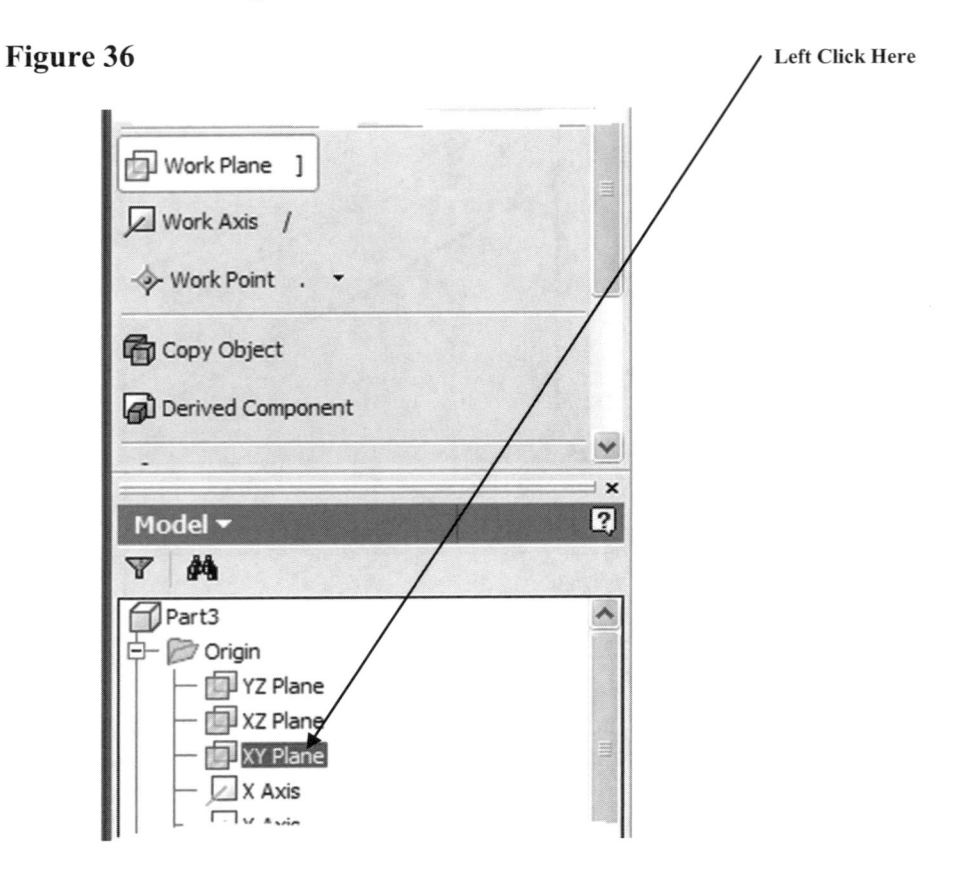

Figure 36

478

40. Move the cursor to the center of the sketch and left click (holding the left mouse button down) dragging the cursor to the lower left portion of the screen. The Offset dialog box will appear. Enter **1.000** as shown in Figure 37 and press the **Enter** key on the keyboard.

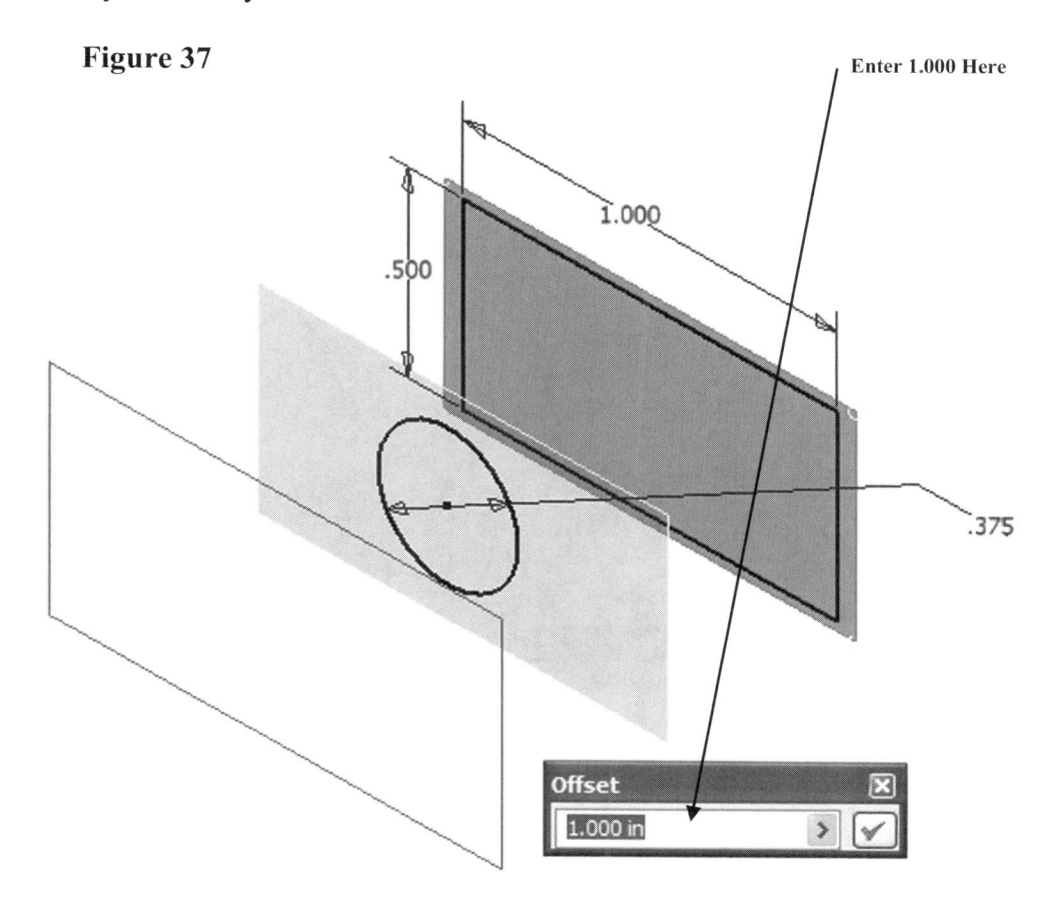

Figure 37

Chapter 9: Introduction to Advanced Commands

41. Move the cursor to the edge of the newly created plane causing the edges to turn red. Small circles will also appear at each corner. After the edges of the plane are highlighted (red), right click once. A pop up menu will appear. Left click on **New Sketch** as shown in Figure 38.

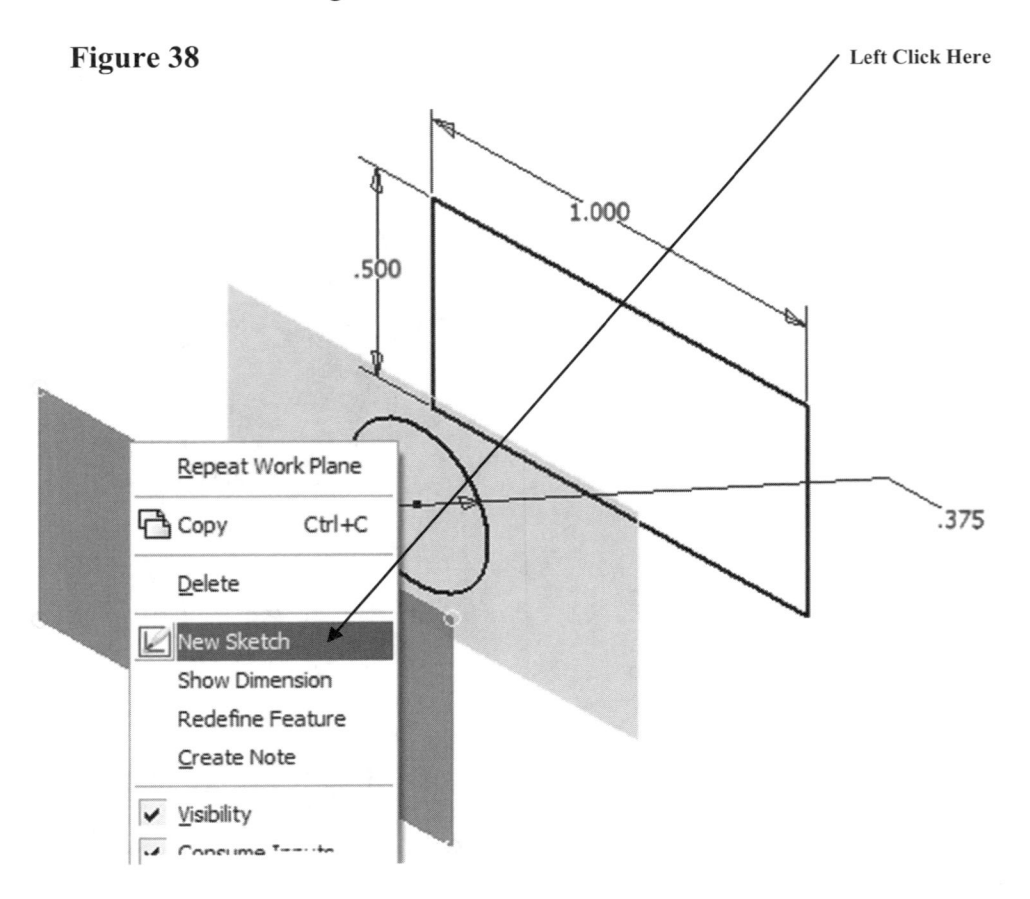

Figure 38

Left Click Here

1.000
.500
.375

Repeat Work Plane
Copy   Ctrl+C
Delete
New Sketch
Show Dimension
Redefine Feature
Create Note
Visibility
Consume Inputs

480

42. Your screen should look similar to Figure 39.

Figure 39

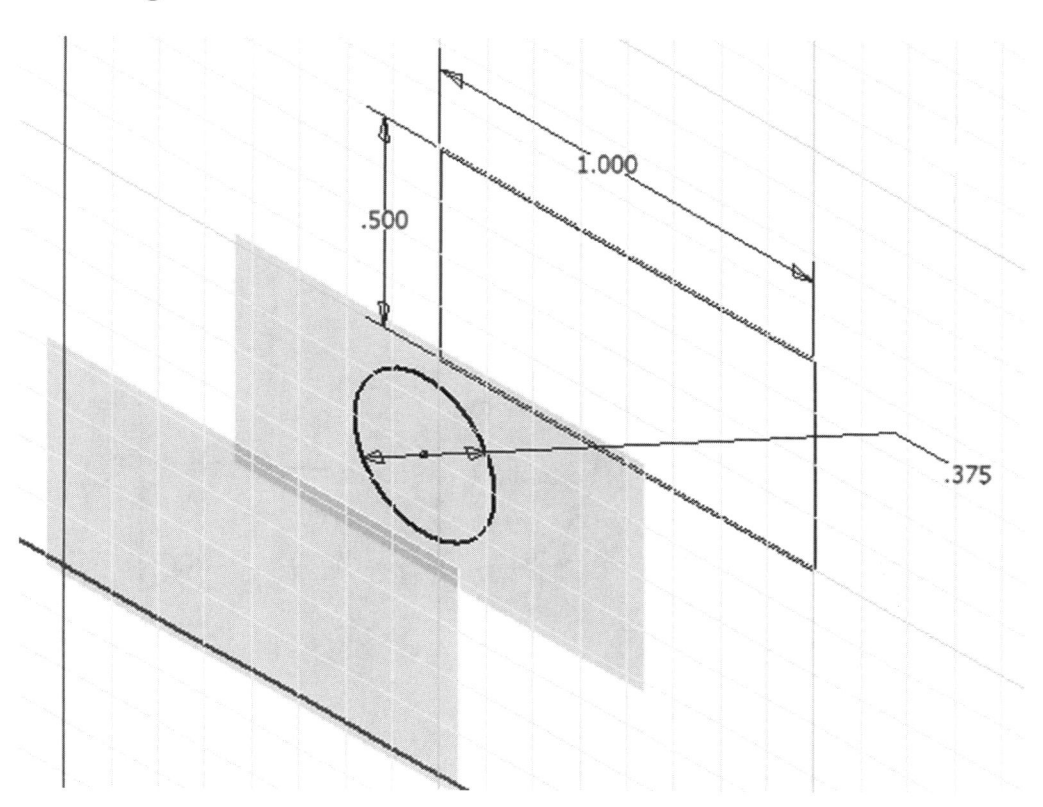

Chapter 9: Introduction to Advanced Commands

43. Complete the sketch shown in Figure 40. Estimate the location of the square and exit the Sketch Panel.

Figure 40

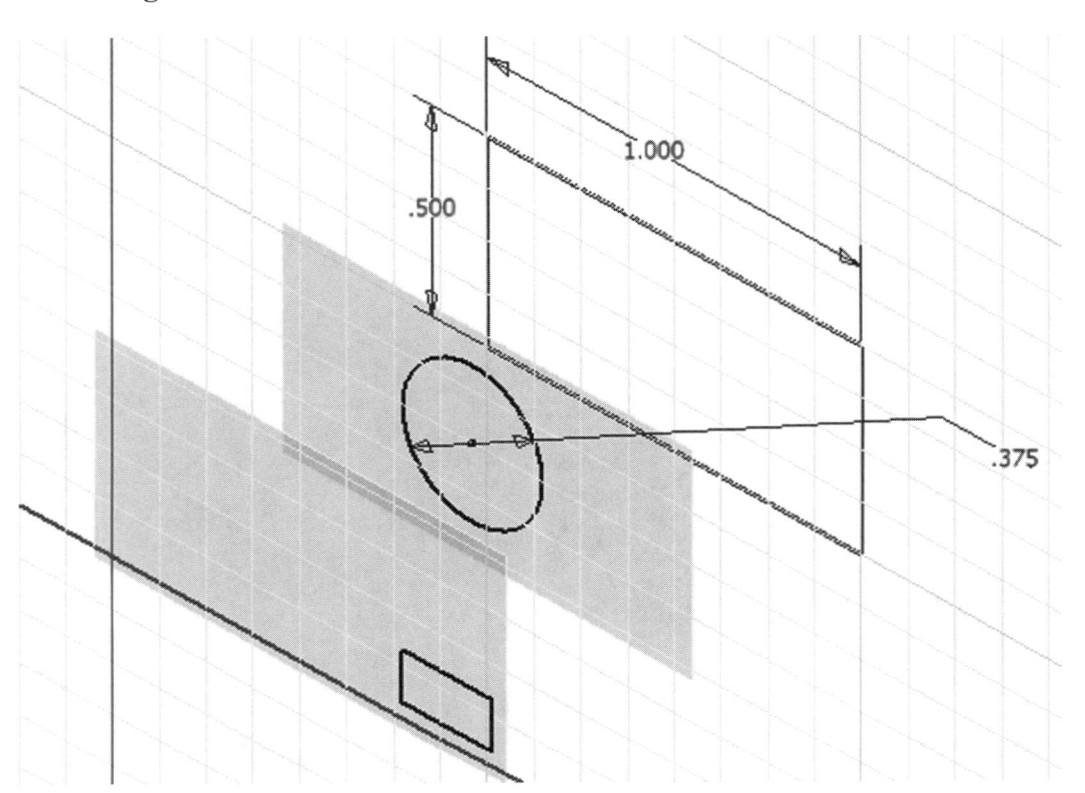

Chapter 9: Introduction to Advanced Commands

44. Move the cursor to the middle left portion of the screen and left click on **Loft** as shown in Figure 41.

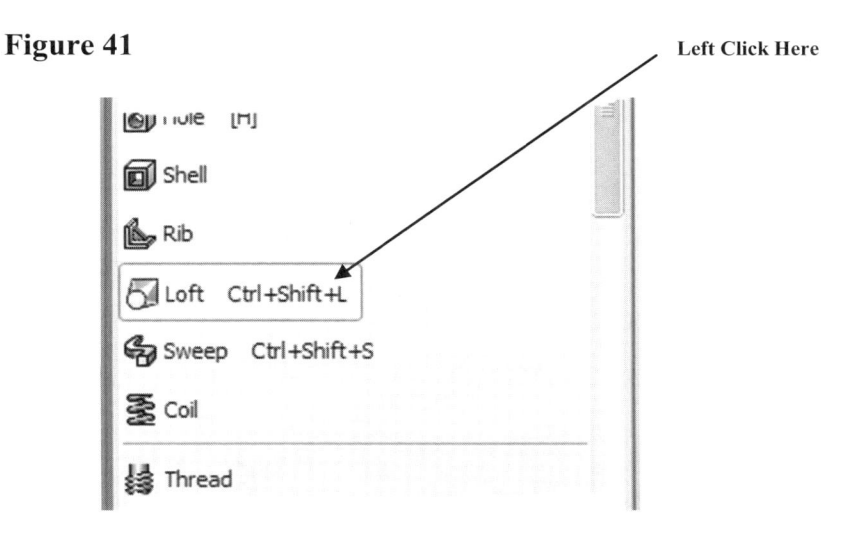

Figure 41

45. The Loft dialog box will appear as shown in Figure 42.

Figure 42

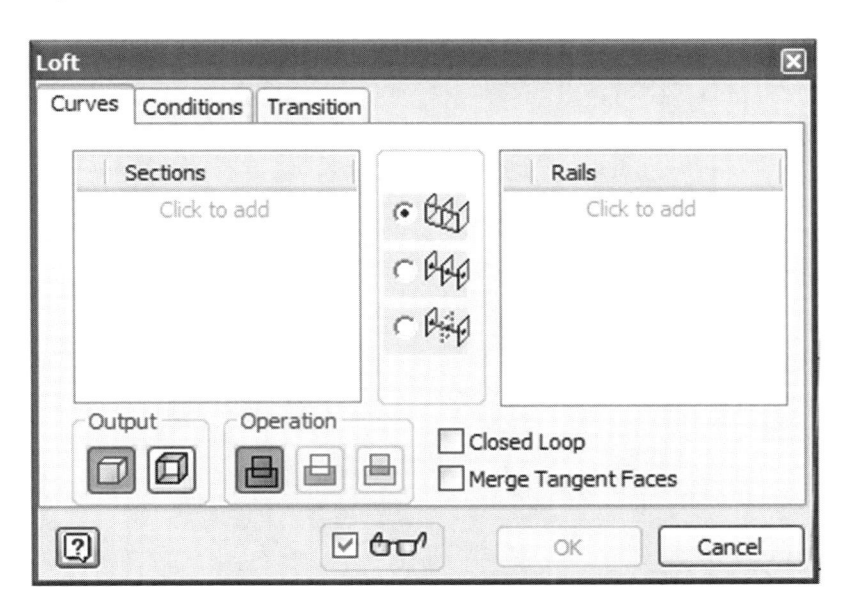

Chapter 9: Introduction to Advanced Commands

46. Left click on each of the sketches as shown in Figure 43.

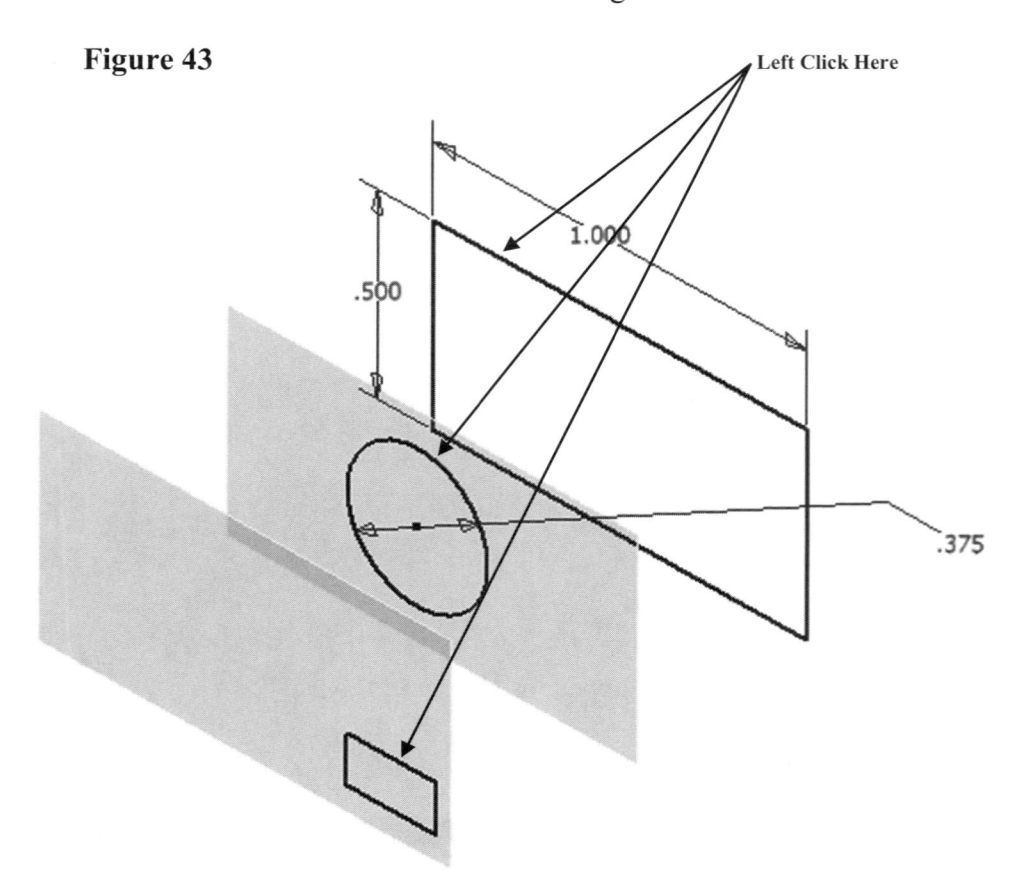

Figure 43

Chapter 9: Introduction to Advanced Commands

47. Inventor will provide a preview of the loft as shown in Figure 44.

Figure 44

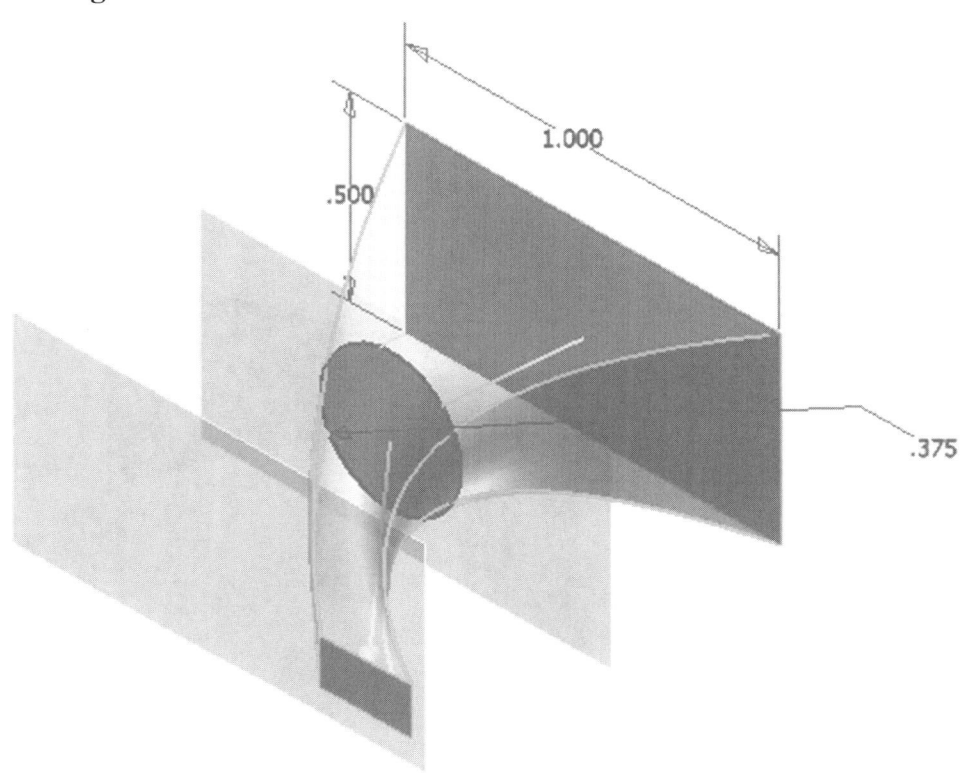

48. Left click on **OK** as shown in Figure 45.

Figure 45

Left Click Here

485

Chapter 9: Introduction to Advanced Commands

49. Your screen should look similar to Figure 46.

Figure 46

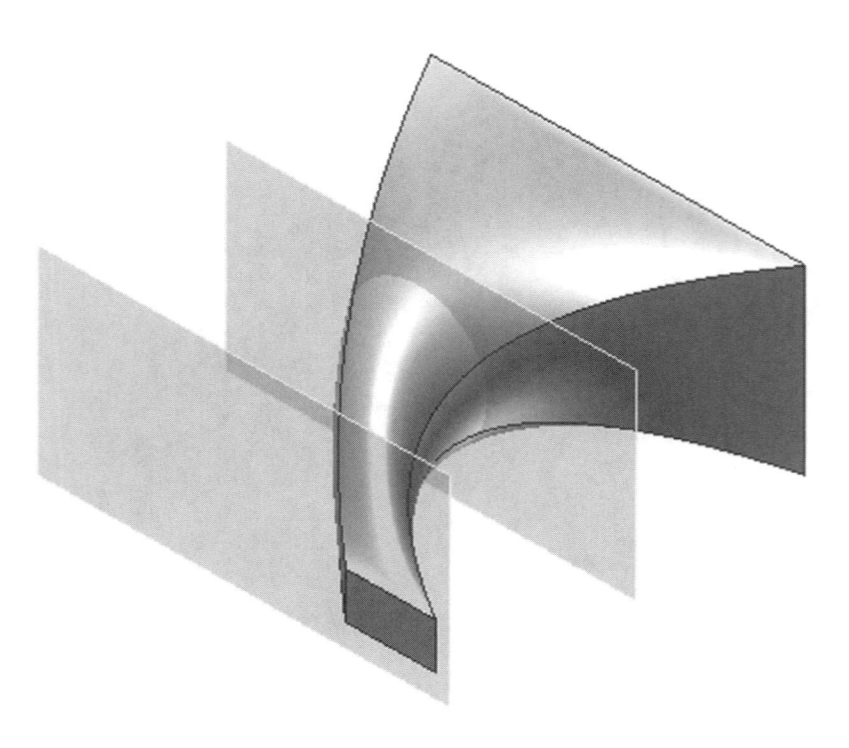

Chapter 9: Introduction to Advanced Commands

50. To hide the work planes, move the cursor over the edge of the work plane causing the edges to turn red. Right click once. A pop up menu will appear. Left click on **Visibility**. Hide both work planes as shown in Figure 47.

Figure 47

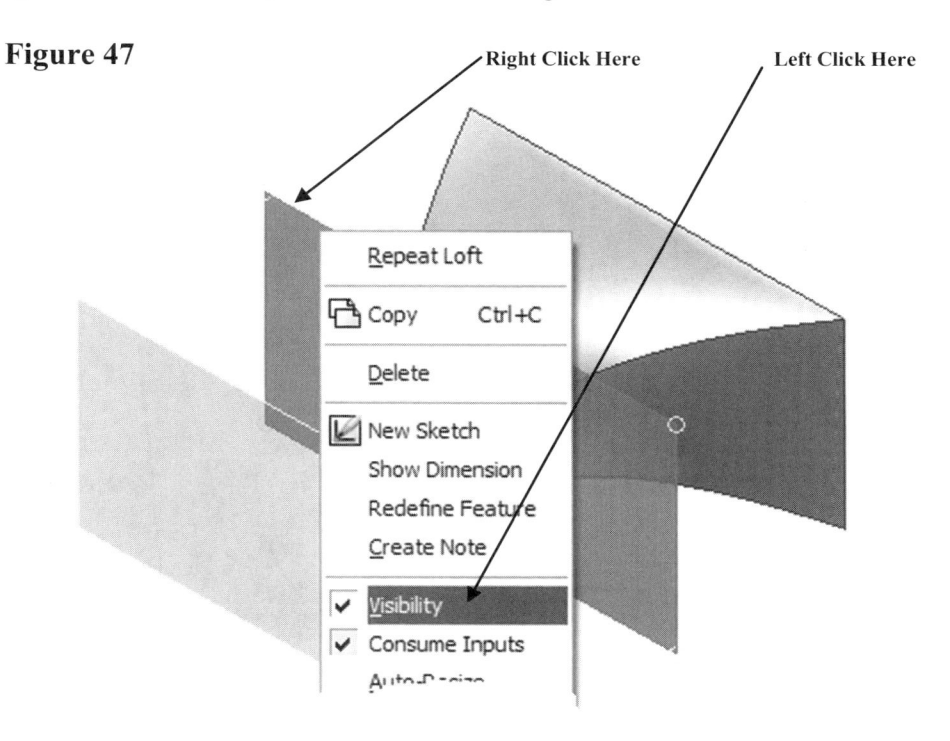

51. Your screen should look similar to Figure 48.

Figure 48

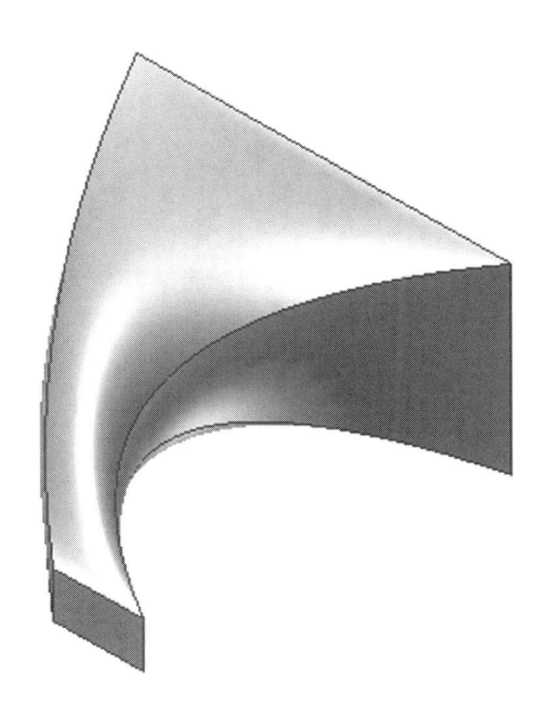

Chapter 9: Introduction to Advanced Commands

52. If more accuracy is required for each sketch, geometry can be projected from one work plane to another as previously described in Chapter 6. Geometry can also be sized and located using the General Dimension command as discussed in previous chapters.

53. Begin a new drawing as shown in Figure 49.

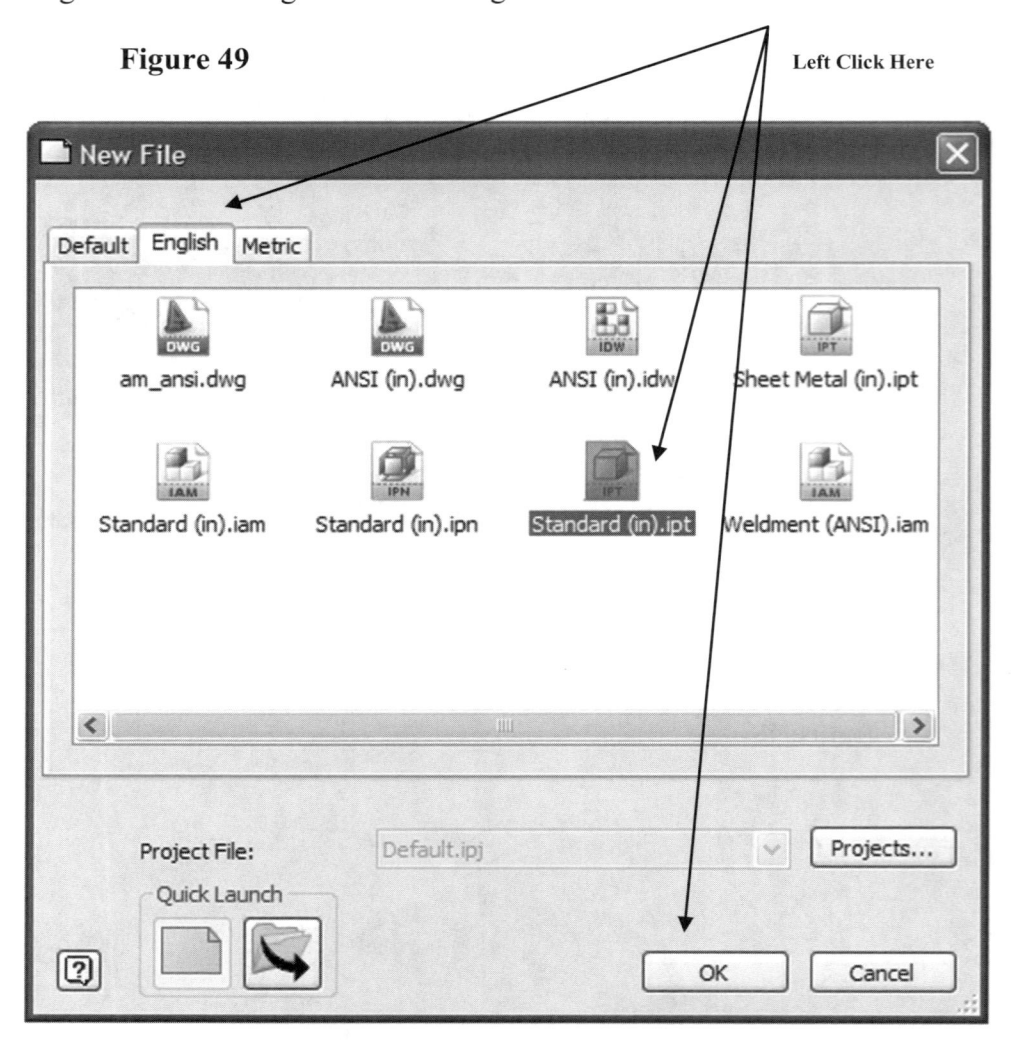

Figure 49

54. Complete the sketch shown in Figure 50 and exit the Sketch Panel.

Figure 50

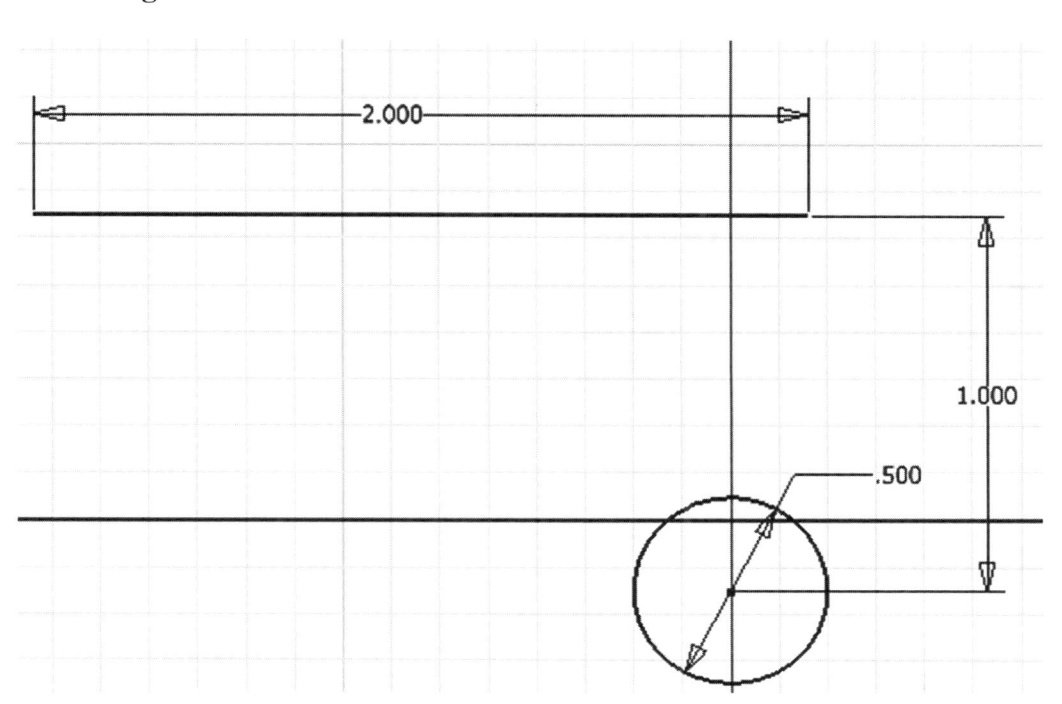

Chapter 9: Introduction to Advanced Commands

55. Move the cursor to the middle left portion of the screen and left click on **Coil**. Left click on the horizontal line above the circle as shown in Figure 51.

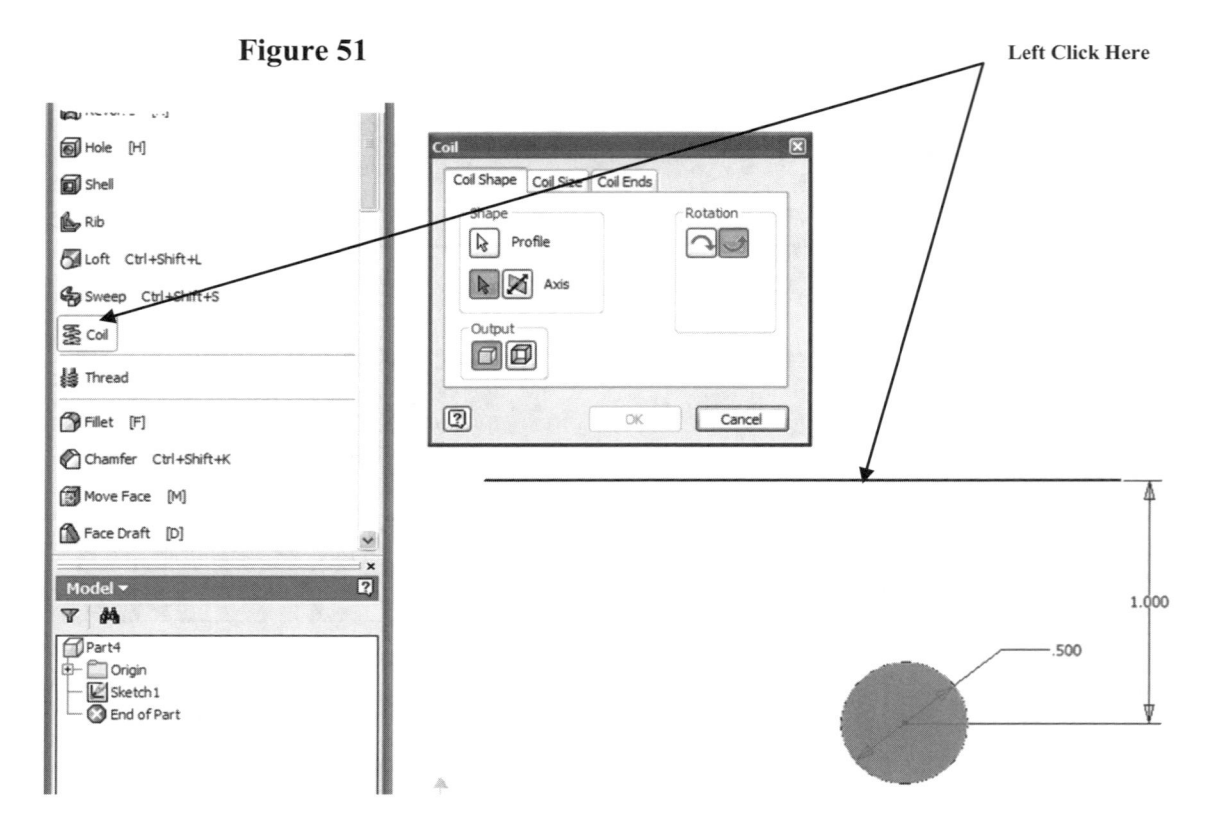

Figure 51

490

56. Inventor will provide a preview of the coil as shown in Figure 52.

Figure 52

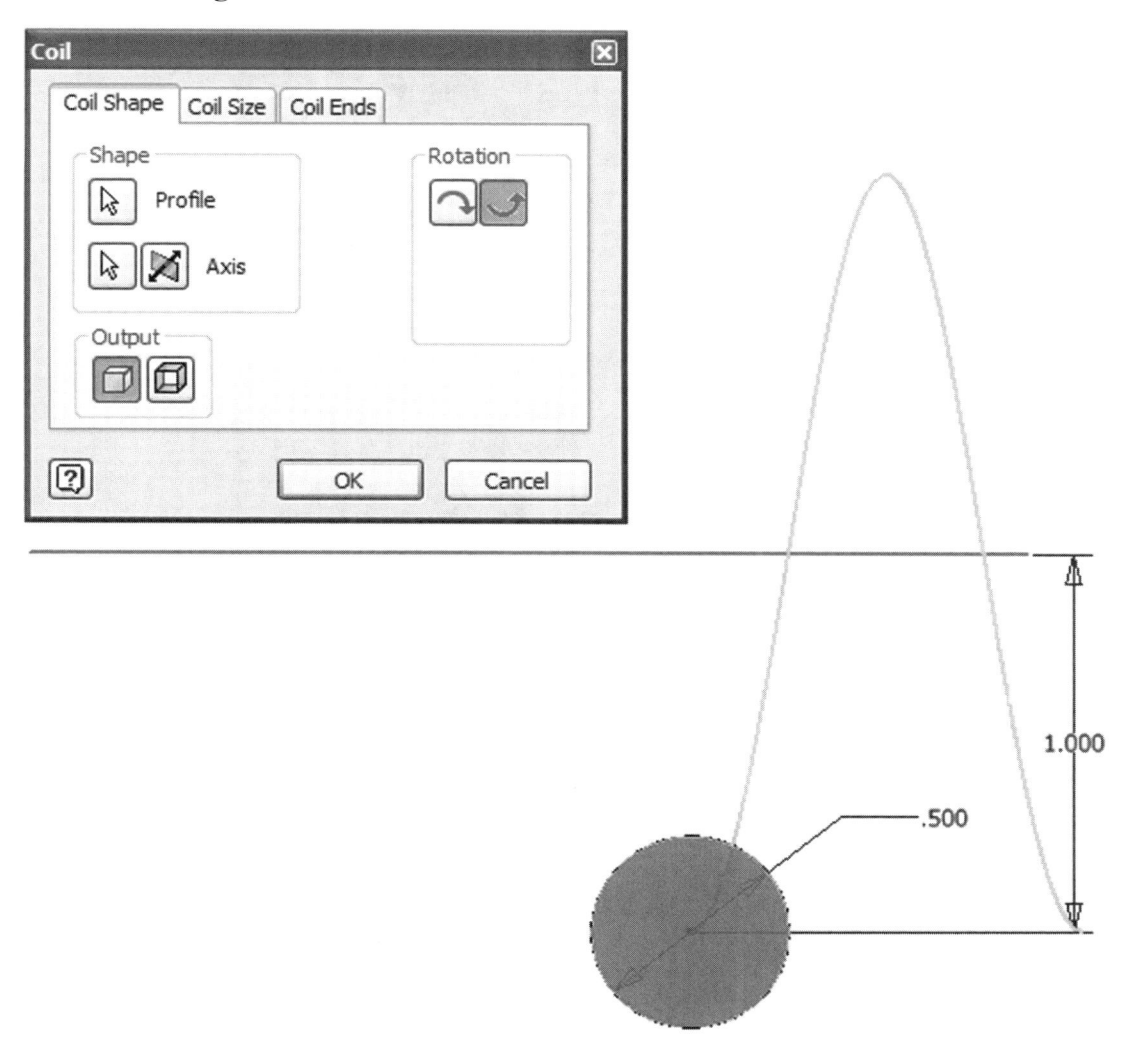

Chapter 9: Introduction to Advanced Commands

57. Left click on the **Coil Size** tab. Under Revolution enter **10**. Left click on **OK** as shown in Figure 53.

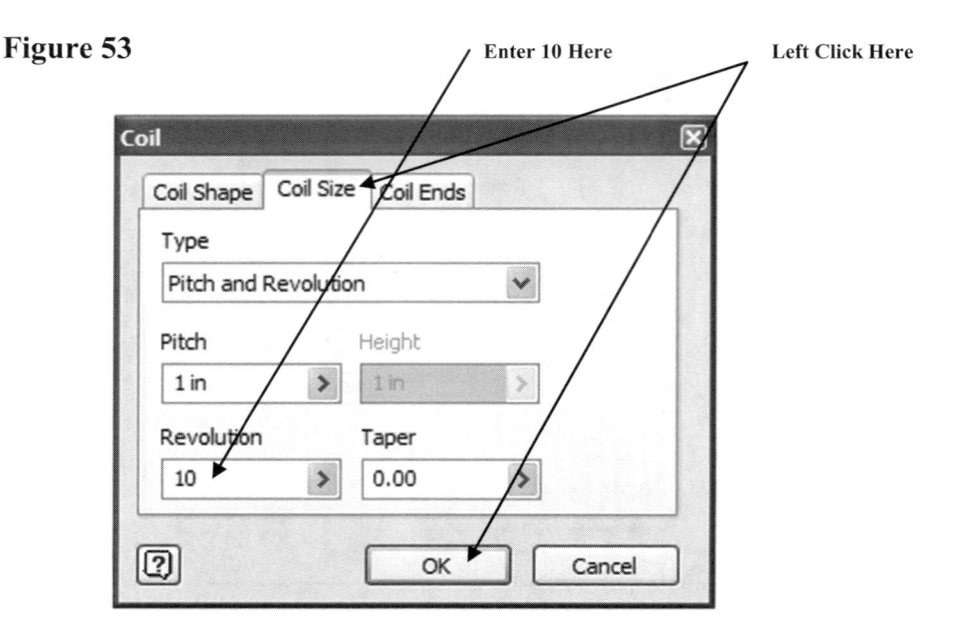

Figure 53

58. Your screen should look similar to Figure 54.

Figure 54

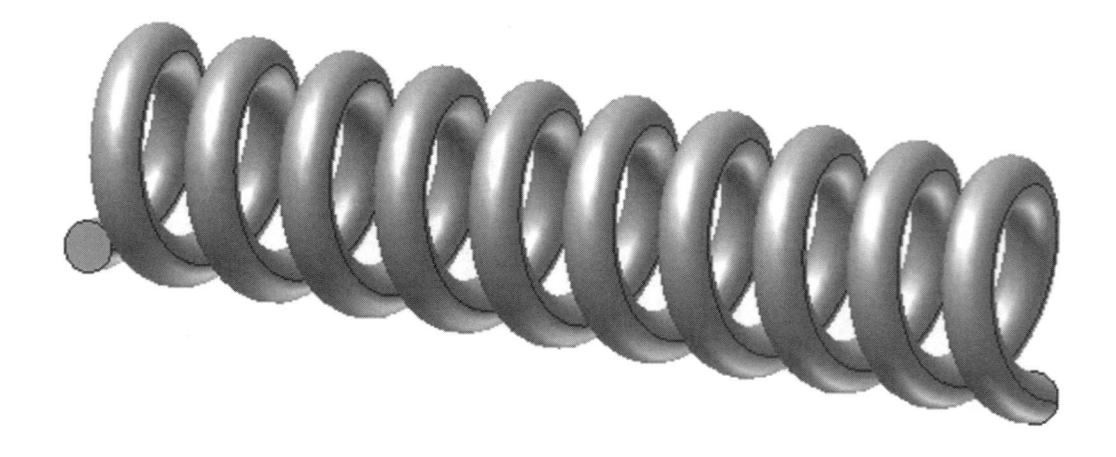

Chapter 10 Introduction to the Design Accelerator

Objectives:
- Learn to Create a Disc Cam
- Learn to edit the Disc Cam
- Learn to constrain the Disc Cam in an Assembly file
- Learn to animate the Disc Cam using the Drive Constraint command

Chapter 10 includes instruction on how to design the parts shown below. This chapter contains a brief introduction to the Design Accelerator. The Design Accelerator contains numerous predefined parts. This chapter will cover one of these parts.

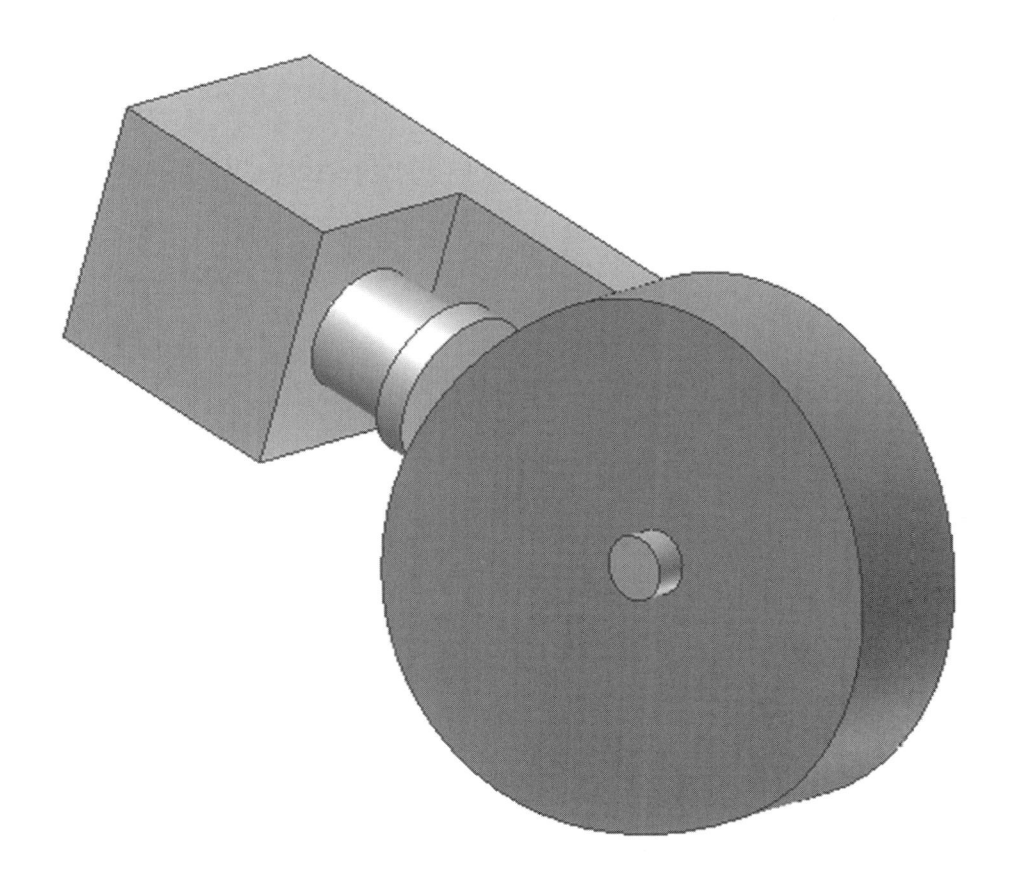

Chapter 10: Introduction to the Design Accelerator

1. Start Inventor by referring to "Chapter 1 Getting Started".

2. After Inventor is running, begin a New Sketch.

3. Complete the sketch shown in Figure 1.

Figure 1

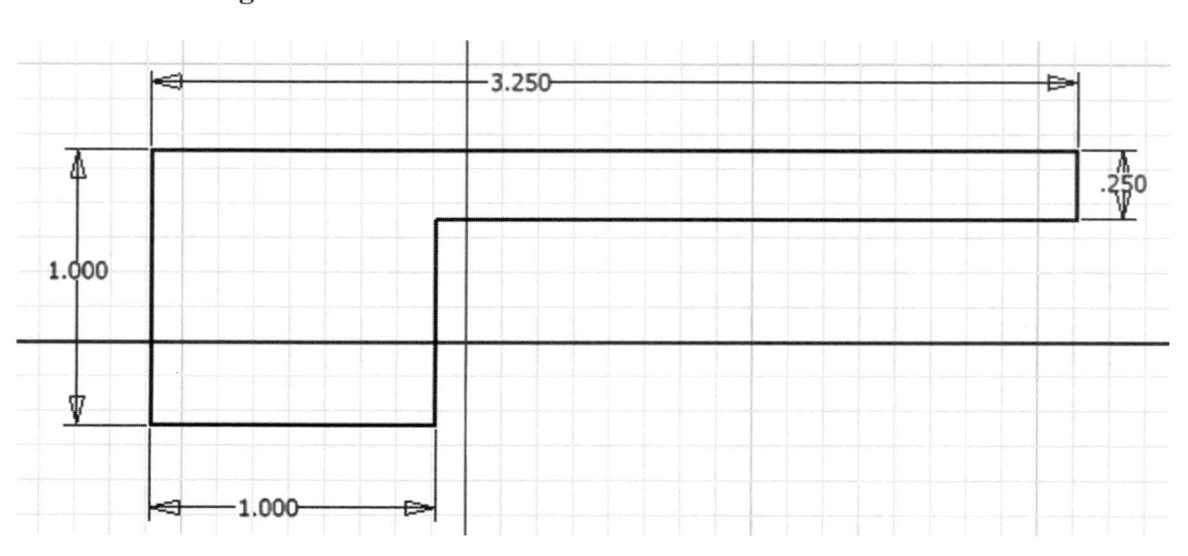

4. Exit the Sketch Panel. Extrude the sketch to a thickness of **1.00** inch as shown in Figure 2.

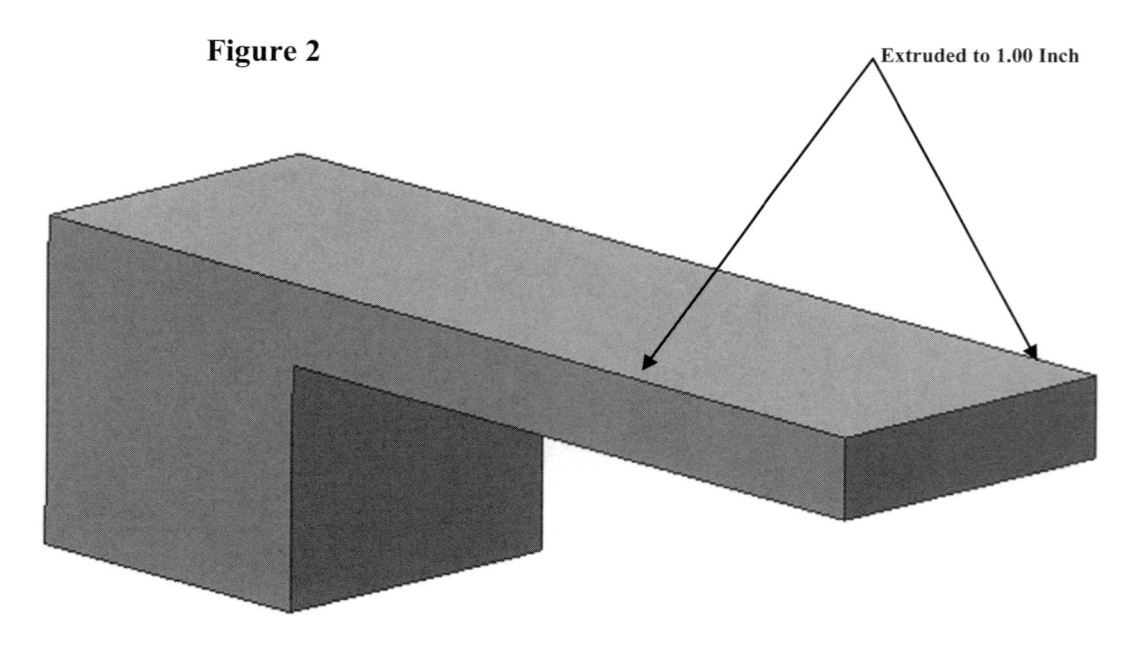

Figure 2 Extruded to 1.00 Inch

Chapter 10: Introduction to the Design Accelerator

5. Use the **Fillet** command (.5 inch fillets) to radius the lower edge(s) as shown in Figure 3.

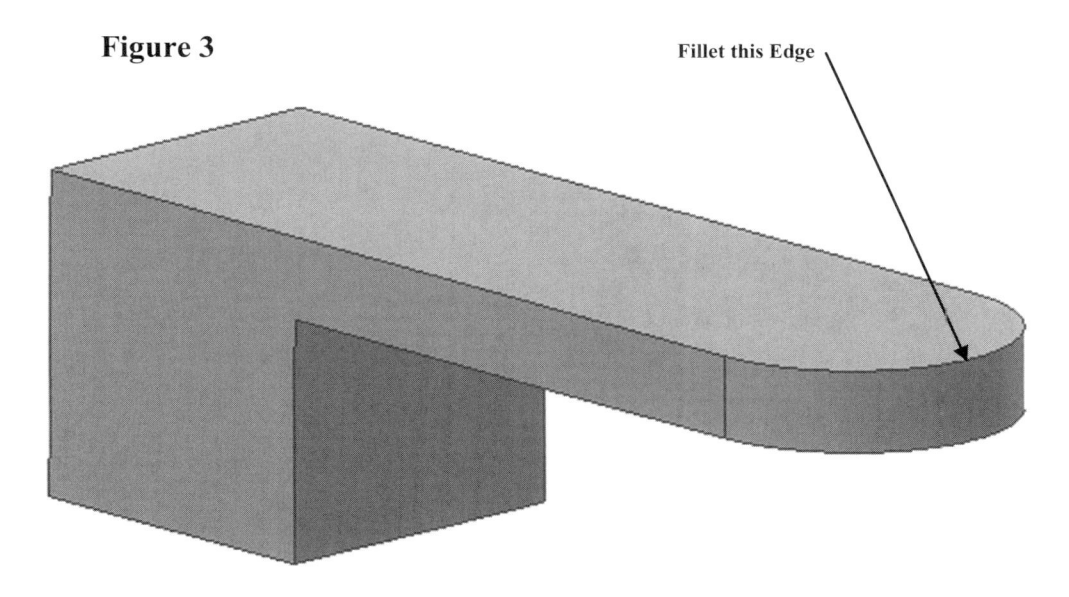

Figure 3

Fillet this Edge

6. Use the **Rotate** command to rotate the part upward as shown in Figure 4.

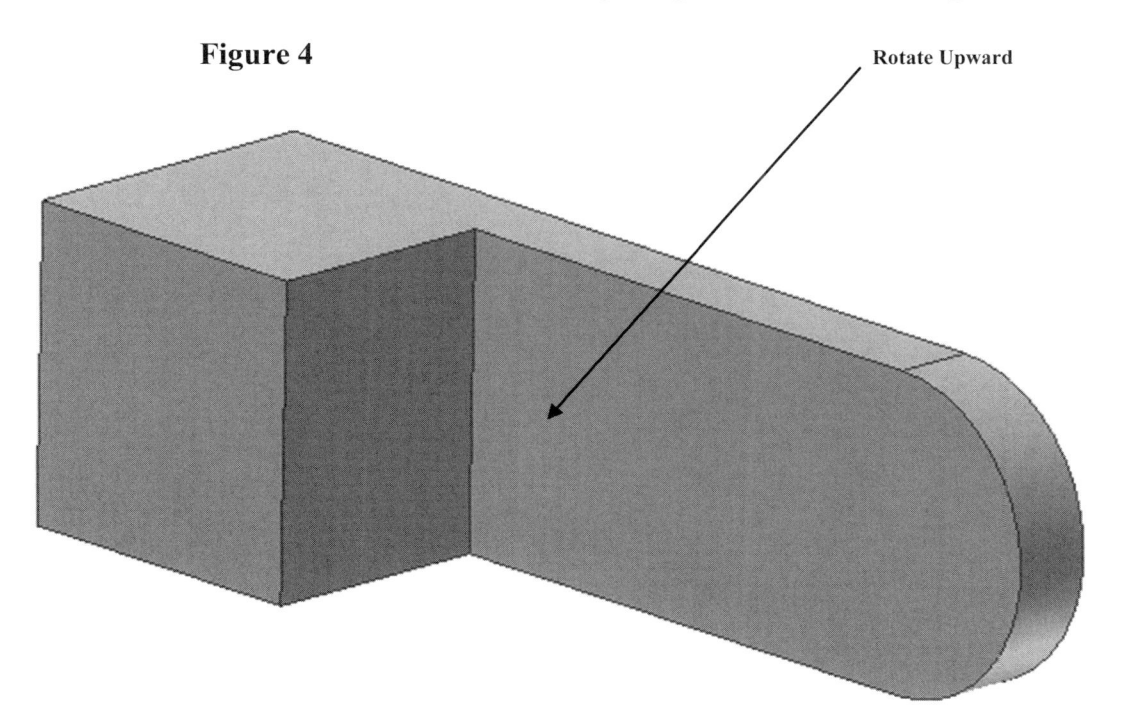

Figure 4

Rotate Upward

Chapter 10: Introduction to the Design Accelerator

7. Complete the sketch as shown in Figure 5. The center of the circle is located on the center of the fillet radius.

Figure 5

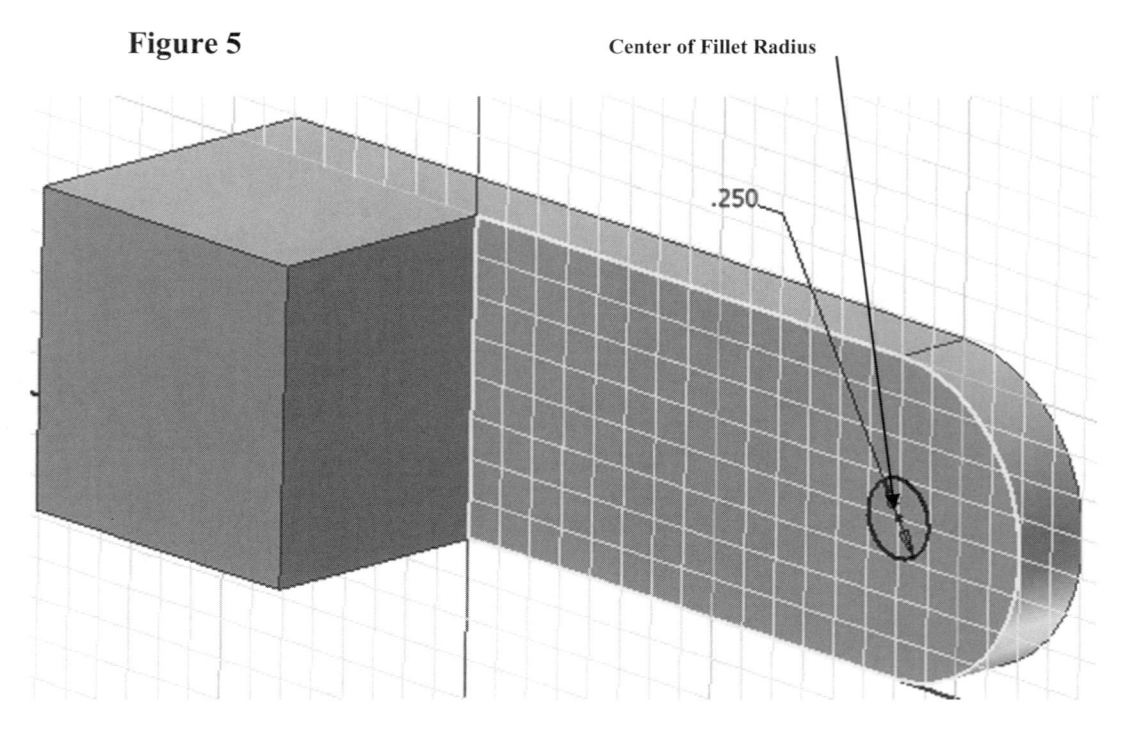

8. Extrude the circle to a distance of **.75** inches as shown in Figure 6.

Figure 6

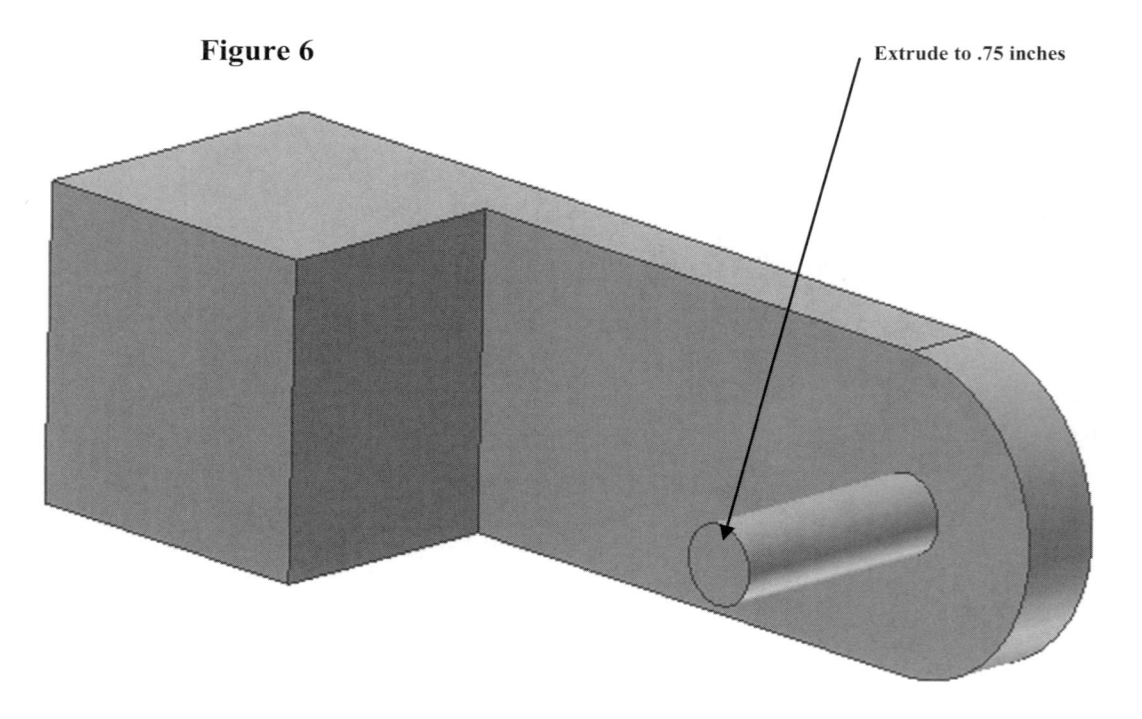

Chapter 10: Introduction to the Design Accelerator

9. Complete the sketch as shown in Figure 7.

   Figure 7

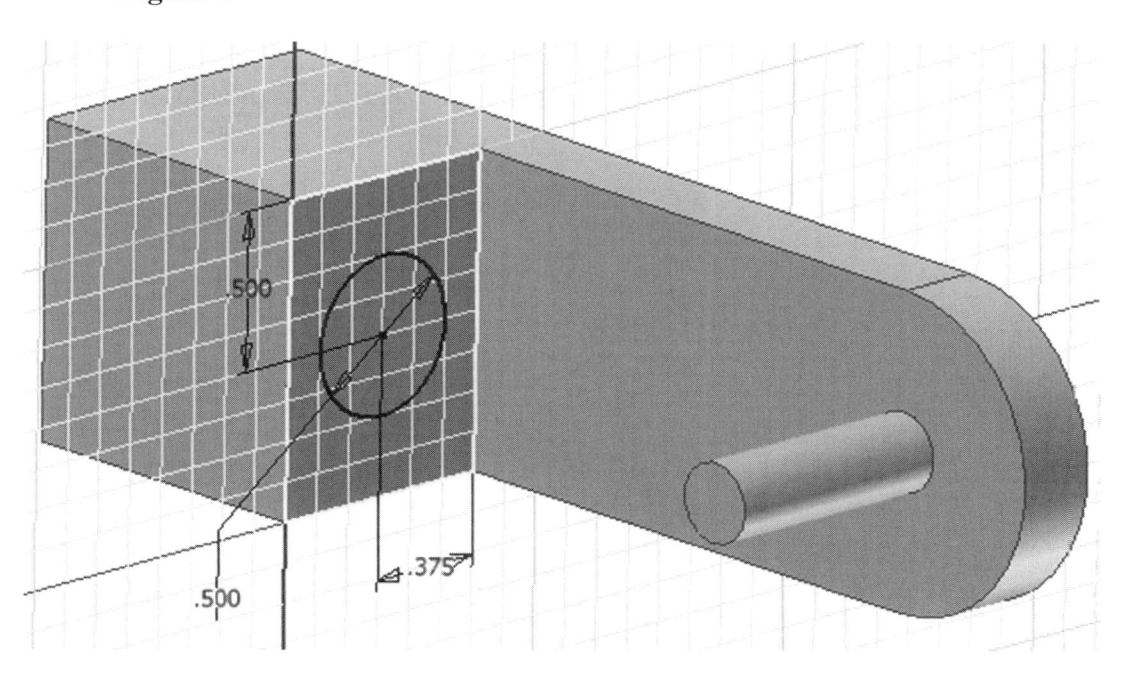

10. Use the "cut" option in the **Extrude** command to cut a hole a distance of 1.00 inch as shown in Figure 8.

    Figure 8   Hole cut 1.00 Inch

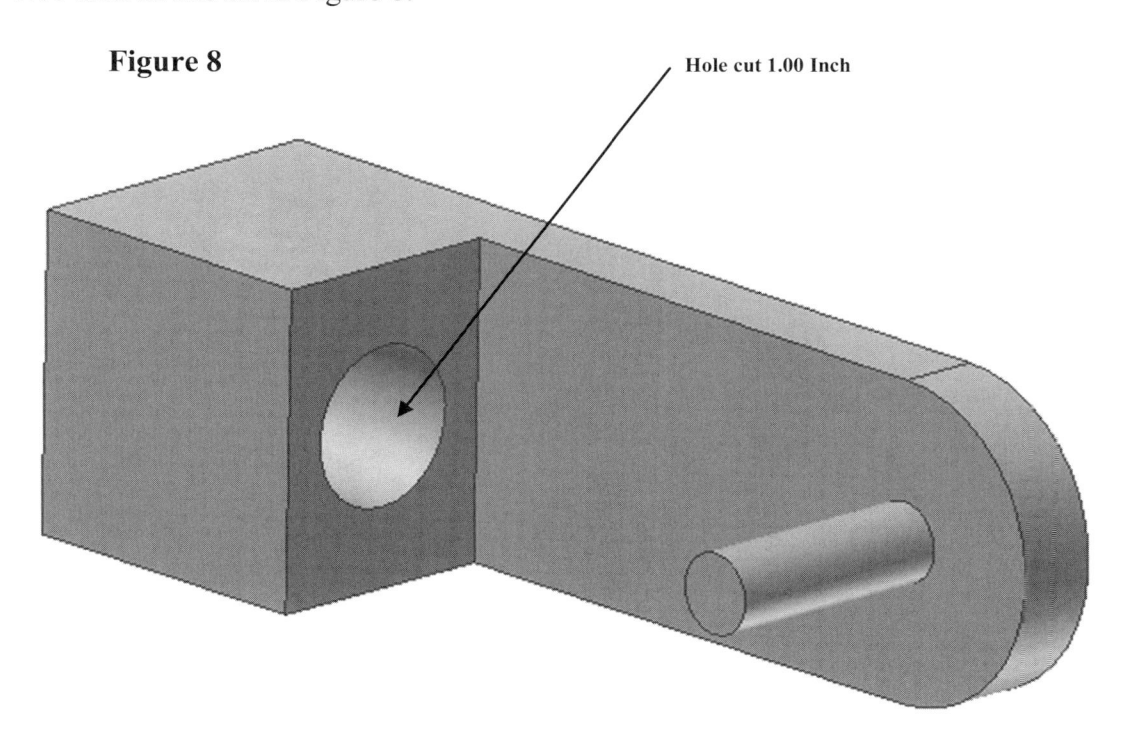

Chapter 10: Introduction to the Design Accelerator

11. Save the part as Camcase1.ipt where it can be easily retrieved later.

12. Begin a new drawing as described in Chapter 1.

13. Complete the sketch shown. Extrude the .500 inch diameter circle to a distance of 1 inch and the .625 inch diameter circle to a distance of .125 inches as shown in Figure 9.

Figure 9

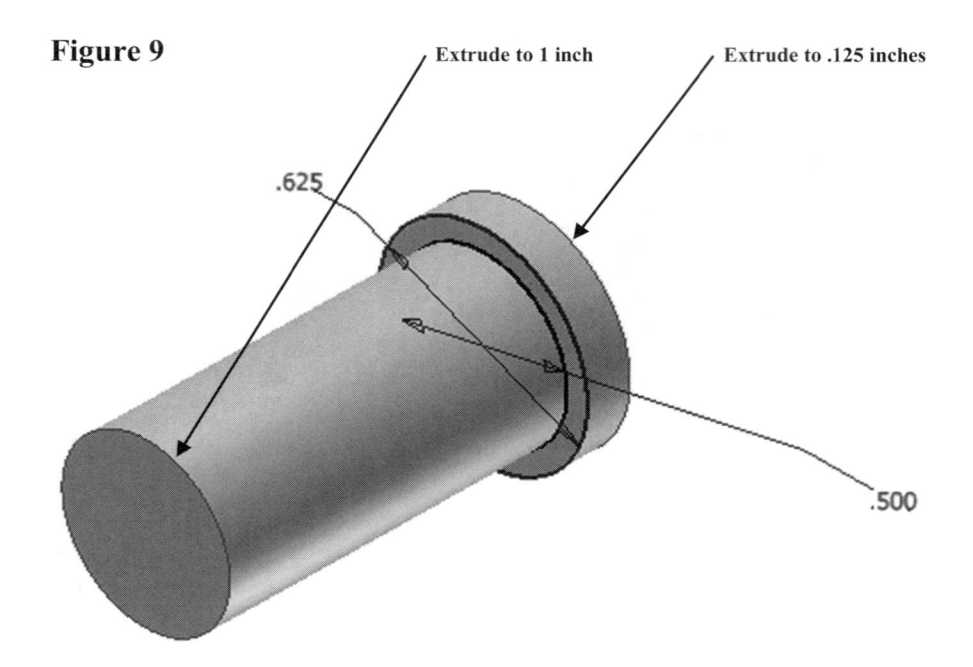

14. The bottom of the part needs to be flat as shown in Figure 10.

Figure 10

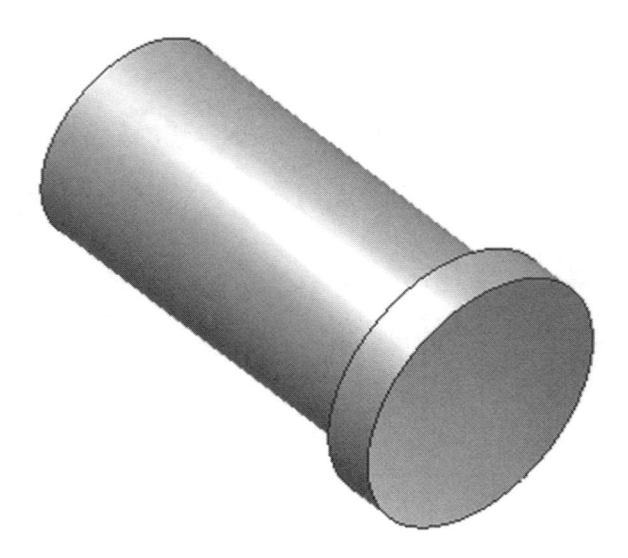

15. Save the part as Lifter1.ipt where it can be easily retrieved later.

16. Begin a new Assembly drawing as described in Chapter 7 and shown in Figure 11.

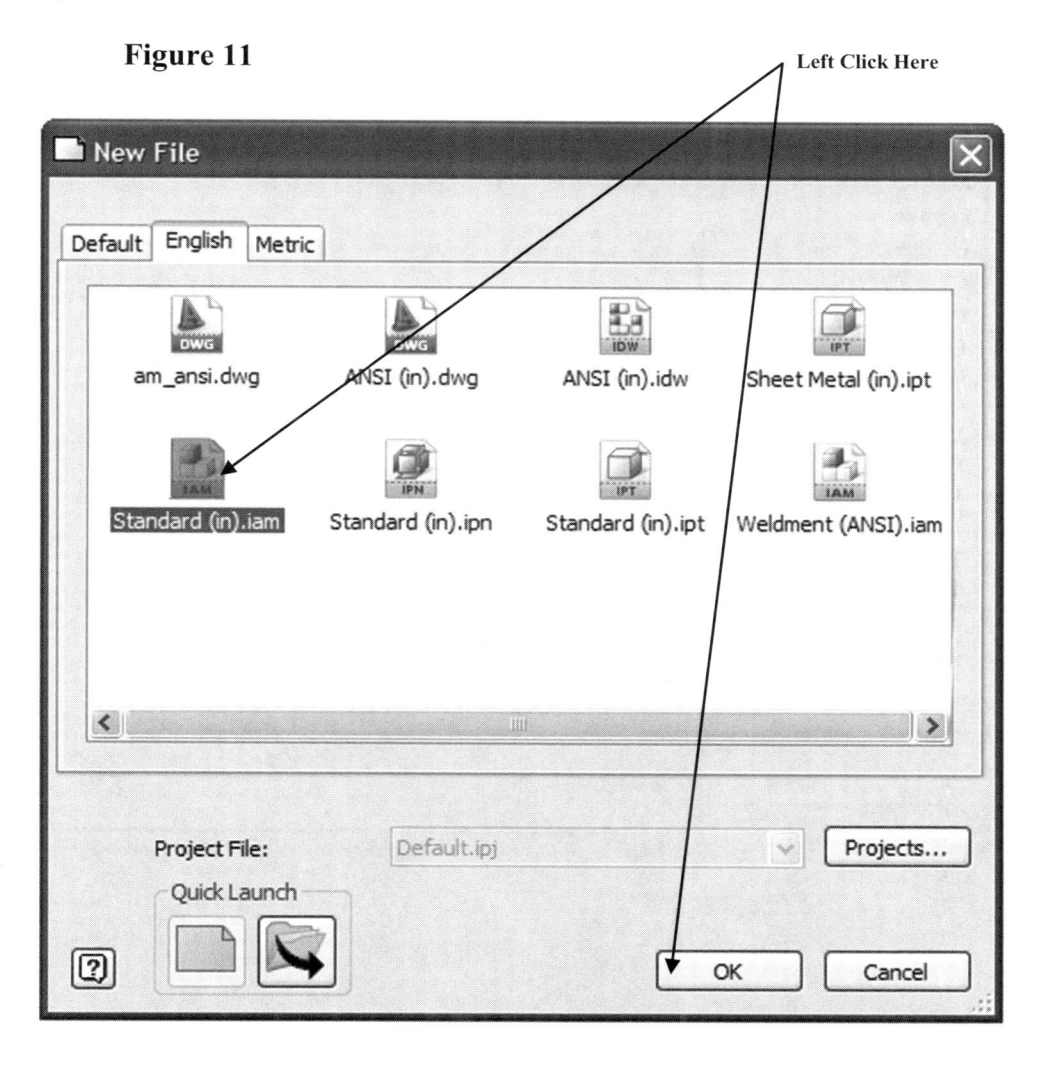

Figure 11

Chapter 10: Introduction to the Design Accelerator

17. The Assembly Panel will appear as shown in Figure 12.

Figure 12

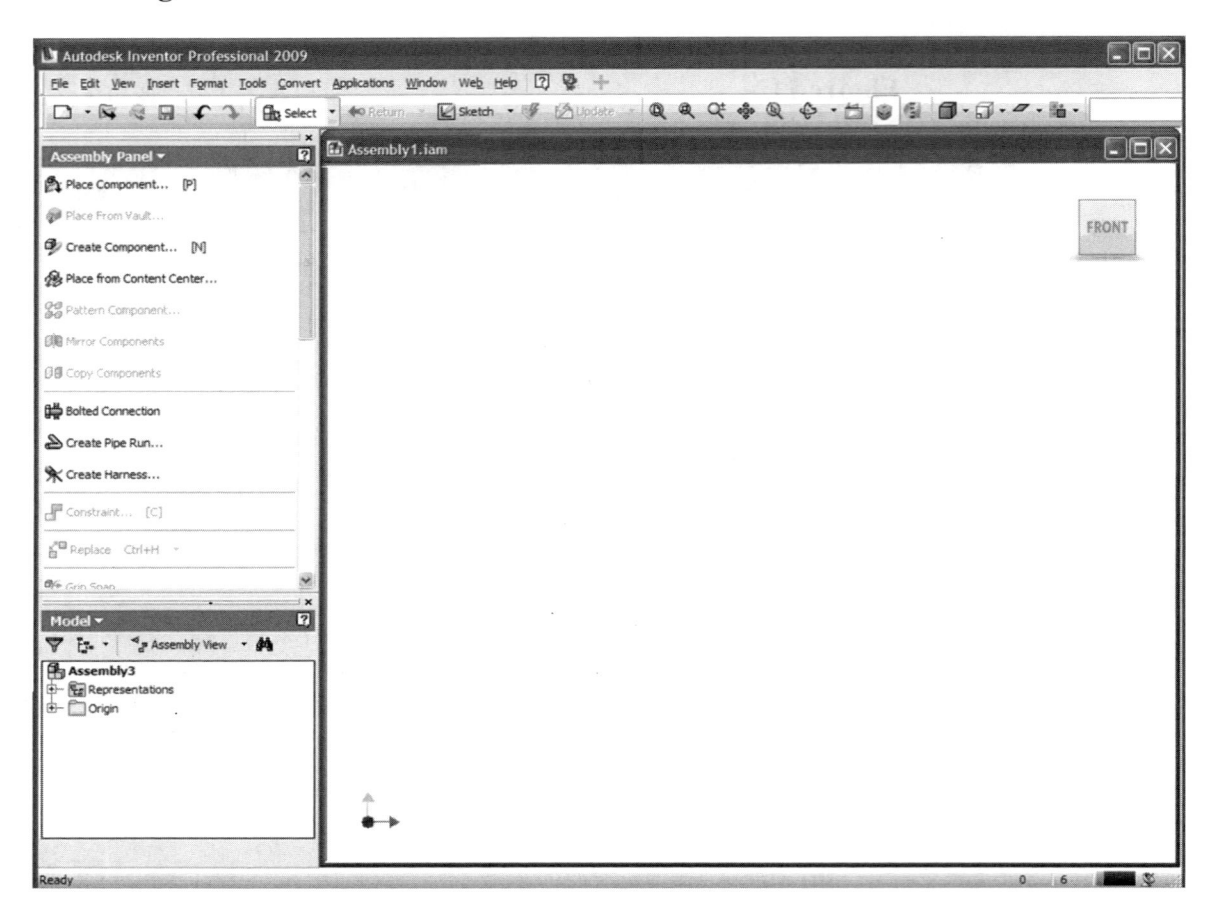

Chapter 10: Introduction to the Design Accelerator

18. Use the **Place Component** command to place the Camcase1.ipt file into the assembly as shown in Figure 13.

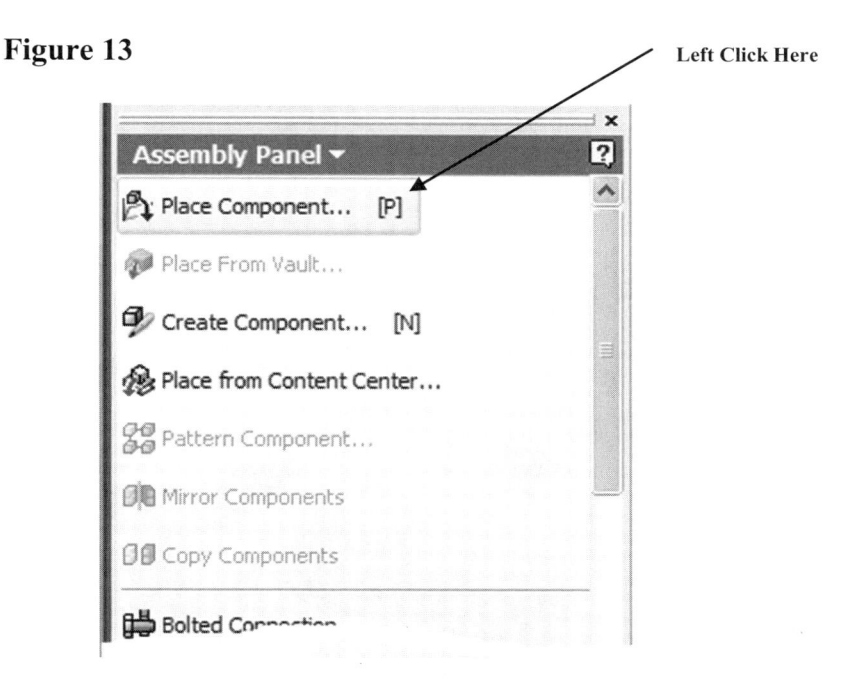

    Figure 13   Left Click Here

19. The Place Component dialog box will appear as shown in Figure 14.

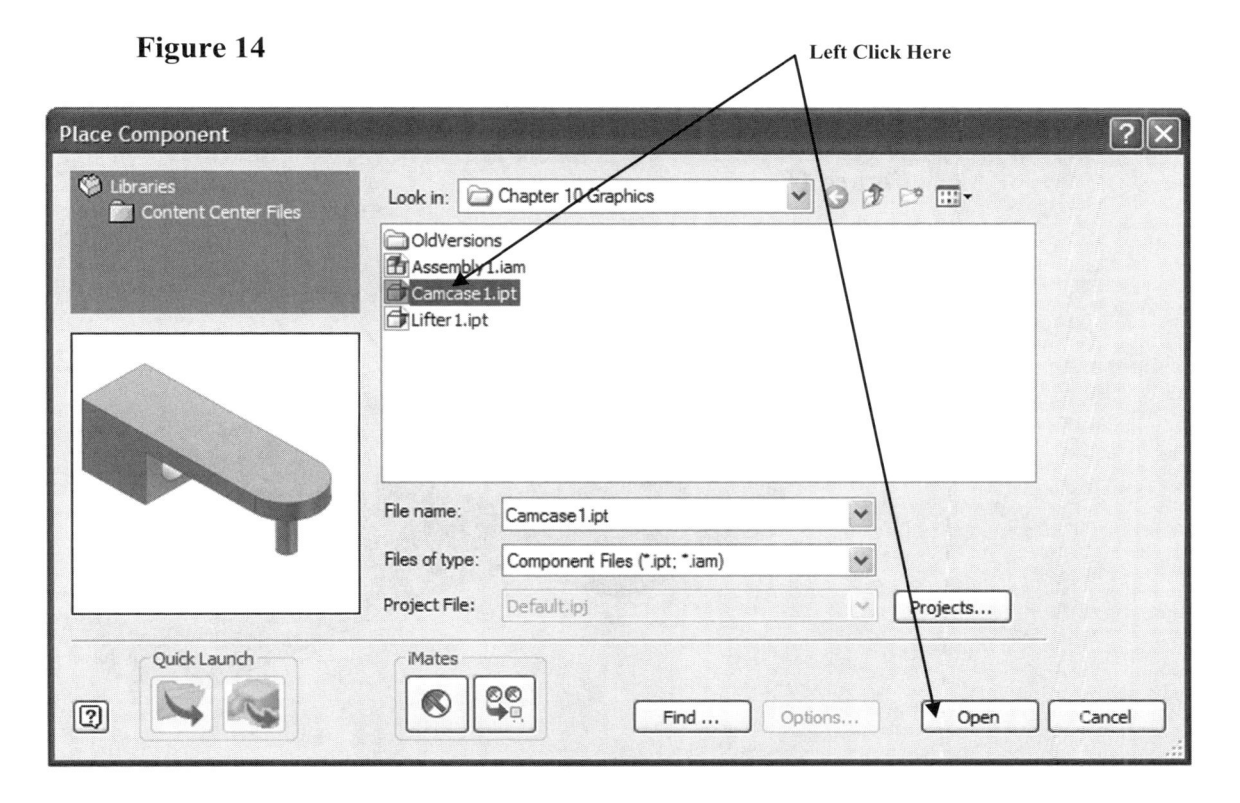

    Figure 14   Left Click Here

Chapter 10: Introduction to the Design Accelerator

20. Repeat the same steps to place the Lifter1.ipt file into the assembly. Your screen should look similar to Figure 15.

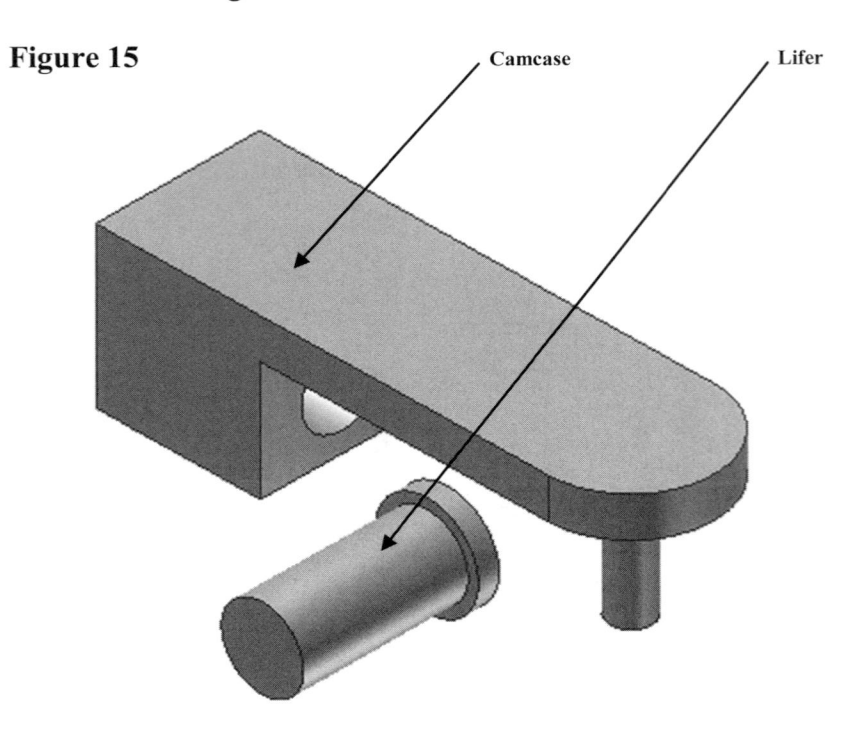

Figure 15

21. Use the **Rotate** command to rotate the case around for better access. Use the **Constraint** command to place the lifter into the lifter bore with the foot towards the bottom of the case as shown in Figure 16.

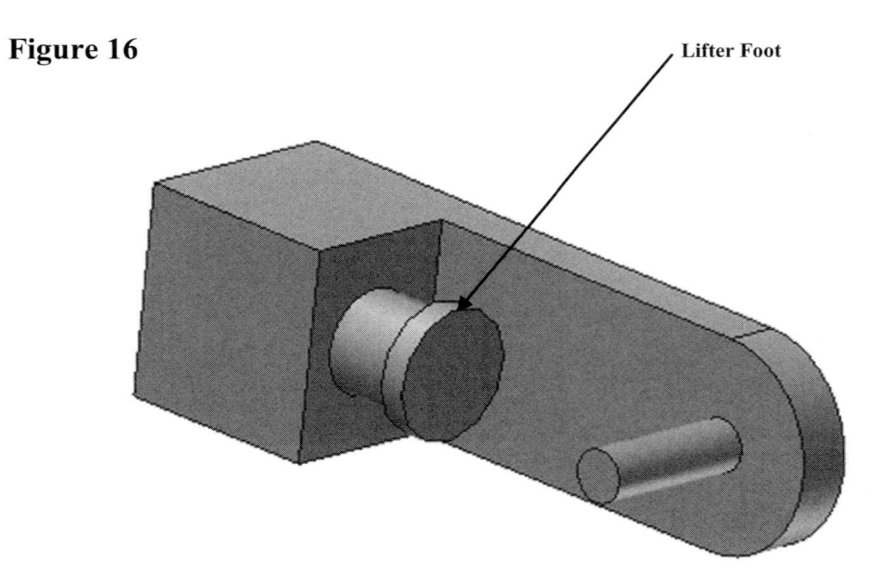

Figure 16

Chapter 10: Introduction to the Design Accelerator

22. Move the cursor to the upper left portion of the screen and left click on the drop down arrow next to Assembly Panel. A drop down menu will appear. Left click on **Design Accelerator** as shown in Figure 17.

Figure 17

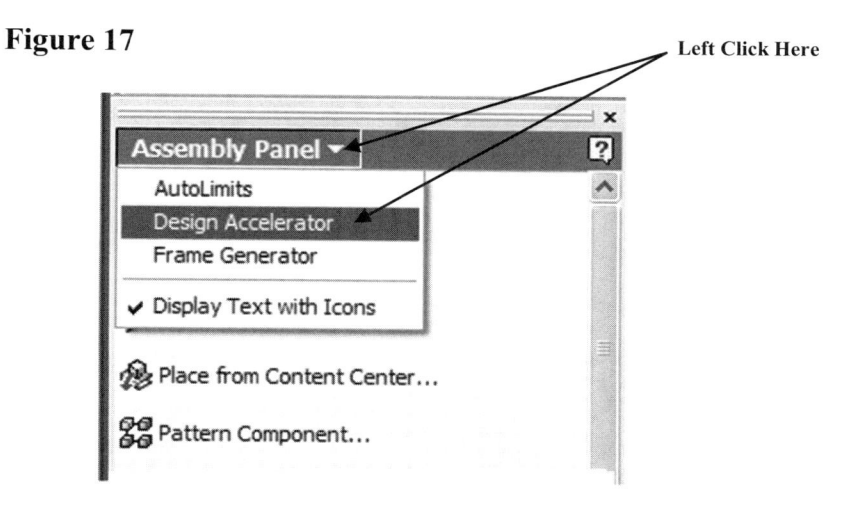

23. The Design Accelerator panel will appear as shown in Figure 18.

Figure 18

503

Chapter 10: Introduction to the Design Accelerator

24. Move the cursor to the upper left portion of the screen and left click on the drop down arrow next to Shaft. A drop down menu will appear. Left click on **Disc Cam** as shown in Figure 19.

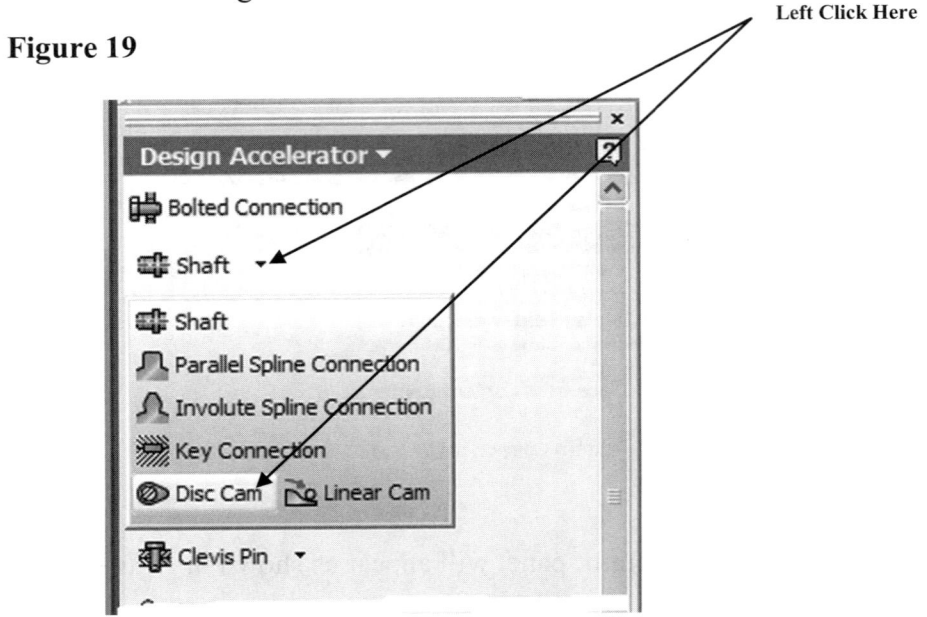

Figure 19

Left Click Here

25. The Disc Cam Component Generator dialog box will appear as shown in Figure 20.

Figure 20

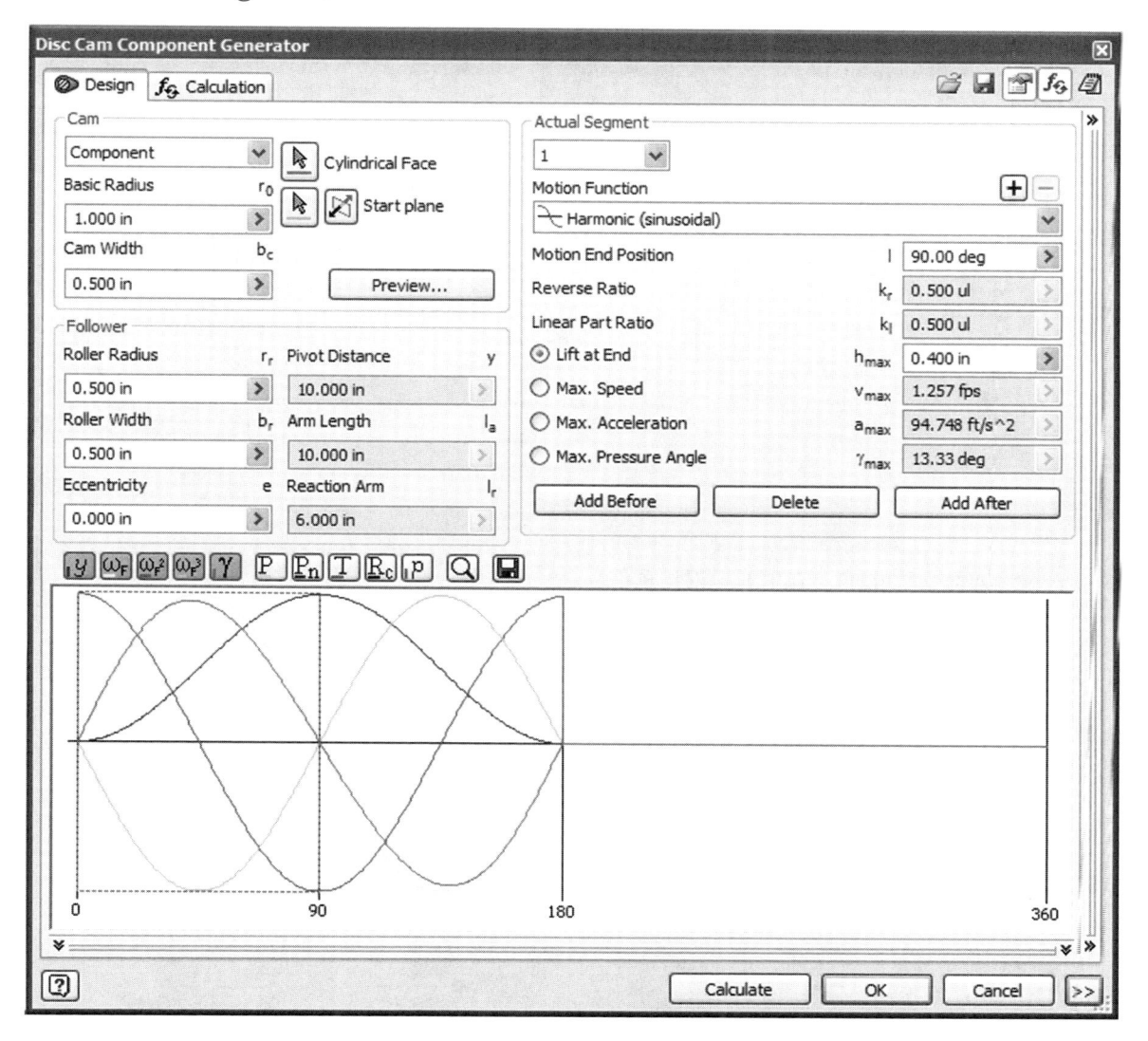

Chapter 10: Introduction to the Design Accelerator

26. Highlight the text below Roller Radius and enter **2.000**. This will create a more pointed disc cam. Left click on **Calculate** and **OK** as shown in Figure 21.

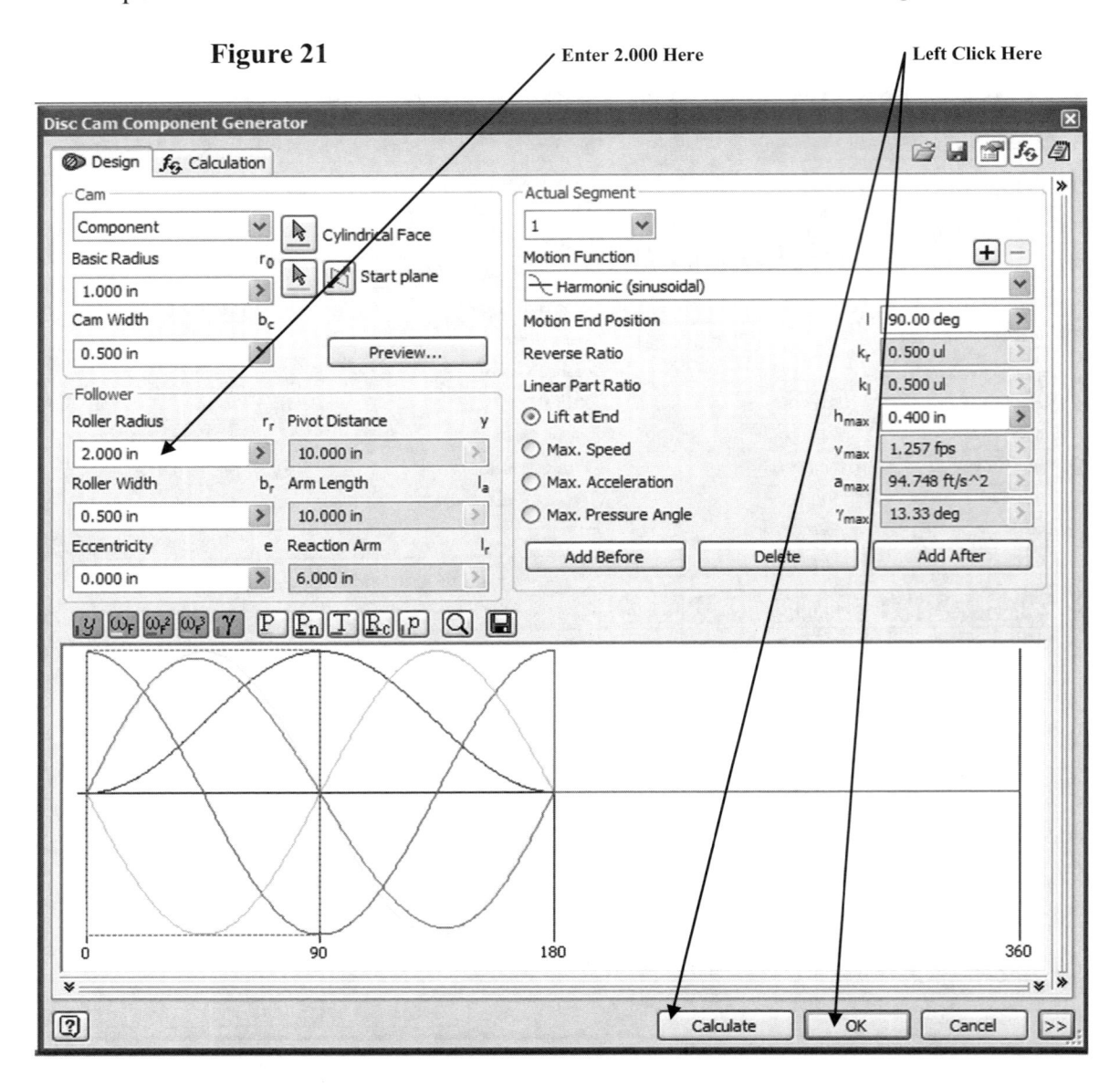

Figure 21

27. The disc cam will be attached to the cursor. Left click as shown in Figure 22.

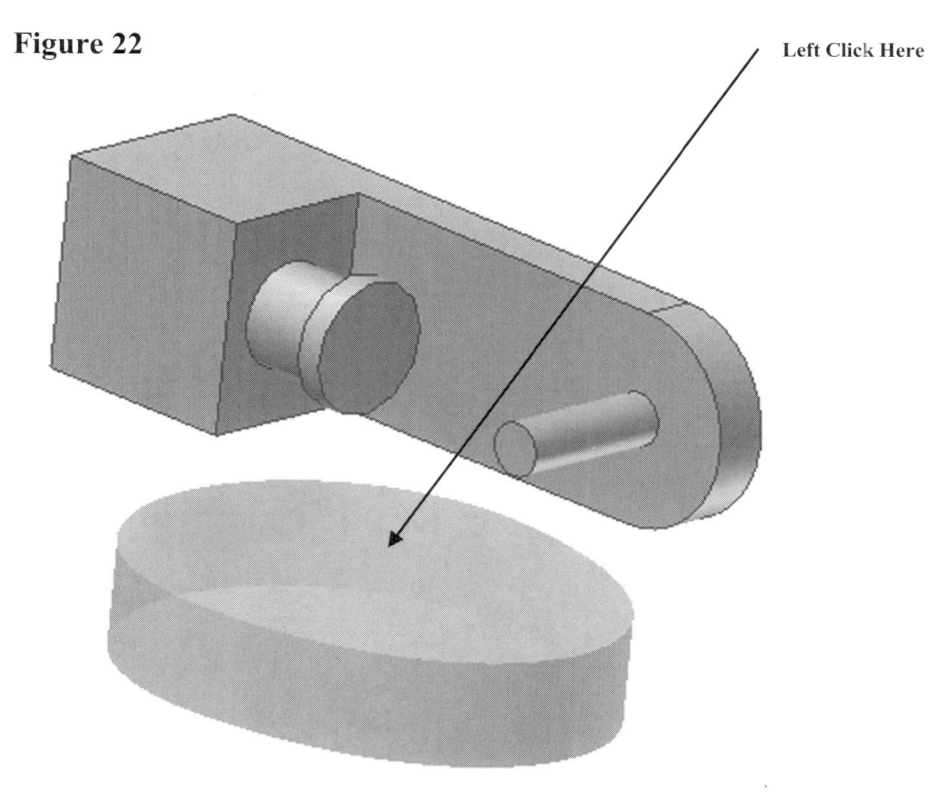

Figure 22

Left Click Here

28. Your screen should look similar to Figure 23.

Figure 23

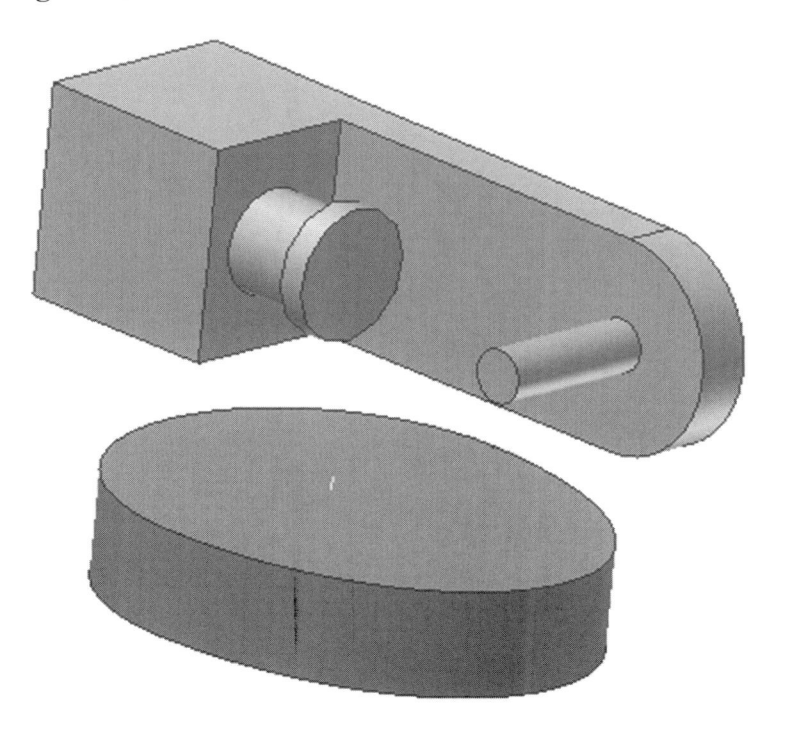

Chapter 10: Introduction to the Design Accelerator

29. The disc cam will need the addition of a center hole and key slot. Move the cursor of the upper face of the disc cam causing the edges to turn red and double click once as shown in Figure 24.

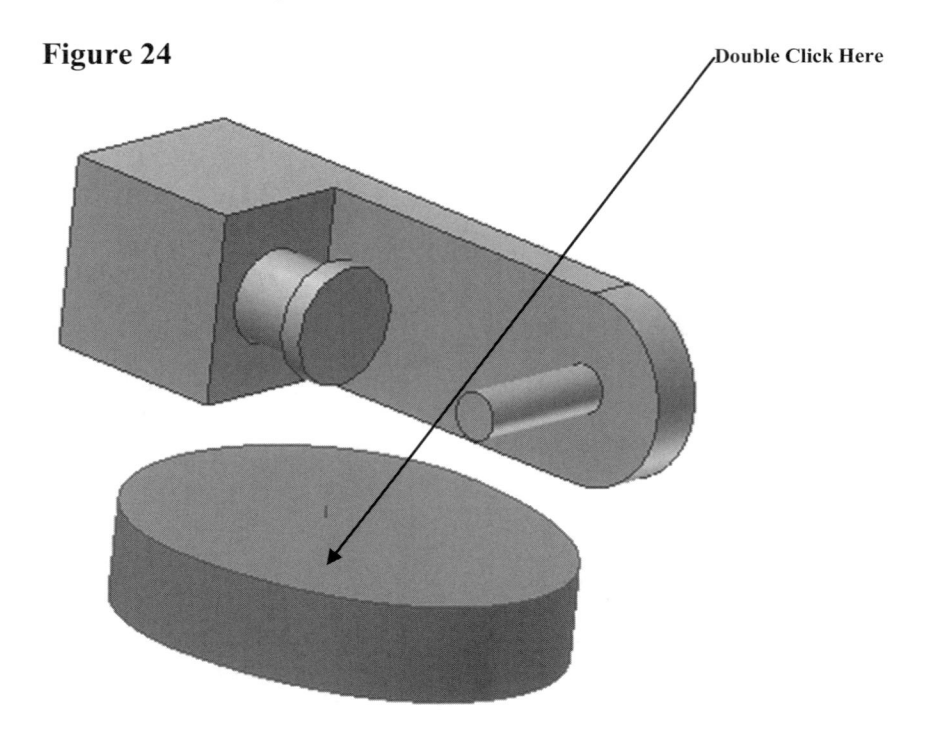

Figure 24

Double Click Here

30. The rest of the parts in the assembly will become inactive as shown in Figure 25.

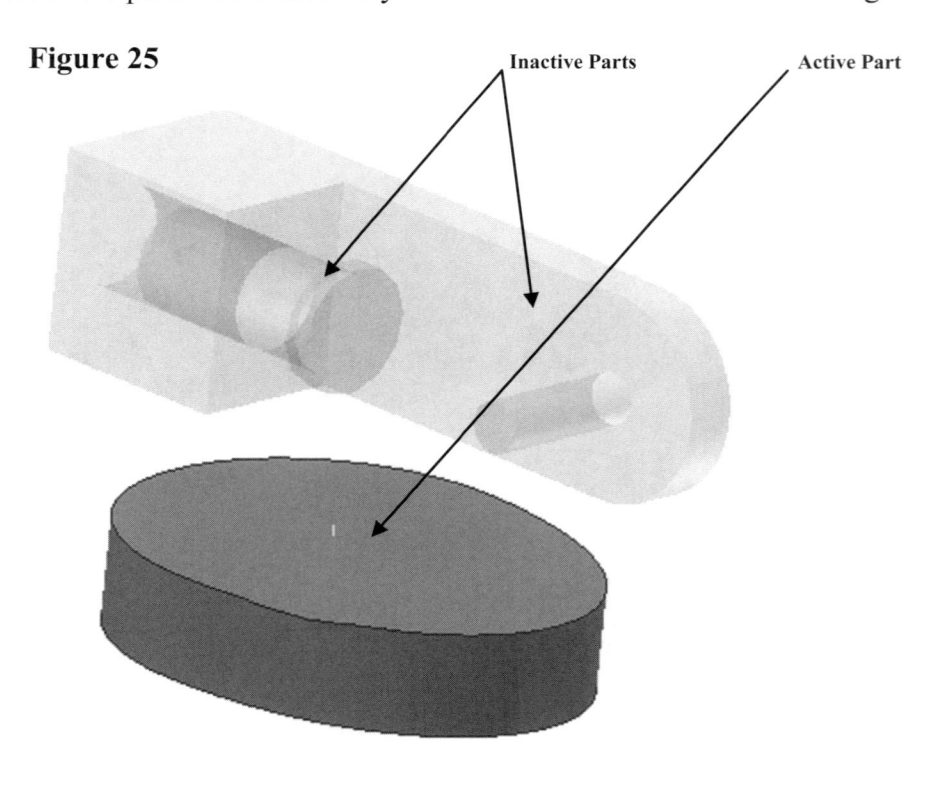

Figure 25

Inactive Parts

Active Part

Chapter 10: Introduction to the Design Accelerator

31. Move the cursor to the upper face of the disc cam causing the edges to turn red and right click once. A pop up menu will appear. Left click on **Edit** as shown in Figure 26.

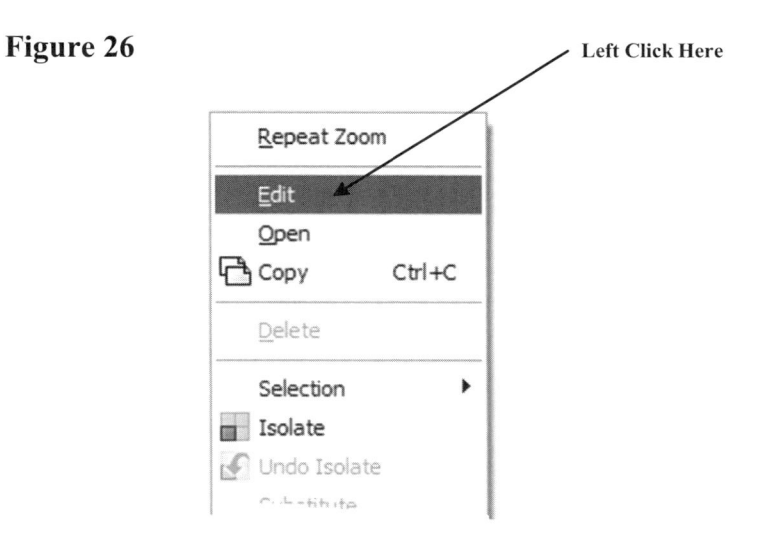

   Figure 26

32. Move the cursor to the upper face of the cam disc causing the edges to turn red and right click once. A pop up menu will appear. Left click on **New Sketch** as shown in Figure 27.

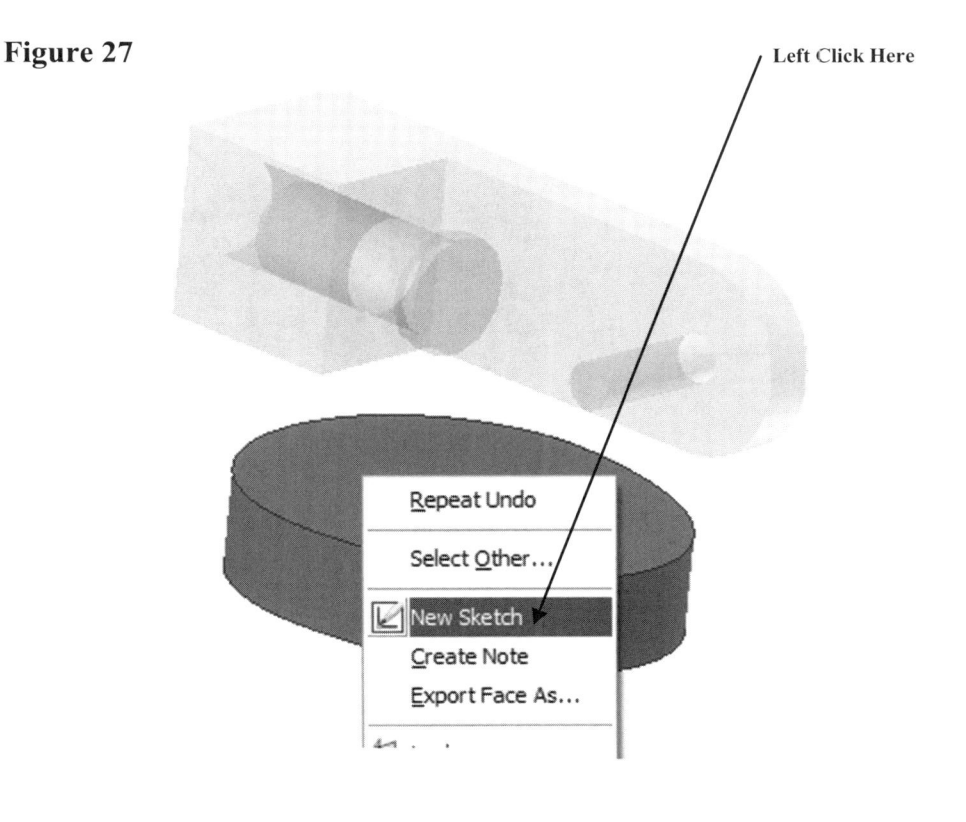

   Figure 27

Chapter 10: Introduction to the Design Accelerator

33. Inventor will return to the Sketch Panel as shown in Figure 28.

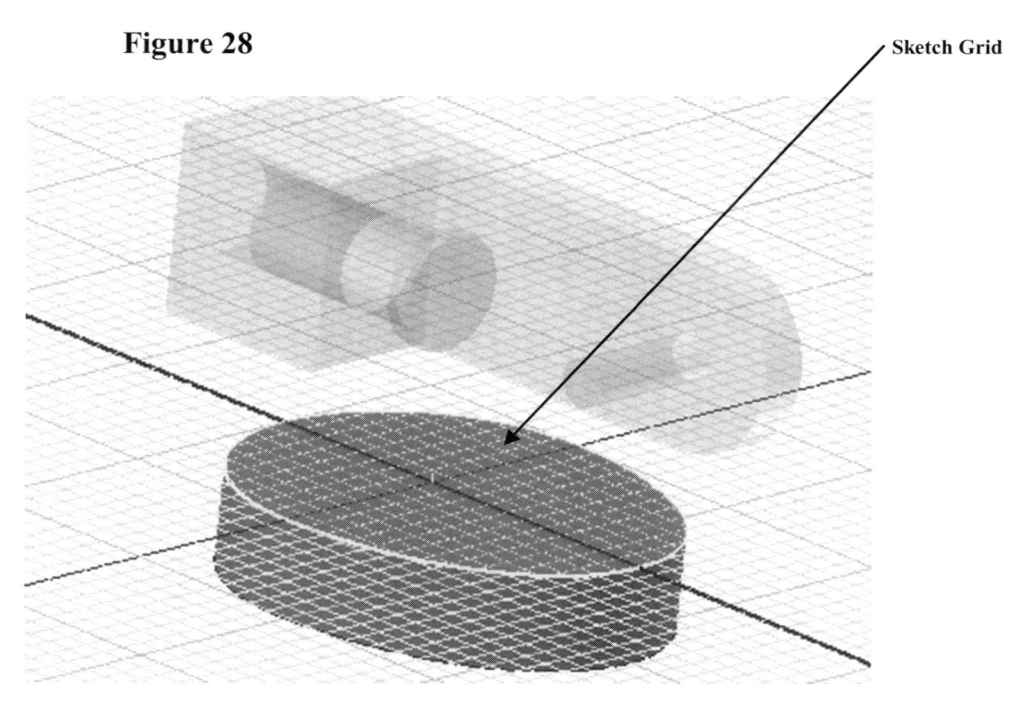

Figure 28

Sketch Grid

34. Use the **Look At** command to gain a perpendicular view of the upper face of the cam disc as shown in Figure 29.

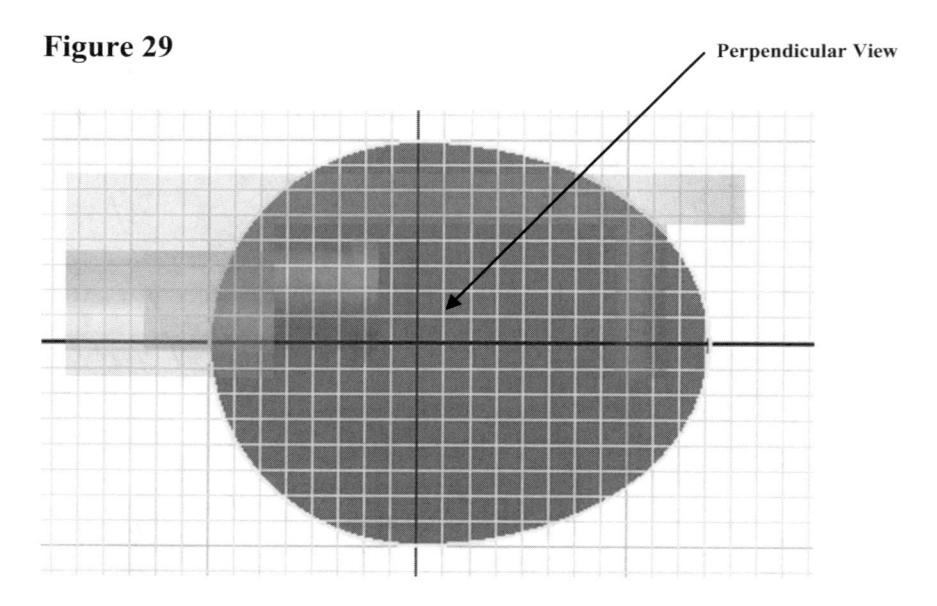

Figure 29

Perpendicular View

510

Chapter 10: Introduction to the Design Accelerator

35. Complete the sketch as shown in Figure 30. Start by drawing a line from the center radius of the disc cam extending to the left side of the cam with a length of 1.000 inch. Use the **General Dimension** command to dimension the line length to 1.000 inch first. The right hand endpoint (beginning endpoint) of this line will become the center of the center hole and key slot.

Figure 30

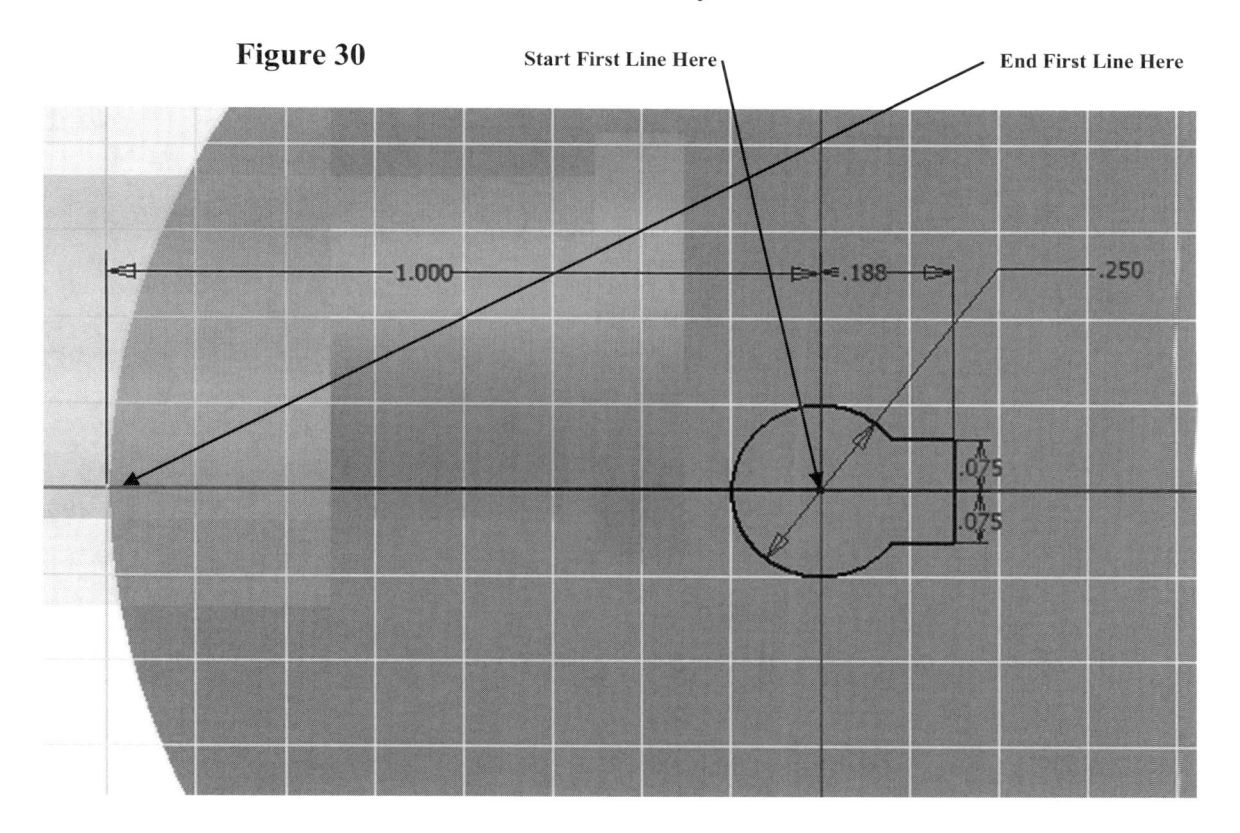

Chapter 10: Introduction to the Design Accelerator

36. Once the sketch is complete, delete the horizontal line that was drawn first as shown in Figure 31. If other dimensions disappear do not be concerned.

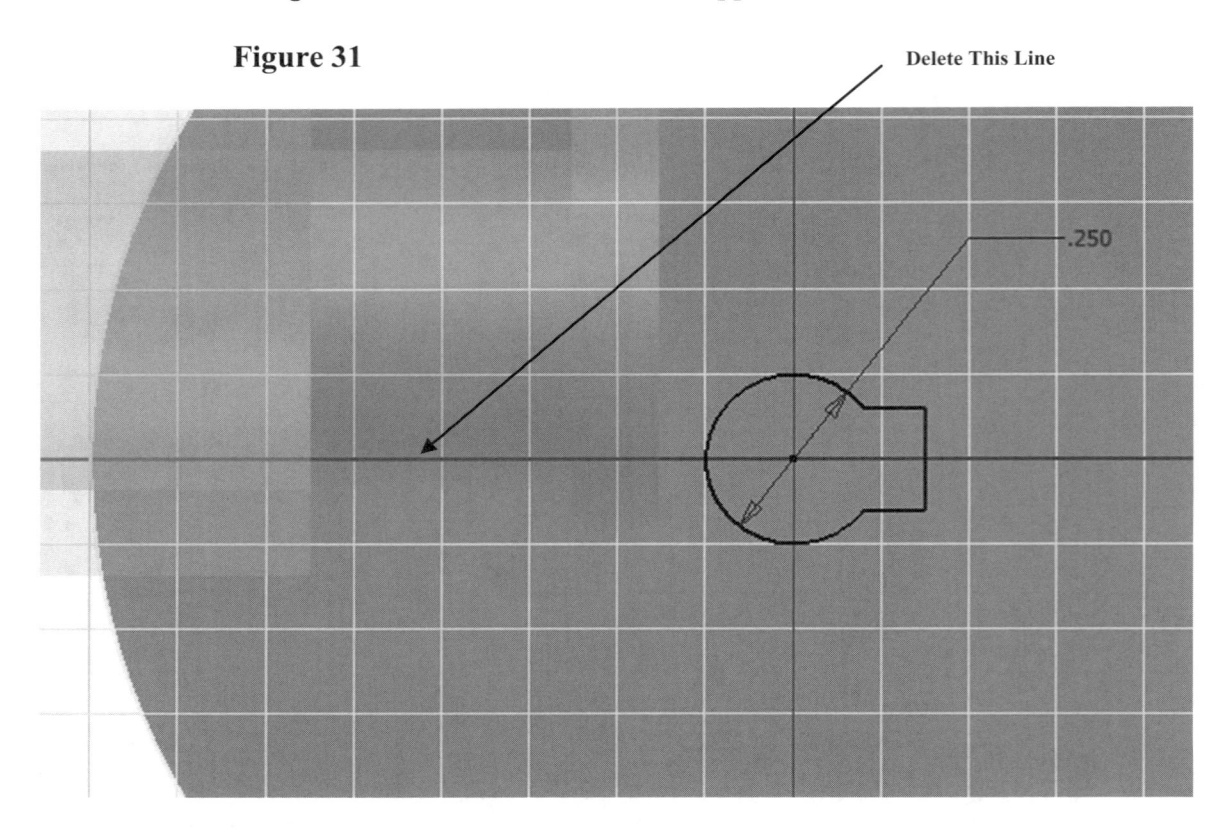

Figure 31

Chapter 10: Introduction to the Design Accelerator

37. Exit the Sketch Panel. Use the **Rotate** command to rotate the part around as shown in Figure 32. Use the **Extrude** command to cut a hole and key slot in the part as shown.

Figure 32

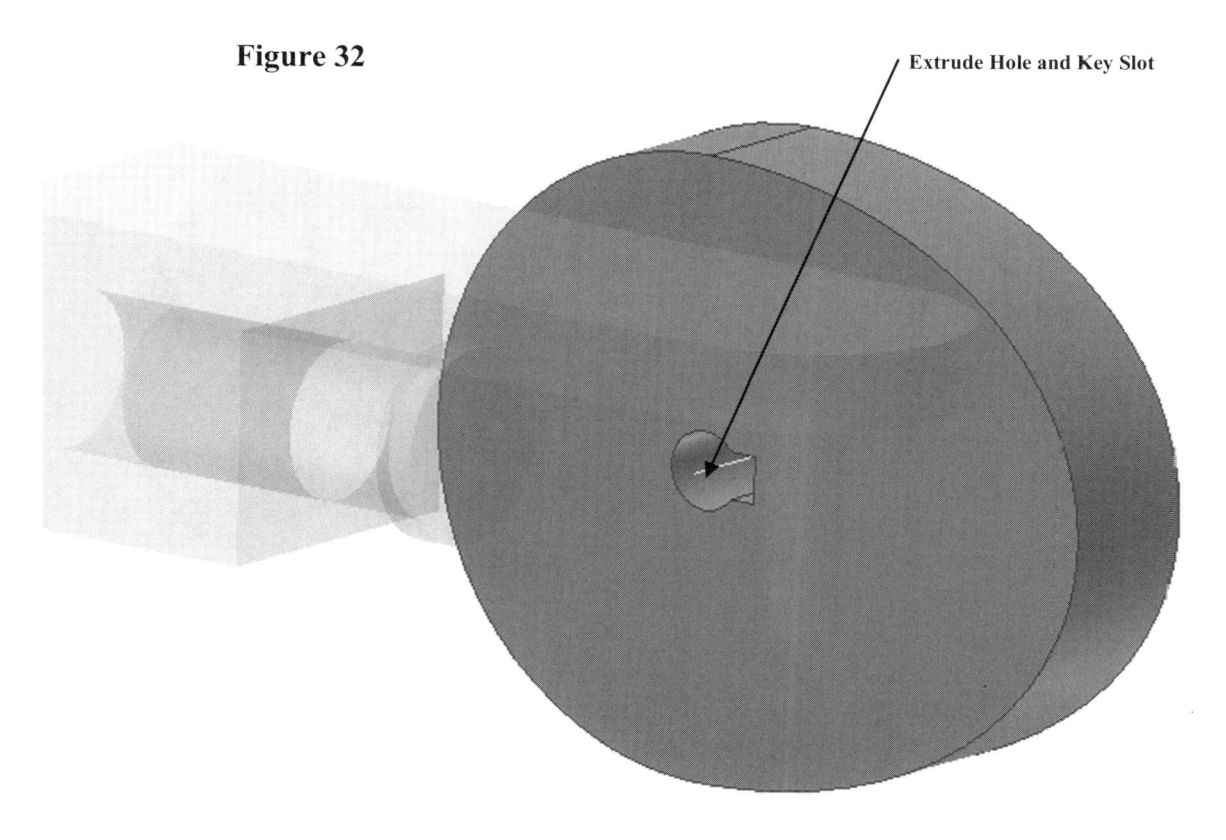

Extrude Hole and Key Slot

38. Move the cursor to the upper middle portion of the screen and left click on **Return** twice as shown in Figure 33.

Figure 33

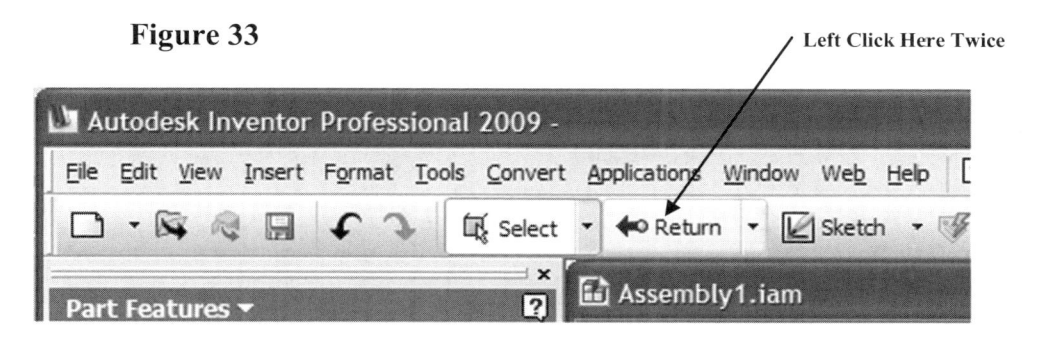

Left Click Here Twice

513

Chapter 10: Introduction to the Design Accelerator

39. Your screen should look similar to Figure 34.

Figure 34

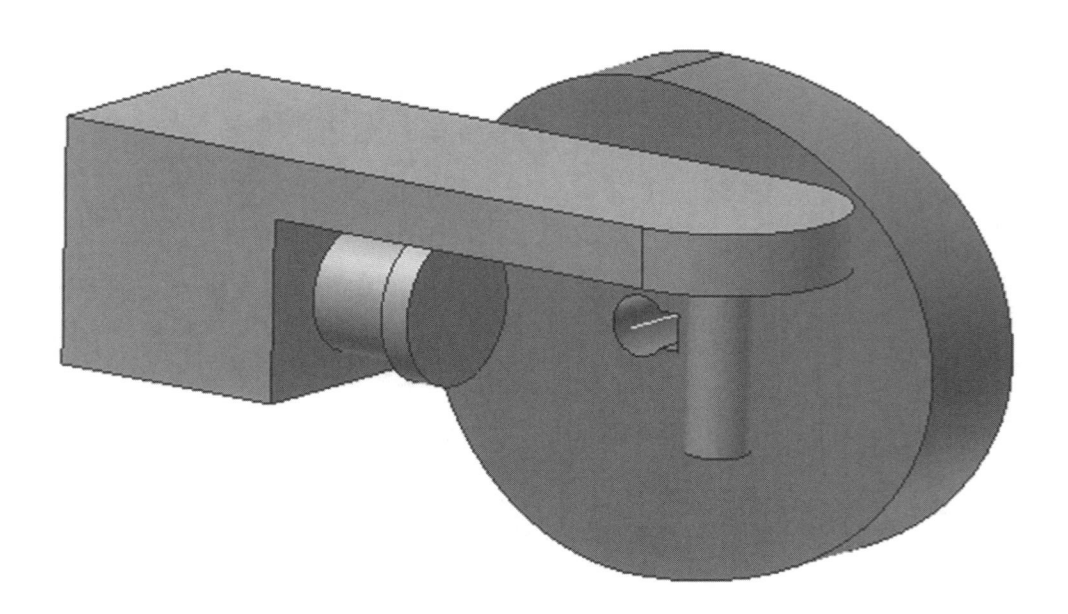

40. Move the cursor to the upper left portion of the screen and left click on the drop down arrow next to Design Accelerator. A drop down menu will appear. Left click on **Assembly Panel** as shown in Figure 35. Inventor will return to the Assembly Panel.

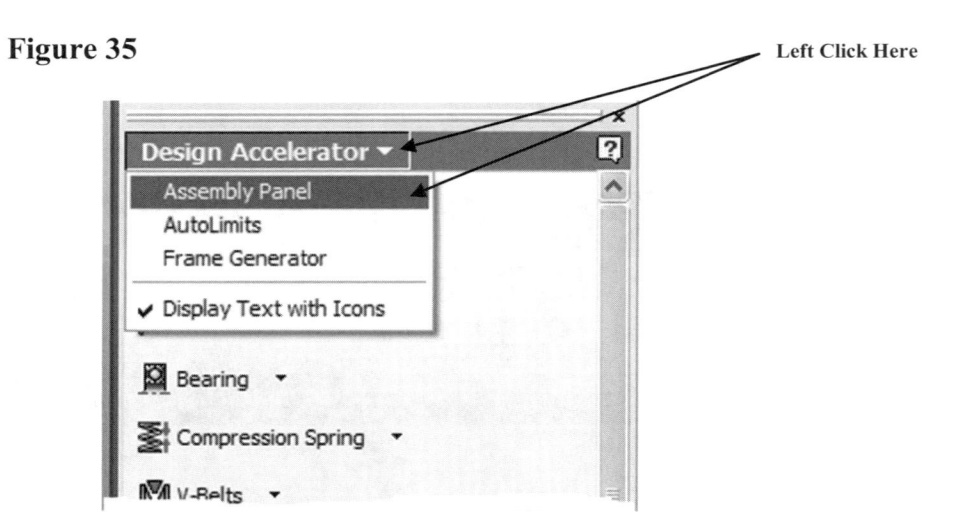

Figure 35   Left Click Here

Chapter 10: Introduction to the Design Accelerator

41. Use the **Constraint** command to constrain the center of the disc cam to the center of the shaft as shown in Figure 36.

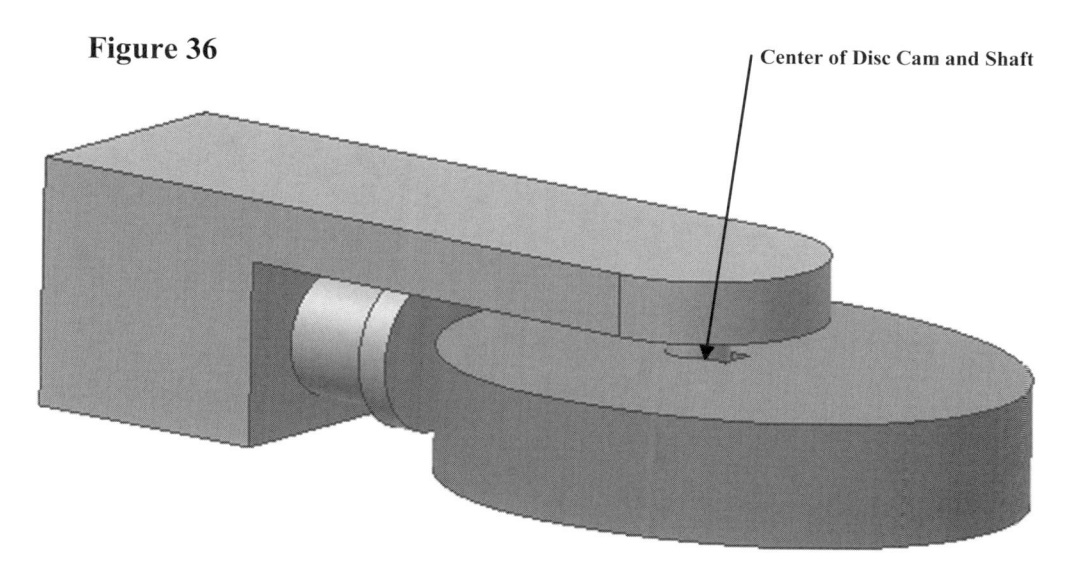

Figure 36

Center of Disc Cam and Shaft

42. Use the **Constraint** command to constrain the disc cam an offset distance of **.125** inches from the inside of the cam case as shown in Figure 37.

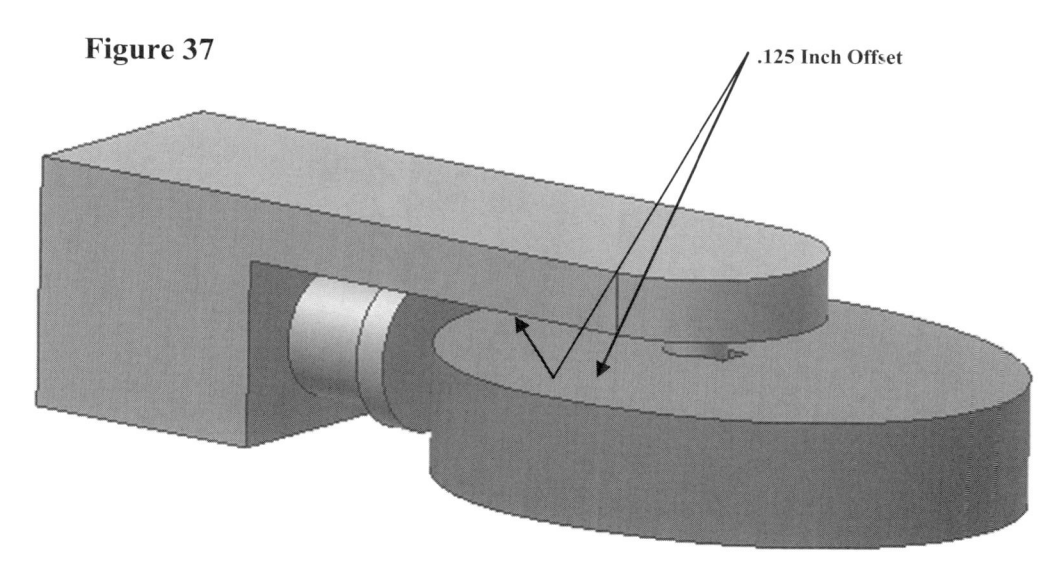

Figure 37

.125 Inch Offset

Chapter 10: Introduction to the Design Accelerator

43. Use the **Rotate** command to rotate the part as shown. The cam disc's location on the shaft should be similar to Figure 38.

Figure 38

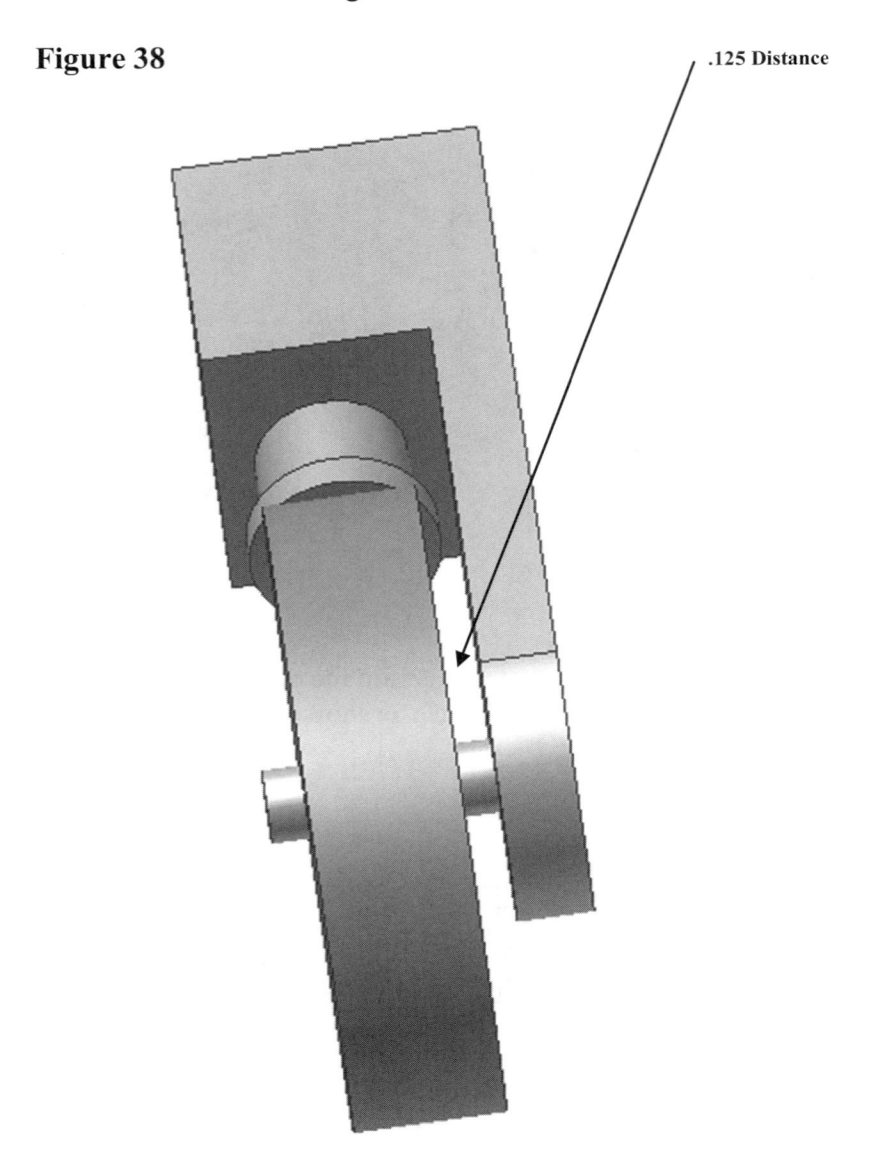

.125 Distance

44. Use the **Rotate** command to rotate the assembly around as shown in Figure 39.

Figure 39

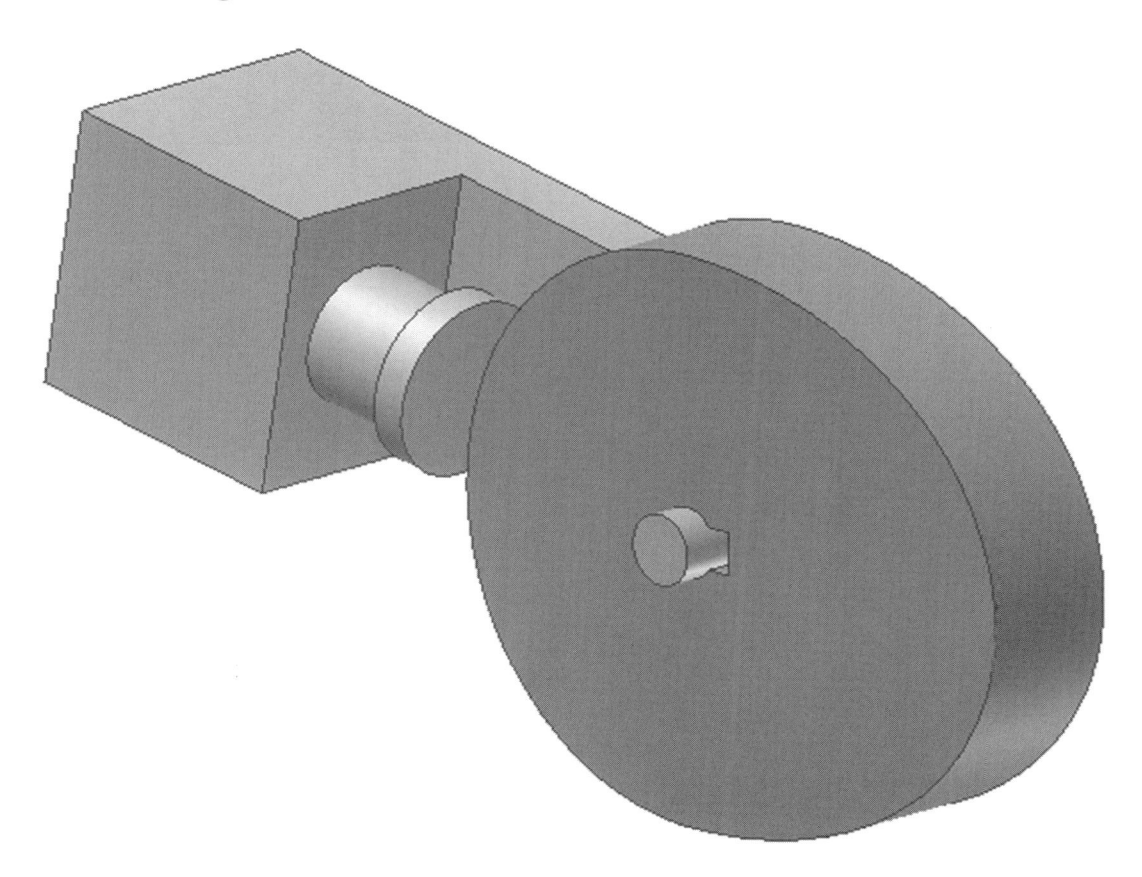

Chapter 10: Introduction to the Design Accelerator

45. Move the cursor to the middle left portion of the screen and left click on **Constraint** as shown in Figure 40.

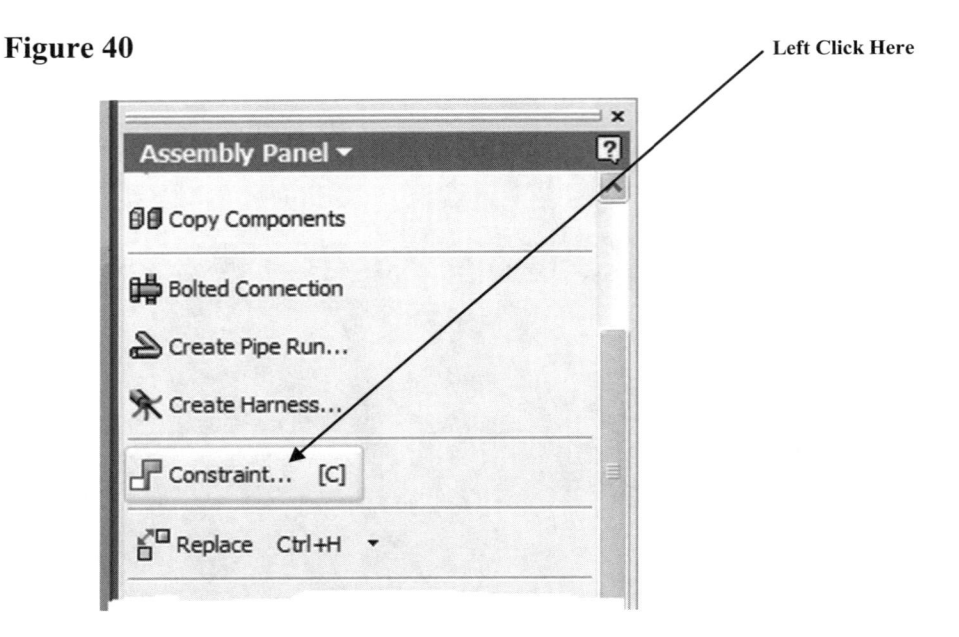

Figure 40   Left Click Here

46. The Place Constraint dialog box will appear. Left click on the **Tangent** icon. Left click on the "Outside" solution as shown in Figure 41.

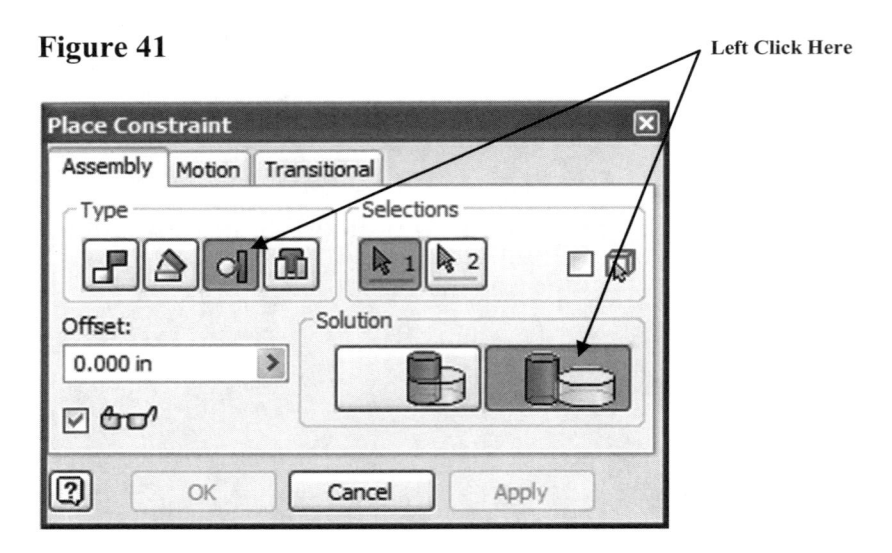

Figure 41   Left Click Here

518

Chapter 10: Introduction to the Design Accelerator

47. Left click on the lifter foot as shown in Figure 42.

Figure 42

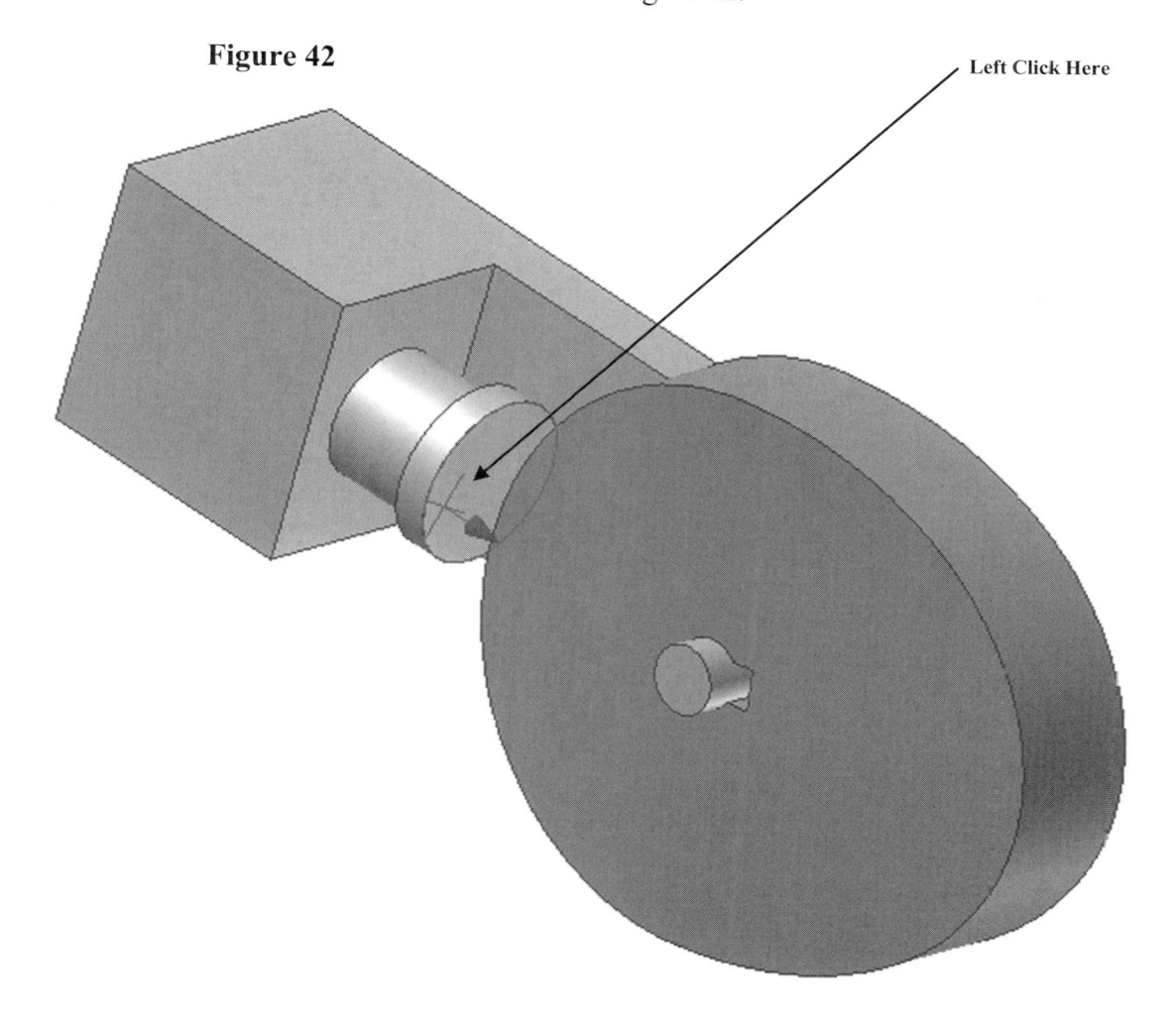

Left Click Here

519

Chapter 10: Introduction to the Design Accelerator

48. Left click on the surface of the disc cam as shown in Figure 43.

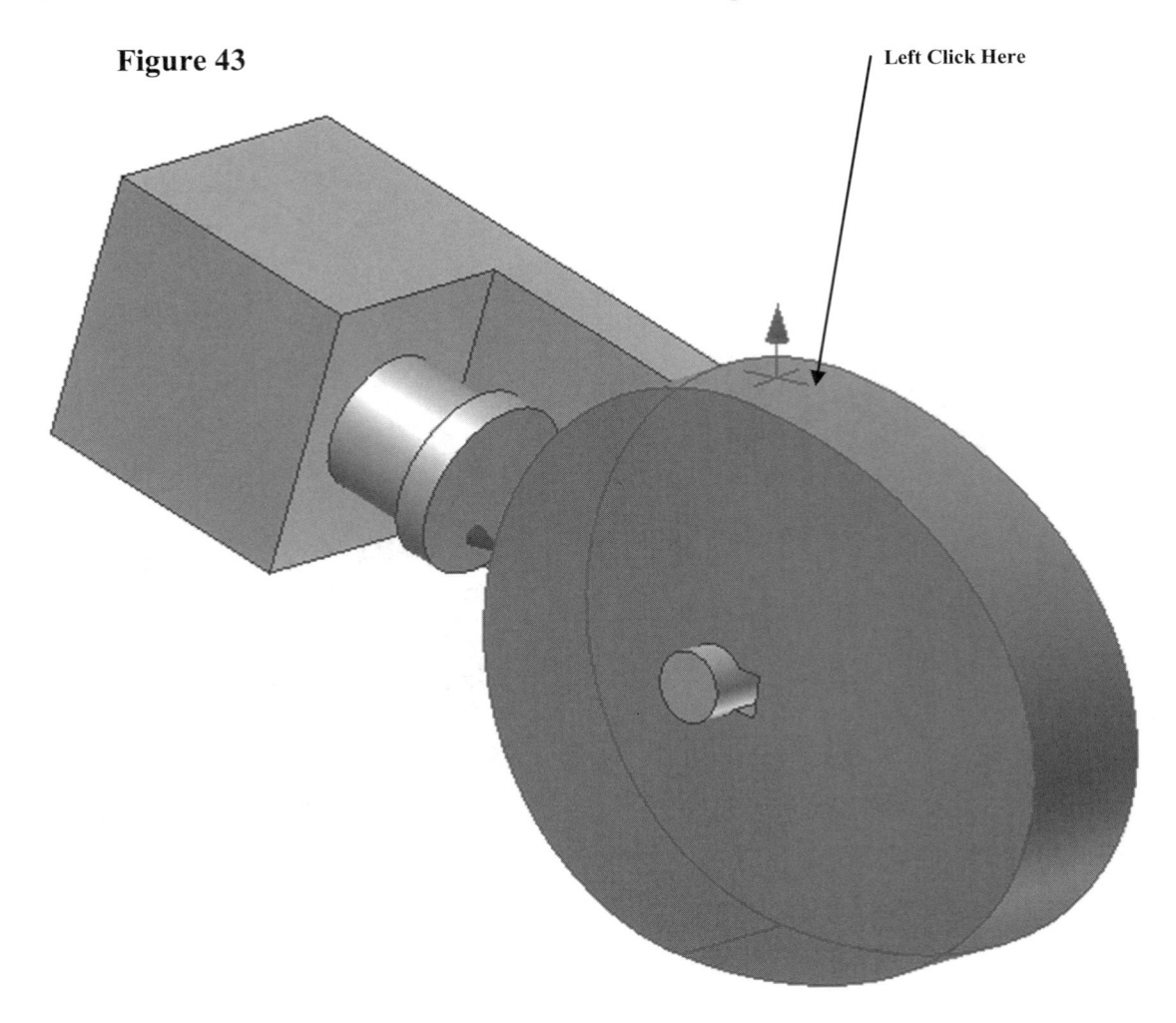

Figure 43

Left Click Here

49. Left click on **OK** as shown in Figure 44.

Figure 44

Left Click Here

Chapter 10: Introduction to the Design Accelerator

50. Use the cursor to rotate the disc cam upward as shown in Figure 45.

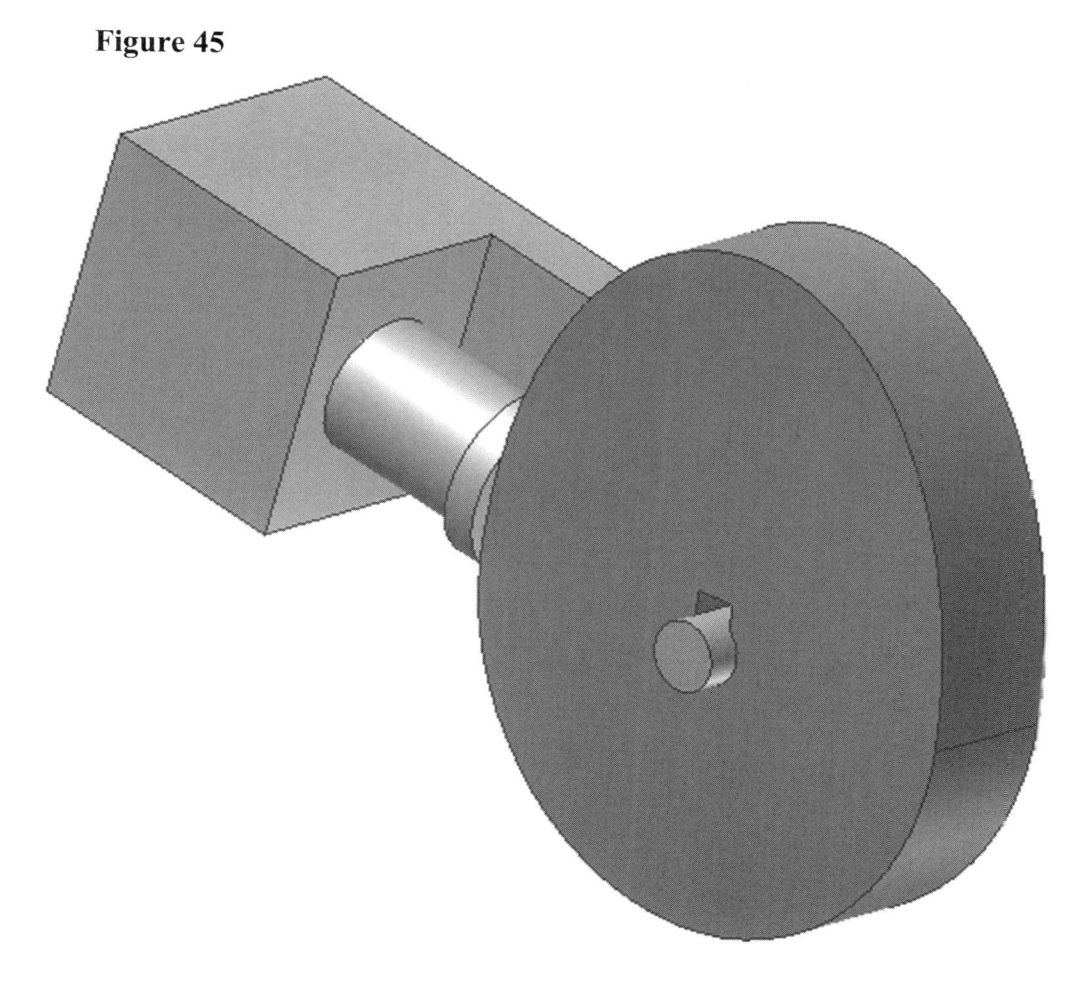

Figure 45

51. Move the cursor to the middle left portion of the screen and left click on **Constraint** as shown in Figure 46.

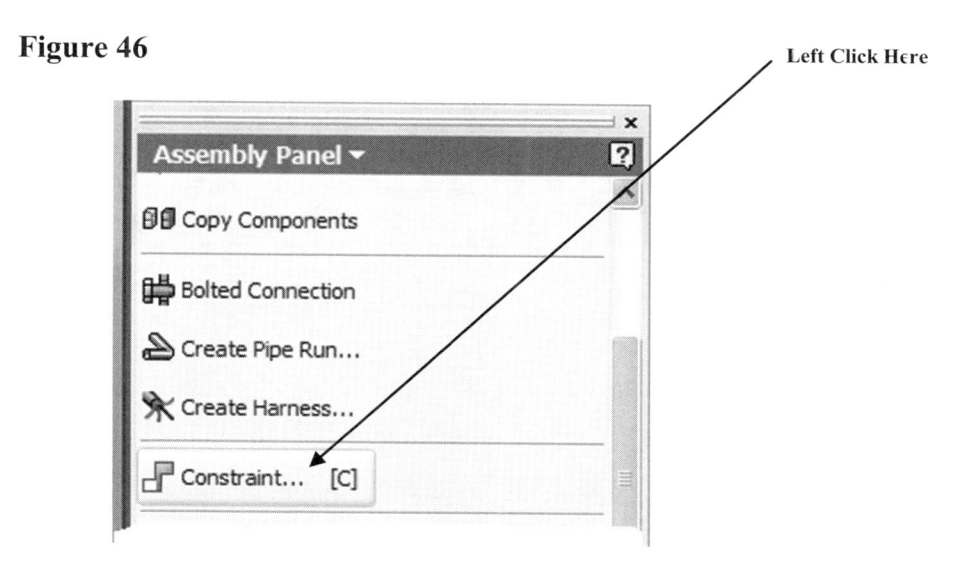

Figure 46

Left Click Here

521

Chapter 10: Introduction to the Design Accelerator

52. The Place Constraint dialog box will appear. Left click on the **Angle** icon. Left click on the "Directed Angle" solution as shown in Figure 47

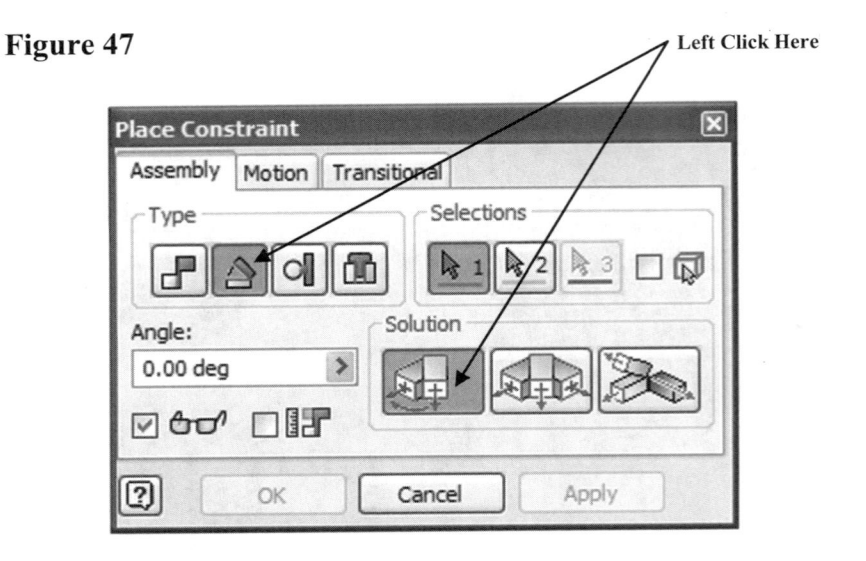

Figure 47

53. Use the **Zoom** command to zoom in on the key slot. Left click on the back of the key slot as shown in Figure 48.

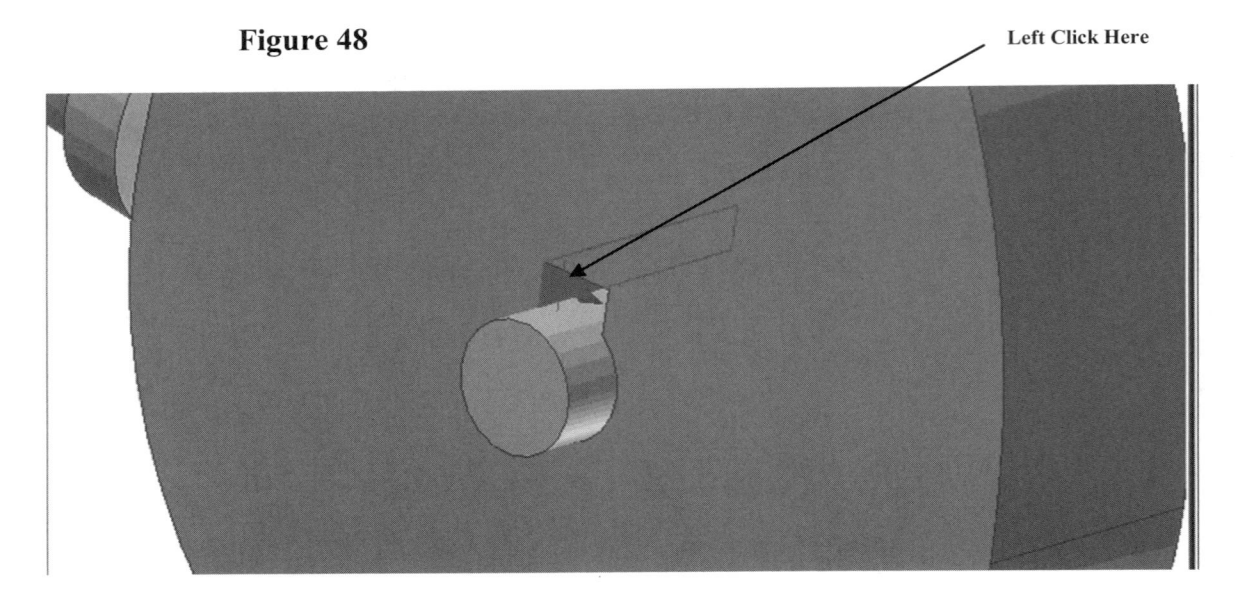

Figure 48

522

Chapter 10: Introduction to the Design Accelerator

54. Left click on the underside of the cam case as shown in Figure 49.

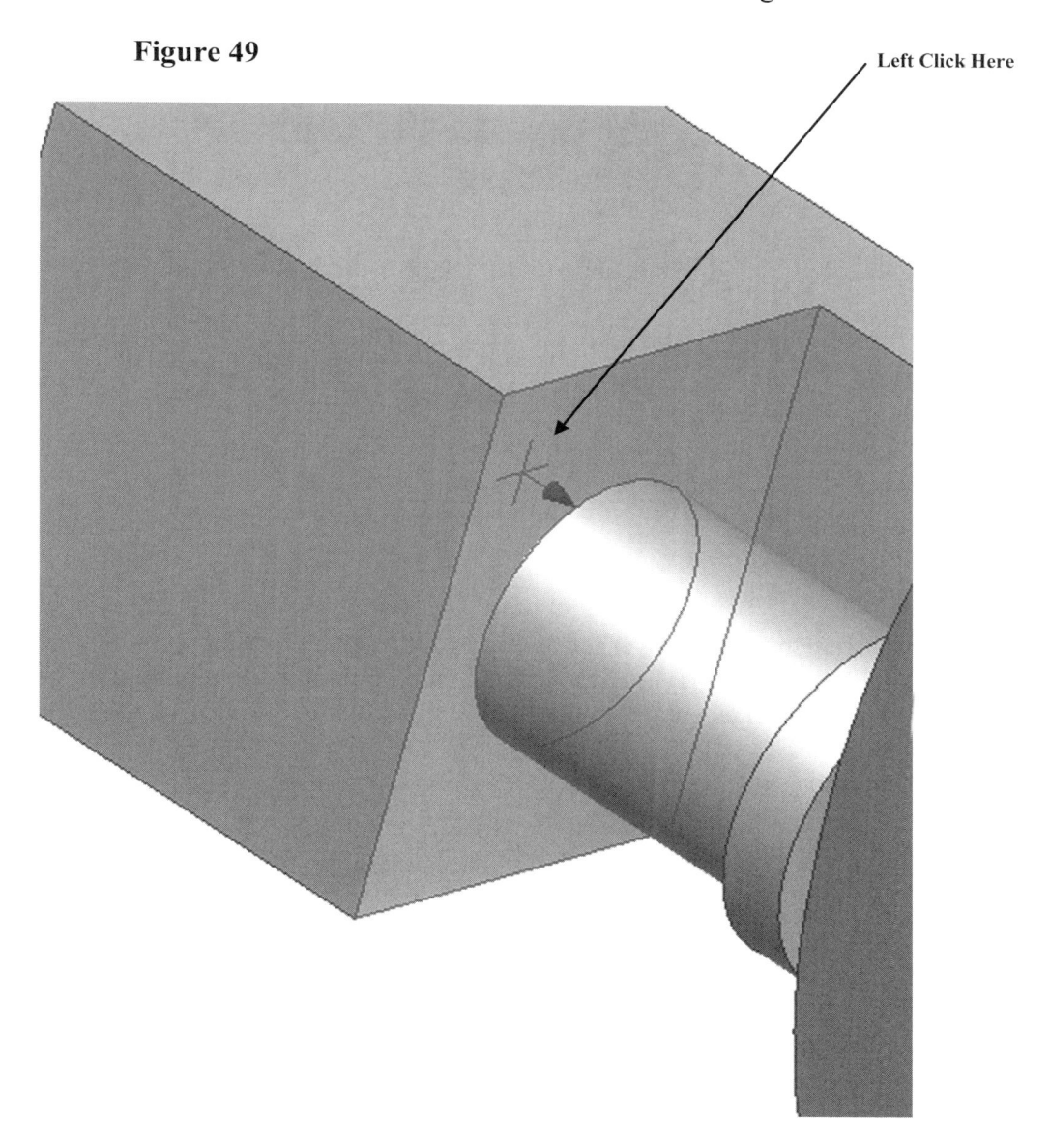

Figure 49

Left Click Here

Chapter 10: Introduction to the Design Accelerator

55. Left click on **OK** as shown in Figure 50.

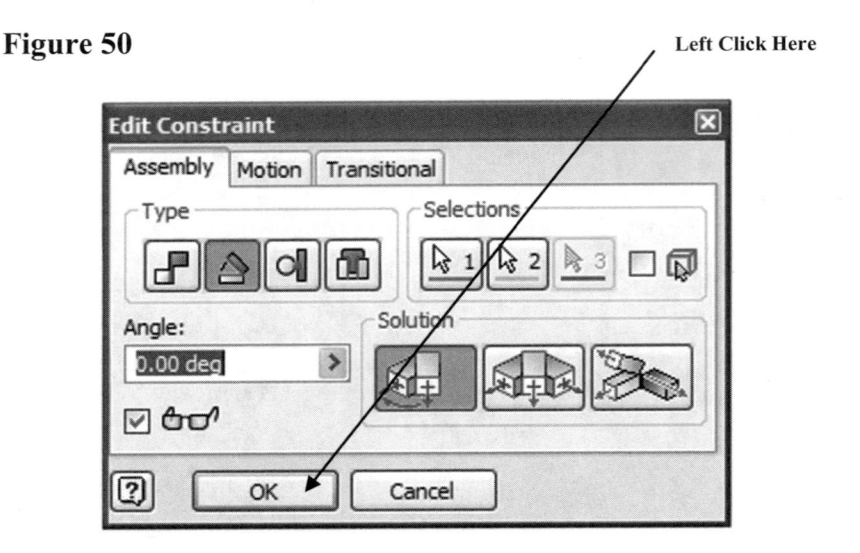

Figure 50

Left Click Here

56. Move the cursor to the lower left portion of the screen to the part tree. Scroll down to **Angle:1** and right click once. A pop up menu will appear. Left click on **Drive Constraint** as shown in Figure 51.

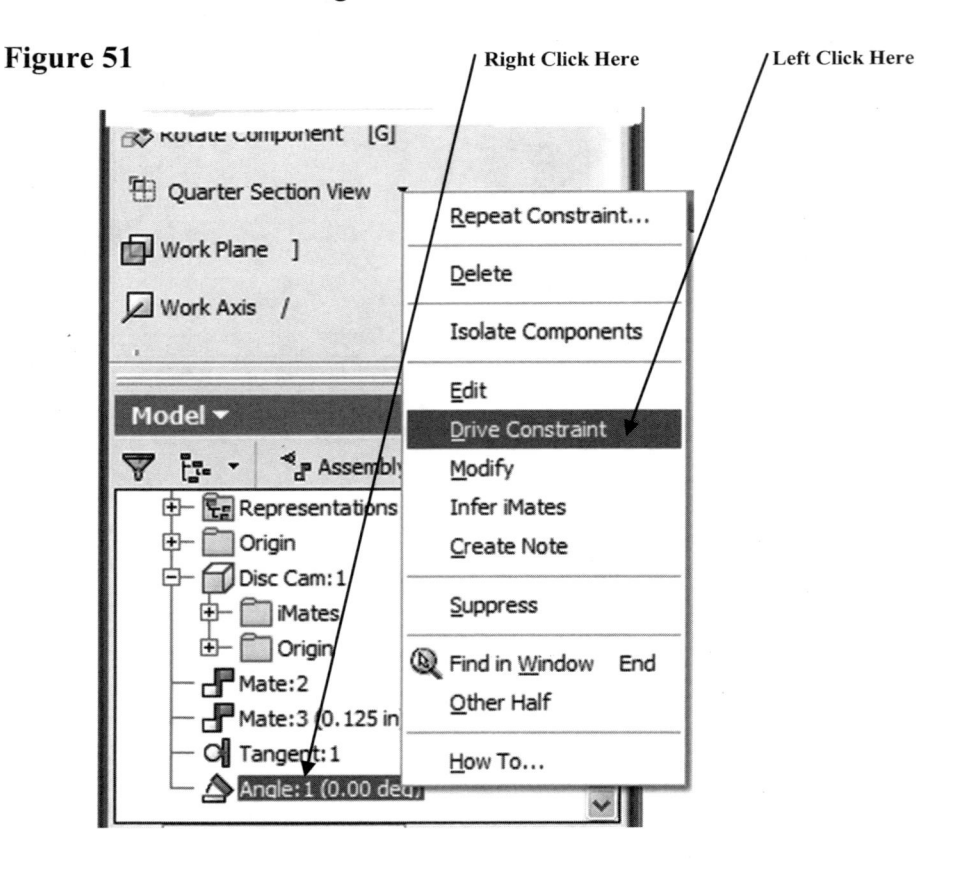

Figure 51

Right Click Here   Left Click Here

524

57. The Drive Constraint dialog box will appear. Enter **0** degrees under "Start". Enter **360000** degrees under "End". Left click on the double arrows at the far lower right corner of the dialog box as shown in Figure 52.

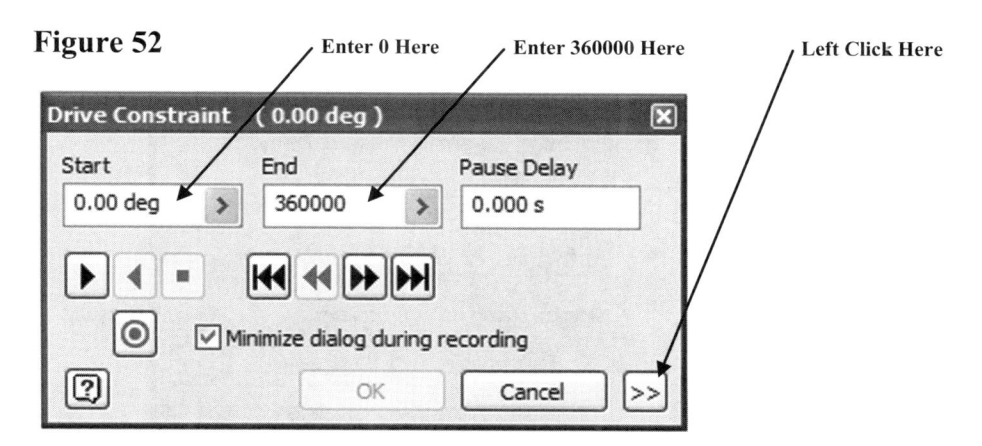

Figure 52

58. The Drive Constraint dialog box will expand providing more options. Enter **10** for the number of degrees as shown in Figure 53.

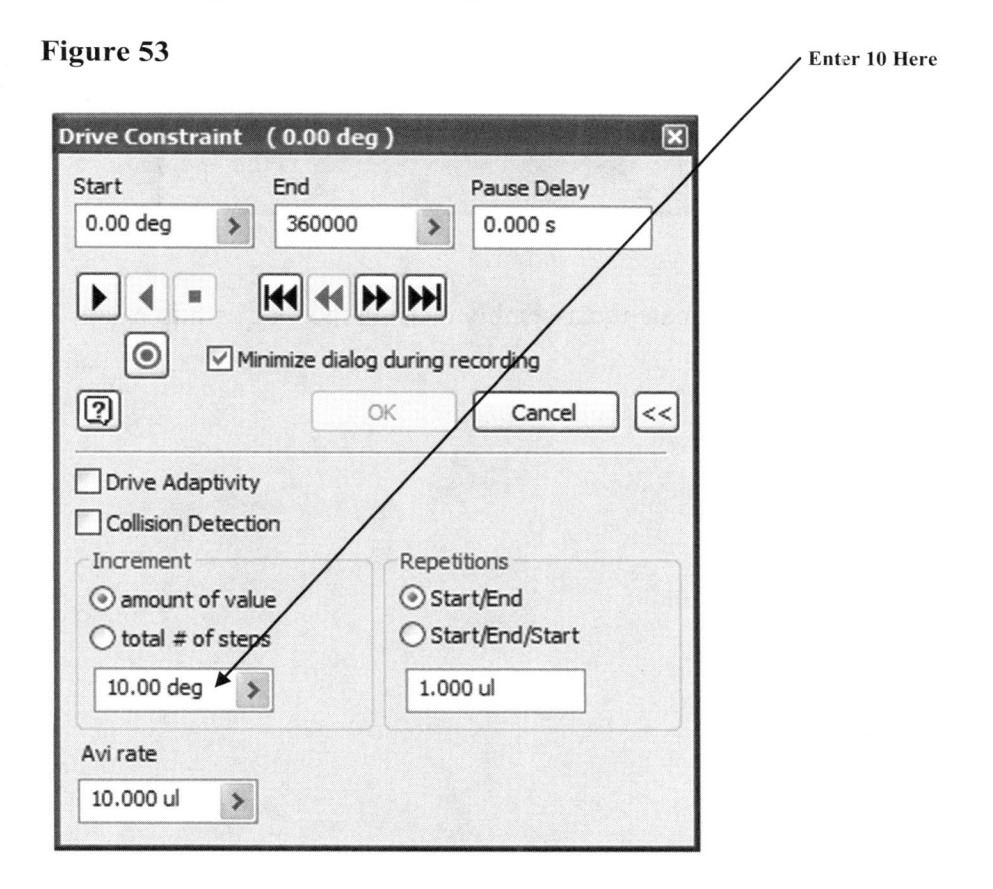

Figure 53

Chapter 10: Introduction to the Design Accelerator

59. Use the **Zoom** option to zoom out. Use the **Pan** option to move the assembly off to the side. Left click on the "Play" icon as shown in Figure 54.

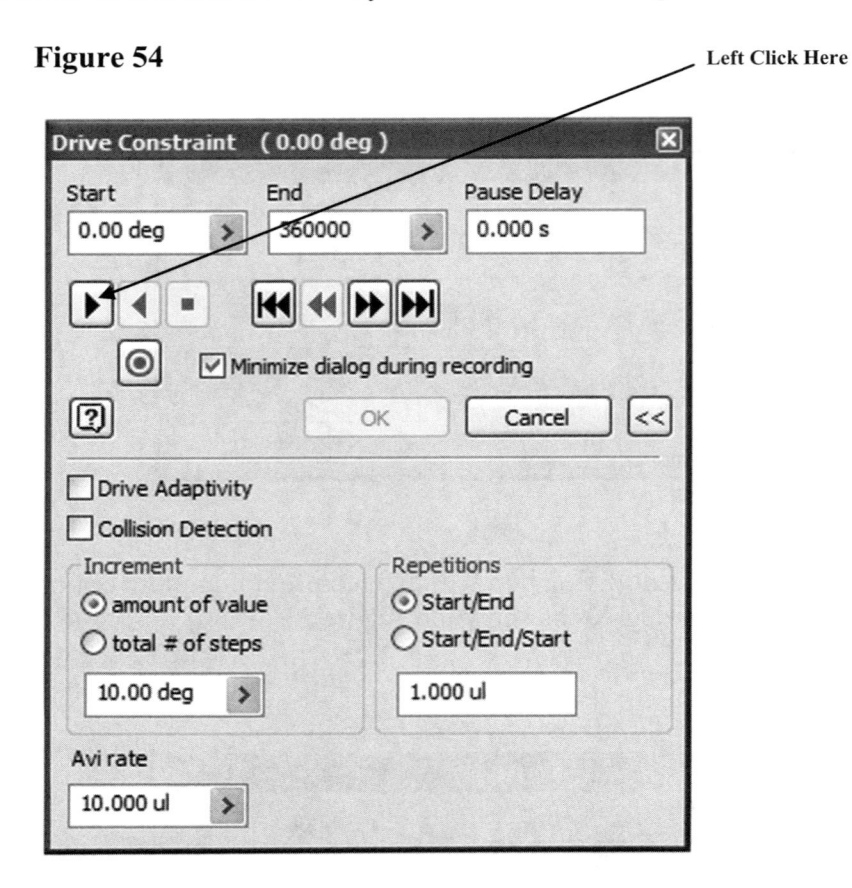

Figure 54

Left Click Here

```
Drive Constraint  ( 0.00 deg )                    [X]
Start            End              Pause Delay
0.00 deg   >    360000    >      0.000 s

[▶] [◀] [■]    [|◀◀] [◀◀] [▶▶] [▶▶|]

[◉]    ☑ Minimize dialog during recording
[?]              OK        Cancel      <<

☐ Drive Adaptivity
☐ Collision Detection
┌Increment─────────┐  ┌Repetitions──────┐
│ ◉ amount of value│  │ ◉ Start/End     │
│ ○ total # of steps│ │ ○ Start/End/Start│
│  10.00 deg   >   │  │  1.000 ul       │
└──────────────────┘  └─────────────────┘
Avi rate
 10.000 ul   >
```

60. Inventor will animate the assembly causing the disc cam to rotate.

Chapter 10: Introduction to the Design Accelerator

61. Left click on the "Stop" icon. The animation will stop. Left click on the "Minimize" icon. The Drive Constraint dialog box will get smaller. Left click on the "Rewind" icon. This will rewind the animation back to 0 degrees as shown in Figure 55. Refer to Chapter 7 for instructions on how to create an .avi or .wmv file.

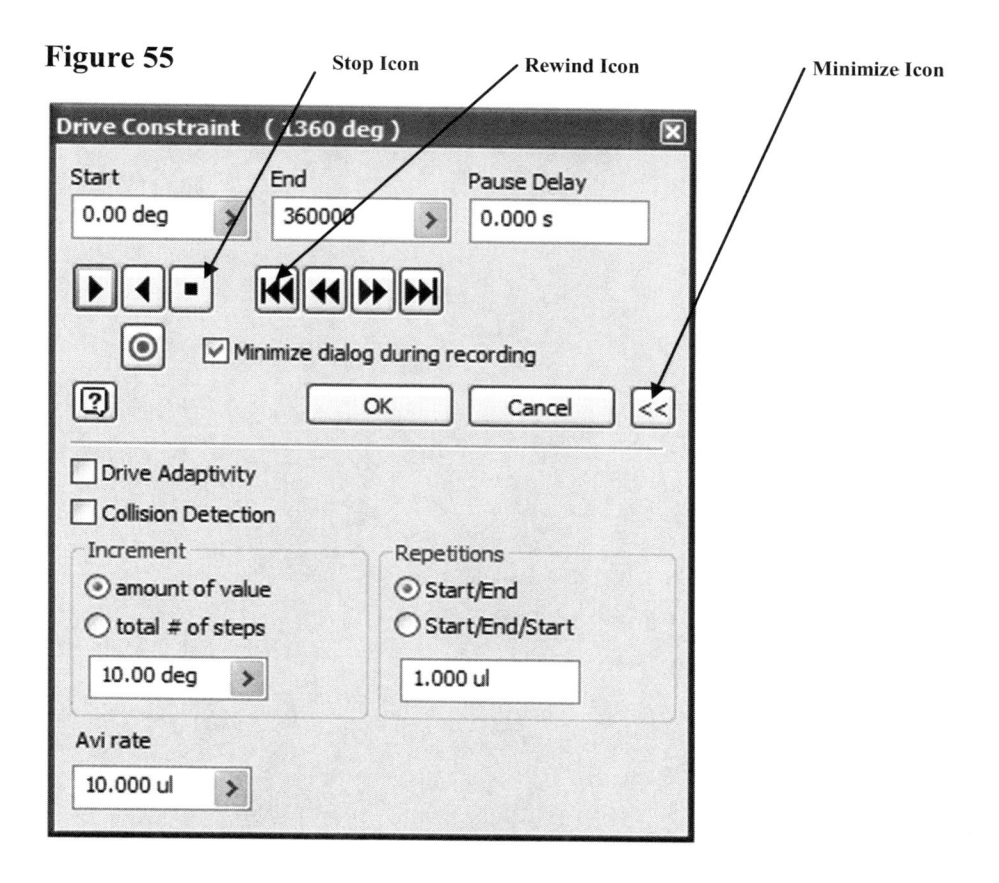

Figure 55

Index

A
Angle Constraint icon, 418
Angle:1, 422
Animate, 452
Apply, 421
As Material, 412
Assembly Panel, 353
Attaching dimension to cursor, 12
Auxiliary View, 187
Auxiliary View dialog box, 188
Axis, 88

B
Base View, 165
Beginning, End point of a line, 7, 68
Bi-directional icon, 300
Blue (Clear/Polished), 414

C
Center Point Circle, 45, 99
Chamfer, 137
Chamfer dialog box, 137
Circular Pattern, 110, 234
Circular Pattern dialog box, 110, 111
Circular Pattern1, 261
Coil, 482
Connected lines, 21
Constraint, 368, 370
Constructing sketch, 6
Continue, 195
Copper (New/Polished), 416
Counter Bore icon, 56
Create, 172
Create Linear Dimension dialog box, 131
Create View, 442
Cut icon, 51, 109

D
Delete dialog box, 192
Deleting a line, 22
Design Accelerator, 503

Dimensioning a line, 11
Direction icon, 109
Drawing Annotation Panel, 197
Drawing View dialog box, 165, 175
Drawing Views Panel, 164, 187, 193
Drive Constraint, 418, 524
Drive Constraint dialog box, 422

Driven dimension, 131

E
Edit Dimension dialog box, 14, 17
Edit Feature, 252, 258
Edit Sketch, 246, 255
Edit text, 268
Edit View, 174, 186
English tab, 5, 163, 441
Error message, 35, 38
Explore icon, 165, 443
Extend, 24
Extrude, 38, 50
Extrude Back, 329
Extrude dialog box, 38, 50
Extrusion1, 251

F
Fillet, 40, 240
Fillet dialog box, 40, 240
Fillet1, 264
Finish Sketch, 34, 49
Flush icon, 380, 383
Format, 198
Format Text dialog box, 206
Front view, 167

G
General Dimension, 12, 15
Green (Clear/Polished), 412
Grounded, 364, 367

H
Hole, 52
Holes dialog box, 56

I
Isometric View, 36, 60

L
Line, 6, 18
Loft command, 477
Look At icon, 93, 144

M
Miniature solid, 175
Minimize icon, 425
Miscellaneous Object (ANSI), 202

N

New icon, 163
New Sketch, 44, 52
Ninety Degree Box, 9
Non-connected lines, 35, 38

O

Occurrence, 266
Open dialog box, 4, 182
Open icon, 182
Opening Inventor, 2
Opens, 35, 38
Orientation, 166
Origin, 285
Over-constrain, 131

P

Pan command, 61
Part Features Panel, 34, 49, 55
Perpendicular symbol, 7-8
Place Component, 353, 356, 357
Place Constraint dialog box, 368, 371
Play icon, 424, 426
Point, Hole Center command, 52
Presentation Panel, 429
Profile icon, 50, 86
Project Geometry, 290
Projected View, 168

R

Radius, 42, 240
Record icon, 426
Return, 404, 410
Revolve, 86
Revolve dialog box, 88
Rewind icon, 425
Rotate Component, 364
Rotate icon, 59, 114
Rotation Axis, 111, 237

S

Save As dialog box, 426
Save dialog box, 428
Scale drop down box, 167, 186
Section View, 193
Section View dialog box, 196
Select Assembly dialog box, 443-444
Shaded Display icon, 288, 301
Shell, 302
Shell dialog box, 302
Sketch, 6, 33
Sketch Panel, 6, 44, 52
Sketch1, 245, 399
Snapped to the intersection of the lines, 9
Solid, 39
Standard (in).iam, 352, 431
Standard (in).ipn, 431
Standard (in) ipt, 5
Starting Inventor, 2
Stop icon, 425
Styles and Standards Editor window, 198
Styles Editor, 198
Suppress, 267
Sweep, 456

T

Text, 205
Text tab, 200
Title block, 164
Trail, 447, 449, 451
Trim, 21
Tweak Component dialog box, 446
Tweak Components, 446
Two Distance Chamfer icon, 137

U

Unground, 364
Update, 250, 253

V

Video (Recording), 426

W

Wireframe Display, 288, 301
Work Planes, 286, 468

X

X axis, 450
XY Plane, 248,

Y

Y axis, 448
YZ Plane, 286

Z

Z axis, 447
Zoom All icon, 61, 116
Zoom icon, 61, 116
Zoom In/Out command, 61, 116
Zoom Window command, 61, 116